2006–2007

59th edition

Editors: Glenda Rollin and Jack Rollin

headline

First published in 2006
by HEADLINE PUBLISHING GROUP

1

Cover photographs Front and spine: Frank Lampard (Chelsea) – *Action Images*; back: Pascal Chimbonda (Wigan Athletic) – *Action Images*.

10-digit ISBN 0 7553 1524 3
13-digit ISBN 978 0 7553 1524 6

Typeset by Wearset Ltd, Boldon, Tyne and Wear

Printed and bound in Great Britain by
Clays Ltd, St Ives plc

Headline's policy is to use papers that are natural, renewable and recyclable products and made from wood grown in sustainable forests. The logging and manufacturing processes are expected to conform to the environmental regulations of the country of origin.

HEADLINE PUBLISHING GROUP
A division of Hodder Headline
338 Euston Road
London NW1 3BH

www.headline.co.uk
www.hodderheadline.com

CONTENTS

European and International Football

Other Football

Information and Records

EDITORIAL

Inevitably the World Cup dominated the summer. While there was considerable scepticism that the soon-to-be-departing Sven-Goran Eriksson would be able to deliver as he had promised, the entire nation with media support was prepared to fly the flag – literally, too.

We exited after losing a penalty shoot-out to Portugal. Had we won, who knows what might have happened in the next match. One thing is certain: there would have been no inquest.

Even before the group stages there were concerns over the selection. With Michael Owen only recently recovered from injury and Wayne Rooney in a tug-of-war tussle with his club Manchester United whether he should be risked so early, the fact remained that the other striking force consisted of Peter Crouch and one-cap Theo Walcott, destined to become the youngest player in the 2006 finals – if he played.

Eriksson has never been an adventurous coach, using substitutions only in clumps. When FIFA decided to restrict their number in friendly internationals, he was at a loss to make more judicious choices. Historically, this was not a first; Alf Ramsey had problems, too, as witness his decisions in the 1970 World Cup when we were leading Germany 2-0 only to lose 3-2, or more importantly in the World Cup qualifying match with Poland in 1973 with a substitution a couple of minutes from the whistle.

Thus with a background of Eriksson having few attacking options and his fingers crossed concerning both Owen and Rooney, he entered the finals in a weak group opposing Trinidad & Tobago, at best filled with non-premiership players, Paraguay not relishing playing in Europe and Sweden, whose claim to fame has been that they have not lost to England since 1968. Second place and still qualifying is the worst that can happen to England.

Eriksson adopted an attack-minded opening with Owen and Crouch up front against Paraguay. A David Beckham free-kick gives us an early lead via an opponent's head. After that it begins to unravel slightly. Owen is taken off, clearly not at his best. For the Trinidad game the same pairing starts with a similar outcome, though this time Wayne Rooney replaces Owen thanks to a media campaign, public support and Eriksson's determination to show he was in charge, not the manager of Manchester United.

Crouch climbs on the back of Gillingham's Brent Sancho for the first of the two late goals, Steven Gerrard whips in another shot. So, with the knock-out stage successfully reached, the match with Sweden is something of a non-event. Time for experiments of course.

Rooney starts in partnership with Owen, who is then cruelly struck down with injury before he has even managed to touch the ball in anger. Crouch comes on as a replacement. We lead from a spectacular goal from Joe Cole, are pulled back level, go ahead again through Gerrard who has taken over from the clearly unhappy Rooney, only to concede another equaliser at the death with the defence having another particularly unhappy evening against Sweden.

It does not matter in the overall scheme of things. We are in the last 16 and face Ecuador whom we only once before met in 1970 away and beaten 2-0. They prove marginally better than Paraguay and again it is a Beckham free-kick which disposes of them. Eriksson takes no chances, selects Rooney to roam alone up front. No place for Crouch.

The quarter-finals beckon and Portugal, masterminded by Luiz Felipe Scolari the coach to whom the England FA said they had not offered Eriksson's job. He had been in charge of Brazil when we lost to them in the last World Cup and was the Portuguese boss when England lost on penalties in Euro 2004!

Would history repeat itself? It did of course. Beforehand, Eriksson opted for the lone Rooney as ranger up front. It ended in tragedy when the striker was alleged to have stamped on Ricardo Carvalho and received a red card, apparently goaded by Cristiano Ronaldo his team mate at Old Trafford. With ten men and Crouch shoved on to plough another lonely furrow, penalties seemed the only way out – one way or another. Only Owen Hargreaves, certainly the best England player in the finals, managed to find the net for us.

The bare facts are that the England players did not produce Premier League form. Perhaps this stage is not conducive to what is required. Naturally we are told there are too many foreigners in our game. They have always been there – Scots, Welsh and Irish before the continental invasion. Could it be we simply cannot produce world class players?

CLUB AND OTHER RECORDS DURING 2005–2006

Arsenal	Thierry Henry overtakes Ian Wright's 185 League and Cup goals and Cliff Bastin's 150 League goals, finishing his League total at 164. Champions League record of 8 successive clean sheets.
Birmingham City	Kenny Cunningham becomes most capped player.
Bolton Wanderers	Enter Europe for first time in UEFA Cup. They sign their 20th different national with Hidetoshi Nakata (Japan).
Charlton Athletic	Most capped player Jonatan Johansson, 41 (70), Finland.
Chelsea	Frank Lampard completes record 164 consecutive League matches. Record transfer fee paid for Andriy Shevchenko £29,500,000 from AC Milan, May 2006. He became overall leading European Cup goalscorer with 52 goals in the Champions League.
Colchester United	Equal record Cup score beating Leamington Spa 9-1 on 5 November 2005.
Darlington	Adrian Webster equals total for Most capped player with 3 from New Zealand.
Derby County	Record crowd 33,475 Derby County Legends v Rangers Legends, May 2006.
Everton	Record transfer fee paid for Andy Johnson £8,500,000 from Crystal Palace, May 2006.
Grimsby Town	John McDermott most League appearances 624.
Lincoln City	Most capped player Gareth McAuley, 5, Northern Ireland.
Manchester United	First Premier League team to score 1000 goals in the competition. Record Premier League attendance 73,006 v Charlton Ath 7 May 2006.
Newcastle United	Alan Shearer overtakes Jackie Milburn's League and Cup record of 200 goals and finishes with a career total of 409 in all competitions.
Peterborough United	Most capped player James Quinn, 9 (46), Northern Ireland.
Portsmouth	Record transfer fee paid for Benjani Mwaruwari £4,100,000 from Auxerre, January 2006.
Port Vale	Most capped player Chris Birchall, 22, Trinidad & Tobago.
Reading	Most League points 106 (English League record).
Rushden & Diamonds	Lee Tomlin becomes youngest Football League player for the club.
Southampton	Youngest League player Theo Walcott, 16 years 143 days v Wolverhampton W, 6 August 2005.
Wigan Athletic	Record transfer fee paid for Emile Heskey £5,500,000 from Birmingham City, July 2006.
Yeovil Town	Arron Davies equals most capped record with his first appearance for Wales.
Celtic	Record Premier League win 8-1 at Dunfermline Ath 19 February 2006.
England	Theo Walcott, England's youngest international 17 years 75 days v Hungary, 30 May 2006.
Wales	Lewin Nyatanga, Wales youngest at 17 years 195 days, overtaken by Gareth Bale at 16 years 315 days.

LEAGUE REVIEW AND CLUB SECTION

Chelsea retained their Premier League title but found it a more difficult campaign than in 2004–05. However their final record would have reflected more favourably had they not relaxed after clinching it.

At a time when they were finding the going tougher and losing interest in all three cup competitions in which they were involved, Chelsea came good again at a crucial moment in the home game with Manchester United on 29 April.

Chelsea gave arguably their most convincing performance of the season and finished worthy 3-0 winners against the only team within possible striking distance of them.

Long gone are the days when a nucleus of players was used to fuel the aspirations of championship contenders. Chelsea have enough for three complete teams as do most of the other leading Premier League clubs.

Twenty-five different players were called upon none of whom managed a full complement of games. John Terry came closest but injury robbed him at the end of playing in every game, missing two, while Frank Lampard with the record for consecutive outings in the competition was similarly hampered and failed to play in three matches.

Lampard was top scorer, too, with 16 League goals while three others reached double figures: Didier Drogba with 12, Hernan Crespo and Eidur Gudjohnsen with ten each. And while the Chelsea defence was as formidable as ever with 20 clean sheets and only the unaccountable lapse at Middlesbrough where they conceded three goals, the attack had its problems. Charlton were the only team to avoid defeat at Stamford Bridge in the Premier League.

The idea of a twin-spearhead featuring Drogba and Crespo did not appear to work well enough, though both had their moments individually of course.

United finished eight points behind in second place in what might be described as a disappointing season for them in terms of League action, such are the pressures in the Premiership. However, Old Trafford had an extension which took its capacity over the 70,000 mark and three of their last four home fixtures were above it.

In spite of this increase, overall attendance figures were slightly down at 12,876,993 compared with 12,881,768 in 2004–05. Arsenal, runners-up the previous season were even pipped for third place by Liverpool, the Gunners' lowest position for ten years.

Still, in their last season at Highbury, Arsenal again had the leading marksman in the Premier League. Thierry Henry hit 27 from 32 games, two of which were as a replacement from the bench. He was also voted Footballer of the Year by the Football Writers' Association. Steven Gerrard of Liverpool was the Professional Footballers' Association choice and Wayne Rooney again won the Young Player award. Jose Mourinho of Chelsea was Manager of the season.

Arsenal were still able to edge their north London rivals Tottenham Hotspur out of a place in the Champions League by two points, Blackburn in sixth place equalled their position of three seasons earlier while Newcastle United were seventh.

Though Wigan Athletic's eventual resting place was tenth, they had had a fine first season in the elite and one which should encourage them considerably for the future.

Sunderland were early casualties in the relegation battle to be joined by the Midland pair Birmingham City and West Bromwich Albion, with Portsmouth effecting another escape act towards the close.

In the Championship, Reading were runaway winners and achieved 106 points, a total previously not reached in any division. After losing their first match at home to Plymouth Argyle they were not beaten again until 17 February at Luton, their only other reverse in the Football League.

They were joined by Sheffield United automatically and by Watford from the play-offs who had actually finished in third place during the season. At the other end of the scale Crewe Alexandra, Millwall and Brighton & Hove Albion were relegated.

Essex teams fared well in League One with Southend United the most consistent of all and Colchester United gaining the first two places and Barnsley taking the play-off berth. However, Swansea City had an inconsistent second half of the season which cost them dearly. Their consolation came from winning what had been the LDV Vans Trophy until the sponsors foundered.

Hartlepool United, Milton Keynes Dons, Swindon Town and Walsall went down, their places being taken by Carlisle United, Northampton Town, Leyton Orient plus Cheltenham Town from the play-offs. Carlisle's feat was outstanding given they were just back from the Conference.

Down to that competition went Oxford United and Rushden & Diamonds with Accrington Stanley and Hereford United rejoining the fold. Ironically it had been Accrington who had gone out of the League in 1962 to be replaced by Oxford.

7

FA Barclaycard Premiership

		P	W	D	L	F	A	W	D	L	F	A	W	D	L	F	A	Gd	Pts
			Home					Away					Total						
1	Chelsea	38	18	1	0	47	9	11	3	5	25	13	29	4	5	72	22	50	91
2	Manchester U	38	13	5	1	37	8	12	3	4	35	26	25	8	5	72	34	38	83
3	Liverpool	38	15	3	1	32	8	10	4	5	25	17	25	7	6	57	25	32	82
4	Arsenal	38	14	3	2	48	13	6	4	9	20	18	20	7	11	68	31	37	67
5	Tottenham H	38	12	5	2	31	16	6	6	7	22	22	18	11	9	53	38	15	65
6	Blackburn R	38	13	3	3	31	17	6	3	10	20	25	19	6	13	51	42	9	63
7	Newcastle U	38	11	5	3	28	15	6	2	11	19	27	17	7	14	47	42	5	58
8	Bolton W	38	11	5	3	29	13	4	6	9	20	28	15	11	12	49	41	8	56
9	West Ham U	38	9	3	7	30	25	7	4	8	22	30	16	7	15	52	55	-3	55
10	Wigan Ath	38	7	3	9	24	26	8	3	8	21	26	15	6	17	45	52	-7	51
11	Everton	38	8	4	7	22	22	6	4	9	12	27	14	8	16	34	49	-15	50
12	Fulham	38	13	2	4	31	21	1	4	14	17	37	14	6	18	48	58	-10	48
13	Charlton Ath	38	8	4	7	22	21	5	4	10	19	34	13	8	17	41	55	-14	47
14	Middlesbrough	38	7	5	7	28	30	5	4	10	20	28	12	9	17	48	58	-10	45
15	Manchester C	38	9	2	8	26	20	4	2	13	17	28	13	4	21	43	48	-5	43
16	Aston Villa	38	6	6	7	20	20	4	6	9	22	35	10	12	16	42	55	-13	42
17	Portsmouth	38	5	7	7	17	24	5	1	13	20	38	10	8	20	37	62	-25	38
18	Birmingham C	38	6	5	8	19	20	2	5	12	9	30	8	10	20	28	50	-22	34
19	WBA	38	6	2	11	21	24	1	7	11	10	34	7	9	22	31	58	-27	30
20	Sunderland	38	1	4	14	12	37	2	2	15	14	32	3	6	29	26	69	-43	15

LEADING GOALSCORERS 2005–06

FA BARCLAYCARD PREMIERSHIP

	League	Carling Cup	FA Cup	Other	Total

Players in this competition scoring ten or more League goals are listed. Other leading scorers classified by total number of goals in all competitions.

	League	Carling Cup	FA Cup	Other	Total
Thierry Henry *(Arsenal)*	27	1	0	5	33
Ruud Van Nistelrooy *(Manchester U)*	21	1	0	2	24
Darren Bent *(Charlton Ath)*	18	2	2	0	22
Frank Lampard *(Chelsea)*	16	0	2	2	20
Wayne Rooney *(Manchester U)*	16	2	0	1	19
Robbie Keane *(Tottenham H)*	16	0	0	0	16
Marlon Harewood *(West Ham U)*	14	0	2	0	16
Ayegbeni Yakubu *(Middlesbrough)*	13	0	4	2	19
Craig Bellamy *(Blackburn R)*	13	2	2	0	17
Didier Drogba *(Chelsea)*	12	0	1	3	16
Henri Camara *(Wigan Ath)*	12	0	0	0	12
Collins John *(Fulham)*	11	0	1	0	12
Mido *(Tottenham H)*	11	0	0	0	11
Steven Gerrard *(Liverpool)*	10	1	4	8	23
Jimmy Floyd Hasselbaink *(Middlesbrough)*	10	1	3	4	18
Hernan Crespo *(Chelsea)*	10	0	1	2	13
Alan Shearer *(Newcastle U)*	10	1	1	0	12
James Beattie *(Everton)*	10	0	0	1	11

In order of total goals:

	League	Carling Cup	FA Cup	Other	Total
Djibril Cisse *(Liverpool)*	9	0	2	8	19
Mark Viduka *(Middlesbrough)*	7	1	2	6	16

Other matches consist of European, Super Cup and Club World Championship games, Football League Trophy, Community Shield and Football League play-offs. Players listed in order of League goals total.

Coca-Cola Football League Championship

		Home					Away					Total						
	P	W	D	L	F	A	W	D	L	F	A	W	D	L	F	A	Gd	Pts
1 Reading	46	19	3	1	58	14	12	10	1	41	18	31	13	2	99	32	67	106
2 Sheffield U	46	15	5	3	43	22	11	7	5	33	24	26	12	8	76	46	30	90
3 Watford	46	11	7	5	39	24	11	8	4	38	29	22	15	9	77	53	24	81
4 Preston NE	46	11	10	2	31	12	9	10	4	28	18	20	20	6	59	30	29	80
5 Leeds U	46	13	7	3	35	18	8	8	7	22	20	21	15	10	57	38	19	78
6 Crystal Palace	46	13	6	4	39	20	8	6	9	28	28	21	12	13	67	48	19	75
7 Wolverhampton W	46	9	10	4	24	18	7	9	7	26	24	16	19	11	50	42	8	67
8 Coventry C	46	12	7	4	39	22	4	8	11	23	43	16	15	15	62	65	-3	63
9 Norwich C	46	12	4	7	34	25	6	4	13	22	40	18	8	20	56	65	-9	62
10 Luton T	46	11	6	6	45	31	6	4	13	21	36	17	10	19	66	67	-1	61
11 Cardiff C	46	10	7	6	32	24	6	5	12	26	35	16	12	18	58	59	-1	60
12 Southampton	46	9	10	4	26	17	4	9	10	23	33	13	19	14	49	50	-1	58
13 Stoke C	46	7	5	11	24	32	10	2	11	30	31	17	7	22	54	63	-9	58
14 Plymouth Arg	46	10	7	6	26	22	3	10	10	13	24	13	17	16	39	46	-7	56
15 Ipswich T	46	8	8	7	28	32	6	6	11	25	34	14	14	18	53	66	-13	56
16 Leicester C	46	8	9	6	30	25	5	6	12	21	34	13	15	18	51	59	-8	54
17 Burnley	46	11	6	6	34	22	3	6	14	12	32	14	12	20	46	54	-8	54
18 Hull C	46	8	8	7	24	21	4	8	11	25	34	12	16	18	49	55	-6	52
19 Sheffield W	46	7	8	8	22	24	6	5	12	17	28	13	13	20	39	52	-13	52
20 Derby Co	46	8	10	5	33	27	2	10	11	20	40	10	20	16	53	67	-14	50
21 QPR	46	7	7	9	24	26	5	7	11	26	39	12	14	20	50	65	-15	50
22 Crewe Alex	46	7	7	9	38	40	2	8	13	19	46	9	15	22	57	86	-29	42
23 Millwall	46	4	8	11	13	27	4	8	11	22	35	8	17	21	35	61	-27	40
24 Brighton & HA	46	4	8	11	21	34	3	9	11	18	37	7	17	22	39	71	-32	38

COCA-COLA FOOTBALL LEAGUE CHAMPIONSHIP

	League	Carling Cup	FA Cup	Other	Total
Players in this competition scoring 12 or more League goals are listed.					
Marlon King *(Watford)*	21	0	0	1	22
Dave Kitson *(Reading)*	18	4	0	0	22
Cameron Jerome *(Cardiff C)*	18	1	1	0	20
(now with Birmingham C.)					
Kevin Doyle *(Reading)*	18	0	1	0	19
Ade Akinbiyi *(Sheffield U)*	15	2	0	0	17
(Includes 12 League and 2 Carling Cup goals for Burnley).					
Andy Johnson *(Crystal Palace)*	15	0	2	0	17
Gary McSheffrey *(Coventry C)*	15	1	1	0	17
Steve Howard *(Luton T)*	14	0	1	0	15
Darius Henderson *(Watford)*	14	0	0	1	15
Ashley Young *(Watford)*	13	1	0	1	15
Clint Morrison *(Crystal Palace)*	13	0	0	0	13
David Healy *(Leeds U)*	12	0	2	0	14
Rob Hulse *(Leeds U)*	12	0	1	1	14
Jason Koumas *(Cardiff C)*	12	1	0	0	13
Dele Adebola *(Coventry C)*	12	0	0	0	12

Coca-Cola Football League Division 1

			Home					Away					Total					
	P	W	D	L	F	A	W	D	L	F	A	W	D	L	F	A	Gd	Pts
1 Southend U	46	13	6	4	37	16	10	7	6	35	27	23	13	10	72	43	29	82
2 Colchester U	46	15	4	4	39	21	7	9	7	19	19	22	13	11	58	40	18	79
3 Brentford	46	10	8	5	35	23	10	8	5	37	29	20	16	10	72	52	20	76
4 Huddersfield T	46	13	6	4	40	25	6	10	7	32	34	19	16	11	72	59	13	73
5 Barnsley	46	11	11	1	37	19	7	7	9	25	25	18	18	10	62	44	18	72
6 Swansea C	46	11	9	3	42	23	7	8	8	36	32	18	17	11	78	55	23	71
7 Nottingham F	46	14	5	4	40	15	5	7	11	27	37	19	12	15	67	52	15	69
8 Doncaster R	46	11	6	6	30	19	9	3	11	25	32	20	9	17	55	51	4	69
9 Bristol C	46	11	7	5	38	22	7	4	12	28	40	18	11	17	66	62	4	65
10 Oldham Ath	46	12	4	7	32	24	6	7	10	26	36	18	11	17	58	60	−2	65
11 Bradford C	46	8	9	6	28	25	6	10	7	23	24	14	19	13	51	49	2	61
12 Scunthorpe U	46	8	8	7	36	33	7	7	9	32	40	15	15	16	68	73	−5	60
13 Port Vale	46	10	5	8	30	26	6	7	10	19	28	16	12	18	49	54	−5	60
14 Gillingham	46	13	4	6	31	21	3	8	12	19	43	16	12	18	50	64	−14	60
15 Yeovil T	46	8	8	7	27	24	7	3	13	27	38	15	11	20	54	62	−8	56
16 Chesterfield	46	6	7	10	31	37	8	7	8	32	36	14	14	18	63	73	−10	56
17 Bournemouth	46	7	11	5	25	20	5	8	10	24	33	12	19	15	49	53	−4	55
18 Tranmere R	46	7	8	8	32	30	6	7	10	18	22	13	15	18	50	52	−2	54
19 Blackpool	46	9	8	6	33	27	3	9	11	23	37	12	17	17	56	64	−8	53
20 Rotherham U	46	7	9	7	31	26	5	7	11	21	36	12	16	18	52	62	−10	52
21 Hartlepool U	46	6	10	7	28	30	5	7	11	16	29	11	17	18	44	59	−15	50
22 Milton Keynes D	46	8	8	7	28	25	4	6	13	17	41	12	14	20	45	66	−21	50
23 Swindon T	46	9	5	9	31	31	2	10	11	15	34	11	15	20	46	65	−19	48
24 Walsall	46	7	7	9	27	34	4	7	12	20	36	11	14	21	47	70	−23	47

COCA-COLA FOOTBALL LEAGUE DIVISION 1

	League	Carling Cup	FA Cup	Other	Total
Freddy Eastwood (Southend U)	23	0	2	0	25
Billy Sharp (Scunthorpe U)	23	0	0	1	24
Lee Trundle (Swansea C)	20	0	0	1	21
James Hayter (Bournemouth)	20	0	0	0	20
Luke Beckett (Oldham Ath)	18	0	0	0	18
Chris Iwelumo (Colchester U)	17	0	2	0	19
Izale McLeod (Milton Keynes D)	17	0	1	0	18
Dean Windass (Bradford C)	16	3	0	1	20
Rory Fallon (Swansea C)	16	0	1	2	19
(Includes 12 League, 1 FA Cup and 1 other goal for Swindon T).					
Chris Greenacre (Tranmere R)	16	0	1	1	18
Steve Brooker (Bristol C)	16	0	0	0	16
Phil Jevons (Yeovil T)	15	0	1	0	16
Paul Hall (Chesterfield)	15	0	0	0	15
Andy Booth (Huddersfield T)	13	0	2	0	15
Darren Byfield (Gillingham)	13	1	0	0	14
Andy Robinson (Swansea C)	12	0	0	6	18
Lloyd Owusu (Brentford)	12	0	2	0	14
Pawel Abbott (Huddersfield T)	12	2	0	0	14
Deon Burton (Rotherham U)	12	1	1	0	14
Marc Richards (Barnsley)	12	0	0	0	12

Coca-Cola Football League Division 2

		Home					Away					Total					
	P	W	D	L	F	A	W	D	L	F	A	W	D	L	F	A	Gd	Pts
1 Carlisle U	46	14	3	6	47	23	11	8	4	37	19	25	11	10	84	42	42	86
2 Northampton T	46	11	8	4	30	15	11	9	3	33	22	22	17	7	63	37	26	83
3 Leyton Orient	46	11	6	6	29	21	11	9	3	38	30	22	15	9	67	51	16	81
4 Grimsby T	46	13	3	7	37	18	9	9	5	27	26	22	12	12	64	44	20	78
5 Cheltenham T	46	10	7	6	39	31	9	8	6	26	22	19	15	12	65	53	12	72
6 Wycombe W	46	9	9	5	41	29	9	8	6	31	27	18	17	11	72	56	16	71
7 Lincoln C	46	9	11	3	37	21	6	10	7	28	32	15	21	10	65	53	12	66
8 Darlington	46	10	7	6	32	26	6	8	9	26	26	16	15	15	58	52	6	63
9 Peterborough U	46	9	7	7	28	21	8	4	11	29	28	17	11	18	57	49	8	62
10 Shrewsbury T	46	10	9	4	33	20	6	4	13	22	35	16	13	17	55	55	0	61
11 Boston U	46	11	5	7	34	28	4	9	10	16	32	15	16	15	50	60	-10	61
12 Bristol R	46	8	6	9	30	29	9	3	11	29	38	17	9	20	59	67	-8	60
13 Wrexham	46	12	6	5	36	19	3	8	12	25	35	15	14	17	61	54	7	59
14 Rochdale	46	8	7	8	34	30	6	7	10	32	39	14	14	18	66	69	-3	56
15 Chester C	46	7	6	10	30	29	7	6	10	23	30	14	12	20	53	59	-6	54
16 Mansfield T	46	9	7	7	37	29	4	8	11	22	37	13	15	18	59	66	-7	54
17 Macclesfield T	46	10	9	4	35	27	2	9	12	25	44	12	18	16	60	71	-11	54
18 Barnet	46	9	8	6	24	22	3	10	10	20	35	12	18	16	44	57	-13	54
19 Bury	46	6	9	8	22	25	6	8	9	23	32	12	17	17	45	57	-12	53
20 Torquay U	46	7	9	7	33	31	6	4	13	20	35	13	13	20	53	66	-13	52
21 Notts Co	46	7	11	5	30	26	5	5	13	18	37	12	16	18	48	63	-15	52
22 Stockport Co	46	7	11	5	34	29	4	8	11	23	49	11	19	16	57	78	-21	52
23 Oxford U	46	7	7	9	25	30	4	9	10	18	27	11	16	19	43	57	-14	49
24 Rushden & D	46	8	5	10	25	31	3	7	13	19	45	11	12	23	44	76	-32	45

COCA-COLA FOOTBALL LEAGUE DIVISION 2

	League	Carling Cup	FA Cup	Other	Total
Karl Hawley (Carlisle U)	22	0	0	4	26
Rickie Lambert (Rochdale)	22	0	0	0	22
Richard Walker (Bristol R)	20	0	0	1	21
Richie Barker (Mansfield T)	18	1	4	0	23
Scott McGleish (Northampton T)	17	1	4	2	24
Tommy Mooney (Wycombe W)	17	1	0	1	19
Junior Agogo (Bristol R)	16	0	2	0	18
Danny Crow (Peterborough U)	15	0	0	2	17
Michael Bridges (Carlisle U)	15	1	0	0	16
(Includes 1 Carling Cup goal for Bristol City).					
Julian Joachim (Boston U)	14	0	2	0	16
Gary Alexander (Leyton Orient)	14	0	0	1	15
Gary Jones (Grimsby T)	13	1	1	2	17
Mark Jones (Wrexham)	13	0	0	2	15
Michael Reddy (Grimsby T)	13	0	0	0	13

FA BARCLAYCARD PREMIERSHIP

HOME TEAM	Arsenal	Aston Villa	Birmingham C	Blackburn R	Bolton W	Charlton Ath	Chelsea	Everton	Fulham	Liverpool
Arsenal	—	5-0	1-0	3-0	1-1	3-0	0-2	2-0	4-1	2-1
Aston Villa	0-0	—	3-1	1-0	2-2	1-0	1-1	4-0	0-0	0-2
Birmingham C	0-2	0-1	—	2-1	1-0	0-1	0-0	0-1	1-0	2-2
Blackburn R	1-0	2-0	2-0	—	0-0	4-1	1-0	0-2	2-1	0-1
Bolton W	2-0	1-1	1-0	0-0	—	4-1	0-2	0-1	2-1	2-2
Charlton Ath	0-1	0-0	2-0	0-2	0-1	—	0-2	0-0	1-1	2-0
Chelsea	1-0	2-1	2-0	4-2	5-1	1-1	—	3-0	3-2	2-0
Everton	1-0	4-1	0-0	1-0	0-4	3-1	1-1	—	3-1	1-3
Fulham	0-4	3-3	0-0	2-1	2-1	2-1	1-0	1-0	—	2-0
Liverpool	1-0	3-1	1-1	1-0	1-0	0-0	1-4	3-1	5-1	—
Manchester C	1-3	3-1	4-1	0-0	0-1	3-2	0-1	2-0	1-2	0-1
Manchester U	2-0	1-0	3-0	1-2	4-1	4-0	1-0	1-1	4-2	1-0
Middlesbrough	2-1	0-4	1-0	0-2	4-3	0-3	3-0	0-1	3-2	0-0
Newcastle U	1-0	1-1	1-0	0-1	3-1	0-0	1-0	2-0	1-1	1-3
Portsmouth	1-1	1-1	1-1	2-2	1-1	1-2	0-2	0-1	1-0	1-3
Sunderland	0-3	1-3	0-1	0-1	0-0	1-3	1-2	0-1	2-1	0-2
Tottenham H	1-1	0-0	2-0	3-2	1-0	3-1	0-2	2-0	1-0	0-0
WBA	2-1	1-2	2-3	2-0	0-0	1-2	1-2	4-0	0-0	0-2
West Ham U	0-0	4-0	3-0	3-1	1-2	0-0	1-3	2-2	2-1	1-2
Wigan Ath	2-3	3-2	1-1	0-3	2-1	3-0	0-1	1-1	1-0	0-1

2005–2006 RESULTS

	Manchester C	Manchester U	Middlesbrough	Newcastle U	Portsmouth	Sunderland	Tottenham H	WBA	West Ham U	Wigan Ath
	1-0	0-0	7-0	2-0	4-0	3-1	1-1	3-1	2-3	4-2
	0-1	0-2	2-3	1-2	1-0	2-1	1-1	0-0	1-2	0-2
	1-2	2-2	0-3	0-0	5-0	1-0	0-2	1-1	1-2	2-0
	2-0	4-3	3-2	0-3	2-1	2-0	0-0	2-0	3-2	1-1
	2-0	1-2	1-1	2-0	1-0	2-0	1-0	2-0	4-1	1-1
	2-5	1-3	2-1	3-1	2-1	2-0	2-3	0-0	2-0	1-0
	2-0	3-0	1-0	3-0	2-0	2-0	2-1	4-0	4-1	1-0
	1-0	0-2	1-0	1-0	0-1	2-2	0-1	2-2	1-2	0-1
	2-1	2-3	1-0	1-0	1-3	2-1	1-0	6-1	1-2	1-0
	1-0	0-0	2-0	2-0	3-0	1-0	1-0	1-0	2-0	3-0
	—	3-1	0-1	3-0	2-1	2-1	0-2	0-0	2-1	0-1
	1-1	—	0-0	2-0	3-0	0-0	1-1	3-0	1-0	4-0
	0-0	4-1	—	1-2	1-1	0-2	3-3	2-2	2-0	2-3
	1-0	0-2	2-2	—	2-0	3-2	3-1	3-0	0-0	3-1
	2-1	1-3	1-0	0-0	—	2-1	0-2	1-0	1-1	0-2
	1-2	1-3	0-3	1-4	1-4	—	1-1	1-1	1-1	0-1
	2-1	1-2	2-0	2-0	3-1	3-2	—	2-1	1-1	2-2
	2-0	1-2	0-2	0-3	2-1	0-1	2-0	—	0-1	1-2
	1-0	1-2	2-1	2-4	2-4	2-0	2-1	1-0	—	0-2
	4-3	1-2	1-1	1-0	1-2	1-0	1-2	0-1	1-2	—

COCA-COLA FOOTBALL LEAGUE

HOME TEAM	Brighton & HA	Burnley	Cardiff C	Coventry C	Crewe Alex	Crystal Palace	Derby Co	Hull C	Ipswich T	Leeds U
Brighton & HA	—	0-0	1-2	2-2	2-2	2-3	0-0	2-1	1-1	2-1
Burnley	1-1	—	3-3	4-0	3-0	0-0	2-2	1-0	3-0	1-2
Cardiff C	1-1	3-0	—	0-0	6-1	1-0	0-0	1-0	2-1	2-1
Coventry C	2-0	1-0	3-1	—	1-1	1-4	6-1	0-2	1-1	1-1
Crewe Alex	2-1	2-1	1-1	4-1	—	2-2	1-1	2-2	1-2	1-0
Crystal Palace	0-1	2-0	1-0	2-0	2-2	—	2-0	2-0	2-2	1-2
Derby Co	1-1	3-0	2-1	1-1	5-1	2-1	—	1-1	3-3	0-0
Hull C	2-0	0-0	2-0	1-2	1-0	1-2	2-1	—	2-0	1-0
Ipswich T	1-2	2-1	1-0	2-2	2-1	0-2	2-0	1-1	—	1-1
Leeds U	3-3	2-0	0-1	3-1	1-0	0-1	3-1	2-0	0-2	—
Leicester C	0-0	0-1	1-2	2-1	1-1	2-0	2-2	3-2	0-0	1-1
Luton T	3-0	2-3	3-3	1-2	4-1	2-0	1-0	2-3	1-0	0-0
Millwall	0-2	1-0	0-0	0-0	1-3	1-1	2-1	1-1	1-2	0-1
Norwich C	3-0	2-1	1-1	1-1	1-1	1-1	2-0	2-1	1-2	0-1
Plymouth Arg	1-0	1-0	0-1	3-1	1-1	2-0	0-2	0-1	2-1	0-3
Preston NE	0-0	0-0	2-1	3-1	1-0	2-0	1-1	3-0	3-1	2-0
QPR	1-1	1-1	1-0	0-1	1-2	1-3	1-1	2-2	2-1	0-1
Reading	5-1	2-1	5-1	2-0	1-0	3-2	5-0	3-1	2-0	1-1
Sheffield U	3-1	3-0	0-0	2-1	0-0	1-0	2-1	3-2	2-0	1-1
Sheffield W	1-1	0-0	1-3	3-2	3-0	0-0	2-1	1-1	0-1	1-0
Southampton	2-1	1-1	3-2	1-1	2-0	0-0	0-0	1-1	0-2	3-4
Stoke C	3-0	1-0	0-3	0-1	2-0	1-3	1-2	0-3	2-2	0-1
Watford	1-1	3-1	2-1	4-0	4-1	1-2	2-2	0-0	2-1	0-0
Wolverhampton W	1-0	0-1	2-0	2-2	1-2	2-1	1-1	1-0	1-0	1-0

CHAMPIONSHIP 2005–2006 RESULTS

Leicester C	Luton T	Millwall	Norwich C	Plymouth Arg	Preston NE	QPR	Reading	Sheffield U	Sheffield W	Southampton	Stoke C	Watford	Wolverhampton W
1-2	1-1	1-2	1-3	2-0	0-0	1-0	0-2	0-1	0-2	0-2	1-5	0-1	1-1
1-0	1-1	2-1	2-0	1-0	0-2	1-0	0-3	1-2	1-2	1-1	1-0	4-1	0-1
1-0	1-2	1-1	0-1	0-2	2-2	0-0	2-5	0-1	1-0	2-1	3-0	1-3	2-2
1-1	1-0	1-0	2-2	3-1	0-1	3-0	1-1	2-0	2-1	1-1	1-2	3-1	2-0
2-2	3-1	4-2	1-2	1-2	0-2	3-4	3-4	1-3	2-0	1-1	1-2	0-0	0-4
2-0	1-2	1-1	4-1	1-0	1-1	2-1	1-1	2-3	2-0	2-0	2-0	3-1	1-1
1-1	1-1	1-0	2-0	1-0	1-1	1-2	2-2	0-1	0-2	2-2	1-2	1-2	0-3
1-1	0-1	1-1	1-1	1-0	1-1	0-0	1-1	1-3	1-0	1-1	0-1	1-2	2-3
2-0	1-0	1-1	0-1	3-1	0-4	2-2	0-3	1-1	2-1	2-2	1-4	0-1	1-1
2-1	2-1	2-1	2-2	0-0	0-0	2-0	1-1	1-1	3-0	2-1	0-0	2-1	2-0
—	0-2	1-1	0-1	1-0	1-2	1-2	1-1	4-2	2-0	0-0	4-2	2-2	1-0
1-2	—	2-1	4-2	1-1	3-0	2-0	3-2	1-1	2-2	3-2	2-3	1-2	1-1
0-1	2-1	—	1-0	1-1	1-2	1-1	0-2	0-4	0-1	0-2	0-1	0-0	0-0
2-1	2-0	1-1	—	2-0	0-3	3-2	0-1	2-1	0-1	3-1	2-1	2-3	1-2
1-0	1-2	0-0	1-1	—	0-0	3-1	0-2	0-0	1-1	2-1	2-1	3-3	2-0
0-0	5-1	2-0	2-0	0-0	—	1-1	0-3	0-0	0-0	1-1	0-1	1-1	2-0
2-3	1-0	1-0	3-0	1-1	0-2	—	1-2	2-1	0-0	1-0	1-2	1-2	0-0
2-0	3-0	5-0	4-0	1-2	2-1	2-1	—	2-1	2-0	2-0	3-1	0-0	1-1
4-1	4-0	2-2	1-3	2-0	2-1	2-3	1-1	—	1-0	3-0	2-1	1-4	1-0
2-1	0-2	1-2	1-0	0-0	2-0	1-1	1-1	1-2	—	0-1	0-2	1-1	0-2
2-0	1-0	2-0	1-0	0-0	0-0	1-1	0-0	0-1	3-0	—	2-0	1-3	0-0
3-2	2-1	2-1	3-1	0-0	0-0	1-2	0-1	1-1	0-0	1-2	—	0-3	1-3
1-2	1-1	0-2	2-1	1-1	1-1	3-0	0-0	2-3	2-1	3-0	1-0	—	3-1
0-0	2-1	1-2	2-0	1-1	1-1	3-1	0-2	0-0	1-3	0-0	0-0	1-1	—

COCA-COLA FOOTBALL LEAGUE

HOME TEAM	Barnsley	Blackpool	Bournemouth	Bradford C	Brentford	Bristol C	Chesterfield	Colchester U	Doncaster R	Gillingham
Barnsley	—	2-2	0-0	0-0	1-1	2-0	1-1	1-0	0-2	1-0
Blackpool	1-1	—	1-3	1-0	0-0	1-1	1-3	1-2	4-2	3-3
Bournemouth	1-1	1-1	—	0-1	2-2	2-0	1-2	1-2	2-1	2-1
Bradford C	0-0	1-0	1-2	—	3-3	1-1	2-0	1-1	2-1	1-0
Brentford	3-1	1-1	0-2	1-1	—	2-3	1-1	0-2	0-1	1-1
Bristol C	3-0	1-1	3-1	0-1	0-1	—	2-4	0-0	0-0	6-0
Chesterfield	0-0	1-1	3-0	1-0	1-3	3-0	—	2-2	0-1	1-1
Colchester U	1-0	3-2	0-1	3-1	1-1	3-2	1-2	—	3-2	5-0
Doncaster R	2-0	0-1	4-2	2-2	0-0	2-0	1-1	0-0	—	2-0
Gillingham	0-3	2-1	1-0	2-1	3-2	1-1	1-0	2-1	1-0	—
Hartlepool U	1-1	0-3	2-1	0-2	1-2	1-2	1-0	0-1	1-1	3-1
Huddersfield T	1-0	2-0	2-2	0-0	3-2	1-0	1-2	2-0	2-2	0-0
Milton Keynes D	0-0	3-0	2-2	2-1	0-1	0-1	0-0	1-1	2-3	1-2
Nottingham F	0-2	1-1	1-1	1-0	1-2	3-1	0-0	1-0	4-0	1-1
Oldham Ath	0-3	3-1	1-0	2-1	0-1	4-3	4-1	1-0	0-1	2-0
Port Vale	3-2	1-2	0-0	0-1	1-0	0-1	3-1	0-1	2-0	0-0
Rotherham U	0-1	4-0	2-0	1-1	2-2	3-1	0-4	1-2	1-0	3-0
Scunthorpe U	2-1	1-0	2-2	0-0	1-3	0-2	2-2	0-0	1-2	1-1
Southend U	1-1	2-1	2-1	1-1	4-1	1-0	0-0	3-1	0-1	0-1
Swansea C	3-1	3-2	1-0	1-1	2-1	7-1	5-1	1-1	1-2	1-2
Swindon T	0-3	0-0	4-2	2-3	1-3	2-1	2-0	1-0	2-1	1-0
Tranmere R	0-1	2-2	0-0	2-2	1-4	0-3	4-1	0-0	0-2	2-2
Walsall	1-2	2-0	0-1	2-2	0-0	0-3	2-3	0-2	1-0	2-0
Yeovil T	2-1	1-1	1-1	0-1	1-2	1-1	1-3	0-0	3-0	4-3

Hartlepool U	Huddersfield T	Milton Keynes D	Nottingham F	Oldham Ath	Port Vale	Rotherham U	Scunthorpe U	Southend U	Swansea C	Swindon T	Tranmere R	Walsall	Yeovil T
1-1	2-2	2-0	2-0	4-0	1-1	1-1	5-2	2-2	2-2	2-0	2-1	2-1	1-0
1-2	0-1	3-2	2-2	1-0	1-0	0-0	5-2	1-2	1-0	0-0	1-1	2-0	2-0
1-1	1-1	2-0	1-1	0-0	1-2	2-0	1-1	1-1	0-1	2-1	0-0	0-0	1-0
0-1	1-2	2-0	1-1	1-4	1-0	1-2	4-2	0-2	1-1	1-1	0-0	2-0	1-1
1-1	2-0	1-0	1-1	3-3	0-1	2-1	2-0	2-0	2-1	0-0	2-0	5-0	3-2
0-1	2-0	2-2	1-1	2-1	4-2	3-1	1-1	0-3	1-0	1-1	1-0	3-0	2-1
3-1	4-3	1-2	1-3	1-1	2-0	0-1	1-2	3-4	0-4	1-1	0-2	2-2	0-3
2-0	1-1	2-0	3-1	0-0	2-1	2-0	1-0	0-3	1-2	1-0	1-0	0-0	3-2
0-1	1-2	1-1	1-2	1-0	1-1	3-1	3-1	2-0	2-1	1-0	0-2	1-0	0-1
1-0	2-0	3-0	1-3	0-1	3-0	1-1	1-3	1-2	1-0	3-0	1-1	0-1	0-0
—	3-1	2-1	3-2	1-1	1-1	0-0	3-3	1-2	2-2	1-1	0-0	1-1	0-1
2-1	—	5-0	2-1	3-2	0-3	4-1	1-4	0-0	3-1	1-1	1-0	3-1	1-2
2-1	2-2	—	1-0	0-1	0-0	1-1	1-0	2-1	1-3	3-1	1-2	2-1	1-1
2-0	2-1	3-0	—	3-0	1-0	2-0	0-1	2-0	1-2	7-1	1-0	1-1	2-1
2-1	0-3	1-2	3-0	—	0-1	0-1	1-1	0-0	1-1	2-2	1-0	2-1	2-0
1-2	1-1	3-1	0-2	2-2	—	2-0	1-2	2-1	3-2	1-1	0-2	3-2	1-0
0-0	1-1	0-0	1-1	2-0	1-1	—	1-1	2-4	2-2	0-1	2-0	1-2	1-2
2-0	2-2	2-0	3-1	4-2	2-0	2-2	—	1-0	2-2	1-2	1-2	1-3	3-4
3-0	1-1	0-0	1-0	2-1	1-2	2-0	3-0	—	1-2	2-0	3-1	0-0	4-1
1-1	2-2	3-1	1-1	0-0	0-0	0-2	2-0	2-2	—	2-1	1-0	1-1	2-0
1-1	0-0	0-1	2-1	2-3	1-2	2-3	1-1	1-2	0-0	—	1-2	1-0	4-2
0-0	2-1	1-2	0-1	4-0	3-0	3-2	0-2	0-0	2-2	1-0	—	1-2	4-1
1-0	1-3	1-1	3-2	0-2	1-1	3-1	2-2	2-2	2-5	1-0	0-0	—	0-2
2-0	1-2	1-1	3-0	0-2	1-0	0-0	0-1	0-2	1-0	0-0	2-2	2-1	—

COCA-COLA FOOTBALL LEAGUE

HOME TEAM	Barnet	Boston U	Bristol R	Bury	Carlisle U	Cheltenham T	Chester C	Darlington	Grimsby T	Leyton Orient
Barnet	—	1-0	1-1	1-1	1-2	1-1	1-3	1-0	0-1	2-3
Boston U	2-1	—	3-1	3-1	0-5	0-0	1-3	0-0	1-1	1-2
Bristol R	2-1	3-1	—	1-0	1-1	0-1	2-1	1-0	1-2	3-3
Bury	0-0	1-1	1-0	—	0-1	0-1	0-0	1-0	1-2	1-2
Carlisle U	1-3	4-2	1-3	4-0	—	1-1	5-0	1-1	1-0	2-3
Cheltenham T	1-1	3-0	2-3	2-1	2-3	—	1-0	1-1	0-3	1-1
Chester C	0-0	0-1	4-0	1-1	2-0	0-1	—	4-4	1-2	0-2
Darlington	2-1	0-0	1-1	2-3	0-5	3-1	1-0	—	0-0	0-1
Grimsby T	3-0	1-0	0-1	2-1	1-2	1-0	1-0	0-1	—	0-1
Leyton Orient	0-0	2-0	2-3	0-1	0-0	1-0	0-1	1-0	0-0	—
Lincoln C	4-1	0-0	1-0	1-1	0-0	0-1	3-1	2-2	5-0	1-1
Macclesfield T	1-1	2-2	2-1	1-0	3-0	2-2	1-0	1-0	1-1	0-0
Mansfield T	4-0	5-0	3-3	0-3	1-1	0-5	1-2	2-2	2-1	0-1
Northampton T	1-2	3-2	4-0	1-1	0-3	1-2	1-0	0-0	0-0	1-1
Notts Co	1-0	1-2	2-0	2-2	0-0	2-3	1-1	3-2	0-1	1-1
Oxford U	2-0	0-0	1-0	2-1	1-0	1-1	0-1	0-2	2-3	2-3
Peterborough U	2-2	0-1	1-2	4-1	1-1	1-0	0-1	2-1	0-1	1-1
Rochdale	1-1	1-1	2-0	1-1	0-2	1-1	2-2	0-2	2-2	2-4
Rushden & D	1-2	1-0	2-3	0-2	0-4	0-1	1-1	1-1	1-1	1-0
Shrewsbury T	2-2	1-1	1-0	0-1	2-1	2-0	3-1	3-1	0-0	3-3
Stockport Co	1-1	0-1	0-1	0-1	0-0	2-2	0-0	0-3	2-1	1-1
Torquay U	0-0	0-0	2-3	0-0	3-4	1-2	0-1	1-2	2-2	2-0
Wrexham	3-1	2-0	1-0	0-0	0-1	2-0	2-1	1-0	1-2	1-2
Wycombe W	1-0	1-1	1-3	4-0	1-1	0-0	3-3	0-1	3-1	4-2

DIVISION 2 2005–2006 RESULTS

Lincoln C	Macclesfield T	Mansfield T	Northampton T	Notts Co	Oxford U	Peterborough U	Rochdale	Rushden & D	Shrewsbury T	Stockport Co	Torquay U	Wrexham	Wycombe W
2-3	1-0	1-0	0-1	2-1	0-0	2-1	1-1	2-1	1-0	0-0	1-0	2-2	0-0
2-1	3-1	2-2	0-1	1-2	1-0	1-0	3-2	2-0	1-1	2-2	2-0	2-1	1-1
0-0	2-3	2-0	0-0	1-2	1-1	2-3	1-2	0-1	2-1	2-2	0-1	2-1	1-2
1-1	0-0	0-0	0-2	2-3	1-1	1-3	2-1	1-1	2-0	0-1	3-2	2-2	2-1
1-0	2-0	1-0	0-1	2-1	2-1	1-0	2-1	5-0	2-2	6-0	1-2	2-1	0-1
4-1	2-2	0-2	3-1	2-0	1-2	2-1	1-1	3-1	1-0	3-3	0-1	2-2	2-1
2-2	2-1	3-1	0-0	0-2	0-1	3-1	2-3	1-2	0-1	1-2	1-1	2-1	1-0
4-2	1-0	4-0	0-1	1-1	1-2	2-1	2-1	1-1	0-1	2-0	3-2	1-1	1-1
3-0	3-1	2-1	1-1	4-0	1-1	1-2	4-1	2-0	1-1	1-3	3-0	2-0	0-1
1-1	2-1	3-1	1-2	1-0	1-0	2-1	1-4	5-1	0-1	2-2	2-1	1-1	1-0
—	2-2	1-1	1-1	2-1	2-1	1-2	1-1	2-2	1-1	2-0	2-0	2-0	1-2
1-1	—	1-1	1-4	0-0	1-1	0-4	1-3	3-1	2-0	6-0	0-2	3-2	2-1
0-0	1-1	—	1-0	2-3	1-0	0-0	1-0	0-1	4-0	2-1	3-0	2-2	2-3
1-1	5-0	1-0	—	2-0	1-0	0-1	2-2	2-0	1-0	2-0	1-0	0-0	0-0
2-1	1-1	2-2	2-2	—	0-0	1-2	1-1	0-0	2-1	2-0	2-2	1-0	1-2
0-1	1-1	1-2	1-3	3-0	—	1-0	1-1	2-2	0-3	1-1	1-0	0-3	2-2
1-1	3-2	2-0	0-1	2-0	0-0	—	3-1	2-0	0-2	2-0	0-0	1-1	0-2
1-2	3-1	2-0	1-1	3-0	0-1	1-0	—	2-1	4-3	0-1	4-1	0-1	1-2
1-1	1-0	1-2	1-3	1-0	3-0	0-2	1-1	—	3-0	3-2	1-0	0-2	1-3
0-1	1-1	0-0	1-1	2-0	2-0	2-1	0-1	4-1	—	2-2	0-1	1-0	1-1
2-3	2-0	2-2	4-2	1-1	2-1	1-1	3-0	2-2	3-1	—	1-1	2-1	3-3
2-1	1-1	0-2	3-3	0-0	3-3	1-0	1-3	2-1	2-1	4-0	—	1-0	2-2
1-1	1-1	4-1	0-1	1-1	1-1	1-1	2-1	2-0	1-2	3-0	4-2	—	2-0
0-3	4-5	2-2	1-1	2-0	2-1	2-2	3-0	0-0	2-0	1-1	0-1	4-1	—

ACCRINGTON STANLEY   FL CHAMPIONSHIP 2

Player	Ht	Wt	Birthplace	D.O.B.	Source
Alcock Danny (G)	5 11	11 03	Staffordshire	15 2 84	Barnsley
Boco Romauld (M)	5 10	10 12		8 7 85	
Brown David (F)	5 10	12 07	Bolton	2 10 78	Hereford U
Cavanagh Peter (D)			Liverpool	14 10 81	Liverpool
Craney Ian (M)			Liverpool	21 7 82	Altrincham
Edwards Phil (D)			Kirkby	8 11 85	Wigan Ath
Jagielka Steve (M)	5 8	11 03	Manchester	10 3 78	Sheffield U
Mangan Andrew (F)	5 9	10 03	Liverpool	30 8 86	Blackpool
Mullin Paul (F)			Bury	16 3 74	Radcliffe Borough
Proctor Andy (M)			Lancashire	13 3 83	
Richardson Leam (D)	5 8	11 04	Blackpool	19 11 79	Leeds
Roberts Gary (M)			Wales	18 3 84	Welshpool T
Todd Andy (M)	6 0	11 03	Nottingham	22 2 79	Burton Alb
Tretton Andy (D)	6 0	11 07	Derby	9 10 76	Hereford U
Ventre Danny (D)				23 1 86	
Welch Michael (D)	6 3	11 12	Crewe	11 1 82	Macclesfield T
Williams Robbie (D)			Liverpool	12 4 79	St Dominics

League Appearances: Alcock, 1; Barry, 26; Boco, 24(6); Bossu, 1; Boyd, 4(2); Brown, D. 26(9); Brown, P. 1(2); Butler, 3; Cavanagh, 19(5); Cook, 1(3); Craney, 38(1); Dibble, 1; Edwards, 27; Elliott, 23; Flynn, 12; Jagielka, 22(8); Jones, 2; Mangan, 5(33); Mullin, 40(1); Navarro, 0(3); O'Neill, 0(3); Proctor, 3(3); Randolph, 14; Richardson, 33; Roberts, 40(2); Todd, 13(1); Tretton, 6(1); Ventre, 10(2); Welch, 32(1); Williams, 35(1).
Goals – League (76): Mullin 14, Craney 13 (1 pen), Roberts 13, Brown D 8 (1 pen), Jagielka 6, Todd 6, Mangan 5, Boco 4, Cavanagh 4 (3 pens), Welch 1, Williams 1, own goal 1.
FA Cup (3): Roberts 2, Welch 1.
Football League Trophy (3): Brown D 1, Mangan 1, Williams 1.
FA Trophy (8): Craney 3, Mullin 3, Boko 1, Brown D 1.
Ground: The Fraser Eagle Stadium, Livingstone Road, Accrington, Lancashire BB5 5BX. Telephone: 01254 356 950.
Record Attendance: 4368 v Colchester U, FA Cup 1st rd, 3 January 2004.).
Capacity: 5057.
Manager: John Coleman.
Secretary: Hannah Bailey.
Most League Goals: 96, Division 3 (N) 1954–55.
Highest League Scorer in Season: George Stewart, 35, 1955–56 and George Hudson, 35, 1960–61.
Most League Goals in Total Aggregate: George Stewart 136, 1954–58.
Most League Appearances: Jim Armstrong, 260, 1927–34.
Colours: Red shirts, white shorts, red stockings.

ARSENAL   FA PREMIERSHIP

Adebayor Emmanuel (F)	6 4	11 08	Lome	26 2 84	Monaco
Aliadiere Jeremie (F)	6 0	11 00	Rambouillet	30 3 83	Scholar
Almunia Manuel (G)	6 3	13 00	Pamplona	19 5 77	Celta Vigo
Bendtner Nicklas (F)	6 2	13 00	Copenhagen	16 1 88	Scholar
Campbell Sol (D)	6 2	15 07	Newham	18 9 74	Tottenham H
Clichy Gael (D)	5 9	10 04	Toulouse	26 7 85	Cannes
Cole Ashley (D)	5 8	10 05	Stepney	20 12 80	Trainee
Connolly Matthew (D)	6 1	11 03	Barnet	24 9 87	Scholar
Cygan Pascal (D)	6 4	13 12	Lens	19 4 74	Lille

20

Diaby Vassirki (M)	6 2	12 04	Paris	11 5 86	Auxerre
Djourou Johan (D)	6 3	13 01	Ivory Coast	18 1 87	Scholar
Eboue Emmanuel (D)	5 10	10 03	Abidjan	4 6 83	Beveren
Fabregas Francesc (M)	5 11	11 01	Vilessoc de Mar	4 5 87	Barcelona
Flamini Mathieu (M)	5 11	11 10	Marseille	7 3 84	Marseille
Garry Ryan (D)	6 0	11 05	Hornchurch	29 9 83	Scholar
Gilbert Kerrea (D)	5 6	11 03	Willesden	28 2 87	Scholar
Henry Thierry (F)	6 2	13 05	Paris	17 8 77	Juventus
Hleb Aleksandr (M)	5 10	11 07	Minsk	1 5 81	Stuttgart
Hoyte Justin (D)	5 11	11 00	Waltham Forest	20 11 84	Scholar
Larsson Sebastian (M)	5 10	11 00	Eskiltuna	6 6 85	Trainee
Lauren Etame-Mayer (D)	5 11	11 07	Londi Kribi	19 1 77	Mallorca
Lehmann Jens (G)	6 4	13 05	Essen	10 11 69	Borussia Dortmund
Ljungberg Frederik (M)	5 9	11 00	Vittsjo	16 4 77	Halmstad
Lupoli Arturo (F)	5 9	10 07	Brescia	24 6 87	Parma
Mannone Vito (G)	6 0	11 08	Desio	2 3 88	Atalanta
Muamba Fabrice (M)	6 1	11 10	DR Congo	6 4 88	Scholar
Poom Mart (G)	6 4	14 02	Tallinn	3 2 72	Sunderland
Reyes Jose Antonio (F)	5 9	12 01	Utrera	1 9 83	Sevilla
Senderos Philippe (D)	6 1	13 10	Geneva	14 2 85	Servette
Silva Gilberto (M)	6 3	12 04	Lagoa da Prata	7 10 76	Atletico Mineiro
Smith Ryan (M)	5 10	11 00	Islington	10 11 86	Scholar
Toure Kolo (D)	5 10	13 08	Ivory Coast	19 3 81	ASEC Mimosas
Van Persie Robin (F)	6 0	11 00	Rotterdam	6 8 83	Feyenoord
Walcott Theo (F)	5 9	11 01	Compton	16 3 89	Southampton

League Appearances: Adebayor, E. 12(1); Bergkamp, D. 8(16); Campbell, S. 20; Clichy, G. 5(2); Cole, A. 9(2); Cygan, P. 11(1); Diaby, V. 9(3); Djourou, J. 6(1); Eboue, E. 11(7); Fabregas, F. 30(5); Flamini, M. 19(12); Gilbert, K. 2; Henry, T. 30(2); Hleb, A. 17(8); Larsson, S. 2(1); Lauren, E. 22; Lehmann, J. 38; Ljungberg, F. 21(4); Lupoli, A. (1); Owusu-Abeyie, Q. (4); Pires, R. 23(10); Reyes, J. 22(4); Senderos, P. 19(1); Silva, G. 33; Song Billong, A. 3(2); Toure, K. 33; Van Persie, R. 13(11).
Goals – League (68): Henry 27 (3 pens), Pires 7 (1 pen), Reyes 5, Van Persie 5, Adebayor 4, Fabregas 3, Hleb 3, Bergkamp 2, Campbell 2, Cygan 2, Senderos 2, Silva 2, Diaby 1, Ljungberg 1, own goals 2.
Carling Cup (10): Van Persie 4 (1 pen), Eboue 1, Henry 1, Lupoli 1, Owusu-Abeyie 1, Reyes 1, Silva 1.
FA Cup (2): Pires 2.
Community Shield (1): Fabregas 1.
Champions League (15): Henry 5, Pires 2 (2 pens), Van Persie 2, Bergkamp 1, Campbell 1, Fabregas 1, Ljungberg 1, Silva 1, Toure 1.
Ground: Emirates Stadium, Drayton Park, London N5. Telephone (020) 7704 4000.
Record Attendance: 73,295 v Sunderland, Div 1, 9 March 1935. **Capacity:** 60,000.
Manager: Arsène Wenger.
Secretary: David Miles.
Most League Goals: 127, Division 1, 1930–31.
Highest League Scorer in Season: Ted Drake, 42, 1934–35.
Most League Goals in Total Aggregate: Thierry Henry, 164, 1999–.
Most Capped Player: Patrick Vieira, 79 (94), France.
Most League Appearances: David O'Leary, 558, 1975–93.
Honours – FA Premier League: Champions – 1997–98, 2001–02, 2003–04. **Football League:** Division 1 Champions – 1930–31, 1932–33, 1933–34, 1934–35, 1937–38, 1947–48, 1952–53, 1970–71, 1988–89, 1990–91. **FA Cup:** Winners – 1929–30, 1935–36, 1949–50, 1970–71, 1978–79, 1992–93, 1997–98, 2001–02, 2002–03, 2004–05. **Football League Cup:** Winners – 1986–87, 1992–93. **European Competitions: European Cup-Winners' Cup:** Winners – 1993–94. **Fairs Cup:** Winners – 1969–70.
Colours: Red shirts with white sleeves, white shorts and stockings.

Player					
Agbonlahor Gabriel (F)	5 11	12 05	Birmingham	13 10 86	Scholar
Angel Juan Pablo (F)	6 0	12 10	Medellin	24 10 75	River Plate
Baros Milan (F)	6 0	12 00	Valasske Mezirici	28 10 81	Liverpool
Barry Gareth (D)	5 11	12 06	Hastings	23 2 81	Trainee
Berger Patrik (M)	6 1	12 06	Prague	10 11 73	Portsmouth
Berson Mathieu (M)	5 9	11 06	Vannes	23 2 80	Nantes
Bouma Wilfred (D)	5 10	13 01	Helmond	15 6 78	PSV Eindhoven
Boyle Lee (M)	5 11	10 08	Donegal	22 1 88	Scholar
Bridges Scott (D)	5 7	13 08	Oxford	3 5 88	Scholar
Cahill Gary (D)	6 2	12 06	Dronfield	19 12 85	Trainee
Davis Steven (M)	5 7	9 07	Ballymena	1 1 85	Scholar
Delaney Mark (D)	6 1	11 07	Haverfordwest	13 5 76	Carmarthen T
Djemba-Djemba Eric (M)	5 9	11 13	Douala	4 5 81	Manchester U
Gardner Craig (M)	5 10	11 13	Solihull	25 11 86	Scholar
Green Paul (D)	5 8	10 04	Birmingham	15 4 87	Scholar
Henderson Stephen (G)	6 3	11 00	Dublin	2 5 88	Scholar
Hendrie Lee (M)	5 10	11 00	Birmingham	18 5 77	Trainee
Hughes Aaron (D)	6 0	11 02	Cookstown	8 11 79	Newcastle U
Laursen Martin (D)	6 2	12 05	Silkeborg	26 7 77	AC Milan
McCann Gavin (M)	5 11	11 00	Blackpool	10 1 78	Sunderland
McGurk Adam (F)	5 9	12 13	St Helier	24 1 89	Scholar
Mellberg Olof (D)	6 1	12 10	Amncharad	3 9 77	Santander
Mikaelsson Tobias (F)	6 3	11 04	Jorlanda	17 11 88	Scholar
Moore Luke (F)	5 11	11 13	Birmingham	13 2 86	Trainee
O'Halloran Stephen (D)	6 0	11 07	Cork	29 11 87	Scholar
Olejnik Robert (G)	6 0	15 06	Vienna	26 11 86	Scholar
Osbourne Isaiah (M)	6 2	12 07	Birmingham	5 11 87	Scholar
Phillips Kevin (F)	5 7	11 00	Hitchin	25 7 73	Southampton
Ridgewell Liam (D)	5 10	10 03	Bexley	21 7 84	Scholar
Samuel J Lloyd (D)	5 11	11 04	Trinidad	29 3 81	Charlton Ath
Sorensen Thomas (G)	6 4	13 10	Fredericia	12 6 76	Sunderland
Taylor Stuart (G)	6 5	13 07	Romford	28 11 80	Arsenal
Tshimanga Christian (M)	5 9	11 10	Kinshasa	16 6 87	Scholar
Whittingham Peter (D)	5 10	9 13	Nuneaton	8 9 84	Trainee
Williams Sam (M)	5 11	10 08	London	9 6 87	Scholar

League Appearances: Agbonlahor, G. 3(6); Angel, J. 12(19); Bakke, E. 8(6); Baros, M. 24(1); Barry, G. 36; Berger, P. 3(5); Bouma, W. 20; Cahill, G. 6(1); Davis, S. 34(1); De la Cruz, U. 4(3); Delaney, M. 12; Djemba-Djemba, E. (4); Gardner, C. 3(5); Hendrie, L. 7(9); Hughes, A. 35; Laursen, M. 1; McCann, G. 32; Mellberg, O. 27; Milner, J. 27; Moore, L. 16(11); Phillips, K. 20(3); Ridgewell, L. 30(2); Samuel, J. 14(5); Solano, N. 2(1); Sorensen, T. 36; Taylor, S. 2; Whittingham, P. 4.

Goals – League (42): Baros 8 (1 pen), Moore 8, Ridgewell 5, Davis 4, Phillips 4, Angel 3, Barry 3, Agbonlahor 1, Cahill 1, Delaney 1, Hendrie 1, McCann 1, Milner 1, own goal 1.

Carling Cup (9): Barry 2 (1 pen), Davis 2, Milner 2, Baros 1, Phillips 1, own goal 1.

FA Cup (6): Baros 3, Davis 2, Barry 1.

Ground: Villa Park, Trinity Road, Birmingham B6 6HE. Telephone (0121) 327 2299.

Record Attendance: 76,588 v Derby Co, FA Cup 6th rd, 2 March 1946.

Capacity: 42,584.

Manager: David O'Leary.

Secretary: Steven Stride.

Most League Goals: 128, Division 1, 1930–31.

Highest League Scorer in Season: 'Pongo' Waring, 49, Division 1, 1930–31.

Most League Goals in Total Aggregate: Harry Hampton, 215, 1904–15.

Most Capped Player: Steve Staunton 64 (102), Republic of Ireland.
Most League Appearances: Charlie Aitken, 561, 1961–76.
Honours – Football League: Division 1 Champions – 1893–94, 1895–96, 1896–97, 1898–99, 1899–1900, 1909–10, 1980–81. Division 2 Champions – 1937–38, 1959–60. Division 3 Champions – 1971–72. **FA Cup:** Winners – 1887, 1895, 1897, 1905, 1913, 1920, 1957. **Football League Cup:** Winners – 1961, 1975, 1977, 1994, 1996. **European Competitions: European Cup:** Winners – 1981–82. **European Super Cup:** Winners: – 1982–83. **Intertoto Cup:** Winners – 2001.
Colours: Claret and blue shirts, white shorts, sky blue stockings with claret top.

BARNET   FL CHAMPIONSHIP 2

Bailey Nicky (M)	5 10	12 08	Putney	10	6 84	Sutton U
Charles Anthony (D)	6 1	12 07	Isleworth	11	3 81	Farnborough T
Devera Joe (D)	6 2	12 00	Southgate	6	2 87	
Flitney Ross (G)	6 3	12 07	Hitchin	1	6 84	Fulham
Graham Richard (F)	5 10	12 03	London	20	3 75	Bristol R
Grazioli Guiliano (F)	5 10	12 00	Marylebone	23	3 75	Bristol R
Gross Adam (D)	5 10	10 09	Thamesmead	16	2 86	Charlton Ath
Hatch Liam (F)	6 4	13 01	Hitchin	3	4 82	Gravesend & Northfleet
Hendon Ian (D)	6 1	13 05	Ilford	5	12 71	Peterborough U
Kandol Tresor (F)	6 0	13 07	Banga	30	8 81	Dagenham & R
King Simon (D)	6 0	13 00	Oxford	11	4 83	Oxford U
Norville Jason (F)	6 0	11 03	Trinidad	9	9 83	Watford
Sinclair Dean (M)	5 10	11 00	St Albans	17	12 84	Norwich C
Warhurst Paul (D)	6 1	13 00	Stockport	26	9 69	Wrexham
Yakubu Ishmail (D)	6 1	12 09	Nigeria	8	4 85	

League Appearances: Bailey, N. 45; Batt, D. 12(10); Bowditch, B. 3(3); Charles, A. 39(1); Clist, S. 12(2); Flitney, R. 35; Fuller, B. 15; Graham, R. 13(2); Grazioli, G. 27(2); Gross, A. 18(2); Hatch, L. 21(14); Hendon, I. 34(1); Hessenthaler, A. 16; Kandol, T. 13; King, S. 31(1); Lee, D. 24(3); Norville, J. 7(15); Reed, M. 4; Roache, L. 2(6); Sinclair, D. 39(5); Soares, L. 14(6); Strevens, B. 31(4); Tynan, S. 7; Varney, A. (1); Vernazza, P. 11(6); Warhurst, P. 7(2); Yakubu, I. 26.
Goals – League (44): Bailey 7 (1 pen), Grazioli 7, Strevens 5, Hendon 4 (4 pens), Kandol 4, Lee 4, Hatch 2, Norville 2, Sinclair 2, Fuller 1, Graham 1, Hessenthaler 1, Roache 1, Soares 1, Yakubu 1, own goal 1.
Carling Cup (7): Lee 2, Bailey 1, Grazioli 1, King 1, Roache 1, Sinclair 1.
FA Cup (0).
Football League Trophy (3): Bailey 1, Norville 1, Sinclair 1.
Ground: Underhill Stadium, Barnet Lane, Barnet, Herts EN5 2BE. Telephone 0870 1700 400.
Record Attendance: 11,026 v Wycombe Wanderers, FA Amateur Cup 4th Round 1951–52. **Capacity:** 4,800.
Manager: Paul Fairclough.
Secretary: Andrew Adie.
Most League Goals: 81, Division 4, 1991–92
Highest League Scorer in Season: Dougie Freedman, 24, Division 3, 1994–95.
Most League Goals in Total Aggregate: Sean Devine, 47, 1995–99.
Most Capped Player: Ken Charlery, 4, St. Lucia.
Most League Appearances: Paul Wilson, 263, 1991–2000.
Honours – Football League: GMVC: Champions – 1990–91. **Football Conference:** Champions – 2004–05. **FA Amateur Cup:** Winners 1945–46.
Colours: Amber with black trim.

Name			Birthplace	Date		Previous Club
Atkinson Rob (M)	6 1	12 00	North Ferriby	29	4 87	Scholar
Austin Neil (D)	5 10	11 09	Barnsley	26	4 83	Trainee
Colgan Nick (G)	6 1	13 06	Drogheda	19	9 73	Hibernian
Devaney Martin (M)	5 11	12 00	Cheltenham	1	6 80	Watford
Flinders Scott (G)	6 4	14 00	Rotherham	12	6 86	Scholar
Harban Thomas (D)	6 0	11 09	Barnsley	12	11 85	Scholar
Hassell Bobby (D)	5 10	12 00	Derby	4	6 80	Trainee
Hayes Paul (F)	6 0	12 12	Dagenham	20	9 83	Scunthorpe U
Heckingbottom Paul (D)	6 0	13 01	Barnsley	17	7 77	Sheffield W
Heslop Simon (M)	5 11	11 00	York	1	5 87	Scholar
Howard Brian (M)	5 8	11 00	Winchester	23	1 83	Swindon T
Jarman Nathan (F)	5 11	11 03	Scunthorpe	19	9 86	Scholar
Joynes Nathan (M)	6 1	12 00	Hoyland	7	8 85	Scholar
Kay Antony (D)	5 11	11 08	Barnsley	21	10 82	Trainee
Laight Ryan (D)	6 2	11 09	Barnsley	16	11 85	Scholar
McParland Anthony (M)	5 7	10 07	Rutherglen	20	9 82	Celtic
McPhail Stephen (M)	5 8	11 04	Westminster	9	12 79	Leeds U
Nardiello Daniel (F)	5 11	11 04	Coventry	22	10 82	Manchester U
Reid Paul (D)	6 2	11 08	Carlisle	18	2 82	Northampton T
Richards Marc (F)	6 2	12 06	Wolverhampton	8	7 82	Northampton T
Shuker Chris (M)	5 5	9 03	Liverpool	9	5 82	Manchester C
Tonge Dale (D)	5 10	10 06	Doncaster	7	5 85	Scholar
Williams Robbie (D)	5 10	11 13	Pontefract	2	10 84	Scholar
Wright Tommy (F)	6 0	12 02	Leicester	28	9 84	Leicester C
Wroe Nicky (M)	5 11	10 02	Sheffield	28	9 85	Scholar

League Appearances: Austin, N. 38; Burns, J. 32(1); Carbon, M. 21(3); Colgan, N. 43; Conlon, B. 8(3); Devaney, M. 34(4); Flinders, S. 3; Hassell, B. 25(3); Hayes, P. 38(7); Heckingbottom, P. 17(1); Howard, B. 25(6); Jarman, N. (9); Kay, A. 33(3); Kell, R. (2); Laight, R. (1); McParland, A. (8); McPhail, S. 30(4); Nardiello, D. 11(23); Reid, P. 31(2); Richards, M. 29(9); Shuker, C. 45(1); Tonge, D. 14(10); Vaughan, T. (1); Watt, S. 3; Williams, R. 13(9); Wright, T. 7(10); Wroe, N. 6(6).
Goals – League (62): Richards 12 (4 pens), Shuker 10, Devaney 6, Hayes 6, Howard 5, Nardiello 5 (1 pen), Burns 3, Hassell 2, McPhail 2, Williams 2 (1 pen), Carbon 1, Conlon 1, Heckingbottom 1, Kay 1, Watt 1, Wright 1, own goals 3.
Carling Cup (2): Burns 2.
FA Cup (8): Hayes 5, Devaney 2, Reid 1.
Football League Trophy (2): Nardiello 1, own goal 1.
Play-Offs (5): Hayes 2 (1 pen), Nardiello 2, Reid 1.
Ground: Oakwell Stadium, Grove St, Barnsley S71 1ET. Telephone (01226) 211 211.
Record Attendance: 40,255 v Stoke C, FA Cup 5th rd, 15 February 1936. **Capacity:** 23,186.
Manager: Andy Ritchie.
Secretary: A. D. Rowing.
Most League Goals: 118, Division 3 (N), 1933–34.
Highest League Scorer in Season: Cecil McCormack, 33, Division 2, 1950–51.
Most League Goals in Total Aggregate: Ernest Hine, 123, 1921–26 and 1934–38.
Most Capped Player: Gerry Taggart, 35 (50), Northern Ireland.
Most League Appearances: Barry Murphy, 514, 1962–78.
Honours – Football League: Division 3 (N) Champions – 1933–34, 1938–39, 1954–55. **FA Cup:** Winners – 1912.
Colours: Red shirts, white shorts, red stockings.

Allen Oliver (F)	5 9	10 05	Essex	7	9 86	
Birley Matt (M)	5 8	11 01	Bromsgrove	26	7 86	Scholar
Bruce Alex (D)	6 0	11 06	Norwich	28	9 84	Blackburn R
Burge Ryan (M)	5 10	10 03	Cheltenham	12	10 88	Scholar
Campbell Dudley (F)	5 10	11 00	London	12	11 81	Brentford
Clemence Stephen (M)	6 0	12 09	Liverpool	31	3 78	Tottenham H
Doyle Colin (G)	6 5	14 05	Cork	12	8 85	Chelsea
Dunn David (M)	5 9	12 03	Gt Harwood	27	12 79	Blackburn R
Forssell Mikael (F)	5 10	10 10	Steinfourt	15	3 81	Chelsea
Gray Julian (M)	6 1	11 00	Lewisham	21	9 79	Crystal Palace
Hall Asa (M)	6 2	11 09	Dudley	29	11 86	Scholar
Harthill Oliver (M)	5 11	11 05	Birmingham	7	9 88	Scholar
Heskey Emile (F)	6 2	13 12	Leicester	11	1 78	Liverpool
Hinks Brett (M)			Birmingham	11	87	Scholar
Howland David (M)	5 11	10 08	Ballynahinch	17	9 86	Scholar
Izzet Muzzy (M)	5 10	10 03	Mile End	31	10 74	Leicester C
Jerome Cameron (F)	6 1	13 06	Huddersfield	14	8 86	Cardiff C
Johnson Damien (M)	5 9	11 09	Lisburn	18	11 78	Blackburn R
Kilkenny Neil (M)	5 8	10 08	Middlesex	19	12 85	Arsenal
McPike James (F)	5 10	11 02	Birmingham	4	10 88	Scholar
Nafti Mehdi (M)	5 9	11 03	Toulouse	20	11 78	Santander
Oji Samuel (D)	6 0	14 05	Westminster	9	10 85	
Painter Marcos (D)	5 11	12 04	Sutton Coldfield	17	8 86	Scholar
Pennant Jermaine (M)	5 9	10 06	Nottingham	15	1 83	Arsenal
Sadler Matthew (D)	5 11	11 08	Birmingham	26	2 85	Scholar
Taylor Maik (G)	6 4	14 02	Hildeshein	4	9 71	Fulham
Taylor Martin (D)	6 4	15 00	Ashington	9	11 79	Blackburn R
Tebily Oliver (D)	6 0	13 05	Abidjan	19	12 75	Celtic
Till Peter (M)	5 11	11 04	Walsall	7	9 85	Scholar
Upson Matthew (D)	6 1	11 04	Eton	18	4 79	Arsenal

League Appearances: Birley, M. (1); Bruce, A. 3(3); Butt, N. 22(2); Campbell, D. 4(7); Clapham, J. 13(3); Clemence, S. 13(2); Cunningham, K. 31; Dunn, D. 8(7); Forssell, M. 10(17); Gray, J. 18(3); Heskey, E. 34; Izzet, M. 10(6); Jarosik, J. 19(5); Johnson, D. 31; Kilkenny, N. 6(12); Latka, M. 6; Lazaridis, S. 11(6); Melchiot, M. 22(1); Morrison, C. (1); Nafti, M. 1; Painter, M. 2(2); Pandiani, W. 7(10); Pennant, J. 35(2); Sadler, M. 8; Sutton, C. 10; Taylor, Maik 34; Taylor, Martin 20(1); Tebily, O. 12(4); Upson, M. 24; Vaesen, N. 4.

Goals – League (28): Jarosik 5, Heskey 4, Butt 3, Forssell 3 (2 pens), Dunn 2, Pandiani 2, Pennant 2, Clapham 1, Gray 1, Melchiot 1, Sutton 1, Upson 1, own goals 2.

Carling Cup (7): Forssell 2 (1 pen), Jarosik 2, Gray 1, Heskey 1, Pennant 1.

FA Cup (6): Forssell 3, Dunn 1, Gray 1, Jarosik 1.

Ground: St Andrews Stadium, Birmingham B9 4NH. Telephone (0871) 226 1875.

Record Attendance: 66,844 v Everton, FA Cup 5th rd, 11 February 1939. **Capacity:** 30,007 (all seated).

Manager: Steve Bruce.

Secretary: Julia Shelton.

Most League Goals: 103, Division 2, 1893–94 (only 28 games).

Highest League Scorer in Season: Joe Bradford, 29, Division 1, 1927–28.

Most League Goals in Total Aggregate: Joe Bradford, 249, 1920–35.

Most Capped Player: Kenny Cunningham, 32 (72), Republic of Ireland.

Most League Appearances: Frank Womack, 491, 1908–28.

Honours – Football League: Division 2 Champions – 1892–93, 1920–21, 1947–48, 1954–55, 1994–95. **Football League Cup:** Winners – 1963. **Leyland Daf Cup:** Winners – 1991. **Auto Windscreens Shield:** Winners – 1995.

Colours: Royal blue shirts with white trim, white shorts with royal blue trim, white stockings with royal blue trim.

Player	Ht	Wt	Birthplace	Date	Previous Club
Ahmed Abdi (M)	5 9	11 05	Cardiff	10 10 88	Scholar
Barker Keith (F)	6 2	12 12	Accrington	21 10 86	Scholar
Bellamy Craig (F)	5 9	10 12	Cardiff	13 7 79	Newcastle U
Bentley David (F)	5 10	11 03	Peterborough	27 8 84	Arsenal
De Vita Raffaele (F)	6 0	11 09	Rome	23 9 87	Scholar
Derbyshire Matt (F)	5 10	11 01	Gt Harwood	14 4 86	Great Harwood T
Douglas Jonathan (M)	6 0	12 07	Clones	22 11 81	Blackpool
Emerton Brett (M)	6 1	13 05	Bankstown	22 2 79	Feyenoord
Enckelman Peter (G)	6 2	12 05	Turku	10 3 77	Aston Villa
Friedel Brad (G)	6 3	14 00	Lakewood	18 5 71	Liverpool
Gallagher Paul (F)	6 1	12 00	Glasgow	9 8 84	Trainee
Garner Joseph (F)			Blackburn	12 4 88	Scholar
Gray Michael (D)	5 8	10 07	Sunderland	3 8 74	Sunderland
Griffiths Rostyn (M)	6 2	12 08	Stoke	10 3 88	Scholar
Hodge Bryan (M)	5 10	12 02	Hamilton	23 9 87	Scholar
Johnson Jemal (F)	5 8	11 09	New Jersey	3 5 84	Scholar
Jones Zak (G)	5 11	12 08	Darwen	24 11 88	Scholar
Kane Tony (D)	5 11	11 00	Belfast	29 8 87	Scholar
Khizanishvili Zurab (D)	6 1	12 08	Tbilisi	6 10 81	Rangers
Kuqi Shefki (F)	6 2	13 13	Albania	10 11 76	Ipswich T
Matteo Dominic (D)	6 1	13 08	Dumfries	28 4 74	Leeds U
McEveley James (D)	6 1	13 03	Liverpool	11 2 85	Trainee
Mokoena Aaron (D)	6 2	14 00	Johannesburg	25 11 80	Genk
Neill Lucas (D)	6 0	12 03	Sydney	9 3 78	Millwall
Nelsen Ryan (D)	5 11	14 02	New Zealand	18 10 77	DC United
Nolan Eddie (D)	6 0	13 05	Waterford	5 8 88	Scholar
O'Keefe Josh (M)	6 1	11 05	Whalley	22 12 88	Scholar
Olsson Martin (D)			Sweden	17 5 88	Hogaborg
Pedersen Morten (F)	5 11	11 00	Vadso	8 9 81	Tromso
Peter Sergio (M)	5 8	11 00	Ludwigshafen	12 10 86	Scholar
Reid Steven (M)	6 0	12 07	Kingston	10 3 81	Millwall
Savage Robbie (M)	5 11	11 00	Wrexham	18 10 74	Birmingham C
Taylor Andy (D)	5 11	11 07	Blackburn	14 3 86	Scholar
Thomas Adam (D)	6 1	11 11	Stockport	1 1 88	Scholar
Thomson Stephen (D)	5 10	12 04	Edinburgh	7 3 88	Scholar
Todd Andy (D)	5 11	13 04	Derby	21 9 74	Charlton Ath
Treacy Keith (M)	5 11	11 11	Dublin	13 9 88	Scholar
Tugay Kerimoglu (M)	5 9	11 07	Istanbul	24 8 70	Rangers

League Appearances: Bellamy, C. 22(5); Bentley, D. 23(6); Dickov, P. 17(4); Emerton, B. 17(13); Flitcroft, G. 1(1); Friedel, B. 38; Gallagher, P. (1); Gray, M. 30; Gresko, V. 1(2); Jansen, M. 1(3); Johnson, J. (3); Khizanishvili, Z. 24(2); Kuqi, S. 15(18); Matteo, D. 6; Mokoena, A. 4(18); Neill, L. 35; Nelsen, R. 31; Pedersen, M. 34; Peter, S. 1(7); Reid, S. 31(3); Savage, R. 34; Sinama-Pongolle, F. 8(2); Thompson, D. 2(4); Todd, A. 20(2); Tugay, K. 23(4).

Goals – League (51): Bellamy 13 (1 pen), Pedersen 9, Kuqi 7, Dickov 5 (2 pens), Reid 4, Bentley 3, Todd 2, Emerton 1, Khizanishvili 1, Neill 1 (pen), Savage 1, Sinama-Pongolle 1, Tugay 1, own goals 2.

Carling Cup (12): Bellamy 2, Dickov 2, Bentley 1, Emerton 1, Khizanishvili 1, Kuqi 1, Neill 1, Pedersen 1, Reid 1, Thompson 1.

FA Cup (5): Bellamy 2, Bentley 1, Neill 1, Todd 1.

Ground: Ewood Park, Blackburn BB2 4JF. Telephone (0870) 111 3232.

Record Attendance: 61,783 v Bolton W, FA Cup 6th rd, 2 March, 1929. **Capacity:** 31,154.

Manager: Mark Hughes.

Secretary: Andrew Pincher.

Most League Goals: 114, Division 2, 1954–55.
Highest League Scorer in Season: Ted Harper, 43, Division 1, 1925–26.
Most League Goals in Total Aggregate: Simon Garner, 168, 1978–92.
Most Capped Player: Henning Berg, 58 (100), Norway.
Most League Appearances: Derek Fazackerley, 596, 1970–86.
Honours – FA Premier League: Champions – 1994–95. **Football League:** Division 1 Champions – 1911–12, 1913–14. Division 2 Champions – 1938–39. Division 3 Champions – 1974–75. **FA Cup:** Winners – 1884, 1885, 1886, 1890, 1891, 1928. **Football League Cup:** Winners – 2002. **Full Members' Cup:** Winners – 1986–87.
Colours: Blue and white halved shirts.

BLACKPOOL   FL CHAMPIONSHIP 1

Bean Marcus (M)	5 11	11 06	Hammersmith	2 11 84	QPR
Blinkhorn Matthew (F)	5 11	10 10	Blackpool	2 3 85	Scholar
Burns Jamie (M)	5 9	10 11	Blackpool	6 3 84	Scholar
Clarke Peter (D)	6 0	12 00	Southport	3 1 82	Everton
Coid Danny (D)	5 11	11 07	Liverpool	3 10 81	Trainee
Donnelly Ciaran (M)	5 9	11 09	Blackpool	2 4 84	Blackburn R
Doughty Phil (D)	6 2	13 02	Kirkham	6 9 86	
Edge Lewis (G)	6 1	12 10	Lancaster	12 1 87	Scholar
Fox David (M)	5 9	11 08	Leek	13 12 83	Manchester U
Jones Lee (G)	6 3	14 04	Pontypridd	9 8 70	Stockport Co
Joseph Marc (D)	6 0	12 05	Leicester	10 11 76	Hull C
Murphy John (F)	6 2	14 00	Whiston	18 10 76	Chester C
Parker Keigan (F)	5 7	10 05	Livington	8 6 82	St Johnstone
Paterson Sean (M)	5 11	11 05	Greenock	26 3 87	Scholar
Prendergast Rory (F)	5 8	12 00	Pontefract	6 4 78	Accrington S
Southern Keith (M)	5 10	12 06	Gateshead	24 4 81	Everton
Vernon Scott (F)	6 1	11 06	Manchester	13 12 83	Oldham Ath
Whittaker Danny (M)	6 0	11 10	Blackpool	13 1 87	Scholar
Wiles Simon (M)	5 11	11 04	Preston	22 4 85	Scholar
Wood Neil (M)	5 10	13 02	Manchester	4 1 83	Coventry C

League Appearances: Armstrong, C. 5; Bean, M. 17; Blinkhorn, M. 4(12); Burns, J. 4(2); Butler, T. 19(5); Clarke, P. 46; Coid, D. 13; Donnelly, C. 17(7); Doolan, J. 15(4); Edge, L. (1); Edwards, R. 28(4); Fox, D. 4(3); Gobern, L. 4(4); Gordon, D. 1; Grayson, S. 8(4); Harkins, G. 4; Jones, L. 31; Joseph, M. 15(1); Kay, M. (1); Kuqi, N. 1(3); Lasley, K. 4(4); McGregor, M. 16(5); Morris, I. 21(9); Murphy, J. 28(6); Parker, K. 36(4); Pogliacomi, L. 15; Prendergast, R. 19(5); Southern, K. 36(6); Stockley, S. 3(4); Taylor, A. 3; Taylor, S. 3(1); Vernon, S. 10(7); Warrender, D. 13(2); Wilcox, J. 26; Wiles, S. 14(13); Williams, G. 6(3); Wood, N. 7; Wright, T. 10(3).
Goals – League (56): Parker 12, Murphy 8, Clarke 6 (3 pens), Wright 6, Morris 3, Wiles 3, Williams 3, Blinkhorn 2, Donnelly 2, Southern 2, Bean 1, Burns 1, Butler 1, Fox 1, Gobern 1, Harkins 1, Vernon 1, own goals 2.
Carling Cup (3): Clarke 1 (pen), Grayson 1, Parker 1.
FA Cup (1): Clarke 1 (pen).
Football League Trophy (5): Blinkhorn 1, Harkins 1, McGregor 1, Southern 1, Vernon 1.
Ground: Bloomfield Road, Seasiders Way, Blackpool FY1 6JJ. Telephone (0870) 443 1953.
Record Attendance: 38,098 v Wolverhampton W, Division 1, 17 September 1955.
Capacity: 9,612.
Manager: Simon Grayson.
Secretary: Matt Williams.
Most League Goals: 98, Division 2, 1929–30.

Highest League Scorer in Season: Jimmy Hampson, 45, Division 2, 1929–30.
Most League Goals in Total Aggregate: Jimmy Hampson, 246, 1927–38.
Most Capped Player: Jimmy Armfield, 43, England.
Most League Appearances: Jimmy Armfield, 568, 1952–71.
Honours – Football League: Division 2 Champions – 1929–30. **FA Cup:** Winners –
1953. **Anglo-Italian Cup:** Winners – 1971. **LDV Vans Trophy:** Winners – 2002, 2004.
Colours: Tangerine shirts, white shorts, tangerine stockings.

BOLTON WANDERERS   FA PREMIERSHIP

Al-Habsi Ali (G)	6 4	12 06	Oman	30 12 81	Lyn
Ben Haim Tal (D)	5 11	11 09	Rishon Le Zion	31 3 82	Maccabi Tel Aviv
Borgetti Jared (F)	6 0	12 04	Culican	14 8 73	Dorados
Davies Kevin (F)	6 0	12 10	Sheffield	26 3 77	Southampton
Diouf El Hadji (F)	5 11	11 11	Dakar	15 1 81	Liverpool
Faye Aboulaye (M)	6 2	13 10	Dakar	26 2 78	Istres
Gardner Ricardo (D)	5 9	11 00	St Andrews	25 9 78	Harbour View
Giannakopoulos Stelios (M)	5 8	11 00	Athens	12 7 74	Olympiakos
Howarth Chris (G)			Bolton	23 5 86	Scholar
Hunt Nicky (D)	6 1	13 08	Westhoughton	3 9 83	Scholar
Jaaskelainen Jussi (G)	6 3	12 10	Mikkeli	19 4 75	VPS
Jaidi Radhi (D)	6 4	14 00	Tunis	30 8 75	Esperance
Nolan Kevin (M)	6 0	14 00	Liverpool	24 6 82	Scholar
O'Brien Joey (M)	6 0	10 13	Dublin	17 2 86	Scholar
Pedersen Henrik (F)	6 1	13 03	Jutland	10 6 75	Silkeborg
Speed Gary (M)	5 10	12 11	Deeside	8 9 69	Newcastle U
Vaz Te Ricardo (F)	6 2	12 07	Lisbon	1 10 86	Scholar
Walker Ian (G)	6 2	13 01	Watford	31 10 71	Leicester C

League Appearances: Ben Haim, T. 32(3); Borgetti, J. 5(14); Campo, I. 8(7);
Davies, K. 37; Diagne-Faye, A. 23(4); Diouf, E. 17(3); Djetou, M. 1(2); Fadiga, K.
5(3); Fernandes, F. (1); Fojut, J. (1); Gardner, R. 27(3); Giannakopoulos, S. 29(5);
Hunt, N. 12(8); Jaaskelainen, J. 38; Jaidi, R. 15(1); Jansen, M. 3(3); N'Gotty, B.
27(2); Nakata, H. 14(7); Nolan, K. 35(1); O'Brien, J. 22(1); Okocha, J. 18(9); Ped-
ersen, H. 15(6); Speed, G. 29(2); Vaz Te, R. 6(16).
Goals – League (49): Giannakopoulos 9, Nolan 9, Davies 7, Speed 4 (2 pens);
Diouf 3, Jaidi 3, Vaz Te 3, Borgetti 2, Campo 2, Diagne-Faye 1, Fadiga 1, Nakata 1,
Okocha 1, Pedersen 1, own goals 2.
Carling Cup (3): Borgetti 2, Vaz Te 1.
FA Cup (5): Giannakopoulos 2, Borgetti 1, Davies 1, Vaz Te 1.
UEFA Cup (9): Borgetti 2, Nolan 2, Diouf 1, Giannakopoulos 1, N'Gotty 1, Vaz
Te 1, own goal 1.
Ground: Reebok Stadium, Burnden Way, Bolton BL6 6JW. Telephone Bolton
(01204) 673 673.
Record Attendance: 69,912 v Manchester C, FA Cup 5th rd, 18 February 1933.
Capacity: 28,101.
Manager: Sam Allardyce.
Secretary: Simon Marland.
Most League Goals: 100, Division 1, 1996–97.
Highest League Scorer in Season: Joe Smith, 38, Division 1, 1920–21.
Most League Goals in Total Aggregate: Nat Lofthouse, 255, 1946–61.
Most Capped Player: Mark Fish, 34 (62), South Africa.
Most League Appearances: Eddie Hopkinson, 519, 1956–70.
Honours – Football League: Division 1 Champions – 1996–97. Division 2
Champions – 1908–09, 1977–78. Division 3 Champions – 1972–73. **FA Cup:**
Winners – 1923, 1926, 1929, 1958. **Sherpa Van Trophy:** Winners – 1989.
Colours: White shirts, white shorts, white stockings.

Canoville Lee (D)	6 1	12 00	Ealing	14 3 81	Torquay U
Clarke Jamie (D)	6 2	12 03	Sunderland	18 9 82	Scholar
Edkins Ashley (M)	5 9	12 02	Coalville	23 12 86	Scholar
Ellender Paul (D)	6 1	12 07	Scunthorpe	21 10 74	Scarborough
Forbes Luke (M)	5 9	10 11	Lincoln	13 2 88	Scholar
Galbraith David (M)	5 8	11 03	Luton	20 12 83	Northampton T
Greaves Mark (D)	6 1	13 00	Hull	22 1 75	Hull C
Holland Chris (M)	5 9	12 13	Clitheroe	11 9 75	Huddersfield T
Hurst Tom (M)	6 1	11 00	Leicester	23 9 87	Scholar
Joachim Julian (F)	5 6	12 02	Boston	20 9 74	Leeds U
Maylett Brad (M)	5 8	10 04	Manchester	24 12 80	Swansea C
McCann Austin (D)	5 9	11 13	Alexandria	21 1 80	Clyde
Norris Rob (M)	5 9	10 03	Nottingham	12 10 87	Scholar
Rusk Simon (M)	5 11	12 08	Peterborough	17 12 81	Peterborough U
Talbot Stewart (M)	6 0	13 07	Birmingham	14 6 73	Brentford
Thomas Danny (M)	5 7	10 10	Leamington Spa	1 5 81	Bournemouth
White Alan (D)	6 3	12 05	Darlington	22 3 76	Leyton Orient
Wright Chris (G)	6 0	13 00	Colchester	27 9 86	Arsenal

League Appearances: Abbey, N. 17; Canoville, L. 42(1); Clare, D. (1); Clarke, J. 12(3); Dudfield, L. 21(15); Edkins, A. (1); Ellender, P. 25; Futcher, B. 13(1); Galbraith, D. 6(6); Greaves, M. 31(3); Green, F. 5(1); Hall, A. 5(7); Holland, C. 29(5); Joachim, J. 41(2); Johnson, G. 3(1); Keene, J. 6; Kuipers, M. 15; Lee, J. 11(6); Logan, C. 13; Maylett, B. 23(15); McCann, A. 31(4); McSporran, J. (2); Melton, S. (3); Noble, D. 10(1); Norris, R. (1); Ross, I. 13(1); Rusk, S. 24(10); Silk, G. 11(3); Talbot, S. 28(2); Thomas, D. 15(20); Till, P. 10(6); Whelan, N. 8(7); White, A. 37; Wright, C. 1.

Goals – League (50): Joachim 14 (1 pen), Dudfield 5, Ross 4 (1 pen), Whelan 4 (1 pen), White 4, Talbot 3, Lee 2, Thomas 2, Canoville 1, Clarke J 1, Ellender 1, Greaves 1, Green 1, Keene 1, Maylett 1, Till 1, own goals 2.

Carling Cup (0).

FA Cup (7): Joachim 2, Futcher 1, Lee 1, Maylett 1, Rusk 1, Talbot 1.

Football League Trophy (2): Maylett 1, White 1.

Ground: Staffsmart Stadium, York Street, Boston, Lincolnshire PE21 6HJ. Telephone (01205) 364 406.

Record Attendance: 10,086 v Corby Town, Friendly, 1955.

Capacity: 6,613.

Manager: Steve Evans.

Secretary: John Blackwell.

Most Capped Player: Andy Kirk, 1, Northern Ireland.

Honours – Nationwide Conference: Champions – 2001–02. **Dr. Martens:** Champions – 1999-2000. Runners-up – 1998–99. **Unibond League:** Runners-up – 1995-96, 1997-98. **Unibond Challenge Cup:** Runners-up – 1996–97. **FA Trophy:** Runners-up – 1984–85. **Northern Premier League:** Champions – 1972–73, 1973–74, 1976–77, 1977–78. **Northern Premier League Cup:** Winners – 1974, 1976. **Northern Premier League Challenge Shield:** Winners – 1974, 1975, 1977, 1978. **Lincolnshire Senior Cup:** Winners – 1935, 1937, 1938, 1946, 1950, 1955, 1956, 1960, 1977, 1979, 1986, 1988, 1989. **Non-League Champions of Champions Cup:** Winners – 1973, 1977. **East Anglian Cup:** – Winners 1961. **Central Alliance League:** Champions – 1961–62. **United Counties League:** Champions – 1965–66. **West Midlands League:** Champions – 1966–67, 1967–68. **Eastern Professional Floodlit Cup:** Winners – 1972.

Colours: Amber and black striped shirts, black shorts with amber stripe, black stockings with yellow top.

AFC BOURNEMOUTH   FL CHAMPIONSHIP 1

Broadhurst Karl (D)	6 1	11 07	Portsmouth	18 3 80	Trainee
Browning Marcus (M)	6 1	12 12	Bristol	22 4 71	Gillingham
Cooke Stephen (M)	5 8	9 02	Walsall	15 2 83	Aston Villa
Cooper Shaun (D)	5 10	10 05	Newport (IW)	5 10 83	Portsmouth
Coutts James (M)	5 6	9 07	Weymouth	15 4 87	Trainee
Cummings Warren (D)	5 9	11 08	Aberdeen	15 10 80	Chelsea
Fletcher Steve (F)	6 2	14 09	Hartlepool	26 7 72	Hartlepool U
Foley-Sheridan Steven (M)	5 4	9 00	Dublin	10 2 86	Aston Villa
Gowling Josh (D)	6 3	12 08	Coventry	29 11 83	Herfolge
Hart Callum (D)	6 0	11 00	Cardiff	21 12 85	Bristol C
Hayter James (F)	5 9	10 13	Sandown (IW)	9 4 79	Trainee
Howe Eddie (D)	5 11	11 07	Amersham	29 11 77	Portsmouth
Maher Shaun (D)	6 1	13 02	Dublin	20 6 78	Bohemians
Moss Neil (G)	6 2	13 10	New Milton	10 5 75	Southampton
O'Connor James (D)	5 10	12 05	Birmingham	20 11 84	Aston Villa
Pitman Brett (M)	6 0	11 00	Jersey	31 1 88	St Paul's, Jersey
Purches Stephen (M)	5 11	11 09	Ilford	14 1 80	West Ham U
Rodrigues Dani (F)	5 11	12 00	Madeira	3 3 80	Yeovil T
Rowe James (M)	5 9	10 00	Frimley	10 3 87	Scholar
Stewart Gareth (G)	6 0	12 08	Preston	3 2 80	Blackburn R
Young Neil (D)	5 9	12 00	Harlow	31 8 73	Tottenham H

League Appearances: Broadhurst, K. 3(4); Brown, A. 3(1); Browning, M. 41(1); Cooke, S. 18(13); Cooper, S. 33(2); Coutts, J. (11); Fletcher, S. 21(6); Foley-Sheridan, S. 33(2); Fordyce, D. 3; Gowling, J. 11(2); Griffiths, A. 6(1); Hart, C. 32(7); Hayter, J. 46; Howe, E. 16(4); Hudson, K. (1); Keene, J. 6(5); Maher, S. 4(2); Moss, N. 4; O'Connor, J. 37(2); Pitman, B. 4(15); Purches, S. 22(4); Rix, B. 7(4); Rodrigues, D. 13(16); Rowe, J. (2); Spicer, J. 4; Stewart, G. 42; Stock, B. 26; Surman, A. 24; Tindall, J. 5(6); Young, N. 42.
Goals – League (49): Hayter 20 (7 pens), Surman 6, Foley-Sheridan 5, Fletcher 4, Rodrigues 3, Stock 3, Cooke 2, Keene 2, Griffiths 1, O'Connor 1, Pitman 1, own goal 1.
Carling Cup (0).
FA Cup (1): Stock 1.
Football League Trophy (4): Keene 2, Cooke 1 (pen), Pitman 1 (pen).
Ground: The Fitness First Stadium at Dean Court, Bournemouth BH7 7AF. Telephone (01202) 726 300.
Record Attendance: 28,799 v Manchester U, FA Cup 6th rd, 2 March 1957.
Capacity: 10,375.
Manager: Sean O'Driscoll.
Secretary: K. R. J. MacAlister.
Most League Goals: 88, Division 3 (S), 1956–57.
Highest League Scorer in Season: Ted MacDougall, 42, 1970–71.
Most League Goals in Total Aggregate: Ron Eyre, 202, 1924–33.
Most Capped Player: Gerry Peyton, 7 (33), Republic of Ireland.
Most League Appearances: Steve Fletcher, 425, 1992–.
Honours – Football League: Division 3 Champions – 1986–87. **Associate Members' Cup:** Winners – 1984.
Colours: Red shirts with three black stripes front and back, black shorts, black stockings.

BRADFORD CITY   FL CHAMPIONSHIP 1

Ainge Simon (D)	6 1	12 02	Bradford	18 2 88	Scholar
Bentham Craig (D)	5 9	11 06	Bingley	7 3 85	Scholar

Name	Ht	Wt	Birthplace	Birthdate	
Bower Mark (D)	5 10	11 00	Bradford	23 1 80	Trainee
Bridge-Wilkinson Marc (M)	5 6	11 00	Coventry	16 3 79	Stockport Co
Brown Joe (M)	5 10	11 04	Bradford	3 4 88	Scholar
Cadamarteri Danny (F)	5 7	13 05	Bradford	12 10 79	Sheffield U
Colbeck Joe (M)	5 10	10 12	Bradford	29 11 86	Scholar
Edghill Richard (D)	5 9	12 01	Oldham	23 9 74	QPR
Emanuel Lewis (D)	5 8	12 01	Bradford	14 10 83	Scholar
Forrest Danny (M)	5 10	11 07	Keighley	23 10 84	Trainee
Howarth Russell (G)	6 2	14 05	York	27 3 82	Tranmere R
McGuire Patrick (M)	5 10	10 07	Bradford	29 7 87	Scholar
Muirhead Ben (M)	5 9	11 02	Doncaster	5 1 83	Manchester U
Penford Thomas (M)	5 10	11 03	Leeds	5 1 85	Scholar
Petta Bobby (M)	5 7	11 05	Rotterdam	6 8 74	Darlington
Ricketts Donovan (G)	6 1	11 05	St James	6 7 77	Village U
Sanasy Kevin (M)	5 8	10 05	Leeds	2 11 84	Scholar
Schumacher Steven (M)	5 10	11 00	Liverpool	30 4 84	Everton
Swift John (M)	5 7	10 06	Leeds	20 9 84	Scholar
Symes Michael (F)	6 3	12 04	Gt Yarmouth	31 10 83	Everton
Wetherall David (D)	6 3	13 12	Sheffield	14 3 71	Leeds U
Windass Dean (F)	5 10	12 03	North Ferriby	1 4 69	Sheffield U

League Appearances: Bentham, C. 6(1); Bower, M. 45; Bridge-Wilkinson, M. 36; Brown, J. 2(11); Cadamarteri, D. 25(14); Claridge, S. 14(12); Colbeck, J. 5(6); Cooke, A. 10(7); Crooks, L. 14(1); Edghill, R. 19; Emanuel, L. 23(14); Holloway, D. 21(3); Howarth, R. 10(1); Kearney, T. 11(4); Morrison, O. 7(3); Muirhead, B. 26(6); Penford, T. 9(1); Petta, B. 23(4); Ricketts, D. 36; Schumacher, S. 24(6); Stewart, D. 20(3); Swift, J. 4(1); Symes, M. 1(2); Taylor, A. 24; Wetherall, D. 46; Wilbraham, A. 5; Windass, D. 40; Wright, J. (1).
Goals – League (51): Windass 16 (3 pens), Bridge-Wilkinson 5 (1 pen), Claridge 5, Wetherall 5, Petta 4, Bower 2, Cadamarteri 2, Emanuel 2, Brown 1, Cooke 1, Edghill 1, Kearney 1, Muirhead 1, Schumacher 1, Stewart 1, Symes 1, Wilbraham 1, own goal 1.
Carling Cup (6): Windass 3, Bridge-Wilkinson 1, Cadamarteri 1, Schumacher 1.
FA Cup (6): Bower 1, Cooke 1, Crooks 1, Edghill 1, Wetherall 1, Windass 1 (pen).
Football League Trophy (2): Brown 2.
Ground: Bradford and Bingley Stadium, Valley Parade, Bradford BD8 7DY. Telephone 0870 822 0000.
Record Attendance: 39,146 v Burnley, FA Cup 4th rd, 11 March 1911. **Capacity:** 25,136.
Manager: Colin Todd.
Secretary: Jon Pollard.
Most League Goals: 128, Division 3 (N), 1928–29.
Highest League Scorer in Season: David Layne, 34, Division 4, 1961–62.
Most League Goals in Total Aggregate: Bobby Campbell, 121, 1981–84, 1984–86.
Most Capped Player: Jamie Lawrence, Jamaica.
Most League Appearances: Cec Podd, 502, 1970–84.
Honours – Football League: Division 2 Champions – 1907–08. Division 3 Champions – 1984–85. Division 3 (N) Champions – 1928–29. **FA Cup:** Winners – 1911.
Colours: Claret and amber.

BRENTFORD   FL CHAMPIONSHIP 1

Name	Ht	Wt	Birthplace	Birthdate	
Brooker Paul (M)	5 8	10 00	Hammersmith	25 11 76	Reading
Charles Darius (M)	5 11	11 10	Ealing	10 12 87	Scholar
Fitzgerald Scott B (D)	6 1	13 00	Westminster	13 8 69	Colchester U
Fitzgerald Scott P (F)	5 11	12 00	Hillingdon	18 11 79	Watford
Frampton Andrew (D)	5 11	10 10	Wimbledon	3 9 79	Crystal Palace
Ide Charlie (M)	5 8	10 06	Sunbury	10 5 88	Scholar

Player					
Lewis Junior (M)	6 2	13 00	Wembley	9 10 73	Hull C
Masters Clark (G)	6 3	13 12	Hastings	31 5 87	Scholar
Moleski George (M)	5 6	10 08	Hillingdon	23 7 87	Scholar
Mousinho John (D)	6 1	12 07	Buckingham	30 4 86	Univ of Notre Dame
Nelson Stuart (G)	6 1	12 12	Stroud	17 9 81	Hucknall T
O'Connor Kevin (F)	5 11	12 00	Blackburn	24 2 82	Trainee
Osborne Karleigh (M)	6 2	12 08	Southall	19 3 88	Scholar
Owusu Lloyd (F)	6 2	14 00	Slough	12 12 76	Reading
Peters Ryan (F)	5 8	10 08	London	21 8 87	Scholar
Rhodes Alex (F)	5 9	10 04	Cambridge	23 1 82	Newmarket T
Skulason Olafur-Ingi (M)	6 0	11 10	Reykjavik	1 4 83	Arsenal
Sodje Sam (D)	6 0	12 00	Greenwich	29 5 79	Margate
Steele Aaron (M)	5 10	12 04	Isleworth	1 2 87	Scholar
Tabb Jay (M)	5 5	9 07	Tooting	21 2 84	Trainee
Tillen Sam (D)	5 10	11 09	Newbury	16 4 85	Chelsea
Turner Michael (D)	6 4	12 06	Lewisham	9 11 83	Charlton Ath
Watts Ryan (M)	5 9	10 10	Greenford	18 5 88	Scholar
Weight Scott (M)	5 11	10 04	Hounslow	3 4 87	Scholar
Willock Calum (F)	6 1	12 08	Lambeth	29 10 81	Peterborough U

League Appearances: Bankole, A. 2; Brooker, P. 32(4); Campbell, D. 13(10); Charles, D. (2); Dobson, M. 3(3); Fitzgerald, S. 3(8); Frampton, A. 36; Gayle, M. 16(8); Hutchinson, E. 17(10); Keenan, J. (3); Lewis, J. 11(3); Mousinho, J. 3(4); Nelson, S. 44(1); Newman, R. 29(1); O'Connor, K. 30; Osborne, K. 1; Owusu, L. 39(3); Peters, R. 1(9); Pratley, D. 25(7); Rankin, I. 31(6); Rhodes, A. 5(12); Skulason, O. 2; Smith, Jamie 7; Sodje, S. 43; Tabb, J. 42; Tillen, S. 20(13); Turner, M. 46; Willock, C. 5(8).

Goals – League (72): Owusu 12 (2 pens), Campbell 9 (2 pens), O'Connor 7 (4 pens), Rankin 7, Tabb 6, Sodje 5, Brooker 4, Pratley 4, Frampton 3, Newman 3, Gayle 2, Hutchinson 2, Turner 2, Fitzgerald 1, Peters 1, Rhodes 1, Willock 1, own goals 2.

Carling Cup (0).

FA Cup (9): Campbell 3, Owusu 2, Rankin 2, O'Connor 1 (pen), Sodje 1.

Football League Trophy (1): Fitzgerald 1.

Play-Offs (1): Tabb 1.

Ground: Griffin Park, Braemar Road, Brentford, Middlesex TW8 0NT. Telephone (0845) 3456 442.

Record Attendance: 39,626 v Preston NE, FA Cup 6th rd, 5 March 1938. **Capacity:** 12,763.

Manager: Leroy Rosenior.

Secretary: Lisa Hall.

Most League Goals: 98, Division 4, 1962–63.

Highest League Scorer in Season: Jack Holliday, 38, Division 3 (S), 1932–33.

Most League Goals in Total Aggregate: Jim Towers, 153, 1954–61.

Most Capped Player: John Buttigieg, 22 (98), Malta.

Most League Appearances: Ken Coote, 514, 1949–64.

Honours – Football League: Division 2 Champions – 1934–35. Division 3 Champions – 1991–92, 1998–99. Division 3 (S) Champions – 1932–33. Division 4 Champions – 1962–63.

Colours: Red, white and black.

BRIGHTON & HOVE ALBION   FL CHAMPIONSHIP 1

Player					
Breach Chris (D)	5 10	12 04	Brighton	19 4 86	Scholar
Butters Guy (D)	6 1	15 05	Hillingdon	30 10 69	Gillingham
Carole Sebastien (M)	5 7	11 05	Pontoise	8 9 82	Chateauroux
Carpenter Richard (M)	6 0	13 03	Sheppey	30 9 72	Cardiff C
Cox Dean (M)	5 4	9 08	Haywards Heath	12 8 87	Scholar

El-Abd Adam (D)	5 10	13 05	Brighton	11 9 84	Scholar
Elphick Tommy (M)	5 11	11 07	Brighton	7 9 87	Scholar
Frutos Alexandre (M)	5 9	10 03	Vitry-le-Francois	23 4 82	Metz
Gatting Joe (D)	5 11	12 04	Brighton	25 11 87	Scholar
Hammond Dean (M)	6 1	11 02	Hastings	7 3 83	Scholar
Hart Gary (F)	5 9	12 07	Harlow	21 9 76	Stansted
Henderson Wayne (G)	5 11	12 02	Dublin	16 9 83	Aston Villa
Hinshelwood Adam (D)	5 11	13 00	Oxford	8 1 84	Scholar
Jarrett Albert (M)	5 11	11 02	Sierra Leone	23 10 84	Dulwich Hamlet
Kazim-Richards Colin (F)	6 1	10 10	Leyton	26 8 86	Bury
Kuipers Michels (G)	6 2	15 00	Amsterdam	26 6 74	Bristol R
Loft Doug (M)	6 0	12 01	Maidstone	25 12 86	Hastings U
Lynch Joel (D)	6 1	12 10	Eastbourne	3 10 87	Scholar
Martin Richard (G)	6 2	12 13	Chelmsford	1 9 87	Scholar
Mayo Kerry (D)	5 9	13 10	Cuckfield	21 9 77	Trainee
Molango Maheta (F)	6 1	12 00	St Imier	24 7 82	VS Burghausen
Oatway Charlie (M)	5 7	11 11	Hammersmith	28 11 73	Brentford
Reid Paul (M)	5 8	12 09	Sydney	6 7 79	Bradford C
Robinson Jake (F)	5 7	10 10	Brighton	23 10 86	Scholar
Sullivan John (M)	5 10	11 04	Brighton	8 3 88	Scholar
Turienzo Federico (F)	6 2	11 13	La Plata	6 2 83	Gimnasia

League Appearances: Blayney, A. 8; Butters, G. 43(2); Carole, S. 34(6); Carpenter, R. 31(1); Chaigneau, F. 1; Cox, D. (1); Dodd, J. 6(1); El-Abd, A. 23(6); Elphick, G. 1(1); Elphick, T. (1); Frutos, A. 27(9); Gatting, J. 5(7); Hammond, D. 40(1); Hart, G. 31(4); Henderson, W. 32; Hinshelwood, A. 10(1); Jarrett, A. 9(2); Kazim-Richards, C. 25(17); Knight, L. 22(3); Kuipers, M. 5; Loft, D. (3); Lynch, J. 16; Mayo, K. 14(4); McCammon, M. 3(4); McPhee, C. 2(5); McShane, P. 38; Nicolas, A. 4(7); Noel-Williams, G. 7; Oatway, C. 17(1); Reid, P. 36(2); Robinson, J. 15(12); Turienzo, F. 1(3).
Goals – League (39): Kazim-Richards 6, Knight 5 (1 pen), Hammond 4, Frutos 3, McShane 3, Butters 2, Carole 2, Noel-Williams 2, Reid 2, Carpenter 1, Hart 1, Loft 1, Lynch 1, Mayo 1, Oatway 1, Robinson 1, own goals 3.
Carling Cup (2): McCammon 1, Robinson 1.
FA Cup (0).
Ground: Withdean Stadium, Tongdean Lane, Brighton. East Sussex BN1 5JD. Telephone (01273) 695 400 (admin offices 44 North Road, Brighton).
Record Attendance: 36,747 v Fulham, Division 2, 27 December 1958 (at Goldstone Ground).
Capacity: 8,850.
Manager: Mark McGhee.
Secretary: Derek J. Allan.
Most League Goals: 112, Division 3 (S), 1955–56.
Highest League Scorer in Season: Peter Ward, 32, Division 3, 1976–77.
Most League Goals in Total Aggregate: Tommy Cook, 114, 1922–29.
Most Capped Player: Steve Penney, 17, Northern Ireland.
Most League Appearances: 'Tug' Wilson, 509, 1922–36.
Honours – Football League: Division 2 Champions – 2001–02. Division 3 Champions – 2000–01. Division 3 (S) Champions – 1957–58. Division 4 Champions – 1964–65.
Colours: Blue and white vertical striped shirts, white shorts, white stockings.

BRISTOL CITY   FL CHAMPIONSHIP 1

Abbey Nathan (G)	6 1	11 13	Islington	11 7 78	Boston U
Basso Adriano (G)	6 1	11 07	Jundiai	18 4 75	Woking
Benyon Elliot (M)			Wycombe	29 8 87	Scholar
Brooker Stephen (F)	5 11	13 13	Newport Pagnell	21 5 81	Port Vale

Brown Scott (M)	5 9	11 00	Runcorn	8 5 85	Scholar
Carey Louis (D)	5 10	12 09	Bristol	20 1 77	Trainee
Cotterill David (F)	5 10	10 11	Cardiff	4 12 87	Scholar
Heywood Matthew (D)	6 3	14 00	Chatham	26 8 79	Swindon T
Keogh Richard (M)	6 0	11 02	Harlow	11 8 86	Stoke C
Lamb Shaun (D)			Bristol	17 11 86	Scholar
Murray Scott (M)	5 8	11 02	Aberdeen	26 5 74	Reading
Myrie-Williams Jennison (F)	5 11	12 08	Lambeth	17 5 88	Scholar
Noble David (M)	6 0	12 04	Hitchin	2 2 82	Boston U
Orr Bradley (M)	6 0	11 11	Liverpool	1 11 82	Newcastle U
Partridge David (D)	6 1	13 06	Westminster	26 11 78	Motherwell
Pearce Sam (G)			Newport	24 2 86	Scholar
Phillips Steve (G)	6 1	13 06	Bath	6 5 78	Paulton R
Russell Alex (M)	5 10	11 07	Crosby	17 3 73	Torquay U
Savage Bas (F)	6 3	13 08	London	7 1 82	Reading
Skuse Cole (M)	6 1	11 05	Bristol	29 3 86	Scholar
Smith Grant (M)	6 1	12 07	Irvine	5 5 80	Swindon T
Stewart Marcus (F)	5 10	11 00	Bristol	7 11 72	Sunderland
Wilkshire Luke (M)	5 9	11 00	Wollongong	2 10 81	Middlesbrough
Woodman Craig (D)	5 8	11 00	Tiverton	22 12 82	Trainee
Wring Danny (M)	5 10	10 03	Portishead	26 10 86	Scholar

League Appearances: Abbey, N. (1); Andrew, C. 1(2); Basso, A. 29; Bridges, M. 4(7); Brooker, S. 34(3); Brown, S. 23(6); Carey, L. 38; Cotterill, D. 37(8); Fontaine, L. 14(1); Fortune, C. 4(2); Gillespie, S. 3(1); Golbourne, S. 4(1); Green, A. 1(1); Heywood, M. 22(2); Joseph, M. 3; Keogh, R. 4(5); Madjo, G. 1(4); McCammon, M. 8(3); Murray, S. 31(6); Myrie-Williams, J. (1); Noble, D. 23(1); Orr, B. 35(3); Partridge, D. 11; Phillips, S. 17(2); Quinn, J. 2(1); Russell, A. 21(6); Sankofa, O. 8; Savage, B. 15(8); Skuse, C. 29(9); Smith, A. 4(7); Smith, J. 4(2); Stewart, M. 16(11); Wilkshire, L. 20(16); Woodman, C. 36(1); Youga, K. 4.
Goals – League (66): Brooker 16, Murray 10 (1 pen), Cotterill 7, Stewart 5 (1 pen), Wilkshire 5, McCammon 4, Russell 4 (2 pens), Carey 3, Heywood 2, Skuse 2 (1 pen), Brown 1, Gillespie 1, Keogh 1, Noble 1, Orr 1, Quinn 1, Savage 1, Woodman 1 (pen).
Carling Cup (2): Bridges 1, Golbourne 1.
FA Cup (0).
Football League Trophy (2): Madjo 1, Murray 1.
Ground: Ashton Gate Stadium, Bristol BS3 2EJ. Telephone (0117) 9630 630.
Record Attendance: 43,335 v Preston NE, FA Cup 5th rd, 16 February 1935.
Capacity: 21,497.
Manager: Gary Johnson.
Secretary: Michelle McDonald.
Most League Goals: 104, Division 3 (S), 1926–27.
Highest League Scorer in Season: Don Clark, 36, Division 3 (S), 1946–47.
Most League Goals in Total Aggregate: John Atyeo, 314, 1951–66.
Most Capped Player: Billy Wedlock, 26, England.
Most League Appearances: John Atyeo, 597, 1951–66.
Honours – Football League: Division 2 Champions – 1905–06. Division 3 (S) Champions – 1922–23, 1926–27, 1954–55. **Welsh Cup:** Winners – 1934. **Anglo-Scottish Cup:** Winners – 1977–78. **Freight Rover Trophy:** Winners – 1985–86. LDV Vans Trophy: Winners – 2002–03.
Colours: Red shirts, white shorts, white stockings.

BRISTOL ROVERS   FL CHAMPIONSHIP 2

Agogo Junior (F)	5 10	11 07	Accra	1 8 79	Barnet
Book Steve (G)	5 11	11 01	Bournemouth	7 7 69	Cirencester T
Campbell Stuart (M)	5 10	10 00	Corby	9 12 77	Grimsby T

Carruthers Chris (M)	5 10	12 00	Kettering	19 8 83	Northampton T
Disley Craig (M)	5 10	10 13	Worksop	24 8 81	Mansfield T
Elliott Steve (D)	6 1	14 00	Derby	29 10 78	Blackpool
Forrester Jamie (F)	5 7	11 00	Bradford	1 11 74	Hull C
Haldane Lewis (F)	6 0	11 03	Trowbridge	13 3 85	Scholar
Hinton Craig (D)	6 0	12 00	Wolverhampton	26 11 77	Kidderminster H
Horsell Martin (G)	6 0	12 00	Torquay	10 12 86	Scholar
Hunt James (M)	5 8	10 03	Derby	17 12 76	Oxford U
Lescott Aaron (M)	5 8	10 09	Birmingham	2 12 78	Stockport Co
Lines Chris (M)	6 2	12 00	Bristol	30 11 85	Filton College
Mullings Darren (M)	6 1	12 00	Bristol	3 3 87	Filton College
Ryan Robbie (D)	5 10	12 05	Dublin	16 5 77	Millwall
Shearer Scott (G)	6 3	12 00	Glasgow	15 2 81	Coventry C
Trollope Paul (M)	6 0	12 06	Swindon	3 6 72	Northampton T
Walker Richard (F)	6 0	12 04	Sutton Coldfield	8 11 77	Oxford U

League Appearances: Agogo, J. 41(1); Anderson, J. 10(2); Bass, J. 7(2); Book, S. 1; Campbell, S. 31(7); Carruthers, C. 39(1); Disley, C. 37(5); Edwards, C. 12(3); Elliott, S. 45; Forrester, J. 3(14); Gibb, A. 21(12); Haldane, L. 19(11); Hinton, C. 34(2); Hunt, J. 40; Igoe, S. 10(1); Leary, M. 12(1); Lescott, A. 35(2); Lines, C. 1(3); Louis, J. 2(6); Mullings, D. (4); Ryan, R. 14; Shearer, S. 45; Somner, M. 1; Walker, R. 44(2); Williams, R. 2(5).
Goals – League (59): Walker 20 (6 pens), Agogo 16 (2 pens), Disley 8, Haldane 3, Elliott 2, Forrester 2, Anderson 1, Campbell 1, Carruthers 1, Edwards 1, Hunt 1, Igoe 1, own goals 2.
Carling Cup (0).
FA Cup (3): Agogo 2, Gibb 1.
Football League Trophy (1): Walker 1.
Ground: The Memorial Stadium, Filton Avenue, Horfield, Bristol BS7 0BF. Telephone (0117) 952 4008.
Record Attendance: 9464 v Liverpool, FA Cup 4th rd, 8 February 1992 (Twerton Park). 38,472 v Preston NE, FA Cup 4th rd, 30 January 1960 (Eastville). 11,433 v Sunderland, League Cup 3rd rd, 31 October 2000 (Memorial Ground).
Capacity: 11,900.
Director of Football: Lennie Lawrence.
Secretary: Rod Wesson.
Most League Goals: 92, Division 3 (S), 1952–53.
Highest League Scorer in Season: Geoff Bradford, 33, Division 3 (S), 1952–53.
Most League Goals in Total Aggregate: Geoff Bradford, 242, 1949–64.
Most Capped Player: Vitalijs Astafjevs, 31 (125), Latvia.
Most League Appearances: Stuart Taylor, 546, 1966–80.
Honours – Football League: Division 3 (S) Champions – 1952–53. Division 3 Champions – 1989–90.
Colours: Blue and white quartered shirts, blue shorts, white stockings.

BURNLEY   FL CHAMPIONSHIP

Branch Graham (M)	6 3	13 11	Liverpool	12 2 72	Stockport Co
Courtney Duane (D)	5 11	11 03	Oldbury	7 1 85	AFC Telford U
Coyne Danny (G)	6 0	12 11	Prestatyn	27 8 83	Leicester C
Crossley Mark (G)	6 0	12 02	Burnley	3 12 87	Scholar
Duff Michael (D)	6 3	12 10	Belfast	11 1 78	Cheltenham T
Elliott Wade (M)	5 10	10 03	Southampton	14 12 78	Bournemouth
Harley Jon (D)	5 8	10 03	Maidstone	26 9 79	Sheffield U
Hyde Micah (M)	5 11	12 03	Newham	10 11 74	Watford
Jensen Brian (G)	6 4	16 09	Copenhagen	8 6 75	WBA
Karbassiyon Daniel (D)	5 8	11 07	Virginia	10 8 84	Arsenal

35

Lafferty Kyle (F)	6 4	11 02	Belfast	21 7 87	Scholar
Mahon Alan (M)	5 8	12 03	Dublin	4 4 78	Wigan Ath
McCann Chris (M)	6 1	11 11	Dublin	21 7 87	Scholar
McGreal John (D)	6 0	12 06	Birkenhead	2 6 72	Ipswich T
Noel-Williams Gifton (F)	6 3	13 06	Islington	21 1 80	Stoke C
O'Connor Gareth (M)	5 10	11 00	Dublin	10 11 78	Bournemouth
O'Connor James (M)	5 8	11 06	Dublin	1 9 79	WBA
Sinclair Frank (D)	5 9	12 03	Lambeth	3 12 71	Leicester C
Spicer John (M)	5 11	11 07	Romford	13 9 83	Bournemouth
Thomas Wayne (D)	6 2	14 12	Gloucester	17 5 79	Stoke C

League Appearances: Akinbiyi, A. 29; Bardsley, P. 6; Bermingham, K. 1(3); Branch, G. 29(8); Courtney, D. 1(6); Coyne, D. 7(1); Duff, M. 39(2); Dyer, N. 4(1); Elliott, W. 23(13); Grant, L. 1; Gray, A. 9; Harley, J. 41; Hyde, M. 39(2); Jensen, B. 38(1); Karbassiyon, D. (5); Lafferty, K. 3(8); Lowe, K. 10(6); Mahon, A. 7(1); McCann, C. 15(8); McGreal, J. 33(2); Noel-Williams, G. 17(12); O'Connor, G. 26(3); O'Connor, J. 46; Ricketts, M. 12(1); Sinclair, F. 36(1); Spicer, J. 22(12); Thomas, W. 12(4).

Goals – League (46): Akinbiyi 12 (1 pen), O'Connor G 7 (4 pens), Elliott 3, Gray 3, O'Connor J 3, Spicer 3, Branch 2, Dyer 2, Harley 2 (1 pen), McCann 2, Noel-Williams 2, Ricketts 2, Lafferty 1, Thomas 1, own goal 1.

Carling Cup (5): Akinbiyi 2, Duff 1, Lowe 1, Spicer 1.

FA Cup (1): O'Connor G 1.

Ground: Turf Moor, Harry Potts Way, Burnley, Lancashire BB10 4BX. Telephone (0870) 443 1882.

Record Attendance: 54,775 v Huddersfield T, FA Cup 3rd rd, 23 February 1924.

Capacity: 22,610.

Manager: Steve Cotterill.

Secretary: Cathy Pickup.

Most League Goals: 102, Division 1, 1960–61.

Highest League Scorer in Season: George Beel, 35, Division 1, 1927–28.

Most League Goals in Total Aggregate: George Beel, 178, 1923–32.

Most Capped Player: Jimmy McIlroy, 51 (55), Northern Ireland.

Most League Appearances: Jerry Dawson, 522, 1907–28.

Honours – Football League: Division 1 Champions – 1920–21, 1959–60. Division 2 Champions – 1897–98, 1972–73. Division 3 Champions – 1981–82. Division 4 Champions – 1991–92. **FA Cup:** Winners – 1913–14. **Anglo-Scottish Cup:** Winners – 1978–79.

Colours: Claret and blue shirts with white trim, claret shorts, claret stockings.

BURY   FL CHAMPIONSHIP 2

Adams Nicky (F)	5 10	11 00	Bolton	16 10 86	Scholar
Barry-Murphy Brian (M)	6 1	13 01	Cork	27 7 78	Sheffield W
Brass Chris (M)	5 10	11 13	Easington	24 7 75	York C
Buchanan David (M)	5 8	10 08	Rochdale	6 5 86	Scholar
Burke Steve (F)	6 0	12 10	Bolton	13 1 88	
Challinor Dave (D)	6 1	12 06	Chester	2 10 75	Stockport Co
Fitzgerald John (D)	6 2	12 13	Dublin	10 2 84	Blackburn R
Flitcroft David (M)	5 11	14 05	Bolton	14 1 74	Macclesfield T
Grundy Aaron (G)	6 1	12 07	Bolton	21 1 88	Scholar
Kennedy Tom (D)	5 10	11 01	Bury	24 6 85	Scholar
Mattis Dwayne (M)	6 1	11 12	Huddersfield	31 7 81	Huddersfield T
Parrish Andy (D)	6 0	11 00	Bolton	22 6 88	
Pugh Marc (M)	5 11	11 04	Burnley	2 4 87	Burnley
Quigley Damien (M)	5 8	11 06	Rochdale	20 9 87	Scholar
Scott Paul (D)	5 11	12 00	Wakefield	5 11 79	Huddersfield T

Smart Allan (F)	6 2	12 07	Perth	8	7 74	Milton Keynes D
Speight Jake (F)	5 7	11 02	Sheffield	28	9 85	Scarborough
Tipton Matt (F)	5 10	11 02	Bangor	29	6 80	Mansfield T
Woodthorpe Colin (D)	6 0	11 08	Ellesmere Port	13	1 69	Stockport Co
Youngs Tom (F)	5 9	11 13	Bury St Edmunds	31	8 79	Leyton Orient

League Appearances: Adams, N. 9(6); Anyinsah, J. 3; Barlow, S. 2(11); Barry-Murphy, B. 35(5); Brass, C. 6(1); Buchanan, D. 22(1); Burke, S. (1); Burns, J. 1; Challinor, D. 46; Daly, J. 11; Dootson, C. 4(1); Edwards, N. 24; Fitzgerald, J. 22(5); Flitcroft, D. 43; Gobern, L. 7; Grundy, A. (1); Hannah, D. 1(1); Hardiker, J. 11; Jarman, N. 1(1); Kennedy, T. 28(5); Marrison, C. 8(8); Mattis, D. 32(4); Newby, J. 4(6); Parrish, A. 6(2); Pugh, M. 3(3); Quigley, D. (1); Reet, D. 6; Ross, I. 6(1); Saunders, B. 1; Schmeichel, K. 15; Scott, P. 40(1); Sedgemore, J. 3(6); Smart, A. 11(2); Speight, J. 7(10); Tipton, M. 15(9); Unsworth, L. (3); Whaley, S. 23; Williams, T. 3; Woodthorpe, C. 31(2); Youngs, T. 16(14).

Goals – League (45): Whaley 7, Mattis 5, Kennedy 4 (3 pens). Reet 4, Barry-Murphy 3, Tipton 3, Youngs 3, Daly 2, Scott 2, Speight 2, Adams 1, Challinor 1, Flitcroft 1, Gobern 1, Newby 1, Pugh 1, Smart 1, own goals 3.

Carling Cup (0).

FA Cup (2): Kennedy 1 (pen), Scott 1.

Football League Trophy (1): Sedgemore 1.

Ground: Gigg Lane, Bury BL9 9HR. Telephone (0161) 764 4881.

Record Attendance: 35,000 v Bolton W, FA Cup 3rd rd, 9 January 1960. **Capacity:** 11,669.

Manager: Chris Casper.

Secretary: Mrs Jill Neville.

Most League Goals: 108, Division 3, 1960–61.

Highest League Scorer in Season: Craig Madden, 35, Division 4, 1981–82.

Most League Goals in Total Aggregate: Craig Madden, 129, 1978–86.

Most Capped Player: Bill Gorman, 11 (13), Republic of Ireland and (4), Northern Ireland.

Most League Appearances: Norman Bullock, 506, 1920–35.

Honours – Football League: Division 2 Champions – 1894–95, 1996–97. Division 3 Champions – 1960–61. **FA Cup:** Winners – 1900, 1903.

Colours: White shirts, royal blue shorts and stockings.

CARDIFF CITY   FL CHAMPIONSHIP

Alexander Neil (G)	6 1	12 08	Edinburgh	10	3 78	Livingston
Ardley Neal (M)	5 10	12 08	Epsom	1	9 72	Watford
Barker Chris (D)	6 2	13 08	Sheffield	2	3 80	Barnsley
Blake Darcy (M)	5 10	12 05	New Tredegar	13	12 88	Scholar
Cooper Kevin (M)	5 8	10 04	Derby	8	2 75	Wolverhampton W
Ferretti Andrea (F)	5 10	11 10	Parma	18	9 86	
Jacobson Joe (D)	5 11	12 06	Cardiff	17	11 86	Scholar
Ledley Joe (M)	6 0	11 07	Cardiff	23	1 87	Scholar
McDonald Curtis (M)	5 10	10 08	Cardiff	24	3 88	Scholar
N'Dumbu Nsungu Guylain (F)	6 1	12 08	Kinshasa	26	12 82	Darlington
Parry Paul (M)	5 11	12 12	Newport	19	8 80	Hereford U
Purse Darren (D)	6 2	12 08	Stepney	14	2 77	WBA
Scimeca Riccardo (D)	6 1	12 09	Leamington Spa	13	6 75	WBA
Thompson Steven (F)	6 2	12 05	Paisley	14	10 78	Rangers
Weston Rhys (D)	6 1	12 12	Kingston	27	10 80	Arsenal
Whitley Jeff (M)	5 8	11 06	Zambia	28	1 79	Sunderland

League Appearances: Alexander, N. 46; Ardley, N. 22(8); Barker, C. 41; Blake, D. (1); Boland, W. 11(4); Cooper, K. 31(5); Cox, N. 21(6); Darlington, J. 7(2); Ferretti, A. (4); Jacobson, J. (1); Jerome, C. 44; Koumas, J. 42(2); Ledley, J. 42; Lee, A. 6(19); Loovens, G. 32(1); McDonald, C. (1); Mulryne, P. 1(3); N'Dumbu Nsungu, G. 4(7); Parry, P. 11(16); Purse, D. 39; Ricketts, M. 17; Scimeca, R. 17(1); Thompson, S. 14; Weston, R. 26(4); Whitley, J. 32(2).
Goals – League (58): Jerome 18, Koumas 12, Purse 5 (3 pens), Ricketts 5, Thompson 4, Ledley 3, Cooper 2, Cox 2, Lee 2, Loovens 2, Parry 1, Scimeca 1, Whitley 1.
Carling Cup (4): Jerome 1, Koumas 1, Ledley 1, Purse 1 (pen).
FA Cup (1): Jerome 1.
Ground: Ninian Park, Cardiff CF11 8SX. Telephone (029) 2022 1001.
Record Attendance: 62,634, Wales v England, 17 October 1959. Capacity: 21,432.
Manager: Dave Jones.
Secretary: Jason Turner.
Most League Goals: 95, Division 3, 2000–01.
Highest League Scorer in Season: Robert Earnshaw, 31, Division 2, 2002–03.
Most League Goals in Total Aggregate: Len Davies, 128, 1920–31.
Most Capped Player: Alf Sherwood, 39 (41), Wales.
Most League Appearances: Phil Dwyer, 471, 1972–85.
Honours – Football League: Division 3 (S) Champions – 1946–47. FA Cup: Winners – 1926–27 (only occasion the Cup has been won by a club outside England). Welsh Cup: Winners – 22 times.
Colours: All royal blue.

CARLISLE UNITED   FL CHAMPIONSHIP 1

Name			Birthplace		Previous club
Aranalde Zigor (D)	6 1	13 03	Ibarra	28 2 73	Sheffield W
Arnison Paul (D)	5 10	10 12	Hartlepool	18 9 77	Hartlepool U
Billy Chris (M)	5 11	11 08	Huddersfield	2 1 73	Bury
Bridges Michael (F)	6 1	10 11	North Shields	5 8 78	Bristol C
Dillon Dan (M)	5 9	10 07	Huntingdon	6 9 86	Scholar
Grand Simon (D)	6 0	10 03	Chorley	23 2 84	Rochdale
Gray Kevin (D)	6 0	14 00	Sheffield	7 1 72	Tranmere R
Hackney Simon (M)	5 8	9 13	Stockport	5 2 84	Woodley Sports
Hawley Karl (F)	5 8	12 02	Walsall	6 12 81	Walsall
Holmes Derek (F)	6 2	13 00	Lanark	18 10 78	Bournemouth
Joyce Luke (M)			Bolton	9 7 87	Wigan Ath
Livesey Danny (D)	6 3	12 10	Salford	31 12 84	Bolton W
Lumsdon Chris (M)	5 11	10 06	Newcastle	15 12 79	Barnsley
McGill Brendan (M)	5 8	9 02	Dublin	22 3 81	Sunderland
Murphy Peter (M)	5 10	12 10	Dublin	27 10 80	Blackburn R
Murray Adam (M)	5 8	10 12	Solihull	30 9 81	Mansfield T
Murray Glenn (F)	6 1	12 12	Maryport	25 9 83	Barrow
Nade Raphael (M)	6 0	12 08	Abidjan	18 10 80	Woking
Simpson Paul (M)	5 8	11 11	Carlisle	26 7 66	Rochdale
Westwood Keiren (G)	6 1	13 10	Manchester	23 10 84	Manchester C
Williams Tony (G)	6 2	13 09	Maesteg	20 9 77	Grimsby T

League Appearances: Andrews, L. 1; Aranalde, Z. 38(1); Arnison, P. 39(2); Beharall, D. 6; Billy, C. 45; Bridges, M. 23(2); Grand, S. 2(6); Gray, K. 44; Hackney, S. 9(21); Hawley, K. 46; Holmes, D. 30(10); Livesey, D. 34(2); Lumsdon, C. 37(1); McClen, J. (2); McGill, B. 18(8); Murphy, P. 38(6); Murray, A. 29(8); Murray, G. 3(23); Nade, R. 10(12); O'Brien, A. 2(3); Rivers, M. 2(2); Simpson, P. 4(5); Westwood, K. 35; Williams, T. 11.
Goals – League (84): Hawley 22, Bridges 15, Holmes 7, Lumsdon 7 (4 pens), Hackney 6, Aranalde 5, Livesey 4, Gray 3, McGill 3, Murray G 3, Grand 2, Murphy 2, Nade 2, Murray A 1, O'Brien 1, own goal 1.
Carling Cup (1): Murray A 1.

FA Cup (0).
Football League Trophy (9): Hawley 4, Grand 1, Holmes 1, Murphy 1, Murray A 1, Murray G 1.
Ground: Brunton Park, Warwick Road, Carlisle CA1 1LL. Telephone (01228) 526 237.
Record Attendance: 27,500 v Birmingham C, FA Cup 3rd rd, 5 January 1957 and v Middlesbrough, FA Cup 5th rd, 7 February 1970. **Capacity:** 16,065.
Manager: Neil McDonald.
Secretary: Mrs Sarah McKnight.
Most League Goals: 113, Division 4, 1963–64.
Highest League Scorer in Season: Jimmy McConnell, 42, Division 3 (N), 1928–29.
Most Goals in Total Aggregate: Jimmy McConnell, 126, 1928–32.
Most Capped Player: Eric Welsh, 4, Northern Ireland.
Most League Appearances: Allan Ross, 466, 1963–79.
Honours – Football League: Division 3 Champions – 1964–65, 1994–95; Championship 2 Champions – 2005–06. **Auto Windscreen Shield:** Winners 1997.
Colours: Blue shirts, white shorts, blue stockings.

CHARLTON ATHLETIC   FA PREMIERSHIP

Ambrose Darren (M)	6 0	11 00	Harlow	29 2 84	Newcastle U
Andersen Stephan (G)	6 2	13 07	Copenhagen	26 11 81	AB Copenhagen
Ashton Nathan (D)	5 8	9 07	Plaistow	30 1 87	Scholar
Bent Darren (F)	5 11	12 07	Wandsworth	6 2 84	Ipswich T
Bent Marcus (F)	6 2	13 03	Hammersmith	19 5 78	Everton
El Karkouri Talal (D)	6 1	12 03	Casablanca	8 7 76	Sunderland
Elliot Rob (G)	6 3	14 10	Chatham	30 4 86	Scholar
Euell Jason (F)	5 11	11 13	Lambeth	6 2 77	Wimbledon
Fortune Jon (D)	6 2	12 12	Islington	23 8 80	Trainee
Gislason Rurik (M)	6 0	11 04	Reykjavik	25 2 88	
Holland Matt (M)	5 10	12 03	Bury	11 4 74	Ipswich T
Hreidarsson Hermann (D)	6 3	12 12	Reykjavik	11 7 74	Ipswich T
Hughes Bryan (M)	5 10	11 08	Liverpool	19 6 76	Birmingham C
Kemenes Szabolcs (G)	6 2	12 12	Budapest	18 5 86	Ferencvaros
Kishishev Radostin (D)	5 11	12 03	Bourgas	30 7 74	Litets Lovech
Lisbie Kevin (F)	5 10	11 06	Hackney	17 10 78	Trainee
Myhre Thomas (G)	6 4	14 02	Sarpsborg	16 10 73	Sunderland
Randolph Darren (G)	6 2	14 00	Dublin	12 5 87	Scholar
Ricketts Mark (D)	6 0	11 02	Sidcup	7 10 84	Scholar
Rommedahl Dennis (F)	5 9	11 08	Copenhagen	22 7 78	PSV Eindhoven
Sam Lloyd (F)	5 8	10 00	Leeds	27 9 84	Scholar
Sankofa Osei (D)	6 0	12 04	London	19 3 85	Scholar
Tanska Jani (D)	6 4	12 12	Anjalankoski	29 7 88	Scholar
Thomas Jerome (M)	5 9	11 09	Brent	23 3 83	Arsenal
Youga Kelly (D)	6 1	12 00	Bangui	22 9 85	Lyon
Young Luke (D)	6 0	12 04	Harlow	19 7 79	Tottenham H

League Appearances: Ambrose, D. 19(9); Andersen, S. 15; Bartlett, S. 6(10); Bent, D. 36; Bent, M. 12(1); Bothroyd, J. 3(15); El Karkouri, T. 4(6); Euell, J. 5(5); Fortune, J. 7(4); Holland, M. 20(3); Hreidarsson, H. 34; Hughes, B. 22(11); Johansson, J. 1(3); Kiely, D. 3; Kishishev, R. 34(3); Lisbie, K. 6); Murphy, D. 17(1); Myhre, T. 20; Perry, C. 27(1); Powell, C. 25(2); Rommedahl, D. 19(2); Sam, L. (2); Sankofa, O. 3(1); Smertin, A. 18; Sorondo, G. 7; Spector, J. 13(7); Thomas, J. 16(9); Young, L. 32.
Goals – League (41): Bent D 18 (3 pens), Murphy 4 (1 pen), Ambrose 3, Hughes 3, Bent M 2, Bothroyd 2, Rommedahl 2, Bartlett 1, Euell 1, Holland 1, Perry 1, Thomas 1, Young 1, own goal 1.
Carling Cup (6): Bent D 2, Ambrose 1, Bothroyd 1, Johansson 1 (pen), Murphy 1.

FA Cup (11): Bothroyd 3, Bent D 2, Hughes 2, Rommedahl 2, Fortune 1, Holland 1.
Ground: The Valley, Floyd Road, Charlton, London SE7 8BL. Telephone (020) 8333 4000.
Record Attendance: 75,031 v Aston Villa, FA Cup 5th rd, 12 February 1938 (at The Valley). **Capacity:** 27,113.
Manager: Iain Dowie.
Secretary: Chris Parkes.
Most League Goals: 107, Division 2, 1957–58.
Highest League Scorer in Season: Ralph Allen, 32, Division 3 (S), 1934–35.
Most League Goals in Total Aggregate: Stuart Leary, 153, 1953–62.
Most Capped Player: Jonatan Johansson, 41 (70), Finland.
Most League Appearances: Sam Bartram, 583, 1934–56.
Honours – Football League: Division 1 Champions – 1999–2000. Division 3 (S) Champions – 1928–29, 1934–35. **FA Cup:** Winners – 1947.
Colours: Red shirts, white shorts, red and white stockings.

CHELSEA   FA PREMIERSHIP

Name			Birthplace			Previous Club
Bridge Wayne (D)	5 10	12 13	Southampton	5 8 80	Southampton
Cech Petr (G)	6 5	14 03	Plzen	20 5 82	Rennes
Cole Carlton (F)	6 3	13 10	Croydon	12 10 83	Scholar
Cole Joe (M)	5 9	11 07	Islington	8 11 81	West Ham U
Crespo Hernan (F)	6 0	12 13	Florida	5 7 75	Internazionale
Cudicini Carlo (G)	6 1	12 06	Milan	6 9 73	Castel di Sangro
Del Horno Asier (D)	5 11	11 12	Portugalete	19 1 81	Athletic Bilbao
Diarra Lassana (M)	5 8	11 02	Paris	10 3 85	Le Havre
Drogba Didier (F)	6 2	13 08	Abidjan	11 3 78	Marseille
Duff Damien (M)	5 9	12 03	Ballyboden	2 3 79	Blackburn R
Elmer Jonas (D)			Zurich	28 2 88	Scholar
Essien Mickael (M)	5 10	13 06	Accra	3 12 82	Lyon
Gallas William (D)	6 0	11 13	Asnieres	17 8 77	Marseille
Geremi (M)	5 10	13 05	Bafoussam	20 12 78	Middlesbrough
Grant Anthony (M)	5 11	11 03	Lambeth	4 6 87	Scholar
Gudjohnsen Eidur (F)	6 1	14 02	Reykjavik	15 9 78	Bolton W
Hollands Danny (M)	6 0	11 11	Ashford (M'sex)	6 11 85	Scholar
Huth Robert (D)	6 3	14 01	Berlin	18 8 84	Scholar
Jarosik Jiri (M)	6 4	13 03	Usti Nad Lebem	27 10 77	CSKA Moscow
Johnson Glen (D)	6 0	12 13	Greenwich	23 8 84	West Ham U
Lampard Frank (M)	6 0	14 01	Romford	20 6 78	West Ham U
Ma Kalambay Yves (G)	6 5	14 10	Brussels	31 1 86	
Makelele Claude (M)	5 7	10 08	Kinshasa	18 2 73	Real Madrid
Mancienne Michael (D)			Isleworth	8 1 88	Scholar
Morais Filipe (M)	5 9	11 10	Lisbon	21 11 85	Scholar
Nuno Morais (D)	6 0	12 05	Penafiel	29 1 84	Penafiel
Paulo Ferreira (D)	6 0	11 13	Cascais	18 1 79	Porto
Pettigrew Adrian (D)	6 0	13 01	Hackney	12 11 86	Scholar
Pidgeley Lenny (G)	6 4	14 07	Isleworth	7 2 84	Scholar
Ricardo Carvalho (D)	6 0	12 06	Amarante	18 5 78	Porto
Robben Arjen (M)	5 11	12 08	Groningen	23 1 84	PSV Eindhoven
Simmonds James (M)			Hammersmith	3 12 87	Scholar
Sinclair Scott (F)	5 10	10 00	Bath	26 3 89	Bristol R
Smith Jimmy (M)	6 0	10 03	Newham	7 1 87	Scholar
Terry John (D)	6 1	13 08	Barking	7 12 80	Trainee
Veron Juan Sebastian (F)	5 11	12 04	La Plata	9 3 75	Manchester U
Worley Harry (D)	6 3	13 00	Warrington	25 11 88	Scholar
Wright-Phillips Shaun (M)	5 5	10 01	Lewisham	25 10 81	Manchester C
Younghusband Phil (F)	5 10	10 08	Ashford	4 8 87	Scholar

League Appearances: Cech, P. 34; Cole, C. (9); Cole, J. 26(8); Crespo, H. 20(10); Cudicini, C. 3(1); Del Horno, A. 25; Diarra, L. 2(1); Drogba, D. 20(9); Duff, D. 18(10); Essien, M. 27(4); Gallas, W. 33(1); Geremi, 8(7); Gudjohnsen, E. 16(10); Huth, R. 7(6); Johnson, G. 4; Lampard, F. 35; Makelele, C. 29(2); Maniche, 3(5); Paulo Ferreira, 18(3); Pidgeley, L. 1; Ricardo Carvalho, 22(2); Robben, A. 21(7); Smith, J. (1); Terry, J. 36; Wright-Phillips, S. 10(17).
Goals – League (72): Lampard 16 (4 pens), Drogba 12, Crespo 10, Cole J 7, Robben 6, Gallas 5, Terry 4, Duff 3, Essien 2, Geremi 2, Gudjohnsen 2, Del Horno 1, Ricardo Carvalho 1, own goal 1.
Carling Cup (1): Terry 1.
FA Cup (12): Cole J 2, Lampard 2 (1 pen), Terry 2, Cole C 1, Crespo 1, Drogba 1, Gudjohnsen 1, Paulo Ferreira 1, Robben 1.
Champions League (9): Crespo 3, Lampard 2 (1 pen), Ricardo Carvalho 2, Cole J 1, Drogba 1, own goal 1.
Community Shield (2): Drogba 2.
Ground: Stamford Bridge, London SW6 1HS. Telephone (0870) 300 1212.
Record Attendance: 82,905 v Arsenal, Division 1, 12 October 1935.
Capacity: 42,294.
Manager: José Mourinho.
Secretary: David Barnard.
Most League Goals: 98, Division 1, 1960–61.
Highest League Scorer in Season: Jimmy Greaves, 41, 1960–61.
Most League Goals in Total Aggregate: Bobby Tambling, 164, 1958–70.
Most Capped Player: Marcel Desailly, 67 (116), France.
Most League Appearances: Ron Harris, 655, 1962–80.
Honours – FA Premier League: Champions – 2004–05, 2005–06. **Football League:** Division 1 Champions – 1954–55. Division 2 Champions – 1983–84, 1988–89. **FA Cup:** Winners – 1970, 1997, 2000. **Football League Cup:** Winners – 1964–65, 1997–98, 2004–05. **Full Members' Cup:** Winners – 1985–86. **Zenith Data Systems Cup:** Winners – 1989–90. **European Cup-Winners' Cup:** Winners – 1970–71, 1997–98. **Super Cup:** Winners – 1999.
Colours: Blue shirts and shorts, white stockings.

CHELTENHAM TOWN FL CHAMPIONSHIP 1

Armstrong Craig (M)	5 11	12 09	South Shields	23 5 75	Bradford C
Bell Mickey (D)	5 9	12 02	Newcastle	15 11 71	Port Vale
Bird David (M)	5 9	12 00	Gloucester	26 12 84	Cinderford T
Brown Scott (G)	6 2	13 01	Wolverhampton	26 4 85	Bristol C
Caines Gavin (D)	6 1	12 00	Birmingham	20 9 83	Scholar
Connolly Adam (M)	5 9	12 04	Manchester	10 4 86	Scholar
Duff Shane (D)	6 1	12 10	Wroughton	2 4 82	Juniors
Finnigan John (M)	5 8	10 09	Wakefield	29 3 76	Lincoln C
Foley Sam (M)			Upton-on-Severn	17 10 86	Scholar
Gallinagh Andy (D)	5 8	11 08	Sutton Coldfield	16 3 85	Stratford T
Gill Jeremy (D)	5 11	12 00	Clevedon	8 9 70	Northampton T
Gillespie Steven (F)	5 9	11 02	Liverpool	4 6 84	Bristol C
Guinan Stephen (F)	6 1	13 02	Birmingham	24 12 75	Shrewsbury T
Higgs Shane (G)	6 3	14 06	Oxford	13 5 77	Bristol R
Lewis Greg (D)			Coleford		Scholar
McCann Grant (M)	5 10	11 00	Belfast	14 4 80	West Ham U
Melligan John (M)	5 9	11 02	Dublin	11 2 82	Wolverhampton W
Musgrove Scott (M)			Stamford	21 6 87	Stoke C
Odejayi Kayode (F)	6 2	12 02	Ibadon	21 2 82	Bristol C
Puddy Will (G)	5 10	11 07	Salisbury	4 10 87	Scholar
Spencer Damien (F)	6 1	14 00	Ascot	19 9 81	Bristol C
Townsend Michael (D)	6 1	13 12	Walsall	17 5 86	Wolverhampton W
Victory Jamie (D)	5 10	12 13	Hackney	14 11 75	Bournemouth

Vincent Ashley (F)	5 10	11 08	Oldbury	26 5 85	Wolverhampton W
Whittington Michael (F)			Bristol		Scholar
Wilson Brian (D)	5 10	11 00	Manchester	9 5 83	Stoke C
Wylde Michael (M)	6 2	13 02	Birmingham	6 1 87	Scholar
Yao Sosthene (M)	5 4	11 09	Ivory Coast	7 8 87	West Ham U

League Appearances: Armstrong, C. 28(6); Bell, M. 7(2); Bird, D. 18(18); Bradshaw, G. (3); Brown, A. 3; Brown, S. 1; Caines, G. 35(4); Connolly, A. 4(1); Duff, S. 18(2); Finnigan, J. 38(1); Gallinagh, A. 1; Gill, J. 41(1); Gillespie, S. 4(10); Guinan, S. 27(3); Higgs, S. 45; McCann, G. 38(1); Melligan, J. 40(2); Odejayi, K. 38(3); Rose, M. 3; Spencer, D. 17(29); Taylor, M. 9(1); Townsend, M. 30(1); Victory, J. 19(3); Vincent, A. 1(12); Wilson, B. 41(2); Wylde, M. (1); Yao, S. (3).
Goals – League (65): Odejayi 11, Wilson 9, McCann 8 (3 pens), Guinan 7, Melligan 6 (1 pen), Gillespie 5, Finnigan 4, Spencer 3, Armstrong 2, Caines 2, Victory 2, Vincent 2, Bird 1 (pen), Connolly 1, own goals 2.
Carling Cup (5): McCann 2, Caines 1, Melligan 1, Victory 1.
FA Cup (7): Odejayi 2, Finnigan 1 (pen), Guinan 1, McCann 1, Melligan 1 (pen), Wilson 1.
Football League Trophy (9): Gillespie 2, Wilson 2, Armstrong 1, Connolly 1, Duff 1, Spicer 1, Victory 1.
Play-Offs (3): Guinan 2, Finnigan 1.
Ground: Whaddon Road, Cheltenham, Gloucester GL52 5NA. Telephone (01242) 573 558.
Record Attendance: at Whaddon Road: 8326 v Reading, FA Cup 1st rd, 17 November 1956; at Cheltenham Athletic Ground: 10,389 v Blackpool, FA Cup 3rd rd, 13 January 1934.
Capacity: 7,013.
Manager: John Ward.
Secretary: Paul Godfrey.
Most League Goals: 66, Division 3, 2001–02.
Highest League Scorer in Season: Julian Alsop, 20, Division 3, 2001–02.
Most League Goals in Total Aggregate: Martin Devaney, 38, 1999–2005.
Most League Appearances: Jamie Victory, 248, 1999–.
Most Capped Player: Grant McCann, 6 (11), Northern Ireland.
Honours – Football Conference: Champions – 1998–99. **FA Trophy:** Winners – 1997–98.
Colours: Red and white striped shirts, white shorts, red stockings.

CHESTER CITY   FL CHAMPIONSHIP 2

Artell Dave (D)	6 3	14 01	Rotherham	22 11 80	Mansfield T
Blundell Greg (F)	5 10	11 06	Liverpool	3 10 77	Doncaster R
Branch Michael (F)	5 10	12 00	Liverpool	18 10 78	Bradford C
Brookfield Ryan (G)	6 0	12 06	Liverpool	10 5 87	
Brown Wayne (G)	6 0	13 11	Southampton	14 1 77	Weston S Mare
Davies Ben (M)	5 7	11 09	Birmingham	27 5 81	Kidderminster H
Harrison Paul (G)	5 9	13 04	Liverpool	18 12 84	Wolverhampton W
Hessey Sean (D)	6 1	12 09	Liverpool	19 9 78	Blackpool
Rutherford Paul (M)	5 9	11 07	Moreton	10 7 87	
Vaughan James (D)	5 10	12 09	Liverpool	6 12 86	Tranmere R
Vaughan Stephen (D)	5 6	11 01	Liverpool	22 1 85	Liverpool

League Appearances: Albrighton, M. 9; Artell, D. 34(3); Asamoah, D. 14(3); Bertos, L. 2(3); Blundell, G. 23(7); Bolland, P. 12(4); Branch, M. 23(4); Brookfield, R. (1); Corden, W. 2; Curle, T. (2); Curtis, T. 34(6); Davies, B. 42(3); Dimech, L. 27(3); Dove, C. 2(3); Drummond, S. 41(1); Edwards, J. 10; El Kholti, A. 7(13); Ellender, P. 5; Gillet, S. 8; Harrison, P. 4; Hessey, S. 17(2); Horwood, E. 1; Lowe, R. 28(4); MacKenzie, C. 30; McNiven, S. 41; Regan, C. 39(2); Richardson, M.

42

22(12); Roberts, M. 1; Robertson, C. (1); Ruddy, J. 4; Rutherford, P. 1(5); Tait, P. 3(6); Vaughan, S. 7(10); Walker, J. 13(8).
Goals – League (53): Lowe 10 (1 pen), Asamoah 8, Blundell 7, Davies 7 (2 pens), Drummond 6, Branch 5 (2 pens), Richardson 4, Artell 2, Bolland 1, Curtis 1, Edwards 1, McNiven 1.
Carling Cup (1): Davies 1.
FA Cup (7): Lowe 3 (1 pen), Richardson 2, Branch 1 (pen), Drummond 1.
Football League Trophy (0).
Ground: Saunders Honda Stadium, Bumpers Lane, Chester CH1 4LT. Telephone (01244) 371 376.
Record Attendance: 20,500 v Chelsea, FA Cup 3rd rd (replay), 16 January 1952 (at Sealand Rd)
Capacity: 6,012.
Manager: Mark Wright.
Secretary: Tony Allan.
Most League Goals: 119, Division 4, 1964–65.
Highest League Scorer in Season: Dick Yates, 36, Division 3 (N), 1946–47.
Most League Goals in Total Aggregate: Stuart Rimmer, 135, 1985–88, 1991–98.
Most Capped Player: Angus Eve, 35 (117), Trinidad & Tobago.
Most League Appearances: Ray Gill, 406, 1951–62.
Honours – Conference: Champions – 2003–04. **Welsh Cup:** Winners – 1908, 1933, 1947. **Debenhams Cup:** Winners 1977.
Colours: Blue and white striped shirts, blue shorts, blue stockings

CHESTERFIELD FL CHAMPIONSHIP 1

Allison Wayne (F)	6 0	15 00	Huddersfield	16 10 68	Sheffield U
Allott Mark (M)	6 0	11 10	Manchester	3 10 77	Oldham Ath
Bailey Alex (D)	5 9	11 03	Newham	21 9 83	Arsenal
Blatherwick Steve (D)	6 2	14 06	Nottingham	20 9 73	Burnley
Davies Gareth (M)	6 0	12 00	Chesterfield	4 2 83	Trainee
Downes Aaron (D)	6 3	13 00	Mudgee	15 5 85	Frickley C
Folan Caleb (F)	6 2	14 00	Leeds	26 10 82	Leeds U
Foyle Ashley (D)	5 11	12 00	Sheffield	17 9 86	Scholar
Hall Paul (M)	5 8	12 00	Manchester	3 7 72	Tranmere R
Hazell Ruben (D)	5 11	12 05	Birmingham	24 4 79	Torquay U
Heath Colin (F)	6 0	11 13	Matlock	31 12 83	Manchester U
Jackson Jamie (F)	5 6	10 04	Sheffield	1 11 86	Scholar
Kovacs Janos (D)	6 4	14 10	Budapest	11 9 85	MTK
Larkin Colin (F)	5 9	11 07	Dundalk	27 4 82	Mansfield T
Nicholson Shane (D)	5 11	12 06	Newark	3 6 70	Tranmere R
Niven Derek (M)	6 0	12 02	Falkirk	12 12 83	Bolton W
O'Hare Alan (D)	6 2	12 08	Drogheda	31 7 82	Bolton W
Roche Barry (G)	6 5	14 08	Dublin	6 4 82	Nottingham F
Smith Adam (M)	5 11	12 00	Huddersfield	20 2 85	Scholar

League Appearances: Allison, W. 26(6); Allott, M. 43; Bailey, A. 17(1); Beckwith, R. 2; Blatherwick, S. 29(1); Clingan, S. 14(7); Davies, G. 13(7); De Bolla, M. 2(2); Downes, A. 20(2); Folan, C. 8(19); Foyle, A. (1); Hall, P. 44(1); Hazell, R. 30(3); Heath, C. 1(3); Hurst, K. 30(7); Jackson, J. (2); Kovacs, J. 9; Lancaster, S. (1); Larkin, C. 31(10); Mugglleton, C. 3; N'Toya. T. 1(3); Nicholson, S. 24(1); Niven, D. 42; O'Hara, J. 19; O'Hare, A. 15(7); Picken, P. 32; Roche, B. 41; Smith, A. 10(16).
Goals – League (63): Hall 15 (2 pens), Allison 11, Larkin 7, Nicholson 5 (3 pens), Niven 5, O'Hara 5, Hurst 4, Allott 3, Smith 3, Blatherwick 2, Clingan 1, De Bolla 1, Picken 1.
Carling Cup (2): Hurst 1, Niven 1.
FA Cup (1): Hurst 1.
Football League Trophy (0).

Ground: Recreation Ground, Chesterfield S40 4SX. Telephone (01246) 209 765.
Record Attendance: 30,968 v Newcastle U, Division 2, 7 April 1939. **Capacity:** 8,502.
Manager: Roy McFarland.
Secretary: Alan Walters.
Most League Goals: 102, Division 3 (N), 1930–31.
Highest League Scorer in Season: Jimmy Cookson, 44, Division 3 (N), 1925–26.
Most League Goals in Total Aggregate: Ernie Moss, 161, 1969–76, 1979–81 and 1984–86.
Most Capped Player: Walter McMillen, 4 (7), Northern Ireland; Mark Williams, 4 (30), Northern Ireland.
Most League Appearances: Dave Blakey, 613, 1948–67.
Honours – Football League: Division 3 (N) Champions – 1930–31, 1935–36. Division 4 Champions – 1969–70, 1984–85. **Anglo-Scottish Cup:** Winners – 1980–81.
Colours: Blue shirts, white shorts, blue stockings.

COLCHESTER UNITED   FL CHAMPIONSHIP

Baldwin Pat (D)	6 3	12 07	City of London	12 11 82	Chelsea
Brown Wayne (D)	6 0	12 06	Barking	20 8 77	Watford
Chilvers Liam (D)	6 2	12 03	Chelmsford	6 11 81	Arsenal
Cousins Mark (G)			Chelmsford	9 1 87	Scholar
Danns Neil (M)	5 8	10 12	Liverpool	23 11 82	Blackburn R
Davison Aidan (G)	6 1	13 12	Sedgefield	11 5 68	Grimsby T
Duguid Karl (M)	5 11	11 06	Hitchin	21 3 78	Trainee
Elokobi George (D)	5 10	13 02	Cameroon	31 1 86	Dulwich Hamlet
Garcia Richard (F)	5 11	12 01	Perth	4 9 81	West Ham U
Gerken Dean (G)	6 1	12 08	Rochford	22 5 85	Scholar
Guy Jamie (M)	6 1	13 00	Barking	1 8 87	Scholar
Halford Greg (D)	6 4	12 10	Chelmsford	8 12 84	Scholar
Iwelumo Chris (F)	6 3	15 03	Coatbridge	1 8 78	Aachen
Izzet Kem (M)	5 7	10 05	Mile End	29 9 80	Charlton Ath
Keith Marino (F)	5 10	12 13	Peterhead	16 12 74	Plymouth Arg
King Robbie (M)	5 11	12 05	Chelmsford	1 10 86	Scholar
Paine Matt (D)	6 1	12 12	Sidcup	22 12 87	Scholar
Pond Russell (M)	5 8	11 10	Leytonstone	27 1 87	Scholar
Richards Garry (D)	6 3	13 00	Romford	11 6 86	Scholar
Thorpe Tony (F)	5 9	12 06	Leicester	10 4 74	Swindon T
Watson Kevin (M)	6 0	12 06	Hackney	3 1 74	Reading
White John (M)	5 10	12 01	Maldon	26 7 86	Scholar

League Appearances: Baldwin, P. 20(5); Brown, W. 38; Campbell-Ryce, J. 1(3); Chilvers, L. 33(1); Clarke, B. 2(4); Cureton, J. 7(1); Danns, N. 38(3); Davison, A. 41; Duguid, K. 26(9); Elokobi, G. 10(2); Garcia, R. 9(13); Gerken, D. 5(2); Guy, J. (2); Halford, G. 45; Howell, D. 1(3); Hunt, S. (2); Iwelumo, C. 46; Izzet, K. 19(14); King, R. (3); Richards, G. 12(3); Stockley, S. 21(6); Thorpe, T. 5(9); Vernon, S. 4(3); Watson, K. 43(1); White, J. 32(3); Williams, G. 6(12); Yeates, M. 42(2).
Goals – League (58): Iwelumo 17 (3 pens), Danns 8, Halford 7, Garcia 5, Yeates 5, Cureton 4, Brown 2, Chilvers 2, Elokobi 1, Stockley 1, Vernon 1, Williams 1, own goals 4.
Carling Cup (0).
FA Cup (17): Danns 5, Cureton 3, Iwelumo 2, Brown 1, Garcia 1, Halford 1, Watson 1, Williams 1, Yeates 1, own goal 1.
Football League Trophy (7): Danns 3, Garcia 2, Duguid 1, Elokobi 1.
Ground: Layer Road Ground, Colchester CO2 7JJ. Telephone (0871) 226 2161.
Record Attendance: 19,072 v Reading, FA Cup 1st rd, 27 Nov, 1948. **Capacity:** 6,189.
Manager: TBC.

Secretary: Miss Caroline Pugh.
Most League Goals: 104, Division 4, 1961–62.
Highest League Scorer in Season: Bobby Hunt, 38, Division 4, 1961–62.
Most League Goals in Total Aggregate: Martyn King, 130, 1956–64.
Most Capped Player: None.
Most League Appearances: Micky Cook, 613, 1969–84.
Honours – GM Vauxhall Conference: Winners – 1991–92. **FA Trophy:** Winners: 1991–92.
Colours: Blue and white vertical striped shirts, white shorts, white stockings.

COVENTRY CITY   FL CHAMPIONSHIP

Name				Birthplace	Date	Previous club
Adebola Dele (F)	6 3	15 00	Lagos	23 6 75	Crystal Palace
Davis Liam (M)	5 9	11 07	Wandsworth	23 11 86	Scholar
Doyle Micky (M)	5 8	11 00	Dublin	8 7 81	Celtic
Giddings Stuart (M)	6 0	11 08	Coventry	27 3 86	Scholar
Hall Marcus (D)	6 1	12 02	Coventry	24 3 76	Stoke C
Heath Matt (D)	6 4	13 13	Leicester	1 11 81	Leicester C
Hughes Stephen (M)	5 9	12 12	Wokingham	18 9 76	Charlton Ath
Hutchison Don (M)	6 1	11 08	Gateshead	9 5 71	Millwall
Impey Andrew (M)	5 8	11 02	Hammersmith	30 9 71	Nottingham F
Ince Clayton (G)	6 3	13 03	Trinidad	13 7 72	Crewe Alex
John Stern (F)	6 0	12 11	Trinidad	30 10 76	Birmingham C
Jorgensen Claus (M)	5 11	11 00	Holstebro	27 4 76	Bradford C
Lynch Ryan (M)	5 11	11 09	Solihull	13 3 87	Scholar
McCrink Paul (M)			Newry	10 11 87	Scholar
McSheffrey Gary (F)	5 8	10 06	Coventry	13 8 82	Trainee
Morrell Andy (F)	5 11	11 06	Doncaster	28 9 74	Wrexham
Osbourne Isaac (M)	5 9	11 11	Birmingham	22 6 86	Scholar
Page Robert (D)	6 0	13 10	Llwynpia	3 9 74	Cardiff C
Reid Craig (F)	5 10	11 10	Coventry	17 12 85	Ipswich T
Scowcroft James (F)	6 1	14 07	Bury St Edmunds	15 11 75	Leicester C
Thornton Kevin (M)	5 7	11 00	Drogheda	9 7 86	Scholar
Whing Andrew (D)	6 0	12 00	Birmingham	20 9 84	Scholar
Williams Adrian (D)	6 2	13 02	Reading	16 8 71	Reading

League Appearances: Adebola, D. 39(5); Bywater, S. 14; Davis, L. (2); Doyle, M. 44; Duffy, R. 30(2); Flood, W. 7(1); Fulop, M. 31; Giddings, S. 1(1); Hall, M. 38(1); Heath, M. 23(2); Hughes, S. 18(1); Hutchison, D. 10(14); Impey, A. 4(12); Ince, C. 1; John, S. 21(4); Jorgensen, C. 15(12); McSheffrey, G. 43; Morrell, A. 10(24); Nalis, L. 5(1); Osbourne, I. 7(3); Page, R. 32; Scowcroft, J. 37(4); Shaw, R. 24(1); Sofiane, Y. (1); Thornton, K. 4(12); Turner, B. (1); Watson, P. 1(2); Whing, A. 24(8); Williams, A. 12(2); Wise, D. 11(2); Wood, N. (4).
Goals – League (62): McSheffrey 15 (3 pens), Adebola 12, John 10, Wise 6, Hutchison 4 (1 pen), Jorgensen 3, Scowcroft 3, Morrell 2, Nalis 2, Flood 1, Heath 1, Page 1, own goals 2.
Carling Cup (3): Heath 1, McSheffrey 1, Morrell 1.
FA Cup (2): John 1, McSheffrey 1.
Ground: Ricoh Arena, Phoenix Way, Foleshill, Coventry CV6 6GE. Telephone (0870) 421 1987.
Record Attendance: 51,455 v Wolverhampton W, Division 2, 29 April 1967 (at Highfield Road). **Capacity:** 32,500.
Manager: Micky Adams.
Secretary: Graham Hover.
Most League Goals: 108, Division 3 (S), 1931–32.
Highest League Scorer in Season: Clarrie Bourton, 49, Division 3 (S), 1931–32.
Most League Goals in Total Aggregate: Clarrie Bourton, 171, 1931–37.
Most Capped Player: Magnus Hedman, 44 (56), Sweden.
Most League Appearances: Steve Ogrizovic, 507, 1984–2000.

Honours – Football League: Division 2 Champions – 1966–67. Division 3 Champions – 1963–64. Division 3 (S) Champions 1935–36. **FA Cup:** Winners – 1986–87.
Colours: Sky blue and white striped shirts with plain sky blue panels on either side, sky blue shorts with white panel on one side and along the top on back, sky blue stockings with white stripe down each calf.

CREWE ALEXANDRA   FL CHAMPIONSHIP 1

Bailey Matt (F)	6 4	11 06	Crewe	12 3 86	Northwich Vic
Bell Lee (M)	5 11	11 00	Alsager	26 1 83	Scholar
Bignot Paul (D)	6 1	12 03	Birmingham	14 2 86	Scholar
Grant Tony (M)	5 9	11 00	Liverpool	14 11 74	Bristol C
Higdon Michael (M)	6 2	11 05	Liverpool	2 9 83	School
Jones Billy (D)	5 11	13 00	Shrewsbury	24 3 87	Scholar
Lloyd Rob (D)	6 0	11 10	Chester	13 8 86	Scholar
Lowe Ryan (F)	5 10	12 08	Liverpool	18 9 78	Chester C
Lunt Kenny (M)	5 10	10 05	Runcorn	20 11 79	Trainee
Maynard Nicky (F)	5 11	11 00	Winsford	11 12 86	Scholar
McCready Chris (D)	6 1	12 05	Ellesmere Port	5 9 81	Scholar
Morris Alex (M)	6 0	11 08	Stoke	5 10 82	Scholar
Moss Darren (D)	5 10	11 00	Wrexham	24 5 81	Shrewsbury T
O'Connor Michael (M)	6 1	11 08	Belfast	6 10 87	Scholar
Otsemobor John (D)	5 10	12 07	Liverpool	23 3 83	Rotherham U
Pope Tom (F)	6 3	11 03	Stoke	27 8 85	Lancaster C
Rix Ben (M)	5 9	11 05	Wolverhampton	11 12 82	Scholar
Roberts Gary (M)	5 8	10 05	Chester	4 2 87	Scholar
Roberts Mark (D)	6 1	12 00	Northwich	16 10 83	Scholar
Rodgers Luke (F)	5 8	11 00	Birmingham	1 1 82	Shrewsbury T
Suhaj Pavol (F)	6 3	12 00	Lipany	16 4 81	Trencin
Sutton Ritchie (D)	6 0	11 05	Stoke	29 4 86	Scholar
Tomlinson Stuart (G)	6 1	11 02	Chester	10 5 85	Scholar
Ugarte Juan (F)	5 10	10 08	San Sebastian	7 11 80	Wrexham
Varney Luke (F)	5 11	11 00	Leicester	28 9 82	Quorn
Vaughan David (M)	5 7	11 00	Abergele	18 2 83	Scholar
Williams Ben (G)	6 0	13 01	Manchester	27 8 82	Manchester U
Williams Owain Fon (G)	6 1	12 09	Gwynedd	17 3 87	Scholar

League Appearances: Bell, L. 14(3); Bignot, P. 4(1); Bougherra, M. 11; Cochrane, J. 2(2); Foster, S. 36(3); Grant, T. 10; Higdon, M. 15(11); Johnson, E. 16(6); Jones, B. 43(1); Jones, S. 36(5); Lunt, K. 43; Maynard, N. (1); McCready, C. 19(6); Moses, A. 12(3); Moss, D. 30(1); O'Connor, M. (2); Otsemobor, J. 16; Rivers, M. 9(8); Rix, B. 1(1); Roberts, G. 27(6); Rodgers, L. 13(13); Suhaj, P. 1(5); Taylor, G. 15; Tomlinson, S. 1(1); Tonkin, A. 27; Turnbull, R. 29; Ugarte, J. (2); Varney, L. 15(12); Vaughan, D. 28(6); Walker, R. 17(1); Williams, B. 16(1).
Goals – League (57): Jones B 6, Rodgers 6, Johnson 5, Jones S 5, Varney 5, Vaughan 5, Lunt 4 (2 pens), Taylor 4, Foster 3, Higdon 3, Rivers 3, Bell 2, Roberts 2, Bougherra 1, Maynard 1, Walker 1, own goal 1.
Carling Cup (1): Walker 1.
FA Cup (1): Jones B 1.
Ground: Alexandria Stadium, Gresty Road, Crewe CW2 6EB. Telephone (01270) 213 014.
Record Attendance: 20,000 v Tottenham H, FA Cup 4th rd, 30 January 1960.
Capacity: 10,046.
Manager: Dario Gradi MBE.
Secretary: Andrew Blakemore.
Most League Goals: 95, Division 3 (N), 1931–32.
Highest League Scorer in Season: Terry Harkin, 35, Division 4, 1964–65.
Most League Goals in Total Aggregate: Bert Swindells, 126, 1928–37.

Most Capped Player: Clayton Ince, 38, Trinidad & Tobago.
Most League Appearances: Tommy Lowry, 436, 1966–78.
Honours – Welsh Cup: Winners – 1936, 1937.
Colours: All red.

CRYSTAL PALACE FL CHAMPIONSHIP

Black Tommy (M)	5 7	11 10	Chigwell	26 11 79	Arsenal
Borrowdale Gary (D)	6 0	12 01	Sutton	16 7 85	Scholar
Boyce Emmerson (D)	6 0	12 03	Aylesbury	24 9 79	Luton T
Butterfield Danny (D)	5 10	11 06	Boston	21 11 79	Grimsby T
Fray Arron (D)	5 11	11 02	Beckenham	1 5 87	Scholar
Freedman Dougie (F)	5 9	12 05	Glasgow	21 1 74	Nottingham F
Grabban Lewis (F)	6 0	11 03	Croydon	12 1 88	Scholar
Granville Danny (D)	6 0	12 00	Islington	19 1 75	Manchester C
Hall Fitz (D)	6 3	13 00	Leytonstone	20 12 80	Southampton
Hall Ryan (M)	5 10	10 04	Dulwich	4 1 88	Scholar
Hudson Mark (D)	6 1	12 01	Guildford	30 3 82	Fulham
Hughes Michael (M)	5 6	10 08	Larne	2 8 71	Wimbledon
Johnson Andy (F)	5 7	10 09	Bedford	10 2 81	Birmingham C
Kiraly Gabor (G)	6 3	13 06	Szombathely	1 4 76	Hertha Berlin
Leigertwood Mikele (D)	6 1	11 04	Enfield	12 11 82	Wimbledon
Macken Jon (F)	5 11	12 04	Manchester	7 9 77	Manchester C
McAnuff Jobi (M)	5 11	11 05	Edmonton	9 11 81	Cardiff C
Morrison Clinton (F)	6 0	12 00	Tooting	14 5 79	Birmingham C
Popovic Tony (D)	6 5	13 01	Australia	7 4 73	Sanfrecce
Reich Marco (M)	6 0	12 00	Meisenheim	30 12 77	Derby Co
Soares Tom (M)	6 0	11 04	Reading	10 7 86	Scholar
Speroni Julian (G)	6 0	11 00	Buenos Aires	18 5 79	Dundee
Togwell Sam (M)	5 11	12 04	Beaconsfield	14 10 84	Scholar
Torghelle Sandor (F)	6 1	13 06	Budapest	5 5 82	MTK
Ward Darren (D)	6 3	11 04	Kenton	13 9 78	Millwall
Watson Ben (M)	5 10	10 11	Camberwell	9 7 85	Scholar

League Appearances: Andrews, W. 5(19); Black, T. (1); Borrowdale, G. 26(4); Boyce, E. 42; Butterfield, D. 9(4); Freedman, D. 19(15); Hall, F. 39; Hudson, M. 8(7); Hughes, M. 30(10); Johnson, A. 30(3); Kiraly, G. 43; Kolkka, J. 1(2); Leigertwood, M. 18(9); Macken, J. 13(11); McAnuff, J. 35(6); Morrison, C. 32(8); Popovic, T. 10; Reich, M. 14(7); Riihilahti, A. 9(6); Soares, T. 38(6); Speroni, J. 3(1); Ward, D. 42(1); Watson, B. 40(2).
Goals – League (67): Johnson 15 (2 pens), Morrison 13, McAnuff 7, Freedman 6 (1 pen), Ward 5, Watson 4, Boyce 2, Hughes 2, Macken 2, Reich 2, Riihilahti 2, Andrews 1, Hall 1, Soares 1, own goals 4.
Carling Cup (7): Reich 2, Freedman 2, Granville 1, Hughes 1, Popovic 1 (pen), own goal 1.
FA Cup (6): Johnson 2 (1 pen), Freedman 1 (pen), Hughes 1, McAnuff 1, Ward 1.
Play-Offs (0).
Ground: Selhurst Park Stadium, Whitehorse Lane, London SE25 6PU. Telephone (020) 8768 6000.
Record Attendance: 51,482 v Burnley, Division 2, 11 May 1979. **Capacity:** 26,225.
Manager: Peter Taylor.
Secretary: Christine Dowdeswell.
Most League Goals: 110, Division 4, 1960–61.
Highest League Scorer in Season: Peter Simpson, 46, Division 3 (S), 1930–31.
Most League Goals in Total Aggregate: Peter Simpson, 153, 1930–36.
Most Capped Player: Aleksandrs Kolinko, 23 (66), Latvia.
Most League Appearances: Jim Cannon, 571, 1973–88.

Honours – Football League: Division 1 – Champions 1993–94. Division 2 Champions – 1978–79. Division 3 (S) 1920–21. **Zenith Data Systems Cup:** Winners – 1991.
Colours: Red and blue vertical striped shirts, red shorts, red stockings.

DARLINGTON   FL CHAMPIONSHIP 2

Clarke Matthew (D)	6 3	13 00	Leeds	18 12 80	Halifax T
Close Brian (D)	5 10	12 00	Belfast	27 1 82	Middlesbrough
Duke David (D)	5 10	11 00	Inverness	7 11 78	Swindon T
Hutchinson Jonathan (D)	5 11	11 11	Middlesbrough	2 4 82	Birmingham C
Jameson Nathan (M)	5 11	12 03	Middlesbrough	20 3 85	Walsall
Janes Alex (D)			York	10 10 87	Scholar
Johnson Simon (F)	5 9	11 09	West Bromwich	9 3 83	Leeds U
Keltie Clark (M)	6 0	11 08	Newcastle	31 8 83	Shildon
Logan Carlos (M)	5 10	12 06	Wythenshawe	7 11 85	Manchester C
Logan Richard (M)	6 0	11 12	Washington	18 2 88	Scholar
Maddison Neil (M)	5 10	12 00	Darlington	2 10 69	Middlesbrough
Martis Shelton (D)	6 0	11 11	Willemstad	29 11 82	Excelsior
McGurk David (D)	6 0	11 10	Middlesbrough	30 9 82	Scholar
McLeod Mark (M)	6 0	12 00	Sunderland	15 12 86	Scholar
Norton Jack (G)	6 0		Middlesbrough	27 3 87	Scholar
Parkin Gavin (F)	6 0		Stockton	19 11 86	Scholar
Peacock Anthony (M)	5 5	11 11	Middlesbrough	6 9 85	Middlesbrough
Russell Sam (G)	6 0	11 00	Middlesbrough	4 10 82	Middlesbrough
Sodje Akpo (F)	6 2	12 08	Greenwich	31 1 81	Huddersfield T
Stamp Phil (M)	5 11	13 05	Middlesbrough	12 12 75	Middlesbrough
Valentine Ryan (D)	5 10	11 05	Wrexham	19 8 82	Everton
Wainwright Neil (M)	6 0	12 00	Warrington	4 11 77	Sunderland

League Appearances: Appleby, M. 18(8); Atieno, T. (3); Bates, G. 6(3); Beaumont, J. (1); Bossu, B. 9; Clarke, M. 42(1); Close, B. 4(2); Cooke, A. 11(3); Dickman, J. 35(3); Duke, D. 17(3); Hopkins, P. 3(2); Hutchinson, J. 19; Jameson, N. 1(4); Johnson, J. 9; Johnson, S. 35(7); Kandol, T. 6(1); Keltie, C. 23(1); Kendrick, J. 21; Knight, D. 3; Lafferty, K. 9; Logan, C. 27(6); Maddison, N. (1); Martis, S. 39(1); McDermott, N. 1(2); McGurk, D. 2(1); McLeod, M. 2(2); N'Dumbu Nsungu, G. 11(10); Peacock, A. 17(10); Russell, S. 30; Schmeichel, K. 4; Sodje, A. 17(19); Stamp, P. 5(3); Stockdale, R. 3; Thomas, S. (6); Valentine, R. 43; Wainwright, N. 23(16); Webster, A. 6(7); Wijnhard, C. 5(3).
Goals – League (58): N'Dumbu Nsungu 10 (3 pens), Sodje 8, Johnson S 7 (3 pens), Logan 4, Clarke 3, Cooke 3, Johnson J 3, Lafferty 3, Wainwright 3, Dickman 2, Kandol 2, Martis 2, Bates 1, Duke 1, Hopkins 1, Stamp 1, Webster 1, Wijnhard 1 (pen), own goals 2.
Carling Cup (1): Logan 1.
FA Cup (0).
Football League Trophy (1): N'Dumbu Nsungu 1 (pen).
Ground: 96.6 TFM Darlington Arena, Neasham Road, Hurworth Moor, Darlington DL2 1GR. Telephone (01325) 387 000.
Record Attendance: 21,023 v Bolton W, League Cup 3rd rd, 14 November 1960.
Capacity: 25,000.
Manager: David Hodgson.
Secretary: Lisa Charlton.
Most League Goals: 108, Division 3 (N), 1929–30.
Highest League Scorer in Season: David Brown, 39, Division 3 (N), 1924–25.
Most League Goals in Total Aggregate: Alan Walsh, 90, 1978–84.
Most Capped Player: Jason Devos, 3 (46), Canada and Adrian Webster, 3, New Zealand.
Most League Appearances: Ron Greener, 442, 1955–68.

Honours – Football League: Division 3 (N) Champions – 1924–25. Division 4 Champions – 1990–91. **GM Vauxhall Conference:** Champions – 1989–90.
Colours: Black and white hooped shirts, black shorts, black stockings.

DERBY COUNTY   FL CHAMPIONSHIP

Name				Birthplace				Previous
Addison Miles (D)	6	2	13 03	Newham	7	1	89	Scholar
Ainsworth Lionel (F)	5	9	9 10	Nottingham	1	10	87	Scholar
Barnes Giles (M)	6	0	12 10	Barking	5	8	88	Scholar
Bisgaard Morten (M)	6	1	12 04	Randers	25	6	74	FC Copenhagen
Boertien Paul (D)	5	10	11 02	Haltwhistle	21	1	79	Carlisle U
Bolder Adam (M)	5	9	10 08	Hull	25	10	80	Hull C
Camp Lee (G)	5	11	11 11	Derby	22	8	84	Scholar
Doyle Nathan (M)	5	10	12 06	Derby	12	1	87	Scholar
Edworthy Marc (D)	5	10	11 11	Barnstaple	24	12	72	Norwich C
Grant Lee (G)	6	3	13 01	Hemel Hempstead	27	1	83	Scholar
Holmes Lee (M)	5	8	10 06	Sutton-in-Ashfield	2	4	87	Scholar
Idiakez Inigo (M)	6	0	12 02	San Sebastian	8	11	73	Rayo Vallecano
Jackson Richard (D)	5	8	12 10	Whitby	18	4	80	Scarborough
Johnson Michael (D)	5	11	11 12	Nottingham	4	7	73	Birmingham C
Johnson Seth (M)	5	10	12 13	Birmingham	12	3	79	Leeds U
Moore Darren (D)	6	2	15 07	Birmingham	22	4	74	WBA
Nyatanga Lewin (D)	6	2	12 08	Burton	18	8	88	Scholar
Peschisolido Paul (F)	5	7	10 12	Scarborough, Can	25	5	71	Sheffield U
Smith Tommy (F)	5	8	11 04	Hemel Hempstead	22	5	80	Sunderland
Thirlwell Paul (M)	5	11	12 08	Springwell	13	2	79	Sheffield U

League Appearances: Addison, M. 2; Ainsworth, L. (2); Barnes, G. 15(4); Bisgaard, M. 25(8); Blackstock, D. 8(1); Bolder, A. 25(10); Camp, L. 40; Davies, A. 22(1); Doyle, N. (4); Edworthy, M. 30; El Hamdaoui, M. 5(4); Emerson, 3(1); Fadiga, K. 2(2); Graham, D. 11(3); Hajto, T. 5; Holdsworth, D. (3); Holmes, L. 9(9); Idiakez, I. 41(1); Jackson, J. 3(3); Jackson, R. 20(6); John, S. 6(1); Johnson, M. 30(1); Johnson, S. 26(4); Kenna, J. 15(1); Lisbie, K. 7; McIndoe, M. 6(2); Mills, P. (1); Moore, D. 14; Nyatanga, L. 23(1); Peschisolido, P. 14(20); Poole, K. 6; Rasiak, G. 6; Smith, T. 43; Thirlwell, P. 15(6); Tudgay, M. 11(10); Whittingham, P. 11; Wright, A. 7.
Goals – League (53): Idiakez 11 (4 pens), Smith 8 (2 pens), Peschisolido 5, Bisgaard 4, Blackstock 3, Davies 3, El Hamdaoui 3, Johnson S 3, Bolder 2, Rasiak 2, Tudgay 2, Barnes 1, Johnson M 1, Lisbie 1, Moore 1, Nyatanga 1, own goals 2.
Carling Cup (0).
FA Cup (3): Peschisolido 2, Smith 1 (pen).
Ground: Pride Park Stadium, Derby DE24 8XL. Telephone (0870) 444 1884.
Record Attendance: Pride Park: 33, 475 Derby Co Legends v Rangers 9 in a row Legends, 1 May 2006 (Ted McMinn Benefit). Baseball Ground: 41,826 v Tottenham H, Division 1, 20 September 1969. **Capacity:** 33,597.
Manager: Billy Davies.
Secretary: Marian McMinn.
Most League Goals: 111, Division 3 (N), 1956–57.
Highest League Scorer in Season: Jack Bowers, 37, Division 1, 1930–31; Ray Straw, 37 Division 3 (N), 1956–57.
Most League Goals in Total Aggregate: Steve Bloomer, 292, 1892–1906 and 1910–14.
Most Capped Players: Deon Burton, 41 (48), Jamaica and Mart Poom, 41 (101), Estonia.
Most League Appearances: Kevin Hector, 486, 1966–78 and 1980–82.
Honours – Football League: Division 1 Champions – 1971–72, 1974–75. Division 2 Champions – 1911–12, 1914–15, 1968–69, 1986–87. Division 3 (N) Champions – 1956–57. **FA Cup:** Winners – 1945–46. **Texaco Cup:** Winners 1972.
Colours: White and black.

DONCASTER ROVERS FL CHAMPIONSHIP 1

Armstrong Alun (F)	6 0	12 00	Gateshead	22 2 75	Rushden & D
Blayney Alan (G)	6 2	13 12	Belfast	9 10 81	Southampton
Brown Adam (M)	5 10	10 07	Sunderland	17 12 87	Scholar
Budtz Jan (G)	6 0	13 05	Denmark	20 4 79	Nordsjaelland
Cockerham Lee (M)	6 3	13 00	Pontefract	12 8 87	Scholar
Coppinger James (F)	5 7	10 03	Middlesbrough	10 1 81	Exeter C
Fenton Nick (D)	6 0	12 02	Preston	23 11 79	Notts Co
Green Paul (M)	5 10	12 00	Pontefract	10 4 83	Trainee
Griffith Anthony (M)			Huddersfield	28 10 86	
Guy Lewis (M)	5 10	10 07	Penrith	27 8 85	Newcastle U
Heffernan Paul (F)	5 10	11 00	Dublin	29 12 81	Bristol C
Lee Graeme (D)	6 2	13 07	Middlesbrough	31 5 78	Sheffield W
McCormack Ross (F)	5 9	11 00	Glasgow	18 8 86	Rangers
McDaid Sean (D)	5 6	9 08	Harrogate	6 3 86	Leeds U
McGuire Phil (D)	5 11	10 06	Glasgow	4 3 80	Aberdeen
McIndoe Michael (M)	5 8	11 00	Edinburgh	2 12 79	Yeovil T
Nelthorpe Craig (M)	5 10	11 00	Doncaster	10 6 87	Scholar
Nielsen Tonny (G)	6 9	13 08	Denmark	10 2 84	Fremad
Pacey Rob (D)	6 4	12 07	Leeds	18 6 87	Scholar
Price Jamie (D)	5 10	11 00	Normanton	27 10 81	Trainee
Ravenhill Ricky (M)	5 10	11 03	Doncaster	16 1 81	Barnsley
Roberts Neil (F)	5 10	11 00	Wrexham	7 4 78	Wigan Ath
Roberts Steve (D)	6 1	11 02	Wrexham	24 2 80	Wrexham
Thornton Sean (M)	5 10	11 00	Drogheda	18 5 83	Sunderland
Warrington Andy (G)	6 3	12 13	Sheffield	10 6 76	York C

League Appearances: Albrighton, M. 16; Armstrong, A. 1(5); Blayney, A. 16; Budtz, J. 20; Coppinger, J. 32(4); Fenton, N. 21(4); Forte, J. 9(4); Fortune-West, L. 16(11); Foster, S. 17; Green, P. 23(11); Griffiths, A. 4; Guy, L. 18(13); Heffernan, P. 22(4); Horlock, K. 13; Hughes, A. 4(2); Lee, G. 20; Marples, S. 12(3); McCormack, R. 12(7); McDaid, S. 35; McGuire, P. 11; McIndoe, M. 29(4); McSporran, J. 2; Mulligan, D. 22(10); Nelthorpe, C. 1; Offiong, R. 2(3); Oji, S. 1(3); Predic, U. 3(3); Price, Jason 11; Ravenhill, R. 23(4); Roberts, N. 17(13); Roberts, S. 23(4); Ryan, T. 7; Seremet, D. 1; Thornton, S. 23(6); Timlin, M. 3; Warrington, A. 9; Wheater, D. 7.

Goals – League (55): Heffernan 8, McIndoe 8 (6 pens), Coppinger 5 (1 pen), Forte 4, McCormack 4 (1 pen), Jason Price 4, Green 3, Guy 3, Ravenhill 3, Fenton 2, Fortune-West 2, Mulligan 2, Roberts N 2, Thornton 2, Lee 1, Roberts S 1, Wheater 1.

Carling Cup (9): Heffernan 3, McIndoe 3 (2 pens), Green 1, Hughes 1, Thornton 1.
FA Cup (7): Heffernan 3, McIndoe 2 (2 pens), Mulligan 2.
Football League Trophy (7): Fortune-West 2, Guy 2, Offiong 1, own goals 2.
Ground: The Earth Stadium, Belle Vue, Doncaster DN4 5HT. Telephone (01302) 539 441.
Record Attendance: 37,149 v Hull C, Division 3 (N), 2 October 1948. **Capacity:** 10,593.
Manager: Dave Penney.
Secretary: David Morris.
Most League Goals: 123, Division 3 (N), 1946–47.
Highest League Scorer in Season: Clarrie Jordan, 42, Division 3 (N) 1946–47.
Most League Goals in Total Aggregate: Tom Keetley, 180, 1923–29.
Most Capped Player: Len Graham, 14, Northern Ireland.
Most League Appearances: Fred Emery, 417, 1925–36.
Honours – Football League: Division 3 Champions – 2003–04. Division 3 (N) Champions – 1934–35, 1946–47, 1949–50. Division 4 Champions – 1965–66, 1968–69. **Football Conference:** Champions – 2002–03.
Colours: Red and white hoops.

EVERTON   FA PREMIERSHIP

Anichebe Victor (F)	6 1	13 00	Nigeria	23 4 88	Scholar
Arteta Mikel (M)	5 9	10 08	San Sebastian	26 3 82	Real Sociedad
Beattie James (F)	6 1	13 06	Lancaster	27 2 78	Southampton
Boyle Patrick (D)	6 0	12 09	Glasgow	20 3 87	Scholar
Cahill Tim (M)	5 10	10 12	Sydney	6 12 79	Millwall
Carsley Lee (M)	5 10	12 04	Birmingham	28 2 74	Coventry C
Davies Simon (M)	5 10	11 07	Haverfordwest	23 10 79	Tottenham H
Downes Aiden (F)				24 7 88	Scholar
Harpur Ryan (M)			Craigavon	1 12 88	Scholar
Hibbert Tony (D)	5 9	11 05	Liverpool	20 2 81	Trainee
Hughes Mark (D)	6 1	13 03	Liverpool	9 12 86	Scholar
Irving John (M)			Liverpool	17 9 88	Scholar
Kearney Alan (M)			Cork	22 9 87	Scholar
Kilbane Kevin (M)	6 1	13 05	Preston	1 2 77	Sunderland
McFadden James (M)	6 0	12 11	Glasgow	14 4 83	Motherwell
Molyneux Lee (D)			Liverpool	24 2 89	Scholar
Morrison Steven (M)			Southport	10 9 88	Scholar
Naysmith Gary (D)	5 9	12 01	Edinburgh	16 11 78	Hearts
Neville Phil (M)	5 11	12 00	Bury	21 1 77	Manchester U
Nuno Valente (D)	6 0	12 03	Lisbon	12 9 74	Porto
Osman Leon (F)	5 8	10 09	Billinge	17 5 81	Trainee
Phelan Scott (M)	5 7	10 07	Liverpool	13 3 88	Scholar
Pistone Alessandro (D)	5 11	11 08	Milan	27 7 75	Newcastle U
Ruddy John (G)	6 3	12 07	St Ives	24 10 86	Cambridge U
Stubbs Alan (D)	6 2	13 12	Kirkby	6 10 71	Celtic
Turner Iain (G)	6 3	12 10	Stirling	26 1 84	Trainee
Van der Meyde Andy (M)	5 10	12 04	Arnhem	30 9 79	Internazionale
Vaughan James (F)	5 11	12 08	Birmingham	14 7 88	Scholar
Vidarsson Bjarni (M)	6 1	11 08	Iceland	5 3 88	Scholar
Weir David (D)	6 5	14 03	Falkirk	10 5 70	Hearts
Wright Richard (G)	6 2	14 04	Ipswich	5 11 77	Arsenal
Yobo Joseph (D)	6 1	13 00	Kano	6 9 80	Marseille

League Appearances: Anichebe, V. (2); Arteta, M. 27(2); Beattie, J. 29(3); Bent, M. 7(11); Cahill, T. 32; Carsley, L. 3(2); Davies, S. 22(8); Ferguson, D. 7(20); Ferrari, M. 6(2); Hibbert, T. 29; Kilbane, K. 21(13); Kroldrup, P. 1; Martyn, N. 20; McFadden, J. 24(8); Naysmith, G. 7; Neville, P. 34; Nuno Valente, 20; Osman, L. 28(7); Pistone, A. 2; Ruddy, J. (1); Stubbs, A. 13(1); Turner, I. 2(1); Van der Meyde, A. 7(3); Vaughan, J. (1); Weir, D. 32(1); Westerveld, S. 2; Wright, R. 14(1); Yobo, J. 29.
Goals – League (34): Beattie 10 (2 pens), Cahill 6, McFadden 6, Osman 4, Anichebe 1, Arteta 1, Bent 1, Davies 1, Ferguson 1, Weir 1, Yobo 1, own goal 1.
Carling Cup (0).
FA Cup (4): Arteta 1 (pen), Cahill 1, McFadden 1, Osman 1.
UEFA Cup (2): Cahill 1, Yobo 1.
Champions League (2): Arteta 1, Beattie 1.
Ground: Goodison Park, Liverpool L4 4EL. Telephone (0870) 442 1878.
Record Attendance: 78,299 v Liverpool, Division 1, 18 September 1948. **Capacity:** 40,394.
Manager: David Moyes.
Secretary: David Harrison.
Most League Goals: 121, Division 2, 1930–31.
Highest League Scorer in Season: William Ralph 'Dixie' Dean, 60, Division 1, 1927–28 (All-time League record).
Most League Goals in Total Aggregate: William Ralph 'Dixie' Dean, 349, 1925–37.
Most Capped Player: Neville Southall, 92, Wales.

51

Most League Appearances: Neville Southall, 578, 1981–98.
Honours – Football League: Division 1 Champions – 1890–91, 1914–15, 1927–28, 1931–32, 1938–39, 1962–63, 1969–70, 1984–85, 1986–87. Division 2 Champions – 1930–31. FA Cup: Winners – 1906, 1933, 1966, 1984, 1995. European Competitions: European Cup-Winners' Cup: Winners – 1984–85.
Colours: Blue shirts, white shorts, white stockings.

FULHAM   FA PREMIERSHIP

Batista Ricardo (G)	6 2	12 06	Portugal	19 11 86	Vitoria Setubal
Boa Morte Luis (F)	5 9	12 06	Lisbon	4 8 77	Southampton
Bocanegra Carlos (D)	5 11	12 07	Alta Loma	25 5 79	Chicago Fire
Brown Michael (M)	5 9	12 04	Hartlepool	25 1 77	Tottenham H
Bullard Jimmy (M)	5 10	11 05	Newham	23 10 78	Wigan Ath
Christanval Philippe (D)	6 2	12 10	Paris	31 8 78	Marseille
Collins Matthew (M)			Merthyr	31 3 86	Scholar
Crossley Mark (G)	6 3	15 09	Barnsley	16 6 69	Middlesbrough
Diop Papa Bouba (M)	6 4	14 12	Dakar	28 1 78	Lens
Drobny Jaroslav (G)	6 4	14 00	Pocatky	19 10 79	Panionios
Ehui Ismael (F)	5 7	10 10	Lille	10 12 86	Scholar
Elliott Simon (M)	6 0	13 02	Wellington	10 6 74	Columbus Crew
Elrich Ahmed (M)	5 11	12 00	Sydney	30 5 81	Busan Icons
Fontaine Liam (D)	6 3	12 02	Beckenham	7 1 86	Trainee
Helguson Heidar (F)	5 10	12 09	Akureyri	22 8 77	Watford
James Chris (M)	5 8	10 12	New Zealand	4 7 87	Scholar
Jensen Claus (M)	6 0	13 01	Nykobing	29 4 77	Charlton Ath
Jensen Niclas (D)	5 9	13 00	Copenhagen	17 8 74	Borussia Dortmund
John Collins (F)	5 11	12 13	Zwandru	17 10 85	Twente
Knight Zat (D)	6 6	15 02	Solihull	2 5 80	Rushall Olympic
Leacock Dean (D)	6 2	12 04	Croydon	10 6 84	Trainee
Legwinski Sylvain (M)	6 1	11 07	Clermont-Ferrand	6 10 73	Bordeaux
Malbranque Steed (M)	5 8	11 07	Mouscron	6 1 80	Lyon
McBride Brian (F)	6 0	12 08	Chicago	19 6 72	Columbus Crew
Milsom Robert (D)			Redhill	2 1 87	Scholar
Moncur Tom (D)			Hackney	23 9 87	Scholar
Niemi Antti (G)	6 1	12 04	Oulu	31 5 72	Southampton
Omozusi Elliot (D)			Hackney	15 12 88	Scholar
Pearce Ian (D)	6 3	15 06	Bury St Edmunds	7 5 74	West Ham U
Pembridge Mark (M)	5 9	11 13	Merthyr	29 11 70	Everton
Pratley Darren (M)	6 1	11 05	Barking	22 4 85	Scholar
Radzinski Tomasz (F)	5 8	11 11	Poznan	14 12 73	Everton
Rehman Zesh (M)	6 2	12 08	Birmingham	14 10 83	Scholar
Rosenior Liam (M)	5 9	11 05	Wandsworth	9 7 84	Bristol C
Timlin Michael (M)	5 9	11 10	Lambeth	19 3 85	Trainee
Volz Moritz (D)	5 8	11 07	Siegen	21 1 83	Arsenal
Warner Tony (G)	6 4	15 06	Liverpool	11 5 74	Cardiff C

League Appearances: Boa Morte, L. 35; Bocanegra, C. 20(1); Bridge, W. 12; Brown, M. 6(1); Christanval, P. 7(8); Crossley, M. 13; Diop, P. 21(1); Elliott, S. 12; Elrich, A. 2(4); Goma, A. 13; Helguson, H. 15(12); Jensen, C. 11; Jensen, N. 14(2); John, C. 16(19); Knight, Z. 29(1); Leacock, D. 5; Legwinski, S. 10(3); Malbranque, S. 32(2); McBride, B. 34(4); Niemi, A. 9; Pearce, I. 10; Pembridge, M. 5; Radzinski, T. 23(10); Rehman, Z. 3; Rosenior, L. 22(2); Volz, M. 23; Warner, T. 16(2).
Goals – League (48): John 11 (1 pen), McBride 9, Helguson 8 (3 pens), Boa Morte 6, Malbranque 6, Diop 2, Jensen C 2, Radzinski 2, Bocanegra 2, own goal 1.
Carling Cup (7): Helguson 2, Boa Morte 1, McBride 1, Radzinski 1, Rehman 1, Rosenior 1.
FA Cup (1): John 1.

Ground: Craven Cottage, Stevenage Road, London SW6 6HH. Telephone: (0870) 442 1222.
Record Attendance: 49,335 v Millwall, Division 2, 8 October 1938. **Capacity:** 22,602.
Manager: Chris Coleman.
Secretary: Zoe Ward.
Most League Goals: 111, Division 3 (S), 1931–32.
Highest League Scorer in Season: Frank Newton, 43, Division 3 (S), 1931–32.
Most League Goals in Total Aggregate: Gordon Davies, 159, 1978–84, 1986–91.
Most Capped Player: Johnny Haynes, 56, England.
Most League Appearances: Johnny Haynes, 594, 1952–70.
Honours – Football League: Division 1 Champions – 2000–01. Division 2 Champions – 1948–49, 1998–99. Division 3 (S) Champions – 1931–32. **European Competitions: Intertoto Cup:** Winners – 2002.
Colours: White shirts, black shorts, white stockings.

GILLINGHAM   FL CHAMPIONSHIP 1

Clohessy Sean (D)	5 11	12 07	Croydon	12 12 86	Arsenal
Collin Frannie (F)	5 10	11 07	Chatham	20 4 87	
Cox Ian (D)	6 1	12 05	Croydon	25 3 71	Burnley
Crichton Paul (G)	6 1	14 04	Pontefract	3 10 68	Accrington S
Crofts Andrew (D)	5 10	11 13	Chatham	29 5 84	Trainee
Flynn Michael (M)	5 10	12 10	Newport	17 10 80	Wigan Ath
Fobi-Edusei Akwasi (M)	5 9	11 00	London	12 9 86	Scholar
Jackman Danny (D)	5 4	10 00	Worcester	3 1 83	Stockport Co
Jarvis Matthew (M)	5 7	11 05	Middlesbrough	22 5 86	Scholar
Johnson Leon (M)	6 0	12 08	London	10 5 81	Southend U
Pouton Alan (M)	6 1	13 06	Newcastle	1 2 77	Grimsby T
Sancho Brent (D)	6 1	14 01	Belmont	13 3 77	Dundee
Spiller Danny (M)	5 8	10 12	Maidstone	10 10 81	Trainee
Stone Craig (M)	6 0	10 05	Gravesend	29 12 88	Scholar

League Appearances: Ashikodi, M. (4); Black, T. 17; Brown, J. 39; Bullock, T. 6; Byfield, D. 27(2); Claridge, S. 1; Clohessy, S. 18(2); Cochrane, J. 5; Collin, F. 1(5); Corneille, M. (2); Cox, I. 36; Crichton, P. 1; Crofts, A. 45; Flynn, M. 30(6); Fobi-Edusei, A. 5(1); Grant, G. 1(9); Harris, N. 28(8); Hessenthaler, A. 14(2); Hislop, S. 2(6); Hope, C. 20(4); Jackman, D. 35(7); Jarvis, M. 30(5); Johnson, L. 25(3); Mulligan, G. 10(3); Pouton, A. 19(4); Rose, R. 13(1); Sancho, B. 16(3); Saunders, M. 3(1); Shields, P. 6(11); Smith, P. 3; Spiller, D. 21(11); Stone, C. (3); Wallis, J. 16(1); Williams, T. 13.
Goals – League (50): Byfield 13 (3 pens), Flynn 6, Harris 6, Black 5, Jarvis 3, Crofts 2, Pouton 2, Sancho 2, Clohessy 1, Cochrane 1, Collin 1, Grant 1, Hessenthaler 1, Hope 1, Johnson 1, Mulligan 1, Shields 1, own goals 2.
Carling Cup (4): Byfield 1, Crofts 1, Jarvis 1, own goal 1.
FA Cup (2): Jarvis 1, Saunders 1.
Football League Trophy (4): Jarvis 2, Collin 1, Jackman 1.
Ground: Priestfield Stadium, Redfern Avenue, Gillingham ME7 4DD. Telephone (01634) 300 000.
Record Attendance: 23,002 v QPR, FA Cup 3rd rd, 10 January 1948. **Capacity:** 11,400.
Manager: Ronnie Jepson.
Secretary: Mrs Gwen E. Poynter.
Most League Goals: 90, Division 4, 1973–74.
Highest League Scorer in Season: Ernie Morgan, 31, Division 3 (S), 1954–55; Brian Yeo, 31, Division 4, 1973–74.
Most League Goals in Total Aggregate: Brian Yeo, 135, 1963–75.

Most Capped Player: Mamady Sidibe 7, Mali.
Most League Appearances: John Simpson, 571, 1957–72.
Honours – Football League: Division 4 Champions – 1963–64.
Colours: Blue with white side and sleeve panel.

GRIMSBY TOWN

FL CHAMPIONSHIP 2

Ashton Paul (G)	6 2	12 08	Nuneaton	25 10 86	Scholar
Barwick Terry (M)	5 11	10 12	Doncaster	11 1 83	Scunthorpe U
Bolland Paul (M)	5 10	10 12	Bradford	23 12 79	Notts Co
Chamberlain Miles (D)	6 0	12 00	Skegness	14 12 86	Scholar
Cohen Gary (F)	5 11	11 02	Ilford	20 1 84	Gretna
Downey Glen (D)	6 1	13 00	Sunderland	20 9 78	Scarborough
Futcher Ben (D)	6 7	12 05	Manchester	20 2 81	Boston U
Hegarty Nick (M)	5 10	11 00	Hemsworth	25 6 86	Scholar
Higgins Ben (M)	5 11	12 00	Grimsby	13 9 87	Scholar
Jones Gary (F)	6 3	15 02	Chester	10 5 75	Tranmere R
Jones Rob (D)	6 7	13 07	Stockton	30 11 79	Stockport Co
Kamudimba Kalala Jean-Paul (M)	5 10	12 02	Lubumbashi	16 2 82	Nice
Lamb Alan (M)	5 10	11 00	Grimsby	20 12 85	Scholar
McDermott John (D)	5 7	11 02	Middlesbrough	3 2 69	Trainee
Mildenhall Steve (G)	6 4	14 01	Swindon	13 5 78	Oldham Ath
Murray Robert (M)	5 8	9 00	Leamington Spa	11 7 88	Scholar
Newey Tom (D)	5 10	10 02	Sheffield	31 10 82	Leyton Orient
North Danny (F)	5 9	12 08	Grimsby	7 9 87	Scholar
Parkinson Andy (F)	5 7	10 07	Liverpool	27 5 79	Sheffield U
Reddy Michael (F)	6 1	13 00	Kilkenny	24 3 80	Sunderland
Richardson Oliver (G)	5 10	12 00	Grimsby	12 2 87	Scholar
Rock Stephen (M)			Grimsby	30 11 87	Scholar
Taylor Andy (M)	6 2	13 00	Grimsby	30 10 88	Scholar
Toner Ciaran (M)	6 1	12 02	Craigavon	30 6 81	Lincoln C
Ward Andrew (M)	6 0	10 12	Grimsby	10 9 86	Scholar
Whittle Justin (D)	6 1	13 00	Derby	18 3 71	Hull C
Woodhouse Curtis (M)	5 8	11 00	Driffield	17 4 80	Hull C

League Appearances: Andrew, C. 3(5); Barwick, T. 2(6); Bloomer, M. 3; Bolland, P. 44; Cohen, G. 32(8); Crane, T. 3(2); Croft, G. 26(7); Downey, G. (1); Francis, S. 5; Futcher, B. 12(3); Goodfellow, M. 8(2); Gritton, M. 7(19); Hegarty, N. (2); Jones, G. 34(6); Jones, R. 38(2); Kamudimba Kalala, J. 14(7); McDermott, J. 32; Mendes, J. 8(7); Mildenhall, S. 46; Newey, T. 35(3); North, D. (1); Parkinson, A. 32(8); Ramsden, S. 8(4); Reddy, M. 42(2); Toner, C. 24(7); Whittle, J. 32; Woodhouse, C. 16.
Goals – League (64): Jones G 13, Reddy 13, Cohen 6, Kamudimba Kalala 5 (4 pens), Bolland 4, Jones R 4, Parkinson 4, Toner 3 (1 pen), Futcher 2, Gritton 2, Andrew 1, Crane 1, Downey 1, Goodfellow 1 (pen), McDermott 1, Mildenhall 1, Newey 1, Woodhouse 1.
Carling Cup (2): Jones G 1, Kamudimba Kalala 1.
FA Cup (1): Jones G 1.
Football League Trophy (1): Ashton 1.
Play-Offs (3): Jones G 2, Futcher 1.
Ground: Blundell Park, Cleethorpes, North-East Lincolnshire DN35 7PY. Telephone (01472) 605 050.
Record Attendance: 31,651 v Wolverhampton W, FA Cup 5th rd, 20 February 1937. **Capacity:** 9,106.
Manager: Graham Rodger.
Secretary: Ian Fleming.
Most League Goals: 103, Division 2, 1933–34.

Highest League Scorer in Season: Pat Glover, 42, Division 2, 1933–34.
Most League Goals in Total Aggregate: Pat Glover, 180, 1930–39.
Most Capped Player: Pat Glover, 7, Wales.
Most League Appearances: John McDermott, 624, 1987–.
Honours – Football League: Division 2 Champions – 1900–01, 1933–34. Division 3
(N) Champions – 1925–26, 1955–56. Division 3 Champions – 1979–80. Division 4
Champions – 1971–72. **League Group Cup:** Winners – 1981–82. **Auto Windscreens
Shield:** Winners – 1997–98.
Colours: Black and white striped shirts, black shorts, white stockings with black trim.

HARTLEPOOL UNITED   FL CHAMPIONSHIP 2

Barron Micky (D)	5 11	11 10	Lumley	22 12 74	Middlesbrough
Boyd Adam (F)	5 9	10 12	Hartlepool	25 5 82	Scholar
Brackstone John (D)	6 0	11 06	Hartlepool	9 2 85	Scholar
Brown James (F)	5 11	11 00	Newcastle	3 1 87	Cramlington J
Bullock Lee (M)	6 0	11 04	Stockton	22 5 81	Cardiff C
Butler Thomas (M)	5 7	10 06	Dublin	25 4 81	Sunderland
Clark Ben (D)	6 1	13 11	Shotley Bridge	24 1 83	Sunderland
Clarke Darrell (M)	5 10	11 05	Mansfield	16 12 77	Mansfield T
Daly Jon (F)	6 3	12 00	Dublin	8 1 83	Stockport Co
Foley David (F)	5 4	8 09	South Shields	12 5 87	Scholar
Humphreys Richie (M)	5 11	12 07	Sheffield	30 11 77	Cambridge U
Jones Carl (D)	6 1	12 02	Sunderland	3 9 86	Chester-le-Street
Konstantopoulos Dimitrios (G)	6 4	14 02	Kalamata	29 11 78	
Llewellyn Chris (F)	5 11	11 06	Swanea	29 8 79	Wrexham
Maidens Michael (M)	5 11	11 04	Middlesbrough	7 5 87	Scholar
Nelson Michael (D)	6 2	13 03	Gateshead	15 3 82	Bury
Porter Joel (F)	5 9	11 13	Adelaide	25 12 78	Sydney Olympic
Proctor Michael (F)	5 11	11 11	Sunderland	3 10 80	Rotherham U
Provett Jim (G)	6 0	13 04	Stockton	22 12 82	Trainee
Robson Matty (D)	5 10	11 02	Durham	23 1 85	Scholar
Strachan Gavin (M)	5 10	11 07	Aberdeen	23 12 78	Southend U
Sweeney Anthony (M)	6 0	11 07	Stockton	5 9 83	Scholar
Tinkler Mark (M)	6 2	12 00	Bishop Auckland	24 10 74	Southend U
Turnbull Stephen (M)	5 10	11 00	South Shields	7 1 87	Scholar
Williams Darren (D)	5 11	11 00	Middlesbrough	28 4 77	Cardiff C
Williams Eifion (F)	5 11	11 02	Angelsey	15 11 75	Torquay U

League Appearances: Barron, M. 13(2); Boyd, A. 12(9); Brackstone, J. 2; Brown,
J. (4); Bullock, L. 22(9); Butler, T. 26(2); Clark, B. 28(4); Clarke, D. 6(6); Collins,
N. 22; Craddock, D. 4; Daly, J. 18(12); Foley. D. 1(10); Humphreys, R. 46; Istead,
S. 4(6); Jones, C. 1; Konstantopoulos, D. 46; Llewellyn, C. 24(5); Maidens, M.
11(9); McDonald, D. 4(1); Nash, G. 3; Nelson, M. 43; Pittman, J. 2(1); Porter, J.
6(2); Proctor, M. 22(4); Robertson, H. 2; Robson, M. 13(6); Strachan, G. 6(3);
Sweeney, A. 34(1); Tinkler, M. 11(4); Turnbull, S. 16(5); Walker, J. 1(3); Williams,
D. 33(6); Williams, E. 24(12).
Goals – League (44): Williams E 7, Porter 5, Sweeney 5, Boyd 4 (1 pen), Bullock
4, Porter 3, Daly 2, Humphreys 2, Istead 2, Nelson 2, Brown 1, Butler 1, Maidens 1,
McDonald 1, Robson 1, Strachan 1, Tinkler 1, own goal 1.
Carling Cup (4): Daly 2, Proctor 2.
FA Cup (3): Butler 1, Llewellyn 1 (pen), Nelson 1.
Football League Trophy (0).
Ground: Victoria Park, Clarence Road, Hartlepool TS24 8BZ. Telephone (01429)
272 584.
Record Attendance: 17,426 v Manchester U, FA Cup 3rd rd, 5 January 1957.
Capacity: 7,691.

Manager: Danny Wilson.
Secretary: Maureen Smith.
Most League Goals: 90, Division 3 (N), 1956–57.
Highest League Scorer in Season: William Robinson, 28, Division 3 (N), 1927–28; Joe Allon, 28, Division 4, 1990–91.
Most League Goals in Total Aggregate: Ken Johnson, 98, 1949–64.
Most Capped Player: Ambrose Fogarty, 1 (11), Republic of Ireland.
Most League Appearances: Wattie Moore, 447, 1948–64.
Honours – Nil.
Colours: Blue and white.

HEREFORD UNITED   FL CHAMPIONSHIP 2

Beckwith Dean (D)	6 3	13 01	Southwark	18	9 83	Gillingham
Ferrell Andy (M)	5 8	11 05	Newcastle	9	1 84	Watford
Fleetwood Stuart (F)	5 9	12 02	Gloucester	23	4 86	Cardiff C
Green Ryan (D)	5 7	10 10	Cardiff	20	10 80	Sheffield W
Ipoua Guy (F)	6 1	13 10	Douala	14	1 76	Doncaster R
James Tony (D)	6 3	14 02	Cardiff	27	6 76	WBA
Jeannin Alex (D)	6 0	11 06	Troyes	30	12 77	Bristol R
Mawson Craig (G)	6 2	13 04	Keighley	16	5 79	Oldham Ath
Mkandawire Tamika (D)	6 0	12 03	Malawi	28	5 83	WBA
Pitman Jamie (M)	5 9	10 09	Trowbridge	6	1 76	Woking
Purdie Rob (F)	5 8	11 02	Leicester	28	9 82	Leicester C
Stanley Colin (M)	5 8	10 08	Bedworth	3	3 83	Telford U
Stansfield Adam (F)	5 11	11 02	Plymouth	10	9 78	Yeovil T
Travis Simon (D)	5 10	11 00	Preston	22	3 77	Stevenage B
Williams Andy (F)	5 11	11 02	Hereford	14	8 86	

League Appearances: Bailey, 5; Beckwith, 29(3); Blewitt, 10(1); Brady, 18(2); Brown, 33; Carey-Bertram, 18(14); Coldicott, 4(1); Evans, 2(5); Ferrell, 30(1); Fleetwood, 13(4); Green, 25(2); Gwynne, 0(1); Ipoua, 13(6); James, 20(3); Jeannin, 37; King, 5; Mawson, 9; Mkandawire, 36(3); Nicolau, 10; Pitman, 14(8); Purdie, 33(7); Stanley, 35(3); Stansfield, 17(6); Taylor, 8(2); Travis, 15(3); Williams, 23(8).
Goals – League (59): Williams 10, Carey-Bertram 8, Ipoua 7, Stansfield 6, Fleetwood 5, Mkandawire 5, Purdie 4 (1 pen), Jeannin 3, Beckwith 2, Ferrell 2, Bailey 1, Green 1, James 1 (pen), King 1, Nicolau 1, Pitman 1, Stanley 1.
FA Cup (2): Barry 1, Stanley 1.
Football League Trophy (5): Mkandawire 2, Carey-Bertram 1, Stansfield 1, own goal 1.
FA Trophy (8): Purdie 2 (1 pen), Stansfield 2, Ipoua 1, Pitman 1, Stanley 1, Williams 1.
Play-Offs (7): Ipoua 2, Williams 2, Green 1, Mkandawire 1, Purdie 1 (pen).
Ground: Edgar Street, Hereford, Herefordshire HR4 9JU. Telephone: (01432) 276 666.
Record Attendance: 18,114 (1958 v Sheffield Wednesday FA Cup Third Round).
Capacity: 8843
Manager: Graham Turner.
Secretary: Mrs Joan Fennessey.
Most League Goals: 86, Division 3, 1975–76.
Highest League Scorer in Season: Dixie McNeil, 35, 1975–76.
Most League Goals in Total Aggregate: Stewart Phillips, 93, 1980–88, 1990–91.
Most Capped Player: Brian Evans, 1 (7) Wales.
Most League Appearances: Mel Pejic, 412, 1980–92.
Honours – Football League: Division 3 Champions – 1975–76. **Welsh Cup:** Winners – 1990.
Colours: White and black shirts, black shorts, white stockings.

HUDDERSFIELD TOWN   FL CHAMPIONSHIP 1

Abbott Pawel (F)	5 7	11 07	York	5 5 82	Preston NE
Adams Danny (D)	5 8	13 05	Manchester	3 1 76	Stockport Co
Ahmed Adnan (M)	5 10	11 12	Burnley	7 6 84	Scholar
Booth Andy (F)	6 1	13 00	Huddersfield	6 12 73	Sheffield W
Brandon Chris (M)	5 8	10 13	Bradford	7 4 76	Chesterfield
Clarke Nathan (D)	6 2	12 00	Halifax	30 11 83	Scholar
Clarke Tom (D)	5 11	12 02	Halifax	21 12 87	Scholar
Collins Michael (M)	6 0	10 12	Halifax	30 4 86	Scholar
Eastwood Simon (G)	6 2	13 00	Luton	26 6 89	Scholar
Hand James (M)	5 9	11 00	Drogheda	22 10 86	Scholar
Hardy Aaron (M)	5 8	11 04	South Elmsall	26 5 86	Scholar
Holdsworth Andy (D)	5 9	11 02	Pontefract	29 1 84	Scholar
Hudson Mark (M)	5 10	11 03	Bishop Auckland	24 10 80	Chesterfield
McAliskey John (F)	6 5	12 07	Huddersfield	2 9 84	Scholar
McCombe John (D)	6 1	14 02	Pontefract	7 5 85	Scholar
McIntosh Martin (D)	6 3	13 07	East Kilbride	19 3 71	Rotherham U
Mirfin David (D)	6 2	14 05	Sheffield	18 4 85	Scholar
Rachubka Paul (G)	6 1	13 01	San Luis Opispo	21 5 81	Charlton Ath
Schofield Danny (F)	5 11	12 00	Doncaster	10 4 80	Brodsworth
Taylor-Fletcher Gary (F)	6 0	11 00	Liverpool	4 6 81	Lincoln C
Walls David (D)	6 0	12 00	Leeds	22 11 86	Scholar
Worthington Jon (M)	5 9	11 05	Dewsbury	16 4 83	Scholar
Young Matthew (M)	5 8	11 03	Leeds	25 10 85	Scholar

League Appearances: Abbott, P. 27(9); Adams, D. 40; Ahmed, A. 4(9); Booth, A. 32(4); Brandon, C. 36(4); Carss, T. 10(7); Clarke, N. 46; Clarke, T. 16(1); Collins, M. 9(8); Graham, D. 15(1); Holdsworth, A. 37(5); Hudson, M. 25(4); McAliskey, J. (9); McCombe, J. 1; McIntosh, M. 20(2); Mendes, J. (5); Mirfin, D. 27(4); Rachubka, P. 34; Schofield, D. 37(4); Senior, P. 12(1); Smith, D. 7(1); Taylor-Fletcher, G. 30(13); Worthington, J. 41; Young, M. (2).
Goals – League (72): Booth 13, Abbott 12 (2 pens), Taylor-Fletcher 10, Graham 9, Schofield 9, McIntosh 4, Worthington 4, Brandon 3 (1 pen), Hudson 3, Clarke T 1, Collins 1, Holdsworth 1, Mirfin 1, own goal 1.
Carling Cup (5): Taylor-Fletcher 3, Abbott 2.
FA Cup (6): Booth 2, Brandon 1, Holdsworth 1, Schofield 1 (pen), Taylor-Fletcher 1.
Football League Trophy (1): Mirfin 1.
Play-Offs (2): Taylor-Fletcher 1, Worthington 1.
Ground: The Galpharm Stadium, Leeds Road, Huddersfield HD1 6PX. Telephone 0870 4444 677.
Record Attendance: 67,037 v Arsenal, FA Cup 6th rd, 27 February 1932.
Capacity: 24,590.
Manager: Peter Jackson.
Secretary: Ann Hough.
Most League Goals: 101, Division 4, 1979–80.
Highest League Scorer in Season: Sam Taylor, 35, Division 2, 1919–20; George Brown, 35, Division 1, 1925–26.
Most League Goals in Total Aggregate: George Brown, 142, 1921–29; Jimmy Glazzard, 142, 1946–56.
Most Capped Player: Jimmy Nicholson, 31 (41), Northern Ireland.
Most League Appearances: Billy Smith, 520, 1914–34.
Honours – Football League: Division 1 Champions – 1923–24, 1924–25, 1925–26. Division 2 Champions – 1969–70. Division 4 Champions – 1979–80. **FA Cup:** Winners – 1922.
Colours: Blue and white striped shirts, white shorts, white stockings.

Andrews Keith (M)	6 0	12 04	Dublin	13 9 80	Wolverhampton W
Ashbee Ian (M)	6 1	13 07	Birmingham	6 9 76	Cambridge U
Aspden Curtis (G)	6 1	11 12	Blackburn	16 11 87	Scholar
Barmby Nick (M)	5 7	11 03	Hull	11 2 74	Leeds U
Burgess Ben (F)	6 4	14 04	Buxton	9 11 81	Stockport Co
Coles Danny (D)	6 1	11 05	Bristol	31 10 81	Bristol C
Collins Sam (D)	6 2	14 03	Pontefract	5 6 77	Port Vale
Cort Leon (D)	6 3	13 01	Bermondsey	11 9 79	Southend U
Dawson Andy (D)	5 10	11 02	Northallerton	20 10 78	Scunthorpe U
Delaney Damien (D)	6 3	14 00	Cork	20 7 81	Leicester C
Duffy Darryl (F)	5 11	12 01	Glasgow	16 4 84	Falkirk
Duke Matt (G)	6 5	13 04	Sheffield	16 7 77	Sheffield U
Elliott Stuart (M)	5 10	11 09	Belfast	23 7 78	Motherwell
Ellison Kevin (M)	6 2	13 04	Liverpool	23 2 79	Chester C
Fagan Craig (F)	5 11	11 08	Birmingham	11 12 82	Colchester U
France Ryan (M)	5 11	11 11	Sheffield	13 12 80	Alfreton T
Fry Russell (M)	6 0	12 01	Hull	4 12 85	Scholar
Green Stuart (M)	5 10	11 01	Whitehaven	15 6 81	Newcastle U
Lynch Mark (D)	5 11	11 03	Manchester	2 9 81	Sunderland
McPhee Stephen (F)	5 7	10 08	Glasgow	5 6 81	Beira Mar
Myhill Boaz (G)	6 3	14 06	Modesto	9 11 82	Aston Villa
Parkin Jon (F)	6 4	13 07	Barnsley	30 12 81	Macclesfield T
Paynter Billy (F)	6 1	14 01	Liverpool	13 7 84	Port Vale
Welsh John (M)	5 7	12 02	Liverpool	10 1 84	Liverpool
Wiseman Scott (D)	6 0	11 06	Hull	9 10 85	Scholar

League Appearances: Andrews, K. 24(2); Ashbee, I. 6; Barmby, N. 21(5); Brown, C. 13; Burgess, B. 3(11); Coles, D. 9; Collins, S. 17; Cort, L. 42; Dawson, A. 17(1); Delaney, D. 45(1); Duffy, D. 5(10); Duke, M. 1(1); Edge, R. 8; Elliott, S. 26(14); Ellison, K. 15(8); Fagan, C. 29(12); France, R. 30(5); Fry, R. (1); Green, S. 20(18); Joseph, M. 2(3); Lynch, M. 15(1); McPhee, S. 2(2); Myhill, B. 45; Noble, M. 4(1); Parkin, J. 18; Paynter, B. 11(11); Price, J. 10(5); Rogers, A. 9; Rui Marques, M. 1; Thelwell, A. 7(2); Welsh, J. 29(3); Wiseman, S. 8(3); Woodhouse, C. 14(4).
Goals – League (49): Elliott 7, Barmby 5, Fagan 5, Parkin 5, Cort 4, Green 4 (1 pen), Duffy 3, Paynter 3, Burgess 2, France 2, Price 2, Welsh 2, Brown 1, Ellison 1, own goals 3.
Carling Cup (1): Price 1.
FA Cup (0).
Ground: Kingston Communications Stadium, The Circle, Walton Street, Hull HU3 6HU. Telephone (0870) 837 0003.
Record Attendance: 55,019 v Manchester U, FA Cup 6th rd, 26 February 1949; 23,495 v Huddersfield T, Division 3, 24 April 2004 at KC Stadium.
Capacity: 25,404.
Manager: Phil Parkinson.
Secretary: Phil Hough.
Most League Goals: 109, Division 3, 1965–66.
Highest League Scorer in Season: Bill McNaughton, 39, Division 3 (N), 1932–33.
Most League Goals in Total Aggregate: Chris Chilton, 195, 1960–71.
Most Capped Player: Theo Whitmore, Jamaica.
Most League Appearances: Andy Davidson, 520, 1952–67.
Honours – Football League: Division 3 (N) Champions – 1932–33, 1948–49. Division 3 Champions – 1965–66.
Colours: Black and amber striped shirts, black shorts with amber trim, black stockings with amber turnover.

Barron Scott (D)	5 9	9 08	Preston	2	9 85	Scholar
Bowditch Dean (F)	5 11	10 08	Bishop's Stortford	15	6 86	Trainee
Brekke-Skard Vemund (M)	5 8	13 03	Norway	11	9 81	Brumunddal
Casement Chris (M)	6 0	12 02	Belfast	12	1 88	Scholar
Clarke Billy (F)	5 7	10 01	Cork	13	12 87	Scholar
Currie Darren (M)	5 10	12 07	Hampstead	29	11 74	Brighton & HA
De Vos Jason (D)	6 4	13 07	London, Can	2	1 74	Wigan Ath
Forster Nicky (F)	5 9	11 05	Caterham	8	9 73	Reading
Garvan Owen (M)	6 0	10 07	Dublin	29	1 88	Scholar
Haynes Danny (F)	5 11	12 04	Peckham	19	1 88	Scholar
Knights Darryl (F)	5 7	10 01	Ipswich	1	5 88	Scholar
Lee Alan (F)	6 2	13 09	Galway	21	8 78	Cardiff C
Naylor Richard (D)	6 1	13 07	Leeds	28	2 77	Trainee
Parkin Sam (F)	6 2	13 00	Roehampton	14	3 81	Swindon T
Peters Jaime (M)	5 7	10 12	Toronto	4	5 87	Moor Green
Price Lewis (G)	6 3	13 06	Poole	19	7 84	Academy
Proudlock Adam (F)	6 0	13 07	Wellington	9	5 81	Sheffield W
Richards Matt (D)	5 8	10 10	Harlow	26	12 84	Scholar
Sito (D)	5 8	11 07	Coruna	21	5 80	Racing Ferrol
Supple Shane (G)	5 11	11 07	Dublin	4	5 87	Scholar
Trotter Liam (M)	6 2	12 02	Ipswich	24	8 88	Scholar
Westlake Ian (M)	5 11	11 00	Clacton	10	11 83	Scholar
Wilnis Fabian (D)	5 8	12 06	Paramaribo	23	8 70	De Graafschap

League Appearances: Barron, S. 14(1); Bowditch, D. 14(7); Brekke-Skard, V. 2(1); Casement, C. 2(3); Clarke, B. 1(1); Collins, A. 2(1); Currie, D. 39(7); De Vos, J. 41; Fish, M. 1; Forster, N. 17(3); Fuller, R. 3; Garvan, O. 29(3); Haynes, D. 6(13); Horlock, K. 13(4); Juan, J. 24(10); Lee, A. 14; Magilton, J. 25(9); McDonald, D. 4(10); McEveley, J. 17(2); Naylor, R. 42; Parkin, S. 17(3); Peters, J. 4(9); Price, L. 25; Proudlock, A. 3(6); Richards, M. 31(7); Sito, 31(7); Supple, S. 21(1); Trotter, L. (1); Westlake, I. 19(7); Williams, G. 12; Wilnis, F. 33(2).

Goals – League (53): Forster 7, Currie 6, Juan 5, Parkin 5, Lee 4, Richards 4 (3 pens), De Vos 3, Garvan 3, Haynes 3, Naylor 3, Fuller 2, Westlake 2, Magilton 1, McDonald 1, McEveley 1, Williams 1, Wilnis 1, own goals 2.

Carling Cup (0).

FA Cup (0).

Ground: Portman Road, Ipswich, Suffolk IP1 2DA. Telephone (01473) 400 500.

Record Attendance: 38,010 v Leeds U, FA Cup 6th rd, 8 March 1975.

Capacity: 30,311.

Manager: Jim Magilton.

Secretary: Sally Webb.

Most League Goals: 106, Division 3 (S), 1955–56.

Highest League Scorer in Season: Ted Phillips, 41, Division 3 (S), 1956–57.

Most League Goals in Total Aggregate: Ray Crawford, 203, 1958–63 and 1966–69.

Most Capped Player: Allan Hunter, 47 (53), Northern Ireland.

Most League Appearances: Mick Mills, 591, 1966–82.

Honours – Football League: Division 1 Champions – 1961–62. Division 2 Champions – 1960–61, 1967–68, 1991–92. Division 3 (S) Champions – 1953–54, 1956–57. **FA Cup:** Winners – 1977–78. **European Competitions: UEFA Cup:** Winners – 1980–81.

Colours: Blue shirts, white shorts, blue stockings.

Name					
Bakke Eirik (M)	6 2	12 10	Sogndal	13 9 77	Sogndal
Bayly Robert (M)			Dublin	22 2 88	Scholar
Beckford Jermaine (F)	6 2	13 02	Ealing	9 12 83	Wealdstone
Bennett Ian (G)	6 0	12 10	Worksop	10 10 71	Birmingham C
Blake Robbie (F)	5 9	12 00	Middlesbrough	4 3 76	Birmingham C
Butler Paul (D)	6 2	15 04	Manchester	2 11 72	Wolverhampton W
Camfield Bailey (D)			Wakefield	22 1 88	Scholar
Crainey Stephen (D)	5 9	12 05	Glasgow	22 6 81	Southampton
Cresswell Richard (F)	6 0	11 08	Bridlington	20 9 77	Preston NE
Derry Shaun (M)	5 10	13 02	Nottingham	6 12 77	Crystal Palace
Einarsson Gylfi (M)	6 0	12 00	Iceland	27 10 78	Lille
Gardner Scott (M)			Luxembourg	1 4 88	Scholar
Gregan Sean (M)	6 2	15 08	Guisborough	29 3 74	WBA
Griffiths Joel (M)	6 0	11 11	Australia	21 8 79	Neuchatel Xamax
Harding Dan (D)	6 0	11 11	Gloucester	23 12 83	Brighton & HA
Healy David (F)	5 8	11 07	Downpatrick	5 8 79	Preston NE
Hird Samuel (D)			Doncaster	7 9 87	
Hulse Rob (F)	6 1	12 04	Crewe	25 10 79	WBA
Kelly Gary (D)	5 10	11 02	Drogheda	9 7 74	Home Farm
Kilgallon Matthew (D)	6 1	12 07	York	8 1 84	Scholar
Lewis Eddie (M)	5 10	11 02	Cerritos	17 5 74	Preston NE
Moore Ian (F)	5 11	12 00	Birkenhead	26 8 76	Burnley
Morris Ian (D)	6 0	11 05	Dublin	27 2 87	Scholar
Parker Ben (D)			Pontefract	8 11 87	Scholar
Pugh Danny (M)	6 0	11 11	Manchester	19 10 82	Manchester U
Richardson Frazer (D)	5 11	12 04	Rotherham	29 10 82	Trainee
Ricketts Michael (F)	6 2	15 10	Birmingham	4 12 78	Middlesbrough
Rothery Gavin (F)			Morley	22 9 87	Scholar
Rui Marques Manuel (D)	5 11	11 13	Luanda	3 9 77	Stuttgart
Stone Steve (F)	5 9	12 07	Gateshead	20 8 71	Portsmouth
Sullivan Neil (G)	6 3	15 08	Sutton	24 2 70	Chelsea
Walton Simon (D)	6 1	13 05	Sherburn-in-Elmet	13 9 87	Scholar
Wilberforce Mark (G)	5 10	11 07	Hull	30 1 87	Scholar
Wright Jermaine (M)	5 10	13 00	Greenwich	21 10 75	Ipswich T

League Appearances: Bakke, E. 7(3); Beckford, J. (5); Bennett, I. 4; Blake, R. 31(10); Butler, P. 44; Crainey, S. 24; Cresswell, R. 12(4); Derry, S. 32(8); Einarsson, G. 6(4); Graham, D. 1(2); Gregan, S. 28; Griffiths, J. (2); Harding, D. 20; Healy, D. 24(18); Hulse, R. 32(7); Kelly, G. 44; Kilgallon, M. 22(3); Lewis, E. 42(1); Miller, L. 26(2); Moore, I. 2(18); Pugh, D. 1(11); Richardson, F. 13(10); Ricketts, M. 1(3); Stone, S. 1(1); Sullivan, N. 42; Walton, S. 3(1); Wright, J. 3.

Goals – League (57): Healy 12 (5 pens), Hulse 12 (1 pen), Blake 11 (3 pens), Cresswell 5, Douglas 5, Lewis 3, Butler 3, Kilgallon 1, Miller 1, Richardson 1, own goal 1.

Carling Cup (4): Cresswell 2, Richardson 1, Ricketts 1.

FA Cup (4): Healy 2 (1 pen), Hulse 1, Kelly 1.

Play-Offs (3): Hulse 1, Lewis 1, Richardson 1.

Ground: Elland Road, Leeds LS11 0ES. Telephone (0113) 367 6000.

Record Attendance: 57,892 v Sunderland, FA Cup 5th rd (replay), 15 March 1967.

Capacity: 39,460.

Manager: Kevin Blackwell. **Secretary:** Alison Royston.

Most League Goals: 98, Division 2, 1927–28.

Highest League Scorer in Season: John Charles, 42, Division 2, 1953–54.

Most League Goals in Total Aggregate: Peter Lorimer, 168, 1965–79 and 1983–86.

Most Capped Player: Lucas Radebe, 58 (70), South Africa.

Most League Appearances: Jack Charlton, 629, 1953–73.

Honours – Football League: Division 1 Champions – 1968–69, 1973–74, 1991–92. Division 2 Champions – 1923–24, 1963–64, 1989–90. **FA Cup:** Winners – 1972. **Football League Cup:** Winners – 1967–68. **European Competitions: European Fairs Cup:** Winners – 1967–68, 1970–71.
Colours: White shirts and shorts with navy blue trim.

LEICESTER CITY   FL CHAMPIONSHIP

De Vries Mark (F)	6 3	12 01	Surinam	24 8 75	Hearts
Dodds Louis (F)	5 10	12 04	Leicester	8 10 86	Scholar
Douglas Rab (G)	6 3	14 12	Lanark	24 4 72	Celtic
Fryatt Matty (F)	5 10	11 00	Nuneaton	5 3 86	Walsall
Gerrbrand Patrik (D)	6 2	12 06	Stockholm	27 4 81	Hammarby
Gradel Max (M)	5 8	12 03	Ivory Coast	30 9 87	
Hamill Joe (M)	5 9	10 10	Airdrie	25 2 84	Hearts
Hammond Elvis (F)	5 10	11 02	Accra	6 10 80	Fulham
Henderson Paul (G)	6 1	12 06	Sydney	22 4 76	Bradford C
Hughes Stephen (M)	5 11	9 06	Motherwell	14 11 82	Rangers
Hume Iain (F)	5 7	11 02	Brampton	31 10 83	Tranmere R
Johansson Nils-Eric (D)	6 1	12 10	Stockholm	13 1 80	Blackburn R
Kisnorbo Patrick (D)	6 1	11 11	Melbourne	24 3 81	Hearts
Logan Conrad (G)	6 0	14 09	Letterkenny	18 4 86	Scholar
Maybury Alan (D)	5 8	11 08	Dublin	8 8 78	Hearts
McCarthy Patrick (D)	6 2	13 07	Dublin	31 5 83	Manchester C
O'Grady Chris (F)	6 3	12 04	Nottingham	25 1 86	Scholar
Porter Levi (F)	5 4	10 05	Leicester	6 4 87	Scholar
Sheehan Alan (D)	5 11	11 02	Athlone	14 9 86	Scholar
Stearman Richard (D)	6 2	10 08	Wolverhampton	19 8 87	Scholar
Sylla Momo (M)	6 0	11 09	Conakry	13 3 77	Celtic
Wesolowski James (D)	5 8	11 11	Sydney	25 8 87	Scholar
Williams Gareth (M)	6 1	12 03	Glasgow	16 12 81	Nottingham F

League Appearances: Brevett, R. (1); Connolly, D. 5; De Vries, M. 20(9); Douglas, R. 32; Dublin, D. 15(6); Fryatt, M. 18(1); Gerrbrand, P. 14(3); Gilbert, P. 4(1); Gudjonsson, J. 40(2); Hamill, J. 7(5); Hammond, E. 15(18); Henderson, P. 14(1); Hughes, S. 28(6); Hume, I. 28(9); Johansson, N. 39; Kisnorbo, P. 36(1); Maybury, A. 40; McCarthy, P. 37(1); O'Grady, C. (13); Sheehan, A. 2; Smith, R. 10(7); Stearman, R. 31(3); Sylla, M. 24(4); Tiatto, D. 11(7); Welsh, A. 4(6); Wesolowski, J. 3(2); Wilcox, J. 3(3); Williams, G. 26(5).
Goals – League (51): Hume 9, Gudjonsson 8 (4 pens), De Vries 6, Fryatt 6, Connolly 4, Hammond 3, Hughes 3, Stearman 3, McCarthy 2, Kisnorbo 1, Maybury 1, O'Grady 1, Smith R 1, Tiatto 1, Welsh 1, Williams 1.
Carling Cup (7): De Vries 2, Gudjonsson 1 (pen), Hamill 1, Johansson 1, Stearman 1, Williams 1.
FA Cup (3): De Vries 1, Hammond 1, Hughes 1.
Ground: The Walkers Stadium, Filbert Way, Leicester LE2 7FL. Telephone (0870) 040 6000.
Record Attendance: 47,298 v Tottenham H, FA Cup 5th rd, 18 February 1928.
Capacity: 32,312.
Manager: Robert Kelly. **Secretary:** Andrew Neville.
Most League Goals: 109, Division 2, 1956–57.
Highest League Scorer in Season: Arthur Rowley, 44, Division 2, 1956–57.
Most League Goals in Total Aggregate: Arthur Chandler, 259, 1923–35.
Most Capped Player: John O'Neill, 39, Northern Ireland.
Most League Appearances: Adam Black, 528, 1920–35.
Honours – Football League: Division 2 Champions – 1924–25, 1936–37, 1953–54, 1956–57, 1970–71, 1979–80. **Football League Cup:** Winners – 1964, 1997, 2000.
Colours: Blue and white.

LEYTON ORIENT   FL CHAMPIONSHIP 1

Alexander Gary (F)	6 0	12 00	Lambeth	15 8 79	Hull C
Barnard Donny (D)	5 9	10 10	Forest Gate	1 7 84	Trainee
Connor Paul (F)	6 2	11 08	Bishop Auckland	12 1 79	Swansea C
Demetriou Jason (M)	5 11	10 08	Newham	18 11 87	Scholar
Duncan Derek (M)	5 9	10 12	Newham	23 4 87	Scholar
Easton Craig (M)	5 11	11 03	Airdrie	26 2 79	Dundee U
Echanomi Efe (M)	5 7	11 07	Nigeria	27 9 86	Scholar
Garner Glyn (G)	6 2	13 11	Pontypool	9 12 76	Bury
Gourgel Nuno (F)			Angola	28 10 87	Scholar
Ibehre Jabo (F)	6 1	12 10	Islington	28 1 83	Trainee
Keith Joe (M)	5 7	11 02	Plaistow	1 10 78	Colchester U
Lockwood Matt (D)	6 0	11 06	Rochford	17 10 76	Bristol R
Mackie John (D)	6 1	12 00	Enfield	5 7 76	Reading
McMahon Daryl (M)	5 11	12 02	Dublin	10 10 83	Port Vale
Miller Justin (D)	6 1	11 07	Johannesburg	16 12 80	Ipswich T
Morris Glenn (G)	5 11	11 00	Woolwich	20 12 83	Scholar
Palmer Aiden (M)	5 8	10 04	Enfield	2 1 87	Scholar
Saah Brian (M)	6 1	11 05	Rush Green	16 12 86	Scholar
Simpson Michael (M)	5 7	10 05	Nottingham	28 2 74	Wycombe W
Smith Dean (D)	6 1	13 10	West Bromwich	19 3 71	Port Vale
Steele Lee (F)	5 8	11 08	Liverpool	2 12 73	Oxford U
Tann Adam (D)	6 0	11 05	Fakenham	12 5 82	Notts Co
Tudor Shane (M)	5 7	11 12	Wolverhampton	10 2 82	Cambridge U
Wallis Scott (M)	5 10	10 10	Enfield	28 6 88	Scholar
Zakuani Gaby (D)	6 0	11 08	Zaire	31 5 86	Scholar

League Appearances: Alexander, G. 42(4); Barnard, D. 14(12); Carlisle, W. 3(9); Connor, P. 15(1); Corden, W. 8; Demetriou, J. 1(2); Dolan, J. 1; Duncan, D. (1); Easton, C. 36(5); Echanomi, E. (16); Garner, G. 43; Hanson, C. (2); Ibehre, J. 22(11); Keith, J. 41(1); Lockwood, M. 42; Mackie, J. 40; McMahon, D. 17(16); Miller, J. 34(2); Morris, G. 3(1); Palmer, A. 3; Saah, B. 2(1); Simpson, M. 45; Steele, L. 14(13); Tann, A. 8(2); Tudor, S. 29(4); Zakuani, G. 43.
Goals – League (67): Alexander 14, Ibehre 8, Lockwood 8 (7 pens), Mackie 6, Connor 5, Easton 4, Steele 4, Tudor 4, Echanomi 3, Corden 2, Keith 2, McMahon 2, Miller 1, Simpson 1, Tann 1, Zakuani 1, own goal 1.
Carling Cup (1): McMahon 1.
FA Cup (6): Steele 2, Easton 1, Keith 1, Mackie 1, Tudor 1.
Football League Trophy (2): Alexander 1, Hanson 1.
Ground: Matchroom Stadium, Brisbane Road, Leyton, London E10 5NE. Telephone 0871 310 1881.
Record Attendance: 34,345 v West Ham U, FA Cup 4th rd, 25 January 1964.
Capacity: 7,872 (rising to approx 9,000 by 2007).
Manager: Martin Ling.
Secretary: Lindsey Freeman.
Most League Goals: 106, Division 3 (S), 1955–56.
Highest League Scorer in Season: Tom Johnston, 35, Division 2, 1957–58.
Most League Goals in Total Aggregate: Tom Johnston, 121, 1956–58, 1959–61.
Most Capped Players: Tunji Banjo, 7 (7), Nigeria; John Chiedozie, 7 (9), Nigeria; Tony Grealish, 7 (45), Eire.
Most League Appearances: Peter Allen, 432, 1965–78.
Honours – Football League: Division 3 Champions – 1969–70. Division 3 (S) Champions – 1955–56.
Colours: All red with white trim.

Bacon Danny (F)	5 10	10 12	Mansfield	20	9 80	Hucknall T
Beevers Lee (D)	6 1	13 00	Doncaster	4 12 83		Boston U
Birch Gary (F)	6 0	12 03	Birmingham	8 10 81		Kidderminster H
Brown Nat (F)	6 2	12 05	Sheffield	15	6 81	Huddersfield T
Cryan Colin (D)	5 9	11 08	Dublin	23	3 81	Sheffield U
Foster Luke (D)	6 2	12 08	Mexborough	8	9 85	Sheffield W
Frecklington Lee (M)	5 8	11 00	Lincoln	8	9 85	Scholar
Gritton Martin (F)	6 1	12 02	Glasgow	1	6 78	Grimsby T
Hughes Jeff (D)	6 1	11 00	Larne	29	5 85	Larne
Kerr Scott (M)	5 9	10 07	Leeds	11 12 81		Scarborough
Marriott Alan (G)	6 0	12 04	Bedford	3	9 78	Tottenham H
Mayo Paul (D)	5 11	11 09	Lincoln	13 10 81		Watford
McAuley Gareth (D)	6 3	13 00	Larne	5 12 79		Coleraine
McCombe Jamie (D)	6 5	12 03	Pontefract	1	1 83	Scunthorpe U
Mettam Leon (F)	5 9	11 01	Lincoln	9 12 86		Scholar
Morgan Paul (D)	6 0	11 03	Belfast	23 10 78		Preston NE
Rayner Simon (G)	6 4	15 00	Vancouver	8	7 83	Port Talbot
Robinson Marvin (F)	5 11	12 13	Crewe	11	4 80	Stockport Co
Ryan Oliver (M)	5 9	11 00	Boston	26	9 85	Scholar
Wilkinson Tom (D)	5 7	11 03	Lincoln	26	9 85	
Yeo Simon (F)	5 10	11 08	Stockport	20 10 73		NZ Knights

League Appearances: Asamoah, D. 19(6); Bacon, D. (1); Beevers, L. 28(5); Birch, G. 23(14); Bloomer, M. 7(5); Brown, N. 37(2); Butcher, R. 4; Cryan, C. 37; Forrester, J. 9; Foster, L. 14(2); Frecklington, L. 3(15); Green, F. 23(5); Gritton, M. 4(6); Hughes, J. 18(4); Keates, D. 19(2); Kerr, S. 41; Logan, R. 8; Marriott, A. 43; Mayo, P. 25(3); McAuley, G. 33(2); McCombe, J. 38; Mettam, L. (1); Molango, M. 5(5); Morgan, P. 19(1); Rayner, S. 3; Robinson, M. 20(12); Robinson, S. 11(1); Ryan, O. 4(6); Stirling, J. (6); Wilkinson, T. (1); Yeo, S. 11(1).

Goals – League (65): Birch 8, Brown 7, Robinson M 7, Forrester 5, McAuley 5, Yeo 5, Keates 4, McCombe 4, Green 3, Mayo 3 (2 pens), Asamoah 2, Frecklington 2, Hughes 2, Kerr 2, Logan 2, Beevers 1, Butcher 1, Foster 1, Gritton 1.

Carling Cup (9): Birch 2, Robinson M 2, Beevers 1, Green 1, Kerr 1, Molango 1, own goal 1.

FA Cup (2): Mayo 1 (pen), Robinson M 1.

Football League Trophy (1): Brown 1.

Play-Offs (1): Robinson M 1.

Ground: Sincil BankStadium, Lincoln LN5 8LD. Telephone (0870) 899 2005.

Record Attendance: 23,196 v Derby Co, League Cup 4th rd, 15 November 1967.

Capacity: 10,127.

Manager: John Schofield.

Secretary: Fran Martin.

Most League Goals: 121, Division 3 (N), 1951–52.

Highest League Scorer in Season: Allan Hall, 41, Division 3 (N), 1931–32.

Most League Goals in Total Aggregate: Andy Graver, 144, 1950–55 and 1958–61.

Most Capped Player: Gareth McAuley, 5, Northern Ireland.

Most League Appearances: Grant Brown, 407, 1989–2002.

Honours – Football League: Division 3 (N) Champions – 1931–32, 1947–48, 1951–52. Division 4 Champions – 1975–76.

Colours: Red and white.

Player			Birthplace		Previous Club
Agger Daniel (D)	6 2	12 06	Hvidovre	12 12 84	Brondby
Anderson Paul (M)	5 9	10 04	Leicester	23 7 88	Hull C
Antwi-Birago Godwin (D)	6 1	13 09	Tafu	7 6 88	San Gregorio
Barragan Juan Antonio (D)	6 1	11 09	Ferrol	12 6 87	Sevilla
Carragher Jamie (D)	5 9	12 01	Liverpool	28 1 78	Trainee
Carson Scott (G)	6 3	13 12	Whitehaven	3 9 85	Leeds U
Cheyrou Bruno (M)	6 1	13 03	Suresnes	10 5 78	Lille
Cisse Djibril (F)	6 0	13 00	Arles	12 8 81	Auxerre
Crouch Peter (F)	6 7	13 03	Macclesfield	30 1 81	Southampton
Diao Salif (M)	6 1	12 08	Kedougou	10 2 77	Sedan
Dudek Jerzy (G)	6 2	12 08	Ribnek	23 3 73	Feyenoord
Finnan Steve (M)	6 0	12 03	Limerick	24 4 76	Fulham
Fowler Robbie (F)	5 10	12 05	Liverpool	9 4 75	Manchester C
Gerrard Steven (M)	6 0	12 05	Whiston	30 5 80	Trainee
Guthrie Danny (M)	5 9	11 06	Shrewsbury	18 4 87	Scholar
Hamann Dietmar (M)	6 2	13 00	Waldasson	27 8 73	Newcastle U
Hamill Adam (M)			Liverpool	25 1 88	Scholar
Hobbs Jack (D)	6 3	13 05	Portsmouth	18 8 88	Lincoln C
Hyypia Sami (D)	6 3	13 09	Porvoo	7 10 73	Willem II
Idrizaj Bezian (F)	6 2	12 02	Austria	12 10 87	LASK Linz
Kewell Harry (M)	5 9	12 06	Sydney	22 9 78	Leeds U
Kirkland Christopher (G)	6 5	14 08	Leicester	2 5 81	Coventry C
Kromkamp Jan (D)	6 3	13 06	Heerenveen	17 8 80	Villarreal
Le Tallec Anthony (M)	6 0	12 00	Hennebont	3 10 84	Le Havre
Luis Garcia (M)	5 6	10 05	Badalona	24 6 78	Barcelona
Mannix David (M)	5 8	11 06	Crewe	24 9 85	Scholar
Martin David (G)	6 1	13 04	Romford	22 1 86	Milton Keynes D
Medjani Carl (D)	6 0	13 04	Lyon	15 5 85	
Mellor Neil (F)	6 0	13 05	Manchester	4 11 82	Scholar
Morientes Fernando (F)	6 0	12 04	Caceres	5 4 76	Real Madrid
O'Donnell Daniel (D)			Liverpool	10 3 86	Scholar
Peltier Lee (F)	5 10	12 00	Liverpool	11 12 86	Scholar
Potter Darren (M)	6 0	10 08	Liverpool	21 12 84	Scholar
Raven David (D)	6 0	11 04	Birkenhead	10 3 85	Scholar
Reina Jose (G)	6 2	14 06	Madrid	31 8 82	Villarreal
Riise John Arne (M)	6 1	14 00	Molde	24 9 80	Monaco
Roque Miguel (M)	6 2	12 03	Tremp	8 7 88	UE Lleida
Sinama-Pongolle	5 7	11 05	Saint-Pierre	20 10 84	Le Havre
Florent (F)					
Sissoko Mohamed (M)	6 2	12 08	Rouen	21 1 85	Valencia
Smith James (M)			Liverpool	17 10 85	Scholar
Traore Djimi (D)	6 2	12 07	Saint-Ouen	1 3 80	Lens
Warnock Stephen (M)	5 7	11 09	Ormskirk	12 12 81	Trainee
Whitbread Zak (D)	6 2	12 07	Houston	4 3 84	Scholar
Xabi Alonso (M)	6 0	12 02	Tolosa	25 11 81	Real Sociedad
Zenden Boudewijn (M)	5 8	11 01	Maastricht	15 8 76	Middlesbrough

League Appearances: Agger, D. 4; Xabi Alonso 29(6); Baros, M. (2); Carragher, J. 36; Cisse, D. 19(14); Crouch, P. 27(5); Dudek, J. 5(1); Finnan, S. 33; Fowler, R. 9(5); Gerrard, S. 32; Hamann, D. 13(4); Hyypia, S. 35(1); Josemi, 3(3); Kewell, H. 22(5); Kromkamp, J. 6(7); Luis Garcia, 15(16); Morientes, F. 20(8); Reina, J. 33; Riise, J. 24(8); Sinama-Pongolle, F. 3(4); Sissoko, M. 21(5); Traore, D. 9(6); Warnock, S. 15(5); Zenden, B. 5(2).

Goals – League (57): Gerrard 10 (2 pens), Cisse 9 (2 pens), Crouch 8, Luis Garcia 7, Fowler 5, Morientes 5, Xabi Alonso 3, Kewell 3, Zenden 2, Hyypia 1, Riise 1, Warnock 1, own goals 2.

Carling Cup (1): Gerrard 1.
FA Cup (20): Gerrard 4 (1 pen), Crouch 3, Riise 3, Cisse 2, Sinama-Pongolle 2, Xabi Alonso 2, Hyypia 1, Luis Garcia 1, Morientes 1, own goal 1.
Champions League (20): Gerrard 7 (1 pen), Cisse 6, Morientes 3, Luis Garcia 2, Carragher 1, Sinama-Pongolle 1.
Super Cup (3): Cisse 2, Luis Garcia 1.
Club World Championship (3): Crouch 2, Gerrard 1.
Ground: Anfield, Anfield Road, Liverpool L4 0TH. Telephone (0151) 263 2361.
Record Attendance: 61,905 v Wolverhampton W, FA Cup 4th rd, 2 February 1952.
Capacity: 45,362.
Manager: Rafael Benitez.
Secretary: William Bryce Morrison.
Most League Goals: 106, Division 2, 1895–96.
Highest League Scorer in Season: Roger Hunt, 41, Division 2, 1961–62.
Most League Goals in Total Aggregate: Roger Hunt, 245, 1959–69.
Most Capped Player: Ian Rush, 67 (73), Wales.
Most League Appearances: Ian Callaghan, 640, 1960–78.
Honours – Football League: Division 1 – Champions 1900–01, 1905–06, 1921–22, 1922–23, 1946–47, 1963–64, 1965–66, 1972–73, 1975–76, 1976–77, 1978–79, 1979–80, 1981–82, 1982–83, 1983–84, 1985–86, 1987–88, 1989–90 (Liverpool have a record number of 18 League Championship wins). Division 2 Champions – 1893–94, 1895–96, 1904–05, 1961–62. **FA Cup:** Winners – 1965, 1974, 1986, 1989, 1992, 2001, 2006. **League Cup:** Winners – 1981, 1982, 1983, 1984, 1995, 2001, 2003. **League Super Cup:** Winners 1985–86. **European Competitions: European Cup:** Winners – 1976–77, 1977–78, 1980–81, 1983–84. **Champions League:** Winners – 2004–05. **UEFA Cup:** Winners – 1972–73, 1975–76, 2001. **Super Cup:** Winners – 1977, 2005.
Colours: Red shirts, red shorts, red stockings.

LUTON TOWN   FL CHAMPIONSHIP

Andrew Calvin (F)	6 0	12 11	Luton	19 12 86	Scholar
Barnett Leon (D)	6 0	12 04	Stevenage	30 11 85	Scholar
Bell David (M)	5 10	11 05	Kettering	21 1 84	Rushden & D
Beresford Marlon (G)	6 1	13 05	Lincoln	2 9 69	Barnsley
Brill Dean (G)	6 2	14 05	Luton	2 12 85	Scholar
Brkovic Ahmet (M)	5 8	11 11	Dubrovnik	23 9 74	Leyton Orient
Coyne Chris (D)	6 2	13 12	Brisbane	20 12 78	Dundee
Davis Sol (D)	5 8	11 13	Cheltenham	4 9 79	Swindon T
Deeney David (D)	5 9	10 06	Bulawayo	12 1 87	Scholar
Edwards Carlos (M)	5 8	11 02	Port of Spain	24 10 78	Wrexham
Feeney Warren (F)	5 10	11 03	Belfast	17 1 81	Stockport Co
Foley Kevin (M)	5 10	11 02	London	1 11 84	Scholar
Heikkinen Markus (D)	6 1	12 13	Katrineholm	13 10 78	Aberdeen
Howard Steve (F)	6 3	15 00	Durham	10 5 76	Northampton T
Keane Keith (M)	5 9	11 02	Luton	20 11 86	Scholar
Leary Michael (M)	6 0	11 11	Ealing	17 4 83	Scholar
Morgan Dean (M)	5 11	13 00	Enfield	3 10 83	Reading
Nicholls Kevin (M)	5 10	12 04	Newham	2 1 79	Wigan Ath
O'Leary Stephen (M)	6 0	11 09	Barnet	12 2 85	Scholar
Perrett Russell (D)	6 1	12 06	Barton-on-Sea	18 6 73	Cardiff C
Robinson Steve (M)	5 9	11 02	Lisburn	10 12 74	Preston NE
Stevens Danny (F)	5 5	9 09	Enfield	26 11 86	Scholar
Underwood Paul (M)	5 11	12 11	Wimbledon	16 8 73	Rushden & D
Vine Rowan (F)	5 11	12 10	Basingstoke	21 9 82	Portsmouth

League Appearances: Andrew, C. (1); Barnett, L. 12(8); Bell, D. 2(7); Beresford, M. 41; Brill, D. 5; Brkovic, A. 39(3); Coyne, C. 28(2); Davies, C. 38(4); Davis, S. 17(4); Edwards, C. 38(4); Feeney, W. 29(13); Foley, K. 35(3); Heikkinen, M. 38(1); Holmes, P. 16(7); Howard, S. 40(3); Keane, K. 5(5); Morgan, D. 25(11); Nicholls, K. 31(1); Perrett, R. 9(2); Robinson, S. 26; Showunmi, E. 15(26); Stevens, D. (1); Underwood, P. 28(1); Vine, R. 21(10).

Goals – League (66): Howard 14, Vine 10 (1 pen), Brkovic 8, Feeney 6, Morgan 6, Nicholls 5 (3 pens), Coyne 2, Edwards 2, Heikkinen 2, Holmes 2, Robinson 2, Andrew 1, Davies 1, Keane 1, Showunmi 1, own goals 3.

Carling Cup (3): Coyne 1, Feeney 1, own goal 1.

FA Cup (3): Howard 1, Nicholls 1 (pen), Robinson 1.

Ground: Kenilworth Stadium, 1 Maple Road, Luton, Beds LU4 8AW. Telephone (01582) 411 622.

Record Attendance: 30,069 v Blackpool, FA Cup 6th rd replay, 4 March 1959.

Capacity: 10,260.

Manager: Mike Newell.

Secretary: Cherry Newbery.

Most League Goals: 103, Division 3 (S), 1936–37.

Highest League Scorer in Season: Joe Payne, 55, Division 3 (S), 1936–37.

Most League Goals in Total Aggregate: Gordon Turner, 243, 1949–64.

Most Capped Player: Mal Donaghy, 58 (91), Northern Ireland.

Most League Appearances: Bob Morton, 494, 1948–64.

Honours – Football League: Championship 1: Winners – 2004–05. Division 2 Champions – 1981–82. Division 4 Champions – 1967–68. Division 3 (S) Champions – 1936–37. **Football League Cup:** Winners – 1987–88.

Colours: White shirts, black shorts, white stockings.

MACCLESFIELD TOWN   FL CHAMPIONSHIP 2

Brightwell Ian (D)	5 10	12 08	Lutterworth	9	4 68	Port Vale
Bullock Martin (M)	5 5	10 07	Derby	5	3 75	Blackpool
Harsley Paul (M)	5 9	11 10	Scunthorpe	29	5 78	Northampton T
McIntyre Kevin (M)	5 11	12 00	Liverpool	23	12 77	Chester C
Miles John (F)	5 10	12 09	Fazackerley	28	9 81	Crewe Alex
Morley Dave (D)	6 3	13 00	St Helens	25	9 77	Doncaster R
Navarro Alan (M)	5 10	11 07	Liverpool	31	5 81	Accrington S
Sandwith Kevin (D)	5 11	12 05	Workington	30	4 78	Lincoln C
Smart Andrew (D)	6 1	14 00	Wythenshawe	17	3 86	Scholar
Swailes Danny (D)	6 3	13 07	Bolton	1	4 79	Bury
Teague Andrew (D)	6 2	12 00	Preston	5	2 86	Scholar
Whitaker Danny (M)	5 10	11 02	Manchester	14	11 80	Wilmslow Sports

League Appearances: Bailey, M. 5; Barras, T. 7; Beresford, D. 9(7); Brightwell, I. 10(1); Briscoe, M. 11(2); Bullock, M. 38(2); Deasy, T. 2(1); Fettis, A. 33; Harsley, P. 45; Lee, T. 11; MacKenzie, N. 4(2); McIntyre, K. 44; McNeil, M. 12; Miles, J. 8(17); Morley, D. 45; Navarro, A. 27; Parkin, J. 9(2); Richardson, M. 8; Russell, A. 12(1); Sandwith, K. 34(1); Smart, A. 7(2); Swailes, D. 39; Teague, A. 23(2); Townson, K. 3(15); Whitaker, D. 41(1); Wijnhard, C. 19(1).

Goals – League (60): Wijnhard 8 (1 pen), Bullock 7, Parkin 7, Harsley 6 (3 pens), McIntyre 5, Miles 4, Whitaker 4, Richardson 3, Sandwith 3, Russell 2, Swailes 2, Townson 2, Briscoe 1, MacKenzie 1, McNeil 1, Morley 1, Teague 1, own goals 2.

Carling Cup (4): Bullock 1, MacKenzie 1, Townson 1, Whitaker 1.

FA Cup (1): Wijnhard 1.

Football League Trophy (14): Wijnhard 3, Parkin 2, Sandwith 2, Beresford 1, Harsley 1, McNeil 1, Smart 1, Teague 1, Townson 1, Whitaker 1.

Ground: Moss Rose Ground, London Road, Macclesfield, Cheshire SK11 0DQ. Telephone (01625) 264 686.

Record Attendance: 9008 v Winsford U, Cheshire Senior Cup 2nd rd, 4 February 1948. **Capacity:** 6,141.
Manager: Brian Horton.
Secretary: Diane Hehir.
Most League Goals: 66, Division 3, 1999–2000.
Highest League Scorer in Season: Jon Parkin, 22, League 2, 2004–05.
Most League Goals in Total Aggregate: Matt Tipton, 41, 2002–05.
Most Capped Player: George Abbey, 10, Nigeria.
Most League Appearances: Darren Tinson, 263, 1997–2003.
Honours – Nil.
Colours: All blue.

MANCHESTER CITY   FA PREMIERSHIP

Barton Joey (M)	5 11	11 09	Huyton	2 9 82	Scholar
Croft Lee (F)	5 9	13 01	Wigan	21 6 85	Scholar
D'Laryea Nathan (D)			Manchester	3 9 85	Scholar
Distin Sylvain (D)	6 3	14 08	Bagnolet	16 12 77	Newcastle U
Dunne Richard (D)	6 2	15 12	Dublin	21 9 79	Everton
Etuhu Calvin (F)			Nigeria	30 5 88	Scholar
Flood Willo (M)	5 6	9 11	Dublin	10 4 85	Trainee
Ireland Stephen (F)	5 8	10 07	Cobh	22 8 86	Scholar
James David (G)	6 5	14 02	Welwyn	1 8 70	West Ham U
Jihai Sun (D)	5 9	12 02	Dalian	30 9 77	Dalian Wanda
Johnson Michael (M)			Urmston	3 3 88	Scholar
Jordan Stephen (D)	6 1	11 13	Warrington	6 3 82	Scholar
Laird Marc (M)			Edinburgh	23 1 86	Scholar
Miller Ishmael (F)	6 3	14 00	Manchester	5 3 87	Scholar
Mills Danny (D)	5 11	12 06	Norwich	18 5 77	Leeds U
Mills Matthew (D)	6 3	12 12	Swindon	14 7 86	Southampton
Onuoha Nedum (D)	6 2	12 04	Warri	12 11 86	Scholar
Reyna Claudio (M)	5 9	11 08	New Jersey	20 7 73	Sunderland
Richards Micah (D)	5 11	13 00	Birmingham	24 6 88	Scholar
Samaras Georgios (F)	6 3	13 07	Heraklion	21 2 85	Heerenveen
Schmeichel Kasper (G)	6 1	13 00	Copenhagen	5 11 86	Scholar
Sibierski Antoine (M)	6 2	12 04	Lille	5 8 74	Lens
Sinclair Trevor (M)	5 9	13 05	Dulwich	2 3 73	West Ham U
Thatcher Ben (D)	5 10	12 07	Swindon	30 11 75	Leicester C
Vassell Darius (F)	5 9	13 00	Birmingham	13 6 80	Aston Villa
Weaver Nick (G)	6 4	14 07	Sheffield	2 3 79	Mansfield T
Wright-Phillips Bradley (M)	5 8	11 00	Lewisham	12 3 85	Scholar

League Appearances: Barton, J. 31; Cole, A. 20(2); Croft, L. 4(17); Distin, S. 31; Dunne, R. 31(1); Flood, W. 1(4); Fowler, R. (4); Ireland, S. 13(11); James, D. 38; Jihai, S. 16(13); Jordan, S. 18; Miller, I. (1); Mills, D. 18; Mills, M. (1); Musampa, K. 24(3); Onuoha, N. 8(2); Reyna, C. 22; Richards, M. 11(2); Riera, A. 12(3); Samaras, G. 10(4); Sibierski, A. 12(12); Sinclair, T. 29(2); Sommeil, D. 14(2); Thatcher, B. 18; Vassell, D. 36; Wright-Phillips, B. 1(17).
Goals – League (43): Cole 9, Vassell 8, Barton 6 (1 pen), Samaras 4, Dunne 3, Sinclair 2, Sibierski 2, Sommeil 2, Croft 1, Fowler 1, Mills D 1, Reyna 1, Riera 1, Wright-Phillips 1.
Carling Cup (1): Vassell 1 (pen).
FA Cup (8): Fowler 3 (1 pen), Cole 1, Musampa 1, Richards 1, Samaras 1, Vassell 1.
Ground: The City of Manchester Stadium, SportCity, Manchester M11 3FF. Telephone (0870) 062 1894.

Record Attendance: 85,569 v Stoke C, FA Cup 6th rd, 3 March 1934 (British record for any game outside London or Glasgow). **Capacity:** 47,500.
Manager: Stuart Pearce.
Secretary: J. B. Halford.
Most League Goals: 108, Division 2, 1926–27, 108, Division 1, 2001–02.
Highest League Scorer in Season: Tommy Johnson, 38, Division 1, 1928–29.
Most League Goals in Total Aggregate: Tommy Johnson, 158, 1919–30.
Most Capped Player: Colin Bell, 48, England.
Most League Appearances: Alan Oakes, 565, 1959–76.
Honours – Football League: Division 1 Champions – 1936–37, 1967–68, 2001–02. Division 2 Champions – 1898–99, 1902–03, 1909–10, 1927–28, 1946–47, 1965–66. **FA Cup winners** 1904, 1934, 1956, 1969. **Football League Cup:** Winners – 1970, 1976. **European Competitions:** European Cup-Winners' Cup: Winners – 1969–70.
Colours: Sky blue shirts, white shorts, sky blue stockings.

MANCHESTER UNITED   FA PREMIERSHIP

Name			Birthplace	Birthdate	Source
Bardsley Phillip (D)	5 11	11 08	Salford	28 6 85	Trainee
Bellion David (F)	6 0	11 09	Sevres	27 11 82	Sunderland
Brown Wes (D)	6 1	13 11	Manchester	13 10 79	Trainee
Campbell Frazier (F)			Huddersfield	13 9 87	Scholar
Cathcart Craig (D)	6 2	11 06	Belfast	6 2 89	Scholar
Eagles Chris (M)	6 0	10 08	Hemel Hempstead	19 11 85	Trainee
Ebanks-Blake Sylvan (F)	5 10	13 04	Cambridge	29 3 86	Scholar
Eckersley Adam (D)	5 9	11 13	Worsley	7 9 85	Scholar
Evans Jonny (D)	6 2	12 02	Belfast	3 1 88	Scholar
Evra Patrice (D)	5 8	11 10	Dakar	15 5 81	Monaco
Ferdinand Rio (D)	6 2	13 12	Peckham	7 11 78	Leeds U
Fletcher Darren (M)	6 0	13 01	Edinburgh	1 2 84	Scholar
Foster Ben (G)	6 2	12 08	Leamington Spa	3 4 83	Stoke C
Gibson Darron (M)	6 0	12 04	Londonderry	25 10 87	Scholar
Giggs Ryan (F)	5 11	11 00	Cardiff	29 11 73	School
Gray David (F)	5 11	11 02	Edinburgh	4 5 88	Scholar
Heaton Tom (G)	6 1	13 12	Chester	15 4 86	Scholar
Heinze Gabriel (D)	5 10	12 04	Crespo	19 4 78	Paris St Germain
Howard Tim (G)	6 3	14 12	New Brunswick	6 3 79	NY/NJ MetroStars
Jones David (M)	5 11	10 00	Southport	4 11 84	Trainee
Jones Richie (M)	6 0	11 00	Manchester	26 9 86	Scholar
Martin Lee (M)	5 10	10 03	Taunton	9 2 87	Scholar
McShane Paul (D)	5 11	11 05	Wicklow	6 1 86	Trainee
Miller Liam (M)	5 8	10 06	Cork	13 2 81	Celtic
N'Galula Floribert (D)			Brussels	7 3 87	Scholar
Neville Gary (D)	5 11	12 04	Bury	18 2 75	Trainee
O'Shea John (D)	6 3	12 10	Waterford	30 4 81	Waterford
Park Ji-Sung (M)	5 9	11 06	Seoul	25 2 81	PSV Eindhoven
Pique Gerard (D)	6 3	12 10	Barcelona	2 2 87	Scholar
Richardson Kieran (M)	5 8	11 00	Greenwich	21 10 84	Scholar
Ronaldo Cristiano (M)	6 1	12 04	Funchal	5 2 85	Sporting Lisbon
Rooney Wayne (F)	5 10	12 04	Liverpool	24 10 85	Everton
Rossi Giuseppe (F)	5 9	11 03	New Jersey	1 2 87	Scholar
Saha Louis (F)	6 1	12 06	Paris	8 8 78	Fulham
Scholes Paul (M)	5 7	11 00	Salford	16 11 74	Trainee
Silvestre Mikael (D)	6 0	13 01	Chambray les Tours	9 8 77	Internazionale
Simpson Danny (D)			Salford	4 1 87	Scholar
Smith Alan (F)	5 10	12 01	Leeds	28 10 80	Leeds U
Solskjaer Ole Gunnar (F)	5 10	11 11	Kristiansund	26 2 73	Molde
Spector Jonathan (D)	6 0	12 08	Chicago	1 3 86	Chicago Sockers
Steele Luke (G)	6 2	12 00	Peterborough	24 9 84	Scholar

Van der Sar Edwin (G) 6 5   14 11   Voorhout   29 10 70   Fulham
Van Nistelrooy Ruud (F) 6 2 12 13   Oss   1 7 76   PSV Eindhoven
Vidic Nemanja (D)   6 1   13 02   Uzice   21 10 81   Spartak Moscow

League Appearances: Bardsley, P. 3(5); Brown, W. 17(2); Evra, P. 7(4); Ferdinand, R. 37; Fletcher, D. 23(4); Giggs, R. 22(5); Heinze, G. 2(2); Howard, T. (1); Keane, R. 4(1); Miller, L. (1); Neville, G. 24(1); O'Shea, J. 34; Park, J. 23(10); Pique, G. 1(2); Richardson, K. 12(10); Ronaldo, C. 24(9); Rooney, W. 34(2); Rossi, G. 1(4); Saha, L. 12(7); Scholes, P. 18(2); Silvestre, M. 30(3); Smith, A. 15(6); Solskjaer, O. (3); Van Nistelrooy, R. 28(7); Van der Sar, E. 38; Vidic, N. 9(2).
Goals – League (72): Van Nistelrooy 21 (2 pens), Rooney 16, Ronaldo 9, Saha 7, Ferdinand 3, Giggs 3, Scholes 2, Fletcher 1, O'Shea 1, Park 1, Richardson 1, Rossi 1, Silvestre 1, Smith 1, own goals 4.
Carling Cup (17): Saha 6, Ronaldo 2 (1 pen), Rooney 2, Ebanks-Blake 1, Miller 1, O'Shea 1, Park 1, Richardson 1, Rossi 1, Van Nistelrooy 1.
FA Cup (8): Richardson 3, Rooney 3, Saha 2, Giggs 1.
Champions League (9): Heinze 2, Van Nistelrooy 2, Giggs 1, Richardson 1, Ronaldo 1, Rooney 1, Scholes 1.
Ground: Old Trafford, Sir Matt Busby Way, Manchester M16 0RA. Telephone (0161) 868 8000.
Record Attendance: 76,962 Wolverhampton W v Grimsby T, FA Cup semi-final. 25 March 1939. **Club record:** 73,006 v Charlton Ath, Premier League, 7 May 2006.
Capacity: 76,212.
Manager: Sir Alex Ferguson CBE.
Secretary: Kenneth R. Merrett.
Most League Goals: 103, Division 1, 1956–57 and 1958–59.
Highest League Scorer in Season: Dennis Viollet, 32, 1959–60.
Most League Goals in Total Aggregate: Bobby Charlton, 199, 1956–73.
Most Capped Player: Bobby Charlton, 106, England.
Most League Appearances: Bobby Charlton, 606, 1956–73.
Honours – FA Premier League: Champions – 1992–93, 1993–94, 1995–96, 1996–97, 1998–99, 1999–2000, 2000–01, 2002–03. **Football League:** Division 1 Champions – 1907–8, 1910–11, 1951–52, 1955–56, 1956–57, 1964–65, 1966–67. Division 2 Champions – 1935–36, 1974–75. **FA Cup:** Winners – 1909, 1948, 1963, 1977, 1983, 1985, 1990, 1994, 1996, 1999, 2004. **Football League Cup:** Winners – 1991–92, 2006. **European Competitions: European Cup:** Champions – 1967–68. **Champions League:** Winners – 1998–99. **European Cup-Winners' Cup:** Winners – 1990–91. **Super Cup:** Winners – 1991. **Inter-Continental Cup:** Winners – 1999.
Colours: Red shirts, white shorts, black stockings.

MANSFIELD TOWN   FL CHAMPIONSHIP 2

Arnold Nathan (F)	5 8	10 07	Mansfield	26 7 87	Rotherham U
Barker Richard (F)	6 1	14 06	Sheffield	30 5 75	Rotherham U
Beardsley Chris (F)	6 0	12 12	Derby	28 2 84	Kidderminster H
Birchall Adam (F)	5 7	10 09	Maidstone	2 12 84	Arsenal
Brown Simon (F)	5 10	11 05	West Bromwich	18 9 83	WBA
Buxton Jake (D)	6 1	13 05	Sutton-in-Ashfield	4 3 85	Scholar
Coke Gilles (M)	6 0	11 11	London	3 6 86	Kingstonian
D'Laryea Jonathan (M)	5 10	12 02	Manchester	3 9 85	Manchester C
Dawson Stephen (M)	5 9	11 09	Dublin	4 12 85	Leicester C
Heron Daniel (M)	5 11	10 09	Cambridge	9 10 86	Scholar
Hjelde Jon Olav (D)	6 2	13 07	Levanger	30 7 72	Nottingham F
Jelleyman Gareth (D)	5 10	11 05	Holywell	14 11 80	Peterborough U
John-Baptiste Alex (D)	5 11	11 11	Sutton-in-Ashfield	31 1 86	Scholar
Langford Michael (G)	5 11	11 02	Wolverhampton	10 5 88	Scholar
Lloyd Callum (M)	5 9	11 04	Nottingham	1 1 86	Scholar
Lonsdale Richard (M)	5 9	10 10	Burton	29 10 87	Scholar

McIntosh Austin (M)	5 11	10 09	Newham	5 11 87	Scholar
Parks Ryan (M)			Mansfield	5 5 87	Scholar
Reet Danny (F)	6 1	14 02	Sheffield	31 1 87	Sheffield W
White Jason (G)	6 2	12 13	Mansfield	28 1 83	Trainee
Wood Chris (M)	6 0	10 11	Worksop	24 1 87	Scholar

League Appearances: Arnold, N. 5(3); Barker, R. 41(2); Beardsley, C. 2(1); Birchall, A. 15(16); Brown, S. 15(14); Buxton, J. 36(3); Coke, G. 33(7); D'Laryea, J. 29; Dawson, S. 31(9); Day, R. 21; Hjelde, J. 30(1); Jacobs, K. 4(1); Jelleyman, G. 33(1); John-Baptiste, A. 40(1); Littlejohn, A. (7); Lloyd, C. 3(9); McLachlan, F. 7(1); Palmer, C. 1; Peers, G. 12(1); Pressman, K. 41; Reet, D. 16(2); Rundle, A. 27(8); Russell, A. 7(11); Talbot, J. 6; Tipton, M. 4; Uhlenbeek, G. 28(12); White, J. 5; Wilson, L. 14(1).

Goals – League (59): Barker 18 (6 pens), Brown 10 (1 pen), Reet 5, Rundle 5, Coke 4, Birchall 2, Day 2, Peers 2, Russell 2, Uhlenbeek 2, Arnold 1, Dawson 1, Hjelde 1, Jelleyman 1, John-Baptiste 1, Wilson 1, own goal 1.

Carling Cup (4): Barker 1, Brown 1, Coke 1, Jelleyman 1.

FA Cup (7): Barker 4 (1 pen), Birchall 1, Brown 1, Coke 1.

Football League Trophy (0).

Ground: Field Mill Ground, Quarry Lane, Mansfield, Nottinghamshire NG18 5DA. Telephone (0870) 756 3160.

Record Attendance: 24,467 v Nottingham F, FA Cup 3rd rd, 10 January 1953.

Capacity: 9,365.

Manager: Peter Shirtliff.

Secretary: Sharon Roberts.

Most League Goals: 108, Division 4, 1962–63.

Highest League Scorer in Season: Ted Harston, 55, Division 3 (N), 1936–37.

Most League Goals in Total Aggregate: Harry Johnson, 104, 1931–36.

Most Capped Player: John McClelland, 6 (53), Northern Ireland.

Most League Appearances: Rod Arnold, 440, 1970–83.

Honours – Football League: Division 3 Champions – 1976–77. Division 4 Champions – 1974–75. **Freight Rover Trophy:** Winners – 1986–87.

Colours: Amber shirts with royal blue trim, royal blue shorts with amber side stripe, amber stockings.

MIDDLESBROUGH   FA PREMIERSHIP

Bates Matthew (D)	5 10	12 03	Stockton	10 12 86	Scholar
Boateng George (M)	5 9	12 06	Nkawkaw	5 9 75	Aston Villa
Cattermole Lee (M)	5 10	11 13	Stockton	21 3 88	Scholar
Christie Malcolm (F)	6 0	12 06	Peterborough	11 4 79	Derby Co
Davies Andrew (D)	6 3	14 08	Stockton	17 12 84	Scholar
Downing Stewart (M)	5 11	10 04	Middlesbrough	22 7 84	Scholar
Ehiogu Ugo (D)	6 2	14 10	Hackney	3 11 72	Aston Villa
Graham Danny (F)	5 11	12 05	Gateshead	12 8 85	Trainee
Hines Sebastian (M)	6 2	12 04	Wetherby	29 5 88	Scholar
Hutchinson Ben (D)			Nottingham	12 87	Arnold T
Johnson Adam (M)	5 9	9 11	Sunderland	14 7 87	Scholar
Jones Brad (G)	6 3	12 01	Armidale	19 3 82	Trainee
Kennedy Jason (M)	6 1	11 10	Stockton	11 9 86	Scholar
Knight David (G)	6 0	11 07	Houghton-le-Spring	15 1 87	Scholar
Liddle Gary (D)	6 1	12 06	Middlesbrough	15 6 86	Scholar
Maccarone Massimo (F)	5 10	12 05	Galliate	6 9 79	Empoli
McMahon Anthony (D)	5 10	11 04	Bishop Auckland	24 3 86	Scholar
Mendieta Gaizka (M)	5 9	11 02	Bilbao	27 3 74	Barcelona
Morrison James (M)	5 10	10 06	Darlington	25 5 86	Trainee
Parlour Ray (M)	5 10	11 12	Romford	7 3 73	Arsenal
Parnaby Stuart (M)	5 11	11 00	Durham City	19 7 82	Trainee
Pogatetz Emanuel (D)	6 2	13 05	Steinbock	16 1 83	Graz

Queudrue Franck (D)	6 1	12 01	Paris	27 8 78	Lens
Riggott Chris (D)	6 2	13 09	Derby	1 9 80	Derby Co
Rochemback Fabio (M)	6 0	13 01	Soledade	10 12 81	Sporting Lisbon
Schwarzer Mark (G)	6 4	14 07	Sydney	6 10 72	Bradford C
Southgate Gareth (D)	6 0	12 03	Watford	3 9 70	Aston Villa
Taylor Andrew (D)	5 10	11 04	Hartlepool	1 8 86	Trainee
Turnbull Ross (G)	6 4	15 00	Bishop Auckland	4 1 85	Trainee
Viduka Mark (F)	6 2	15 01	Melbourne	9 10 75	Leeds U
Walker Josh (M)	5 11	11 13	Newcastle	21 2 89	Scholar
Wheater David (D)	6 4	12 12	Redcar	14 2 87	Scholar
Yakubu Ayegbeni (F)	6 0	14 07	Benin City	22 11 82	Portsmouth

League Appearances: Bates, M. 12(4); Boateng, G. 25(1); Cattermole, L. 10(4); Christie, M. 3(3); Cooper, C. (1); Craddock, T. (1); Davies, A. 4(8); Doriva, 19(8); Downing, S. 11(1); Ehiogu, U. 16(2); Graham, D. 1(2); Hasselbaink, J. 12(10); Job, J. (1); Johnson, A. 8(5); Jones, B. 9; Kennedy, J. 1(2); Maccarone, M. 6(11); McMahon, T. 3; Mendieta, G. 15(2); Morrison, J. 21(3); Nemeth, S. 1(4); Parlour, R. 11(2); Parnaby, S. 19(1); Pogatetz, E. 21(3); Queudrue, F. 26(3); Reiziger, M. 4; Riggott, C. 22; Rochemback, F. 22; Schwarzer, M. 27; Southgate, G. 24; Taylor, A. 7(6); Turnbull, R. 2; Viduka, M. 19(8); Walker, J. (1); Wheater, D. 4(2); Xavier, A. 4; Yakubu, A. 29(5).
Goals – League (48): Yakubu 13 (3 pens), Hasselbaink 9 (1 pen), Viduka 7, Queudrue 3, Boateng 2, Maccarone 2 (1 pen), Mendieta 2, Parnaby 2, Rochemback 2, Cattermole 1, Downing 1, Johnson 1, Morrison 1, Pogatetz 1, own goal 1.
Carling Cup (3): Hasselbaink 1, Nemeth 1, Viduka 1.
FA Cup (14): Yakubu 4 (1 pen), Hasselbaink 3, Viduka 2, Mendieta 1, Morrison 1, Parnaby 1, Riggott 1, Rochemback 1.
UEFA Cup (20): Viduka 6, Maccarone 5, Hasselbaink 4, Yakubu 2 (1 pen), Boateng 1, Parnaby 1, Riggott 1.
Ground: Riverside Stadium, Middlesbrough, TS3 6RS. Telephone (0870) 421 1986.
Record Attendance: Ayresome Park: 53,536 v Newcastle U, Division 1, 27 December 1949. Riverside Stadium: 34,814 v Newcastle U, FA Premier League, 5 March 2003. **Capacity:** 35,041.
Manager: Gareth Southgate.
Secretary: Karen Nelson.
Most League Goals: 122, Division 2, 1926–27.
Highest League Scorer in Season: George Camsell, 59, Division 2, 1926–27 (Second Division record).
Most League Goals in Total Aggregate: George Camsell, 325, 1925–39.
Most Capped Player: Wilf Mannion, 26, England.
Most League Appearances: Tim Williamson, 563, 1902–23.
Honours – Football League: Division 1 Champions 1994–95. Division 2 Champions 1926–27, 1928–29, 1973–74. **Football League Cup:** Winners – 2004. **Amateur Cup:** Winners – 1895, 1898. **European Competition:** UEFA Cup: Runners-up: 2005–06.
Anglo-Scottish Cup: Winners – 1975–76.
Colours: Red with white chest band and gold trim.

MILLWALL   FL CHAMPIONSHIP 1

Braniff Kevin (F)	5 11	10 03	Belfast	4 3 83	Scholar
Cogan Barry (F)	5 9	9 0	Sligo	4 11 84	Scholar
Craig Tony (D)	6 0	10 03	Greenwich	20 4 85	Scholar
Dunne Alan (D)	5 10	10 13	Dublin	23 8 82	Trainee
Elliott Marvin (M)	6 0	12 02	Wandsworth	15 9 84	Scholar
Grant Gavin (F)	5 11	11 00	Wembley	27 3 84	Gillingham
Hayles Barry (F)	5 10	12 11	Lambeth	17 5 72	Sheffield U
Hendry Will (M)	5 11	12 10	Slough	10 11 86	Scholar
Lawrence Matthew (D)	6 1	12 12	Northampton	19 6 74	Wycombe W

Livermore David (M)	5 11	12 02	Edmonton	20 5 80	Trainee
May Ben (F)	6 3	12 12	Gravesend	10 3 84	Juniors
Morris Jody (F)	5 5	10 03	Hammersmith	22 12 78	Rotherham U
Phillips Mark (D)	6 2	11 00	Lambeth	27 1 82	Scholar
Pooley Dean (D)	6 1	11 02	Sidcup	10 9 86	Scholar
Powel Berry (F)	6 2	13 00	Utrecht	2 5 80	Den Bosch
Robinson Paul (D)	6 1	11 09	Barnet	7 1 82	Scholar
Williams Marvin (M)	5 11	11 06	Sydenham	12 8 87	Scholar

League Appearances: Asaba, C. 17(4); Braniff, K. 9(6); Cameron, C. 5; Cogan, B. 6(8); Craig, T. 26(2); Doyle, C. 14; Dunne, A. 40; Dyer, B. 9(1); Dyer, L. 2(4); Elliott, M. 33(6); Fangueiro, C. 1(8); Hayles, B. 21(2); Healy, J. 1); Hendry, W. 2(1); Hutchison, D. 7(4); Ifil, P. 16; Igoe, S. 3(2); Jones, P. 3; Lawrence, M. 30(1); Livermore, D. 41; Marshall, A. 29; May, B. 24(15); Morris, J. 24; Peeters, B. (2); Phillips, M. 19(3); Pooley, D. (1); Powel, B. 8(4); Robinson, P. 29(3); Robinson, T. (1); Serioux, A. 2(3); Simpson, J. 8(5); Vincent, J. 18(1); Whitbread, Z. 25; Williams, A. 12; Williams, M. 8(14); Wright, J. 15.
Goals – League (35): May 10, Hayles 4 (1 pen), Williams M 4, Asaba 3, Dyer B 2, Elliott 2, Hutchison 2, Livermore 2, Wright 2, Powel 1, Simpson 1, Williams A 1, own goal 1.
Carling Cup (9): Dunne 2, Asaba 1, Elliott 1, Fangueiro 1, Hayles 1, Livermore 1, May 1, Robinson 1.
FA Cup (1): Williams M.
Ground: The Den, Zampa Road, London SE16 3LN. Telephone (020) 7232 1222.
Record Attendance: 20,093 v Arsenal, FA Cup 3rd rd, 10 January 1994. **Capacity:** 20,146.
Manager: Nigel Spackman.
Secretary: Yvonne Haines.
Most League Goals: 127, Division 3 (S), 1927–28.
Highest League Scorer in Season: Richard Parker, 37, Division 3 (S), 1926–27.
Most League Goals in Total Aggregate: Teddy Sheringham, 93, 1984–91 and Neil Harris, 93, 1995–2004.
Most Capped Player: Eamonn Dunphy, 22 (23), Republic of Ireland.
Most League Appearances: Barry Kitchener, 523, 1967–82.
Honours – Football League: Division 2 Champions – 1987–88, 2000–01. Division 3 (S) Champions – 1927–28, 1937–38. Division 4 Champions – 1961–62. **Football League Trophy:** Winners – 1982–83.
Colours: Blue and white shirts, blue and shite shorts, blue stockings.

MILTON KEYNES DONS   FL CHAMPIONSHIP 2

Baker Matt (G)	6 0	14 00	Harrogate	18 12 79	Wrexham
Baldock Sam (F)	5 7	10 07	Buckingham	15 3 89	Scholar
Chorley Ben (M)	6 3	13 02	Sidcup	30 9 82	Arsenal
Crooks Leon (M)	6 0	11 12	Greenwich	21 11 85	Scholar
Edds Gareth (D)	5 11	11 01	Sydney	3 2 81	Bradford C
Harding Ben (M)	5 10	11 02	Carshalton	6 9 84	Scholar
Kamara Malvin (M)	5 11	13 00	London	17 11 83	Scholar
Lewington Dean (D)	5 11	11 07	Kingston	18 5 84	Scholar
McKoy Nick (M)	6 0	12 06	Newham	3 9 86	Scholar
McLeod Izale (F)	6 1	11 02	Perry Bar	15 10 84	Derby Co
Mitchell Paul (M)	5 9	12 01	Manchester	26 8 81	Scholar
Morgan Craig (D)	6 0	11 04	St Asaph	18 6 85	Wrexham
Platt Clive (F)	6 4	12 07	Wolverhampton	27 10 77	Peterborough U
Small Wade (M)	5 8	11 05	Croydon	23 2 84	Scholar
Smith Gary (M)	5 8	10 09	Middlesbrough	30 1 84	Middlesbrough
Taylor Scott (F)	5 10	11 04	Chertsey	5 5 76	Plymouth Arg
Wilbraham Aaron (F)	6 3	12 04	Knutsford	21 10 79	Hull C

League Appearances: Baker, M. 37; Batista, R. 9; Carrilho, M. 1(2); Chorley, B. 25(1); Crooks, L. 22(1); Edds, G. 32(9); Harding, B. 8(2); Kamara, M. 6(17); Lewington, D. 44; McClenahan, T. 24(5); McKoy, N. 5(11); McLeod, I. 33(6); Mills, P. 16; Mitchell, P. 39; Morais, F. 11(2); Morgan, C. 38(2); Oyedele, S. 2(1); Palmer, S. 1(1); Partridge, D. 18; Platt, C. 34(6); Puncheon, J. 1; Quinn, S. 13(2); Ricketts, M. 4(1); Rizzo, N. 15(14); Small, W. 24(4); Smith, G. 18(7); Taylor, S. 10(7); Wilbraham, A. 16(15).

Goals – League (45): McLeod 17 (2 pens), Platt 6, Wilbraham 4, Edds 3, Smith 3 (1 pen), Taylor 3, Harding 2, Kamara 2, Rizzo 2 (1 pen), Lewington 1, Mills 1, Small 1.

Carling Cup (0).

FA Cup (8): Edds 2, Platt 2, McLeod 1 (pen), Rizzo 1, Smith 1, own goal 1.

Football League Trophy (7): Smith 3 (1 pen), Wilbraham 2, Mills 1, Small 1.

Ground: The National Hockey Stadium, Silbury Boulevard, Milton Keynes, Buckinghamshire MK9 1FA. Telephone (01908) 607 090.

Record Attendance: 30,115 v Manchester U, FA Premier League, 9 May 1993 (at Selhurst Park). **Capacity:** 8,836.

Manager: Martin Allen.

Football Operations Manager: Kirstine Nicholson.

Most League Goals: 97, Division 3, 1983–84.

Highest League Scorer in Season: Alan Cork, 29, 1983–84.

Most League Goals in Total Aggregate: Alan Cork, 145, 1977–92.

Most Capped Player: Kenny Cunningham, 40 (72), Republic of Ireland.

Most League Appearances: Alan Cork, 430, 1977–92.

Honours – Football League: Division 4 Champions – 1982–83. **FA Cup:** Winners – 1987–88.

Colours: All white.

NEWCASTLE UNITED   FA PREMIERSHIP

Name	Ht	DoB	Birthplace	Signed	From
Ameobi Foluwashola (F)	6 3	11 13	Zaria	12 10 81	Trainee
Atkin Liam (M)	6 2	12 03	Ashington	12 12 86	Scholar
Babayaro Celestine (D)	5 9	12 06	Kaduna	29 8 78	Chelsea
Boumsong Jean-Alain (D)	6 3	13 03	Douala	14 12 79	Rangers
Bowyer Lee (M)	5 9	10 12	Canning Town	3 1 77	West Ham U
Bramble Titus (D)	6 2	13 10	Ipswich	31 7 81	Ipswich T
Butt Nicky (M)	5 10	11 05	Manchester	21 1 75	Manchester U
Carr Stephen (D)	5 9	12 02	Dublin	29 8 76	Tottenham H
Chopra Michael (F)	5 9	10 03	Newcastle	23 12 83	Scholar
Clark Lee (M)	5 8	11 07	Wallsend	27 10 72	Fulham
Dyer Kieron (M)	5 8	10 00	Ipswich	29 12 78	Ipswich T
Edgar David (D)	6 2	12 13	Ontario	19 5 87	Scholar
Elliott Robbie (D)	5 10	10 12	Gosforth	25 12 73	Bolton W
Emre Belezoglu (M)	5 8	10 10	Istanbul	7 9 80	Internazionale
Faye Amdy (M)	6 1	12 04	Dakar	12 3 77	Portsmouth
Gate Kris (D)	5 7	10 03	Newcastle	1 1 85	Scholar
Given Shay (G)	6 0	13 03	Lifford	20 4 76	Blackburn R
Harper Steve (G)	6 2	13 10	Easington	14 3 75	Seaham Red Star
Huntington Paul (D)	6 3	12 08	Carlisle	17 9 87	Scholar
Krul Tim (G)	6 2	11 08	Den Haag	3 4 88	Den Haag
Luque Alberto (F)	6 0	11 11	Barcelona	11 3 78	La Coruna
Milner James (M)	5 10	11 00	Leeds	4 1 86	Leeds U
Moore Craig (D)	6 1	12 00	Canterbury, Aus	12 12 75	M'gladbach
N'Zogbia Charles (M)	5 9	11 00	Le Havre	28 5 86	Le Havre
O'Brien Alan (M)	5 10	10 10	Dublin	20 2 85	Scholar
Owen Michael (F)	5 8	10 12	Chester	14 12 79	Liverpool
Parker Scott (M)	5 9	11 10	Lambeth	13 10 80	Chelsea
Pattison Matt (M)	5 9	11 00	Johannesburg	27 10 86	Scholar

Ramage Peter (D)	6 1	11 03	Whitley Bay	22 11 83	Trainee
Shanks Chris (D)	6 0	11 00	Ashington	16 10 86	Scholar
Solano Nolberto (M)	5 8	10 07	Callao	12 12 74	Aston Villa
Taylor Steven (D)	6 1	13 01	Greenwich	23 1 86	Trainee
Viana Hugo (M)	5 9	11 09	Barcelos	15 1 83	Sporting Lisbon

League Appearances: Ameobi, F. 25(5); Babayaro, C. 26(2); Boumsong, J. 30(3); Bowyer, L. 18(10); Bramble, T. 21(3); Carr, S. 19; Chopra, M. 6(7); Clark, L. 8(14); Dyer, K. 4(7); Elliott, R. 14(3); Emre, B. 19(1); Faye, A. 14(8); Given, S. 38; Jenas, J. 3(1); Luque, A. 6(8); Milner, J. 1(2); Moore, C. 8; N'Zogbia, C. 27(5); O'Brien, A. 3(1); Owen, M. 10(1); Parker, S. 26; Pattison, M. 2(1); Ramage, P. 23; Shearer, A. 31(1); Solano, N. 27(2); Taylor, S. 12.
Goals – League (47): Shearer 10 (4 pens), Ameobi 9 (1 pen), Owen 7, Solano 6, N'Zogbia 5, Bramble 2, Emre 2, Bowyer 1, Chopra 1, Clark 1, Luque 1, Parker 1, own goal 1.
Carling Cup (1): Shearer 1.
FA Cup (4): Chopra 1, Dyer 1, Parker 1, Shearer 1.
Ground: St James' Park, Newcastle-upon-Tyne NE1 4ST. Telephone (0191) 201 8400.
Record Attendance: 68,386 v Chelsea, Division 1, 3 Sept 1930. **Capacity:** 52,387.
Manager: Glenn Roeder.
Secretary: Russell Cushing.
Most League Goals: 98, Division 1, 1951–52.
Highest League Scorer in Season: Hughie Gallacher, 36, Division 1, 1926–27.
Most League Goals in Total Aggregate: Jackie Milburn, 177, 1946–57.
Most Capped Player: Shay Given, 67 (76), Republic of Ireland.
Most League Appearances: Jim Lawrence, 432, 1904–22.
Honours – Football League: Division 1 – Champions 1904–05, 1906–07, 1908–09, 1926–27, 1992–93. Division 2 Champions – 1964–65. **FA Cup:** Winners – 1910, 1924, 1932, 1951, 1952, 1955. **Texaco Cup:** Winners – 1973–74, 1974–75. **European Competitions: European Fairs Cup:** Winners – 1968–69. **Anglo-Italian Cup:** Winners – 1973.
Colours: Black and white striped shirts, black shorts, black stockings.

NORTHAMPTON TOWN   FL CHAMPIONSHIP 1

Bojic Pedj (D)	5 11	11 12	Sydney	9 4 84	Sydney Olympic
Bonner Tom (D)	6 0	11 06	Sydenham	6 2 88	Scholar
Bunn Mark (G)	6 0	12 02	Camden	16 11 84	Scholar
Chambers Luke (D)	6 1	11 13	Kettering	29 8 85	Scholar
Cross Scott (M)	5 10	11 00	Northampton	30 10 87	Scholar
Crowe Jason (D)	5 9	10 09	Sidcup	30 9 78	Grimsby T
Doig Chris (D)	6 2	12 06	Dumfries	13 2 81	Nottingham F
Dolman Liam (D)			Brixworth	26 9 87	Scholar
Dyche Sean (D)	6 0	13 10	Kettering	28 6 71	Watford
Gearing Matthew (F)	5 7	11 07	Northampton	11 9 86	Scholar
Gilligan Ryan (M)	5 10	11 07	Swindon	18 1 87	Watford
Graham Luke (D)	6 2	13 04	Kettering	27 4 86	Scholar
Harper Lee (G)	6 1	15 06	Chelsea	30 10 71	Walsall
Hunt David (D)	5 10	11 08	Dulwich	10 9 82	Leyton Orient
Jess Eion (M)	5 10	11 06	Aberdeen	13 12 70	Nottingham F
Johnson Brad (M)	6 0	12 10	Hackney	28 4 87	Cambridge U
Johnson Brett (D)	6 1	13 00	Hammersmith	15 8 85	Aldershot T
Kirk Andy (F)	5 11	11 07	Belfast	29 5 79	Boston U
Low Josh (F)	6 2	14 03	Bristol	15 2 79	Oldham Ath
McGleish Scott (F)	5 9	11 09	Barnet	10 2 74	Colchester U
Murray Fred (D)	5 10	11 12	Tipperary	22 5 82	Cambridge U
Smith Martin (F)	5 11	12 07	Sunderland	13 11 74	Huddersfield T

Taylor Ian (M)   6 2   11 06 Birmingham   4 6 68 Derby Co
Westwood Ashley (D)   6 0   12 09 Bridgnorth   31 8 76 Sheffield W

League Appearances: Bojic, P. 18(18); Chambers, L. 42(1); Cross, S. (4); Crowe, J. 41; Doig, C. 36(2); Dudfield, L. 2(4); Dyche, S. 34(1); Galbraith, D. 1(3); Gilligan, R. 4(19); Hand, J. 8(3); Harper, L. 46; Hunt, D. 35(5); Jess, E. 35(3); Johnson, Brad 1(2); Johnson, Brett 2(4); Johnson, G. 22(2); Kirk, A. 20(9); Lee, J. 8(3); Low, J. 29(6); McGleish, S. 39(3); Mendes, J. 9(3); Mikolanda, P. 2; Rowson, D. 13(16); Sabin, E. 4(2); Smith, M. 22(4); Taylor, I. 33; Westwood, A. (3).
Goals – League (63): McGleish 17 (2 pens), Kirk 8 (2 pens), Taylor 7, Low 5, Bojic 4, Gilligan 4, Hunt 3, Smith 3, Crowe 2, Doig 2, Mendes 2, Dudfield 1, Jess 1, Johnson G 1, Lee 1, own goals 2.
Carling Cup (3): Kirk 1, McGleish 1, Sabin 1 (pen).
FA Cup (8): McGleish 4 (1 pen), Bojic 1, Doig 1, Low 1, Smith 1.
Football League Trophy (7): Cross 2, McGleish 2, Bojic 1, Kirk 1, Mendes 1.
Ground: Sixfields Stadium, Upton Way, Northampton NN5 5QA. Telephone 0870 822 1997.
Record Attendance: (at County Ground): 24,523 v Fulham, Division 1, 23 April 1966; (at Sixfields Stadium): 7,557 v Manchester C, Division 2, 26 September 1998.
Capacity: 7,653.
Manager: John Gorman.
Secretary: Norman Howells.
Most League Goals: 109, Division 3, 1962–63 and Division 3 (S), 1952–53.
Highest League Scorer in Season: Cliff Holton, 36, Division 3, 1961–62.
Most League Goals in Total Aggregate: Jack English, 135, 1947–60.
Most Capped Player: Edwin Lloyd Davies, 12 (16), Wales.
Most League Appearances: Tommy Fowler, 521, 1946–61.
Honours – Football League: Division 3 Champions – 1962–63. Division 4 Champions – 1986–87.
Colours: Claret shirts, white shorts, claret stockings.

NORWICH CITY   FL CHAMPIONSHIP

Cave-Brown Andrew (D)   5 10   12 02   Gravesend   5 8 88   Scholar
Colin Jurgen (D)   5 10   11 10   Utrecht   20 1 81   PSV Eindhoven
Doherty Gary (D)   6 2   13 04   Carndonagh   31 1 80   Tottenham H
Drury Adam (D)   5 10   11 08   Cottenham   29 8 78   Peterborough U
Earnshaw Robert (F)   5 6   9 09   Mulfulira   6 4 81   WBA
Edworthy Marc (D)   5 8   10 05   Barnstaple   24 12 72   Wolverhampton W
Etuhu Dickson (M)   6 2   13 04   Kano   8 6 82   Preston NE
Fleming Craig (D)   5 11   12 05   Halifax   6 10 71   Oldham Ath
Gallacher Paul (G)   6 0   12 00   Glasgow   16 8 79   Dundee U
Green Robert (G)   6 3   13 01   Chertsey   18 1 80   Trainee
Henderson Ian (F)   5 9   10 12   Thetford   24 1 85   Scholar
Huckerby Darren (F)   5 10   12 02   Nottingham   23 4 76   Manchester C
Hughes Andy (M)   5 11   12 01   Stockport   2 1 78   Reading
Jarrett Jason (M)   6 1   13 10   Bury   14 9 79   Wigan Ath
Jarvis Rossi (D)   5 11   11 12   Fakenham   11 3 88   Scholar
Jarvis Ryan (F)   6 0   11 05   Fakenham   11 7 86   Scholar
Lewis Joe (G)   6 5   11 12   Bury St Edmunds   6 10 87   Scholar
Louis-Jean Mathieu (D) 5 9   11 07   Mont-St-Aignan   22 2 76   Nottingham F
McKenzie Leon (F)   5 10   10 06   Croydon   17 5 78   Peterborough U
McVeigh Paul (F)   5 6   10 12   Belfast   6 12 77   Tottenham H
Robinson Carl (M)   5 11   12 08   Llandrindod Wells 13 10 76   Sunderland
Safri Youssef (M)   5 8   11 00   Casablanca   13 1 77   Coventry C
Shackell Jason (D)   6 3   12 09   Hitchin   27 9 83   Scholar
Spillane Michael (M)   5 9   11 10   Cambridge   23 3 89   Scholar
Thorne Peter (F)   6 1   13 13   Manchester   21 6 73   Cardiff C

League Appearances: Ashton, D. 28; Brennan, J. 12(6); Charlton, S. 17(4); Colin, J. 24(1); Davenport, C. 14(1); Doherty, G. 39(3); Drury, A. 39; Earnshaw, R. 13(2); Etuhu, D. 15(4); Fleming, C. 31(5); Gallacher, P. 4; Green, R. 42; Henderson, I. 8(16); Huckerby, D. 39(4); Hughes, A. 35(1); Jarrett, J. 6(5); Jarvis, Rossi (3); Jarvis, Ryan 1(3); Johansson, J. 6(6); Lisbie, K. 4(2); Louis-Jean, M. 2; Marney, D. 12(1); McKenzie, L. 11(9); McVeigh, P. 22(14); Rehman, Z. 5; Robinson, C. 18(4); Safri, Y. 25(5); Shackell, J. 16(1); Spillane, M. 2; Thorne, P. 11(10); Wright, D. 5.
Goals – League (56): Ashton 10, Earnshaw 8, Huckerby 8, McVeigh 7 (1 pen), McKenzie 4 (1 pen) Johansson 3, Hughes 2, Charlton 1, Davenport 1, Doherty 1, Fleming 1, Henderson 1, Ryan Jarvis 1, Lisbie 1, Safri 1, Thorne 1, own goals 5.
Carling Cup (4): Ashton 1, Huckerby 1 (pen), McKenzie 1, own goal 1.
FA Cup (1): McVeigh 1 (pen).
Ground: Carrow Road, Norwich NR1 1JE. Telephone (01603) 760 760.
Record Attendance: 43,984 v Leicester C, FA Cup 6th rd, 30 March 1963.
Capacity: 26,034.
Manager: Nigel Worthington.
Secretary: Kevan Platt.
Most League Goals: 99, Division 3 (S), 1952–53.
Highest League Scorer in Season: Ralph Hunt, 31, Division 3 (S), 1955–56.
Most League Goals in Total Aggregate: Johnny Gavin, 122, 1945–54, 1955–58.
Most Capped Player: Mark Bowen, 35 (41), Wales.
Most League Appearances: Ron Ashman, 592, 1947–64.
Honours – Football League: Division 1 Champions – 2003–04. Division 2 Champions – 1971–72, 1985–86. Division 3 (S) Champions – 1933–34. **Football League Cup:** Winners – 1962, 1985.
Colours: Yellow shirts, green shorts, yellow stockings.

NOTTINGHAM FOREST   FL CHAMPIONSHIP 1

Bastians Felix (M)	6 2	12 00	Bochum	9	5 88	Scholar
Beaumont James (M)	5 7	10 10	Stockton	11	12 84	Newcastle U
Bennett Julian (D)	6 1	13 00	Nottingham	17	12 84	Walsall
Breckin Ian (D)	6 2	13 05	Rotherham	24	2 75	Wigan Ath
Clingan Sammy (M)	5 11	11 06	Belfast	13	1 84	Wolverhampton W
Commons Kris (M)	5 6	9 08	Nottingham	30	8 83	Stoke C
Cullingworth James (M)			Nottingham	18	9 87	Scholar
Cullip Danny (D)	6 0	12 12	Bracknell	17	9 76	Sheffield U
Curtis John (D)	5 10	11 07	Nuneaton	3	9 78	Portsmouth
Dobie Scott (F)	6 1	12 05	Workington	10	10 78	Millwall
Eaden Nicky (D)	5 9	12 02	Sheffield	12	12 72	Wigan Ath
Fernandez Vincent (D)	6 3	10 11	Lyon	19	9 86	Scholar
Friio David (M)	6 0	11 05	Thionville	17	2 73	Plymouth Arg
Gamble Paddy (G)			Nottingham	1	9 88	Scholar
Gardner Ross (M)	5 8	10 06	South Shields	15	12 85	Newcastle U
Glass Matt (F)			Swindon	28	5 88	Scholar
Harris Neil (F)	5 11	12 00	Orsett	12	7 77	Millwall
Holt Gary (M)	6 0	12 00	Irvine	9	3 73	Norwich C
Holt Grant (F)	6 1	14 02	Carlisle	12	4 81	Rochdale
James Kevin (M)	5 7	11 12	Southwark	3	1 80	Gillingham
Johnson David (F)	5 6	12 00	Kingston, Jam	15	8 76	Ipswich T
Lester Jack (F)	5 9	12 08	Sheffield	8	10 75	Sheffield U
Maloney Brendan (M)			Enfield	18	1 89	Scholar
Morgan Wes (D)	6 2	14 00	Nottingham	21	1 84	Scholar
Mullarkey Sam (M)			Lincoln	24	9 87	Scholar
Padula Gino (D)	5 9	12 11	Buenos Aires	11	7 76	QPR
Pedersen Rune (G)	6 3	13 08	Copenhagen	9	10 79	Aarhus
Perch James (D)	5 11	11 05	Mansfield	29	9 85	Scholar

Pittman Jon-Paul (F)	5 9	11 00	Oklahoma City	24 10 86	Scholar
Power Alan (M)			Dublin	23 1 88	Scholar
Roberts Dale (M)	6 3	11 06	Horden	22 10 86	Scholar
Rogers Alan (D)	5 9	12 10	Liverpool	3 1 77	Leicester C
Southall Nicky (M)	5 11	12 04	Stockton	28 1 72	Gillingham
Thompson John (D)	6 0	12 01	Dublin	12 10 81	Home Farm
Tyson Nathan (F)	5 10	10 02	Reading	4 5 82	Wycombe W
Vickerton Martin (D)	5 10	11 02	Nottingham	24 6 87	Scholar
Weir-Daley Spencer (F)	5 9	10 11	Leicester	5 9 85	Scholar

League Appearances: Bastians, F. 2(9); Bennett, J. 18; Bopp, E. 2(10); Breckin, I. 46; Clingan, S. 14(1); Commons, K. 36(1); Cullip, D. 10(1); Curtis, J. 27; Dadi, E. (5); Dobie, S. 6(2); Eaden, N. 26(2); Fernandez, V. (1); Friio, D. 11(6); Gardner, R. 6(6); Gerrard, P. 21(1); Harris, N. (1); Holt, Gary 23(3); Holt, Grant 18(1); Hoult, R. 8; Johnson, D. 12(5); Lester, J. 15(23); Morgan, W. 41(2); Padula, G. 3; Pedersen, R. 17(1); Perch, J. 34(4); Southall, N. 37(3); Taylor, G. 17(3); Thompson, J. 28(7); Tyson, N. 28; Vickerton, M. (1); Weir-Daley, S. (6).
Goals – League (67): Tyson 10, Breckin 8, Commons 8, Southall 8, Lester 5 (2 pens), Grant Holt 4, Taylor 4 (1 pen), Johnson 3, Perch 3, Thompson 3, Bennett 2, Dobie 2, Morgan 2, Bopp 1 (pen), Friio 1, Weir-Daley 1, own goals 2.
Carling Cup (2): Breckin 2.
FA Cup (3): Taylor 2, Gary Holt 1.
Football League Trophy (2): Bopp 1, Weir-Daly 1.
Ground: The City Ground, Nottingham NG2 5FJ. Telephone (0115) 982 4444.
Record Attendance: 49,946 v Manchester U, Division 1, 28 October 1967.
Capacity: 30,602.
Manager: Colin Calderwood.
Football Administrator: Jane Carnelly.
Most League Goals: 110, Division 3 (S), 1950–51.
Highest League Scorer in Season: Wally Ardron, 36, Division 3 (S), 1950–51.
Most League Goals in Total Aggregate: Grenville Morris, 199, 1898–1913.
Most Capped Player: Stuart Pearce, 76 (78), England.
Most League Appearances: Bob McKinlay, 614, 1951–70.
Honours – Football League: Division 1 – Champions 1977–78, 1997–98. Division 2 Champions – 1906–07, 1921–22. Division 3 (S) Champions – 1950–51. **FA Cup:** Winners – 1898, 1959. **Football League Cup:** Winners – 1977–78, 1978–79, 1988–89, 1989–90. **Anglo-Scottish Cup:** Winners – 1976–77. **Simod Cup:** Winners – 1989. **Zenith Data Systems Cup:** Winners – 1991–92. **European Competitions: European Cup:** Winners – 1978–79, 1979–80. **Super Cup:** Winners – 1979–80.
Colours: Red shirts, white shorts, red stockings.

NOTTS COUNTY   FL CHAMPIONSHIP 2

Baudet Julien (D)	6 3	15 03	St Martin D'heres	13 1 79	Rotherham U
Edwards Mike (D)	6 1	13 01	North Ferriby	25 4 80	Grimsby T
Frost Stef (M)	6 2	11 05	Eastwood	3 7 89	Scholar
Martin Dan (D)	6 1	12 13	Derby	27 9 86	Scholar
Needham Liam (M)	6 1	12 02	Sheffield	19 10 85	Gainsborough T
Palmer Chris (M)	5 7	11 00	Derby	16 10 83	Derby Co
Pilkington Kevin (G)	6 1	13 00	Hitchin	8 3 74	Mansfield T
Pipe David (M)	5 10	12 04	Caerphilly	5 11 83	Coventry C
Rhodes Chris (M)	5 9	10 12	Mansfield	9 1 87	Scholar
Sheridan Jake (M)	5 9	11 06	Nottingham	8 7 86	Dunkirk
Sissoko Noe (M)	6 3	14 00	Bamako	2 6 83	Creteil
Whitlow Mike (D)	6 0	13 03	Northwich	13 1 68	Sheffield U
Wilson Kelvin (D)	6 1	11 13	Nottingham	3 9 85	Scholar

League Appearances: Baudet, J. 42; Berry, T. 4(1); Chillingworth, D. 8(5); Crooks, L. 18; Dadi, E. 9(2); De Bolla, M. 8(6); Doyle, N. 12; Edwards, M. 45(1); Friars, E. 5; Frost, S. (4); Gill, M. 7(7); Gordon, G. 4(2); Hurst, G. 15(3); Long, S. 7(12); Marshall, S. 1; Martin, D. 16(6); McGoldrick, D. 4(2); McMahon, L. 23(6); Needham, L. 21(1); O'Callaghan, B. 30(3); Palmer, C. 25(4); Pilkington, K. 45; Pipe, D. 43; Scoffham, S. 22(8); Sheridan, J. 13(14); Sissoko, N. 1(2); Tann, A. 4(1); Ullathorne, R. 31(2); White, A. 10(16); Williams, M. (1); Wilson, K. 33(1); Zadkovich, R. (1).
Goals – League (48): Hurst 9, Edwards 7, Baudet 6 (4 pens), Scoffham 5, Martin 4, Chillingworth 2, Dadi 2 (2 pens), Pipe 2, White 2, Crooks 1, De Bolla 1, Friars 1, Long 1, O'Callaghan 1, Palmer 1, Sheridan 1, Wilson 1, own goal 1.
Carling Cup (1): Palmer 1.
FA Cup (3): Baudet 1, McMahon 1, Tann 1.
Football League Trophy (2): Long 1, McMahon 1 (pen).
Ground: Meadow Lane Stadium, Meadow Lane, Nottingham NG2 3HJ. Telephone (0115) 952 9000.
Record Attendance: 47,310 v York C, FA Cup 6th rd, 12 March 1955. **Capacity:** 20,300.
Manager: Steve Thompson.
Secretary: Tony Cuthbert.
Most League Goals: 107, Division 4, 1959–60.
Highest League Scorer in Season: Tom Keetley, 39, Division 3 (S), 1930–31.
Most League Goals in Total Aggregate: Les Bradd, 124, 1967–78.
Most Capped Player: Kevin Wilson, 15 (42), Northern Ireland.
Most League Appearances: Albert Iremonger, 564, 1904–26.
Honours – Football League: Division 2 Champions – 1896–97, 1913–14, 1922–23. Division 3 Champions – 1997–98. Division 3 (S) Champions – 1930–31, 1949–50. Division 4 Champions – 1970–71. **FA Cup:** Winners – 1893–94. **Anglo-Italian Cup:** Winners – 1995.
Colours: Black and white striped shirts, black shorts, black stockings.

OLDHAM ATHLETIC   FL CHAMPIONSHIP 1

Butcher Richard (M)	6 0	13 01	Peterborough	22	1 81	Lincoln C
Day Chris (G)	6 2	13 07	Whipps Cross	28	7 75	QPR
Eardley Ian (M)			Llandudno	6	11 88	Scholar
Edwards Paul (M)	5 11	10 12	Manchester	1	1 80	Blackpool
Forbes Terrell (D)	5 11	12 07	Southwark	17	8 81	Grimsby T
Griffin Adam (D)	5 7	10 03	Manchester	26	8 84	Scholar
Haining Will (D)	6 0	11 00	Glasgow	2	10 82	Scholar
Hall Chris (F)	6 1	11 04	Manchester	27	11 86	Scholar
Hughes Mark (M)	5 10	12 05	Dungannon	16	9 83	Tottenham H
Liddell Andy (F)	5 7	11 11	Leeds	28	6 73	Sheffield U
Owen Gareth (D)	6 1	11 07	Stoke	21	9 82	Stoke C
Porter Chris (F)	6 1	12 09	Wigan	12	12 83	Bury
Scott Rob (D)	6 0	12 09	Epsom	15	8 73	Rotherham U
Smith Terry (G)	6 0	11 00	Chester	16	9 87	Scholar
Stam Stefan (D)	6 2	13 00	Amersfoort	14	9 79	Huizen
Swailes Chris (D)	6 2	13 09	Gateshead	19	10 70	Rotherham U
Taylor Chris (M)	5 11	11 00	Oldham	20	12 86	
Taylor Jason (M)	6 1	11 03	Ashton-under-Lyne	28	1 87	Scholar
Tierney Marc (D)	5 11	11 02	Manchester	7	9 86	Trainee
Warne Paul (M)	5 10	11 07	Norwich	8	5 73	Rotherham U
Wellens Richard (M)	5 9	11 06	Manchester	26	3 80	Blackpool
Wolfenden Matthew (M)	5 9	11 01	Oldham	23	7 87	Scholar

League Appearances: Beckett, L. 27(7); Bonner, M. 5(2); Branston, G. 38; Butcher, R. 32(4); Day, C. 30; Eardley, I. 1; Edwards, P. 29(5); Eyres, D. 15(6); Facey, D. (3); Forbes, T. 33(6); Grant, A. 2; Grant, L. 16; Haining, W. 13(2); Hall, C. 3(14); Hall, D. 9(1); Hughes, M. 30(3); Killen, C. 10(2); Liddell, A. 29; Owen, G.

17; Porter, C. 18(13); Scott, R. 19(2); Stam, S. 9(4); Swailes, C. 14(1); Taylor, C. 11(3); Tierney, M. 13(6); Warne, P. 38(2); Wellens, R. 45; Wolfenden, M. (1).
Goals – League (58): Beckett 18 (4 pens), Liddell 9 (2 pens), Warne 9, Porter 7, Butcher 4, Wellens 4, Killen 2, Bonner 1, Branston 1, Eyres 1, Hughes 1, Scott 1.
Carling Cup (0).
FA Cup (6): Porter 2, Eyres 1, Hall C 1, Liddell 1 (pen), Warne 1.
Football League Trophy (1): Liddell 1 (pen).
Ground: Boundary Park, Furtherwood Road, Oldham OL1 2PA. Telephone (0871) 226 2235.
Record Attendance: 46,471 v Sheffield W, FA Cup 4th rd. 25 January 1930.
Capacity: 13,624.
Manager: John Sheridan.
Secretary: Alan Hardy.
Most League Goals: 95, Division 4, 1962–63.
Highest League Scorer in Season: Tom Davis, 33, Division 3 (N), 1936–37.
Most League Goals in Total Aggregate: Roger Palmer, 141, 1980–94.
Most Capped Player: Gunnar Halle, 24 (64), Norway.
Most League Appearances: Ian Wood, 525, 1966–80.
Honours – Football League: Division 2 Champions – 1990–91, Division 3 (N) Champions – 1952–53. Division 3 Champions – 1973–74.
Colours: Royal blue shirts with white trim, royal blue shorts with white trim, white stockings.

OXFORD UNITED   CONFERENCE

Name					
Basham Steve (F)	5 11	12 04	Southampton	2 12 77	Preston NE
Beechers Billy (M)	5 9	11 10	Oxford	1 6 87	Scholar
Burgess Andy (M)	6 2	11 12	Bedford	10 8 81	Rushden & D
Dempster John (D)	6 1	11 07	Kettering	1 4 83	Rushden & D
Franklin Tom (D)	6 1	12 00	Oxford	12 5 89	Scholar
Hargreaves Chris (M)	6 0	12 13	Cleethorpes	12 5 72	Brentford
Mansell Lee (D)	5 10	11 10	Gloucester	28 10 82	Luton T
McCoy Kyle (F)	5 7	10 07	Oxford	13 9 87	Scholar
Odubade Yemi (F)	5 7	11 07	Lagos	4 7 84	Eastbourne B
Sills Tim (F)	6 1	14 00	Romsey	10 9 79	Aldershot T
Weedon Ben (D)	5 9	11 00	Oxford	30 3 89	Scholar
Willmott Chris (D)	6 2	13 08	Bedford	30 9 77	Northampton T

League Appearances: Ashton, J. 32(1); Basham, S. 30(10); Beechers, B. (1); Bradbury, L. 18(4); Brooks, J. 4(5); Burgess, A. 12(4); Campbell, A. 3(2); Davies, C. 10(10); Dempster, J. 6; E'Beyer, M. 3(3); Fitzgerald, S. 2(1); Gemmill, S. (1); Goodhind, W. 4(2); Gray, S. 10; Griffin, A. 8(1); Guatelli, A. 4; Hackett, C. 19(2); Hargreaves, C. 34(1); Horsted, L. 1(3); Hughes, R. (3); Mansell, L. 44; Morgan, D. 1(2); N'Toya, T. 7(1); Odubade, Y. 4(4); Quinn, B. 44; Roach, N. 1(6); Robinson, M. 44; Roget, L. 32(1); Sabin, E. 28(1); Sills, T. 9(4); Smith, J. 5(1); Stirling, J. 6(4); Tardif, C. 10(1); Turley, B. 32(1); Weedon, B. 1(1); Willmott, C. 38(3).
Goals – League (43): Basham 8 (3 pens), Bradbury 5 (2 pens), N'Toya 4 (1 pen), Davies 2, Hackett 2, Quinn 2, Roget 2, Willmott 2, Ashton 1, Burgess 1, E'Beyer 1, Fitzgerald 1, Hargreaves 1, Mansell 1, Morgan 1, Odubade 1, Sills 1.
Carling Cup (0).
FA Cup (6): Basham 5 (1 pen), Sabin 1.
Football League Trophy (3): Mansell 1, Roget 1, Sabin 1.
Ground: The Kassam Stadium, Grenoble Road, Oxford OX4 4XP. Telephone (01865) 337 500.
Record Attendance: 22,730 (at Manor Ground) v Preston NE, FA Cup 6th rd, 29 February 1964. **Capacity:** 12,500.
Manager: Jim Smith.
Secretary: Mick Brown.

Most League Goals: 91, Division 3, 1983–84.
Highest League Scorer in Season: John Aldridge, 30, Division 2, 1984–85.
Most League Goals in Total Aggregate: Graham Atkinson, 77, 1962–73.
Most Capped Player: Jim Magilton, 18 (52), Northern Ireland.
Most League Appearances: John Shuker, 478, 1962–77.
Honours – Football League: Division 2 Champions – 1984–85. Division 3 Champions – 1967–68, 1983–84. **Football League Cup:** Winners – 1985–86.
Colours: Yellow shirts with navy trim, navy shorts with yellow trim, navy stockings with yellow trim.

PETERBOROUGH UNITED FL CHAMPIONSHIP 2

Name	ft	in			Birthplace				Previous club
Arber Mark (D)	6	1	12	11	Johannesburg	8	10	77	Oldham Ath
Benjamin Trevor (F)	6	2	13	07	Kettering	8	2	79	Coventry C
Bolland Phil (D)	6	4	13	03	Liverpool	26	8	76	Chester C
Carden Paul (M)	5	9	11	10	Liverpool	29	3	79	Chester C
Crow Danny (F)	5	10	11	00	Great Yarmouth	26	1	86	Norwich C
Day Jamie (M)	5	9	10	06	Wycombe	7	5	86	Scholar
Fry Adam (M)	5	8	10	07	Bedford	9	2	85	Scholar
Gain Peter (M)	5	9	11	07	Hammersmith	11	11	76	Lincoln C
Holden Dean (D)	6	1	12	04	Salford	15	9	79	Oldham Ath
Huke Shane (M)	5	11	12	07	Reading	2	10	85	Scholar
Kennedy Peter (D)	5	11	11	11	Lisburn	10	9	73	Wigan Ath
McShane Luke (G)	6	1	10	09	Peterborough	6	11	85	Scholar
Newton Adam (M)	5	10	11	00	Ascot	4	12	80	West Ham U
Plummer Chris (D)	6	2	12	12	Isleworth	12	10	76	QPR
Quinn James (M)	6	1	12	10	Coventry	15	12	74	Sheffield W
Ryan Tim (D)	5	10	11	00	Stockport	10	12	74	Doncaster R
Semple Ryan (M)	5	11	10	11	Belfast	4	7	85	Scholar
St Ledger-Hall Sean (D)	6	0	11	09	Solihull	28	12	84	Scholar
Tyler Mark (G)	5	11	12	00	Norwich	2	4	77	Trainee

League Appearances: Arber, M. 46; Benjamin, T. 5(15); Bolland, P. 17; Boucaud, A. 2(1); Burton, S. 17(2); Carden, P. 42; Crow, D. 34(4); Day, J. 19(6); Farrell, D. 19(10); Gain, P. 37; Hand, J. 9; Harrison, L. 6; Holden, D. 34(1); Huke, S. 3; Kennedy, P. 10(4); Kuqi, N. 1; Logan, R. 13(15); Miller, A. 2; Newton, A. 36(4); Opara, L. 2(6); Plummer, C. 16(6); Quinn, J. 21(3); Ryan, T. 6(1); Semple, R. 11(17); St Ledger-Hall, S. 43; Thorpe, L. 6; Tyler, M. 40; Willock, C. 9(6).
Goals – League (57): Crow 15 (1 pen), Quinn 7 (1 pen), Farrell 6, Logan 4, Gain 3, Holden 3, Newton 3, Semple 3, Willock 3, Arber 2, Burton 2 (1 pen), Benjamin 1, Day 1, Opara 1, Plummer 1, St Ledger-Hall 1, own goal 1.
Carling Cup (1): Plummer 1.
FA Cup (0).
Football League Trophy (5): Crow 2, Benjamin 1 (pen), Hand 1, Logan 1.
Ground: London Road Stadium, Peterborough PE2 8AL. Telephone (01733) 563 947.
Record Attendance: 30,096 v Swansea T, FA Cup 5th rd, 20 February 1965.
Capacity: 15,460.
Manager: Keith Alexander.
Secretary: Mary Faxon.
Most League Goals: 134, Division 4, 1960–61.
Highest League Scorer in Season: Terry Bly, 52, Division 4, 1960–61.
Most League Goals in Total Aggregate: Jim Hall, 122, 1967–75.
Most Capped Player: James Quinn, 9 (46), Northern Ireland.
Most League Appearances: Tommy Robson, 482, 1968–81.
Honours – Football League: Division 4 Champions – 1960–61, 1973–74.
Colours: All blue.

PLYMOUTH ARGYLE   FL CHAMPIONSHIP

Name			Birthplace			
Aljofree Hasney (D)	6 0	12 03	Manchester	11 7 78	Dundee U
Barness Anthony (D)	5 10	13 01	Lewisham	25 3 73	Bolton W
Bouzsaky Akos (M)	5 11	11 09	Hungary	7 5 82	MTK
Capaldi Tony (M)	6 0	12 00	Porsgrunn	12 8 81	Birmingham C
Chadwick Nick (F)	5 11	10 09	Stoke	26 10 82	Everton
Connolly Paul (D)	6 0	11 10	Liverpool	29 9 83	Scholar
Debbage James (G)	6 3	12 09	Cramlington		Scholar
Dickson Ryan (M)	5 10	11 05	Saltash	14 12 86	Scholar
Djordjic Bojan (M)	5 10	11 01	Belgrade	6 2 82	Rangers
Doumbe Stephen (D)	6 1	12 05	Paris	28 0 79	Hibernian
Hodges Lee (M)	6 0	12 01	Epping	4 9 73	Reading
Larrieu Romain (G)	6 2	13 00	Mont-de-Marsan	31 8 76	ASOA Valence
McCormick Luke (G)	6 0	13 12	Coventry	15 8 83	Scholar
Nalis Lilian (M)	6 1	11 00	Nogent sur Marne	29 9 71	Sheffield U
Norris David (M)	5 7	11 06	Peterborough	22 2 81	Bolton W
Sawyer Gary (D)			Bideford	5 7 85	Scholar
Summerfield Luke (M)	6 0	11 00	Ivybridge	6 12 87	Scholar
Wotton Paul (D)	5 11	11 01	Plymouth	17 8 77	Trainee
Zebroski Chris (F)	6 1	11 08	Swindon	29 10 86	Scholar

League Appearances: Aljofree, H. 36(1); Barness, A. 33(3); Brevett, R. 12(1); Buzsaky, A. 16(18); Capaldi, T. 38(3); Chadwick, N. 26(11); Clarke, L. 5; Connolly, P. 27(4); Derbyshire, M. 2(10); Djordjic, B. 9(13); Doumbe, S. 43; Evans, M. 36(9); Gudjonsson, B. 6(4); Hodges, L. 12(1); Jarrett, J. 7; Larrieu, R. 45; Lasley, K. (5); McCormick, L. 1; Mendes, N. 2; Nalis, L. 20; Norris, D. 44(1); Pericard, V. 14(1); Pulis, A. (5); Reid, R. (1); Taylor, S. 8(10); Ward, E. 15(1); West, T. 4; Wotton, P. 45; Zebroski, C. (4).
Goals – League (39): Wotton 8 (5 pens), Chadwick 5, Buzsaky 4, Evans 4, Pericard 4, Capaldi 3, Norris 2, Aljofree 1, Djordjic 1, Doumbe 1, Nalis 1, Taylor 1, Ward 1, own goals 3.
Carling Cup (3): Buzsaky 1, Taylor 1, Wotton 1 (pen).
FA Cup (0).
Ground: Home Park, Plymouth, Devon PL2 3DQ. Telephone (01752) 562 561.
Record Attendance: 43,596 v Aston Villa, Division 2, 10 October 1936.
Capacity: 20,922.
Manager: Ian Holloway.
Secretary: Carole Rowntree.
Most League Goals: 107, Division 3 (S), 1925–26 and 1951–52.
Highest League Scorer in Season: Jack Cock, 32, Division 3 (S), 1926–27.
Most League Goals in Total Aggregate: Sammy Black, 180, 1924–38.
Most Capped Player: Moses Russell, 20 (23), Wales.
Most League Appearances: Kevin Hodges, 530, 1978–92.
Honours – Football League: Division 2 Champions – 2003–04. Division 3 (S) Champions – 1929–30, 1951–52. Division 3 Champions – 1958–59, 2001–02.
Colours: Green shirts, white shorts, green stockings.

PORTSMOUTH   FA PREMIERSHIP

Name			Birthplace			
Ashdown Jamie (G)	6 1	13 05	Reading	30 11 80	Reading
Davis Sean (M)	5 10	12 00	Clapham	20 9 79	Tottenham H
Duffy Richard (D)	5 10	9 05	Swansea	30 8 85	Swansea C
Fordyce Daryl (M)	6 0	11 08	Belfast	2 1 87	Scholar
Griffin Andy (D)	5 9	10 10	Billinge	7 3 79	Newcastle U
Harris Scott (M)			Worthing	24 7 85	Scholar
Hughes Richard (M)	6 0	13 03	Glasgow	25 6 79	Bournemouth

Keene James (F)	5 11	11 08	Wells	26 12 85	Scholar
Lua-Lua Lomano (F)	5 8	12 00	Kinshasa	28 12 80	Newcastle U
Mbesuma Collins (F)	6 0	12 04	Luanshya	3 2 84	Kaizer Chiefs
Mornar Ivica (F)	6 2	13 01	Split	12 1 74	Anderlecht
Mwaruwari Benjamin (F)	6 2	12 03	Harare	13 8 78	Auxerre
O'Brien Andy (D)	6 2	11 13	Harrogate	29 6 79	Newcastle U
O'Neil Gary (M)	5 10	11 00	Beckenham	18 5 83	Trainee
Pamarot Noe (D)	5 11	13 07	Fontenay-sous-Bois	14 4 79	Tottenham H
Pedro Mendes (M)	5 9	12 04	Guimaraes	26 2 79	Tottenham H
Primus Linvoy (D)	5 10	12 04	Forest Gate	14 9 73	Reading
Priske Brian (D)	6 3	12 02	Horsens	14 5 77	Genk
Songo'o Frank (M)	6 2	12 06	Yaounde	14 5 87	Barcelona
Stefanovic Dejan (D)	6 2	13 01	Belgrade	28 10 74	Vitesse
Taylor Matthew (F)	5 11	12 03	Oxford	27 11 81	Luton T
Todorov Svetoslav (F)	6 0	12 02	Dobrich	30 8 78	West Ham U
Viafara John (M)	6 0	13 01	Robles	27 10 78	Once Caldas
Wilson Marc (M)	6 2	12 07	Belfast	17 8 87	Scholar

League Appearances: Ashdown, J. 17; Cisse, A. 2(1); D'Alessandro, A. 13; Dario Silva, D. 13; Davis, S. 16(1); Diao, S. 7(4); Griffin, A. 20(2); Hughes, R. 21(5); Karadas, A. 4(13); Kiely, D. 15; Koroman, O. 1(2); Lua-Lua, L. 24(1); Mbesuma, C. (4); Mornar, I. 1(1); Mwaruwari, B. 16; O'Brien, A. 29; O'Neil, G. 36; Olisadebe, E. (2); Pamarot, N. 4(4); Pedro Mendes, 14; Pericard, V. 3(3); Primus, L. 20; Priske, B. 26(4); Robert, L. 13(4); Routledge, W. 3(10); Skopelitis, G. (5); Songo'o, F. (2); Stefanovic, D. 27(1); Taylor, M. 32(2); Todorov, S. 6(18); Viafara, J. 10(4); Vignal, G. 13(1); Vukic, Z. 6(3); Westerveld, S. 6.

Goals – League (37): Lua-Lua 7, O'Neil 6, Taylor 6 (2 pens), Todorov 4, Pedro Mendes 3, Dario Silva 2, D'Alessandro 1, Davis 1, Karadas 1, Koroman 1, Mwaruwari 1, Robert 1, Viafara 1, Vukic 1, own goal 1.

Carling Cup (2): O'Neil 1, Taylor 1 (pen).

FA Cup (2): Dario Silva 1, Davis 1.

Ground: Fratton Park, Frogmore Road, Portsmouth, Hampshire PO4 8RA. Telephone (02392) 731 204.

Record Attendance: 51,385 v Derby Co, FA Cup 6th rd, 26 February 1949.

Capacity: 20,328.

Manager: Harry Redknapp.

Secretary: Paul Weld.

Most League Goals: 97, Division 1, 2002–03.

Highest League Scorer in Season: Guy Whittingham, 42, Division 1, 1992–93.

Most League Goals in Total Aggregate: Peter Harris, 194, 1946–60.

Most Capped Player: Jimmy Dickinson, 48, England.

Most League Appearances: Jimmy Dickinson, 764, 1946–65.

Honours – Football League: Division 1 Champions – 1948–49, 1949–50, 2002–03. Division 3 (S) Champions – 1923–24. Division 3 Champions – 1961–62, 1982–83.

FA Cup: Winners – 1939.

Colours: Blue shirts, white shorts, red stockings.

PORT VALE   FL CHAMPIONSHIP 1

Abbey George (D)	5 9	10 08	Port Harcourt	20 10 78	Macclesfield T
Anyon Joe (G)	6 1	12 11	Blackpool	29 12 86	Scholar
Birchall Chris (M)	5 9	13 02	Stafford	5 5 84	Scholar
Briscoe Louie (F)	6 0	12 00	Burton	2 4 88	Scholar
Cardle Joe (M)	5 8	9 05	Blackpool	27 2 87	Scholar
Constantine Leon (F)	6 2	12 00	Hackney	24 2 78	Torquay U
Dinning Tony (M)	6 0	13 05	Wallsend	12 4 75	Wigan Ath
Goodlad Mark (G)	6 2	14 00	Barnsley	9 9 79	Nottingham F
Holmes Daniel (M)	6 0	12 00	Burton	17 11 86	Scholar

Husbands Michael (F)	5 8	10 10	Birmingham	13 11 83	Rushall Olympic
Lowndes Nathan (F)	5 10	12 06	Salford	2 6 77	Plymouth Arg
McGregor Mark (D)	5 11	11 05	Chester	16 2 77	Blackpool
Prosser Luke (M)	6 3	10 05	Hertfordshire	28 5 88	Scholar
Walsh Michael (D)	6 0	13 10	Rotherham	5 8 77	Scunthorpe U

League Appearances: Abbey, G. 19(1); Bell, M. 14(1); Birchall, C. 23(8); Briscoe, L. (4); Cardle, J. 1(5); Clarke, D. (1); Collins, S. 15; Constantine, L. 30; Cornes, C. 7(3); Cummins, M. 36(3); Dinning, T. 33(2); Doherty, S. 3(3); Fortune, C. 20(5); Goodlad, M. 46; Hulbert, R. (1); Husbands, M. 6(18); Innes, M. 17(6); James, C. 30(5); Lowndes, N. 30(5); Matthews, L. (3); McGregor, M. 14; Mulligan, G. 8(2); Paynter, B. 16; Pilkington, G. 46; Porter, A. 2; Rowland, S. 13(5); Sam, H. (4); Smith, J. 18(9); Sonner, D. 25(4); Talbot, J. 4(1); Togwell, S. 26(1); Walsh, M. 4.
Goals – League (49): Constantine 10 (1 pen), Cummins 10, Lowndes 5, Husbands 4 (1 pen), Cornes 3, Bell 2, Dinning 2 (1 pen), Fortune 2, Paynter 2, Pilkington 2, Togwell 2, Birchall 1, Mulligan 1, Smith 1, Sonner 1, own goal 1.
Carling Cup (1): Cummins 1.
FA Cup (7): Constantine 2, Togwell 2, Birchall 1, Husbands 1, Lowndes 1.
Football League Trophy (1): Smith 1.
Ground: Vale Park, Hamil Road, Burslem, Stoke-on-Trent ST6 1AW. Telephone (01782) 655 800.
Record Attendance: 49,768 v Aston Villa, FA Cup 5th rd, 20 February 1960.
Capacity: 18,982.
Manager: Martin Foyle.
Secretary: Bill Lodey.
Most League Goals: 110, Division 4, 1958–59.
Highest League Scorer in Season: Wilf Kirkham 38, Division 2, 1926–27.
Most League Goals in Total Aggregate: Wilf Kirkham, 154, 1923–29, 1931–33.
Most Capped Player: Chris Birchall, 22, Trinidad & Tobago.
Most League Appearances: Roy Sproson, 761, 1950–72.
Honours – Football League: Division 3 (N) Champions – 1929–30, 1953–54. Division 4 Champions – 1958–59. **Autoglass Trophy:** Winners – 1993. **LDV Vans Trophy:** Winners – 2001
Colours: White shirts with gold and black trim, black shorts with white and gold trim, black stockings.

PRESTON NORTH END   FL CHAMPIONSHIP

Agyemang Patrick (F)	6 1	13 10	Walthamstow	29 9 80	Gillingham
Alexander Graham (D)	5 10	12 02	Coventry	10 10 71	Luton T
Anyinsah Joe (M)	5 8	11 00	Bristol	8 10 84	Bristol C
Beattie Warren (M)	5 8	10 12	Preston	18 10 86	Scholar
Davidson Callum (D)	5 10	11 00	Stirling	25 6 76	Leicester C
Davis Claude (D)	6 2	13 09	Jamaica	6 3 79	Portmore U
Dichio Danny (F)	6 3	12 03	Hammersmith	19 10 74	Millwall
Hibbert Dave (F)	6 2	12 00	Eccleshall	28 1 86	Port Vale
Hill Matt (D)	5 8	11 13	Bristol	26 3 81	Bristol C
Lonergan Andrew (G)	6 2	13 00	Preston	19 10 83	Scholar
Lucketti Chris (D)	6 1	13 00	Littleborough	28 9 71	Huddersfield T
Mawene Youl (D)	6 1	13 00	Caen	16 7 79	Derby Co
McCormack Alan (M)	5 8	11 05	Dublin	10 1 84	
McKenna Paul (M)	5 8	11 00	Eccleston	20 10 77	Trainee
Mears Tyrone (D)	6 1	11 10	Stockport	18 2 83	Manchester C
Nash Carlo (G)	6 3	15 03	Bolton	13 9 73	Middlesbrough
Neal Chris (G)	6 2	12 04	St Albans	23 10 85	Scholar
Neal Lewis (M)	5 10	11 02	Leicester	14 7 81	Stoke C
Nowland Adam (M)	5 11	11 06	Preston	6 7 81	Nottingham F
Nugent Dave (F)	5 11	12 00	Liverpool	2 5 85	Bury

O'Neil Brian (M)	6 1	12 04	Paisley	6 9 72	Derby Co
Ormerod Brett (F)	5 11	11 12	Blackburn	18 10 76	Southampton
Sedgwick Chris (M)	6 0	12 01	Sheffield	28 4 80	Rotherham U
Smith Andy (F)	5 11	11 10	Lisburn	25 9 80	Glentoran
Stock Brian (M)	5 11	11 02	Winchester	24 12 81	Bournemouth
Whaley Simon (M)	5 10	11 11	Bolton	7 6 85	Bury

League Appearances: Agyemang, P. 19(23); Alexander, G. 39(1); Anyinsah, J. (3); Cresswell, R. 3; Davidson, C. 26(1); Davis, C. 37(3); Dichio, D. 18(15); Etuhu, D. 6(7); Hibbert, D. (10); Hill, M. 24(2); Jarrett, J. 8(2); Johnson, J. 2(1); Jones, D. 21(3); Lucketti, C. 23(5); Mawene, Y. 26(4); McKenna, P. 40(1); Mears, T. 27(5); Nash, C. 46; Neal, L. 13(11); Nowland, A. 9(4); Nugent, D. 27(5); O'Neil, B. 22(3); Ormerod, B. 13(2); Sedgwick, C. 39(7); Stewart, M. 4; Stock, B. 4(2); Whaley, S. 7(9); Wilson, K. 3(3).

Goals – League (59): Nugent 10, Agyemang 6, Davidson 4, Ormerod 4, Sedgwick 4 (1 pen), Alexander 3 (3 pens), Davis 3, Jones 3, Nowland 3, Whaley 3, Etuhu 2, McKenna 2, Mears 2, Neal L 2, Jarrett 1, Johnson 1, Lucketti 1, Mawene 1, O'Neil 1, Stock 1, own goals 2.

Carling Cup (2): Alexander 1 (pen), Dichio 1.
FA Cup (5): Dichio 2, Alexander 1, O'Neil 1, Sedgwick 1.
Play-Offs (1): Nugent 1.
Ground: Sir Tom Finney Way, Deepdale, Preston PR1 6RU. Telephone (0870) 442 1964.
Record Attendance: 42,684 v Arsenal, Division 1, 23 April 1938. **Capacity:** 20,600.
Manager: Paul Simpson.
Secretary: Janet Parr.
Most League Goals: 100, Division 2, 1927–28 and Division 1, 1957–58.
Highest League Scorer in Season: Ted Harper, 37, Division 2, 1932–33.
Most League Goals in Total Aggregate: Tom Finney, 187, 1946–60.
Most Capped Player: Tom Finney, 76, England.
Most League Appearances: Alan Kelly, 447, 1961–75.
Honours – Football League: Division 1 Champions – 1888–89 (first champions), 1889–90. Division 2 Champions – 1903–04, 1912–13, 1950–51, 1999–2000. Division 3 Champions – 1970–71, 1995–96. **FA Cup:** Winners – 1889, 1938.
Colours: White shirts, blue shorts, white stockings.

QUEENS PARK RANGERS   FL CHAMPIONSHIP

Ainsworth Gareth (M)	5 10	12 05	Blackburn	10 5 73	Cardiff C
Baidoo Shabazz (M)	5 8	10 07	Hackney	13 4 88	Scholar
Bailey Stefan (M)	5 11	12 08	London	10 11 87	Scholar
Bignot Marcus (D)	5 7	11 04	Birmingham	22 8 74	Rushden & D
Bircham Marc (M)	5 11	11 06	Hammersmith	11 5 78	Millwall
Cole Jake (G)	6 2	13 00	Hammersmith	11 9 85	Scholar
Cook Lee (M)	5 8	11 10	Hammersmith	3 8 82	Watford
Doherty Tom (M)	5 8	10 06	Bristol	17 3 79	Bristol C
Donnelly Scott (M)	5 8	11 10	Hammersmith	25 12 87	Scholar
Evatt Ian (D)	6 3	13 12	Coventry	19 11 81	Chesterfield
Furlong Paul (F)	6 0	13 11	London	1 10 68	Birmingham C
Gallen Kevin (F)	5 11	13 05	Hammersmith	21 9 75	Barnsley
Hislop Matthew (D)	5 11	12 00	Wolverhampton	31 1 87	Arsenal
Howell Andrew (D)			Gt Yarmouth	18 3 89	Scholar
Johnson Ryan (D)			Dartford	15 1 87	Scholar
Jones Paul (G)	6 3	15 02	Chirk	18 4 67	Wolverhampton W
Jones Ray (F)	6 4	14 05	East Ham	28 8 88	Scholar
Kanyuka Patrick (D)	6 0	12 06	Kinshasa	19 7 87	
Lomas Steve (M)	6 0	12 08	Hannover	18 1 74	West Ham U
Milanese Mauro (D)	6 1	13 01	Trieste	17 9 71	Perugia

Moore Stefan (F)	5 10	10 12	Birmingham	28	9 83	Aston Villa
Mulholland Scott (M)	5 8	10 05	Bexley Heath	7	9 86	Scholar
Munday Jonathan (D)				13	4 88	
Nygaard Marc (F)	6 5	14 05	Copenhagen	1	9 76	Brescia
Rose Matthew (D)	5 11	12 02	Dartford	24	9 75	Arsenal
Rowlands Martin (M)	5 9	10 10	Hammersmith	8	2 79	Brentford
Royce Simon (G)	6 2	12 10	Forest Gate	9	9 71	Charlton Ath
Shimmin Dominic (D)	6 0	12 06	Bermondsey	13 10 87		Arsenal
Shittu Dan (D)	6 2	16 03	Lagos	2	9 80	Charlton Ath
Thomas Sean (G)	6 1	12 03	Edgware	5	9 87	Scholar
Townsend Luke (M)	6 0	11 10	Guildford	28	9 86	Scholar
Ukah Ugo (D)	6 0	12 11	Parma	18	1 84	Pro Vasto

League Appearances: Ainsworth, G. 33(10); Baidoo, S. 6(9); Bailey, S. 5; Barnes, P. 1; Bean, M. 4(5); Bignot, M. 44; Bircham, M. 24(2); Brown, A. 1(1); Clarke, L. 1; Cole, J. 1(2); Cook, L. 34(6); Doherty, T. 14(1); Donnelly, S. 3(5); Dyer, L. 15; Evatt, I. 21(6); Furlong, P. 31(6); Gallen, K. 18; Hislop, M. 1; Jones, P. 14; Jones, R. (2); Kus, M. 3; Langley, R. 22(11); Lomas, S. 18(3); Lowe, K. 1; Milanese, M. 22(4); Miller, A. 1; Moore, S. 11(14); Nygaard, M. 20(7); Rose, M. 15; Rowlands, M. 12(2); Royce, S. 30; Santos, G. 25(6); Shimmin, D. 1(1); Shittu, D. 45; Sturridge, D. 6(3); Taylor, A. 1(2); Ukah, U. (1); Youssouf, S. 2(4).
Goals – League (50): Ainsworth 9, Nygaard 9 (1 pen), Furlong 7, Cook 4, Gallen 4 (1 pen), Shittu 4, Langley 3 (2 pens), Baidoo 2, Bircham 2, Moore 2, Rowlands 2, Santos 1, own goal 1.
Carling Cup (0).
FA Cup (0).
Ground: Loftus Road Stadium, South Africa Road, Shepherds Bush, London W12 7PA. Telephone (020) 8743 0262.
Record Attendance: 35,353 v Leeds U, Division 1, 27 April 1974. **Capacity:** 18,769.
Manager: Gary Waddock (caretaker).
Secretary: Sheila Marson.
Most League Goals: 111, Division 3, 1961–62.
Highest League Scorer in Season: George Goddard, 37, Division 3 (S), 1929–30.
Most League Goals in Total Aggregate: George Goddard, 172, 1926–34.
Most Capped Player: Alan McDonald, 52, Northern Ireland.
Most League Appearances: Tony Ingham, 519, 1950–63.
Honours – Football League: Division 2 Champions – 1982–83. Division 3 (S) Champions – 1947–48. Division 3 Champions – 1966–67. **Football League Cup:** Winners – 1966–67.
Colours: Blue and white hooped shirts, white shorts, white stockings.

READING   FA PREMIERSHIP

Brown Aaron (D)	6 4	14 07	Birmingham	23	6 83	Tamworth
Convey Bobby (M)	5 9	11 04	Philadelphia	27	5 83	DC United
Cox Simon (M)	5 10	10 12	Reading	28	4 87	Scholar
Doyle Kevin (F)	5 11	12 06	Adamstown	18	9 83	Cork C
Federici Adam (G)	6 2	14 02	Nowra	31	1 85	
Golbourne Scott (M)	5 8	11 08	Bristol	29	2 88	Bristol C
Gunnarsson Brynjar (M)	6 1	12 01	Reykjavik	16 10 75		Watford
Hahnemann Marcus (G)	6 3	16 04	Seattle	15	6 72	Fulham
Halls John (M)	6 0	11 11	Islington	14	2 82	Stoke C
Harper James (M)	5 10	11 02	Chelmsford	9 11 80		Arsenal
Hayes Jonathan (M)	5 7	11 00	Dublin	9	7 87	Scholar
Hunt Steve (M)	5 9	10 10	Port Laoise	1	8 80	Brentford
Ingimarsson Ivar (D)	6 0	12 07	Reykjavik	20	8 77	Wolverhampton W
Kitson Dave (F)	6 3	13 00	Hitchin	21	1 80	Cambridge U
Lita Leroy (F)	5 7	11 12	DR Congo	28 12 84		Bristol C
Little Glen (M)	6 3	13 00	Wimbledon	15 10 75		Burnley

Name			Birthplace		Previous club
Long Shane (F)	5 10	11 02	Kilkenny	22 1 87	Cork C
Makin Chris (D)	5 11	11 02	Manchester	8 5 73	Leicester C
Murty Graeme (D)	5 10	11 10	Saltburn	13 11 74	York C
Osano Curtis (M)	5 11	11 04	Nakuru	8 3 87	Scholar
Oster John (M)	5 9	10 08	Boston	8 12 78	Burnley
Shorey Nicky (D)	5 9	10 10	Romford	19 2 81	Leyton Orient
Sidwell Steven (M)	5 10	11 00	Wandsworth	14 12 82	Arsenal
Sinnott Conor (M)	6 0	11 05	Wexford	19 1 86	Bray W
Sonko Ibrahima (D)	6 3	13 07	Bignola	22 1 81	Brentford
Stack Graham (G)	6 2	12 07	Hampstead	26 9 81	Arsenal

League Appearances: Baradji, S. (1); Convey, B. 45; Cox, S. (2); Dobson, M. (1); Doyle, K. 41(4); Golbourne, S. (1); Gunnarsson, B. 19(10); Hahnemann, M. 45; Halls, J. 1; Harper, J. 44(1); Hunt, S. 3(35); Ingimarsson, I. 46; Kitson, D. 27(7); Lita, L. 22(4); Little, G. 34(1); Long, S. (10); Makin, C. 11(1); Murty, G. 40; Obinna, E. (6); Oster, J. 11(22); Shorey, N. 40; Sidwell, S. 29(4); Sonko, I. 46; Stack, G. 1.

Goals – League (99): Doyle 18 (1 pen), Kitson 18 (4 pens), Lita 11, Sidwell 10, Convey 7, Harper 7, Little 5, Gunnarsson 4, Long 3, Sonko 3, Hunt 2, Ingimarsson 2, Shorey 2, Halls 1, Murty 1 (pen), Oster 1, own goals 4.

Carling Cup (6): Kitson 4, Lita 1, Oster 1.

FA Cup (6): Lita 3, Doyle 1 (pen), Hunt 1, Long 1.

Ground: Madejski Stadium, Junction 11, M4, Reading, Berkshire RG2 0FL. Telephone (0118) 968 1100.

Record Attendance: 33,042 v Brentford, FA Cup 5th rd, 19 February 1927.

Capacity: 24,225.

Manager: Steve Coppell.

Secretary: Sue Hewett.

Most League Goals: 112, Division 3 (S), 1951–52.

Highest League Scorer in Season: Ronnie Blackman, 39, Division 3 (S), 1951–52.

Most League Goals in Total Aggregate: Ronnie Blackman, 158, 1947–54.

Most Capped Player: Jimmy Quinn, 17 (46), Northern Ireland.

Most League Appearances: Martin Hicks, 500, 1978–91.

Honours – Football League: Championship Champions – 2005–06. Division 2 Champions – 1993–94. Division 3 Champions – 1985–86. Division 3 (S) Champions – 1925–26. Division 4 Champions – 1978–79. **Simod Cup:** Winners – 1987–88.

Colours: Blue and white hooped shirts, blue shorts, blue stockings.

ROCHDALE   FL CHAMPIONSHIP 2

Name			Birthplace		Previous club
Boardman Jon (D)	6 2	12 09	Reading	27 1 81	Woking
Brown Gary (D)	5 6	10 00	Darwen	29 10 85	Scholar
Christie Iyseden (F)	5 10	12 02	Coventry	14 11 76	Kidderminster H
Coleman Theo (M)	5 11	10 07	Manchester	5 5 89	Scholar
Cooksey Ernie (M)	5 9	11 12	Bishops Stortford	17 9 78	Oldham Ath
Dagnall Chris (F)	5 8	12 03	Liverpool	15 4 86	Tranmere R
Doolan John (M)	6 1	13 00	Liverpool	7 5 74	Blackpool
Gilks Matthew (G)	6 3	13 09	Rochdale	4 6 82	Scholar
Goodall Alan (D)	5 9	11 06	Birkenhead	2 12 81	Bangor C
Goodhind Warren (D)	5 11	11 02	Johannesburg	16 8 77	Cambridge U
Jackson Mark (D)	5 11	12 00	Barnsley	30 9 77	Kidderminster H
Jaszczun Tommy (M)	5 11	12 09	Kettering	16 9 77	Northampton T
Jones Gary (M)	5 11	12 05	Birkenhead	3 6 77	Barnsley
Lambert Ricky (M)	6 2	12 01	Liverpool	16 2 82	Stockport Co
Moyo-Modise Clive (F)	5 10	11 00	London	20 9 87	
Ramsden Simon (D)	6 0	12 06	Bishop Auckland	17 12 81	Grimsby T
Thompson Joe (M)	6 0	9 07	Rochdale	5 3 89	Scholar
Williams Matt (M)	5 11	12 00	Bury	21 6 88	Scholar
Woodhall Danny (G)	6 1	12 07	West Birch	10 12 87	Scholar

League Appearances: Bayliss, D. 4; Boardman, J. 17(4); Brisco, N. 14(2); Brown, G. 6(10); Cartwright, L. 21(6); Christie, I. 10(4); Clarke, J. 21(1); Coleman, T. 1; Cooksey, E. 27(7); Dagnall, C. 15(6); Doolan, J. 16(2); Gallimore, T. 32(2); Gilks, M. 46; Goodall, A. 37(3); Goodhind, W. 10; Griffiths, G. 29; Holt, G. 21; Jackson, M. 12; Jaszczun, T. 12(5); Jones, G. 42; Kitchen, B. 3(5); Lambert, R. 43(3); McArdle, R. 16(3); Moyo-Modise, C. 1(8); Ramsden, S. 15; Sturrock, B. 15(16); Tait, P. 4(7); Thompson, J. (1); Warner, S. 16(8).

Goals – League (66): Lambert 22 (4 pens), Holt 14 (5 pens), Sturrock 6, Jones 4 (1 pen), Cooksey 3, Dagnall 3, Goodall 3, Christie 2, Griffiths 2, Boardman 1, Cartwright 1, McArdle 1, Ramsden 1, Tait 1, Warner 1, own goal 1.

Carling Cup (0).

FA Cup (0).

Football League Trophy (5): Tait 2, Holt 1 (pen), own goals 2.

Ground: Spotland Stadium, Sandy Lane, Rochdale OL11 5DS. Telephone (0870) 822 1907.

Record Attendance: 24,231 v Notts Co, FA Cup 2nd rd, 10 December 1949.

Capacity: 10,208.

Manager: Steve Parkin.

Secretary: Colin Garlick.

Most League Goals: 105, Division 3 (N), 1926–27.

Highest League Scorer in Season: Albert Whitehurst, 44, Division 3 (N), 1926–27.

Most League Goals in Total Aggregate: Reg Jenkins, 119, 1964–73.

Most Capped Player: Leo Bertos, 6 (7), New Zealand.

Most League Appearances: Graham Smith, 317, 1966–74.

Honours – Nil.

Colours: All blue.

ROTHERHAM UNITED   FL CHAMPIONSHIP 1

Barker Shaun (D)	6 3	12 09	Nottingham	19 9 82	Scholar
Boulding Mick (F)	5 10	11 05	Sheffield	8 2 76	Barnsley
Brogan Stephen (D)	5 7	10 04	Rotherham	12 4 88	Scholar
Butler Martin (F)	5 11	12 09	Wordsley	15 9 74	Reading
Campbell-Ryce Jamal (F)	5 7	11 10	Lambeth	6 4 83	Charlton Ath
Cutler Neil (G)	6 1	12 00	Cannock	3 9 76	Stockport Co
Duncum Sam (M)	5 9	11 02	Sheffield	18 2 87	Scholar
Hedge Jonathan (G)	6 2	13 02	Rotherham	19 7 88	Scholar
Hoskins Will (F)	5 11	11 08	Nottingham	6 5 86	Scholar
Hurst Paul (D)	5 5	10 03	Sheffield	25 9 74	Trainee
Keane Michael (M)	5 7	13 07	Dublin	29 12 82	Hull C
King Liam (F)	5 9	10 02	Rotherham	3 12 87	Scholar
Montgomery Gary (G)	6 2	13 06	Leamington Spa	8 10 82	Coventry C
Mullin John (M)	6 1	12 09	Bury	11 8 75	Burnley
Murdock Colin (D)	6 2	13 00	Ballymena	2 7 75	Crewe Alex
Newsham Mark (M)	5 10	9 11	Hatfield	24 3 87	Scholar
Robertson Gregor (D)	6 0	12 04	Edinburgh	19 1 84	Nottingham F
Shaw Paul (F)	5 11	12 04	Burnham	4 9 73	Sheffield U
Taylor Ryan (F)	6 2	10 10	Rotherham	4 5 88	Scholar
Whittington Lee (M)	5 8	9 13	Sheffield	10 5 87	Scholar
Williamson Lee (M)	5 10	10 04	Derby	7 6 82	Northampton T
Worrell David (D)	5 11	12 04	Dublin	12 1 78	Plymouth Arg

League Appearances: Barker, S. 42(1); Brogan, S. (3); Burton, D. 24; Butler, M. 33(6); Campbell-Ryce, J. 4(3); Conlon, B. 3; Cutler, N. 22; Duncum, S. 1; Evans, P. 4; Forte, J. 8(3); Gilchrist, P. 9(2); Hoskins, W. 7(16); Hurst, P. 28(3); Keane, M. 26(2); Leadbitter, G. 3(2); McLaren, P. 35(4); Minto, S. 5(1); Monkhouse, A. 7(5); Montgomery, G. 24; Mullin, J. 40(3); Murdock, C. 39; Newsham, M. (3);

Otsemobor, J. 4(6); Quinn, S. 16; Robertson, G. 30(5); Shaw, P. 15(2); Taylor, R. (1); Williamson, L. 37; Worrell, D. 40(1).
Goals – League (52): Burton 12 (3 pens), Butler 7, Forte 4, Hoskins 4, Shaw 4, Williamson 4, Barker 3, McLaren 3, Mullin 2, Murdock 2, Conlon 1, Leadbitter 1, Monkhouse 1, Robertson 1, own goals 3.
Carling Cup (3): Burton 1, Otsemobor 1, own goal 1.
FA Cup (3): McLaren 2, Burton 1.
Football League Trophy (4): Butler 1, Evans 1, Hoskins 1, Newsham 1.
Ground: Millmoor, Rotherham S60 1RH. Telephone (01709) 512 434.
Record Attendance: 25,170 v Sheffield U, Division 2, 13 December 1952. **Capacity:** 8,200.
Manager: Alan Knill.
Most League Goals: 114, Division 3 (N), 1946–47.
Highest League Scorer in Season: Wally Ardron, 38, Division 3 (N), 1946–47.
Most League Goals in Total Aggregate: Gladstone Guest, 130, 1946–56.
Most Capped Player: Shaun Goater, 14 (19), Bermuda.
Most League Appearances: Danny Williams, 459, 1946–62.
Honours – Football League: Division 3 Champions – 1980–81. Division 3 (N) Champions – 1950–51. Division 4 Champions – 1988–89. **Auto Windscreens Shield:** Winners – 1996.
Colours: Red shirts with white sleeves, white shorts, red stockings.

RUSHDEN & DIAMONDS   CONFERENCE

Berry Tyrone (F)	5 8	10 03	Brixton	11 3 87	Crystal Palace
Bolt Alex (M)	5 8	10 00		11 6 89	Scholar
Chillingworth Daniel (F)	6 0	12 06	Cambridge	13 9 81	Cambridge U
Grainger Daniel (D)	5 10	10 10	Thrapston	15 10 86	Scholar
Gulliver Phil (D)	6 2	14 09	Bishop Auckland	12 9 82	Middlesbrough
Hatswell Wayne (D)	6 0	13 10	Swindon	8 2 75	Kidderminster H
Hunter Barry (D)	6 4	12 06	Coleraine	18 11 68	Reading
Ioannou Nicky (M)	5 11	11 00	Camden	3 7 87	Scholar
Jackson Simeon (M)	5 8	11 00	Kingston, Jam	28 3 87	Scholar
Josephs Ricardo (M)	5 11	12 06	Jamaica	17 1 87	Scholar
Kelly Marcus (M)	5 7	10 00	Ketteringham	16 3 86	Juniors
Lambley Lawrence (M)	5 10	12 00		20 6 89	Scholar
Langdon Dominic (M)	6 2	11 00		14 9 88	Scholar
Okuonghae Magnus (F)	6 3	13 04	Nigeria	16 2 86	Scholar
Pearson Greg (F)	6 0	12 00	Birmingham	3 4 85	West Ham U
Reynolds Ben (M)	5 10	10 00		27 9 88	Scholar
Savage David (M)	6 2	13 05	Dublin	30 7 73	Bristol R
Shaw Tom (M)	6 0	10 00	Nottingham	1 12 86	Scholar
Stead Jon (M)	5 11	11 00	Peterborough	6 1 88	Scholar
Tomlin Lee (F)	5 11	11 00	Leicester	12 1 89	
Turner John (F)	5 10	11 00	Harrow	12 2 86	Cambridge U
Tynan Scott (G)	6 2	13 03	Huyton	27 11 83	Barnet
Udoji Ugo (M)			Greenwich	9 1 89	Scholar
Wark Scott (M)	6 3	13 04	Glasgow	9 6 87	Scholar
Woodman Andy (G)	6 3	15 08	Camberwell	11 8 71	Barnsley

League Appearances: Allen, G. 5; Armstrong, A. 6(3); Bell, D. 13(1); Berry, T. 13(7); Broughton, D. 32(5); Bull, R. 19; Burgess, A. 7(2); Caskey, D. 17(1); Castle, P. 1; Chillingworth, D. 3(3); Crane, D. 8; Dempster, J. 13(1); Gier, R. 34(1); Grainger, D. 2(12); Gulliver, P. 40; Hatswell, W. 17; Hawkins, P. 20(1); Hunter, B. (5); Jackson, S. 8(6); Joseph, R. 1; Kelly, M. 39(2); McCafferty, N. 19(4); Mikolanda, P. 7(2); Mills, G. 7(4); Nicholls, A. 26(4); O'Grady, C. 20(2); Okuonghae, M. 15(6); Pearson, G. 16(6); Ruddy, J. 3; Savage, D. 30(2); Shaw, T. (1); Stokes, T. 18(1); Taylor, J. 4(8); Tomlin, L. 4(17); Turner, J. 4(7); Tynan, S. 13(1); Woodman, A. 3; Young, J. 19(1).

Goals – League (44): Broughton 10 (1 pen), Jackson 5, Gulliver 4, O'Grady 4, Bell 3, Dempster 3, Kelly 3, Savage 2, Allen 1, Caskey 1, Grainger 1, Hatswell 1, Mikolanda 1, Okuonghae 1, Pearson 1, Taylor 1, Turner 1, own goal 1.
Carling Cup (0).
FA Cup (1): Armstrong 1.
Football League Trophy (1): Pearson 1.
Ground: Nene Park, Irthlingborough, Northants NN9 5QF. Telephone (01933) 652 000.
Record Attendance: 6,431 v Leeds U, FA Cup 3rd rd, 2 January 1999.
Capacity: 6,441
Manager: Paul Hart.
Secretary: Helen Thompson.
Most League Goals: 73, Division 3, 2002–03.
Highest League Scorer in Season: Onandi Lowe, 19, Division 3, 2001–02.
Most League Appearances: Andy Burgess, 147, 2001–06.
Most Capped Player: Onandi Lowe, 9, Jamaica.
Honours – Football League: Division 3 Champions – 2002–03. **Conference:** Champions – 2000–01. **Southern League Midland Division:** Champions – 1993–94. **Premier Division:** Champions – 1995–96. **FA Trophy:** Semi-finalists – 1994. **Northants FA Hillier Senior Cup:** Winners – 1993–94, 1998–99. **Maunsell Premier Cup:** Winners – 1994–95, 1998–99.
Colours: Red shirts, red shorts, red stockings.

SCUNTHORPE UNITED   FL CHAMPIONSHIP 1

Name	Ht	Wt	Birthplace	Born	Previous Club
Allanson Ashley (M)	5 11	12 00	Hull	13 11 86	Hull C
Baraclough Ian (M)	6 1	12 02	Leicester	4 12 70	Notts Co
Beagrie Peter (M)	5 8	12 00	Middlesbrough	28 11 65	Wigan Ath
Butler Andy (D)	6 2	14 02	Doncaster	4 11 83	Scholar
Byrne Cliff (D)	6 0	12 11	Dublin	27 4 82	Sunderland
Crosby Andy (D)	6 2	13 07	Rotherham	3 3 73	Oxford U
Foster Steve (D)	6 1	13 00	Mansfield	3 12 74	Doncaster R
Goodwin Jim (M)	5 9	12 01	Waterford	20 11 81	Stockport Co
Hinds Richard (D)	6 2	12 02	Sheffield	22 8 80	Hull C
Keogh Andrew (F)	6 0	11 06	Dublin	16 5 86	Leeds U
MacKenzie Neil (M)	6 2	12 05	Birmingham	15 4 76	Macclesfield T
Ridley Lee (D)	5 9	11 09	Scunthorpe	5 12 81	Scholar
Sharp Billy (F)	5 9	11 00	Sheffield	5 2 86	Sheffield U
Smith Rob (M)	6 0	12 06	Newcastle	22 10 86	Scholar
Sparrow Matt (M)	5 11	11 06	Wembley	3 10 81	Scholar
Taylor Cleveland (M)	5 8	10 07	Leicester	9 9 83	Bolton W
Torpey Steve (F)	6 3	14 13	Islington	8 12 70	Bristol C
Twibey Dean (D)	5 9	10 05	Pontefract	6 9 86	Scholar
Williams Marcus (D)	5 10	10 07	Doncaster	8 4 86	Scholar

League Appearances: Allanson, A. (1); Baraclough, I. 37(1); Beagrie, P. 21(9); Butler, A. 15(1); Byrne, C. 25(7); Corden, W. 5(4); Crosby, A. 38(4); Ehui, I. (3); Evans, T. 18; Foster, S. 18; Goodwin, J. 10(3); Hinds, R. 42; Johnson, T. 3(11); Keogh, A. 40(5); MacKenzie, N. 12(2); Musselwhite, P. 28; Parton, A. 3(3); Ridley, L. 2(1); Rose, M. 15; Ryan, R. 7(6); Sharp, B. 35(2); Sparrow, M. 30(9); Stanton, N. 21(1); Taylor, C. 31(14); Till, P. 6(2); Timlin, M. (1); Torpey, S. 16(10); Williams, M. 28(1).
Goals – League (68): Sharp 23 (3 pens), Keogh 11, Hinds 6, Beagrie 5 (4 pens), Sparrow 5, Baraclough 3, Crosby 3 (1 pen), Taylor 3, Goodwin 2, MacKenzie 2, Butler 1, Byrne 1, Johnson 1, Ridley 1, Torpey 1.
Carling Cup (2): Hinds 1, Ryan 1.
FA Cup (5): Keogh 3, Baraclough 1, Johnson 1.
Football League Trophy (4): Crosby 1 (pen), Johnson 1, Keogh 1, Sharp 1.

Ground: Glanford Park, Doncaster Road, Scunthorpe DN15 8TD. Telephone (01724) 747 671.
Record Attendance: Old Showground: 23,935 v Portsmouth, FA Cup 4th rd, 30 January 1954. Glanford Park: 8,775 v Rotherham U, Division 4, 1 May 1989.
Capacity: 9,182.
Manager: Brian Laws.
Most League Goals: 88, Division 3 (N), 1957–58.
Highest League Scorer in Season: Barrie Thomas, 31, Division 2, 1961–62.
Most League Goals in Total Aggregate: Steve Cammack, 110, 1979–81, 1981–86.
Most Capped Player: None.
Most League Appearances: Jack Brownsword, 595, 1950–65.
Honours – Football League: Division 3 (N) Champions – 1957–58.
Colours: Claret and blue.

SHEFFIELD UNITED   FA PREMIERSHIP

Player	Ht	Wt	Birthplace	DOB	Previous
Akinbiyi Ade (F)	6 1	13 08	Hackney	10 10 74	Burnley
Annerson Jamie (G)			Sheffield	21 6 88	Oldham Ath
Armstrong Chris (D)	5 9	11 00	Newcastle	5 8 82	Scholar
Ashmore James (M)	5 8	11 00	Sheffield	2 3 86	Scholar
Barnes Phil (G)	6 2	15 04	Sheffield	2 3 79	Blackpool
Beckett Luke (F)	5 11	11 02	Sheffield	25 11 76	Stockport Co
Binnion Travis (M)	5 10	11 02	Derby	10 11 86	Scholar
Bromby Leigh (D)	6 0	12 04	Dewsbury	2 6 80	Sheffield W
Forte Jonathan (M)	6 0	12 06	Sheffield	25 7 86	Scholar
Francis Simon (D)	6 0	14 09	Nottingham	16 2 85	Bradford C
Geary Derek (D)	5 6	10 08	Dublin	19 6 80	Sheffield W
Gillespie Keith (M)	5 10	11 03	Larne	18 2 75	Leicester C
Gyaki Ryan (G)	5 10	11 02	Toronto	6 12 85	Scholar
Haidong Hao (F)	5 11	11 00	Qingdao	9 5 70	Dalian Shide
Hill Shane (M)			London	5 8 87	Scholar
Horwood Evan (D)	6 0	10 06	Billingham	10 3 86	Scholar
Hurst Kevan (M)	5 10	11 07	Chesterfield	27 8 85	Scholar
Ifill Paul (M)	6 0	12 09	Brighton	20 10 79	Millwall
Jagielka Phil (D)	5 11	14 00	Manchester	17 8 82	Scholar
Kabba Steven (F)	5 8	12 06	Lambeth	7 3 81	Crystal Palace
Kenny Paddy (G)	6 0	15 10	Halifax	17 5 78	Bury
Kozluk Rob (D)	5 8	11 07	Sutton-in-Ashfield	5 7 77	Derby Co
Law Nicky (M)	5 10	11 06	Nottingham	29 3 88	Scholar
Marrison Colin (F)	6 1	12 05	Sheffield	23 9 85	Scholar
McFadzean Kyle (D)	6 1	13 04	Sheffield	20 2 87	Scholar
Montgomery Nick (M)	5 8	12 08	Leeds	28 10 81	Scholar
Morgan Chris (D)	6 0	13 06	Barnsley	9 11 77	Barnsley
Quinn Alan (M)	5 9	11 09	Dublin	13 6 79	Sheffield W
Quinn Stephen (M)	5 6	9 08	Dublin	4 4 86	Scholar
Robertson Chris (D)	6 3	11 08	Dundee	11 10 86	Scholar
Roma Dominic (D)	5 9	12 08	Sheffield	29 11 85	Scholar
Ross Ian (M)	5 10	11 00	Sheffield	13 1 86	Scholar
Shipperley Neil (F)	6 1	13 12	Chatham	30 10 74	Crystal Palace
Tonge Michael (M)	5 10	12 06	Manchester	7 4 83	Scholar
Travis Nicky (M)	6 0	12 01	Sheffield	12 3 87	Scholar
Unsworth Dave (D)	6 1	13 07	Chorley	16 10 73	Portsmouth
Webber Danny (F)	5 10	11 04	Manchester	28 12 81	Watford
Wright Alan (D)	5 3	9 13	Ashton-under-Lyme	28 9 71	Middlesbrough

League Appearances: Akinbiyi, A. 10(5); Armstrong, C. 21(3); Bromby, L. 35; Collins, N. 2; Deane, B. 2; Dyer, B. 3(2); Flitcroft, G. 3(3); Forte, J. (1); Francis, S. (1); Geary, D. 17(3); Gillespie, K. 8(22); Gray, A. 1; Harley, J. 4; Horsfield, G. 1(2); Ifill, P. 28(11); Jagielka, P. 46; Kabba, S. 21(13); Kenny, P. 46; Kozluk, R.

21(6); Lucketti, C. 2(1); Montgomery, N. 34(5); Morgan, C. 37(2); Nalis, L. 3(1); Pericard, V. 3(8); Quinn, A. 23(4); Shaw, P. (1); Shipperley, N. 34(5); Short, C. 20(3); Tonge, M. 23(7); Unsworth, D. 33(1); Webber, D. 24(11); Wright, A. 3(3).
Goals – League (76): Shipperley 11, Webber 10, Ifill 9, Kabba 9 (1 pen), Jagielka 8, Quinn 4, Unsworth 4 (1 pen), Akinbiyi 3, Morgan 3, Tonge 3, Armstrong 2, Pericard 2, Bromby 1, Dyer 1, Gray 1 (pen), Montgomery 1, Short 1, own goals 3.
Carling Cup (1): Ross 1.
FA Cup (1): Kabba 1.
Ground: Bramall Lane Ground, Cherry Street, Bramall Lane, Sheffield S2 4SU. Telephone (0870) 787 1960.
Record Attendance: 68,287 v Leeds U, FA Cup 5th rd, 15 February 1936.
Capacity: 30,864.
Manager: Neil Warnock.
Secretary: Donna Fletcher.
Most League Goals: 102, Division 1, 1925–26.
Highest League Scorer in Season: Jimmy Dunne, 41, Division 1, 1930–31.
Most League Goals in Total Aggregate: Harry Johnson, 205, 1919–30.
Most Capped Player: Billy Gillespie, 25, Northern Ireland.
Most League Appearances: Joe Shaw, 629, 1948–66.
Honours – Football League: Division 1 Champions – 1897–98. Division 2 Champions – 1952–53. Division 4 Champions – 1981–82. **FA Cup:** Winners – 1899, 1902, 1915, 1925.
Colours: Red and white striped shirts, black shorts, black stockings.

SHEFFIELD WEDNESDAY				FL CHAMPIONSHIP	
Adams Steve (M)	6 0	12 01	Plymouth	25 9 80	Plymouth Arg
Adamson Chris (G)	6 2	13 07	Ashington	4 11 78	St Patrick's Ath
Brunt Chris (M)	6 1	13 02	Belfast	14 12 84	Middlesbrough
Bullen Lee (D)	6 1	12 08	Edinburgh	29 3 71	Dunfermline Ath
Burton Deon (F)	5 9	11 09	Ashford	25 10 76	Rotherham U
Collins Patrick (D)	6 2	12 07	Newcastle	4 2 85	Sunderland
Corr Barry (F)	6 3	12 07	Co Wicklow	2 4 85	Leeds U
Coughlan Graham (D)	6 2	13 07	Dublin	18 11 74	Plymouth Arg
Gilbert Peter (D)	5 11	12 00	Newcastle	31 7 83	Leicester C
Graham David (F)	5 10	11 02	Edinburgh	6 10 78	Wigan Ath
Hills John (D)	5 9	12 08	St Annes-on-Sea	21 4 78	Gillingham
Kirby Ben (G)	6 1	12 02	Reading	16 3 87	Scholar
Lucas David (G)	6 1	13 06	Preston	23 11 77	Preston NE
MacLean Steve (F)	5 10	12 01	Edinburgh	23 8 82	Scunthorpe U
McAllister Sean (M)	5 8	10 07	Bolton	15 8 87	Scholar
McArdle Rory (D)	6 1	11 11	Sheffield	1 5 87	Scholar
O'Brien Burton (M)	5 10	11 09	South Africa	10 6 81	Livingston
Partridge Richie (M)	5 8	11 00	Dublin	12 9 80	Liverpool
Rocastle Craig (M)	6 1	12 13	Lewisham	17 8 81	Chelsea
Simek Frankie (D)	6 0	11 06	St Louis	13 10 84	Arsenal
Spurr Tommy (D)	6 1	11 05	Leeds	13 9 87	Scholar
Talbot Drew (F)	5 10	11 00	Barnsley	19 7 86	Trainee
Tudgay Marcus (F)	5 10	12 04	Worthing	3 2 83	Derby Co
Whelan Glenn (M)	5 11	12 07	Dublin	13 1 84	Manchester C
Wood Richard (D)	6 3	12 03	Ossett	5 7 85	Scholar

League Appearances: Adams, S. 8; Adamson, C. 5; Agbonlahor, G. 4(4); Best, L. 5(8); Bischoff, M. 4; Brunt, C. 35(9); Bullen, L. 12(16); Burton, D. 15(2); Carson, S. 9; Collins, P. 3; Corr, B. 7(9); Coughlan, G. 33; Diallo, D. 8(3); Eagles, C. 21(4); Folly, Y. 14; Gilbert, P. 17; Graham, D. 19(5); Heckingbottom, P. 4; Hills, J. 26(1); Lee, G. 14(1); Lucas, D. 18; MacLean, S. 4(2); McAllister, S. 1(1); McGovern, J. 3(4); Murphy, D. 4; O'Brien, B. 34(10); Partridge, R. 6(12); Peacock, L. 19(3); Proudlock, A. (6); Rocastle, C. 14(3); Ross, M. 1; Simek, F. 42(1); Spurr, T. 2; Tudgay, M. 14(4); Weaver, N. 14; Whelan, G. 40(3); Wood, R. 27(3).

Goals – League (39): Brunt 7 (1 pen), Tudgay 5, Coughlan 4, Burton 3, Eagles 3, Best 2, Graham 2, MacLean 2 (2 pens), O'Brien 2, Peacock 2, Lee 1, Simek 1, Whelan 1, Wood 1, own goals 3.
Carling Cup (6): Proudlock 2, Coughlan 1, Graham 1, Partridge 1, Peacock 1.
FA Cup (2): Heckingbottom 2.
Ground: Hillsborough, Sheffield S6 1SW. Telephone 0870 999 1867.
Record Attendance: 72,841 v Manchester C, FA Cup 5th rd, 17 February 1934.
Capacity: 39,812.
Manager: Paul Sturrock.
Secretary: Kaven Walker.
Most League Goals: 106, Division 2, 1958–59.
Highest League Scorer in Season: Derek Dooley, 46, Division 2, 1951–52.
Most League Goals in Total Aggregate: Andy Wilson, 199, 1900–20.
Most Capped Player: Nigel Worthington, 50 (66), Northern Ireland.
Most League Appearances: Andy Wilson, 501, 1900–20.
Honours – Football League: Division 1 Champions – 1902–03, 1903–04, 1928–29, 1929–30. Division 2 Champions – 1899–1900, 1925–26, 1951–52, 1955–56, 1958–59.
FA Cup: Winners – 1896, 1907, 1935. **Football League Cup:** Winners – 1990–91.
Colours: Blue and white striped shirts, black shorts, blue stockings.

SHREWSBURY TOWN   FL CHAMPIONSHIP 2

Name						
Adaggio Marco (F)	5 8	12 04	Malaga	6 10 87		
Ashton Neil (M)	5 8	12 04	Liverpool	15 1 85	Tranmere R	
Burton Sagi (D)	6 2	14 02	Birmingham	25 11 77	Peterborough U	
Cadwallader Gav (D)	6 2	12 01	Shrewsbury	18 4 86		
Cowan Gavin (D)	6 4	12 06	Hanover	24 5 81	Canvey Island	
Cronin Lance (G)	6 1	12 00	Brighton	11 9 85	Crystal Palace	
Edwards Dave (M)	5 11	11 05	Shrewsbury	3 2 86	Trainee	
Hart Joe (G)	6 3	13 03	Shrewsbury	19 4 87	Trainee	
Herd Ben (D)	5 9	10 12	Welwyn	21 6 85	Watford	
Hogg Steven (M)	6 3	11 11	Heywood	1 10 85	Manchester U	
Hope Richard (D)	6 2	12 06	Stockton	22 6 78	Chester C	
Hurst Glynn (F)	5 10	11 06	Barnsley	17 1 76	Notts Co	
Langmead Kelvin (F)	6 1	12 00	Coventry	23 3 85	Preston NE	
McMenamin Colin (F)	5 10	10 12	Glasgow	12 2 81	Livingston	
Sorvel Neil (M)	5 10	11 04	Whiston	2 3 73	Crewe Alex	
Stallard Mark (F)	6 0	13 09	Derby	24 10 74	Barnsley	
Tolley Jamie (M)	6 0	11 03	Ludlow	12 5 83	Trainee	
Whitehead Stuart (D)	6 0	12 02	Bromsgrove	17 7 77	Darlington	

League Appearances: Adaggio, M. (5); Ashton, N. 39(5); Burton, S. 15(1); Cadwallader, G. (2); Cowan, G. 9(6); Darby, D. 7(4); Denny, J. 7(7); Edwards, D. 27(3); Evans, R. 2(4); Hart, J. 46; Herd, B. 45(1); Hogg, S. 7(5); Hope, R. 42; Hurst, G. 15(1); Jackson, M. 2(3); Langmead, K. 29(13); Leslie, S. (1); Lyng, C. (1); McClen, J. 4; McMenamin, C. 40(3); Sharp, K. 27(3); Smith, B. 9(3); Sorvel, N. 44(1); Stallard, M. 25(12); Tolley, J. 30(6); Walton, D. 15(1); Whitehead, S. 20(3).
Goals – League (55): McMenamin 10 (5 pens), Langmead 9, Stallard 6, Burton 4 (1 pen), Sorvel 4, Tolley 4, Hurst 3, Darby 2, Edwards 2, Herd 2, Hope 2, Walton 2, Ashton 1, Cowan 1, Sharp 1 (pen), Smith 1, own goal 1.
Carling Cup (3): Denny 2, Stallard 1.
FA Cup (5): Edwards 2, Hope 1, McMenamin 1 (pen), Tolley 1.
Football League Trophy (0).
Ground: Gay Meadow, Abbey Foregate, Shrewsbury, Shropshire SY2 6AB. Telephone (01743) 360 111.
Record Attendance: 18,917 v Walsall, Division 3, 26 April 1961. **Capacity:** 8,000.
Manager: Gary Peters.
Secretary: John W. Howarth.

Most League Goals: 101, Division 4, 1958–59.
Highest League Scorer in Season: Arthur Rowley, 38, Division 4, 1958–59.
Most League Goals in Total Aggregate: Arthur Rowley, 152, 1958–65 (completing his League record of 434 goals).
Most Capped Player: Jimmy McLaughlin, 5 (12), Northern Ireland; Bernard McNally, 5, Northern Ireland.
Most League Appearances: Mickey Brown, 418, 1986–91; 1992–94; 1996–2001.
Honours – Football League: Division 3 Champions – 1978–79, 1993–94. **Welsh Cup:** Winners – 1891, 1938, 1977, 1979, 1984, 1985.
Colours: Blue and amber.

SOUTHAMPTON   FL CHAMPIONSHIP

Name	Ht	Wt	Birthplace	Date	Club/Status
Baird Chris (D)	5 10	11 11	Ballymoney	25 2 82	Scholar
Belmandi Djamel (M)	5 7	11 00	Champigny-sur-Marne	27 3 76	Manchester C
Best Leon (F)	6 1	13 03	Nottingham	19 9 86	Scholar
Bialkowski Bartosz (G)	6 3	12 10	Braniewo	6 7 87	Gornik Zabrze
Blackstock Dexter (F)	6 2	13 00	Oxford	20 5 86	Scholar
Condesso Feliciano (M)	6 0	11 13	Congo	6 4 87	
Cranie Martin (D)	6 1	12 09	Yeovil	23 9 86	Scholar
Critchell Kyle (D)	6 0	12 02	Dorchester	18 1 87	Scholar
Dutton-Black Josh (M)			Oxford	29 12 87	Scholar
Dyer Nathan (M)	5 5	9 00	Trowbridge	29 11 87	Scholar
Folly Yoann (M)	5 9	11 04	Togo	6 6 85	St Etienne
Fuller Ricardo (F)	6 3	12 10	Kingston	31 10 79	Portsmouth
Gillett Simon (M)	5 6	11 07	Oxford	6 11 85	Scholar
Higginbotham Danny (D)	6 2	12 01	Manchester	29 12 78	Derby Co
James Lloyd (M)	5 11	11 01	Bristol	16 2 88	Scholar
Jones Kenwyne (F)	6 2	13 06	Trinidad & Tobago	5 10 84	W Connection
Lallana Adam (M)			Southampton	10 5 88	Scholar
Lundekvam Claus (D)	6 3	13 05	Austevoll	22 2 73	Brann
McGoldrick David (F)	6 1	11 10	Nottingham	29 11 87	Notts Co
Miller Kevin (M)	6 1	13 00	Falmouth	15 3 69	Bristol R
Oakley Matthew (M)	5 10	12 06	Peterborough	17 8 77	Trainee
Ostlund Alexander (D)	5 11	11 13	Akersborg	2 11 78	Feyenoord
Poke Michael (G)	6 1	13 12	Staines	21 11 85	Trainee
Powell Darren (D)	6 2	13 07	Hammersmith	10 3 76	Crystal Palace
Prutton David (M)	5 10	13 00	Hull	12 9 81	Nottingham F
Rudd Sean (D)	6 2	11 03	Oxford	23 10 87	Scholar
Smith Paul (G)	6 3	14 00	Epsom	17 12 79	Brentford
Sparv Tim (M)	6 4	12 05	Vasa	20 2 87	Scholar
Surman Andrew (M)	6 0	11 09	Johannesburg	20 8 86	Trainee
Svensson Michael (D)	6 2	12 02	Sweden	25 11 75	Troyes
Van Damme Jelle (D)	6 4	13 01	Lokeren	10 10 83	Ajax

League Appearances: Baird, C. 16(1); Bale, G. 2; Belmandi, D. 21(1); Best, L. 1(2); Bialkowski, B. 5; Blackstock, D. 7(12); Brennan, J. 13(1); Chaplow, R. 11; Cranie, M. 7(4); Delap, R. 12(4); Dyer, N. 10(7); Folly, Y. 2; Fuller, R. 21(9); Hajto, T. 15(5); Higginbotham, D. 37; Jones, K. 17(17); Kenton, D. 12(1); Kosowski, K. 12(6); Lundekvam, C. 34; Madsen, P. 8(1); McCann, N. 7(4); McGoldrick, D. 1; Miller, K. 7; Mills, J. 3(1); Niemi, A. 25; Oakley, M. 29; Ormerod, B. 13(6); Ostlund, A. 10(2); Pahars, M. 5(3); Potter, D. 8(2); Powell, D. 24(1); Prutton, D. 14(3); Quashie, N. 24; Rasiak, G. 12(1); Smith, P. 9; Surman, A. 11(1); Svensson, M. 7; Walcott, T. 13(8); Wise, D. 8(3); Wright, J. 13.

Goals – League (49): Fuller 9, Jones 4 (1 pen), Quashie 4 (2 pens), Rasiak 4 (1 pen), Walcott 4, Belmandi 3, Blackstock 3, Higginbotham 3 (1 pen), Madsen 2, Oakley 2, Surman 2, Chaplow 1, Kosowski 1, Lundekvam 1, Ormerod 1, Pahars 1, Powell 1, Wise 1, own goals 2.

Carling Cup (3): Blackstock 1, Dyer 1, Ormerod 1.
FA Cup (5): Jones 1, Kenton 1, Prutton 1, Quashie 1, Walcott.
Ground: St Mary's Stadium, Britannia Road, Southampton SO14 5FP. Telephone (0870) 220 0000.
Record Attendance: 32,104 v Liverpool, FA Premier League, 18 January 2003.
Capacity: 32,689.
Manager: George Burley.
Secretary: Liz Coley.
Most League Goals: 112, Division 3 (S), 1957–58.
Highest League Scorer in Season: Derek Reeves, 39, Division 3, 1959–60.
Most League Goals in Total Aggregate: Mike Channon, 185, 1966–77, 1979–82.
Most Capped Player: Peter Shilton, 49 (125), England.
Most League Appearances: Terry Paine, 713, 1956–74.
Honours – Football League: Division 3 (S) Champions – 1921–22. Division 3 Champions – 1959–60. **FA Cup:** Winners – 1975–76.
Colours: Red and white striped shirts, black shorts, white stockings.

SOUTHEND UNITED   FL CHAMPIONSHIP

Ademeno Charles (F)	5 10	11 13	Milton Keynes	12 12 88	Scholar
Barrett Adam (D)	6 1	12 09	Dagenham	29 11 79	Bristol R
Bentley Mark (M)	6 2	13 04	Hertford	7 1 78	Dagenham & R
Bradbury Lee (F)	6 0	12 07	Isle of Wight	3 7 75	Oxford U
Cole Mitchell (M)	5 11	11 05	City of London	6 10 85	Grays Ath
Eastwood Freddy (F)	5 11	12 00	Epsom	29 10 83	Grays Ath
Flahavan Darryl (G)	5 11	12 06	Southampton	28 11 78	Woking
Gower Mark (M)	5 8	12 02	Edmonton	5 10 78	Barnet
Gray Wayne (F)	5 10	13 05	Dulwich	7 11 80	Wimbledon
Guttridge Luke (M)	5 5	8 06	Barnstaple	27 3 82	Cambridge U
Hunt Lewis (D)	5 11	12 09	Birmingham	25 8 82	Derby Co
Jupp Duncan (D)	6 1	12 12	Guildford	25 1 75	Luton T
Lawson James (M)	5 9	10 03	Basildon	21 1 87	Scholar
Maher Kevin (M)	6 0	12 00	Ilford	17 10 76	Tottenham H
Moussa Franck (M)	5 8	10 08	Brussels	24 9 87	Scholar
Pettefer Carl (M)	5 8	10 06	Burnham	22 3 81	Portsmouth
Prior Spencer (D)	6 3	13 00	Rochford	22 4 71	Cardiff C
Smith Jay (M)	5 7	10 11	London	24 9 81	Aston Villa
Sodje Efe (D)	6 1	12 00	Greenwich	5 10 72	Yeovil T
Wilson Che (D)	5 9	12 01	Ely	17 1 79	Cambridge C
Wright Mark (M)			London	20 1 87	Scholar

League Appearances: Ademeno, C. (1); Barrett, A. 45; Bentley, M. 20(13); Bradbury, L. 11(4); Campbell-Ryce, J. 7(6); Cole, M. 19(10); Eastwood, F. 34(6); Edwards, A. 19(1); Flahavan, D. 43; Goater, S. 28(6); Gower, M. 34(6); Gray, W. 23(16); Griemink, B. 3; Guttridge, L. 41; Hunt, L. 23(7); Jupp, D. 29; Lawson, J. 7(16); Maher, K. 44; Moussa, F. (1); Pettefer, C. 5(6); Prior, S. 15(2); Smith, J. 3(10); Sodje, E. 12(1); Wilson, C. 41(3).
Goals – League (72): Eastwood 23 (1 pen), Goater 11 (2 pens), Gray 9 (3 pens), Gower 6, Bentley 5, Guttridge 5, Barrett 3, Lawson 2, Wilson 2, Bradbury 1, Cole 1, Maher 1, Smith 1, Sodje 1, own goal 1.
Carling Cup (0).
FA Cup (2): Eastwood 2.
Football League Trophy (0).
Ground: Roots Hall, Victoria Avenue, Southend-on-Sea SS2 6NQ. Telephone (01702) 304 050.
Record Attendance: 31,090 v Liverpool FA Cup 3rd rd, 10 January 1979. **Capacity:** 12,268.
Manager: Steve Tilson.

Secretary: Mrs Helen Norbury.
Most League Goals: 92, Division 3 (S), 1950–51.
Highest League Scorer in Season: Jim Shankly, 31, 1928–29; Sammy McCrory, 1957–58, both in Division 3 (S).
Most League Goals in Total Aggregate: Roy Hollis, 122, 1953–60.
Most Capped Player: George Mackenzie, 9, Eire.
Most League Appearances: Sandy Anderson, 452, 1950–63.
Honours – Football League: Championship 1 Champions – 2005–06. Division 4 Champions – 1980–81.
Colours: All navy blue with white panel on sleeve.

STOCKPORT COUNTY   FL CHAMPIONSHIP 2

Player					
Allen Damien (M)	5 11	11 04	Cheadle	1 8 86	Scholar
Bramble Tes (F)	6 2	13 05	Ipswich	20 7 80	Southend U
Briggs Keith (M)	6 0	11 05	Glossop	11 12 81	Norwich C
Clare Rob (D)	6 2	13 00	Belper	28 2 83	Blackpool
Coward Chris (F)	6 1	11 07	Manchester	23 7 89	Scholar
Crowther Ryan (M)	5 11	11 00	Stockport	17 9 88	Scholar
Dickinson Liam (F)	6 4	11 07	Salford	4 10 85	Woodley Sports
Duncan Craig (G)	6 1	11 07	Manchester	17 10 87	Scholar
Ellis Dan (M)	5 10	12 07	Stockport	18 11 88	Scholar
Foster Liam (M)	5 10	11 02	Eccles	4 9 87	Scholar
Le Fondre Adam (F)	5 9	11 04	Stockport	2 12 86	Scholar
Malcolm Michael (F)	5 10	11 07	Wembley	13 10 85	Tottenham H
Raynes Michael (M)	6 2	12 02	Wythenshawe	15 10 87	Scholar
Robinson Mark (D)	5 9	11 00	Guisborough	24 7 81	Hereford U
Spencer James (G)	6 3	15 04	Stockport	11 4 85	Trainee
Tunnicliffe James (D)	6 4	12 03	Denton	17 1 89	Scholar
Turnbull Paul (M)	5 10	11 02	Stockport	23 1 89	Scholar
Williams Ashley (D)	6 0	11 02	Wolverhampton	23 8 84	Hednesford T

League Appearances: Allen, D. 13(9); Beharall, D. 10(2); Boshell, D. 28(5); Bramble, T. 33(4); Briggs, K. 39(2); Clare, R. 31(3); Collins, A. 2(1); Crowe, D. 1(5); Crowther, R. (1); Dickinson, L. 12(9); Dje, L. 5(2); Dolan, J. 2; Duke, M. 3; Easter, J. 18(1); Ellis, D. (3); Foster, L. (1); Greenwood, R. 17(5); Griffin, A. 20(1); Griffin, D. 4; Hamshaw, M. 35(4); Hughes, M. 3; Ikeme, C. 9; Le Fondre, A. 4(18); Malcolm, M. 10(13); O'Connor, K. 6(1); Raynes, M. 23(2); Robinson, M. 46; Singh, H. 19(5); Smylie, D. 1(2); Spencer, J. 34; Strachan, G. 4; Symes, M. 1(1); Taylor, J. 9; Tunnicliffe, J. (1); Vaughan, T. 10; Ward, J. 7(2); Williams, A. 33(3); Williams, C. 1(2); Wolski, M. 14(6).
Goals – League (57): Easter 8 (1 pen), Dickinson 7, Le Fondre 6 (1 pen), Bramble 5, Hamshaw 5, Briggs 4, Malcolm 3, Clare 2, Griffin A 2, Robinson 2 (2 pens), Boshell 1, Hughes 1, O'Connor 1, Raynes 1, Singh 1, Vaughan 1, Ward 1, Williams A 1, Wolski 1, own goals 4.
Carling Cup (2): Boshell 1, Le Fondre 1.
FA Cup (6): Easter 3, Briggs 2, Wolski 1.
Football League Trophy (1): own goal 1.
Ground: Edgeley Park, Hardcastle Road, Edgeley, Stockport, Cheshire SK3 9DD. Telephone (0161) 286 8888.
Record Attendance: 27,833 v Liverpool, FA Cup 5th rd, 11 February 1950.
Capacity: 10,641.
Manager: Jim Gannon.
Secretary: Kevan Taylor.
Most League Goals: 115, Division 3 (N), 1933–34.
Highest League Scorer in Season: Alf Lythgoe, 46, Division 3 (N), 1933–34.
Most League Goals in Total Aggregate: Jack Connor, 132, 1951–56.
Most Capped Player: Jarkko Wiss, 9 (36), Finland.
Most League Appearances: Andy Thorpe, 489, 1978–86, 1988–92.

Honours – Football League: Division 3 (N) Champions – 1921–22, 1936–37. Division 4 Champions – 1966–67.
Colours: Blue shirts with white chestband, blue shorts, white stockings.

STOKE CITY   FL CHAMPIONSHIP

Player		Ht	Birthplace	Birthday	Club
Bangoura Sambegou (F)	6 0	12 02	Guinea	3 4 82	Standard Liege
Brammer Dave (M)	5 10	12 00	Bromborough	28 2 75	Crewe Alex
Broomes Marlon (D)	6 0	12 12	Birmingham	28 11 77	Preston NE
Buxton Lewis (D)	6 1	13 10	Newport (IW)	10 12 83	Portsmouth
Chadwick Luke (M)	5 11	11 08	Cambridge	18 11 80	West Ham U
Dickinson Carl (D)	6 0	12 00	Swadlincote	31 3 87	Scholar
Duberry Michael (D)	6 1	14 09	Enfield	14 10 75	Leeds U
Duggan Robert (G)	6 1	12 07	Dublin	1 4 87	Scholar
Eustace John (M)	5 11	11 12	Solihull	3 11 79	Coventry C
Garret Robert (M)	5 6	10 04	Belfast	5 5 88	Scholar
Harper Kevin (F)	5 6	12 00	Oldham	15 1 76	Portsmouth
Hazley Matthew (M)	5 10	12 03	Banbridge	30 12 87	Scholar
Henry Karl (M)	6 0	12 00	Wolverhampton	26 11 82	Trainee
Hill Clint (D)	6 0	11 06	Liverpool	19 10 78	Oldham Ath
Hoefkens Carl (D)	6 1	12 13	Lier	6 10 78	Beerschot
Kopteff Peter (M)	5 11	11 11	Helsingfors	10 4 79	Viking
Paterson Martin (M)	5 9	11 05	Tunstall	13 5 87	Scholar
Pulis Anthony (M)	5 10	11 10	Bristol	21 7 84	Portsmouth
Rooney Adam (F)	5 10	12 03	Dublin	21 4 87	Scholar
Russell Darel (M)	6 0	11 09	Mile End	22 10 80	Norwich C
Sidibe Mamady (F)	6 4	12 02	Bamako	18 12 79	Gillingham
Sigurdsson Hannes (F)	6 2	13 02	Reykjavik	10 4 83	Viking
Simonsen Steve (G)	6 2	12 00	South Shields	3 4 79	Everton
Sweeney Peter (M)	6 0	12 11	Glasgow	25 9 84	Millwall
Wilkinson Andy (D)	5 11	11 00	Stone	6 8 84	Scholar

League Appearances: Bangoura, S. 23(1); Brammer, D. 38(2); Broomes, M. 36(1); Buxton, L. 25(7); Chadwick, L. 33(3); De Goey, E. 1(1); Dickinson, C. 4(1); Duberry, M. 41; Dyer, B. 2(9); Gallagher, P. 32(5); Garret, R. (2); Halls, J. 13; Harper, K. 5(9); Hazley, M. (1); Henry, K. 11(13); Hill, C. 12(1); Hoefkens, C. 44; Junior, 16(6); Kolar, M. 12(2); Kopteff, P. 3(3); Paterson, M. 2(1); Rooney, A. 2(3); Russell, D. 35(2); Sidibe, M. 37(5); Sigurdsson, H. 10(13); Simonsen, S. 45; Skoko, J. 9; Sweeney, P. 8(9); Taggart, G. 3; Wilkinson, A. 4(2).
Goals – League (54): Gallagher 11 (1 pen), Bangoura 9, Sidibe 6, Rooney 4, Hoefkens 3 (2 pens), Russell 3, Broomes 2, Chadwick 2, Halls 2, Skoko 2, Brammer 1, Buxton 1, Duberry 1, Harper 1, Kolar 1, Sigurdsson 1, Sweeney 1, Taggart 1, own goals 2.
Carling Cup (1): Brammer 1 (pen).
FA Cup (3): Chadwick 1, Gallagher 1, Sidibe 1.
Ground: Britannia Stadium, Stanley Matthews Way, Stoke-on-Trent ST4 4EG. Telephone (01782) 592 222.
Record Attendance: 51,380 v Arsenal, Division 1, 29 March 1937. **Capacity:** 28,218.
Manager: Tony Pulis.
Secretary: Diane Richardson.
Most League Goals: 92, Division 3 (N), 1926–27.
Highest League Scorer in Season: Freddie Steele, 33, Division 1, 1936–37.
Most League Goals in Total Aggregate: Freddie Steele, 142, 1934–49.
Most Capped Player: Gordon Banks, 36 (73), England.
Most League Appearances: Eric Skeels, 506, 1958–76.
Honours – Football League: Division 2 Champions – 1932–33, 1962–63, 1992–93. Division 3 (N) Champions – 1926–27. **Football League Cup:** Winners – 1971–72. **Autoglass Trophy:** Winners – 1992. **Auto Windscreens Shield:** Winners – 2000.
Colours: Red and white striped shirts, white shorts with red trim, white stockings with red trim.

Alnwick Ben (G)	6 2	13 12	Prudhoe	1	1 87	Scholar
Arca Julio (M)	5 9	11 13	Quilmes	31	1 81	Argentinos Juniors
Bassila Christian (M)	6 4	13 01	Paris	5 10 77		Strasbourg
Brown Chris (F)	6 3	13 08	Doncaster	11 12 84		Trainee
Caldwell Steven (D)	6 2	13 13	Stirling	12	9 80	Newcastle U
Collins Danny (D)	6 2	12 00	Buckley	6	8 80	Chester C
Collins Neill (D)	6 3	13 00	Troon	2	9 83	Dumbarton
Davis Kelvin (G)	6 1	11 05	Bedford	29	9 76	Ipswich T
Delap Rory (M)	6 3	13 00	Sutton Coldfield	6	7 76	Southampton
Elliott Stephen (F)	5 8	11 08	Dublin	6	1 84	Manchester C
Kyle Kevin (F)	6 3	14 08	Stranraer	7	6 81	Ayr Boswell
Lawrence Liam (M)	5 11	12 06	Retford	14 12 81		Mansfield T
Leadbitter Grant (M)	5 9	11 06	Sunderland	7	1 86	Trainee
McCartney George (D)	5 11	11 03	Belfast	29	4 81	Trainee
Miller Tommy (M)	6 0	11 07	Easington	8	1 79	Ipswich T
Murphy Daryl (F)	6 2	13 12	Waterford	15	3 83	Waterford
Nosworthy Nayron (D)	6 0	12 08	Brixton	11 10 80		Gillingham
Smith Daniel (D)	5 9	10 10	Sunderland	5 10 86		Scholar
Smith Kevin (F)	5 11	11 09	Edinburgh	20	3 87	Leeds U
Stead Jon (F)	6 3	13 03	Huddersfield	7	4 83	Blackburn R
Welsh Andy (F)	5 8	9 06	Manchester	24 11 83		Stockport Co
Whitehead Dean (M)	5 11	12 06	Oxford	12	1 82	Oxford U
Wright Stephen (D)	6 0	12 00	Liverpool	8	2 80	Liverpool

League Appearances: Alnwick, B. 5; Arca, J. 22(2); Bassila, C. 12(1); Breen, G. 33(2); Brown, C. 10(3); Caldwell, S. 23(1); Collins, D. 22(1); Davis, K. 33; Delap, R. 5(1); Elliott, S. 11(4); Gray, A. 13(8); Hoyte, J. 27; Kyle, K. 9(4); Lawrence, L. 19(10); Le Tallec, A. 12(15); Leadbitter, G. 8(4); McCartney, G. 13; Miller, T. 27(2); Murphy, D. 5(13); Nosworthy, N. 24(6); Robinson, C. 3(2); Smith, D. 1(2); Stead, J. 21(9); Stubbs, A. 8(2); Welsh, A. 12(2); Whitehead, D. 37; Woods, M. 1(6); Wright, S. 2.
Goals – League (26): Lawrence 3, Le Tallec 3, Miller 3, Whitehead 3 (2 pens), Elliott 2, Arca 1, Breen 1, Brown 1, Collins D 1, Delap 1, Gray 1, Hoyte 1, Kyle 1, Murphy 1, Stead 1, Stubbs 1, own goal 1.
Carling Cup (1): Le Tallec 1.
FA Cup (4): Arca 1, Collins N 1, Le Tallec 1, Whitehead 1.
Ground: Stadium of Light, Sunderland, Tyne and Wear SR5 1SU. Telephone (0191) 551 5000.
Record Attendance: 75,118 v Derby Co, FA Cup 6th rd replay, 8 March 1933 (Roker Park). 48,353 v Liverpool, FA Premier League, 13 April 2002 (Stadium of Light). **Capacity:** 49,000.
Manager: TBC.
Secretary: TBC.
Most League Goals: 109, Division 1, 1935–36.
Highest League Scorer in Season: Dave Halliday, 43, Division 1, 1928–29.
Most League Goals in Total Aggregate: Charlie Buchan, 209, 1911–25.
Most Capped Player: Charlie Hurley, 38 (40), Republic of Ireland.
Most League Appearances: Jim Montgomery, 537, 1962–77.
Honours – Football League: Championship – Winners – 2004–05. Division 1 Champions – 1891–92, 1892–93, 1894–95, 1901–02, 1912–13, 1935–36, 1995–96, 1998–99. Division 2 Champions – 1975–76. Division 3 Champions – 1987–88. **FA Cup:** Winners – 1937, 1973.
Colours: Red and white striped shirts, black shorts, black and red stockings.

Akinfenwa Adebayo (F)	5 11	13 07	Nigeria	10 5 82	Torquay U
Austin Kevin (D)	6 2	15 00	Hackney	12 2 73	Bristol R
Britton Leon (M)	5 6	10 00	Merton	16 9 82	West Ham U
Fallon Rory (F)	6 2	11 09	Gisbourne	20 3 82	Swindon T
Gueret Willy (G)	6 2	14 01	Saint Claude	3 8 73	Millwall
Iriekpen Ezomo (D)	6 1	12 02	East London	14 5 82	West Ham U
Knight Leon (F)	5 5	9 06	Hackney	16 9 82	Brighton & HA
MacDonald Shaun (M)	6 1	11 04	Swansea	17 6 88	Scholar
McLeod Kevin (M)	5 11	12 00	Liverpool	12 9 80	QPR
Monk Garry (D)	6 1	13 00	Bedford	6 3 79	Barnsley
O'Leary Kristian (M)	6 0	12 09	Port Talbot	30 8 77	Trainee
Ricketts Sam (D)	6 0	12 11	Aylesbury	11 10 81	Oxford U
Robinson Andy (M)	5 8	11 04	Birkenhead	3 11 79	Cammell Laird
Tate Alan (D)	6 1	13 05	Easington	2 9 82	Manchester U
Trundle Lee (F)	6 0	13 03	Liverpool	10 10 76	Wrexham
Tudur-Jones Owain (M)	6 2	12 00	Bangor	15 10 84	Bangor C
Watt Steven (D)	6 2	12 09	Aberdeen	1 5 85	Chelsea
Way Darren (M)	5 7	11 00	Plymouth	21 11 79	Yeovil T
Williams Tom (M)	5 11	12 06	Carshalton	8 7 80	Gillingham

League Appearances: Akinfenwa, A. 29(5); Anderson, I. (5); Austin, K. 23(3); Bean, M. 9; Britton, L. 36(2); Connor, P. 5(8); Edwards, C. 1(1); Fallon, R. 12(5); Forbes, A. 12(17); Goodfellow, M. 5(6); Gueret, W. 46; Iriekpen, E. 28; Knight, L. 10(7); Lowe, K. 4; Macdonald, S. 2(5); Martinez, R. 34(5); McLeod, K. 23(6); Monk, G. 33; Nugent, K. (1); O'Leary, K. 12(3); Ricketts, S. 43(1); Robinson, A. 29(10); Tate, A. 42(1); Thorpe, L. (3); Trundle, L. 34(2); Tudur-Jones, O. 17(4); Watt, S. 2; Way, D. 2(3); Williams, T. 13(4).

Goals – League (78): Trundle 20 (3 pens), Robinson 12 (2 pens), Akinfenwa 9, Knight 8, McLeod 7, Britton 4, Fallon 4, Forbes 4, Tudur-Jones 3, Martinez 2, Bean 1, Connor 1, Monk 1, O'Leary 1, Ricketts 1.

Carling Cup (1): Akinfenwa 1.

FA Cup (0).

Football League Trophy (17): Akinfenwa 5, Robinson 5, Knight 2, Britton 1, Connor 1, Forbes 1, Monk 1, Trundle 1.

Play-Offs (5): Knight 2, Fallon 1, Ricketts 1, Robinson 1.

Ground: Liberty Stadium, Landore, Swansea SA1 2FA. Telephone (01792) 616 600.

Record Attendance: 32,796 v Arsenal, FA Cup 4th rd, 17 February 1968 (at Vetch Field). **Capacity:** 20,520.

Director of Football: Kenny Jackett.

Secretary: Jackie Rockey.

Most League Goals: 90, Division 2, 1956–57.

Highest League Scorer in Season: Cyril Pearce, 35, Division 2, 1931–32.

Most League Goals in Total Aggregate: Ivor Allchurch, 166, 1949–58, 1965–68.

Most Capped Player: Ivor Allchurch, 42 (68), Wales.

Most League Appearances: Wilfred Milne, 585, 1919–37.

Honours – Football League: Division 3 Champions – 1999–2000. Division 3 (S) Champions – 1924–25, 1948–49. **Autoglass Trophy:** Winners – 1994, 2006. **Football League Trophy:** Winners – 2006. **Welsh Cup:** Winners – 11 times.

Colours: All white.

Brown Aaron (M)	5 10	11 11	Bristol	14 3 80	QPR
Bulman Matty (G)	6 0	11 05	Swindon	14 10 86	Scholar
Caton Andy (M)	6 0	12 03	Oxford	3 12 87	Scholar
Comyn-Platt Charlie (D)	6 2	12 00	Salford	2 10 85	Bolton W
Cureton Jamie (F)	5 8	10 07	Bristol	28 8 75	QPR
Evans Rhys (G)	6 1	12 02	Swindon	27 1 82	Chelsea
Gurney Andy (D)	5 7	10 08	Bristol	25 1 74	Swansea C
Henry Leigh (D)			Swindon	?? 10 86	Scholar
Holgate Ashan (F)	6 2	12 00	Swindon	9 11 86	Scholar
Ifil Jerel (D)	6 1	12 11	Wembley	27 6 82	Watford
Jutkiewicz Lucas (F)	6 1	12 11	Southampton	20 3 89	Scholar
Nicholas Andrew (D)	6 0	12 10	Liverpool	10 10 83	Liverpool
O'Hanlon Sean (D)	6 1	12 05	Southport	2 1 83	Everton
Peacock Lee (F)	6 0	12 08	Paisley	9 10 76	Sheffield W
Pook Michael (M)	5 11	11 10	Swindon	22 10 85	Scholar
Roberts Chris (F)	5 9	13 02	Cardiff	22 10 79	Bristol C
Shakes Ricky (M)	5 10	12 00	Brixton	26 1 85	Bolton W
Smith Jack (D)	5 11	11 05	Hemel Hempsted	14 10 83	Watford
Stroud David (M)	5 10	12 04	Swindon	10 11 87	Scholar
Wells Ben (M)	5 9	10 07	Basingstoke	26 3 88	Scholar
Whalley Gareth (M)	5 10	11 06	Manchester	19 12 73	Wigan Ath

League Appearances: Benjamin, T. 5(3); Bouazza, H. 11(2); Brown, A. 23(4); Collins, P. 13; Comyn-Platt, C. 13(9); Cureton, J. 22(8); Diagouraga, T. 5(3); Evans, R. 32; Fallon, R. 25; Gurney, A. 24(4); Heath, C. 8(3); Heaton, T. 14; Holgate, A. 2(4); Ifil, J. 34(2); Jarrett, A. 2(4); Jenkins, S. 17(7); Jutkiewicz, L. 3(2); McDermott, N. 9(4); McPhee, C. 6(2); Miglioranzi, S. 22(5); Mikolanda, P. 1(4); Nicholas, A. 31(2); Nicolau, N. 3(2); O'Hanlon, S. 40; Peacock, L. 11(4); Pook, M. 26(4); Reeves, A. 1; Roberts, C. 4(17); Shakes, R. 26(11); Smith, J. 38; Smith, P. 5(4); Stroud, D. 1(1); Summerbee, N. 1; Thorpe, T. 6(1); Wells, B. (4); Whalley, G. 23(1).

Goals – League (46): Fallon 12, Cureton 7, O'Hanlon 4, Roberts 3 (1 pen), Shakes 3, Benjamin 2 (1 pen), Bouazza 2 (1 pen), Brown 2, McDermott 2, Peacock 2, Comyn-Platt 1, Gurney 1 (pen), Heath 1, Jenkins 1, Miglioranzi 1, Thorpe 1, own goal 1.

Carling Cup (1): Pook 1.

FA Cup (3): Comyn-Platt 1, Fallon 1 (pen), Gurney 1.

Football League Trophy (3): Bouazza 1, Fallon 1, Roberts 1.

Ground: County Ground, County Road, Swindon SN1 2ED. Telephone (0870) 443 1969.

Record Attendance: 32,000 v Arsenal, FA Cup 3rd rd, 15 January 1972. **Capacity:** 14,255.

Manager: Dennis Wise.

Secretary: Linda Birrell.

Most League Goals: 100, Division 3 (S), 1926–27.

Highest League Scorer in Season: Harry Morris, 47, Division 3 (S), 1926–27.

Most League Goals in Total Aggregate: Harry Morris, 216, 1926–33.

Most Capped Player: Rod Thomas, 30 (50), Wales.

Most League Appearances: John Trollope, 770, 1960–80.

Honours – Football League: Division 2 Champions – 1995–96. Division 4 Champions – 1985–86. **Football League Cup:** Winners – 1968–69. **Anglo-Italian Cup:** Winners – 1970.

Colours: Red shirts with white and green, red shorts with white stripe, red stockings with white turnover.

TORQUAY UNITED   FL CHAMPIONSHIP 2

Bedeau Anthony (F)	5 9	12 00	Hammersmith	24 3 79	Trainee
Garner Darren (M)	5 10	12 02	Plymouth	10 12 71	Rotherham U
Hewlett Matt (M)	6 1	12 07	Bristol	25 2 76	Swindon T
Hill Kevin (F)	5 11	11 00	Exeter	6 3 76	Torrington
Hockley Matthew (D)	5 10	12 07	Paignton	5 6 82	Trainee
Marriott Andy (G)	6 0	12 04	Sutton-in-Ashfield	11 10 70	Bury
Osei-Kuffour Jo (F)	5 8	12 00	Edmonton	17 11 81	Arsenal
Phillips Martin (M)	5 8	10 03	Exeter	13 3 76	Plymouth Arg
Taylor Craig (D)	6 1	13 00	Plymouth	24 1 74	Plymouth Arg
Villis Matt (D)	6 2	12 00	Bridgwater	13 4 84	Plymouth Arg
Woods Steve (D)	6 0	12 05	Northwich	15 12 76	Chesterfield

League Appearances: Afful, L. (5); Andrews, L. 6(1); Bedeau, A. 26(5); Coleman, L. 7(7); Connell, A. 12(10); Constantine, L. 10(5); Flynn, P. 1; Garner, D. 40(3); Hancox, R. (1); Hewlett, M. 18(6); Hill, K. 41(1); Hockley, M. 25(11); Hollands, D. 10; Lawless, A. 11(3); Lloyd, A. 19(1); Lockwood, A. 9; Marriott, A. 46; McAliskey, J. 3; McGlinchey, B. 4(1); Osei-Kuffour, J. 34(9); Phillips, M. 23(3); Priso, C. 1(2); Reed, S. 11; Robinson, P. 12(9); Sako, M. 10(15); Sharp, J. 30(2); Sow, M. 9(2); Stonebridge, I. 3; Taylor, C. 27(4); Thorpe, L. 10; Villis, M. 11(1); Woodman, C. 2; Woods, S. 35(3).
Goals – League (53): Bedeau 9 (1 pen), Hill 9, Osei-Kuffour 8, Connell 7, Lockwood 3, Phillips 3, Robinson 3 (1 pen), Sako 3, Thorpe 3, Garner 2, Constantine 1, Hewlett 1, Hollands 1.
Carling Cup (0).
FA Cup (3): Bedeau 2, Stonebridge 1.
Football League Trophy (1): Osei Kuffour 1.
Ground: Plainmoor Ground, Torquay, Devon TQ1 3PS. Telephone (01803) 328 666.
Record Attendance: 21,908 v Huddersfield T, FA Cup 4th rd, 29 January 1955.
Capacity: 6,285.
Manager: Ian Atkins.
Secretary: Deborah Hancox.
Most League Goals: 89, Division 3 (S), 1956–57.
Highest League Scorer in Season: Sammy Collins, 40, Division 3 (S), 1955–56.
Most League Goals in Total Aggregate: Sammy Collins, 204, 1948–58.
Most Capped Player: Rodney Jack, St Vincent.
Most League Appearances: Dennis Lewis, 443, 1947–59.
Honours – Nil.
Colours: Yellow shirts with royal blue sleeves, yellow shorts, yellow stockings.

TOTTENHAM HOTSPUR   FA PREMIERSHIP

Barcham Andy (F)	5 8	11 10	Basildon	16 12 86	Scholar
Barnard Lee (F)	5 10	10 10	Romford	18 7 84	Trainee
Burch Rob (G)	6 2	12 13	Yeovil	8 10 83	Trainee
Button David (G)	6 3	13 00	Stevenage	27 2 89	Scholar
Carrick Michael (M)	6 1	11 10	Wallsend	28 7 81	West Ham U
Daniels Charlie (M)	6 1	12 12	Harlow	7 9 86	Scholar
Davenport Calum (D)	6 4	14 00	Bedford	1 1 83	Coventry C
Davids Edgar (M)	5 7	10 10	Paramaribo	13 3 73	Internazionale
Davis Jamie (M)	5 7	10 10	Braintree	25 10 88	Scholar
Dawkins Simon (F)	5 10	11 01	Edgware	1 12 87	Scholar
Dawson Michael (D)	6 2	12 02	Northallerton	18 11 83	Nottingham F
Defendi Rodrigo (D)	6 2	13 01	Ribeirao Preto	16 6 86	Cruzeiro
Defoe Jermain (F)	5 7	10 04	Beckton	7 10 82	West Ham U

El Hamdaoui Mounir (F)	6 0	13 05	Rotterdam	14 7 84	Excelsior
Forecast Tommy (G)	6 6	11 10	Newham	15 10 86	Scholar
Fulop Marton (G)	6 3	12 08	Budapest	3 5 83	MTK
Gardner Anthony (D)	6 3	14 00	Stafford	19 9 80	Port Vale
Ghali Hossam (M)	5 11	12 04	Cairo	15 12 81	Feyenoord
Hallfredsson Emil (M)	6 1	13 01	Iceland	29 6 84	FH
Huddlestone Tom (M)	6 2	11 02	Nottingham	28 12 86	Derby Co
Ifil Phil (D)	5 9	10 08	Willesden	18 11 86	Scholar
Jenas Jermaine (M)	5 11	11 00	Nottingham	18 2 83	Newcastle U
Keane Robbie (F)	5 9	12 06	Dublin	8 7 80	Leeds U
Kelly Stephen (D)	6 1	12 01	Dublin	6 9 83	Juniors
King Ledley (D)	6 2	14 05	Bow	12 10 80	Trainee
Lee Charlie (M)	5 11	11 07	Whitechapel	5 1 87	Scholar
Lee Young-Pyo (D)	5 8	10 10	Hong Chung	23 4 77	PSV Eindhoven
Lennon Aaron (M)	5 6	10 03	Leeds	16 4 87	Leeds U
Lewis Stuart (M)	5 10	11 06	Welwyn	15 10 87	Scholar
Maghoma Jacques (M)	5 9	11 06	Lubumbashi	23 10 87	Scholar
Marney Dean (M)	5 9	11 04	Barking	31 1 84	Scholar
Martin Joe (M)	6 0	12 13	Dagenham	29 11 88	Scholar
McKenna Kieran (M)	5 10	10 07	London	14 5 86	Academy
Mills Leigh (D)	6 2	13 00	Winchester	8 2 88	Scholar
Murphy Danny (M)	5 10	11 09	Chester	18 3 77	Charlton Ath
O'Hara Jamie (M)	5 11	12 04	Dartford	25 9 86	Scholar
Reid Andy (F)	5 8	11 02	Dublin	29 7 82	Nottingham F
Robinson Paul (G)	6 4	15 07	Beverley	15 10 79	Leeds U
Routledge Wayne (M)	5 6	11 02	Sidcup	7 1 85	Crystal Palace
Stalteri Paul (D)	5 11	11 13	Toronto	18 10 77	Werder Bremen
Tainio Teemu (M)	5 9	11 09	Tornio	27 11 79	Auxerre
Yeates Mark (F)	5 9	10 07	Dublin	11 1 85	Trainee
Ziegler Reto (M)	6 0	12 06	Nyon	16 1 86	Grasshoppers

League Appearances: Barnard, L. (3); Brown, M. 2(7); Carrick, M. 35; Davenport, C. 1(3); Davids, E. 28(3); Dawson, M. 31(1); Defoe, J. 23(13); Edman, E. 3; Gardner, A. 16(1); Huddlestone, T. (4); Jackson, J. (1); Jenas, J. 30; Kanoute, F. (1); Keane, R. 25(11); Kelly, S. 9; King, L. 26; Lee, Y. 31; Lennon, A. 21(6); Mido, 24(3); Murphy, D. 2(8); Naybet, N. 2(1); Pamarot, N. (2); Pedro Mendes, 3(3); Rasiak, G. 4(4); Reid, A. 7(6); Robinson, P. 38; Routledge, W. 2(1); Stalteri, P. 33; Tainio, T. 22(2).
Goals – League (53): Keane 16 (3 pens), Mido 11 (1 pen), Defoe 9, Jenas 6, King 3, Carrick 2, Lennon 2, Davids 1, Stalteri 1, Tainio 1, own goal 1.
Carling Cup (0).
FA Cup (2): Jenas 1, Stalteri 1.
Ground: White Hart Lane, Bill Nicholson Way, 748 High Road, Tottenham, London N17 0AP. Telephone (0870) 420 5000.
Record Attendance: 75,038 v Sunderland, FA Cup 6th rd, 5 March 1938.
Capacity: 36,237.
Head Coach: Martin Jol.
Secretary: John Alexander.
Most League Goals: 115, Division 1, 1960–61.
Highest League Scorer in Season: Jimmy Greaves, 37, Division 1, 1962–63.
Most League Goals in Total Aggregate: Jimmy Greaves, 220, 1961–70.
Most Capped Player: Pat Jennings, 74 (119), Northern Ireland.
Most League Appearances: Steve Perryman, 655, 1969–86.
Honours – Football League: Division 1 Champions – 1950–51, 1960–61. Division 2 Champions – 1919–20, 1949–50. **FA Cup:** Winners – 1901 (as non-League club), 1921, 1961, 1962, 1967, 1981, 1982, 1991. **Football League Cup:** Winners – 1970–71, 1972–73, 1998–99. **European Competitions: European Cup-Winners' Cup:** Winners – 1962–63. **UEFA Cup:** Winners – 1971–72, 1983–84.
Colours: White shirts, navy shorts, white stockings.

TRANMERE ROVERS   FL CHAMPIONSHIP 1

Achterberg John (G)	6 1	13 00	Utrecht	8 7 71	Eindhoven
Brown Paul (M)	5 8	12 02	Liverpool	10 9 84	Scholar
Davies Steve (F)	6 0	12 00	Liverpool	29 12 87	Scholar
Goodison Ian (D)	6 1	12 06	St James, Jam	21 11 72	Seba U
Greenacre Chris (F)	5 9	12 09	Halifax	23 12 77	Stoke C
Harrison Danny (M)	5 11	12 04	Liverpool	4 11 82	Scholar
Henry Paul (M)	5 8	11 06	Liverpool	28 1 88	Scholar
James Oliver (D)	6 0	11 10	Birkenhead	30 1 87	Scholar
Jennings Steven (M)	5 7	11 07	Liverpool	28 10 84	Scholar
Jones Mike (M)			Birkenhead	15 8 87	Scholar
Linwood Paul (D)	6 2	13 04	Birkenhead	24 10 83	Scholar
McAteer Jason (M)	5 9	11 05	Birkenhead	18 6 71	Sunderland
Roberts Gareth (D)	5 8	11 00	Wrexham	6 2 78	Liverpool
Sharps Ian (D)	6 3	13 05	Warrington	23 10 80	Trainee
Tremarco Carl (D)	5 10	12 02	Liverpool	11 10 85	Scholar
Zola Makongo Calvin (F)	6 3	13 07	Kinshasa	31 12 84	Newcastle U

League Appearances: Achterberg, J. 19; Aiston, S. 23(13); Bruce, A. 10(1); Dagnall, C. (6); Davies, S. 6(16); Facey, D. 30(7); Francis, S. 16(1); Goodison, I. 32(6); Greenacre, C. 45; Harrison, D. 26(9); Hume, I. 5(1); Jackson, M. 41; James, O. (1); Jennings, S. 24(14); Jones, M. 1; Linwood, P. 12(2); McAteer, J. 23(6); Murray, M. 2; O'Leary, S. 19(2); Rankine, M. 20(4); Raven, D. 11; Roberts, G. 44; Seremet, D. 13; Sharps, I. 39; Summerbee, N. 4(2); Tremarco, C. 14(4); Whitmore, T. (4); Wilson, S. 12; Zola, C. 15(7).
Goals – League (50): Greenacre 16 (2 pens), Facey 8, Zola 4, Aiston 3, Jackson 3, O'Leary 3, Davies 2, Harrison 2, Roberts 2, Francis 1, Goodison 1, Hume 1, Jennings 1, Sharps 1, Tremarco 1, own goal 1.
Carling Cup (1): Sharps 1.
FA Cup (1): Greenacre 1.
Football League Trophy (5): Facey 1, Greenacre 1 (pen), Harrison 1, Jennings 1, Rankine 1.
Ground: Prenton Park, Prenton Road West, Birkenhead, Merseyside CH42 9PY. Telephone (0870) 460 3333.
Record Attendance: 24,424 v Stoke C, FA Cup 4th rd, 5 February 1972.
Capacity: 16,567.
Manager: Ronnie Moore.
Secretary: Mick Horton.
Most League Goals: 111, Division 3 (N), 1930–31.
Highest League Scorer in Season: Bunny Bell, 35, Division 3 (N), 1933–34.
Most League Goals in Total Aggregate: Ian Muir, 142, 1985–95.
Most Capped Player: John Aldridge, 30 (69), Republic of Ireland.
Most League Appearances: Harold Bell, 595, 1946–64 (incl. League record 401 consecutive appearances).
Honours – Football League: Division 3 (N) Champions – 1937–38. **Welsh Cup:** Winners – 1935. **Leyland Daf Cup:** Winners – 1990.
Colours: White shirts with reflex blue trim, white shorts with reflex blue trim, white stockings with reflex blue trim.

WALSALL   FL CHAMPIONSHIP 2

Barrowman Andrew (F)	5 11	11 06	Wishaw	27 11 84	Mansfield T
Bradley Mark (D)	6 0	11 05	Dudley	14 1 88	Scholar
Constable James (F)	6 2	12 12	Malmesbury	4 10 84	Chippenham T
Dann Scott (D)	6 2	12 00	Liverpool	14 2 87	Scholar

Deakin Graham (M)	5 10	11 05	Birmingham	24 4 87	Scholar
Demontagnac Ishmel (F)	5 10	11 05	Newham	15 6 88	Charlton Ath
Fox Daniel (D)	5 11	12 06	Winsford	29 5 86	Everton
Gerrard Anthony (D)	6 2	13 07	Liverpool	6 2 86	Everton
Gilmartin Rene (G)	6 5	13 06	Islington	31 5 87	St Patrick's BC
Keates Dean (M)	5 6	10 06	Walsall	30 6 78	Lincoln C
McDermott David (M)	5 5	10 00	Stourbridge	6 2 88	Scholar
McKeown James (G)	6 1	13 07	Birmingham	24 7 89	Scholar
Nicholls Alex (F)	5 10	11 00	Stourbridge	19 12 87	Scholar
Pead Craig (M)	5 9	11 06	Bromsgrove	15 9 81	Coventry C
Roper Ian (D)	6 3	14 00	Nuneaton	20 6 77	Trainee
Smith Emmanuel (D)	6 2	12 03	Birmingham	8 11 88	Scholar
Standing Michael (M)	5 10	10 07	Shoreham	20 3 81	Bradford C
Sztybel Jay (M)	5 9	11 00	Redditch	11 10 87	Scholar
Taylor Kris (M)	5 9	11 05	Stafford	12 1 84	Manchester U
Tilt Luke (G)	6 1	12 00	Dudley	18 6 88	Scholar
Westwood Chris (D)	5 11	12 10	Dudley	13 2 77	Hartlepool U
Wrack Darren (M)	5 9	12 02	Cleethorpes	5 5 76	Grimsby T
Wright Mark (M)	5 11	11 00	Wolverhampton	24 2 82	Scholar

League Appearances: Atieno, T. 1(1); Barrowman, A. 10(3); Bennett, J. 17(2); Bradley, M. (3); Broad, J. 2; Claridge, S. 7; Constable, J. 7(10); Demontagnac, I. 14(10); Devlin, P. 8; Fitzgerald, S. 1(4); Fox, D. 33; Fryatt, M. 23; Gerrard, A. 32(2); Gillett, S. 2; Gilmartin, R. 2; Harkness, J. 1; Husbands, M. 1(3); James, K. 12(3); Keates, D. 14; Kinsella, M. 6(3); Larrosa, R. 2(5); Leary, M. 12(3); Leitao, J. 20(3); McDermott, D. (1); Merson, P. 6(1); Mills, P. 14; Murphy, J. 14; Nicholls, A. 4(4); Oakes, A. 25; Osborn, S. 27(5); Pead, C. 38(1); Roper, I. 24(1); Ruddy, J. 5; Skora, E. 4; Smith, G. 13; Smith, P. 8; Standing, M. 10(10); Staunton, S. 5(2); Sztybel, J. 1; Taylor, D. 4(7); Taylor, K. 15(7); Tilt, L. (1); Timm, M. 6(3); Westwood, C. 26(3); Wrack, D. 7; Wright, M. 23(7).

Goals – League (47): Fryatt 11 (4 pens), Leitao 5, Constable 3, Smith G 3, Westwood 3, Demontagnac 2, Keates 2 (1 pen), Osborn 2, Skora 2, Taylor K 2, Wright 2, Barrowman 1, Bennett 1, Claridge 1, Devlin 1, James 1, Leary 1, Smith P 1, Timm 1, own goals 2.

Carling Cup (0).

FA Cup (8): James 3, Fryatt 2 (1 pen), Kinsella 1, Leary 1, Leitao 1.

Football League Trophy (6): Constable 2, Bennett 1, Fryatt 1, Leitao 1, Nicholls 1.

Ground: Bescot Stadium, Bescot Crescent, Walsall WS1 4SA. Telephone (0870) 442 0442.

Record Attendance: 11,037 v Wolverhampton W, Division 1, 11 January 2003.

Capacity: 11,126.

Manager: Richard Money.

Secretary: K. R. Whalley.

Most League Goals: 102, Division 4, 1959–60.

Highest League Scorer in Season: Gilbert Alsop, 40, Division 3 (N), 1933–34 and 1934–35.

Most League Goals in Total Aggregate: Tony Richards, 184, 1954–63; Colin Taylor, 184, 1958–63, 1964–68, 1969–73.

Most Capped Player: Mick Kearns, 15 (18), Republic of Ireland.

Most League Appearances: Colin Harrison, 467, 1964–82.

Honours – Football League: Division 4 Champions – 1959–60.

Colours: Red shirts, white shorts, red stockings.

WATFORD   FA PREMIERSHIP

Bangura Al Hassan (M)	5 8	10 07	Sierra Leone	24 1 88	Scholar
Blizzard Dominic (M)	6 2	13 05	High Wycombe	2 9 83	Scholar
Bouazza Hameur (F)	5 11	12 01	Evry	22 2 85	Scholar

Campana Alex (M)	5 11	12 01	Harrow	11 10 88	Scholar
Carlisle Clarke (D)	6 2	14 11	Preston	14 10 79	Leeds U
Chamberlain Alec (G)	6 2	14 00	March	20 6 64	Sunderland
Chambers James (D)	5 10	12 05	Sandwell	20 11 80	WBA
DeMerit Jay (D)	6 1	13 05	Wisconsin	4 12 79	Northwood
Diagouraga Toumani (M)	6 2	11 05	Paris	10 6 87	Scholar
Doyley Lloyd (M)	5 10	12 05	Whitechapel	1 12 82	Scholar
Ferdinand Les (F)	5 11	13 05	Acton	8 12 66	Reading
Francis Fran (M)	6 2	14 03	Jamaica	18 1 87	Stoke C
Gill Ben (M)	5 9	10 11	Harrow	9 10 87	Scholar
Grant Joel (F)	6 0	12 01	Acton	26 8 87	Scholar
Henderson Darius (F)	6 3	14 03	Sutton	7 9 81	Gillingham
King Marlon (F)	5 10	12 10	Dulwich	26 4 80	Nottingham F
Lee Richard (G)	6 0	13 03	Oxford	5 10 82	Scholar
Mackay Malky (D)	6 2	14 07	Bellshill	19 2 72	West Ham U
Mahon Gavin (M)	6 0	13 00	Birmingham	2 1 77	Brentford
Mariappa Adrian (D)	5 10	11 12	Harrow	3 10 86	Scholar
McNamee Anthony (M)	5 6	9 11	Lambeth	13 7 84	Scholar
Osborne Junior (M)	5 10	12 03	Watford	12 2 88	Scholar
Robinson Theo (M)	5 11	11 00	Birmingham	22 1 89	Scholar
Spring Matthew (M)	5 11	12 05	Harlow	17 11 79	Leeds U
Stewart Jordan (D)	6 0	12 09	Birmingham	3 3 82	Leicester C
Young Ashley (M)	5 9	9 13	Stevenage	9 7 85	Juniors

League Appearances: Agbonlahor, G. 1(1); Bangura, A. 11(24); Benjamin, T. 2; Blizzard, D. 9(1); Bouazza, H. 3(11); Carlisle, C. 30(2); Chamberlain, A. 2(1); Chambers, J. 26(12); DeMerit, J. 27(5); Devlin, P. 21(2); Diagouraga, T. 1; Doyley, L. 40(4); Eagles, C. 16(1); Fletcher, C. 3; Foster, B. 44; Francis, F. (1); Grant, J. 2(5); Henderson, D. 27(3); King, M. 40(1); MacKay, M. 35(3); Mahon, G. 35(3); Mariappa, A. 1(2); McNamee, A. 26(12); Osborne, J. 1; Robinson, T. (1); Spring, M. 36(3); Stewart, J. 29(6); Young, A. 38(1).

Goals – League (77): King 21 (1 pen), Henderson 14, Young 13, Spring 8, Carlisle 3, Eagles 3, MacKay 3, Mahon 3, DeMerit 2, Devlin 2, Bangura 1, Bouazza 1, McNamee 1, own goals 2.

Carling Cup (5): Carlisle 2, Blizzard 1, Bouazza 1 (pen), Young 1.

FA Cup (0).

Play-Offs (6): Demerit 1, Henderson 1 (pen), King 1, Spring 1, Young 1, own goal 1.

Ground: Vicarage Road Stadium, Vicarage Road, Watford, Herts WD18 0ER. Telephone (0870) 111 1881.

Record Attendance: 34,099 v Manchester U, FA Cup 4th rd (replay), 3 February 1969. **Capacity:** 19,920.

Manager: Adrian Boothroyd.

Secretary: Michelle Ives.

Most League Goals: 92, Division 4, 1959–60.

Highest League Scorer in Season: Cliff Holton, 42, Division 4, 1959–60.

Most League Goals in Total Aggregate: Luther Blissett, 148, 1976–83, 1984–88, 1991–92.

Most Capped Player: John Barnes, 31 (79), England and Kenny Jackett, 31, Wales.

Most League Appearances: Luther Blissett, 415, 1976–83, 1984–88, 1991–92.

Honours – Football League: Division 3 Champions – 1968–69. Division 2 Champions – 1997–98. Division 4 Champions – 1977–78.

Colours: Yellow shirts, red shorts, red stockings.

WEST BROMWICH ALBION   FL CHAMPIONSHIP

| Albrechtsen Martin (D) | 6 1 | 12 13 | Copenhagen | 30 3 80 | FC Copenhagen |
| Carter Darren (M) | 6 2 | 12 11 | Solihull | 18 12 83 | Birmingham C |

Chaplow Richard (M)	5 9	9 03	Accrington	2 2 85	Burnley
Clement Neil (D)	6 0	12 03	Reading	3 10 78	Chelsea
Davies Curtis (D)	6 2	11 13	Waltham Forest	15 3 85	Luton T
Davies Rob (M)	5 9	11 02	Tywyn	24 3 87	Scholar
Ellington Nathan (F)	5 10	13 01	Bradford	2 7 81	Wigan Ath
Elvins Rob (F)				17 9 86	Scholar
Forsyth Jeff (D)	5 10	12 02		14 10 87	Scholar
Gaardsoe Thomas (D)	6 2	12 08	Randers	23 11 79	Ipswich T
Gera Zoltan (M)	6 0	11 11	Pecs	22 4 79	Ferencvaros
Greening Jonathan (M)	5 11	11 00	Scarborough	2 1 79	Middlesbrough
Hodgkiss Jared (M)	5 6	11 02	Stafford	15 11 86	Scholar
Horsfield Geoff (F)	5 10	11 02	Barnsley	1 11 73	Wigan Ath
Hoult Russell (G)	6 3	14 09	Ashby	22 11 72	Portsmouth
Inamoto Junichi (M)	6 0	11 11	Cogoshima	18 9 79	Fulham
Kamara Diomansy (F)	6 0	11 05	Paris	8 11 80	Portsmouth
Koumas Jason (M)	5 10	11 02	Wrexham	25 9 79	Tranmere R
Kuszczak Tomasz (G)	6 3	13 03	Krosno Odrzansia	20 3 82	Hertha Berlin
Nicholson Stuart (F)	5 10	11 09	Newcastle	3 2 86	Scholar
Quashie Nigel (M)	6 0	13 10	Peckham	20 7 78	Southampton
Robinson Paul (D)	5 9	11 12	Watford	14 12 78	Watford
Wallwork Ronnie (M)	5 10	12 09	Manchester	10 9 77	Manchester U

League Appearances: Albrechtsen, M. 26(5); Campbell, K. 19(10); Carter, D. 11(9); Chaplow, R. 4(3); Clement, N. 29(2); Davies, C. 33; Earnshaw, R. 4(8); Ellington, N. 15(16); Gaardsoe, T. 7; Gera, Z. 12(3); Greening, J. 37(1); Hodgkiss, J. (1); Horsfield, G. 10(8); Hoult, R. (1); Inamoto, J. 16(6); Johnson, A. 8; Kamara, D. 21(5); Kanu, N. 17(8); Kirkland, C. 10; Kozak, J. 4(2); Kuszczak, T. 28; Martinez, W. 11(1); Moore, D. 3(2); Nicholson, S. (4); Quashie, N. 9; Robinson, P. 33; Scimeca, R. 2; Wallwork, R. 31; Watson, S. 28(2).
Goals – League (31): Ellington 5 (1 pen), Kanu 5, Horsfield 4, Campbell 3, Davies 2, Gera 2, Greening 2, Albrechtsen 1, Carter 1, Clement 1, Earnshaw 1, Kamara 1, Martinez 1, Quashie 1, Watson 1.
Carling Cup (8): Ellington 3, Earnshaw 2, Inamoto 1, Kamara 1, Kanu 1.
FA Cup (3): Chaplow 2, Gera 1 (pen).
Ground: The Hawthorns, West Bromwich, West Midlands B71 4LF. Telephone (0870) 066 8888
Record Attendance: 64,815 v Arsenal, FA Cup 6th rd, 6 March 1937. **Capacity:** 28,000.
Manager: Bryan Robson.
Secretary: John Evans.
Most League Goals: 105, Division 2, 1929–30.
Highest League Scorer in Season: William 'Ginger' Richardson, 39, Division 1, 1935–36.
Most League Goals in Total Aggregate: Tony Brown, 218, 1963–79.
Most Capped Player: Stuart Williams, 33 (43), Wales.
Most League Appearances: Tony Brown, 574, 1963–80.
Honours – Football League: Division 1 Champions – 1919–20. Division 2 Champions – 1901–02, 1910–11. **FA Cup:** Winners – 1888, 1892, 1931, 1954, 1968.
Football League Cup: Winners – 1965–66.
Colours: Navy blue and white striped shirts, white shorts, navy blue stockings.

WEST HAM UNITED   FA PREMIERSHIP

Ashton Dean (F)	6 2	14 07	Crewe	24 11 83	Norwich C
Benayoun Yossi (M)	5 10	11 00	Beer Sheva	6 6 80	Santander
Bywater Steve (G)	6 2	12 00	Manchester	7 6 81	Manchester C
Carroll Roy (G)	6 2	13 12	Enniskillen	30 9 77	Manchester U
Clarke Clive (D)	5 11	12 03	Dublin	14 1 80	Stoke C

Cohen Chris (M)	5 11	10 11	Norwich	5 3 87	Scholar
Collins James (D)	6 2	14 05	Newport	23 8 83	Cardiff C
Dailly Christian (D)	6 1	12 10	Dundee	23 10 73	Blackburn R
Ephraim Hogan (F)	5 9	10 06	Islington	31 3 88	Scholar
Etherington Matthew (M)	5 10	10 12	Truro	14 8 81	Tottenham H
Ferdinand Anton (D)	6 2	11 00	Peckham	18 2 85	Trainee
Fitzgerald Lorcan (D)	5 9	10 09	Republic of Ireland	3 1 89	Scholar
Fletcher Carl (M)	5 10	11 07	Camberley	7 4 80	Bournemouth
Gabbidon Daniel (D)	6 0	13 05	Cwmbran	8 8 79	Cardiff C
Harewood Marlon (F)	6 1	13 07	Hampstead	25 8 79	Nottingham F
Hislop Shaka (G)	6 4	14 04	Hackney	22 2 69	Portsmouth
Katan Yaniv (F)	6 1	12 13	Haifa	27 1 81	Maccabi Haifa
Konchesky Paul (D)	5 10	11 07	Barking	15 5 81	Charlton Ath
Mullins Hayden (M)	5 11	11 12	Reading	27 3 79	Crystal Palace
Newton Shaun (M)	5 8	11 00	Camberwell	20 8 75	Wolverhampton W
Noble Mark (M)	5 11	12 00	West Ham	8 5 87	Scholar
Reid Kyel (M)	5 10	12 05	Deptford	26 11 87	Scholar
Reo-Coker Nigel (M)	5 8	12 03	Southwark	14 5 84	Wimbledon
Sheringham Teddy (F)	6 0	12 05	Highams Park	2 4 66	Portsmouth
Stokes Tony (M)	5 10	11 10	Bethnal Green	7 1 87	Scholar
Tomkins James (D)	6 3	11 10	Basildon	29 3 89	Scholar
Walker Jim (G)	5 11	13 04	Sutton-in-Ashfield	9 7 73	Walsall
Ward Elliott (D)	6 2	13 00	Harrow	19 1 85	Scholar
Zamora Bobby (F)	6 1	11 11	Reading	16 1 81	Tottenham H

League Appearances: Aliadiere, J. 1(6); Ashton, D. 9(2); Bellion, D. 2(6); Benayoun, Y. 30(4); Bywater, S. (1); Carroll, R. 19; Clarke, C. 2; Collins, J. 13(1); Dailly, C. 6(16); Etherington, M. 33; Ferdinand, A. 32(1); Fletcher, C. 6(6); Gabbidon, D. 31(1); Harewood, M. 31(6); Hislop, S. 16; Katan, Y. 2(4); Konchesky, P. 36(1); Mullins, H. 35; Newton, S. 8(18); Noble, M. 4(1); Reid, K. 1(1); Reo-Coker, N. 31; Repka, J. 19; Scaloni, L. 13; Sheringham, T. 15(11); Walker, J. 3; Ward, E. 3(1); Zamora, B. 17(17).

Goals – League (52): Harewood 14 (2 pens), Sheringham 6 (1 pen), Zamora 6, Benayoun 5, Reo-Coker 5, Ashton 3, Collins 3, Etherington 2, Ferdinand 2, Fletcher 1, Konchesky 1, Newton 1, own goals 4.

Carling Cup (4): Zamora 2, Bellion 1, Dailly 1.

FA Cup (14): Ashton 3, Harewood 2, Zamora 2, Etherington 1, Konchesky 1, Mullins 1, Sheringham 1 (pen), own goal 3.

Ground: The Boleyn Ground, Green Street, Upton Park, London E13 9AZ. Telephone (020) 8548 2748.

Record Attendance: 42,322 v Tottenham H, Division 1, 17 October 1970. **Capacity:** 35,303.

Manager: Alan Pardew.

Secretary: Peter Barnes.

Most League Goals: 101, Division 2, 1957–58.

Highest League Scorer in Season: Vic Watson, 42, Division 1, 1929–30.

Most League Goals in Total Aggregate: Vic Watson, 298, 1920–35.

Most Capped Player: Bobby Moore, 108, England.

Most League Appearances: Billy Bonds, 663, 1967–88.

Honours – Football League: Division 2 Champions – 1957–58, 1980–81. **FA Cup:** Winners – 1964, 1975, 1980. **European Competitions: European Cup-Winners' Cup:** Winners – 1964–65. **Intertoto Cup:** Winners – 1999.

Colours: Claret shirts with sky blue sleeves, white shorts and sky blue stockings.

WIGAN ATHLETIC   FA PREMIERSHIP

Baines Leighton (D)	5 8	11 10	Liverpool	11 12 84	Trainee
Camara Henri (F)	5 9	10 08	Dakar	10 5 77	Wolverhampton W

Name			Birthplace	Date	Club
Chimbonda Pascal (D)	5 10	11 05	Les Abymes	21 2 79	Bastia
Connolly David (F)	5 9	11 00	Willesden	6 6 77	Leicester C
De Zeeuw Arjan (D)	6 0	13 06	Castricum	16 4 70	Portsmouth
Filan John (G)	6 2	14 06	Sydney	8 2 70	Blackburn R
Francis Damien (M)	6 0	11 10	Wandsworth	27 2 79	Norwich C
Jackson Matt (D)	6 1	14 00	Leeds	19 10 71	Norwich C
Johansson Andreas (M)	5 11	12 05	Vanersborg	5 7 78	Djurgaarden
Kavanagh Graham (M)	5 10	13 02	Dublin	2 12 73	Cardiff C
McCulloch Lee (F)	6 1	13 00	Bellshill	14 5 78	Motherwell
McMillan Steve (D)	5 9	11 12	Edinburgh	19 1 76	Motherwell
Pollitt Mike (G)	6 4	15 03	Farnworth	29 2 72	Rotherham U
Roberts Jason (F)	6 0	12 06	Park Royal	25 1 78	WBA
Scharner Paul (D)	6 3	12 09	Scheibbs	11 3 80	Brann
Skoko Josip (M)	5 9	12 02	Mount Gambier	10 12 75	Genclerbirligi
Taylor Ryan (M)	5 8	10 04	Liverpool	19 8 84	Tranmere R
Teale Gary (F)	5 11	12 00	Glasgow	21 7 78	Ayr U
Wright David (D)	5 11	11 00	Warrington	1 5 80	Crewe Alex

League Appearances: Baines, L. 35(2); Bullard, J. 35(1); Camara, H. 25(4); Chimbonda, P. 37; Connolly, D. 4(13); De Zeeuw, A. 31; Filan, J. 15; Francis, D. 16(4); Henchoz, S. 26; Jackson, M. 11(5); Johansson, A. 6(10); Kavanagh, G. 32(3); Mahon, A. 5(1); McCulloch, L. 27(3); McMillan, S. (2); Mellor, N. 3; Pollitt, M. 23(1); Roberts, J. 34; Scharner, P. 14(2); Skoko, J. 3(2); Taylor, R. 3(8); Teale, G. 20(4); Thompson, D. 7(3); Wright, D. 1(1); Ziegler, R. 5(5).

Goals – League (45): Camara 12, Roberts 8 (1 pen), McCulloch 5, Bullard 4, Johansson 4, Scharner 3, Chimbonda 2, Thompson 2, Connolly 1, Francis 1, Mahon 1, Mellor 1, own goal 1.

Carling Cup (9): Roberts 4, Johansson 2, Connolly 1 (pen), Scharner 1, Taylor 1 (pen).

FA Cup (4): Roberts 2, Connolly 1, Johansson 1.

Ground: JJB Stadium, Robin Park, Newtown, Wigan WN5 0UZ. Telephone (01942) 774 000.

Record Attendance: 27,526 v Hereford U, FA Cup 2nd rd, 12 December 1953 (at Springfield Park). **Capacity:** 25,138.

Manager: Paul Jewell.

Secretary: Stuart Hayton.

Most League Goals: 84, Division 3, 1996–97.

Highest League Scorer in Season: Graeme Jones, 31, Division 3, 1996–97.

Most League Goals in Total Aggregate: Andy Liddell, 70, 1998–2004.

Most Capped Player: Roy Carroll, 9 (17), Northern Ireland.

Most League Appearances: Kevin Langley, 317, 1981–86, 1990–94.

Honours – Football League: Division 2 Champions – 2002–03. Division 3 Champions – 1996–97. **Freight Rover Trophy:** Winners – 1984–85. **Auto Windscreens Shield:** Winners – 1998–99.

Colours: Blue shirts, blue shorts, white stockings.

WOLVERHAMPTON WANDERERS   FL CHAMPIONSHIP

Name			Birthplace	Date	Club
Clarke Leon (F)	6 2	14 02	Birmingham	10 2 85	Trainee
Clyde Mark (D)	6 2	12 04	Limavady	27 12 82	Scholar
Cornes Christopher (M)			Worcester	20 12 86	Scholar
Cort Carl (F)	6 4	12 07	Southwark	1 11 77	Newcastle U
Craddock Jody (D)	6 2	12 00	Bromsgrove	25 7 75	Sunderland
Davies Mark (M)	5 11	11 08	Willenhall	18 2 88	Scholar
Edwards Rob (D)	6 1	11 10	Telford	25 12 82	Aston Villa
Frankowski Tomasz (F)	5 8	10 01	Poland	16 8 74	Elche
Gobern Lewis (M)	5 10	11 07	Birmingham	28 1 85	Scholar
Gyepes Gabor (D)	6 3	13 01	Hungary	26 6 81	Ferencvaros

Player			Birthplace			Previous Club
Hennessey Wayne (G)			Anglesey	24	1 87	Scholar
Ikeme Carl (G)	6 2	13 09	Sutton Coldfield	8	6 86	Scholar
Jones Daniel (D)	6 2	13 00	Rowley Regis	14	7 86	Scholar
Lescott Jolean (D)	6 2	14 00	Birmingham	16	8 82	Trainee
Little Mark (D)			Worcester	20	8 88	Scholar
Lowe Keith (D)	6 2	13 03	Wolverhampton	13	9 85	Scholar
McNamara Jackie (M)	5 9	10 04	Glasgow	24	10 73	Celtic
Murray Matt (G)	6 4	13 10	Solihull	2	5 81	Trainee
Naylor Lee (D)	5 10	12 00	Bloxwich	19	3 80	Trainee
O'Connor Kevin (M)	5 11	12 02	Dublin	19	10 85	Scholar
Oakes Michael (G)	6 2	14 00	Northwich	30	10 73	Aston Villa
Olofinjana Seyi (M)	6 2	13 05	Nigeria	30	6 80	Brann
Ricketts Rohan (M)	5 10	11 07	Clapham	22	12 82	Tottenham H
Riley Martin (D)			Wolverhampton	5	12 86	Scholar
Rosa Denes (M)	5 8	10 05	Hungary	7	4 77	Ferencvaros
Seol Ki-Hyun (F)	6 2	12 08	Seoul	18	1 79	Anderlecht

League Appearances: Aliadiere, J. 12(2); Anderton, D. 20(4); Cameron, C. 20(7); Clarke, L. 10(14); Cort, C. 24(7); Craddock, J. 17(1); Davies, M. 12(8); Edwards, R. 39(3); Frankowski, T. 12(4); Ganea, V. 11(7); Gobern, L. (1); Gyepes, G. 19(1); Huddlestone, T. 12(1); Ince, P. 15(3); Jones, D. 1; Kennedy, M. 37(3); Lescott, J. 46; Lowe, K. 3; McNamara, J. 9(1); Miller, K. 33(2); Murray, M. 1; Naylor, L. 38(2); Ndah, G. 6(8); Oakes, M. 16(1); Olofinjana, S. 6(7); Postma, S. 29; Ricketts, R. 17(8); Rosa, D. 6(3); Ross, M. 13(5); Seol, K. 22(10).
Goals – League (50): Cort 11, Miller 10 (3 pens) Cameron 4, Ganea 4, Seol 4, Ince 3, Aliadiere 2, Kennedy 2, Rosa 2, Anderton 1, Clarke 1, Davies 1, Huddlestone 1, Lescott 1, Naylor 1, Ndah 1, own goal 1.
Carling Cup (6): Cameron 2, Miller 2, Anderton 1, Ganea 1.
FA Cup (1): Clarke 1.
Ground: Molineux, Waterloo Road, Wolverhampton WV1 4QR. Telephone (0870) 442 0123.
Record Attendance: 61,315 v Liverpool, FA Cup 5th rd, 11 February 1939.
Capacity: 29,277.
Manager: TBC.
Secretary: Richard Skirrow.
Most League Goals: 115, Division 2, 1931–32.
Highest League Scorer in Season: Dennis Westcott, 38, Division 1, 1946–47.
Most League Goals in Total Aggregate: Steve Bull, 250, 1986–99.
Most Capped Player: Billy Wright, 105, England (70 consecutive).
Most League Appearances: Derek Parkin, 501, 1967–82.
Honours – Football League: Division 1 Champions – 1953–54, 1957–58, 1958–59. Division 2 Champions – 1931–32, 1976–77. Division 3 (N) Champions – 1923–24. Division 3 Champions – 1988–89. Division 4 Champions – 1987–88. **FA Cup:** Winners – 1893, 1908, 1949, 1960. **Football League Cup:** Winners – 1973–74, 1979–80. **Texaco Cup:** Winners – 1971. **Sherpa Van Trophy:** Winners – 1988.
Colours: Gold and black.

WREXHAM   FL CHAMPIONSHIP 2

Player			Birthplace			Previous Club
Crowell Matt (M)	5 11	10 10	Bridgend	3	7 84	Southampton
Done Matt (M)	5 10	10 04	Oswestry	22	6 88	Scholar
Evans Gareth (D)	6 1	12 12	Wrexham	10	1 87	Scholar
Ferguson Darren (M)	6 0	11 10	Glasgow	9	2 72	Wolverhampton W
Harris Mark (D)	5 11	10 10	Liverpool	15	8 83	Scholar
Holt Andy (M)	6 1	12 07	Stockport	21	5 78	Hull C
Ingham Michael (G)	6 4	13 10	Preston	7	9 80	Sunderland
Jones Mark (M)	5 11	10 12	Wrexham	15	8 83	Scholar
Jones Michael (M)	6 3	13 00	Liverpool	3	12 87	Scholar

Lawrence Dennis (D)	6 7	11 13	Trinidad	1	8 74	Defence Force
Mackin Levi (M)	6 1	12 00	Chester	4	4 86	Scholar
McEvilly Lee (F)	6 0	13 00	Liverpool	15	4 82	Accrington S
Pejic Shaun (D)	6 0	11 07	Hereford	16	11 82	Trainee
Spender Simon (D)	5 11	11 00	Mold	15	11 85	Scholar
Walters Jon (F)	6 0	12 06	Birkenhead	20	9 83	Hull C
Williams Danny (M)	6 1	13 00	Wrexham	12	7 79	Bristol R
Williams Marc (F)	5 10	11 12	Colwyn Bay	27	7 88	Scholar
Williams Mike (D)	5 11	12 00	Colwyn Bay	27	10 86	Scholar

League Appearances: Bayliss, D. 21(1); Bennett, D. 20(13); Crowell, M. 26(3); Derbyshire, M. 16; Done, M. 1(5); Ferguson, D. 36(3); Foy, R. 7(10); Holt, A. 35(1); Ingham, M. 40; Jones, Mark 42; Jones, Michael 6(1); Lawrence, D. 38(1); Linwood, P. 8(1); Mackin, L. 3(14); McEvilly, L. 15(8); Pejic, S. 26; Reed, J. (3); Roche, L. 17; Smith, A. 15(5); Spender, S. 15(4); Ugarte, J. 2; Walters, J. 33(5); Warhurst, P. 6(5); Whitley, J. 10; Williams, D. 45; Williams, Marc 2(2); Williams, Mike 7(5); Williams, S. 14(1).
Goals – League (61): Mark Jones 13, Derbyshire 10, McEvilly 7 (1 pen), Walters 5, Williams D 4, Crowell 3 (2 pens), Foy 3, Holt 3, Bennett 2, Ferguson 2, Lawrence 2, Spender 2, Williams S 2, Roche 1, Warhurst 1, own goal 1.
Carling Cup (0).
FA Cup (1): McEvilly 1.
Football League Trophy (3): Mark Jones 2, Ferguson 1.
Ground: Racecourse Ground, Mold Road, Wrexham LL11 2AH. Telephone (01978) 262 129.
Record Attendance: 34,445 v Manchester U, FA Cup 4th rd, 26 January 1957.
Capacity: 15,500.
Manager: Denis Smith.
Secretary: Geraint Parry.
Most League Goals: 106, Division 3 (N), 1932–33.
Highest League Scorer in Season: Tom Bamford, 44, Division 3 (N), 1933–34.
Most League Goals in Total Aggregate: Tom Bamford, 175, 1928–34.
Most Capped Player: Joey Jones, 29 (72), Wales.
Most League Appearances: Arfon Griffiths, 592, 1959–61, 1962–79.
Honours – Football League: Division 3 Champions – 1977–78. **LDV Vans Trophy:** Winners – 2004–05. **Welsh Cup:** Winners – 22 times.
Colours: Red shirts, white shorts, red stockings.

WYCOMBE WANDERERS　　FL CHAMPIONSHIP 2

Antwi Will (D)	6 2	12 08	Epsom	19	10 82	Aldershot T
Anya Ikechi (M)	5 5	11 04	Glasgow	3	1 88	Scholar
Betsy Kevin (M)	6 1	12 00	Seychelles	20	3 78	Oldham Ath
Bloomfield Matt (M)	5 9	11 00	Ipswich	8	2 84	Ipswich T
Burnell Joe (M)	5 8	12 00	Bristol	10	10 80	Bristol C
Cadmore Tom (D)			Rickmansworth	26	1 88	Scholar
Christon Lewis (M)			Milton Keynes	21	1 89	Scholar
Dixon Jonny (F)	5 9	11 01	Murcia	16	1 84	Scholar
Easter Jermaine (F)	5 9	12 02	Cardiff	15	1 82	Stockport
Easton Clint (M)	5 11	11 00	Barking	1	10 77	Norwich C
Faulkner James (F)			Aylesbury	22	11 87	Scholar
Gregory Steven (D)	6 1	12 04	Haddenham	19	3 87	Scholar
Griffin Charlie (F)	6 0	12 07	Bath	25	6 79	Forest Green R
Johnson Roger (D)	6 3	11 00	Ashford	28	4 83	Trainee
Lee Robert (M)	5 10	11 10	Plaistow	1	2 66	Oldham Ath
Martin Russell (M)	6 0	11 08	Brighton	4	1 86	Lewes
Mooney Tommy (F)	5 10	13 05	Billingham	11	8 71	Oxford U
Oakes Stefan (M)	6 1	13 07	Leicester	6	9 78	Notts Co

Senda Danny (M)	5 10	10 02	Harrow	17 4 81	Southampton
Stonebridge Ian (F)	6 0	11 04	Lewisham	30 8 81	Plymouth Arg
Talia Frank (G)	6 1	13 06	Melbourne	20 7 72	Reading
Torres Sergio (M)	6 2	12 04	Mar del Plata	8 11 83	Basingstoke T
Williams Steve (G)	6 6	13 10	Oxford	21 4 83	Scholar
Williamson Mike (D)	6 4	13 03	Stoke	8 11 83	Southampton

League Appearances: Antwi, W. 5; Anya, I. (2); Betsy, K. 41(1); Bloomfield, M. 35(4); Bowditch, D. 9(2); Burnell, J. 27(6); Collins, A. 3(2); Dixon, J. (17); Duke, M. 5; Easter, J. 8(7); Easton, C. 40(4); Gregory, S. (1); Griffin, C. 13(9); Johnson, R. 45; Keogh, R. 2(1); Lee, R. 28(3); Lonergan, A. 2; Martin, R. 11(12); Mooney, T. 44(1); Oakes, S. 31(6); Senda, D. 44; Stonebridge, I. 8(19); Talia, F. 35; Torres, S. 13(11); Turner, I. 3; Tyson, N. 15; Williams, S. 1; Williamson, M. 38(1).
Goals – League (72): Mooney 17 (3 pens), Tyson 11 (1 pen), Betsy 8, Johnson 7, Bloomfield 5, Williamson 5, Griffin 3, Martin 3, Easter 2, Oakes 2, Stonebridge 2, Bowditch 1, Collins 1, Easton 1, Torres 1, own goals 3.
Carling Cup (6): Tyson 2, Dixon 1, Johnson 1, Mooney 1, Stonebridge 1.
FA Cup (1): Burnell 1.
Football League Trophy (6): Griffin 4 (1 pen), Easton 2.
Play-Offs (1): Mooney 1.
Ground: Adams Park, Hillbottom Road, Sands, High Wycombe HP12 4HJ. Telephone (01494) 472 100.
Record Attendance: 9,650 v Wimbledon, FA Cup 5th rd, 17 February 2001.
Manager: Paul Lambert.
Secretary: Keith J. Allen.
Most League Goals: 72, Championship 2, 2005–06.
Highest League Goalscorer in Season: Sean Devine, 23, 1999–2000.
Most League Goals in Total Aggregate: Nathan Tyson, 42, 2005–06.
Most Capped Player: Mark Rogers, 7, Canada.
Most League Appearances: Steve Brown, 371, 1994–2004.
Honours – GM Vauxhall Conference: Winners – 1993. **FA Trophy:** Winners – 1991, 1993.
Colours: Light blue and dark blue quarters.

YEOVIL TOWN   FL CHAMPIONSHIP 1

Amankwaah Kevin (D)	6 1	12 12	Harrow	19 5 82	Bristol C
Barker Danny (G)	6 1	11 05	Oxford	30 1 87	
Barry Anthony (M)	5 7	10 00	Liverpool	29 5 86	Accrington S
Davies Arron (M)	5 9	11 00	Cardiff	22 6 84	Southampton
Guyett Scott (D)	6 2	13 06	Ascot	20 1 76	Chester C
Harrold Matt (F)	6 1	11 10	Leyton	25 7 84	Brentford
Jevons Phil (F)	5 11	12 00	Liverpool	1 8 79	Grimsby T
Jones Nathan (M)	5 6	10 06	Rhondda	28 5 73	Brighton & HA
Lindegaard Andy (F)	5 8	11 04	Taunton	10 9 80	Westland Sport
Lockwood Adam (D)	6 0	12 07	Wakefield	26 10 81	Reading
McCallum Gavin (M)	5 9	12 00	Mississauga	24 8 87	
Miles Colin (D)	6 0	13 10	Edmonton	6 9 78	Morton
Poole David (M)	5 8	12 00	Manchester	25 11 84	Manchester U
Ramos Francisco (G)	6 3	12 08	Lisbon	9 10 83	
Skiverton Terry (D)	6 1	13 06	Mile End	26 6 75	Wycombe W
Terry Paul (M)	5 10	12 06	Barking	3 4 79	Dagenham & R
Thomas Bradley (D)	6 2	13 00	Forest Green	29 3 84	Eastleigh
Weale Chris (G)	6 2	13 03	Yeovil	9 2 82	Juniors
Webb Daniel (F)	6 1	11 08	Poole	2 7 83	Cambridge U

League Appearances: Alvarez, L. 4; Amankwaah, K. 38; Barry, A. 4; Bastianini, P. 15(5); Cohen, C. 29(1); Collis, S. 21(2); Davies, A. 27(12); Doherty, T. 1; Fontaine, L. 10; Gall, K. 11(26); Guyett, S. 16(5); Harrold, M. 28(14); Jevons, P. 35(3); Johnson, L. 26; Jones, N. 37(6); Lindegaard, A. 14(9); Lockwood, A. 18(2); Melono, A. 1; Miles, C. 18(12); Oliver, L. (3); Poole, D. 20(5); Rocastle, C. 5(3); Rose, M. (1); Skiverton, T. 36; Sodje, E. 17(2); Terry, P. 34(8); Way, D. 15; Weale, C. 25; Webb, D. (4); Williams, D. (1); Wilson, M. 1(1).

Goals – League (54): Jevons 15 (4 pens), Harrold 9, Davies 8, Skiverton 6, Bastianini 3, Gall 2, Johnson 2, Poole 2, Alvarez 1, Amankwaah 1, Cohen 1, Sodje 1, Terry 1, Way 1, own goal 1.

Carling Cup (3): Davies 1, Gall 1, Way 1.

FA Cup (5): Davies 1, Jevons 1, Johnson 1, Terry 1, Way 1.

Football League Trophy (0).

Ground: Huish Park, Lufton Way, Yeovil, Somerset BA22 8YF. Telephone (01935) 423 662.

Record Attendance: 8,612 v Arsenal, FA Cup 3rd rd, 2 January 1993 (16,318 v Sunderland at Huish). **Capacity:** 9,665.

Manager: Russell Slade.

Secretary: Jean Cotton.

Most League Goals: 90, FL Championship 2, 2004–05.

Highest League Goalscorer in Season: Phil Jevons, 27, 2004–05.

Most League Goals in Total Aggregate: Phil Jevons, 42, 2004–06.

Most Capped Player: Andrejs Stolcers, 1 (81), Latvia and Arron Davies, 1, Wales.

Most League Appearances: Lee Johnson, 115, 2003–06.

Honours – Football League: Championship 2 – Winners 2004–05. **Football Conference:** Champions – 2002–03. **FA Trophy:** Winners 2001–02.

Colours: Green and white hooped shirts, white shorts, white stockings.

LEAGUE POSITIONS: FA PREMIER from 1992–93 and DIVISION 1 1980–81 to 1991–92

	2004–05	2003–04	2002–03	2001–02	2000–01	1999–2000	1998–99	1997–98	1996–97	1995–96	1994–95	1993–94	1992–93
Arsenal	2	1	2	1	2	2	2	1	3	5	12	4	10
Aston Villa	10	6	16	8	8	6	6	7	5	4	18	10	2
Barnsley	–	–	–	–	–	–	19	–	–	–	–	–	–
Birmingham C	12	10	13	–	–	–	–	–	–	–	–	–	–
Blackburn R	15	15	6	10	–	–	19	6	13	7	1	2	4
Bolton W	6	8	17	16	–	–	–	18	–	20	–	–	–
Bradford C	–	–	–	–	20	17	–	–	–	–	–	–	–
Brighton & HA	–	–	–	–	–	–	–	–	–	–	–	–	–
Charlton Ath	11	7	12	14	9	–	18	–	–	–	–	–	–
Chelsea	1	2	4	6	6	5	3	4	6	11	11	14	11
Coventry C	–	–	–	–	19	14	15	11	17	16	16	11	15
Crystal Palace	18	–	–	–	–	–	–	20	–	–	19	–	20
Derby Co	–	–	–	19	17	16	8	9	12	–	–	–	–
Everton	4	17	7	15	16	13	14	17	15	6	15	17	13
Fulham	13	9	14	13	–	–	–	–	–	–	–	–	–
Ipswich T	–	–	–	18	5	–	–	–	–	–	22	19	16
Leeds U	–	19	15	5	4	3	4	5	11	13	5	5	17
Leicester C	–	18	–	20	13	8	10	10	9	–	21	–	–
Liverpool	5	4	5	2	3	4	7	3	4	3	4	8	6
Luton T	–	–	–	–	–	–	–	–	–	–	–	–	–
Manchester C	8	16	9	–	18	–	–	–	–	18	17	16	9
Manchester U	3	3	1	3	1	1	1	2	1	1	2	1	1
Middlesbrough	7	11	11	12	14	12	9	–	19	12	–	–	21
Millwall	–	–	–	–	–	–	–	–	–	–	–	–	–
Newcastle U	14	5	3	4	11	11	13	13	2	2	6	3	–
Norwich C	19	–	–	–	–	–	–	–	–	–	20	12	3
Nottingham F	–	–	–	–	–	–	20	–	20	9	3	–	22
Notts Co	–	–	–	–	–	–	–	–	–	–	–	–	–
Oldham Ath	–	–	–	–	–	–	–	–	–	–	–	21	19
Oxford U	–	–	–	–	–	–	–	–	–	–	–	–	–
Portsmouth	16	13	–	–	–	–	–	–	–	–	–	–	–
QPR	–	–	–	–	–	–	–	–	–	19	8	9	5
Sheffield U	–	–	–	–	–	–	–	–	–	–	–	20	14
Sheffield W	–	–	–	–	19	12	16	16	7	15	13	7	7
Southampton	20	12	8	11	10	15	17	12	16	17	10	18	18
Stoke C	–	–	–	–	–	–	–	–	–	–	–	–	–
Sunderland	–	–	20	17	7	7	–	–	18	–	–	–	–
Swansea C	–	–	–	–	–	–	–	–	–	–	–	–	–
Swindon T	–	–	–	–	–	–	–	–	–	–	–	22	–
Tottenham H	9	14	10	9	12	10	11	14	10	8	7	15	8
Watford	–	–	–	–	–	20	–	–	–	–	–	–	–
WBA	17	–	19	–	–	–	–	–	–	–	–	–	–
West Ham U	–	–	18	7	15	9	5	8	14	10	14	13	–
Wimbledon	–	–	–	–	–	18	16	15	8	14	9	6	12
Wolverhampton W	–	20	–	–	–	–	–	–	–	–	–	–	–

1991–92	1990–91	1989–90	1988–89	1987–88	1986–87	1985–86	1984–85	1983–84	1982–83	1981–82	1980–81	
4	1	4	1	6	4	7	7	6	10	5	3	Arsenal
7	17	2	17	–	22	16	10	10	6	11	1	Aston Villa
–	–	–	–	–	–	–	–	–	–	–	–	Barnsley
–	–	–	–	–	–	21	–	20	17	16	13	Birmingham C
–	–	–	–	–	–	–	–	–	–	–	–	Blackburn R
–	–	–	–	–	–	–	–	–	–	–	–	Bolton W
–	–	–	–	–	–	–	–	–	–	–	–	Bradford C
–	–	–	–	–	–	–	–	–	22	13	19	Brighton & HA
–	–	19	14	17	19	–	–	–	–	–	–	Charlton Ath
14	11	5	–	18	14	6	6	–	–	–	–	Chelsea
19	16	12	7	10	10	17	18	19	19	14	16	Coventry C
10	3	15	–	–	–	–	–	–	–	–	22	Crystal Palace
–	20	16	5	15	–	–	–	–	–	–	–	Derby Co
12	9	6	8	4	1	2	1	7	7	8	15	Everton
–	–	–	–	–	–	–	–	–	–	–	–	Fulham
–	–	–	–	–	–	20	17	12	9	2	2	Ipswich T
1	4	–	–	–	–	–	–	–	–	20	9	Leeds U
–	–	–	–	20	19	15	15	–	–	–	21	Leicester C
6	2	1	2	1	2	1	2	1	1	1	5	Liverpool
20	18	17	16	9	7	9	13	16	18	–	–	Luton T
5	5	14	–	–	21	15	–	–	20	10	12	Manchester C
2	6	13	11	2	11	4	4	4	3	3	8	Manchester U
–	–	–	18	–	–	–	–	–	–	22	14	Middlesbrough
–	–	20	10	–	–	–	–	–	–	–	–	Millwall
–	–	–	20	8	17	11	14	–	–	–	–	Newcastle U
18	15	10	4	14	5	–	20	14	14	–	20	Norwich C
8	8	9	3	3	8	8	9	3	5	12	7	Nottingham F
21	–	–	–	–	–	–	–	21	15	15	–	Notts Co
17	–	–	–	–	–	–	–	–	–	–	–	Oldham Ath
–	–	–	–	21	18	18	–	–	–	–	–	Oxford U
–	–	–	–	19	–	–	–	–	–	–	–	Portsmouth
11	12	11	9	5	16	13	19	5	–	–	–	QPR
9	13	–	–	–	–	–	–	–	–	–	–	Sheffield U
3	–	18	15	11	13	5	8	–	–	–	–	Sheffield W
16	14	7	13	12	12	14	5	2	12	7	6	Southampton
–	–	–	–	–	–	–	22	18	13	18	11	Stoke C
–	19	–	–	–	–	–	21	13	16	19	17	Sunderland
–	–	–	–	–	–	–	–	–	21	6	–	Swansea C
–	–	–	–	–	–	–	–	–	–	–	–	Swindon T
15	10	3	6	13	3	10	3	8	4	4	10	Tottenham H
–	–	–	–	20	9	12	11	11	2	–	–	Watford
–	–	–	–	–	–	22	12	17	11	17	4	WBA
22	–	–	19	16	15	3	16	9	8	9	–	West Ham U
13	7	8	12	7	6	–	–	–	–	–	–	Wimbledon
–	–	–	–	–	–	–	22	–	21	18		Wolverhampton W

LEAGUE POSITIONS: DIVISION 1 from 1992–93, CHAMPIONSHIP from 2004–05 and DIVISION 2 1980–81 to 1991–92

	2004–05	2003–04	2002–03	2001–02	2000–01	1999–2000	1998–99	1997–98	1996–97	1995–96	1994–95	1993–94	1992–93
Aston Villa	–	–	–	–	–	–	–	–	–	–	–	–	–
Barnsley	–	–	–	23	16	4	13	–	2	10	6	18	13
Birmingham C	–	–	–	5	5	5	4	7	10	15	–	22	19
Blackburn R	–	–	–	–	2	11	–	–	–	–	–	–	–
Bolton W	–	–	–	–	3	6	6	–	1	–	3	14	–
Bournemouth	–	–	–	–	–	–	–	–	–	–	–	–	–
Bradford C	–	23	19	15	–	–	2	13	21	–	–	–	–
Brentford	–	–	–	–	–	–	–	–	–	–	–	–	22
Brighton & HA	20	–	23	–	–	–	–	–	–	–	–	–	–
Bristol C	–	–	–	–	–	–	24	–	–	–	23	13	15
Bristol R	–	–	–	–	–	–	–	–	–	–	–	–	24
Burnley	13	19	16	7	7	–	–	–	–	22	–	–	–
Bury	–	–	–	–	–	–	22	17	–	–	–	–	–
Cambridge U	–	–	–	–	–	–	–	–	–	–	–	–	23
Cardiff C	16	13	–	–	–	–	–	–	–	–	–	–	–
Carlisle U	–	–	–	–	–	–	–	–	–	–	–	–	–
Charlton Ath	–	–	–	–	–	1	–	4	15	6	15	11	12
Chelsea	–	–	–	–	–	–	–	–	–	–	–	–	–
Coventry C	19	12	20	11	–	–	–	–	–	–	–	–	–
Crewe Alex	21	18	–	22	14	19	18	11	–	–	–	–	–
Crystal Palace	–	6	14	10	21	15	14	–	6	3	–	1	–
Derby Co	4	20	18	–	–	–	–	–	–	2	9	6	8
Fulham	–	–	–	–	1	9	–	–	–	–	–	–	–
Gillingham	22	21	11	12	13	–	–	–	–	–	–	–	–
Grimsby T	–	–	24	19	18	20	11	–	22	17	10	16	9
Huddersfield T	–	–	–	–	22	8	10	16	20	8	–	–	–
Hull C	–	–	–	–	–	–	–	–	–	–	–	–	–
Ipswich T	3	5	7	–	–	3	3	5	4	7	–	–	–
Leeds U	14	–	–	–	–	–	–	–	–	–	–	–	–
Leicester C	15	–	2	–	–	–	–	–	–	5	–	4	6
Leyton Orient	–	–	–	–	–	–	–	–	–	–	–	–	–
Luton T	–	–	–	–	–	–	–	–	–	24	16	20	20
Manchester C	–	–	–	1	–	2	–	22	14	–	–	–	–
Mansfield T	–	–	–	–	–	–	–	–	–	–	–	–	–
Middlesbrough	–	–	–	–	–	–	–	2	–	–	1	9	–
Millwall	10	10	9	4	–	–	–	–	–	22	12	3	7
Newcastle U	–	–	–	–	–	–	–	–	–	–	–	–	1
Norwich C	–	1	8	6	15	12	9	15	13	16	–	–	–
Nottingham F	23	14	6	16	11	14	–	1	–	–	–	–	–
Notts Co	–	–	–	–	–	–	–	–	–	24	7	17	
Oldham Ath	–	–	–	–	–	–	–	–	23	18	14	–	–
Oxford U	–	–	–	–	–	23	12	17	–	–	23	14	
Peterborough U	–	–	–	–	–	–	–	–	–	–	–	24	10
Plymouth Arg	17	–	–	–	–	–	–	–	–	–	–	–	–
Port Vale	–	–	–	–	–	23	21	19	8	12	17	–	–
Portsmouth	–	–	1	17	20	18	19	20	7	21	18	17	3
Preston NE	5	15	12	8	4	–	–	–	–	–	–	–	–
QPR	11	–	–	–	23	10	20	21	9	–	–	–	–
Reading	7	9	4	–	–	–	–	24	18	19	2	–	–

114

	1991–92	1990–91	1989–90	1988–89	1987–88	1986–87	1985–86	1984–85	1983–84	1982–83	1981–82	1980–81
Aston Villa	–	–	–	–	2	–	–	–	–	–	–	–
Barnsley	16	8	19	7	14	11	12	11	14	10	6	–
Birmingham C	–	–	–	23	19	19	–	2	–	–	–	–
Blackburn R	6	19	5	5	5	12	19	5	6	11	10	4
Bolton W	–	–	–	–	–	–	–	–	–	22	19	18
Bournemouth	–	–	22	12	17	–	–	–	–	–	–	–
Bradford C	–	–	23	14	4	10	13	–	–	–	–	–
Brentford	–	–	–	–	–	–	–	–	–	–	–	–
Brighton & HA	23	6	18	19	–	22	11	6	9	–	–	–
Bristol C	17	9	–	–	–	–	–	–	–	–	–	21
Bristol R	13	13	–	–	–	–	–	–	–	–	–	22
Burnley	–	–	–	–	–	–	–	–	–	21	–	–
Bury	–	–	–	–	–	–	–	–	–	–	–	–
Cambridge U	5	–	–	–	–	–	–	22	12	14	13	
Cardiff C	–	–	–	–	–	–	21	15	–	20	19	–
Carlisle U	–	–	–	–	–	–	20	16	7	14	–	–
Charlton Ath	7	16	–	–	–	–	2	17	13	17	13	–
Chelsea	–	–	–	1	–	–	–	1	18	12	12	
Coventry C	–	–	–	–	–	–	–	–	–	–	–	–
Crewe Alex	–	–	–	–	–	–	–	–	–	–	–	–
Crystal Palace	–	–	–	3	6	6	5	15	18	15	15	–
Derby Co	3	–	–	–	–	1	–	–	20	13	16	6
Fulham	–	–	–	–	–	22	9	11	4	–	–	
Gillingham	–	–	–	–	–	–	–	–	–	–	–	–
Grimsby T	19	–	–	–	–	21	15	10	5	19	17	7
Huddersfield T	–	–	–	–	23	17	16	13	12	–	–	–
Hull C	–	24	14	21	15	14	6	–	–	–	–	–
Ipswich T	1	14	9	8	8	5	–	–	–	–	–	–
Leeds U	–	–	1	10	7	4	14	7	10	8	–	–
Leicester C	4	22	13	15	13	–	–	–	–	3	8	–
Leyton Orient	–	–	–	–	–	–	–	–	–	–	22	17
Luton T	–	–	–	–	–	–	–	–	–	–	1	5
Manchester C	–	–	–	2	9	–	–	3	4	–	–	–
Mansfield T	–	–	–	–	–	–	–	–	–	–	–	–
Middlesbrough	2	7	21	–	3	–	21	19	17	16	–	–
Millwall	15	5	–	–	1	16	9	–	–	–	–	–
Newcastle U	20	11	3	–	–	–	–	–	3	5	9	11
Norwich C	–	–	–	–	–	–	1	–	–	–	3	–
Nottingham F	–	–	–	–	–	–	–	20	–	–	–	2
Notts Co	–	4	–	–	–	–	–	–	–	–	–	–
Oldham Ath	–	1	8	16	10	3	8	14	19	7	11	15
Oxford U	21	10	17	17	–	–	–	1	–	–	–	–
Peterborough U	–	–	–	–	–	–	–	–	–	–	–	–
Plymouth Arg	22	18	16	18	16	7	–	–	–	–	–	–
Port Vale	24	15	11	–	–	–	–	–	–	–	–	–
Portsmouth	9	17	12	20	–	2	4	4	16	–	–	–
Preston NE	–	–	–	–	–	–	–	–	–	–	–	20
QPR	–	–	–	–	–	–	–	–	–	1	5	8
Reading	–	–	–	–	22	13	–	–	–	–	–	–

	2004-05	2003-04	2002-03	2001-02	2000-01	1999-2000	1998-99	1997-98	1996-97	1995-96	1994-95	1993-94	1992-93
Rotherham U	24	17	15	21	–	–	–	–	–	–	–	–	–
Sheffield U	8	8	3	13	10	16	8	6	5	9	8	–	–
Sheffield W	–	–	22	20	17	–	–	–	–	–	–	–	–
Shrewsbury T	–	–	–	–	–	–	–	–	–	–	–	–	–
Southend U	–	–	–	–	–	–	–	–	24	14	13	15	18
Stockport Co	–	–	–	24	19	17	16	8	–	–	–	–	–
Stoke C	12	11	21	–	–	–	–	23	12	4	11	10	–
Sunderland	1	3	–	–	–	–	1	3	–	1	20	12	21
Swansea C	–	–	–	–	–	–	–	–	–	–	–	–	–
Swindon T	–	–	–	–	–	24	17	18	19	–	21	–	5
Tranmere R	–	–	–	–	24	13	15	14	11	13	5	5	4
Walsall	–	22	17	18	–	22	–	–	–	–	–	–	–
Watford	18	16	13	14	9	–	5	–	–	23	7	19	16
WBA	–	2	–	2	6	21	12	10	16	11	19	21	–
West Ham U	6	4	–	–	–	–	–	–	–	–	–	–	2
Wigan Ath	2	7	–	–	–	–	–	–	–	–	–	–	–
Wimbledon	–	24	10	9	8	–	–	–	–	–	–	–	–
Wolverhampton W	9	–	5	3	12	7	7	9	3	20	4	8	11
Wrexham	–	–	–	–	–	–	–	–	–	–	–	–	–

LEAGUE POSITIONS: DIVISION 2 from 1992–93, LEAGUE 1 from 2004–05 and DIVISION 3 1980–81 to 1991–92

	2004-05	2003-04	2002-03	2001-02	2000-01	1999-2000	1998-99	1997-98	1996-97	1995-96	1994-95	1993-94	1992-93
Aldershot	–	–	–	–	–	–	–	–	–	–	–	–	–
Barnet	–	–	–	–	–	–	–	–	–	–	–	24	–
Barnsley	13	12	19	–	–	–	–	–	–	–	–	–	–
Birmingham C	–	–	–	–	–	–	–	–	–	–	1	–	–
Blackpool	16	14	13	16	–	22	14	12	7	3	12	20	18
Bolton W	–	–	–	–	–	–	–	–	–	–	–	–	2
Bournemouth	8	9	–	21	7	16	7	9	16	14	19	17	17
Bradford C	11	–	–	–	–	–	–	–	–	6	14	7	10
Brentford	4	17	16	3	14	17	–	21	4	15	2	16	–
Brighton & HA	–	4	–	1	–	–	–	–	–	23	16	14	9
Bristol C	7	3	3	7	9	9	–	2	5	13	–	–	–
Bristol R	–	–	–	–	21	7	13	5	17	10	4	8	–
Burnley	–	–	–	–	–	2	15	20	9	17	–	6	13
Bury	–	–	–	22	16	15	–	–	1	–	–	–	–
Cambridge U	–	–	–	24	19	19	–	–	–	–	20	10	–
Cardiff C	–	–	6	4	–	21	–	–	–	–	22	19	–
Carlisle U	–	–	–	–	–	–	–	23	–	21	–	–	–

1991–92	1990–91	1989–90	1988–89	1987–88	1986–87	1985–86	1984–85	1983–84	1982–83	1981–82	1980–81	
–	–	–	–	–	–	–	–	–	20	7	–	Rotherham U
–	–	2	–	21	9	7	18	–	–	–	–	Sheffield U
–	3	–	–	–	–	–	–	2	6	4	10	Sheffield W
–	–	–	22	18	18	17	8	8	9	18	14	Shrewsbury T
12	–	–	–	–	–	–	–	–	–	–	–	Southend U
–	–	–	–	–	–	–	–	–	–	–	–	Stockport Co
–	–	24	13	11	8	10	–	–	–	–	–	Stoke C
18	–	6	11	–	20	18	–	–	–	–	–	Sunderland
–	–	–	–	–	–	–	21	–	–	–	3	Swansea C
8	21	4	6	12	–	–	–	–	–	–	–	Swindon T
14	–	–	–	–	–	–	–	–	–	–	–	Tranmere R
–	–	–	24	–	–	–	–	–	–	–	–	Walsall
10	20	15	4	–	–	–	–	–	–	2	9	Watford
–	23	20	9	20	15	–	–	–	–	–	–	WBA
–	2	7	–	–	–	–	–	–	–	–	1	West Ham U
–	–	–	–	–	–	–	–	–	–	–	–	Wigan Ath
–	–	–	–	–	–	3	12	–	–	–	–	Wimbledon
11	12	10	–	–	–	–	22	–	2	–	–	Wolverhampton W
–	–	–	–	–	–	–	–	–	–	21	16	Wrexham

1991–92	1990–91	1989–90	1988–89	1987–88	1986–87	1985–86	1984–85	1983–84	1982–83	1981–82	1980–81	
–	–	–	24	20	–	–	–	–	–	–	–	Aldershot
–	–	–	–	–	–	–	–	–	–	–	–	Barnet
–	–	–	–	–	–	–	–	–	–	–	2	Barnsley
2	12	7	–	–	–	–	–	–	–	–	–	Birmingham C
–	–	23	19	10	9	12	–	–	–	–	23	Blackpool
13	4	6	10	–	21	18	17	10	–	–	–	Bolton W
8	9	–	–	–	1	15	10	17	14	–	–	Bournemouth
16	8	–	–	–	–	–	1	7	12	–	–	Bradford C
1	6	13	7	12	11	10	13	20	9	8	9	Brentford
–	–	–	–	2	–	–	–	–	–	–	–	Brighton & HA
–	–	2	11	5	6	9	5	–	–	23	–	Bristol C
–	–	1	5	8	19	16	6	5	7	15	–	Bristol R
–	–	–	–	–	–	–	21	12	–	1	8	Burnley
21	7	5	13	14	16	20	–	–	–	–	–	Bury
–	1	–	–	–	–	–	24	–	–	–	–	Cambridge U
–	–	21	16	–	–	22	–	–	–	2	–	Cardiff C
–	–	–	–	–	22	–	–	–	–	2	19	Carlisle U

LEAGUE POSITIONS: DIVISION 2 from 1992–93, LEAGUE 1 from 2004–05 and DIVISION 3 1980–81 to 1991–92 (cont.)

	2004-05	2003-04	2002-03	2001-02	2000-01	1999-2000	1998-99	1997-98	1996-97	1995-96	1994-95	1993-94	1992-93
Charlton Ath	–	–	–	–	–	–	–	–	–	–	–	–	–
Cheltenham T	–	–	21	–	–	–	–	–	–	–	–	–	–
Chester C	–	–	–	–	–	–	–	–	–	–	23	–	24
Chesterfield	17	20	20	18	–	24	9	10	10	7	–	–	–
Colchester U	15	11	12	15	17	18	18	–	–	–	–	–	–
Crewe Alex	–	–	2	–	–	–	–	–	6	5	3	–	–
Darlington	–	–	–	–	–	–	–	–	–	–	–	–	–
Derby Co	–	–	–	–	–	–	–	–	–	–	–	–	–
Doncaster R	10	–	–	–	–	–	–	–	–	–	–	–	–
Exeter C	–	–	–	–	–	–	–	–	–	–	–	22	19
Fulham	–	–	–	–	–	1	6	–	–	–	–	21	12
Gillingham	–	–	–	–	–	3	4	8	11	–	–	–	–
Grimsby T	–	21	–	–	–	–	–	3	–	–	–	–	–
Hartlepool U	6	6	–	–	–	–	–	–	–	–	–	–	–
Huddersfield T	9	–	22	6	–	–	–	–	–	–	5	11	15
Hull C	2	–	–	–	–	–	–	–	–	24	8	9	20
Leyton Orient	–	–	–	–	–	–	–	–	–	–	24	18	7
Lincoln C	–	–	–	–	–	23	–	–	–	–	–	–	–
Luton T	1	10	9	–	22	13	12	17	3	–	–	–	–
Macclesfield T	–	–	–	–	–	–	24	–	–	–	–	–	–
Manchester C	–	–	–	–	–	–	3	–	–	–	–	–	–
Mansfield T	–	–	23	–	–	–	–	–	–	–	–	–	22
Middlesbrough	–	–	–	–	–	–	–	–	–	–	–	–	–
Millwall	–	–	–	–	1	5	10	18	14	–	–	–	–
Newport Co	–	–	–	–	–	–	–	–	–	–	–	–	–
Northampton T	–	–	24	20	18	–	22	4	–	–	–	–	–
Notts Co	–	23	15	19	8	8	16	–	24	4	–	–	–
Oldham Ath	19	15	5	9	15	14	20	13	–	–	–	–	–
Oxford U	–	–	–	–	24	20	–	–	–	–	2	7	–
Peterborough U	23	18	11	17	12	–	–	–	21	19	15	–	–
Plymouth Arg	–	1	8	–	–	–	–	22	19	–	21	3	14
Portsmouth	–	–	–	–	–	–	–	–	–	–	–	–	–
Port Vale	18	7	17	14	11	–	–	–	–	–	–	2	3
Preston NE	–	–	–	–	–	1	5	15	15	–	–	–	21
QPR	–	2	4	8	–	–	–	–	–	–	–	–	–
Reading	–	–	–	2	3	10	11	–	–	–	–	1	8
Rotherham U	–	–	–	–	2	–	–	–	23	16	17	15	11
Rushden & D	–	22	–	–	–	–	–	–	–	–	–	–	–
Scunthorpe U	–	–	–	–	–	23	–	–	–	–	–	–	–
Sheffield U	–	–	–	–	–	–	–	–	–	–	–	–	–
Sheffield W	5	16	–	–	–	–	–	–	–	–	–	–	–
Shrewsbury T	–	–	–	–	–	–	–	–	22	18	18	–	–
Southend U	–	–	–	–	–	–	–	24	–	–	–	–	–
Stockport Co	24	19	14	–	–	–	–	–	2	9	11	4	6
Stoke C	–	–	–	5	5	6	8	–	–	–	–	–	1
Sunderland	–	–	–	–	–	–	–	–	–	–	–	–	–
Swansea C	–	–	–	–	23	–	–	–	–	22	10	13	5
Swindon T	12	5	10	13	20	–	–	–	–	–	1	–	–
Torquay U	21	–	–	–	–	–	–	–	–	–	–	–	–

1991–92	1990–91	1989–90	1988–89	1987–88	1986–87	1985–86	1984–85	1983–84	1982–83	1981–82	1980–81	
–	–	–	–	–	–	–	–	–	–	–	3	Charlton Ath
–	–	–	–	–	–	–	–	–	–	–	–	Cheltenham T
18	19	16	8	15	15	–	–	–	–	24	18	Chester C
–	–	–	22	18	17	17	–	–	24	11	5	Chesterfield
–	–	–	–	–	–	–	–	–	–	–	22	Colchester U
–	22	12	–	–	–	–	–	–	–	–	–	Crewe Alex
24	–	–	–	–	23	13	–	–	–	–	–	Darlington
–	–	–	–	–	–	3	7	–	–	–	–	Derby Co
–	–	–	24	13	11	14	–	23	19	–	–	Doncaster R
20	16	–	–	–	–	–	–	24	19	18	11	Exeter C
9	21	20	4	9	18	–	–	–	–	3	13	Fulham
–	–	–	23	13	5	5	4	8	13	6	15	Gillingham
–	3	–	22	–	–	–	–	–	–	–	–	Grimsby T
11	–	–	–	–	–	–	–	–	–	–	–	Hartlepool U
3	11	8	14	–	–	–	3	–	3	17	4	Huddersfield T
14	–	–	–	–	–	–	3	4	–	–	24	Hull C
10	13	14	–	–	–	–	22	11	20	–	–	Leyton Orient
–	–	–	–	–	–	21	19	14	6	4	–	Lincoln C
–	–	–	–	–	–	–	–	–	–	–	–	Luton T
–	–	–	–	–	–	–	–	–	–	–	–	Macclesfield T
–	–	–	–	–	–	–	–	–	–	–	–	Manchester C
–	24	15	15	19	10	–	–	–	–	–	–	Mansfield T
–	–	–	–	–	2	–	–	–	–	–	–	Middlesbrough
–	–	–	–	–	–	–	2	9	17	9	16	Millwall
–	–	–	–	23	19	18	13	4	16	12	–	Newport Co
–	–	22	20	6	–	–	–	–	–	–	–	Northampton T
–	–	3	9	4	7	8	–	–	–	–	–	Notts Co
–	–	–	–	–	–	–	–	–	–	–	–	Oldham Ath
–	–	–	–	–	–	–	–	1	5	5	14	Oxford U
6	–	–	–	–	–	–	–	–	–	–	–	Peterborough U
–	–	–	–	–	–	2	15	19	8	10	7	Plymouth Arg
–	–	–	–	–	–	–	–	–	1	13	6	Portsmouth
–	–	–	3	11	12	–	–	23	–	–	–	Port Vale
17	17	19	6	16	–	–	23	16	16	14	–	Preston NE
–	–	–	–	–	–	–	–	–	–	–	–	QPR
12	15	10	18	–	–	1	9	–	21	12	10	Reading
–	23	9	–	21	14	14	12	18	–	–	1	Rotherham U
–	–	–	–	–	–	–	–	–	–	–	–	Rushden & D
–	–	–	–	–	–	–	21	–	–	–	–	Scunthorpe U
–	–	–	2	–	–	–	–	3	11	–	21	Sheffield U
–	–	–	–	–	–	–	–	–	–	–	–	Sheffield W
22	18	11	–	–	–	–	–	–	–	–	–	Shrewsbury T
–	2	–	21	17	–	–	–	22	15	7	–	Southend U
5	–	–	–	–	–	–	–	–	–	–	–	Stockport Co
4	14	–	–	–	–	–	–	–	–	–	–	Stoke C
–	–	–	–	1	–	–	–	–	–	–	–	Sunderland
19	20	17	12	–	–	24	20	–	–	–	–	Swansea C
–	–	–	–	–	3	–	–	–	–	22	17	Swindon T
23	–	–	–	–	–	–	–	–	–	–	–	Torquay U

LEAGUE POSITIONS: DIVISION 2 from 1992–93, LEAGUE 1 from 2004–05 and DIVISION 3 1980–81 to 1991–92 (cont.)

	2004-05	2003-04	2002-03	2001-02	2000-01	1999-2000	1998-99	1997-98	1996-97	1995-96	1994-95	1993-94	1992-93
Tranmere R	3	8	7	12	–	–	–	–	–	–	–	–	–
Walsall	14	–	–	–	4	–	2	19	12	11	–	–	–
Watford	–	–	–	–	–	–	1	13	–	–	–	–	–
WBA	–	–	–	–	–	–	–	–	–	–	–	–	4
Wigan Ath	–	–	1	10	6	4	6	11	–	–	–	–	23
Wimbledon	20†	–	–	–	–	–	–	–	–	–	–	–	–
Wolverhampton W	–	–	–	–	–	–	–	–	–	–	–	–	–
Wrexham	22	13	–	23	10	11	17	7	8	8	13	12	–
Wycombe W	–	24	18	11	13	12	19	14	18	12	6	–	–
York C	–	–	–	–	–	21	16	20	20	9	5	–	

† As Milton Keynes D

LEAGUE POSITIONS: DIVISION 3 from 1992–93, LEAGUE 2 from 2004–05 and DIVISION 4 1980–81 to 1991–92

	2004-05	2003-04	2002-03	2001-02	2000-01	1999-2000	1998-99	1997-98	1996-97	1995-96	1994-95	1993-94	1992-93
Aldershot	–	–	–	–	–	–	–	–	–	–	–	–	–
Barnet	–	–	–	–	24	6	16	7	15	9	11	–	3
Blackpool	–	–	–	–	7	–	–	–	–	–	–	–	–
Bolton W	–	–	–	–	–	–	–	–	–	–	–	–	–
Boston U	16	11	15	–	–	–	–	–	–	–	–	–	–
Bournemouth	–	–	4	–	–	–	–	–	–	–	–	–	–
Bradford C	–	–	–	–	–	–	–	–	–	–	–	–	–
Brentford	–	–	–	–	–	–	1	–	–	–	–	–	–
Brighton & HA	–	–	–	–	1	11	17	23	23	–	–	–	–
Bristol C	–	–	–	–	–	–	–	–	–	–	–	–	–
Bristol R	12	15	20	23	–	–	–	–	–	–	–	–	–
Burnley	–	–	–	–	–	–	–	–	–	–	–	–	–
Bury	17	12	7	–	–	–	–	–	–	3	4	13	7
Cambridge U	24	13	12	–	–	–	2	16	10	16	–	–	–
Cardiff C	–	–	–	–	2	–	3	21	7	22	–	–	1
Carlisle U	–	23	22	17	22	23	23	–	3	–	1	7	18
Cheltenham T	14	14	–	4	9	8	–	–	–	–	–	–	–
Chester C	20	–	–	–	–	24	14	14	6	8	–	2	–
Chesterfield	–	–	–	–	3	–	–	–	–	–	3	8	12
Colchester U	–	–	–	–	–	–	–	4	8	7	10	17	10
Crewe Alex	–	–	–	–	–	–	–	–	–	–	–	3	6

*Record expunged

	1991–92	1990–91	1989–90	1988–89	1987–88	1986–87	1985–86	1984–85	1983–84	1982–83	1981–82	1980–81
Tranmere R	–	5	4	–	–	–	–	–	–	–	–	–
Walsall	–	–	24	–	3	8	6	11	6	10	20	20
Watford	–	–	–	–	–	–	–	–	–	–	–	–
WBA	7	–	–	–	–	–	–	–	–	–	–	–
Wigan Ath	15	10	18	17	7	4	4	16	15	18	–	–
Wimbledon	–	–	–	–	–	–	–	2	–	21	–	–
Wolverhampton W	–	–	–	1	–	–	23	–	–	–	–	–
Wrexham	–	–	–	–	–	–	–	–	–	22	–	–
Wycombe W	–	–	–	–	–	–	–	–	–	–	–	–
York C	–	–	–	23	20	7	8	–	–	–	–	–

	1991–92	1990–91	1989–90	1988–89	1987–88	1986–87	1985–86	1984–85	1983–84	1982–83	1981–82	1980–81
Aldershot	*	23	22	–	–	6	16	13	5	18	16	6
Barnet	7	–	–	–	–	–	–	–	–	–	–	–
Blackpool	4	5	–	–	–	–	2	6	21	12	–	–
Bolton W	–	–	–	3	–	–	–	–	–	–	–	–
Boston U	–	–	–	–	–	–	–	–	–	–	–	–
Bournemouth	–	–	–	–	–	–	–	–	–	–	4	13
Bradford C	–	–	–	–	–	–	–	–	–	–	2	14
Brentford	–	–	–	–	–	–	–	–	–	–	–	–
Brighton & HA	–	–	–	–	–	–	–	4	14	–	–	–
Bristol C	–	–	–	–	–	–	–	–	–	–	–	–
Bristol R	–	–	–	–	–	–	–	–	–	–	–	–
Burnley	1	6	16	16	10	22	14	–	–	–	–	–
Bury	–	–	–	–	–	–	4	15	5	9	12	–
Cambridge U	–	–	6	8	15	11	22	–	–	–	–	–
Cardiff C	9	13	–	–	2	13	–	–	–	–	–	–
Carlisle U	22	20	8	12	23	–	–	–	–	–	–	–
Cheltenham T	–	–	–	–	–	–	–	–	–	–	–	–
Chester C	–	–	–	–	–	2	16	24	13	–	–	–
Chesterfield	13	18	7	–	–	–	1	13	–	–	–	–
Colchester U	–	–	24	22	9	5	6	7	8	6	6	–
Crewe Alex	6	–	–	3	17	17	12	10	16	23	24	18

LEAGUE POSITIONS: DIVISION 3 from 1992–93, LEAGUE 2 from 2004–05 and DIVISION 4 1980–81 to 1991–92 (cont.)

	2004–05	2003–04	2002–03	2001–02	2000–01	1999–2000	1998–99	1997–98	1996–97	1995–96	1994–95	1993–94	1992–93
Darlington	8	18	14	15	20	4	11	19	18	5	20	21	15
Doncaster R	–	1	–	–	–	–	–	24	19	13	9	15	16
Exeter C	–	–	23	16	19	21	12	15	22	14	22	–	–
Fulham	–	–	–	–	–	–	–	–	2	17	8	–	–
Gillingham	–	–	–	–	–	–	–	–	–	2	19	16	21
Grimsby T	18	–	–	–	–	–	–	–	–	–	–	–	–
Halifax T	–	–	–	24	23	18	10	–	–	–	–	–	22
Hartlepool U	–	–	2	7	4	7	22	17	20	20	18	–	–
Hereford U	–	–	–	–	–	–	–	–	24	6	16	20	17
Huddersfield T	–	4	–	–	–	–	–	–	–	–	–	–	–
Hull C	–	2	13	11	6	14	21	22	17	–	–	–	–
Kidderminster H	23	16	11	10	16	–	–	–	–	–	–	–	–
Leyton Orient	11	19	18	18	5	19	6	11	16	21	–	–	–
Lincoln C	6	7	6	22	18	15	–	3	9	18	12	18	8
Luton T	–	–	–	2	–	–	–	–	–	–	–	–	–
Macclesfield T	5	20	16	13	14	13	–	2	–	–	–	–	–
Maidstone U	–	–	–	–	–	–	–	–	–	–	–	–	–
Mansfield T	13	5	–	3	13	17	8	12	11	19	6	12	–
Newport Co	–	–	–	–	–	–	–	–	–	–	–	–	–
Northampton T	7	6	–	–	–	3	–	–	4	11	17	22	20
Notts Co	19	–	–	–	–	–	–	1	–	–	–	–	–
Oxford U	15	9	8	21	–	–	–	–	–	–	–	–	–
Peterborough U	–	–	–	–	–	5	9	10	–	–	–	–	–
Plymouth Arg	–	–	–	1	12	12	13	–	–	4	–	–	–
Port Vale	–	–	–	–	–	–	–	–	–	–	–	–	–
Preston NE	–	–	–	–	–	–	–	–	–	1	5	5	–
Reading	–	–	–	–	–	–	–	–	–	–	–	–	–
Rochdale	9	21	19	5	8	10	19	18	14	15	15	9	11
Rotherham U	–	–	–	–	–	2	5	9	–	–	–	–	–
Rushden & D	22	–	1	6	–	–	–	–	–	–	–	–	–
Scarborough	–	–	–	–	–	–	24	6	12	23	21	14	13
Scunthorpe U	2	22	5	8	10	–	4	8	13	12	7	11	14
Sheffield U	–	–	–	–	–	–	–	–	–	–	–	–	–
Shrewsbury T	21	–	24	9	15	22	15	13	–	–	–	1	9
Southend U	4	17	17	12	11	16	18	–	–	–	–	–	–
Stockport Co	–	–	–	–	–	–	–	–	–	–	–	–	–
Swansea C	3	10	21	20	–	1	7	20	5	–	–	–	–
Swindon T	–	–	–	–	–	–	–	–	–	–	–	–	–
Torquay U	–	3	9	19	21	9	20	5	21	24	13	6	19
Tranmere R	–	–	–	–	–	–	–	–	–	–	–	–	–
Walsall	–	–	–	–	–	–	–	–	–	–	2	10	5
Wigan Ath	–	–	–	–	–	–	–	–	1	10	14	19	–
Wimbledon	–	–	–	–	–	–	–	–	–	–	–	–	–
Wolverhampton W	–	–	–	–	–	–	–	–	–	–	–	–	–
Wrexham	–	–	3	–	–	–	–	–	–	–	–	–	2
Wycombe W	10	–	–	–	–	–	–	–	–	–	–	4	–
Yeovil T	1	8	–	–	–	–	–	–	–	–	–	–	–
York C	–	24	10	14	17	20	–	–	–	–	–	–	4

1991-92	1990-91	1989-90	1988-89	1987-88	1986-87	1985-86	1984-85	1983-84	1982-83	1981-82	1980-81	Club
–	1	–	24	13	–	–	3	14	17	13	8	Darlington
21	11	20	23	–	–	–	–	2	–	–	3	Doncaster R
–	–	1	13	22	14	21	18	–	–	–	–	Exeter C
–	–	–	–	–	–	–	–	–	–	–	–	Fulham
11	15	14	–	–	–	–	–	–	–	–	–	Gillingham
–	–	2	9	–	–	–	–	–	–	–	–	Grimsby T
20	22	23	21	18	15	20	21	21	11	19	23	Halifax T
–	3	19	19	16	18	7	19	23	22	14	9	Hartlepool U
17	17	17	15	19	16	10	5	11	24	10	22	Hereford U
–	–	–	–	–	–	–	–	2	8	–	–	Huddersfield T
–	–	–	–	–	–	–	–	–	–	–	–	Hull C
–	–	–	–	–	–	–	–	–	–	–	–	Kidderminster H
–	–	–	6	8	7	5	–	–	–	–	–	Leyton Orient
10	14	10	10	–	24	–	–	–	–	–	2	Lincoln C
–	–	–	–	–	–	–	–	–	–	–	–	Luton T
–	–	–	–	–	–	–	–	–	–	–	–	Macclesfield T
18	19	5	–	–	–	–	–	–	–	–	–	Maidstone U
3	–	–	–	–	–	3	14	19	10	20	7	Mansfield T
–	–	–	–	24	–	–	–	–	–	–	–	Newport Co
16	10	–	–	–	1	8	23	18	15	22	10	Northampton T
–	–	–	–	–	–	–	–	–	–	–	–	Notts Co
–	–	–	–	–	–	–	–	–	–	–	–	Oxford U
–	4	9	17	7	10	17	11	7	9	5	5	Peterborough U
–	–	–	–	–	–	–	–	–	–	–	–	Plymouth Arg
–	–	–	–	–	–	4	12	–	3	7	19	Port Vale
–	–	–	–	–	2	23	–	–	–	–	–	Preston NE
–	–	–	–	–	–	–	–	3	–	–	–	Reading
8	12	12	18	21	21	18	17	22	20	21	15	Rochdale
2	–	–	1	–	–	–	–	–	–	–	–	Rotherham U
–	–	–	–	–	–	–	–	–	–	–	–	Rushden & D
12	9	18	5	12	–	–	–	–	–	–	–	Scarborough
5	8	11	4	4	8	15	9	–	4	23	16	Scunthorpe U
–	–	–	–	–	–	–	–	–	–	1	–	Sheffield U
–	–	–	–	–	–	–	–	–	–	–	–	Shrewsbury T
–	–	3	–	–	3	9	20	–	–	–	1	Southend U
–	2	4	20	20	19	11	22	12	16	18	20	Stockport Co
–	–	–	6	12	–	–	–	–	–	–	–	Swansea C
–	–	–	–	–	–	1	8	17	8	–	–	Swindon T
–	7	15	14	5	23	24	24	9	12	15	17	Torquay U
–	–	–	2	14	20	19	6	10	19	11	21	Tranmere R
15	16	–	–	–	–	–	–	–	–	–	–	Walsall
–	–	–	–	–	–	–	–	–	–	3	11	Wigan Ath
–	–	–	–	–	–	–	–	–	1	–	4	Wimbledon
–	–	–	–	1	4	–	–	–	–	–	–	Wolverhampton W
14	24	21	7	11	9	13	15	20	–	–	–	Wrexham
–	–	–	–	–	–	–	–	–	–	–	–	Wycombe W
–	–	–	–	–	–	–	–	–	–	–	–	Yeovil T
19	21	13	11	–	–	–	–	1	7	17	24	York C

LEAGUE CHAMPIONSHIP HONOURS

FA PREMIER LEAGUE

Maximum points: 126

	First	*Pts*	*Second*	*Pts*	*Third*	*Pts*
1992–93	Manchester U	84	Aston Villa	74	Norwich C	72
1993–94	Manchester U	92	Blackburn R	84	Newcastle U	77
1994–95	Blackburn R	89	Manchester U	88	Nottingham F	77

Maximum points: 114

1995–96	Manchester U	82	Newcastle U	78	Liverpool	71
1996–97	Manchester U	75	Newcastle U*	68	Arsenal*	68
1997–98	Arsenal	78	Manchester U	77	Liverpool	65
1998–99	Manchester U	79	Arsenal	78	Chelsea	75
1999–00	Manchester U	91	Arsenal	73	Leeds U	69
2000–01	Manchester U	80	Arsenal	70	Liverpool	69
2001–02	Arsenal	87	Liverpool	80	Manchester U	77
2002–03	Manchester U	83	Arsenal	78	Newcastle U	69
2003–04	Arsenal	90	Chelsea	79	Manchester U	75
2004–05	Chelsea	95	Arsenal	83	Manchester U	77
2005–06	Chelsea	91	Manchester U	83	Liverpool	82

FOOTBALL LEAGUE CHAMPIONSHIP

Maximum points: 138

2004–05	Sunderland	94	Wigan Ath	87	Ipswich T††	85
2005–06	Reading	106	Sheffield U	90	Watford	81

DIVISION 1

Maximum points: 138

1992–93	Newcastle U	96	West Ham U*	88	Portsmouth††	88
1993–94	Crystal Palace	90	Nottingham F	83	Millwall††	74
1994–95	Middlesbrough	82	Reading††	79	Bolton W	77
1995–96	Sunderland	83	Derby Co	79	Crystal Palace††	75
1996–97	Bolton W	98	Barnsley	80	Wolverhampton W††	76
1997–98	Nottingham F	94	Middlesbrough	91	Sunderland††	90
1998–99	Sunderland	105	Bradford C	87	Ipswich T††	86
1999–00	Charlton Ath	91	Manchester C	89	Ipswich T	87
2000–01	Fulham	101	Blackburn R	91	Bolton W	87
2001–02	Manchester C	99	WBA	89	Wolverhampton W††	86
2002–03	Portsmouth	98	Leicester C	92	Sheffield U††	80
2003–04	Norwich C	94	WBA	86	Sunderland††	79

FOOTBALL LEAGUE CHAMPIONSHIP 1

Maximum points: 138

2004–05	Luton T	98	Hull C	86	Tranmere R††	79
2005–06	Southend U	82	Colchester U	79	Brentford††	76

DIVISION 2

Maximum points: 138

1992–93	Stoke C	93	Bolton W	90	Port Vale††	89
1993–94	Reading	89	Port Vale	88	Plymouth Arg††	85
1994–95	Birmingham C	89	Brentford††	85	Crewe Alex††	83
1995–96	Swindon T	92	Oxford U	83	Blackpool††	82
1996–97	Bury	84	Stockport Co	82	Luton T††	78
1997–98	Watford	88	Bristol C	85	Grimsby T	72

	First	Pts	Second	Pts	Third	Pts
1998–99	Fulham	101	Walsall	87	Manchester C	82
1999–00	Preston NE	95	Burnley	88	Gillingham	85
2000–01	Millwall	93	Rotherham U	91	Reading††	86
2001–02	Brighton & HA	90	Reading	84	Brentford*††	83
2002–03	Wigan Ath	100	Crewe Alex	86	Bristol C††	83
2003–04	Plymouth Arg	90	QPR	83	Bristol C††	82

FOOTBALL LEAGUE CHAMPIONSHIP 2
Maximum points: 138

	First	Pts	Second	Pts	Third	Pts
2004–05	Yeovil T	83	Scunthorpe U*	80	Swansea C	80
2005–06	Carlisle U	86	Northampton T	83	Leyton Orient	81

DIVISION 3
Maximum points: 126

	First	Pts	Second	Pts	Third	Pts
1992–93	Cardiff C	83	Wrexham	80	Barnet	79
1993–94	Shrewsbury T	79	Chester C	74	Crewe Alex	73
1994–95	Carlisle U	91	Walsall	83	Chesterfield	81

Maximum points: 138

	First	Pts	Second	Pts	Third	Pts
1995–96	Preston NE	86	Gillingham	83	Bury	79
1996–97	Wigan Ath*	87	Fulham	87	Carlisle U	84
1997–98	Notts Co	99	Macclesfield T	82	Lincoln C	75
1998–99	Brentford	85	Cambridge U	81	Cardiff C	80
1999–00	Swansea C	85	Rotherham U	84	Northampton T	82
2000–01	Brighton & HA	92	Cardiff C	82	Chesterfield¶	80
2001–02	Plymouth Arg	102	Luton T	97	Mansfield T	79
2002–03	Rushden & D	87	Hartlepool U	85	Wrexham	84
2003–04	Doncaster R	92	Hull C	88	Torquay U*	81

* Won or placed on goal average (ratio)/goal difference.
†† Not promoted after play-offs. ¶ 9 pts deducted for irregularities.

FOOTBALL LEAGUE
Maximum points: a 44; b 60

	First	Pts	Second	Pts	Third	Pts
1888–89a	Preston NE	40	Aston Villa	29	Wolverhampton W	28
1889–90a	Preston NE	33	Everton	31	Blackburn R	27
1890–91a	Everton	29	Preston NE	27	Notts Co	26
1891–92b	Sunderland	42	Preston NE	37	Bolton W	36

DIVISION 1 to 1991–92
Maximum points: a 44; b 52; c 60; d 68; e 76; f 84; g 126; h 120; k 114.

	First	Pts	Second	Pts	Third	Pts
1892–93c	Sunderland	48	Preston NE	37	Everton	36
1893–94c	Aston Villa	44	Sunderland	38	Derby Co	36
1894–95c	Sunderland	47	Everton	42	Aston Villa	39
1895–96c	Aston Villa	45	Derby Co	41	Everton	39
1896–97c	Aston Villa	47	Sheffield U*	36	Derby Co	36
1897–98c	Sheffield U	42	Sunderland	37	Wolverhampton W*	35
1898–99d	Aston Villa	45	Liverpool	43	Burnley	39
1899–1900d	Aston Villa	50	Sheffield U	48	Sunderland	41
1900–01d	Liverpool	45	Sunderland	43	Notts Co	40
1901–02d	Sunderland	44	Everton	41	Newcastle U	37
1902–03d	The Wednesday	42	Aston Villa*	41	Sunderland	41
1903–04d	The Wednesday	47	Manchester C	44	Everton	43
1904–05d	Newcastle U	48	Everton	47	Manchester C	46
1905–06e	Liverpool	51	Preston NE	47	The Wednesday	44

	First	Pts	Second	Pts	Third	Pts
1906–07e	Newcastle U	51	Bristol C	48	Everton*	45
1907–08e	Manchester U	52	Aston Villa*	43	Manchester C	43
1908–09e	Newcastle U	53	Everton	46	Sunderland	44
1909–10e	Aston Villa	53	Liverpool	48	Blackburn R*	45
1910–11e	Manchester U	52	Aston Villa	51	Sunderland*	45
1911–12e	Blackburn R	49	Everton	46	Newcastle U	44
1912–13e	Sunderland	54	Aston Villa	50	Sheffield W	49
1913–14e	Blackburn R	51	Aston Villa	44	Middlesbrough*	43
1914–15e	Everton	46	Oldham Ath	45	Blackburn R*	43
1919–20f	WBA	60	Burnley	51	Chelsea	49
1920–21f	Burnley	59	Manchester C	54	Bolton W	52
1921–22f	Liverpool	57	Tottenham H	51	Burnley	49
1922–23f	Liverpool	60	Sunderland	54	Huddersfield T	53
1923–24f	Huddersfield T*	57	Cardiff C	57	Sunderland	53
1924–25f	Huddersfield T	58	WBA	56	Bolton W	55
1925–26f	Huddersfield T	57	Arsenal	52	Sunderland	48
1926–27f	Newcastle U	56	Huddersfield T	51	Sunderland	49
1927–28f	Everton	53	Huddersfield T	51	Leicester C	48
1928–29f	Sheffield W	52	Leicester C	51	Aston Villa	50
1929–30f	Sheffield W	60	Derby Co	50	Manchester C*	47
1930–31f	Arsenal	66	Aston Villa	59	Sheffield W	52
1931–32f	Everton	56	Arsenal	54	Sheffield W	50
1932–33f	Arsenal	58	Aston Villa	54	Sheffield W	51
1933–34f	Arsenal	59	Huddersfield T	56	Tottenham H	49
1934–35f	Arsenal	58	Sunderland	54	Sheffield W	49
1935–36f	Sunderland	56	Derby Co*	48	Huddersfield T	48
1936–37f	Manchester C	57	Charlton Ath	54	Arsenal	52
1937–38f	Arsenal	52	Wolverhampton W	51	Preston NE	49
1938–39f	Everton	59	Wolverhampton W	55	Charlton Ath	50
1946–47f	Liverpool	57	Manchester U*	56	Wolverhampton W	56
1947–48f	Arsenal	59	Manchester U*	52	Burnley	52
1948–49f	Portsmouth	58	Manchester U*	53	Derby Co	53
1949–50f	Portsmouth*	53	Wolverhampton W	53	Sunderland	52
1950–51f	Tottenham H	60	Manchester U	56	Blackpool	50
1951–52f	Manchester U	57	Tottenham H*	53	Arsenal	53
1952–53f	Arsenal*	54	Preston NE	54	Wolverhampton W	51
1953–54f	Wolverhampton W	57	WBA	53	Huddersfield T	51
1954–55f	Chelsea	52	Wolverhampton W*	48	Portsmouth*	48
1955–56f	Manchester U	60	Blackpool*	49	Wolverhampton W	49
1956–57f	Manchester U	64	Tottenham H*	56	Preston NE	56
1957–58f	Wolverhampton W	64	Preston NE	59	Tottenham H	51
1958–59f	Wolverhampton W	61	Manchester U	55	Arsenal*	50
1959–60f	Burnley	55	Wolverhampton W	54	Tottenham H	53
1960–61f	Tottenham H	66	Sheffield W	58	Wolverhampton W	57
1961–62f	Ipswich T	56	Burnley	53	Tottenham H	52
1962–63f	Everton	61	Tottenham H	55	Burnley	54
1963–64f	Liverpool	57	Manchester U	53	Everton	52
1964–65f	Manchester U*	61	Leeds U	61	Chelsea	56
1965–66f	Liverpool	61	Leeds U*	55	Burnley	55
1966–67f	Manchester U	60	Nottingham F*	56	Tottenham H	56
1967–68f	Manchester C	58	Manchester U	56	Liverpool	55
1968–69f	Leeds U	67	Liverpool	61	Everton	57
1969–70f	Everton	66	Leeds U	57	Chelsea	55
1970–71f	Arsenal	65	Leeds U	64	Tottenham H*	52

	First	Pts	Second	Pts	Third	Pts
1971–72f	Derby Co	58	Leeds U*	57	Liverpool*	57
1972–73f	Liverpool	60	Arsenal	57	Leeds U	53
1973–74f	Leeds U	62	Liverpool	57	Derby Co	48
1974–75f	Derby Co	53	Liverpool*	51	Ipswich T	51
1975–76f	Liverpool	60	QPR	59	Manchester U	56
1976–77f	Liverpool	57	Manchester C	56	Ipswich T	52
1977–78f	Nottingham F	64	Liverpool	57	Everton	55
1978–79f	Liverpool	68	Nottingham F	60	WBA	59
1979–80f	Liverpool	60	Manchester U	58	Ipswich T	53
1980–81f	Aston Villa	60	Ipswich T	56	Arsenal	53
1981–82g	Liverpool	87	Ipswich T	83	Manchester U	78
1982–83g	Liverpool	82	Watford	71	Manchester U	70
1983–84g	Liverpool	80	Southampton	77	Nottingham F*	74
1984–85g	Everton	90	Liverpool*	77	Tottenham H	77
1985–86g	Liverpool	88	Everton	86	West Ham U	84
1986–87g	Everton	86	Liverpool	77	Tottenham H	71
1987–88h	Liverpool	90	Manchester U	81	Nottingham F	73
1988–89k	Arsenal*	76	Liverpool	76	Nottingham F	64
1989–90k	Liverpool	79	Aston Villa	70	Tottenham H	63
1990–91k	Arsenal†	83	Liverpool	76	Crystal Palace	69
1991–92g	Leeds U	82	Manchester U	78	Sheffield W	53

No official competition during 1915–19 and 1939–46; Regional Leagues operating.
* Won or placed on goal average (ratio)/goal difference.
† 2 pts deducted

DIVISION 2 to 1991–92

Maximum points: a 44; b 56; c 60; d 68; e 76; f 84; g 126; h 132; k 138.

	First	Pts	Second	Pts	Third	Pts
1892–93a	Small Heath	36	Sheffield U	35	Darwen	30
1893–94b	Liverpool	50	Small Heath	42	Notts Co	39
1894–95c	Bury	48	Notts Co	39	Newton Heath*	38
1895–96c	Liverpool*	46	Manchester C	46	Grimsby T*	42
1896–97c	Notts Co	42	Newton Heath	39	Grimsby T	38
1897–98c	Burnley	48	Newcastle U	45	Manchester C	39
1898–99d	Manchester C	52	Glossop NE	46	Leicester Fosse	45
1899–1900d	The Wednesday	54	Bolton W	52	Small Heath	46
1900–01d	Grimsby T	49	Small Heath	48	Burnley	44
1901–02d	WBA	55	Middlesbrough	51	Preston NE*	42
1902–03d	Manchester C	54	Small Heath	51	Woolwich A	48
1903–04d	Preston NE	50	Woolwich A	49	Manchester U	48
1904–05d	Liverpool	58	Bolton W	56	Manchester U	53
1905–06e	Bristol C	66	Manchester U	62	Chelsea	53
1906–07e	Nottingham F	60	Chelsea	57	Leicester Fosse	48
1907–08e	Bradford C	54	Leicester Fosse	52	Oldham Ath	50
1908–09e	Bolton W	52	Tottenham H*	51	WBA	51
1909–10e	Manchester C	54	Oldham Ath*	53	Hull C*	53
1910–11e	WBA	53	Bolton W	51	Chelsea	49
1911–12e	Derby Co*	54	Chelsea	54	Burnley	52
1912–13e	Preston NE	53	Burnley	50	Birmingham	46
1913–14e	Notts Co	53	Bradford PA*	49	Woolwich A	49
1914–15e	Derby Co	53	Preston NE	50	Barnsley	47
1919–20f	Tottenham H	70	Huddersfield T	64	Birmingham	56
1920–21f	Birmingham*	58	Cardiff C	58	Bristol C	51
1921–22f	Nottingham F	56	Stoke C*	52	Barnsley	52
1922–23f	Notts Co	53	West Ham U*	51	Leicester C	51

127

	First	Pts	Second	Pts	Third	Pts
1923–24f	Leeds U	54	Bury*	51	Derby Co	51
1924–25f	Leicester C	59	Manchester U	57	Derby Co	55
1925–26f	Sheffield W	60	Derby Co	57	Chelsea	52
1926–27f	Middlesbrough	62	Portsmouth*	54	Manchester C	54
1927–28f	Manchester C	59	Leeds U	57	Chelsea	54
1928–29f	Middlesbrough	55	Grimsby T	53	Bradford PA*	48
1929–30f	Blackpool	58	Chelsea	55	Oldham Ath	53
1930–31f	Everton	61	WBA	54	Tottenham H	51
1931–32f	Wolverhampton W	56	Leeds U	54	Stoke C	52
1932–33f	Stoke C	56	Tottenham H	55	Fulham	50
1933–34f	Grimsby T	59	Preston NE	52	Bolton W*	51
1934–35f	Brentford	61	Bolton W*	56	West Ham U	56
1935–36f	Manchester U	56	Charlton Ath	55	Sheffield U*	52
1936–37f	Leicester C	56	Blackpool	55	Bury	52
1937–38f	Aston Villa	57	Manchester U*	53	Sheffield U	53
1938–39f	Blackburn R	55	Sheffield U	54	Sheffield W	53
1946–47f	Manchester C	62	Burnley	58	Birmingham C	55
1947–48f	Birmingham C	59	Newcastle U	56	Southampton	52
1948–49f	Fulham	57	WBA	56	Southampton	55
1949–50f	Tottenham H	61	Sheffield W*	52	Sheffield U*	52
1950–51f	Preston NE	57	Manchester C	52	Cardiff C	50
1951–52f	Sheffield W	53	Cardiff C*	51	Birmingham C	51
1952–53f	Sheffield U	60	Huddersfield T	58	Luton T	52
1953–54f	Leicester C*	56	Everton	56	Blackburn R	55
1954–55f	Birmingham C*	54	Luton T*	54	Rotherham U	54
1955–56f	Sheffield W	55	Leeds U	52	Liverpool*	48
1956–57f	Leicester C	61	Nottingham F	54	Liverpool	53
1957–58f	West Ham U	57	Blackburn R	56	Charlton Ath	55
1958–59f	Sheffield W	62	Fulham	60	Sheffield U*	53
1959–60f	Aston Villa	59	Cardiff C	58	Liverpool*	50
1960–61f	Ipswich T	59	Sheffield U	58	Liverpool	52
1961–62f	Liverpool	62	Leyton Orient	54	Sunderland	53
1962–63f	Stoke C	53	Chelsea*	52	Sunderland	52
1963–64f	Leeds U	63	Sunderland	61	Preston NE	56
1964–65f	Newcastle U	57	Northampton T	56	Bolton W	50
1965–66f	Manchester C	59	Southampton	54	Coventry C	53
1966–67f	Coventry C	59	Wolverhampton W	58	Carlisle U	52
1967–68f	Ipswich T	59	QPR*	58	Blackpool	58
1968–69f	Derby Co	63	Crystal Palace	56	Charlton Ath	50
1969–70f	Huddersfield T	60	Blackpool	53	Leicester C	51
1970–71f	Leicester C	59	Sheffield U	56	Cardiff C*	53
1971–72f	Norwich C	57	Birmingham C	56	Millwall	55
1972–73f	Burnley	62	QPR	61	Aston Villa	50
1973–74f	Middlesbrough	65	Luton T	50	Carlisle U	49
1974–75f	Manchester U	61	Aston Villa	58	Norwich C	53
1975–76f	Sunderland	56	Bristol C*	53	WBA	53
1976–77f	Wolverhampton W	57	Chelsea	55	Nottingham F	52
1977–78f	Bolton W	58	Southampton	57	Tottenham H*	56
1978–79f	Crystal Palace	57	Brighton & HA*	56	Stoke C	56
1979–80f	Leicester C	55	Sunderland	54	Birmingham C*	53
1980–81f	West Ham U	66	Notts Co	53	Swansea C*	50
1981–82g	Luton T	88	Watford	80	Norwich C	71
1982–83g	QPR	85	Wolverhampton W	75	Leicester C	70
1983–84g	Chelsea*	88	Sheffield W	88	Newcastle U	80

	First	Pts	Second	Pts	Third	Pts
1984–85g	Oxford U	84	Birmingham C	82	Manchester C	74
1985–86g	Norwich C	84	Charlton Ath	77	Wimbledon	76
1986–87g	Derby Co	84	Portsmouth	78	Oldham Ath††	75
1987–88h	Millwall	82	Aston Villa*	78	Middlesbrough	78
1988–89k	Chelsea	99	Manchester C	82	Crystal Palace	81
1989–90k	Leeds U*	85	Sheffield U	85	Newcastle U††	80
1990–91k	Oldham Ath	88	West Ham U	87	Sheffield W	82
1991–92k	Ipswich T	84	Middlesbrough	80	Derby Co	78

No official competition during 1915–19 and 1939–46; Regional Leagues operating.
* Won or placed on goal average (ratio)/goal difference.
†† Not promoted after play-offs.

DIVISION 3 to 1991–92
Maximum points: 92; 138 from 1981–82.

1958–59	Plymouth Arg	62	Hull C	61	Brentford*	57
1959–60	Southampton	61	Norwich C	59	Shrewsbury T*	52
1960–61	Bury	68	Walsall	62	QPR	60
1961–62	Portsmouth	65	Grimsby T	62	Bournemouth*	59
1962–63	Northampton T	62	Swindon T	58	Port Vale	54
1963–64	Coventry C*	60	Crystal Palace	60	Watford	58
1964–65	Carlisle U	60	Bristol C*	59	Mansfield T	59
1965–66	Hull C	69	Millwall	65	QPR	57
1966–67	QPR	67	Middlesbrough	55	Watford	54
1967–68	Oxford U	57	Bury	56	Shrewsbury T	55
1968–69	Watford*	64	Swindon T	64	Luton T	61
1969–70	Orient	62	Luton T	60	Bristol R	56
1970–71	Preston NE	61	Fulham	60	Halifax T	56
1971–72	Aston Villa	70	Brighton & HA	65	Bournemouth*	62
1972–73	Bolton W	61	Notts Co	57	Blackburn R	55
1973–74	Oldham Ath	62	Bristol R*	61	York C	61
1974–75	Blackburn R	60	Plymouth Arg	59	Charlton Ath	55
1975–76	Hereford U	63	Cardiff C	57	Millwall	56
1976–77	Mansfield T	64	Brighton & HA	61	Crystal Palace*	59
1977–78	Wrexham	61	Cambridge U	58	Preston NE*	56
1978–79	Shrewsbury T	61	Watford*	60	Swansea C	60
1979–80	Grimsby T	62	Blackburn R	59	Sheffield W	58
1980–81	Rotherham U	61	Barnsley*	59	Charlton Ath	59
1981–82	Burnley*	80	Carlisle U	80	Fulham	78
1982–83	Portsmouth	91	Cardiff C	86	Huddersfield T	82
1983–84	Oxford U	95	Wimbledon	87	Sheffield U*	83
1984–85	Bradford C	94	Millwall	90	Hull C	87
1985–86	Reading	94	Plymouth Arg	87	Derby Co	84
1986–87	Bournemouth	97	Middlesbrough	94	Swindon T	87
1987–88	Sunderland	93	Brighton & HA	84	Walsall	82
1988–89	Wolverhampton W	92	Sheffield U*	84	Port Vale	84
1989–90	Bristol R	93	Bristol C	91	Notts Co	87
1990–91	Cambridge U	86	Southend U	85	Grimsby T*	83
1991–92	Brentford	82	Birmingham C	81	Huddersfield T	78

* Won or placed on goal average (ratio)/goal difference.

DIVISION 4 (1958–1992)
Maximum points: 92; 138 from 1981–82.

1958–59	Port Vale	64	Coventry C*	60	York C	60
1959–60	Walsall	65	Notts Co*	60	Torquay U	60

129

	First	Pts	Second	Pts	Third	Pts
1960–61	Peterborough U	66	Crystal Palace	64	Northampton T*	60
1961–62†	Millwall	56	Colchester U	55	Wrexham	53
1962–63	Brentford	62	Oldham Ath*	59	Crewe Alex	59
1963–64	Gillingham*	60	Carlisle U	60	Workington	59
1964–65	Brighton & HA	63	Millwall*	62	York C	62
1965–66	Doncaster R*	59	Darlington	59	Torquay U	58
1966–67	Stockport Co	64	Southport*	59	Barrow	59
1967–68	Luton T	66	Barnsley	61	Hartlepools U	60
1968–69	Doncaster R	59	Halifax T	57	Rochdale*	56
1969–70	Chesterfield	64	Wrexham	61	Swansea U	60
1970–71	Notts Co	69	Bournemouth	60	Oldham Ath	59
1971–72	Grimsby T	63	Southend U	60	Brentford	59
1972–73	Southport	62	Hereford U	58	Cambridge U	57
1973–74	Peterborough U	65	Gillingham	62	Colchester U	60
1974–75	Mansfield T	68	Shrewsbury T	62	Rotherham U	59
1975–76	Lincoln C	74	Northampton T	68	Reading	60
1976–77	Cambridge U	65	Exeter C	62	Colchester U*	59
1977–78	Watford	71	Southend U	60	Swansea C*	56
1978–79	Reading	65	Grimsby T*	61	Wimbledon*	61
1979–80	Huddersfield T	66	Walsall	64	Newport Co	61
1980–81	Southend U	67	Lincoln C	65	Doncaster R	56
1981–82	Sheffield U	96	Bradford C*	91	Wigan Ath	91
1982–83	Wimbledon	98	Hull C	90	Port Vale	88
1983–84	York C	101	Doncaster R	85	Reading*	82
1984–85	Chesterfield	91	Blackpool	86	Darlington	85
1985–86	Swindon T	102	Chester C	84	Mansfield T	81
1986–87	Northampton T	99	Preston NE	90	Southend U	80
1987–88	Wolverhampton W	90	Cardiff C	85	Bolton W	78
1988–89	Rotherham U	82	Tranmere R	80	Crewe Alex	78
1989–90	Exeter C	89	Grimsby T	79	Southend U	75
1990–91	Darlington	83	Stockport Co*	82	Hartlepool U	82
1991–92§	Burnley	83	Rotherham U*	77	Mansfield T	77

* Won or placed on goal average (ratio)/goal difference.

†*Maximum points:* 88 owing to Accrington Stanley's resignation. ††*Not promoted after play-offs.*

§*Maximum points:* 126 owing to Aldershot being expelled.

DIVISION 3—SOUTH (1920–1958)
1920–21 Season as Division 3.
Maximum points: a 84; b 92.

	First	Pts	Second	Pts	Third	Pts
1920–21a	Crystal Palace	59	Southampton	54	QPR	53
1921–22a	Southampton*	61	Plymouth Arg	53	Portsmouth	53
1922–23a	Bristol C	59	Plymouth Arg*	53	Swansea T	53
1923–24a	Portsmouth	59	Plymouth Arg	55	Millwall	54
1924–25a	Swansea T	57	Plymouth Arg	56	Bristol C	53
1925–26a	Reading	57	Plymouth Arg	56	Millwall	53
1926–27a	Bristol C	62	Plymouth Arg	60	Millwall	56
1927–28a	Millwall	65	Northampton T	55	Plymouth Arg	53
1928–29a	Charlton Ath*	54	Crystal Palace	54	Northampton T*	52
1929–30a	Plymouth Arg	68	Brentford	61	QPR	51
1930–31a	Notts Co	59	Crystal Palace	51	Brentford	50
1931–32a	Fulham	57	Reading	55	Southend U	53
1932–33a	Brentford	62	Exeter C	58	Norwich C	57
1933–34a	Norwich C	61	Coventry C*	54	Reading*	54

	First	Pts	Second	Pts	Third	Pts
1934–35a	Charlton Ath	61	Reading	53	Coventry C	51
1935–36a	Coventry C	57	Luton T	56	Reading	54
1936–37a	Luton T	58	Notts Co	56	Brighton & HA	53
1937–38a	Millwall	56	Bristol C	55	QPR*	53
1938–39a	Newport Co	55	Crystal Palace	52	Brighton & HA	49
1939–46	Competition cancelled owing to war.					
1946–47a	Cardiff C	66	QPR	57	Bristol C	51
1947–48a	QPR	61	Bournemouth	57	Walsall	51
1948–49a	Swansea T	62	Reading	55	Bournemouth	52
1949–50a	Notts Co	58	Northampton T*	51	Southend U	51
1950–51b	Nottingham F	70	Norwich C	64	Reading*	57
1951–52b	Plymouth Arg	66	Reading*	61	Norwich C	61
1952–53b	Bristol R	64	Millwall*	62	Northampton T	62
1953–54b	Ipswich T	64	Brighton & HA	61	Bristol C	56
1954–55b	Bristol C	70	Leyton Orient	61	Southampton	59
1955–56b	Leyton Orient	66	Brighton & HA	65	Ipswich T	64
1956–57b	Ipswich T*	59	Torquay U	59	Colchester U	58
1957–58b	Brighton & HA	60	Brentford*	58	Plymouth Arg	58

* Won or placed on goal average (ratio).

DIVISION 3—NORTH (1921–1958)
Maximum points: a 76; b 84; c 80; d 92.

	First	Pts	Second	Pts	Third	Pts
1921–22a	Stockport Co	56	Darlington*	50	Grimsby T	50
1922–23a	Nelson	51	Bradford PA	47	Walsall	46
1923–24b	Wolverhampton W	63	Rochdale	62	Chesterfield	54
1924–25b	Darlington	58	Nelson*	53	New Brighton	53
1925–26b	Grimsby T	61	Bradford PA	60	Rochdale	59
1926–27b	Stoke C	63	Rochdale	58	Bradford PA	55
1927–28b	Bradford PA	63	Lincoln C	55	Stockport Co	54
1928–29g	Bradford C	63	Stockport Co	62	Wrexham	52
1929–30b	Port Vale	67	Stockport Co	63	Darlington*	50
1930–31b	Chesterfield	58	Lincoln C	57	Wrexham*	54
1931–32c	Lincoln C*	57	Gateshead	57	Chester	50
1932–33b	Hull C	59	Wrexham	57	Stockport Co	54
1933–34b	Barnsley	62	Chesterfield	61	Stockport Co	59
1934–35b	Doncaster R	57	Halifax T	55	Chester	54
1935–36b	Chesterfield	60	Chester*	55	Tranmere R	55
1936–37b	Stockport Co	60	Lincoln C	57	Chester	53
1937–38b	Tranmere R	56	Doncaster R	54	Hull C	53
1938–39b	Barnsley	67	Doncaster R	56	Bradford C	52
1939–46	Competition cancelled owing to war.					
1946–47b	Doncaster R	72	Rotherham U	60	Chester	56
1947–48b	Lincoln C	60	Rotherham U	59	Wrexham	50
1948–49b	Hull C	65	Rotherham U	62	Doncaster R	50
1949–50b	Doncaster R	55	Gateshead	53	Rochdale*	51
1950–51d	Rotherham U	71	Mansfield T	64	Carlisle U	62
1951–52d	Lincoln C	69	Grimsby T	66	Stockport Co	59
1952–53d	Oldham Ath	59	Port Vale	58	Wrexham	56
1953–54d	Port Vale	69	Barnsley	58	Scunthorpe U	57
1954–55d	Barnsley	65	Accrington S	61	Scunthorpe U*	58
1955–56d	Grimsby T	68	Derby Co	63	Accrington S	59
1956–57d	Derby Co	63	Hartlepools U	59	Accrington S*	58
1957–58d	Scunthorpe U	66	Accrington S	59	Bradford C	57

* Won or placed on goal average (ratio).

131

PROMOTED AFTER PLAY-OFFS

(Not accounted for in previous section)

1986–87 Aldershot to Division 3.
1987–88 Swansea C to Divison 3.
1988–89 Leyton Orient to Division 3.
1989–90 Cambridge U to Division 3; Notts Co to Division 2; Sunderland to Division 1.
1990–91 Notts Co to Division 1; Tranmere R to Division 2; Torquay U to Division 3.
1991–92 Blackburn R to Premier League; Peterborough U to Division 1.
1992–93 Swindon T to Premier League; WBA to Division 1; York C to Division 2.
1993–94 Leicester C to Premier League; Burnley to Division 1; Wycombe W to Division 2.
1994–95 Huddersfield T to Division 1.
1995–96 Leicester C to Premier League; Bradford C to Division 1; Plymouth Arg to Division 2.
1996–97 Crystal Palace to Premier League; Crewe Alex to Division 1; Northampton T to Division 2.
1997–98 Charlton Ath to Premier League; Colchester U to Division 2.
1998–99 Watford to Premier League; Scunthorpe to Division 2.
1999–00 Peterborough U to Division 2.
2000–01 Walsall to Division 1; Blackpool to Division 2.
2001–02 Birmingham C to Premier League; Stoke C to Division 1; Cheltenham T to Division 2.
2002–03 Wolverhampton W to Premier League; Cardiff C to Division 1; Bournemouth to Division 2.
2003–04 Crystal Palace to Premier League; Brighton & HA to Division 1; Huddersfield T to Division 2.
2004–05 West Ham U to Premier League; Sheffield W to Football League Championship, Southend U to Football League Championship 1.
2005–06 Watford to Premier League; Barnsley to Football League Championship; Cheltenham T to Football League Championship 1.

RELEGATED CLUBS

FA PREMIER LEAGUE TO DIVISION 1

1992–93 Crystal Palace, Middlesbrough, Nottingham F.
1993–94 Sheffield U, Oldham Ath, Swindon T.
1994–95 Crystal Palace, Norwich C, Leicester C, Ipswich T.
1995–96 Manchester C, QPR, Bolton W.
1996–97 Sunderland, Middlesbrough, Nottingham F.
1997–98 Bolton W, Barnsley, Crystal Palace.
1998–99 Charlton Ath, Blackburn R, Nottingham F.
1999–90 Wimbledon, Sheffield W, Watford.
2000–01 Manchester C, Coventry C, Bradford C.
2001–02 Ipswich T, Derby Co, Leicester C.
2002–03 West Ham U, WBA, Sunderland.
2003–04 Leicester C, Leeds U, Wolverhampton W.

FA PREMIER LEAGUE TO FOOTBALL LEAGUE CHAMPIONSHIP

2004–05 Crystal Palace, Norwich C, Southampton.
2005–06 Birmingham C, WBA, Sunderland.

DIVISION 1 TO DIVISION 2

1898–99 Bolton W and Sheffield W
1899–1900 Burnley and Glossop
1900–01 Preston NE and WBA
1901–02 Small Heath and Manchester C
1902–03 Grimsby T and Bolton W
1903–04 Liverpool and WBA
1904–05 League extended. Bury and
Notts Co, two bottom clubs in
First Division, re-elected.
1905–06 Nottingham F and
Wolverhampton W
1906–07 Derby Co and Stoke C
1907–08 Bolton W and Birmingham C
1908–09 Manchester C and Leicester Fosse
1909–10 Bolton W and Chelsea
1910–11 Bristol C and Nottingham F
1911–12 Preston NE and Bury
1912–13 Notts Co and Woolwich Arsenal
1913–14 Preston NE and Derby Co
1914–15 Tottenham H and Chelsea*
1919–20 Notts Co and Sheffield W
1920–21 Derby Co and Bradford PA
1921–22 Bradford C and Manchester U
1922–23 Stoke C and Oldham Ath
1923–24 Chelsea and Middlesbrough
1924–25 Preston NE and Nottingham F
1925–26 Manchester C and Notts Co
1926–27 Leeds U and WBA
1927–28 Tottenham H and Middlesbrough
1928–29 Bury and Cardiff C
1929–30 Burnley and Everton
1930–31 Leeds U and Manchester U
1931–32 Grimsby T and West Ham U
1932–33 Bolton W and Blackpool
1933–34 Newcastle U and Sheffield U

1934–35 Leicester C and Tottenham H
1935–36 Aston Villa and Blackburn R
1936–37 Manchester U and Sheffield W
1937–38 Manchester C and WBA
1938–39 Birmingham C and Leicester C
1946–47 Brentford and Leeds U
1947–48 Blackburn R and Grimsby T
1948–49 Preston NE and Sheffield U
1949–50 Manchester C and Birmingham C
1950–51 Sheffield W and Everton
1951–52 Huddersfield T and Fulham
1952–53 Stoke C and Derby Co
1953–54 Middlesbrough and Liverpool
1954–55 Leicester C and Sheffield W
1955–56 Huddersfield T and Sheffield U
1956–57 Charlton Ath and Cardiff C
1957–58 Sheffield W and Sunderland
1958–59 Portsmouth and Aston Villa
1959–60 Luton T and Leeds U
1960–61 Preston NE and Newcastle U
1961–62 Chelsea and Cardiff C
1962–63 Manchester C and Leyton Orient
1963–64 Bolton W and Ipswich T
1964–65 Wolverhampton W and
Birmingham C
1965–66 Northampton T and Blackburn R
1966–67 Aston Villa and Blackpool
1967–68 Fulham and Sheffield U
1968–69 Leicester C and QPR
1969–70 Sunderland and Sheffield W
1970–71 Burnley and Blackpool
1971–72 Huddersfield T and Nottingham F
1972–73 Crystal Palace and WBA
1973–74 Southampton, Manchester U,
Norwich C

1974–75	Luton T, Chelsea, Carlisle U
1975–76	Wolverhampton W, Burnley, Sheffield U
1976–77	Sunderland, Stoke C, Tottenham H
1977–78	West Ham U, Newcastle U, Leicester C
1978–79	QPR, Birmingham C, Chelsea
1979–80	Bristol C, Derby Co, Bolton W
1980–81	Norwich C, Leicester C, Crystal Palace
1981–82	Leeds U, Wolverhampton W, Middlesbrough
1982–83	Manchester C, Swansea C, Brighton & HA
1983–84	Birmingham C, Notts Co, Wolverhampton W
1984–85	Norwich C, Sunderland, Stoke C
1985–86	Ipswich T, Birmingham C, WBA
1986–87	Leicester C, Manchester C, Aston Villa
1987–88	Chelsea**, Portsmouth, Watford, Oxford U
1988–89	Middlesbrough, West Ham U, Newcastle U
1989–90	Sheffield W, Charlton Ath, Millwall
1990–91	Sunderland and Derby Co
1991–92	Luton T, Notts Co, West Ham U
1992–93	Brentford, Cambridge U, Bristol R
1993–94	Birmingham C, Oxford U, Peterborough U
1994–95	Swindon T, Burnley, Bristol C, Notts Co
1995–96	Millwall, Watford, Luton T
1996–97	Grimsby T, Oldham Ath, Southend U
1997–98	Manchester C, Stoke C, Reading
1998–99	Bury, Oxford U, Bristol C
1999–00	Walsall, Port Vale, Swindon T
2000–01	Huddersfield T, QPR, Tranmere R
2001–02	Crewe Alex, Barnsley, Stockport Co
2002–03	Sheffield W, Brighton & HA, Grimsby T
2003–04	Walsall, Bradford C, Wimbledon

**Relegated after play-offs.
*Subsequently re-elected to Division 1 when League was extended after the War.

FOOTBALL LEAGUE CHAMPIONSHIP TO FOOTBALL LEAGUE CHAMPIONSHIP 1

2004–05	Gillingham, Nottingham F, Rotherham U.
2005–06	Crewe Alex, Millwall, Brighton & HA.

DIVISION 2 TO DIVISION 3

1920–21	Stockport Co
1921–22	Bradford PA and Bristol C
1922–23	Rotherham Co and Wolverhampton W
1923–24	Nelson and Bristol C
1924–25	Crystal Palace and Coventry C
1925–26	Stoke C and Stockport Co
1926–27	Darlington and Bradford C
1927–28	Fulham and South Shields
1928–29	Port Vale and Clapton Orient
1929–30	Hull C and Notts Co
1930–31	Reading and Cardiff C
1931–32	Barnsley and Bristol C
1932–33	Chesterfield and Charlton Ath
1933–34	Millwall and Lincoln C
1934–35	Oldham Ath and Notts Co
1935–36	Port Vale and Hull C
1936–37	Doncaster R and Bradford C
1937–38	Barnsley and Stockport Co
1938–39	Norwich C and Tranmere R
1946–47	Swansea T and Newport Co
1947–48	Doncaster R and Millwall
1948–49	Nottingham F and Lincoln C
1949–50	Plymouth Arg and Bradford PA
1950–51	Grimsby T and Chesterfield
1951–52	Coventry C and QPR
1952–53	Southampton and Barnsley
1953–54	Brentford and Oldham Ath
1954–55	Ipswich T and Derby Co
1955–56	Plymouth Arg and Hull C
1956–57	Port Vale and Bury
1957–58	Doncaster R and Notts Co
1958–59	Barnsley and Grimsby T
1959–60	Bristol C and Hull C
1960–61	Lincoln C and Portsmouth
1961–62	Brighton & HA and Bristol R
1962–63	Walsall and Luton T
1963–64	Grimsby T and Scunthorpe U
1964–65	Swindon T and Swansea T
1965–66	Middlesbrough and Leyton Orient
1966–67	Northampton T and Bury
1967–68	Plymouth Arg and Rotherham U
1968–69	Fulham and Bury
1969–70	Preston NE and Aston Villa
1970–71	Blackburn R and Bolton W
1971–72	Charlton Ath and Watford

1972–73 Huddersfield T and Brighton & HA
1973–74 Crystal Palace, Preston NE, Swindon T
1974–75 Millwall, Cardiff C, Sheffield W
1975–76 Oxford U, York C, Portsmouth
1976–77 Carlisle U, Plymouth Arg, Hereford U
1977–78 Blackpool, Mansfield T, Hull C
1978–79 Sheffield U, Millwall, Blackburn R
1979–80 Fulham, Burnley, Charlton Ath
1980–81 Preston NE, Bristol C, Bristol R
1981–82 Cardiff C, Wrexham, Orient
1982–83 Rotherham U, Burnley, Bolton W
1983–84 Derby Co, Swansea C, Cambridge U
1984–85 Notts Co, Cardiff C, Wolverhampton W
1985–86 Carlisle U, Middlesbrough, Fulham
1986–87 Sunderland**, Grimsby T, Brighton & HA
1987–88 Huddersfield T, Reading, Sheffield U**
1988–89 Shrewsbury T, Birmingham C, Walsall
1989–90 Bournemouth, Bradford C, Stoke C

1990–91 WBA and Hull C
1991–92 Plymouth Arg, Brighton & HA, Port Vale
1992–93 Preston NE, Mansfield T, Wigan Ath, Chester C
1993–94 Fulham, Exeter C, Hartlepool U, Barnet
1994–95 Cambridge U, Plymouth Arg, Cardiff C, Chester C, Leyton Orient
1995–96 Carlisle U, Swansea C, Brighton & HA, Hull C
1996–97 Peterborough U, Shrewsbury T, Rotherham U, Notts Co
1997–98 Brentford, Plymouth Arg, Carlisle U, Southend U
1998–99 York C, Northampton T, Lincoln C, Macclesfield T
1999–00 Cardiff C, Blackpool, Scunthorpe U, Chesterfield
2000–01 Bristol R, Luton T, Swansea C, Oxford U
2001–02 Bournemouth, Bury, Wrexham, Cambridge U
2002–03 Cheltenham T, Huddersfield T, Mansfield T, Northampton T
2003–04 Grimsby T, Rushden & D, Notts Co, Wycombe W

FOOTBALL LEAGUE CHAMPIONSHIP 1 TO FOOTBALL LEAGUE CHAMPIONSHIP 2

2004–05 Torquay U, Wrexham, Peterborough U, Stockport Co.
2005–06 Hartlepool U, Milton Keynes D, Swindon T, Walsall.

DIVISION 3 TO DIVISION 4

1958–59 Rochdale, Notts Co, Doncaster R, Stockport Co
1959–60 Accrington S, Wrexham, Mansfield T, York C
1960–61 Chesterfield, Colchester U, Bradford C, Tranmere R
1961–62 Newport Co, Brentford, Lincoln C, Torquay U
1962–63 Bradford PA, Brighton & HA, Carlisle U, Halifax T
1963–64 Millwall, Crewe Alex, Wrexham, Notts Co
1964–65 Luton T, Port Vale, Colchester U, Barnsley
1965–66 Southend U, Exeter C, Brentford, York C
1966–67 Doncaster R, Workington, Darlington, Swansea T
1967–68 Scunthorpe U, Colchester U, Grimsby T, Peterborough U (demoted)

1968–69 Oldham Ath, Crewe Alex, Hartlepool, Northampton T
1969–70 Bournemouth, Southport, Barrow, Stockport Co
1970–71 Reading, Bury, Doncaster R, Gillingham
1971–72 Mansfield T, Barnsley, Torquay U, Bradford C
1972–73 Rotherham U, Brentford, Swansea C, Scunthorpe U
1973–74 Cambridge U, Shrewsbury T, Southport, Rochdale
1974–75 Bournemouth, Tranmere R, Watford, Huddersfield T
1975–76 Aldershot, Colchester U, Southend U, Halifax T
1976–77 Reading, Northampton T, Grimsby T, York C
1977–78 Port Vale, Bradford C, Hereford U, Portsmouth

1978–79 Peterborough U, Walsall, Tranmere R, Lincoln C
1979–80 Bury, Southend U, Mansfield T, Wimbledon
1980–81 Sheffield U, Colchester U, Blackpool, Hull C
1981–82 Wimbledon, Swindon T, Bristol C, Chester
1982–83 Reading, Wrexham, Doncaster R, Chesterfield
1983–84 Scunthorpe U, Southend U, Port Vale, Exeter C
1984–85 Burnley, Orient, Preston NE, Cambridge U

1985–86 Lincoln C, Cardiff C, Wolverhampton W, Swansea C
1986–87 Bolton W**, Carlisle U, Darlington, Newport Co
1987–88 Doncaster R, York C, Grimsby T, Rotherham U**
1988–89 Southend U, Chesterfield, Gillingham, Aldershot
1989–90 Cardiff C, Northampton T, Blackpool, Walsall
1990–91 Crewe Alex, Rotherham U, Mansfield T
1991–92 Bury, Shrewsbury T, Torquay U, Darlington

**Relegated after play-offs.

LEAGUE STATUS FROM 1986–87

RELEGATED FROM LEAGUE	PROMOTED TO LEAGUE
1986–87 Lincoln C	Scarborough
1987–88 Newport Co	Lincoln C
1988–89 Darlington	Maidstone U
1989–90 Colchester U	Darlington
1990–91 —	Barnet
1991–92 —	Colchester U
1992–93 Halifax T	Wycombe W
1993–94 —	—
1994–95 —	
1995–96 —	—
1996–97 Hereford U	Macclesfield T
1997–98 Doncaster R	Halifax T
1998–99 Scarborough	Cheltenham T
1999–2000 Chester C	Kidderminster H
2000–01 Barnet	Rushden & D
2001–02 Halifax T	Boston U
2002–03 Shrewsbury T, Exeter C	Yeovil T, Doncaster R
2003–04 Carlisle U, York C	Chester C, Shrewsbury T
2004–05 Kidderminster H, Cambridge U	Barnet, Carlisle U
2005–06 Oxford U, Rushden & D	Accrington S, Hereford U

LEAGUE TITLE WINS

FA PREMIER LEAGUE – Manchester U 8, Arsenal 3, Chelsea 2, Blackburn R 1.

FOOTBALL LEAGUE CHAMPIONSHIP – Reading 1, Sunderland 1.

LEAGUE DIVISION 1 – Liverpool 18, Arsenal 10, Everton 9, Sunderland 8, Aston Villa 7, Manchester U 7, Newcastle U 5, Sheffield W 4, Huddersfield T 3, Leeds U 3, Manchester C 3, Portsmouth 3, Wolverhampton W 3, Blackburn R 2, Burnley 2, Derby Co 2, Nottingham F 2, Preston NE 2, Tottenham H 2; Bolton W, Charlton Ath, Chelsea, Crystal Palace, Fulham, Ipswich T, Middlesbrough, Norwich C, Sheffield U, WBA 1 each.

FOOTBALL LEAGUE CHAMPIONSHIP 1 – Luton T 1, Southend U 1.

LEAGUE DIVISION 2 – Leicester C 6, Manchester C 6, Birmingham C (one as Small Heath) 5, Sheffield W 5, Derby Co 4, Liverpool 4, Preston NE 4, Ipswich T 3, Leeds U 3, Middlesbrough 3, Notts Co 3, Stoke C 3, Aston Villa 2, Bolton W 2, Burnley 2, Bury 2, Chelsea 2, Fulham 2, Grimsby T 2, Manchester U 2, Millwall 2, Norwich C 2, Nottingham F 2, Tottenham H 2, WBA 2, West Ham U 2, Wolverhampton W 2; Blackburn R, Blackpool, Bradford C, Brentford, Brighton & HA, Bristol C, Coventry C, Crystal Palace, Everton, Huddersfield T, Luton T, Newcastle U, Plymouth Arg, QPR, Oldham Ath, Oxford U, Reading, Sheffield U, Sunderland, Swindon T, Watford, Wigan Ath 1 each.

FOOTBALL LEAGUE CHAMPIONSHIP 2 – Carlisle U 1, Yeovil T 1.

LEAGUE DIVISION 3 – Brentford 2, Carlisle U 2, Oxford U 2, Plymouth Arg 2, Portsmouth 2, Preston NE 2, Shrewsbury T 2; Aston Villa, Blackburn R, Bolton W, Bournemouth, Bradford C, Brighton & HA, Bristol R, Burnley, Bury, Cambridge U, Cardiff C, Coventry C, Doncaster R, Grimsby T, Hereford U, Hull C, Leyton Orient, Mansfield T, Northampton T, Notts Co, Oldham Ath, QPR, Reading, Rotherham U, Rushden & D Southampton, Sunderland, Swansea C, Watford, Wigan Ath, Wolverhampton W, Wrexham 1 each.

LEAGUE DIVISION 4 – Chesterfield 2, Doncaster R 2, Peterborough U 2; Brentford, Brighton & HA, Burnley, Cambridge U, Darlington, Exeter C, Gillingham, Grimsby T, Huddersfield T, Lincoln C, Luton T, Mansfield T, Millwall, Northampton T, Notts Co, Port Vale, Reading, Rotherham U, Sheffield U, Southend U, Southport, Stockport Co, Swindon T, Walsall, Watford, Wimbledon, Wolverhampton W, York C 1 each.

DIVISION 3 (South) – Bristol C 3, Charlton Ath 2, Ipswich T 2, Millwall 2, Notts Co 2, Plymouth Arg 2, Swansea T 2; Brentford, Brighton & HA, Bristol R, Cardiff C, Coventry C, Crystal Palace, Fulham, Leyton Orient, Luton T, Newport Co, Norwich C, Nottingham F, Portsmouth, QPR, Reading, Southampton 1 each.

DIVISION 3 (North) – Barnsley 3, Doncaster R 3, Lincoln C 3, Chesterfield 2, Grimsby T 2, Hull C 2, Port Vale 2, Stockport Co 2; Bradford C, Bradford PA, Darlington, Derby Co, Nelson, Oldham Ath, Rotherham U, Scunthorpe U, Stoke C, Tranmere R, Wolverhampton W 1 each.

FOOTBALL LEAGUE PLAY-OFFS 2005–2006

CHAMPIONSHIP FIRST LEG

Leeds U	(0) 1	Preston NE	(0) 1
Crystal Palace	(0) 0	Watford	(0) 3

CHAMPIONSHIP SECOND LEG

Preston NE	(0) 0	Leeds U	(0) 2
Watford	(0) 0	Crystal Palace	(0) 0

CHAMPIONSHIP FINAL Sunday, 21 May 2006 *(at Millennium Stadium)*

Leeds U (0) 0

Watford (1) 3 *(Demerit 25, Sullivan 57 (og), Henderson 84 (pen))*   64,736

Leeds U: Sullivan; Kelly, Kilgallon, Derry, Butler, Gregan (Bakke), Douglas, Richardson (Blake), Hulse, Miller (Healy), Lewis.
Watford: Foster; Doyley, Stewart, Spring, Mackay, Demerit, Chambers (Bangoura), Mahon, Henderson, King, Young.
Referee: M. Dean (Wirral).

LEAGUE 1 FIRST LEG

Barnsley	(0) 0	Huddersfield T	(0) 1
Swansea C	(0) 1	Brentford	(1) 1

LEAGUE 1 SECOND LEG

Brentford	(0) 0	Swansea C	(2) 2
Huddersfield T	(0) 1	Barnsley	(0) 3

LEAGUE 1 FINAL Saturday, 27 May 2006 *(at Millennium Stadium)*

Swansea C (2) 2 *(Fallon 28, Robinson 40)*

Barnsley (1) 2 *(Hayes 19, Nardiello 62)*   55,419

Swansea C: Gueret; Ricketts, Austin, O'Leary, Monk, Tate, Britton, Tudur-Jones, Knight (Trundle), Fallon (Akinfenwa), Robinson (McLeod).
Barnsley: Colgan; Hassell, Heckingbottom, Howard (Tonge), Reid, Kay, Devaney, Nardiello (Shuker), Hayes, Richards (Wright), McPhail.
aet; Barnsley won 4-3 on penalties.
Referee: L. Mason (Lancashire).

LEAGUE 2 FIRST LEG

Lincoln C	(0) 0	Grimsby T	(1) 1
Wycombe W	(0) 1	Cheltenham T	(1) 2

LEAGUE 2 SECOND LEG

Grimsby T	(0) 2	Lincoln C	(1) 1
Cheltenham T	(0) 0	Wycombe W	(0) 0

LEAGUE 2 FINAL Sunday, 28 May 2006 *(at Millennium Stadium)*

Grimsby T (0) 0

Cheltenham T (0) 1 *(Guinan 63)*   29,196

Grimsby T: Mildenhall; Croft (Futcher), Newey, Woodhouse, Whittle, Jones R, Mendes (Goodfellow), Bolland, Parkinson, Jones G, Reddy (Cohen).
Cheltenham T: Higgs; Gill, Armstrong (Bell), McCann, Caines, Duff, Vincent (Spencer), Finnigan, Gillespie (Odejayi), Guinan, Wilson.
Referee: P. Taylor (Hertfordshire).

LEAGUE ATTENDANCES 2005–2006

FA BARCLAYCARD PREMIERSHIP ATTENDANCES

	Average Gate			Season 2005–06	
	2004–05	2005–06	+/–%	Highest	Lowest
Arsenal	37,978	38,186	+0.55	38,389	37,867
Aston Villa	37,354	34,059	–8.82	42,551	26,422
Birmingham City	28,760	27,392	–4.76	29,312	24,010
Blackburn Rovers	22,314	21,015	–5.82	29,142	16,953
Bolton Wanderers	26,006	25,265	–2.85	27,718	22,733
Charlton Athletic	26,403	26,196	–0.78	27,111	23,453
Chelsea	41,870	41,902	+0.08	42,321	40,652
Everton	36,834	36,860	+0.07	40,158	34,333
Fulham	19,838	20,654	+4.11	22,486	16,550
Liverpool	42,587	44,236	+3.87	44,983	42,293
Manchester City	45,192	42,856	–5.17	47,192	40,256
Manchester United	67,871	68,765	+1.32	73,006	67,684
Middlesbrough	31,965	28,463	–10.96	31,908	25,971
Newcastle United	51,844	52,032	+0.36	52,327	50,451
Portsmouth	20,072	19,840	–1.16	20,240	19,030
Sunderland	28,821	33,904	+17.64	44,003	28,226
Tottenham Hotspur	35,883	36,074	+0.53	36,247	35,427
West Bromwich Albion	25,987	25,404	–2.24	27,623	23,144
West Ham United	27,403	33,743	+23.14	34,970	29,582
Wigan Athletic	11,571	20,610	+78.12	25,023	16,641

FOOTBALL LEAGUE CHAMPIONSHIP ATTENDANCES

	Average Gate			Season 2005–06	
	2004–05	2005–06	+/–%	Highest	Lowest
Brighton & Hove Albion	6,434	6,802	+5.7	7,999	5,859
Burnley	12,466	12,462	0.0	17,912	10,431
Cardiff City	12,976	11,720	–9.7	16,403	8,724
Coventry City	16,048	21,302	+32.7	26,851	16,156
Crewe Alexandra	7,403	6,732	–9.1	8,942	5,686
Crystal Palace	24,108	19,457	–19.3	23,843	17,291
Derby County	25,219	24,166	–4.2	30,391	21,434
Hull City	18,027	19,841	+10.1	23,486	17,698
Ipswich Town	25,651	24,253	–5.5	29,184	22,551
Leeds United	29,207	22,355	–23.5	27,843	18,353
Leicester City	24,137	22,234	–7.9	25,578	18,856
Luton Town	7,940	9,139	+15.1	10,248	7,474
Millwall	11,699	9,529	–18.5	13,209	7,108
Norwich City	24,354	24,952	+2.5	27,470	23,838
Plymouth Argyle	16,428	13,776	–16.1	17,726	10,460
Preston North End	13,889	14,617	+5.2	19,350	12,453
Queens Park Rangers	16,056	13,441	–16.3	16,152	10,901
Reading	17,169	20,207	+17.7	23,845	14,027
Sheffield United	19,594	23,650	+20.7	30,558	17,739
Sheffield Wednesday	23,100	24,853	+7.6	33,439	20,244
Southampton	30,610	23,614	–22.9	30,173	19,086
Stoke City	16,456	14,432	–12.3	20,408	10,121
Watford	14,290	15,415	+7.9	19,842	11,358
Wolverhampton Wanderers	26,620	23,624	–11.3	27,980	21,683

Premiership and Football League attendance averages and highest crowd figures for 2005–06 are unofficial. The official Premiership total was 12,876,993.

FOOTBALL LEAGUE CHAMPIONSHIP 1 ATTENDANCES

	Average Gate			Season 2005–06	
	2004–05	2005–06	+/–%	Highest	Lowest
Barnsley	9,779	9,054	–7.4	13,263	6,996
Blackpool	6,032	5,820	–3.5	8,541	4,326
AFC Bournemouth	7,123	6,458	–9.3	9,359	5,191
Bradford City	8,839	8,265	–6.5	15,608	6,745
Brentford	6,082	6,775	+11.4	9,903	5,131
Bristol City	11,391	11,725	+2.9	15,889	9,103
Chesterfield	4,961	4,772	–3.8	7,073	3,445
Colchester United	3,534	3,969	+12.3	5,920	2,721
Doncaster Rovers	6,886	6,139	–10.8	8,299	4,262
Gillingham	8,528	6,671	–21.8	8,128	4,861
Hartlepool United	5,182	4,812	–7.1	6,895	3,375
Huddersfield Town	11,905	13,058	+9.7	19,052	10,304
Milton Keynes Dons FC	4,896	5,776	+18.0	8,426	4,423
Nottingham Forest	23,608	20,257	–14.2	28,193	16,237
Oldham Athletic	6,462	5,797	–10.3	7,772	3,878
Port Vale	4,973	4,657	–6.4	6,793	3,452
Rotherham United	6,272	5,306	–15.4	7,625	3,537
Scunthorpe United	5,178	5,171	–0.1	7,152	3,786
Southend United	6,077	8,053	+32.5	11,387	5,261
Swansea City	8,458	14,112	+66.8	19,288	11,028
Swindon Town	5,835	5,951	+2.0	8,985	4,139
Tranmere Rovers	9,044	7,211	–20.3	9,152	6,210
Walsall	6,085	5,392	–11.4	8,703	4,293
Yeovil Town	6,320	6,668	+5.5	9,579	5,048

FOOTBALL LEAGUE CHAMPIONSHIP 2 ATTENDANCES

	Average Gate			Season 2005–06	
	2004–05	2005–06	+/–%	Highest	Lowest
Barnet	2,512	2,578	+2.6	3,873	1,366
Boston United	2,932	2,519	–14.1	4,476	1,651
Bristol Rovers	7,077	5,989	–15.4	7,551	4,836
Bury	3,032	2,594	–14.4	4,276	1,673
Carlisle United	5,513	7,218	+30.9	13,467	5,190
Cheltenham Town	3,648	3,453	–5.3	6,005	2,531
Chester City	2,812	2,964	+5.4	4,801	1,806
Darlington	4,245	4,199	–1.1	8,640	2,905
Grimsby Town	4,943	5,151	+4.2	8,458	3,658
Leyton Orient	3,712	4,699	+26.6	6,720	3,463
Lincoln City	4,927	4,739	–3.8	7,182	2,956
Macclesfield Town	2,272	2,275	+0.1	4,553	1,576
Mansfield Town	4,092	3,560	–13.0	6,444	2,357
Northampton Town	5,927	5,935	+0.1	7,114	5,012
Notts County	5,384	5,467	+1.5	9,817	3,710
Oxford United	5,347	5,443	+1.8	12,243	3,702
Peterborough United	4,341	4,364	+0.5	8,637	2,833
Rochdale	2,690	2,808	+4.4	4,439	1,769
Rushden & Diamonds	3,321	3,162	–4.8	5,211	2,216
Shrewsbury Town	4,251	3,997	–6.0	6,249	2,469
Stockport County	5,000	4,772	–4.6	10,006	3,460
Torquay United	3,511	2,851	–18.8	5,697	2,010
Wrexham	4,751	4,478	–5.7	7,240	3,195
Wycombe Wanderers	4,937	5,445	+10.3	7,134	4,166

TRANSFERS 2005–2006

JUNE 2005	From	To
2 Bent, Darren	Ipswich Town	Charlton Athletic
7 Campbell, Dudley J.	Yeading	Brentford
29 Doherty, Thomas	Bristol City	Queens Park Rangers
6 Evatt, Ian R.	Chesterfield	Queens Park Rangers
8 Heffernan, Paul	Bristol City	Doncaster Rovers
16 Lynch, Mark J.	Sunderland	Hull City
3 Macken, Jonathan P.	Manchester City	Crystal Palace
14 Moore, Stefan	Aston Villa	Queens Park Rangers
15 Parker, Scott M.	Chelsea	Newcastle United
30 Pollitt, Michael F.	Rotherham United	Wigan Athletic
16 Stead, Jonathan	Blackburn Rovers	Sunderland
10 Van der Sar, Edwin	Fulham	Manchester United
11 Vernon, Scott M.	Oldham Athletic	Blackpool
29 Villis, Matthew	Plymouth Argyle	Torquay United
1 Webber, Daniel V.	Watford	Sheffield United
9 Wellens, Richard P.	Blackpool	Oldham Athletic

JULY 2005		
11 Ambrose, Darren	Newcastle United	Charlton Athletic
8 Artell, David J.	Mansfield Town	Chester City
7 Bellamy, Craig D.	Newcastle United	Blackburn Rovers
28 Blake, Robert J.	Birmingham City	Leeds United
15 Blundell, Gregg	Doncaster Rovers	Chester City
5 Breckin, Ian	Wigan Athletic	Nottingham Forest
26 Bridges, Michael	Sunderland	Bristol City
20 Carruthers, Christopher P.A.	Northampton Town	Bristol Rovers
5 Carter, Darren A.	Birmingham City	West Bromwich Albion
21 Cole, Andrew A.	Fulham	Manchester City
14 Cole, Mitchell J.	Grays Athletic	Southend United
26 Coles, Daniel R.	Bristol City	Hull City
12 Coughlan, Graham	Plymouth Argyle	Sheffield Wednesday
20 Crouch, Peter J.	Southampton	Liverpool
2 Davis, Kelvin G.	Ipswich Town	Sunderland
14 Dichio, Daniele S.E.	Millwall	Preston North End
1 Eaden, Nicholas J.	Wigan Athletic	Nottingham Forest
4 Forssell, Mikael K.	Chelsea	Birmingham City
19 Foster, Benjamin	Stoke City	Manchester United
27 Gilbert, Peter	Plymouth Argyle	Leicester City
22 Gunnarsson, Brynjar B.	Watford	Reading
8 Hargreaves, Christian	Brentford	Oxford United
13 Harrold, Matthew	Brentford	Yeovil
11 Heath, Matthew P.	Leicester City	Coventry City
7 Helguson, Heidar	Watford	Fulham
30 Huddlestone, Thomas A.	Derby County	Tottenham Hotspur
21 Hughes, Andrew J.	Reading	Norwich City
21 Hulse, Robert W.	West Bromwich Albion	Leeds United
7 Johnson, Brett	Aldershot Town	Northampton Town
5 Konchesky, Paul M.	Charlton Athletic	West Ham United
14 Lennon, Aaron J.	Leeds United	Tottenham Hotspur
14 Lita, Leroy	Bristol City	Reading
4 Louis-Jean, Matthieu	Nottingham Forest	Norwich City
15 Martin, Daniel A.	Derby County	Notts County
20 Nade, Raphael	Woking	Carlisle United
7 O'Brien, Andrew J.	Newcastle United	Portsmouth
25 Parkin, Sam	Swindon Town	Ipswich Town
6 Phillips, Kevin	Southampton	Aston Villa
22 Prendergast, Rory	Accrington Stanley	Blackpool
6 Purser, Wayne M.	Peterborough United	Weymouth
22 Rodgers, Luke J.	Shrewsbury Town	Crewe Alexandra
20 Shipperley, Neil J.	Crystal Palace	Sheffield United
15 Stewart, Jordan B.	Leicester City	Watford
13 Talbot, Stewart D.	Brentford	Boston United
13 Taylor, Ryan A.	Tranmere Rovers	Wigan Athletic
19 Thornton, Sean	Sunderland	Doncaster Rovers

27	Vassell, Darius	Aston Villa	Manchester City
22	Vine, Rowan	Portsmouth	Luton Town
12	Williamson, Lee	Northampton Town	Rotherham United
19	Wright-Phillips, Shaun C.	Manchester City	Chelsea
13	Yakubu, Ayegbeni	Portsmouth	Middlesbrough

TEMPORARY TRANSFERS

14	Beckett, Luke J.	Sheffield United	Oldham Athletic
6	Davies, Andrew	Middlesbrough	Derby County
26	Denton, Samuel E.	Bradford City	Harrogate Town
15	Diouf, El Hadji O.	Liverpool	Bolton Wanderers
1	Duffy, Richard	Portsmouth	Coventry City
26	Eagles, Christopher M.	Manchester United	Sheffield Wednesday
30	Elebert, David	Preston North End	Scarborough
6	Johnson, Edward W.	Manchester United	Crewe Alexandra
12	King, Marlon F.	Nottingham Forest	Watford
18	Kirkland, Christopher E.	Liverpool	West Bromwich Albion
26	McArdle, Rory A.	Sheffield Wednesday	Rochdale
7	Robert, Laurent	Newcastle United	Portsmouth
6	Sawyer, Gary D.	Plymouth Argyle	Exeter City
5	Smertin, Alexei	Chelsea	Charlton Athletic
11	Spector, Jonathan M.	Manchester United	Charlton Athletic
18	Stack, Graham	Arsenal	Reading
1	Symes, Michael	Bradford City	Macclesfield Town
21	Young, Jamie	Reading	Rushden & Diamonds

AUGUST 2005

22	Anderton, Darren R.	Birmingham City	Wolverhampton Wanderers
25	Asaba, Carl	Stoke City	Millwall
23	Baros, Milan	Liverpool	Aston Villa
3	Broomes, Marlon C.	Preston North End	Stoke City
8	Camara, Henri	Wolverhampton Wanderers	Wigan Athletic
8	Carlisle, Clarke J.	Leeds United	Watford
31	Clare, Daryl A.	Boston United	Crawley Town
1	Clarke, Clive	Stoke City	West Ham United
31	Connolly, David J.	Leicester City	Wigan Athletic
31	Courtney, Duane	AFC Telford United	Burnley
24	Cresswell, Richard P.W.	Preston North End	Leeds United
5	Cullip, Daniel	Sheffield United	Nottingham Forest
25	Dadi, Eugene	Tranmere Rovers	Nottingham Forest
31	Davies, Curtis E.	Luton Town	West Bromwich Albion
11	De Zeeuw, Arjan	Portsmouth	Wigan Athletic
24	Devaney, Martin T.	Watford	Barnsley
15	Ellington, Nathan L.F.	Wigan Athletic	West Bromwich Albion
5	Francis, Damien J.	Norwich City	Wigan Athletic
5	Fuller, Ricardo	Portsmouth	Southampton
11	Graham, David	Wigan Athletic	Sheffield Wednesday
11	Gray, Andrew D.	Sheffield United	Sunderland
31	Hammond, Elvis Z.	Fulham	Leicester City
30	Harley, Jon	Sheffield United	Burnley
4	Henderson, Darius A.	Gillingham	Watford
6	Hughes, Aaron W.	Newcastle United	Aston Villa
31	Hume, Iain	Tranmere Rovers	Leicester City
31	Jenas, Jermaine A.	Newcastle United	Tottenham Hotspur
31	Johnson, Gavin	Boston United	Northampton Town
25	Morrison, Clinton	Birmingham City	Crystal Palace
11	Murphy, Joseph	West Bromwich Albion	Sunderland
3	Neal, Lewis	Stoke City	Preston North End
4	Neville, Philip	Manchester United	Everton
30	Nowland, Adam C.	Nottingham Forest	Preston North End
19	Pogliacomi, Leslie A.	Oldham Athletic	Blackpool
31	Sabin, Eric	Northampton Town	Oxford United
18	Sharp, William	Sheffield United	Scunthorpe United
31	Solano, Nolberto A.	Aston Villa	Newcastle United
25	Spicer, John W.	AFC Bournemouth	Burnley
19	Spring, Matthew	Leeds United	Watford
31	Thirlwell, Paul	Sheffield United	Derby County
26	Torres, Sergio P.	Basingstoke Town	Wycombe Wanderers

| 17 Unsworth, David G. | Portsmouth | Sheffield United |
| 31 Williams, Thomas A. | Barnsley | Gillingham |

TEMPORARY TRANSFERS

25 Aliadiere, Jeremie	Arsenal	West Ham United
4 Andrew, Calvin H.	Luton Town	Grimsby Town
12 Angel, Mark	Kings Lynn	Cambridge United
12 Anyon, Joseph	Port Vale	Stafford Rangers
15 Ashikodi, Moses	West Ham United	Gillingham
1 Atieno, Taiwo L.	Walsall	Kidderminster Harriers
31 Bakke, Eirik	Leeds United	Aston Villa
17 Bellion, David	Manchester United	West Ham United
31 Bentley, David M.	Arsenal	Blackburn Rovers
31 Bermingham, Karl	Manchester City	Burnley
4 Best, Leon J.	Southampton	Sheffield Wednesday
12 Blewitt, Darren L.	West Ham United	Hereford United
12 Bond, Andrew M.	Crewe Alexandra	Lancaster City
19 Bossu, Bertrand	Darlington	Accrington Stanley
22 Brooks, Jamie P.	Oxford United	Slough Town
21 Brown, Paul H.	Tranmere Rovers	Accrington Stanley
10 Brown, Wayne L.	Chester City	Hereford United
1 Bruce, Alex	Birmingham City	Tranmere Rovers
31 Burch, Robert K.	Tottenham Hotspur	Bristol City
4 Butt, Nicholas	Newcastle United	Birmingham City
3 Bywater, Stephen	West Ham United	Coventry City
5 Carlisle, Clarke J.	Leeds United	Watford
4 Chadwick, Luke H.	West Ham United	Stoke City
2 Clarke, Ryan J.	Bristol Rovers	Forest Green Rovers
31 Clingan, Samuel G.	Wolverhampton Wanderers	Chesterfield
26 Coleman, Dean S.	Walsall	Hailsowen Town
12 Collins, Neill	Sunderland	Hartlepool United
3 Collins, Patrick	Sheffield Wednesday	Swindon Town
28 Cornes, Christopher R.	Wolverhampton Wanderers	Port Vale
31 Denton, Samuel E.	Bradford City	Guiseley
31 Derbyshire, Matthew	Blackburn Rovers	Plymouth Argyle
3 Diao, Salif	Liverpool	Portsmouth
10 Dormand, James	Birmingham City	Tamworth
19 Douglas, Jonathan	Blackburn Rovers	Leeds United
5 Duke, Matthew	Hull City	Stockport County
2 Fish, Mark A.	Charlton Athletic	Ipswich Town
18 Flood, William	Manchester City	Coventry City
31 Foley-Sheridan, Steven	Aston Villa	AFC Bournemouth
31 Forte, Jonathan	Sheffield United	Doncaster Rovers
2 Foster, Benjamin	Manchester United	Watford
30 Fox, Michael J.S.	Chesterfield	Belper Town
29 Gallagher, Paul	Blackburn Rovers	Stoke City
12 Gordon, Christopher	Lincoln City	Gainsborough Trinity
9 Graham, Luke	Northampton Town	Forest Green Rovers
11 Guyett, Scott B.	Yeovil Town	Aldershot Town
12 Haldane, Lewis O.	Bristol Rovers	Forest Green Rovers
19 Hammond, Elvis Z.	Fulham	Leicester City
19 Harkness, Jonathan	Walsall	Cambridge United
26 Harley, Jon	Sheffield United	Burnley
31 Harper, Adrian	Sheffield United	Scarborough
27 Harris, Neil	Nottingham Forest	Gillingham
19 Heath, Colin	Manchester United	Swindon Town
19 Heaton, Thomas D.	Manchester United	Swindon Town
4 Henderson, Wayne	Aston Villa	Brighton & Hove Albion
5 Horwood, Evan D.	Sheffield United	Scunthorpe United
9 Howell, Simeon	Reading	Forest Green Rovers
31 Hoyte, Justin R.	Arsenal	Sunderland
7 Hurst, Kevan	Sheffield United	Chesterfield
31 Ikeme, Carl	Wolverhampton Wanderers	Stockport County
22 Jarosik, Jiri	Chelsea	Birmingham City
3 Jones, David F.L.	Manchester United	Preston North End
22 Jones, Paul S.	Wolverhampton Wanderers	Millwall
30 Jubb, Anthony P.	Chesterfield	Belper Town
8 Keenan, Joseph J.	Chelsea	Brentford

3	Le Tallec, Anthony	Liverpool	Sunderland
31	Leary, Michael	Luton Town	Bristol Rovers
25	Lee, Richard A.	Watford	Blackburn Rovers
26	Lowe, Keith S.	Wolverhampton Wanderers	Burnley
2	Marney, Dean E.	Tottenham Hotspur	Norwich City
18	McClenahan, Trent	West Ham United	Milton Keynes Dons
31	McDermott, Neale T.	Fulham	Swindon Town
30	McEveley, James	Blackburn Rovers	Ipswich Town
6	McGurk, David	Darlington	York City
12	McPhee, Christopher S.	Brighton & Hove Albion	Aldershot Town
19	McShane, Luke	Peterborough United	Gravesend & Northfleet
4	McShane, Paul D.	Manchester United	Brighton & Hove Albion
31	Mills, Pablo	Derby County	Milton Keynes Dons
2	Milner, James P.	Newcastle United	Aston Villa
5	Molango, Maheta	Brighton & Hove Albion	Lincoln City
31	Nethercott, Stuart	Wycombe Wanderers	Woking
26	Nowland, Adam C.	Nottingham Forest	Preston North End
12	O'Grady, Christopher	Leicester City	Rushden & Diamonds
31	Oliver, Luke	Yeovil Town	Woking
3	Palmer, Jermaine	Grimsby Town	Scarborough
18	Picken, Philip J.	Manchester United	Chesterfield
8	Platt, Sean	Walsall	Willenhall Town
20	Poke, Michael H.	Southampton	Oldham Athletic
31	Poom, Mart	Sunderland	Arsenal
19	Postma, Stefan	Aston Villa	Wolverhampton Wanderers
30	Pratley, Darren	Fulham	Brentford
26	Randolph, Darren E.	Charlton Athletic	Accrington Stanley
31	Rankine, Michael	Scunthorpe United	Barrow
31	Rasiak, Grzegorz	Derby County	Tottenham Hotspur
15	Reed, Stephen	Yeovil Town	Woking
25	Rose, Michael C.	Yeovil Town	Cheltenham Town
26	Ross, Ian	Sheffield United	Boston United
31	Scully, Anthony D.T.	Notts County	Exeter City
3	Surman, Andrew R.	Southampton	AFC Bournemouth
2	Taylor, Andrew D.	Middlesbrough	Bradford City
5	Thelwell, Paul	Sheffield United	Derby County
2	Turnbull, Ross	Middlesbrough	Crewe Alexandra
26	Vaughan, Anthony J.	Barnsley	Stockport County
9	Vaughan, Lee	Walsall	Willenhall Town
5	Vincent, Jamie R.	Derby County	Millwall
26	Welsh, John J.	Liverpool	Hull City
31	Williams, Ryan N.	Bristol Rovers	Aldershot Town
31	Wright, Jake M.	Bradford City	Halifax Town
31	Wright, Thomas	Leicester City	Blackpool
5	Yeates, Mark	Tottenham Hotspur	Colchester United

SEPTEMBER 2005

12	Rasiak, Grzegorz	Derby County	Tottenham Hotspur

TEMPORARY TRANSFERS

22	Agbonlahor, Gabriel	Aston Villa	Watford
8	Bacon, Daniel S.	Lincoln City	Burton Albion
26	Bailey, Matthew	Crewe Alexandra	Hereford United
1	Baradji, Sekou	West Ham United	Reading
21	Benjamin, Trevor J.	Peterborough United	Watford
19	Bermingham, Karl	Manchester City	Burnley
23	Berry, Tyrone	Crystal Palace	Notts County
31	Blayney, Alan	Southampton	Brighton & Hove Albion
16	Boucaud, Andre	Peterborough United	Aldershot Town
2	Broad, Joseph R.	Walsall	Redditch United
20	Brooks, Jamie P.	Oxford United	Slough Town
23	Brown, Aaron	Queens Park Rangers	Cheltenham Town
8	Brown, Christopher	Sunderland	Hull City
30	Burch, Robert K.	Tottenham Hotspur	Bristol City
9	Campbell, Darren	Reading	Tamworth
27	Campbell-Ryce, Jamal	Rotherham United	Southend United
15	Castle, Peter	Reading	St Albans City
27	Clarke, Darrell J.	Hartlepool United	Port Vale

144

29	Cornes, Christopher R.	Wolverhampton Wanderers	Port Vale
12	Davenport, Calum R.P.	Tottenham Hotspur	Norwich City
27	Dyer, Lloyd	West Bromwich Albion	Queens Park Rangers
16	El Hamdaoui, Mounir	Tottenham Hotspur	Derby County
14	Fadiga, Khalilou	Bolton Wanderers	Derby County
15	Fletcher, Carl N.	West Ham United	Watford
21	Flood, William	Manchester City	Coventry City
2	Fontaine, Liam V.H.	Fulham	Yeovil Town
27	Forte, Jonathan	Sheffield United	Doncaster Rovers
26	Francis, Simon C.	Sheffield United	Grimsby Town
23	Frecklington, Lee	Lincoln City	Stamford
5	Friars, Emmett	Notts County	AFC Telford United
8	Gallagher, Paul	Blackburn Rovers	Stoke City
30	Gillett, Simon J.	Southampton	Walsall
14	Guyett, Scott B.	Yeovil Town	Aldershot Town
11	Haldane, Lewis O.	Bristol Rovers	Forest Green Rovers
23	Hand, Jamie	Watford	Peterborough United
1	Harris, Neil	Nottingham Forest	Gillingham
15	Hoult, Russell	West Bromwich Albion	Nottingham Forest
16	Husbands, Michael P.	Rushall Olympic	Walsall
12	Ifil, Phillip	Tottenham Hotspur	Millwall
11	Jackson, Johnnie	Tottenham Hotspur	Derby County
16	John, Stern	Coventry City	Derby County
26	Jones, Paul S.	Wolverhampton Wanderers	Millwall
13	Keene, James D.	Portsmouth	AFC Bournemouth
23	Leadbitter, Grant	Sunderland	Rotherham United
15	Lindegaard, Andrew	Yeovil Town	Crawley Town
9	Lisbie, Kevin	Charlton Athletic	Norwich City
30	McAliskey, John	Huddersfield Town	Torquay United
23	McGoldrick, David J.	Southampton	Notts County
14	McPhee, Christopher S.	Brighton & Hove Albion	Aldershot Town
22	Mikolanda, Petr	West Ham United	Northampton Town
16	Miller, Adam E.	Queens Park Rangers	Peterborough United
23	Morris, Ian	Leeds United	Blackpool
30	O'Brien, Alan	Newcastle United	Carlisle United
16	Palmer, Jermaine	Grimsby Town	York City
14	Pericard, Vincent D.P.	Portsmouth	Sheffield United
12	Platt, Sean	Walsall	Willenhall Town
23	Quinn, Stephen	Sheffield United	Milton Keynes Dons
23	Randolph, Darren E.	Charlton Athletic	Accrington Stanley
22	Rankine, Michael	Scunthorpe United	Barrow
27	Ross, Ian	Sheffield United	Boston United
27	Ruddy, John T.G.	Everton	Walsall
27	Sankofa, Osey O.K.	Charlton Athletic	Bristol City
23	Sanna, Christopher	Stoke City	Watford
8	Saunders, Mark P.	Gillingham	Welling United
23	Scully, Anthony D.T.	Notts County	Exeter City
30	Smith, Ryan C.M.	Arsenal	Leicester City
13	Vaughan, Lee	Walsall	Willenhall Town
7	Wallis, Jonathan	Gillingham	Hastings United
15	Whittingham, Peter	Aston Villa	Derby County
22	Williams, Adrian	Coventry City	Millwall
2	Williams, Dale T.	Yeovil Town	Tiverton Town
29	Wright, Jake M.	Bradford City	Halifax Town
13	Wright, Jermaine M.	Leeds United	Millwall

OCTOBER 2005

TEMPORARY TRANSFERS

28	Agbonlahor, Gabriel	Aston Villa	Sheffield Wednesday
23	Andrew, Calvin H.	Luton Town	Grimsby Town
27	Anyon, Joseph	Port Vale	Harrogate Town
13	Armstrong, Christopher	Sheffield United	Blackpool
26	Bailey, Matthew	Crewe Alexandra	Hereford United
7	Bell, Lee	Crewe Alexandra	Burton Albion
28	Bevan, Scott	Milton Keynes Dons	Tamworth
27	Blackstock, Dexter A.	Southampton	Derby County

145

17 Blayney, Alan	Southampton	Brighton & Hove Albion
7 Bouazza, Hameur	Watford	Swindon Town
26 Brooks, Jamie P.	Oxford United	Slough
6 Butcher, Richard T.	Oldham Athletic	Lincoln City
7 Coleman, Omari	Lincoln City	Aldershot Town
14 Conlon, Barry J.	Barnsley	Rotherham United
21 Cureton, Jamie	Swindon Town	Colchester United
28 Dann, Scott	Walsall	Redditch United
20 D'Laryea, Jonathan A.	Manchester City	Mansfield Town
18 Dolan, Joseph	Leyton Orient	Stockport County
31 Dyer, Lloyd	West Bromwich Albion	Queens Park Rangers
28 Dyer, Nathan A.J.	Southampton	Burnley
16 Edwards, Philip	Wigan Athletic	Accrington Stanley
26 Frecklington, Lee	Lincoln City	Stamford
4 Friars, Emmett	Notts County	AFC Telford United
28 Fulop, Marton	Tottenham Hotspur	Coventry City
21 Hand, Jamie	Watford	Peterborough United
27 Hardiker, John	Bury	Morecambe
28 Harkness, Jonathan	Walsall	Halesowen Town
28 Harley, Ryan B.	Bristol City	Forest Green Rovers
17 Hoult, Russell	West Bromwich Albion	Nottingham Forest
25 Huddlestone, Thomas A.	Tottenham Hotspur	Wolverhampton Wanderers
13 Husbands, Michael P.	Rushall Olympic	Port Vale
10 Jackson, Mark	Preston North End	Shrewsbury Town
21 Johnson, Jemal J.	Blackburn Rovers	Preston North End
31 Jones, Paul S.	Wolverhampton Wanderers	Millwall
4 Kay, Jamie	Stockport County	Woodleigh Sports
17 Keene, James D.	Portsmouth	AFC Bournemouth
21 Leadbitter, Grant	Sunderland	Rotherham United
4 Leary, Michael	Luton Town	Bristol Rovers
10 Lee, Kevin	Wigan Athletic	Accrington Stanley
13 Lindegaard, Andrew	Yeovil Town	Crawley Town
8 Lonergan, Andrew	Preston North End	Wycombe Wanderers
14 Lowe, Keith S.	Wolverhampton Wanderers	Burnley
14 Mendes, Albert J.H.A.	Huddersfield Town	Northampton Town
24 Morris, Ian	Leeds United	Blackpool
25 Mulligan, Gary	Sheffield United	Port Vale
27 Mullins, John	Reading	Kidderminster Harriers
21 Murphy, Joseph	Sunderland	Walsall
14 Nalis, Lilian B.P.	Sheffield United	Coventry City
21 O'Leary, Stephen	Luton Town	Tranmere Rovers
4 Oliver, Luke	Yeovil Town	Woking
21 Palmer, Jermaine	Grimsby Town	Hinckley United
28 Poke, Michael H.	Southampton	Northampton Town
10 Proudlock, Adam D.	Sheffield Wednesday	Ipswich Town
21 Quinn, James S.	Peterborough United	Bristol City
30 Randolph, Darren E.	Charlton Athletic	Accrington Stanley
14 Rankine, Michael	Scunthorpe United	Barrow
14 Rix, Benjamin	Crewe Alexandra	Scarborough
20 Robinson, Trevor K.	Millwall	Tamworth
27 Rose, Jason	Millwall	Aldershot Town
27 Ross, Ian	Sheffield United	Boston United
28 Ross, Maurice	Sheffield Wednesday	Wolverhampton Wanderers
21 Sanna, Christopher	Stoke City	Watford
4 Saunders, Ben	Doncaster Rovers	Worksop Town
28 Smith, Paul W.	Walsall	Gillingham
8 Strachan, Gavin D.	Hartlepool United	Stockport County
28 Thorne, Emerson A.	Wigan Athletic	Derby County
6 Till, Peter	Birmingham City	Scunthorpe United
21 Tomlinson, Ezekiel	Stockport County	AFC Telford United
21 Warrender, Daniel J.	Manchester City	Blackpool
28 Watt, Steven	Chelsea	Barnsley
14 Wijnhard, Clyde	Darlington	Macclesfield Town
21 Wilson, Kyle P.	Crewe Alexandra	Altrincham
13 Youga, Kelly A.	Charlton Athletic	Bristol City

NOVEMBER 2005

TEMPORARY TRANSFERS

24 Abbey, Nathanael	Boston United	Leyton Orient
25 Agbonlahor, Gabriel	Aston Villa	Sheffield Wednesday
18 Anaclet, Edward B.	Southampton	Tamworth
11 Andrews, Lee D.	Carlisle United	York City
10 Armstrong, Christopher	Sheffield United	Blackpool
23 Barwick, Terence P.	Grimsby Town	York City
6 Bell, Lee	Crewe Alexandra	Burton Albion
28 Bevan, Scott	Milton Keynes Dons	Tamworth
28 Blackstock, Dexter A.	Southampton	Derby County
7 Bouazza, Hameur	Watford	Swindon Town
4 Breach, Christopher B.	Brighton & Hove Albion	Bognor Regis Town
15 Bridges, Michael	Bristol City	Carlisle United
18 Broad, Joseph R.	Walsall	Redditch United
24 Brown, Aaron	Tamworth	Reading
24 Brown, Aaron	Queens Park Rangers	Swindon Town
9 Cohen, Christopher D.	West Ham United	Yeovil Town
24 Coleman, Omari	Lincoln City	Gravesend & Northfleet
2 Collins, Sam	Port Vale	Hull City
21 Constable, James A.	Chippenham Town	Walsall
4 Constantine, Leon	Torquay United	Port Vale
3 Cornes, Christopher R.	Wolverhampton Wanderers	Port Vale
18 Cureton, Jamie	Swindon Town	Colchester United
18 Dann, Scott	Walsall	Redditch United
24 De Bolla, Mark	Chesterfield	Notts County
24 D'Laryea, Jonathan A.	Manchester City	Mansfield Town
24 Dobson, Michael W.	Brentford	Reading
24 Dolan, Joseph	Leyton Orient	Fisher Athletic
24 Doyle, Colin	Birmingham City	Millwall
24 Drench, Steven M.	Blackburn Rovers	Morecambe
4 Dyer, Bruce A.	Stoke City	Millwall
28 Dyer, Lloyd	West Bromwich Albion	Queens Park Rangers
25 Dyer, Nathan A.J.	Southampton	Burnley
14 Edwards, Philip	Wigan Athletic	Accrington Stanley
23 Elliot, Robert	Charlton Athletic	Accrington Stanley
11 Etuhu, Dixon P.	Preston North End	Norwich City
18 Evans, Paul S.	Nottingham Forest	Rotherham United
23 Fitzgerald, Scott	Brentford	Oxford United
18 Forte, Jonathan	Sheffield United	Doncaster Rovers
10 Fortune, Clayton A.	Bristol City	Port Vale
10 Fowler, Lee A.	Huddersfield Town	Scarborough
18 Francis, Simon C.	Sheffield United	Tranmere Rovers
23 Frecklington, Lee	Lincoln City	Stamford
24 Gilbert, Peter	Leicester City	Sheffield Wednesday
10 Gillespie, Steven	Bristol City	Cheltenham Town
24 Gobern, Lewis T.	Wolverhampton Wanderers	Blackpool
24 Graham, Daniel A.W.	Middlesbrough	Derby County
15 Grant, Lee A.	Derby County	Burnley
22 Green, Francis	Lincoln City	Boston United
10 Griffin, Adam	Oldham Athletic	Oxford United
24 Hand, Jamie	Watford	Peterborough United
11 Harding, Benjamin S.	Milton Keynes Dons	Forest Green Rovers
15 Harkins, Gary	Blackburn Rovers	Blackpool
24 Horwood, Evan D.	Sheffield United	York City
23 Huddlestone, Thomas A.	Tottenham Hotspur	Wolverhampton Wanderers
21 Husbands, Michael P.	Rushall Olympic	Port Vale
24 Hutchison, Donald	Millwall	Coventry City
24 Jarrett, Jason L.	Norwich City	Plymouth Argyle
24 Johnson, Bradley	Northampton Town	Gravesend & Northfleet
24 Johnson, Brett	Northampton Town	Gravesend & Northfleet
24 Jones, Zachariah S.	Blackburn Rovers	Southampton
10 Joseph, Marc E.	Hull City	Bristol City
11 Kandol, Tresor O.	Dagenham & Redbridge	Darlington
8 Kay, Jamie	Stockport County	Woodleigh Sports
21 Keene, James D.	Portsmouth	AFC Bournemouth
9 Keogh, Richard J.	Bristol City	Wycombe Wanderers
22 Knowles, Daniel	Gillingham	East Thurrock United

24	Koo-Boothe, Nathan	Milton Keynes Dons	Grays Athletic
24	Kuipers, Michael	Brighton & Hove Albion	Boston United
7	Leary, Michael	Luton Town	Bristol Rovers
2	Lloyd, Anthony	Huddersfield Town	Torquay United
18	Lloyd, Callum	Mansfield Town	Alfreton Town
24	Lloyd, Robert F.	Crewe Alexandra	Witton Albion
18	Lockwood, Adam B.	Yeovil Town	Torquay United
24	Logan, Richard J.	Peterborough United	Lincoln City
24	MacKenzie, Neil	Macclesfield Town	Scunthorpe United
11	Madjo, Guy B.	Bristol City	Forest Green Rovers
24	Martin, Richard W.	Brighton & Hove Albion	Kingstonian
24	Maynard, Nicholas D.	Crewe Alexandra	Witton Albion
17	McDonald, Dean L.	Ipswich Town	Hartlepool United
24	Melton, Stephen	Boston United	Tamworth
17	Mendes, Albert J.H.A.	Huddersfield Town	Northampton Town
24	Mikolanda, Petr	West Ham United	Swindon Town
4	Miller, Liam W.	Manchester United	Leeds United
23	Morgan, Daniel F.	Oxford United	Basingstoke Town
23	Morris, Ian	Leeds United	Blackpool
24	Motteram, Carl	Birmingham City	Tamworth
28	Mulligan, Gary	Sheffield United	Port Vale
29	Mullins, John	Reading	Kidderminster Harriers
24	Murphy, Darryl	Sunderland	Sheffield Wednesday
21	Murphy, Joseph	Sunderland	Walsall
23	Noble, David J.	Boston United	Bristol City
24	Oji, Samuel U.U.	Birmingham City	Doncaster Rovers
8	Oliver, Luke	Yeovil Town	Woking
24	Parton, Andrew	Scunthorpe United	Scarborough
9	Paynter, William P.	Port Vale	Hull City
28	Pidgeley, Leonard J.	Chelsea	Millwall
17	Poke, Michael H.	Southampton	Northampton Town
24	Pope, Thomas J.	Crewe Alexandra	Lancaster City
24	Prendergast, Rory	Blackpool	Halifax Town
2	Quinn, Stephen	Sheffield United	Milton Keynes Dons
4	Reet, Daniel	Sheffield Wednesday	Bury
3	Ricketts, Mark J.	Charlton Athletic	Milton Keynes Dons
23	Rigoglioso, Adriano	Doncaster Rovers	Southport
23	Roach, Neville	Eastleigh	Oxford United
22	Roberts, Mark A.	Crewe Alexandra	Southport
24	Robinson, Carl P.	Sunderland	Norwich City
3	Robinson, Steven E.	Lincoln City	Worksop Town
10	Ruddy, John T.G.	Everton	Rushden & Diamonds
18	Russell, Allan	Macclesfield Town	Mansfield Town
4	Ryan, Oliver	Lincoln City	Ilkeston Town
1	Sankofa, Osey O.K.	Charlton Athletic	Bristol City
24	Saunders, Ben	Doncaster Rovers	Worksop Town
24	Savage, Basir M.	Coventry City	Bristol City
24	Scully, Anthony D.T.	Notts County	Crawley Town
4	Sedgemore, Jake O.	Bury	Burton Albion
23	Seremet, Dino	Luton Town	Doncaster Rovers
11	Skora, Eric	Preston North End	Walsall
24	Speight, Jake	Scarborough	Bury
4	Stonebridge, Ian R.	Wycombe Wanderers	Torquay United
24	Sutton, Ritchie A.	Crewe Alexandra	Leek Town
6	Till, Peter	Birmingham City	Scunthorpe United
10	Togwell, Samuel J.	Crystal Palace	Port Vale
9	Turner, Iain R.	Everton	Wycombe Wanderers
11	Tyson, Nathan	Wycombe Wanderers	Nottingham Forest
17	Vernazza, Paulo A.P.	Rotherham United	Barnet
24	Vincent, Ashley D.	Cheltenham Town	Aldershot Town
22	Ward, Elliott L.	West Ham United	Plymouth Argyle
15	Warrender, Daniel J.	Manchester City	Blackpool
4	Weaver, Nicholas	Manchester City	Sheffield Wednesday
24	Whitbread, Zak B.	Liverpool	Millwall
24	Wilcox, Jason M.	Leicester City	Blackpool
4	Wilkinson, Neil	Hartlepool United	Blyth Spartans
9	Williams, Gavin J.	West Ham United	Ipswich Town
18	Wilson, Kyle P.	Crewe Alexandra	Altrincham

4	Winter, James H.	Hartlepool United	Gateshead
3	Woodman, Craig A.	Bristol City	Torquay United
17	Wright, David	Wigan Athletic	Norwich City
1	Wright, Jake M.	Bradford City	Halifax Town
10	Youga, Kelly A.	Charlton Athletic	Bristol City

DECEMBER 2005

28	Diouf, El Hadji O.	Liverpool	Bolton Wanderers

TEMPORARY TRANSFERS

19	Anaclet, Edward B.	Southampton	Tamworth
12	Andrews, Lee D.	Carlisle United	York City
16	Appleby, Andrew	Hartlepool United	Blyth Spartans
16	Breach, Christopher B.	Brighton & Hove Albion	Bognor Regis Town
23	Brooks, Jamie P.	Oxford United	Brackley Town
2	Chilaka, Chibuzor	Notts County	Hinckley United
8	Cohen, Christopher D.	West Ham United	Yeovil Town
23	Coleman, Omari	Lincoln City	Gravesend & Northfleet
2	Corneille, Mark	Gillingham	Eastbourne Borough
30	Crane, Anthony S.	Grimsby Town	Worksop Town
16	D'Laryea, Jonathan A.	Manchester City	Mansfield Town
30	Dolan, Joseph	Leyton Orient	Fisher Athletic
23	Doyle, Colin	Birmingham City	Millwall
22	Drench, Steven M.	Blackburn Rovers	Morecambe
12	Edwards, Philip	Wigan Athletic	Accrington Stanley
30	Elliot, Robert	Charlton Athletic	Accrington Stanley
29	Foley-Sheridan, Steven	Aston Villa	AFC Bournemouth
10	Fowler, Lee A.	Huddersfield Town	Scarborough
19	Francis, Simon C.	Sheffield United	Tranmere Rovers
23	Grant, Lee A.	Derby County	Burnley
23	Hardiker, John	Bury	Morecambe
16	Harding, Benjamin S.	Milton Keynes Dons	Forest Green Rovers
16	Hicks, David	Northampton Town	Hitchin Town
12	Johnson, Bradley	Northampton Town	Gravesend & Northfleet
23	Johnson, Brett	Northampton Town	Gravesend & Northfleet
30	Johnson, Edward W.	Manchester United	Crewe Alexandra
15	Joseph, Marc E.	Hull City	Bristol City
8	Kay, Jamie	Stockport County	Woodley Sports
30	Kennedy, Luke D.	Rushden & Diamonds	Cambridge City
30	Knight, David	Middlesbrough	Darlington
22	Knowles, Daniel	Gillingham	East Thurrock United
5	Lamb, Alan	Grimsby Town	Eastwood Town
19	Lloyd, Robert F.	Crewe Alexandra	Witton Albion
12	Lockwood, Adam B.	Yeovil Town	Torquay United
24	Logan, Conrad	Leicester City	Boston United
18	Logan, Richard J.	Peterborough United	Lincoln City
12	Martin, Richard W.	Brighton & Hove Albion	Kingstonian
4	Maynard, Nicholas D.	Crewe Alexandra	Witton Albion
30	McClenahan, Trent	West Ham United	Milton Keynes Dons
30	Melton, Stephen	Boston United	Tamworth
23	Morgan, Daniel F.	Oxford United	Basingstoke Town
28	Nethercott, Stuart	Wycombe Wanderers	Woking
2	Palmer, Jermaine	Grimsby Town	Hinckley United
29	Picken, Philip J.	Manchester United	Chesterfield
20	Platt, Sean	Walsall	Hednesford Town
20	Poom, Mart	Sunderland	Arsenal
23	Pope, Thomas J.	Crewe Alexandra	Lancaster City
29	Prendergast, Rory	Blackpool	Halifax Town
5	Reet, Daniel	Sheffield Wednesday	Bury
7	Ricketts, Mark J.	Charlton Athletic	Milton Keynes Dons
1	Robinson, Steven E.	Lincoln City	Worksop Town
16	Ruddy, John T.G.	Everton	Chester City
5	Ryan, Oliver	Lincoln City	Ilkeston Town
16	Saunders, Ben	Doncaster Rovers	Worksop Town
2	Sedgemore, Jake O.	Bury	Burton Albion
30	Smith, Ryan C.M.	Arsenal	Leicester City
5	Stonebridge, Ian R.	Wycombe Wanderers	Torquay United
21	Sutton, Ritchie A.	Crewe Alexandra	Leek Town

28 Turnbull, Ross	Middlesbrough	Crewe Alexandra
20 Ward, Elliot L.	West Ham United	Plymouth Argyle
19 Warrender, Daniel J.	Manchester City	Blackpool
18 Weaver, Nicholas	Manchester City	Sheffield Wednesday
23 Wilcox, Jason M.	Leicester City	Blackpool
2 Wilkinson, Neil	Hartlepool United	Blyth Spartans
7 Williams, Christopher	Stockport County	Leigh RMI
6 Williams, Gavin J.	West Ham United	Ipswich Town
22 Wilson, Kyle P.	Crewe Alexandra	Barrow
22 Winters, Thomas R.	Oxford United	Brackley Town

JANUARY 2006

27 Akinbiyi, Adeola P.	Burnley	Sheffield United
24 Ashton, Dean	Norwich City	West Ham United
31 Barrowman, Andrew	Birmingham City	Walsall
23 Bean, Marcus T.	Queens Park Rangers	Blackpool
12 Bell, David A.	Rushden & Diamonds	Luton Town
10 Bennett, Julian L.	Walsall	Nottingham Forest
17 Bent, Marcus N.	Everton	Charlton Athletic
31 Bentley, David M.	Arsenal	Blackburn Rovers
31 Berry, Tyrone	Crystal Palace	Rushden & Diamonds
5 Blayney, Alan	Southampton	Doncaster Rovers
1 Brown, Aaron	Tamworth	Reading
3 Brown, Aaron	Queens Park Rangers	Swindon Town
31 Brown, Michael R.	Tottenham Hotspur	Fulham
13 Burgess, Andrew J.	Rushden & Diamonds	Oxford United
1 Burton, Deon J.	Rotherham United	Sheffield Wednesday
31 Campbell, Dudley J.	Brentford	Birmingham City
31 Castle, Peter	Reading	Rushden & Diamonds
5 Chadwick, Luke H.	West Ham United	Stoke City
31 Christie, Iyseden	Kidderminster Harriers	Rochdale
20 Clarke, Jamie W.	Rochdale	Boston United
24 Clingan, Samuel G.	Wolverhampton Wanderers	Nottingham Forest
2 Collins, Sam	Port Vale	Hull City
1 Constable, James A.	Chippenham Town	Walsall
3 Constantine, Leon	Torquay United	Port Vale
17 Crane, Anthony S.	Grimsby Town	Worksop Town
12 Da Silva Mendes, Pedro M.	Tottenham Hotspur	Portsmouth
16 Dagnall, Christopher	Tranmere Rovers	Rochdale
12 Davis, Sean	Tottenham Hotspur	Portsmouth
31 Delap, Rory J.	Southampton	Sunderland
30 Dempster, John	Rushden & Diamonds	Oxford United
30 Dyer, Lloyd	West Bromwich Albion	Millwall
3 Earnshaw, Robert	West Bromwich Albion	Norwich City
31 Easter, Jermaine	Stockport County	Wycombe Wanderers
11 Edwards, Philip	Wigan Athletic	Accrington Stanley
3 Etuhu, Dixon P.	Preston North End	Norwich City
28 Foley-Sheridan, Steven	Aston Villa	AFC Bournemouth
30 Fowler, Robert B.	Manchester City	Liverpool
10 Fryatt, Matthew C.	Walsall	Leicester City
12 Futcher, Benjamin P.	Boston United	Grimsby Town
5 Gilbert, Peter	Leicester City	Sheffield Wednesday
31 Gillespie, Steven	Bristol City	Cheltenham Town
3 Golbourne, Scott J.	Bristol City	Reading
31 Gritton, Martin	Grimsby Town	Lincoln City
19 Halls, John	Stoke City	Reading
20 Hatswell, Wayne	Kidderminster Harriers	Rushden & Diamonds
18 Heckingbottom, Paul	Sheffield Wednesday	Barnsley
31 Jackson, Mark G.	Kidderminster Harriers	Rochdale
12 Joseph, Marc E.	Hull City	Blackpool
30 Kandol, Tresor O.	Dagenham & Redbridge	Barnet
25 Kiely, Dean L.	Charlton Athletic	Portsmouth
3 King, Marlon F.	Nottingham Forest	Watford
12 Lee, Graeme B.	Sheffield Wednesday	Doncaster Rovers
9 Lee, Jason	Boston United	Northamptonn Town
6 Lloyd, Anthony	Huddersfield Town	Torquay United
1 MacKenzie, Neil	Macclesfield Town	Scunthorpe United
13 Martin, David E.	Milton Keynes Dons	Liverpool

18	McGregor, Mark D.T.	Blackpool	Port Vale
31	Mills, Matthew C.	Southampton	Manchester City
26	Moore, Darren M.	West Bromwich Albion	Derby County
31	Murphy, Daniel B.	Charlton Athletic	Tottenham Hotspur
10	Niemi, Antti	Southampton	Fulham
10	Noble, David J.	Boston United	Bristol City
26	Odubade, Yemi	Eastbourne Borough	Oxford United
27	Oliver, Luke	Yeovil Town	Stevenage Borough
30	Ormerod, Brett R.	Southampton	Preston North End
18	Otsemobor, John	Rotherham United	Crewe Alexandra
12	Pamarot, Noe	Tottenham Hotspur	Portsmouth
12	Parkin, Jonathan	Macclesfield Town	Hull City
2	Paynter, William P.	Port Vale	Hull City
10	Postma, Stefan	Aston Villa	Wolverhampton Wanderers
24	Price, Jason	Hull City	Doncaster Rovers
1	Proudlock, Adam D.	Sheffield Wednesday	Ipswich Town
31	Quashie, Nigel F.	Southampton	West Bromwich Albion
30	Ramsden, Simon	Grimsby Town	Rochdale
13	Reet, Daniel	Sheffield Wednesday	Mansfield Town
17	Robinson, Carl P.	Sunderland	Norwich City
26	Ross, Maurice	Sheffield Wednesday	Wolverhampton Wanderers
30	Sills, Timothy	Aldershot Town	Oxford United
25	Smith, Kevin	Leeds United	Sunderland
11	Sodje, Efetobore	Yeovil Town	Southend United
3	Speight, Jake	Scarborough	Bury
1	Stack, Graham	Arsenal	Reading
16	Stock, Brian B.	AFC Bournemouth	Preston North End
20	Stubbs, Alan	Sunderland	Everton
17	Taylor, Scott J.	Plymouth Argyle	Milton Keynes Dons
30	Thomas, Bradley M.	Eastleigh	Yeovil Town
5	Tudgay, Marcus	Derby County	Sheffield Wednesday
31	Turner, John A.J.	Cambridge United	Rushden & Diamonds
20	Tynan, Scott J.	Barnet	Rushden & Diamonds
3	Tyson, Nathan	Wycombe Wanderers	Nottingham Forest
23	Warrender, Daniel J.	Manchester City	Blackpool
2	Welsh, John J.	Liverpool	Hull City
9	Whaley, Simon	Bury	Preston North End
4	Williams, Gavin J.	West Ham United	Ipswich Town
31	Willock, Calum	Peterborough United	Brentford
31	Wood, Neil A.	Coventry City	Blackpool
27	Woodhouse, Curtis	Hull City	Grimsby Town
1	Wright, Thomas	Leicester City	Barnsley

TEMPORARY TRANSFERS

6	Adaggio, Marco	Shrewsbury Town	AFC Telford United
27	Afful, Leslie S.	Exeter City	Torquay United
30	Andrew, Calvin H.	Luton Town	Bristol City
31	Angus, Stevland D.	Grays Athletic	Barnet
13	Asamoah, Derek	Lincoln City	Chester City
12	Bailey, Matthew	Crewe Alexandra	Southport
20	Bean, Marcus T.	Queens Park Rangers	Blackpool
31	Benjamin, Trevor J.	Peterborough United	Swindon Town
13	Berry, Tyrone	Crystal Palace	Rushden & Diamonds
1	Best, Leon J.	Southampton	Sheffield Wednesday
27	Black, Thomas R.	Crystal Palace	Gillingham
1	Bloomer, Matthew	Lincoln City	Grimsby Town
27	Bowditch, Dean	Ipswich Town	Wycombe Wanderers
20	Bridge, Wayne M.	Chelsea	Fulham
13	Castle, Peter	Reading	Rushden & Diamonds
31	Cecila Batista, Ricardo J.	Fulham	Milton Keynes Dons
31	Clarke, Leon M.	Wolverhampton Wanderers	Queens Park Rangers
31	Cohen, Christopher D.	West Ham United	Yeovil Town
13	Collins, Aiden	Ipswich Town	Wycombe Wanderers
21	Corden, Simon W.	Scunthorpe United	Chester City
4	Corneille, Mark	Gillingham	Eastbourne Borough
19	Craddock, Darren	Hartlepool United	York City
9	Crooks, Lee R.	Bradford City	Notts County
20	Dadi, Eugene	Nottingham Forest	Notts County

13	Dagnall, Christopher	Tranmere Rovers	Rochdale
30	Dixon, Jonathan J.	Wycombe Wanderers	Aldershot Town
31	Dobson, Michael W.	Brentford	Reading
20	Doolan, John	Blackpool	Rochdale
20	Dootson, Craig R.	Bury	Hinckley United
12	Doyle, Colin	Birmingham City	Millwall
31	Drench, Steven M.	Blackburn Rovers	Morecambe
13	Duke, Matthew	Hull City	Wycombe Wanderers
6	Eagles, Christopher M.	Manchester United	Watford
30	Easter, Jermaine	Stockport County	Wycombe Wanderers
20	Edwards, Andrew D.	Southend United	Grays Athletic
31	El Hamdaoui, Mounir	Tottenham Hotspur	Derby County
23	Elphick, Gary	Brighton & Hove Albion	Aldershot Town
12	Flitcroft, Garry W.	Blackburn Rovers	Sheffield United
31	Folly, Yoann	Southampton	Sheffield Wednesday
16	Fontaine, Liam V.H.	Fulham	Bristol City
9	Forte, Jonathan	Sheffield United	Rotherham United
10	Fortune, Clayton A.	Bristol City	Port Vale
4	Fowler, Lee A.	Huddersfield Town	Scarborough
23	Francis, Simon C.	Sheffield United	Tranmere Rovers
12	Fuller, Barry M.	Charlton Athletic	Barnet
30	Fulop, Marton	Tottenham Hotspur	Coventry City
31	Gallagher, Paul	Blackburn Rovers	Stoke City
1	Gillespie, Steven	Bristol City	Cheltenham Town
4	Gobern, Lewis T.	Wolverhampton Wanderers	Blackpool
1	Graham, Daniel A.W.	Middlesbrough	Derby County
23	Graham, David	Sheffield Wednesday	Huddersfield Town
13	Grant, Anthony P.S.	Chelsea	Oldham Athletic
31	Grant, Lee A.	Derby County	Oldham Athletic
20	Green, Adam	Fulham	Bristol City
20	Griffin, Adam	Oldham Athletic	Stockport County
6	Hall, Asa	Birmingham City	Boston United
12	Hayes, Jonathan	Reading	Forest Green Rovers
13	Heckingbottom, Paul	Sheffield Wednesday	Barnsley
19	Hicks, David	Northampton Town	Hitchin Town
1	Hopkins, Paul D.	Everton	Darlington
31	Horwood, Evan D.	Sheffield United	Chester City
13	Howarth, Christopher	Bolton Wanderers	Stockport County
5	Huddlestone, Thomas A.	Tottenham Hotspur	Wolverhampton Wanderers
20	Hurst, Kevan	Sheffield United	Chesterfield
5	Hutchison, Donald	Millwall	Coventry City
20	Ifil, Phillip	Tottenham Hotspur	Millwall
12	Igoe, Samuel	Millwall	Bristol Rovers
4	James, Kevin E.	Nottingham Forest	Walsall
25	Jarman, Nathan G.	Barnsley	Bury
26	Jarrett, Albert O.	Brighton & Hove Albion	Swindon Town
21	Jaszczun, Antony J.	Rochdale	Cambridge United
1	Johansson, Jonatan L.	Charlton Athletic	Norwich City
18	Johnson, Bradley	Northampton Town	Gravesend & Northfleet
20	Johnson, Brett	Northampton Town	Grays Athletic
26	Jones, Zachariah S.	Blackburn Rovers	Southampton
10	Joseph, Marc E.	Hull City	Blackpool
13	Keene, James D.	Portsmouth	Boston United
31	Kell, Richard	Barnsley	Scarborough
6	Knight, David	Middlesbrough	Darlington
24	Knowles, Daniel	Gillingham	East Thurrock United
23	Kuqi, Njazi	Birmingham City	Blackpool
6	Lafferty, Kyle	Burnley	Darlington
5	Lamb, Alan	Grimsby Town	Eastwood Town
31	Lapham, Kyle J.	Swindon Town	Cirencester Town
6	Leary, Michael	Luton Town	Walsall
18	Lee, Thomas E.	Manchester United	Macclesfield Town
6	Logan, Conrad	Leicester City	Boston United
31	Lowe, Keith S.	Wolverhampton Wanderers	Queens Park Rangers
12	Marrison, Colin	Sheffield United	Bury
16	Martin, Richard W.	Brighton & Hove Albion	Kingstonian
2	McArdle, Rory A.	Sheffield Wednesday	Rochdale
26	McCombe, John	Huddersfield Town	Torquay United

24	McGurk, David	Darlington	York City
1	McShane, Paul D.	Manchester United	Brighton & Hove Albion
19	Mellor, Neil A.	Liverpool	Wigan Athletic
18	Mendes, Albert J.H.A.	Huddersfield Town	Grimsby Town
27	Mikolanda, Petr	West Ham United	Rushden & Diamonds
6	Miller, Liam W.	Manchester United	Leeds United
27	Morais, Filipe A.	Chelsea	Milton Keynes Dons
1	Morris, Ian	Leeds United	Blackpool
31	Mulligan, Gary	Sheffield United	Gillingham
20	Mullins, John	Reading	Kidderminster Harriers
26	Nade, Raphael	Carlisle United	Weymouth
12	Nash, Gerard	Ipswich Town	Hartlepool United
27	Nicolau, Nicky G.	Swindon Town	Hereford United
20	N'Toya, Zoa T.	Chesterfield	York City
13	O'Hara, Jamie	Tottenham Hotspur	Chesterfield
20	O'Leary, Stephen	Luton Town	Tranmere Rovers
31	Osborne, Junior	Watford	Kidderminster Harriers
31	Palmer, Jermaine	Grimsby Town	Kettering Town
19	Partridge, David W.	Bristol City	Milton Keynes Dons
3	Pittman, Jon P.	Nottingham Forest	Hartlepool United
18	Poke, Thomas J.	Crewe Alexandra	Lancaster City
26	Potter, Darren M.	Liverpool	Southampton
10	Pratley, Darren	Fulham	Brentford
21	Quinn, Stephen	Sheffield United	Rotherham United
31	Raven, David H.	Liverpool	Tranmere Rovers
20	Rayner, Simon	Lincoln City	Alfreton Town
31	Reed, Matthew	West Ham United	Barnet
31	Rehman, Zeshan	Fulham	Norwich City
9	Ricketts, Mark J.	Charlton Athletic	Milton Keynes Dons
31	Ricketts, Michael B.	Leeds United	Burnley
31	Rix, Benjamin	Crewe Alexandra	AFC Bournemouth
20	Roach, Neville	Eastleigh	Oxford United
20	Roache, Lee P.	Barnet	Yeading
31	Roberts, Mark A.	Crewe Alexandra	Chester City
3	Roberts, Mark A.	Crewe Alexandra	Southport
31	Robertson, Christopher	Sheffield United	Chester City
1	Robinson, Trevor K.	Millwall	Cambridge United
20	Rogers, Alan	Nottingham Forest	Hull City
1	Rose, Michael C.	Yeovil Town	Scunthorpe United
30	Routledge, Wayne N.A.	Tottenham Hotspur	Portsmouth
1	Saunders, Ben	Doncaster Rovers	Bury
9	Scarsella, David D.A.	Barnsley	Tooting & Mitcham United
13	Schmeichel, Kasper	Manchester City	Darlington
3	Sedgemore, Jacob O.	Bury	Burton Albion
1	Seremet, Dino	Luton Town	Tranmere Rovers
12	Silk, Gary L.	Portsmouth	Boston United
31	Sinama-Pongolle, Florent	Liverpool	Blackburn Rovers
12	Smith, Dan	Sunderland	Huddersfield Town
11	Smith, Grant G.	Bristol City	Walsall
5	Sodje, Efetobore	Yeovil Town	Southend United
14	Stock, Brian B.	AFC Bournemouth	Preston North End
6	Stokes, Tony	West Ham United	Rushden & Diamonds
31	Symes, Michael	Bradford City	Stockport County
13	Taylor, Andrew	Blackburn Rovers	Queens Park Rangers
6	Taylor, Daryl S.	Walsall	Hereford United
17	Taylor, Gareth K.	Nottingham Forest	Crewe Alexandra
12	Taylor, Kris	Walsall	Burton Albion
24	Taylor, Sean	Sunderland	Blackpool
12	Till, Peter	Birmingham City	Boston United
6	Timm, Mads	Manchester United	Walsall
5	Togwell, Samuel J.	Crystal Palace	Port Vale
1	Tudgay, Marcus	Derby County	Sheffield Wednesday
6	Turner, John A.J.	Cambridge United	Rushden & Diamonds
20	Varney, Alexander	Charlton Athletic	Barnet
6	Vaughan, Lee	Walsall	AFC Telford United
1	Walker, James L.N.	Charlton Athletic	Hartlepool United
26	Ward, Elliott L.	West Ham United	Plymouth Argyle
20	Watkins, Robert J.	Fulham	Gravesend & Northfleet

3	Weaver, Nicholas	Manchester City	Sheffield Wednesday
4	Whitbread, Zak B.	Liverpool	Millwall
31	White, Andrew	Notts County	Kidderminster Harriers
10	Williams, Anthony S.	Carlisle United	Bury
20	Williams, Matthew	Notts County	Tamworth
22	Wilson, Kyle P.	Crewe Alexandra	Barrow
20	Winters, Thomas R.	Oxford United	Brackley Town
19	Wood, Neil A.	Coventry City	Blackpool
23	Ziegler, Reto	Tottenham Hotspur	Wigan Athletic

FEBRUARY 2006

TEMPORARY TRANSFERS

24	Albrighton, Mark	Doncaster Rovers	Chester City
13	Aliadiere, Jeremie	Arsenal	Wolverhampton Wanderers
27	Andrew, Calvin H.	Luton Town	Bristol City
9	Anyinsah, Joseph G.	Preston North End	Bury
23	Anyon, Joseph	Port Vale	Harrogate Town
4	Barnes, Philip K.	Sheffield United	Queens Park Rangers
28	Black, Thomas R.	Crystal Palace	Gillingham
27	Bowditch, Dean	Ipswich Town	Wycombe Wanderers
27	Brevett, Rufus E.	Plymouth Argyle	Leicester City
17	Brown, Aaron	Reading	AFC Bournemouth
24	Cecila Baptista, Ricardo J.	Fulham	Milton Keynes Dons
8	Chaplow, Richard D.	West Bromwich Albion	Southampton
13	Chillingworth, Daniel T.	Rushden & Diamonds	Notts County
9	Cochrane, Justin v.	Crewe Alexandra	Gillingham
15	Collins, Aiden	Ipswich Town	Wycombe Wanderers
17	Collins, Neill	Sunderland	Sheffield United
24	Cooke, Andrew R.	Bradford City	Darlington
8	Corneille, Mark	Gillingham	Folkestone Invicta
24	Doyle, Nathan	Derby County	Notts County
24	Ehui, Ismael	Fulham	Scunthorpe United
24	Ellender, Paul	Boston United	Chester City
16	Fitzgerald, Scott	Brentford	Walsall
10	Fordyce, Daryl T.	Portsmouth	AFC Bournemouth
6	Forte, Jonathan	Sheffield United	Rotherham United
24	Fuller, Barry M.	Charlton Athletic	Barnet
24	Fuller, Ricardo	Southampton	Ipswich Town
10	Goodhind, Warren	Rochdale	Oxford United
14	Hand, Jamie	Fisher Athletic	Northampton Town
28	Harthill, Oliver	Birmingham City	Alvechurch
17	Healy, Joe B.	Millwall	Walton & Hersham
10	Horlock, Kevin	Ipswich Town	Doncaster Rovers
13	Horsfield, Geoffrey M.	West Bromwich Albion	Sheffield United
13	Hughes, Mark A.	Everton	Stockport County
13	Igoe, Samuel	Millwall	Bristol Rovers
21	Jarrett, Albert O.	Brighton & Hove Albion	Swindon Town
27	Johnson, Thomas	Scunthorpe United	Tamworth
16	Kuipers, Michael	Brighton & Hove Albion	Boston United
9	Lafferty, Kyle	Burnley	Darlington
8	Lamb, Alan	Grimsby Town	Eastwood Town
10	Lasley, Keith	Plymouth Argyle	Blackpool
1	Lee, Thomas E.	Manchester United	Macclesfield Town
22	Lisbie, Kevin	Charlton Athletic	Derby County
17	Makabu-Ma-Kalamby, Yves	Chelsea	Watford
13	Marrison, Colin	Sheffield United	Bury
17	McCammon, Mark J.	Brighton & Hove Albion	Bristol City
13	McDermott, Neale T.	Fulham	Darlington
24	McSporran, Jermaine	Doncaster Rovers	Boston United
10	Mills, Pablo	Derby County	Portsmouth
12	Nade, Raphael	Carlisle United	Weymouth
27	Nix, Kyle	Sheffield United	Barnsley
8	Noble, Mark	West Ham United	Hull City
10	Oyedele, Ade S.	Milton Keynes Dons	Woking
20	Pearson, Gregory	Rushden & Diamonds	Hucknall Town
10	Pericard, Vincent D.P.	Portsmouth	Plymouth Argyle
19	Quinn, Stephen	Sheffield United	Rotherham United

154

8 Rasiak, Grzegorz	Tottenham Hotspur	Southampton
22 Rayner, Simon	Lincoln City	Alfreton Town
24 Roache, Lee P.	Barnet	Yeading
16 Roma, Dominic	Sheffield United	Tamworth
23 Schmeichel, Kasper	Manchester City	Bury
8 Skoko, Josip	Wigan Athletic	Stoke City
17 Smikle, Brian J.	West Bromwich Albion	Halifax Town
15 Smith, Daniel	Sunderland	Huddersfield Town
18 Smylie, Daryl	Newcastle United	Stockport County
24 Stockdale, Robert K.	Hull City	Darlington
9 Talbot, Jason C.	Mansfield Town	Port Vale
15 Taylor, Andrew	Blackburn Rovers	Blackpool
24 Taylor, Sean	Sunderland	Blackpool
24 Timlin, Michael	Fulham	Scunthorpe United
17 Watkins, Robert J.	Fulham	Gravesend & Northfleet
23 Westerveld, Sander	Portsmouth	Everton
10 Wheater, David J.	Middlesbrough	Doncaster Rovers
15 Wilkinson, Neil	Hartlepool United	Blyth Spartans
16 Williams, Christopher	Stockport County	Northwich Victoria
27 Williams, Matthew	Notts County	Tamworth
24 Willis, Paul	Liverpool	Stockport County
20 Wilson, Kyle P.	Crewe Alexandra	Barrow
9 Wilson, Laurence T.	Everton	Mansfield Town
23 Wright, Alan	Sheffield United	Derby County
8 Wright, Jermaine M.	Leeds United	Southampton

MARCH 2006

20 Beckford, Jermaine P.	Wealdstone	Leeds United
31 Makofo, Serge	Milton Keynes Dons	Kettering Town

TEMPORARY TRANSFERS

24 Albrighton, Mark	Doncaster Rovers	Chester City
23 Aliadiere, Jeremie	Arsenal	Wolverhampton Wanderers
23 Alsop, Sam	Birmingham City	Yeovil Town
17 Andrews, Lee D.	Carlisle United	Torquay United
28 Anyon, Joseph	Port Vale	Harrogate Town
31 Appleby, Andrew	Hartlepool United	Blyth Spartans
22 Atieno, Taiwo L.	Walsall	Darlington
10 Bailey, Matthew	Crewe Alexandra	Lancaster City
16 Bardsley, Philip A.	Manchester United	Burnley
23 Beaumont, James	Nottingham Forest	Darlington
17 Beckwith, Robert	Luton Town	Chesterfield
10 Bischoff, Mikkel	Manchester City	Sheffield Wednesday
2 Bloomer, Matthew	Lincoln City	Cambridge United
17 Bond, Clay	Plymouth Argyle	Torquay United
23 Bowditch, Ben E.	Barnet	Yeading
10 Bradshaw, Gary	Cheltenham Town	North Ferriby United
24 Breach, Christopher B.	Brighton & Hove Albion	Bognor Regis Town
23 Brevett, Rufus E.	Plymouth Argyle	Leicester City
23 Burns, Jamie D.	Blackpool	Bury
3 Cameron, Colin	Wolverhampton Wanderers	Millwall
23 Campbell-Ryce, Jamal	Rotherham United	Colchester United
10 Carson, Scott P.	Liverpool	Sheffield Wednesday
17 Chillingworth, Daniel T.	Rushden & Diamonds	Notts County
23 Claridge, Stephen E.	Bradford City	Walsall
23 Clarke, Leon M.	Wolverhampton Wanderers	Plymouth Argyle
23 Clarke, William C.	Ipswich Town	Colchester United
14 Cochrane, Justin V.	Crewe Alexandra	Gillingham
23 Coleman, Liam	Torquay United	Forest Green Rovers
16 Collins, Aiden	Ipswich Town	Stockport County
14 Cooke, Andrew R.	Bradford City	Darlington
23 Corden, Wayne	Scunthorpe United	Leyton Orient
17 Daly, Jonathan M.	Hartlepool United	Bury
13 Dann, Scott	Walsall	Hednesford Town
23 Diagouraga, Toumani	Watford	Swindon Town
3 Doherty, Thomas	Queens Park Rangers	Yeovil Town
16 Dove, Craig	Chester City	Forest Green Rovers
24 Doyle, Nathan	Derby County	Notts County

21	Edwards, Jake	Exeter City	Chester City
24	Ehui, Ismael	Fulham	Scunthorpe United
23	Forrester, Jamie	Bristol Rovers	Lincoln City
13	Forte, Jonathan	Sheffield United	Rotherham United
30	Friars, Emmett	Notts County	Alfreton Town
25	Fuller, Barry M.	Charlton Athletic	Barnet
23	Gobern, Lewis T.	Wolverhampton Wanderers	Bury
23	Goodhind, Warren	Rochdale	Oxford United
13	Graham, Daniel A.W.	Middlesbrough	Leeds United
17	Gray, Andrew D.	Sunderland	Burnley
13	Griffiths, Anthony J.	Doncaster Rovers	Oxford United
23	Guatelli, Andrea	Portsmouth	Oxford United
4	Hall, Asa	Birmingham City	Boston United
20	Healy, Joe B.	Millwall	Walton & Hersham
23	Hegarty, Nick	Grimsby Town	Willenhall Town
20	Hollands, Daniel T.	Chelsea	Torquay United
17	Horlock, Kevin	Ipswich Town	Doncaster Rovers
23	Horsted, Liam A.	Portsmouth	Oxford United
23	Jackson, Mark	Preston North End	Southport
7	Jarrett, Jason L.	Norwich City	Preston North End
17	Johnson, Jemal J.	Blackburn Rovers	Darlington
9	Jordan, Michael W.	Arsenal	Yeovil Town
21	Kuipers, Michael	Brighton & Hove Albion	Boston United
17	Kuqi, Njazi	Birmingham City	Peterborough United
1	Lapham, Kyle J.	Swindon Town	Cirencester Town
23	Lee, Kevin	Wigan Athletic	Blackpool
16	Lee, Thomas E.	Manchester United	Macclesfield Town
22	Lisbie, Kevin	Charlton Athletic	Derby County
8	Lucketti, Christopher J.	Preston North End	Sheffield United
23	Mahon, Alan	Wigan Athletic	Burnley
23	Marques, Rui M.	Leeds United	Hull City
13	Marrison, Colin	Sheffield United	Bury
23	McCammon, Mark J.	Brighton & Hove Albion	Bristol City
8	McIndoe, Michael	Doncaster Rovers	Derby County
23	McLachlan, Fraser	Mansfield Town	Morecambe
2	McNeil, Mathew	Hyde United	Macclesfield Town
23	McPhee, Christopher S.	Brighton & Hove Albion	Swindon Town
23	Morais, Filipe A.	Chelsea	Milton Keynes Dons
17	Mulligan, Gary	Sheffield United	Gillingham
23	Murray, Matthew W.	Wolverhampton Wanderers	Tranmere Rovers
24	Nade, Raphael	Carlisle United	Weymouth
23	Nash, Gerard	Ipswich Town	Southend United
23	Newby, Jon P.R.	Bury	Kidderminster Harriers
23	Noble, Mark	West Ham United	Hull City
23	Noel-Williams, Gifton R.	Burnley	Brighton & Hove Albion
23	N'Toya, Zoa	Chesterfield	Oxford United
23	O'Connor, Kevin J.A.	Wolverhampton Wanderers	Stockport County
23	Opara, Lloyd	Cheshunt	Peterborough United
29	Pope, Thomas J.	Crewe Alexandra	Stafford Rangers
10	Pulis, Anthony J.	Stoke City	Plymouth Argyle
23	Rayner, Simon	Lincoln City	Alfreton Town
7	Reed, Matthew	West Ham United	Barnet
3	Reed, Stephen	Yeovil Town	Torquay United
23	Richardson, Marcus G.	Chester City	Macclesfield Town
8	Rix, Benjamin	Crewe Alexandra	AFC Bournemouth
9	Roberts, Mark A.	Crewe Alexandra	Southport
23	Rocastle, Craig A.	Sheffield Wednesday	Yeovil Town
21	Roma, Dominic	Sheffield United	Tamworth
23	Ross, Ian	Sheffield United	Bury
28	Schmeichel, Kasper	Manchester City	Bury
23	Sherlock, James	Gainsborough Trinity	Lincoln City
17	Smikle, Brian J.	West Bromwich Albion	Halifax Town
14	Smith, James A.	Bristol City	Brentford
23	Smith, Jay A.	Southend United	Oxford United
21	Stewart, Marcus P.	Bristol City	Preston North End
17	Stockley, Sam J.	Colchester United	Blackpool
30	Sutton, Ritchie A.	Crewe Alexandra	Stafford Rangers
6	Taylor, Andrew	Blackburn Rovers	Blackpool
4	Taylor, Daryl S.	Walsall	Hereford United
17	Taylor, Jason J.F.	Oldham Athletic	Stockport County
3	Taylor, Michael	Cheltenham Town	Forest Green Rovers
23	Timlin, Michael	Fulham	Doncaster Rovers

17	Vernon, Scott M.	Blackpool	Colchester United
15	Vincent, Jamie R.	Yeovil Town	Millwall
7	Ward, Jamie J.	Aston Villa	Stockport County
1	Welsh, Andrew P.D.	Sunderland	Leicester City
10	Wheater, David J.	Middlesbrough	Doncaster Rovers
3	Wilbraham, Aaron	Milton Keynes Dons	Bradford City
31	Wilkinson, Jack L.	Hartlepool United	Newcastle Benfield (Bay
	Plastics)		
30	Wilkinson, Neil	Hartlepool United	Whitby Town
17	Williams, Gareth A.	Colchester United	Blackpool
10	Wilson, Kelvin J.	Notts County	Preston North End
9	Wilson, Lawrence T.	Everton	Mansfield Town
9	Wilson, Marc D.	Portsmouth	Yeovil Town
23	Wright, Alan	Sheffield United	Derby County
4	Wright, Jermaine M.	Leeds United	Southampton

APRIL 2006
TEMPORARY TRANSFERS

7	Bischoff, Mikkel	Manchester City	Sheffield Wednesday
5	Bloomer, Matthew	Lincoln City	Cambridge United
6	Bradshaw, Gary	Cheltenham Town	North Ferriby United
2	Cameron, Colin	Wolverhampton Wanderers	Millwall
7	Carson, Scott P.	Liverpool	Sheffield Wednesday
16	Cooke, Andrew R.	Bradford City	Darlington
27	Forrester, Jamie	Bristol Rovers	Lincoln City
11	Johnson, Jemal J.	Blackburn Rovers	Darlington
10	Jordan, Michael W.	Arsenal	Yeovil Town
20	Logan, Conrad	Leicester City	Boston United
11	Mapes, Charles E.	Yeading	Yeovil Town
20	Mulligan, Gary	Sheffield United	Gillingham
7	Reed, Matthew	West Ham United	Barnet
4	Reed, Stephen	Yeovil Town	Torquay United
7	Rix, Benjamin	Crewe Alexandra	AFC Bournemouth
23	Ross, Ian	Sheffield United	Bury
23	Schmeichel, Kasper	Manchester City	Bury
18	Smikle, Brian J.	West Bromwich Albion	Halifax Town
19	Smith, James A.	Bristol City	Brentford
25	Taylor, Jason J.F.	Oldham Athletic	Stockport County
7	Taylor, Michael	Cheltenham Town	Forest Green Rovers
10	Ward, Jamie J.	Aston Villa	Stockport County
11	Wilson, Marc D.	Portsmouth	Yeovil Town

MAY 2006

18	Bullard, James R.	Wigan Athletic	Fulham
31	Hart, Charles (Joe) J.J.	Shrewsbury Town	Manchester City
26	Jarrett, Jason L.	Norwich City	Preston North End
24	Mahon, Alan	Wigan Athletic	Burnley
19	O'Connor, James F.E.	AFC Bournemouth	Doncaster Rovers
2	Rasiak, Grzegorz	Tottenham Hotspur	Southampton
2	Sandell, Andrew C.	Bath City	Bristol Rovers
16	Sherlock, James	Gainsborough Trinity	Lincoln City
26	Wilson, Kelvin J.	Notts County	Preston North End

TEMPORARY TRANSFERS

5	Logan, Conrad	Leicester City	Boston United
9	Pratley, Darren	Fulham	Brentford
9	Smith, James A.	Bristol City	Brentford
3	Stewart, Marcus P.	Bristol City	Preston North End

FOREIGN TRANSFERS 2005–2006

JULY 2005		*From*	*To*
27	Barragan-Fernandez, Antoni	Sevilla	Liverpool
25	Belozoglu, Emre	Internazionale	Newcastle United
27	Benayoun, Yossi	Racing Santander	West Ham United
25	Borgetti, Jared	Pachucha	Bolton Wanderers
26	Chimbonda, Pascal	Bastia	Wigan Athletic
1	Del Horno, Asier	Athletic Bilbao	Chelsea
22	Diarra, Lassana	Le Havre	Chelsea
15	Drobny, Jaroslav	Panionios	Fulham
13	Elrich, Ahmed	Busan Icons	Fulham
25	Karadas, Azar	Benfica	Portsmouth

22 Kroldrup, Per	Udinese	Everton
15 Mannone, Vito	Atalanta	Arsenal
1 Moore, Craig	Borrusia Munchengladbach	Newcastle United
11 Park, Ji-Sung	PSV Eindhoven	Manchester United
6 Reina, Jose	Villarreal	Liverpool
19 Sissoko, Mohamed	Valencia	Liverpool
11 Stalteri, Paul	Werder Bremen	Tottenham Hotspur
12 Tainio, Teema	Auxerre	Tottenham Hotspur
21 Viafara, John	Once Caldas	Portsmouth
28 Westerveld, Sander	Real Sociedad	Portsmouth

AUGUST 2005

8 Antwi, Godwin	Zaragoza	Liverpool
24 Bassila, Christian	Strasbourg	Sunderland
30 Bouma, Wilfred	PSV Eindhoven	Aston Villa
22 Brandao, Goncalo	Belenenses	Charlton Athletic
5 Davids, Edgar	Internazionale	Tottenham Hotspur
19 Essien, Michael	Lyon	Chelsea
26 Ferrari, Matteo	Roma	Everton
1 Gislason, Rurik	HJK Helsinki	Charlton Athletic
5 Hleb, Alexandr	Stuttgart	Arsenal
18 Hussian, Yasser	Al Sadd	Manchester City
30 Idrizaj, Besian	Linz	Liverpool
31 Khizanishvili, Zurab	Rangers	Blackburn Rovers
1 Krul, Tim	Den Haag	Newcastle United
31 Lee, Yong-Pyo	PSV Eindhoven	Tottenham Hotspur
26 Luque, Alberto	La Coruna	Newcastle United
3 Mbesuma, Collins	Kaizer Chiefs	Portsmouth
30 Nuno Valente	Porto	Everton
23 Mikolanda, Petr	Viktoria Zizkov	West Ham United
23 Nakata, Hidetoshi	Fiorentina	Bolton Wanderers
25 Pogatetz, Emanuel	Leverkusen	Middlesbrough
23 Priske, Brian	Genk	Portsmouth
31 Rochemback, Fabio	Sporting Lisbon	Middlesbrough
8 Roque, Miguel	Lleida	Liverpool
31 Dario Silva, Debray	Sevilla	Portsmouth
31 Skoko, Josip	Genclerbirligi	Wigan Athletic
16 Song, Alexandre	Bastia	Arsenal
31 Van der Meyde, Andy	Internazionale	Everton
31 Vukic, Zvonimir	Shakhtar Donetsk	Portsmouth

JANUARY 2006

13 Adebayor, Emmanuel	Monaco	Arsenal
12 Agger, Daniel	Brondby	Liverpool
10 Al-Habsi, Ali	Lyn	Bolton Wanderers
31 D'Alessandro, Andreas	Wolfsburg	Portsmouth
31 Diaby, Vassiriki	Auxerre	Arsenal
6 Elliott, Simon	Columbus Crew	Fulham
10 Evra, Patrice	Monaco	Manchester United
31 Ghali, Hossan	Feyenoord	Tottenham Hotspur
1 Haapala, Tuomas	MyPa	Manchester City
10 Hojsted, Ingi	B36 Torshavn	Birmingham City
3 Katan, Yaniv	Maccabi Haifa	West Ham United
30 Koroman, Ognjien	Terek Groznyi	Portsmouth
25 Kozak, Jan	Artmedia	West Bromwich Albion
4 Kromkamp, Jan	Villarreal	Liverpool
31 Latka, Martin	Slavia Prague	Birmingham City
4 Maniche	Dynamo Moscow	Chelsea
6 Mwaruwari, Benjamin	Auxerre	Portsmouth
4 Olisadebe, Emanuel	Panathinaikos	Portsmouth
31 Olsson, Martin	Hogaborgs	Blackburn Rovers
31 Perez, Oscar	Cordoba	Bolton Wanderers
5 Riera, Alberto	Espanyol	Manchester City
31 Samaras, Georgios	Heerenveen	Manchester City
6 Scharner, Paul	Brann	Wigan Athletic
4 Vidic, Nemanja	Spartak Moscow	Manchester United

158

FA CUP REVIEW 2005–2006

An FA Cup final fit for a new Wembley was staged at the Millennium Stadium. Indeed it was good enough to have been held at any outstanding venue with Liverpool and West Ham United sharing goals before a penalty shoot-out ruined it again.

Liverpool who invariably succeed with spot kicks duly did so and though the purists may have pointed to two defensive errors and a fluke which gave the Hammers their trio of goals while two blistering strikes from Steven Gerrard lit up the afternoon for the Merseysiders, the Londoners might well have snatched it late on.

Unfortunately for them, the rebound fell to Marlon Harewood who was injured and only able to offer a token swing at it and the chance was lost.

Six goals apart it was the best final for years, Liverpool recovering from two defensive blunders to level the scores only to find themselves trailing again until they equalised on the stroke of full-time with West Ham thinking it was theirs after all.

The extra period brought tired limbs and had the game carried on Liverpool appeared to have more injury problems than their opponents. History, of course, is invariably only concerned with facts.

When the first round proper began in November with the remnants of the minnows coming into contact with the Football League clubs there were immediate surprises. Tamworth won at Bournemouth, Burscough dumped Gillingham and replays gave Eastbourne another crack at Oxford, similarly Weymouth against Forest, Burton with Peterborough, even Harrogate against Torquay and Chasetown causing Oldham problems. Halifax, too, earned a second bite at Rushden.

Parity for the middle classes was somewhat restored when Colchester United created their biggest FA Cup win whacking Leamington 9-1.

Replays wiped out the aspirations of Weymouth, Halifax and Harrogate (on penalties), Eastbourne and Chasetown. Not so Burton Albion who edged out Posh to grab a second round tie with Burscough and a 4-1 win. Tamworth, too, battled on taking Hartlepool United out of the competition. Otherwise only Stevenage drawing with Northampton raised an eyebrow before losing the replay.

However, suffice to say that several other non-league clubs had managed to avoid League opposition and were still in contention when the third round arrived. One such club Northwich were drawn at Sunderland, Nuneaton at home to Middlesbrough, Tamworth at Stoke while Burton had the plum of the pickings at home to Manchester United.

Only Northwich lost, the other three forced replays before bowing out Nuneaton 5-2, money spinning Burton 5-0 at Old Trafford but Tamworth only losing on penalties. Moreover, the arrival of Premier League teams produced high profile casualties as well.

Leyton Orient won at Fulham, Leicester found a late winner to oust Tottenham. Liverpool discovered themselves 3-1 down at Luton before staging a 5-3 victory, Robbie Fowler destined to be re-united at Anfield, hit a hat-trick for Manchester City against Scunthorpe.

Torquay held Birmingham in Devon, Reading earned a replay at West Bromwich while another non-Premier team performance concerned Colchester winning at Sheffield United. Wigan had to rely on penalties in their replay with Leeds while Leroy Lita's treble gave Reading the edge in the second game. Torquay lost at Birmingham.

Round Four was not short of a mild shock either, Brentford edging out Sunderland, Reading held Birmingham before losing the replay and Arsenal fell to a late goal at Bolton.

Fifth round Liverpool faced old foes in Manchester United and won with a Peter Crouch goal. Colchester caused a heart flutter at Chelsea taking an own goal lead before losing 3-1 and Charlton accounted for Brentford, the least of the upstarts.

Replays saw 2-1 wins for both Manchester City over Aston Villa and West Ham against Bolton. Against tradition and due to the crowded calendar, all four sixth round ties were played midweek on different days. A Dean Ashton brace gave the Hammers a win at Manchester City, then came Liverpool's 7-0 thrashing of Birmingham at St Andrews, an early John Terry goal for Chelsea disposing of Newcastle and Charlton going scoreless with Middlesbrough, before Boro won the replay 4-2.

In the semi-finals Liverpool again had the Indian sign on Chelsea who suffered Jose Mourinho's wrong starting line-up and they only came into the game when it was virtually lost, while one goal was enough for West Ham against Middlesbrough.

Thus in the chronological sequence of events, Liverpool had earlier defeated Luton, Portsmouth, Manchester United and Birmingham, while West Ham's other victims had been Norwich, Blackburn, Bolton and Manchester City. The scene was set for a memorable final which it was at least until the end of extra time!

THE FA CUP 2005–2006

FIRST ROUND

Cambridge C	(0) 0	Hereford U	(0) 1
Merthyr T	(1) 1	Walsall	(2) 2
Port Vale	(1) 2	Wrexham	(0) 1
Barnet	(0) 0	Southend U	(1) 1
Barnsley	(1) 1	Darlington	(0) 0
Bournemouth	(1) 1	Tamworth	(1) 2
Bristol C	(0) 0	Notts Co	(1) 2
Burnham	(0) 1	Aldershot T	(0) 3
Burscough	(1) 3	Gillingham	(0) 2
Bury	(0) 2	Scunthorpe U	(2) 2
Cheltenham T	(0) 1	Carlisle U	(0) 0
Chester C	(0) 2	Folkestone I	(1) 1
Chippenham T	(0) 1	Worcester C	(1) 1
Colchester U	(2) 9	Leamington	(0) 1
Eastbourne B	(0) 1	Oxford U	(0) 1
Grimsby T	(0) 1	Bristol R	(1) 2
Hartlepool U	(1) 2	Dagenham & R	(1) 1
Histon	(1) 4	Hednesford T	(0) 0
Kettering T	(1) 1	Stevenage B	(2) 3
Leyton Orient	(0) 0	Chesterfield	(0) 0
Lincoln C	(1) 1	Milton Keynes D	(1) 1
Macclesfield T	(0) 1	Yeovil T	(0) 1
Morecambe	(0) 1	Northwich Vic	(2) 3
Nottingham F	(1) 1	Weymouth	(0) 1
Nuneaton B	(2) 2	Ramsgate	(0) 0
Peterborough U	(0) 0	Burton A	(0) 0
Rochdale	(0) 0	Brentford	(1) 1
Rotherham U	(2) 3	Mansfield T	(2) 4
Shrewsbury T	(3) 4	Braintree T	(0) 1
Southport	(0) 1	Woking	(1) 1
Stockport Co	(1) 2	Swansea C	(0) 0
Swindon T	(1) 2	Boston U	(2) 2
Torquay U	(0) 1	Harrogate T	(1) 1
Wycombe W	(0) 1	Northampton T	(0) 3
York C	(0) 0	Grays Ath	(1) 3
Bradford C	(0) 2	Tranmere R	(1) 1
Chasetown	(1) 1	Oldham Ath	(1) 1
Doncaster R	(1) 4	Blackpool	(0) 1
Halifax T	(1) 1	Rushden & D	(1) 1
Huddersfield T	(1) 4	Welling U	(0) 1

FIRST ROUND REPLAYS

Weymouth	(0) 0	Nottingham F	(0) 2
Worcester C	(0) 1	Chippenham T	(0) 0
Harrogate T	(0) 0	Torquay U	(0) 0
(aet; Torquay U won 6-5 on penalties.)			
Milton Keynes D	(2) 2	Lincoln C	(1) 1
Rushden & D	(0) 0	Halifax T	(0) 0
(aet; Rushden & D won 5-4 on penalties.)			
Scunthorpe U	(0) 1	Bury	(0) 0
(aet).			
Woking	(0) 1	Southport	(0) 0
(aet).			
Yeovil T	(1) 4	Macclesfield T	(0) 0
Boston U	(4) 4	Swindon T	(0) 1

Burton Alb	(0) 1	Peterborough U	(0) 0
Chesterfield	(1) 1	Leyton Orient	(2) 2
Oldham Ath	(1) 4	Chasetown	(0) 0
Oxford U	(2) 3	Eastbourne B	(0) 0

SECOND ROUND

Mansfield T	(2) 3	Grays Ath	(0) 0
Port Vale	(0) 1	Bristol R	(0) 1
Aldershot T	(0) 0	Scunthorpe U	(1) 1
Barnsley	(1) 1	Bradford C	(0) 1
Burton Alb	(0) 0	Burscough	(0) 0
(Postponed; waterlogged pitch.)			
Cheltenham T	(1) 1	Oxford U	(0) 1
Chester C	(1) 3	Nottingham F	(0) 0
Hartlepool U	(0) 1	Tamworth	(1) 2
Hereford U	(0) 0	Stockport Co	(1) 2
Nuneaton B	(1) 2	Histon	(2) 2
Oldham Ath	(0) 1	Brentford	(0) 1
Rushden & D	(0) 0	Leyton Orient	(0) 1
Shrewsbury T	(1) 1	Colchester U	(1) 2
Southend U	(0) 1	Milton Keynes D	(1) 2
Stevenage B	(1) 2	Northampton T	(0) 2
Torquay U	(1) 2	Notts Co	(0) 1
Walsall	(1) 2	Yeovil T	(0) 0
Woking	(0) 0	Northwich Vic	(0) 0
Boston U	(0) 1	Doncaster R	(1) 2
Worcester C	(0) 0	Huddersfield T	(0) 1
Burton Alb	(3) 4	Burscough	(0) 1

SECOND ROUND REPLAYS

Bradford C	(1) 3	Barnsley	(0) 5
(aet).			
Brentford	(0) 1	Oldham Ath	(0) 0
Bristol R	(0) 0	Port Vale	(1) 1
Northampton T	(2) 2	Stevenage B	(0) 0
Northwich Vic	(1) 2	Woking	(1) 1
Oxford U	(0) 1	Cheltenham T	(0) 2
Histon	(0) 1	Nuneaton B	(1) 2

THIRD ROUND

Port Vale	(0) 2	Doncaster R	(1) 1
Arsenal	(2) 2	Cardiff C	(0) 1
Barnsley	(0) 1	Walsall	(0) 1
Blackburn R	(2) 3	QPR	(0) 0
Brighton & HA	(0) 0	Coventry C	(0) 1
Chelsea	(1) 2	Huddersfield T	(0) 1
Cheltenham T	(0) 2	Chester C	(0) 2
Crystal Palace	(2) 4	Northampton T	(1) 1
Derby Co	(1) 2	Burnley	(1) 1
Hull C	(0) 0	Aston Villa	(0) 1
Ipswich T	(0) 0	Portsmouth	(1) 1
Luton T	(2) 3	Liverpool	(1) 5
Manchester C	(0) 3	Scunthorpe U	(1) 1
Millwall	(1) 1	Everton	(0) 1
Newcastle U	(0) 1	Mansfield T	(0) 0
Norwich C	(0) 1	West Ham U	(1) 2
Nuneaton B	(0) 1	Middlesbrough	(1) 1
Preston NE	(0) 2	Crewe Alex	(1) 1
Sheffield U	(1) 1	Colchester U	(1) 2

Sheffield W	(1) 2	Charlton Ath	(3) 4
Southampton	(1) 4	Milton Keynes D	(0) 3
Stockport Co	(1) 2	Brentford	(1) 3
Stoke C	(0) 0	Tamworth	(0) 0
Torquay U	(0) 0	Birmingham C	(0) 0
WBA	(0) 1	Reading	(0) 1
Watford	(0) 0	Bolton W	(2) 3
Wigan Ath	(0) 1	Leeds U	(0) 1
Wolverhampton W	(1) 1	Plymouth Arg	(0) 0
Burton Alb	(0) 0	Manchester U	(0) 0
Fulham	(0) 1	Leyton Orient	(2) 2
Leicester C	(1) 3	Tottenham H	(2) 2
Sunderland	(2) 3	Northwich Vic	(0) 0

THIRD ROUND REPLAYS

Birmingham C	(0) 2	Torquay U	(0) 0
Chester C	(0) 0	Cheltenham T	(0) 1
Leeds U	(1) 3	Wigan Ath	(1) 3
(aet; Wigan Ath won 4-2 on penalties.)
| Middlesbrough | (2) 5 | Nuneaton B | (0) 2 |
| Reading | (0) 3 | WBA | (2) 2 |
(aet.)
| Tamworth | (1) 1 | Stoke C | (0) 1 |
(aet; Stoke C won 5-4 on penalties.)
Walsall	(0) 2	Barnsley	(0) 0
Everton	(0) 1	Millwall	(0) 0
Manchester U	(2) 5	Burton Alb	(0) 0

FOURTH ROUND

Aston Villa	(0) 3	Port Vale	(0) 1
Bolton W	(0) 1	Arsenal	(0) 0
Brentford	(0) 2	Sunderland	(0) 1
Charlton Ath	(1) 2	Leyton Orient	(0) 1
Cheltenham T	(0) 0	Newcastle U	(2) 2
Colchester U	(1) 3	Derby Co	(0) 1
Coventry C	(0) 1	Middlesbrough	(0) 1
Everton	(1) 1	Chelsea	(0) 1
Leicester C	(0) 0	Southampton	(0) 1
Manchester C	(0) 1	Wigan Ath	(0) 0
Preston NE	(1) 1	Crystal Palace	(1) 1
Reading	(1) 1	Birmingham C	(0) 1
Stoke C	(1) 2	Walsall	(0) 1
West Ham U	(2) 4	Blackburn R	(1) 2
Portsmouth	(0) 1	Liverpool	(2) 2
Wolverhampton W	(0) 0	Manchester U	(2) 3

FOURTH ROUND REPLAYS

Birmingham C	(1) 2	Reading	(0) 1
Crystal Palace	(1) 1	Preston NE	(1) 2
Chelsea	(3) 4	Everton	(0) 1
Middlesbrough	(1) 1	Coventry C	(0) 0

FIFTH ROUND

Bolton W	(0) 0	West Ham U	(0) 0
Charlton Ath	(2) 3	Brentford	(0) 1
Liverpool	(1) 1	Manchester U	(0) 0
Newcastle U	(0) 1	Southampton	(0) 0
Aston Villa	(0) 1	Manchester C	(0) 1

Chelsea	(1) 3	Colchester U	(1) 1
Preston NE	(0) 0	Middlesbrough	(0) 2
Stoke C	(0) 0	Birmingham C	(0) 1

FIFTH ROUND REPLAYS

| Manchester C | (1) 2 | Aston Villa | (0) 1 |
| West Ham U | (1) 2 | Bolton W | (1) 1 |

SIXTH ROUND

Manchester C	(0) 1	West Ham U	(1) 2
Birmingham C	(0) 0	Liverpool	(3) 7
Chelsea	(1) 1	Newcastle U	(0) 0
Charlton Ath	(0) 0	Middlesbrough	(0) 0

SIXTH ROUND REPLAY

| Middlesbrough | (2) 4 | Charlton Ath | (1) 2 |

SEMI-FINAL

| Chelsea | (0) 1 | Liverpool | (1) 2 |
| Middlesbrough | (0) 0 | West Ham U | (0) 1 |

THE FA CUP FINAL

Saturday, 13 May 2005

(at Millennium Stadium, Cardiff, attendance 74,000)

Liverpool (1) 3   West Ham U (2) 3

Liverpool: Reina; Finnan, Riise, Xabi Alonso (Kromkamp), Carragher, Hyypia, Sissoko, Gerrard, Crouch (Hamann), Cisse, Kewell (Morientes).

Scorers: Cisse 32, Gerrard 54, 90.

West Ham U: Hislop; Scaloni, Konchesky, Gabbidon, Ferdinand, Fletcher (Dailly), Benayoun, Reo-Coker, Harewood, Ashton (Zamora), Etherington (Sheringham).

Scorers: Carragher 21 (og), Ashton 28, Konchesky 64.

aet; Liverpool won 3-1 on penalties: Hamann scored; Zamora saved; Hyypia saved; Sheringham scored; Gerrard scored; Konchesky saved; Riise scored; Ferdinand saved.

Referee: A. Wiley (Staffordshire).

PAST FA CUP FINALS

Details of one goalscorer is not available in 1878.

1872	The Wanderers ....1 *Betts*	Royal Engineers 0		
1873	The Wanderers ....2 *Kinnaird, Wollaston*	Oxford University 0		
1874	Oxford University..................2 *Mackarness, Patton*	Royal Engineers 0		
1875	Royal Engineers ....1 *Renny-Tailyour*	Old Etonians ....1* *Bonsor*		
Replay	Royal Engineers ....2 *Renny-Tailyour, Stafford*	Old Etonians 0		
1876	The Wanderers ....1 *Edwards*	Old Etonians ....1* *Bonsor*		
Replay	The Wanderers ....3 *Wollaston, Hughes 2*	Old Etonians 0		
1877	The Wanderers ....2 *Lindsay, Kenrick*	Oxford University ....1* *Kinnaird (og)*		
1878	The Wanderers ....3 *Kenrick 2, Kinnaird*	Royal Engineers ....1 *Unknown*		
1879	Old Etonians ....1 *Clerke*	Clapham Rovers 0		
1880	Clapham Rovers ....1 *Lloyd-Jones*	Oxford University 0		
1881	Old Carthusians ....3 *Wyngard, Parry, Todd*	Old Etonians 0		
1882	Old Etonians ....1 *Anderson*	Blackburn Rovers..............................0		
1883	Blackburn Olympic ....2 *Costley, Matthews*	Old Etonians ....1* *Goodhart*		
1884	Blackburn Rovers.................2 *Sowerbutts, Forrest*	Queen's Park, Glasgow ....1 *Christie*		
1885	Blackburn Rovers.................2 *Forrest, Brown*	Queen's Park, Glasgow 0		
1886	Blackburn Rovers.................0	West Bromwich Albion 0		
Replay	Blackburn Rovers.................2 *Brown, Sowerbutts*	West Bromwich Albion 0		
1887	Aston Villa ....2 *Hunter, Hodgetts*	West Bromwich Albion 0		
1888	West Bromwich Albion ....2 *Woodhall, Bayliss*	Preston NE ....1 *Dewhurst*		
1889	Preston NE ....3 *Dewhurst, J. Ross, Thompson*	Wolverhampton W..............................0		
1890	Blackburn Rovers.................6 *Walton, John Southworth, Lofthouse, Townley 3*	Sheffield W ....1 *Bennett*		
1891	Blackburn Rovers.................3 *Dewar, John Southworth, Townley*	Notts Co...1 *Oswald*		
1892	West Bromwich Albion ....3 *Geddes, Nicholls, Reynolds*	Aston Villa 0		
1893	Wolverhampton W................1 *Allen*	Everton 0		

1894	Notts Co 4		Bolton W 1	
	Watson, Logan 3		*Cassidy*	
1895	Aston Villa 1		West Bromwich Albion 0	
	J. Devey			
1896	Sheffield W 2		Wolverhampton W 1	
	Spiksley 2		*Black*	
1897	Aston Villa 3		Everton 2	
	Campbell, Wheldon,		*Boyle, Bell*	
	Crabtree			
1898	Nottingham F 3		Derby Co 1	
	Cape 2, McPherson		*Bloomer*	
1899	Sheffield U 4		Derby Co 1	
	Bennett, Beers, Almond,		*Boag*	
	Priest			
1900	Bury 4		Southampton 0	
	McLuckie 2, Wood, Plant			
1901	Tottenham H 2		Sheffield U 2	
	Brown 2		*Bennett, Priest*	
Replay	Tottenham H 3		Sheffield U 1	
	Cameron, Smith, Brown		*Priest*	
1902	Sheffield U 1		Southampton 1	
	Common		*Wood*	
Replay	Sheffield U 2		Southampton 1	
	Hedley, Barnes		*Brown*	
1903	Bury 6		Derby Co 0	
	Ross, Sagar, Leeming 2,			
	Wood, Plant			
1904	Manchester C 1		Bolton W 0	
	Meredith			
1905	Aston Villa 2		Newcastle U 0	
	Hampton 2			
1906	Everton 1		Newcastle U 0	
	Young			
1907	Sheffield W 2		Everton 1	
	Stewart, Simpson		*Sharp*	
1908	Wolverhampton W 3		Newcastle U 1	
	Hunt, Hedley, Harrison		*Howey*	
1909	Manchester U 1		Bristol C 0	
	A. Turnbull			
1910	Newcastle U 1		Barnsley 1	
	Rutherford		*Tufnell*	
Replay	Newcastle U 2		Barnsley 0	
	Shepherd 2 (1 pen)			
1911	Bradford C 0		Newcastle U 0	
Replay	Bradford C 1		Newcastle U 0	
	Speirs			
1912	Barnsley 0		West Bromwich Albion 0	
Replay	Barnsley 1		West Bromwich Albion 0*	
	Tufnell			
1913	Aston Villa 1		Sunderland 0	
	Barber			
1914	Burnley 1		Liverpool 0	
	Freeman			
1915	Sheffield U 3		Chelsea 0	
	Simmons, Masterman, Kitchen			

1920	Aston Villa 1	Huddersfield T...................................0*
	Kirton	
1921	Tottenham H......................1	Wolverhampton W............................0
	Dimmock	
1922	Huddersfield T 1	Preston NE 0
	Smith (pen)	
1923	Bolton W 2	West Ham U 0
	Jack, J.R. Smith	
1924	Newcastle U 2	Aston Villa 0
	Harris, Seymour	
1925	Sheffield U..........................1	Cardiff C 0
	Tunstall	
1926	Bolton W 1	Manchester C 0
	Jack	
1927	Cardiff C 1	Arsenal 0
	Ferguson	
1928	Blackburn Rovers.................3	Huddersfield T...................................1
	Roscamp 2, McLean	*A. Jackson*
1929	Bolton W 2	Portsmouth...0
	Butler, Blackmore	
1930	Arsenal................................2	Huddersfield T...................................0
	James, Lambert	
1931	West Bromwich Albion 2	Birmingham 1
	W.G. Richardson 2	*Bradford*
1932	Newcastle U 2	Arsenal 1
	Allen 2	*John*
1933	Everton 3	Manchester C 0
	Stein, Dean, Dunn	
1934	Manchester C 2	Portsmouth...1
	Tilson 2	*Rutherford*
1935	Sheffield W 4	West Bromwich Albion 2
	Rimmer 2, Palethorpe,	*Boyes, Sandford*
	Hooper	
1936	Arsenal................................1	Sheffield U 0
	Drake	
1937	Sunderland 3	Preston NE...1
	Gurney, Carter, Burbanks	*F. O'Donnell*
1938	Preston NE 1	Huddersfield T...................................0*
	Mutch (pen)	
1939	Portsmouth..........................4	Wolverhampton W............................1
	Parker 2, Barlow,	*Dorsett*
	Anderson	
1946	Derby Co 4	Charlton Ath......................................1*
	H. Turner (og), Doherty,	*H. Turner*
	Stamps 2	
1947	Charlton Ath 1	Burnley 0*
	Duffy	
1948	Manchester U 4	Blackpool 2
	Rowley 2, Pearson,	*Shimwell (pen), Mortensen*
	Anderson	
1949	Wolverhampton W 3	Leicester C 1
	Pye 2, Smyth,	*Griffiths*
1950	Arsenal................................2	Liverpool 0
	Lewis 2	

1951	Newcastle U 2	Blackpool 0
	Milburn 2	
1952	Newcastle U 1	Arsenal 0
	G. Robledo	
1953	Blackpool...................................4	Bolton W 3
	Mortensen 3, Perry	*Lofthouse, Moir, Bell*
1954	West Bromwich Albion 3	Preston NE 2
	Allen 2 (1 pen), Griffin	*Morrison, Wayman*
1955	Newcastle U 3	Manchester C...................................1
	Milburn, Mitchell,	*Johnstone*
	Hannah	
1956	Manchester C.............................3	Birmingham C..................................1
	Hayes, Dyson, Johnstone	*Kinsey*
1957	Aston Villa 2	Manchester U 1
	McParland 2	*T. Taylor*
1958	Bolton W 2	Manchester U 0
	Lofthouse 2	
1959	Nottingham F 2	Luton T 1
	Dwight, Wilson	*Pacey*
1960	Wolverhampton W 3	Blackburn Rovers.............................0
	McGrath (og), Deeley 2	
1961	Tottenham H..............................2	Leicester C 0
	Smith, Dyson	
1962	Tottenham H..............................3	Burnley 1
	Greaves, Smith,	*Robson*
	Blanchflower (pen)	
1963	Manchester U............................3	Leicester C 1
	Herd 2, Law	*Keyworth*
1964	West Ham U...............................3	Preston NE 2
	Sissons, Hurst, Boyce	*Holden, Dawson*
1965	Liverpool 2	Leeds U 1*
	Hunt, St John	*Bremner*
1966	Everton 3	Sheffield W 2
	Trebilcock 2, Temple	*McCalliog, Ford*
1967	Tottenham H..............................2	Chelsea 1
	Robertson, Saul	*Tambling*
1968	West Browmich Albion 1	Everton 0*
	Astle	
1969	Manchester C............................1	Leicester C 0
	Young	
1970	Chelsea......................................2	Leeds U 2*
	Houseman, Hutchinson	*Charlton, Jones*
Replay	Chelsea......................................2	Leeds U 1*
	Osgood, Webb	*Jones*
1971	Arsenal......................................2	Liverpool 1*
	Kelly, George	*Heighway*
1972	Leeds U......................................1	Arsenal 0
	Clarke	
1973	Sunderland 1	Leeds U 0
	Porterfield	
1974	Liverpool 3	Newcastle 0
	Keegan 2, Heighway	
1975	West Ham U...............................2	Fulham 0
	A. Taylor 2	

1976	Southampton 1	Manchester U 0
	Stokes	
1977	Manchester U 2	Liverpool 1
	Pearson, J. Greenhoff	*Case*
1978	Ipswich T 1	Arsenal 0
	Osborne	
1979	Arsenal......................................3	Manchester U 2
	Talbot, Stapleton,	*McQueen, McIlroy*
	Sunderland	
1980	West Ham U.............................1	Arsenal 0
	Brooking	
1981	Tottenham H...........................1	Manchester C............................1*
	Hutchison (og)	*Hutchison*
Replay	Tottenham H...........................3	Manchester C............................2
	Villa 2, Crooks	*MacKenzie, Reeves (pen)*
1982	Tottenham H...........................1	QPR 1*
	Hoddle	*Fenwick*
Replay	Tottenham H...........................1	QPR 0
	Hoddle (pen)	
1983	Manchester U 2	Brighton & HA..........................2*
	Stapleton, Wilkins	*Smith, Stevens*
Replay	Manchester U 4	Brighton & HA..........................0
	Robson 2, Whiteside, Muhren (pen)	
1984	Everton 2	Watford 0
	Sharp, Gray	
1985	Manchester U 1	Everton 0*
	Whiteside	
1986	Liverpool 3	Everton 1
	Rush 2, Johnston	*Lineker*
1987	Coventry C 3	Tottenham H.............................2*
	Bennett, Houchen,	*C. Allen, Kilcline (og)*
	Mabbutt (og)	
1988	Wimbledon 1	Liverpool 0
	Sanchez	
1989	Liverpool 3	Everton 2*
	Aldridge, Rush 2	*McCall 2*
1990	Manchester U 3	Crystal Palace 3*
	Robson, Hughes 2	*O'Reilly, Wright 2*
Replay	Manchester U 1	Crystal Palace 0
	Martin	
1991	Tottenham H...........................2	Nottingham F............................1*
	Stewart, Walker (og)	*Pearce*
1992	Liverpool 2	Sunderland 0
	Thomas, Rush	
1993	Arsenal......................................1	Sheffield W...............................1*
	Wright	*Hirst*
Replay	Arsenal......................................2	Sheffield W...............................1*
	Wright, Linighan	*Waddle*
1994	Manchester U 4	Chelsea 0
	Cantona 2 (2 pens),	
	Hughes, McClair	
1995	Everton 1	Manchester U 0
	Rideout	
1996	Manchester U 1	Liverpool 0
	Cantona	

1997	Chelsea.............................2	Middlesbrough.................................0
	Di Matteo, Newton	
1998	Arsenal.............................2	Newcastle U 0
	Overmars, Anelka	
1999	Manchester U.......................2	Newcastle U 0
	Sheringham, Scholes	
2000	Chelsea.............................1	Aston Villa 0
	Di Matteo	
2001	Liverpool 2	Arsenal 1
	Owen 2	*Ljungberg*
2002	Arsenal.............................2	Chelsea
	Parlour, Ljungberg	
2003	Arsenal.............................1	Southampton.................................0
	Pires	
2004	Manchester U.......................3	Millwall 0
	Ronaldo, Van Nistelrooy 2 (1 pen)	
2005	Arsenal.............................0	Manchester U 0*
	Arsenal won 5-4 on penalties	
2006	Liverpool 3	West Ham U 3*
	Cisse, Gerrard 2	*Carragher (og), Ashton, Konchesky*
	Liverpool won 3-1 on penalties	

After extra time

SUMMARY OF FA CUP WINNERS SINCE 1872

Manchester United	11
Arsenal	10
Tottenham Hotspur	8
Aston Villa	7
Liverpool	7
Blackburn Rovers	6
Newcastle United	6
Everton	5
The Wanderers	5
West Bromwich Albion	5
Bolton Wanderers	4
Manchester City	4
Sheffield United	4
Wolverhampton Wanderers	4
Chelsea	3
Sheffield Wednesday	3
West Ham United	3
Bury	2
Nottingham Forest	2
Old Etonians	2
Preston North End	2
Sunderland	2
Barnsley	1
Blackburn Olympic	1
Blackpool	1
Bradford City	1
Burnley	1
Cardiff City	1
Charlton Athletic	1
Clapham Rovers	1
Coventry City	1
Derby County	1
Huddersfield Town	1
Ipswich Town	1
Leeds United	1
Notts County	1
Old Carthusians	1
Oxford University	1
Portsmouth	1
Royal Engineers	1
Southampton	1
Wimbledon	1

APPEARANCES IN FA CUP FINAL

Arsenal	17
Manchester United	17
Liverpool	13
Newcastle United	13
Everton	12
Aston Villa	10
West Bromwich Albion	10
Tottenham Hotspur	9
Blackburn Rovers	8
Manchester City	8
Wolverhampton Wanderers	8
Bolton Wanderers	7
Chelsea	7
Preston North End	7
Old Etonians	6
Sheffield United	6
Sheffield Wednesday	6
Huddersfield Town	5
The Wanderers	5
West Ham United	5
Derby County	4
Leeds United	4
Leicester City	4
Oxford University	4
Royal Engineers	4
Southampton	4
Sunderland	4
Blackpool	3
Burnley	3
Nottingham Forest	3
Portsmouth	3
Barnsley	2
Birmingham City	2
Bury	2
Cardiff City	2
Charlton Athletic	2
Clapham Rovers	2
Notts County	2
Queen's Park (Glasgow)	2
Blackburn Olympic	1
Bradford City	1
Brighton & Hove Albion	1
Bristol City	1
Coventry City	1
Crystal Palace	1
Fulham	1
Ipswich Town	1
Luton Town	1
Middlesbrough	1
Millwall	1
Old Carthusians	1
Queen's Park Rangers	1
Watford	1
Wimbledon	1

CARLING CUP REVIEW 2005–2006

Just because Wigan Athletic were beaten 4-0 in the Carling Cup final by Manchester United, it should not overshadow their achievement as newcomers to the Premier League. Most pre-season opinion was that they would be relegation fodder.

Though the second half of their season did not match the first, Wigan had the cup run. Of course raised eyebrows are the norm in the first round rather than gasps from fallen giants. Cheltenham took five goals off Brentford, Yeovil won at Ipswich, Lincoln had a nap and themselves against Crewe and Macclesfield surprised Forest in Nottingham.

Veteran Dean Windass was a treble shooter for Bradford City at Rochdale in another 5-0 romp, Wolves similarly disposed of Chester 5-1. Naturally the second round was a different ball game.

Tottenham provided the first really surprising casualty given they turned out a truly representative team at Grimsby where a late strike from Jean-Paul Kamudimba Kalala sent them heading south. Portsmouth had less of a journey but the same outcome when they lost in extra time at Gillingham.

Heroics at Doncaster where Rovers forced Manchester City into extra time and then won 3-0 on penalties, courtesy of shot-stopper substitute goalkeeper Jan Budtz who only came on in overtime for the injured Andy Warrington.

However, there was also a game of nine goals and another of eleven. Fulham edged Lincoln 5-4 during the extra period but the sensation was at Wycombe where Aston Villa found themselves 3-1 down at the interval, only to score seven times in the second half for an incredible 8-3 comeback.

Meanwhile Wigan had started quietly enough with a 1-0 victory over Bournemouth leaving it until the 86th minute to score.

Enter the European committed clubs in round three and the team who were to become the Latics' opponents in the final, Manchester United. Already a thankless task for Barnet at Old Trafford was amplified when they had goalkeeper Ross Flitney sent off for handling the ball outside his area. So 4-1 was not horrific.

While Villa were restricted to one goal by Burnley's defence, Liverpool were caught at Crystal Palace losing 2-1, Chelsea lost on penalties to Charlton and Wigan eased past Watford 3-0.

Grimsby found Newcastle tougher than Spurs and there were away day successes for West Bromwich Albion at Fulham and Middlesbrough at Everton. Arsenal's three second half goals were sufficient at Sunderland.

Round four and shocks for earlier winners. Villa went down 3-0 at Doncaster who had their third different goalkeeper. Blackburn gave Charlton a two-goal start and beat them 3-2, Boro settled Crystal Palace by the odd goal in three and Manchester United had a comfortable 3-1 win over Albion.

Three goals separated Arsenal and Reading, the latter with the consolation that they were heading for the Premier League the following season. Birmingham were pushed all the way at Millwall before emerging in the penalty shoot-out, Bolton nudged through in extra time against Leicester and Wigan kept another clean sheet with their third home draw of the competition, beating Newcastle with a late penalty.

Quarter-final time and Wigan were favoured once more with being drawn out of the hat first. Lancastrian neighbours Bolton were their opponents and a brace from Jason Roberts plus a further sound defensive display shot them into the semi-final.

Two goals for Louis Saha helped Manchester United to a 3-1 win at Birmingham, Paul Dickov left it late to put Middlesbrough out for Blackburn and for once the goalkeeping heroism was to thwart Doncaster against Arsenal, the Gunners prevailing on spot kicks after a 2-2 draw.

Semi-final time in the Carling Cup comes in January. Arsenal probably did not relish having to face Wigan given their other commitments, but at least the first leg was away. Paul Scharner's goal for the Latics gave them a slender lead. The following day Blackburn and Manchester United were involved in a 1-1 draw, thus the outcome was still in the balance.

At Highbury, Arsenal took a crucial lead it seemed when Thierry Henry scored in the 65th minute to ensure both teams were level on aggregate. And when Robin Van Persie put Arsenal ahead in the 108th minute, the tie seemed to be slipping away from Wigan's grasp.

But with seconds ticking away Roberts came to the rescue for Wigan and his goal ensured their final place on away goals.

In the final at Cardiff, Manchester United took the lead through Wayne Rooney, Saha and Cristiano Ronaldo made it three before Rooney added his second for the 4-0 win. Yet Wigan had done enough for overall congratulations.

CARLING CUP 2005–2006

FIRST ROUND

Southend U	(0) 0	Southampton	(2) 3
Blackpool	(2) 2	Hull C	(1) 1
Bristol C	(1) 2	Barnet	(1) 4
Burnley	(0) 2	Carlisle U	(0) 1
Bury	(0) 0	Leicester C	(2) 3
Cheltenham T	(1) 5	Brentford	(0) 0
Crystal Palace	(0) 3	Walsall	(0) 0
Gillingham	(0) 1	Oxford U	(0) 0
Hartlepool U	(1) 3	Darlington	(0) 1
Ipswich T	(0) 0	Yeovil T	(1) 2
Leeds U	(2) 2	Oldham Ath	(0) 0
Leyton Orient	(0) 1	Luton T	(1) 3
Lincoln C	(2) 5	Crewe Alex	(1) 1
Mansfield T	(1) 1	Stoke C	(1) 1
(aet; Mansfield T won 3-0 on penalties.)			
Millwall	(0) 2	Bristol R	(0) 0
Milton Keynes D	(0) 0	Norwich C	(0) 1
(aet.)			
Northampton T	(1) 3	QPR	(0) 0
Nottingham F	(1) 2	Macclesfield T	(2) 3
Plymouth Arg	(2) 2	Peterborough U	(1) 1
Preston NE	(0) 2	Barnsley	(0) 2
(aet; Barnsley won 5-4 on penalties.)			
Reading	(1) 3	Swansea C	(1) 1
(aet.)			
Rochdale	(0) 0	Bradford C	(2) 5
Rotherham U	(1) 3	Port Vale	(1) 1
Scunthorpe U	(0) 2	Tranmere R	(0) 1
Sheffield U	(0) 1	Boston U	(0) 0
Shrewsbury T	(1) 3	Brighton & HA	(1) 2
(aet.)			
Stockport Co	(1) 2	Sheffield W	(1) 4
(aet.)			
Swindon T	(0) 1	Wycombe W	(1) 3
Watford	(2) 3	Notts Co	(0) 1
Wolverhampton W	(1) 5	Chester C	(0) 1
Wrexham	(0) 0	Doncaster R	(0) 1
Chesterfield	(1) 2	Huddersfield T	(1) 4
Colchester U	(0) 0	Cardiff C	(2) 2
Derby Co	(0) 0	Grimsby T	(1) 1
Rushden & D	(0) 0	Coventry C	(2) 3
Torquay U	(0) 0	Bournemouth	(0) 0
(aet; Bournemouth won 4-3 on penalties.)			

SECOND ROUND

Barnet	(1) 2	Plymouth Arg	(1) 1
Burnley	(1) 3	Barnsley	(0) 0

Cardiff C	(0) 2	Macclesfield T	(1) 1
Charlton Ath	(1) 3	Hartlepool U	(1) 1
Crystal Palace	(0) 1	Coventry C	(0) 0
Gillingham	(1) 3	Portsmouth	(1) 2
Grimsby T	(0) 1	Tottenham H	(0) 0
Leicester C	(1) 2	Blackpool	(0) 1
Mansfield T	(0) 1	Southampton	(0) 0
Norwich C	(1) 2	Northampton T	(0) 0
Reading	(0) 1	Luton T	(0) 0
Rotherham U	(0) 0	Leeds U	(2) 2
Scunthorpe U	(0) 0	Birmingham C	(1) 2
Sheffield W	(0) 2	West Ham U	(1) 4
Shrewsbury T	(0) 0	Sheffield U	(0) 0
(aet; Sheffield U won 4-3 on penalties.)			
Sunderland	(0) 1	Cheltenham T	(0) 0
(aet.)			
WBA	(2) 4	Bradford C	(1) 1
Watford	(1) 2	Wolverhampton W	(1) 1
(aet.)			
Wigan Ath	(0) 1	Bournemouth	(0) 0
Wycombe W	(3) 3	Aston Villa	(1) 8
Yeovil T	(0) 1	Millwall	(0) 2
Blackburn R	(1) 3	Huddersfield T	(0) 1
Doncaster R	(0) 1	Manchester C	(0) 1
(aet; Doncaster R won 3-0 on penalties.)			
Fulham	(2) 5	Lincoln C	(0) 4
(aet.)			

THIRD ROUND

Aston Villa	(1) 1	Burnley	(0) 0
Blackburn R	(0) 3	Leeds U	(0) 0
Crystal Palace	(1) 2	Liverpool	(1) 1
Doncaster R	(0) 2	Gillingham	(0) 0
Fulham	(0) 2	WBA	(1) 3
(aet.)			
Mansfield T	(0) 2	Millwall	(1) 3
Reading	(0) 2	Sheffield U	(0) 0
Sunderland	(0) 0	Arsenal	(0) 3
Wigan Ath	(0) 3	Watford	(0) 0
(aet.)			
Birmingham C	(1) 2	Norwich C	(1) 1
Bolton W	(0) 1	West Ham U	(0) 0
Cardiff C	(0) 0	Leicester C	(1) 1
Chelsea	(1) 1	Charlton Ath	(1) 1
(aet; Charlton Ath won 5-4 on penalties.)			
Everton	(0) 0	Middlesbrough	(1) 1
Grimsby T	(0) 0	Newcastle U	(0) 1
Manchester U	(2) 4	Barnet	(0) 1

FOURTH ROUND

Arsenal	(2) 3	Reading	(0) 0
Doncaster R	(1) 3	Aston Villa	(0) 0

173

Millwall	(0) 2	Birmingham C	(1) 2

(aet; Birmingham C won 4-3 on penalties.)

Bolton W	(0) 2	Leicester C	(0) 1
Charlton Ath	(1) 2	Blackburn R	(0) 3
Manchester U	(2) 3	WBA	(0) 1
Middlesbrough	(0) 2	Crystal Palace	(1) 1
Wigan Ath	(0) 1	Newcastle U	(0) 0

QUARTER-FINALS

Birmingham C	(0) 1	Manchester U	(0) 3
Wigan Ath	(2) 2	Bolton W	(0) 0
Doncaster R	(1) 2	Arsenal	(0) 2

(aet; Arsenal won 3-1 on penalties.)

Middlesbrough	(0) 0	Blackburn R	(0) 1

SEMI-FINALS FIRST LEG

Wigan Ath	(0) 1	Arsenal	(0) 0
Blackburn R	(1) 1	Manchester U	(1) 1

SEMI-FINALS SECOND LEG

Arsenal	(0) 2	Wigan Ath	(0) 1
Manchester U	(1) 2	Blackburn R	(1) 1

CARLING CUP FINAL

Sunday, 26 February 2006

(at Millennium Stadium, Cardiff, attendance 66,866)

Manchester U (1) 4   Wigan Ath (0) 0

Manchester U: Van der Sar; Neville, Silvestre (Evra), Park, Brown (Vidic), Ferdinand, Ronaldo (Richardson), O'Shea, Saha, Rooney, Giggs.
Scorers: Rooney 33, 61, Saha 55, Ronaldo 59.

Wigan Ath: Pollitt (Filan); Chimbonda, Baines, Kavanagh (Ziegler), Henchoz (McCulloch), De Zeeuw, Teale, Bullard, Camara, Roberts, Scharner.

Referee: A. Wiley (Staffordshire).

PAST LEAGUE CUP FINALS

Played as two legs up to 1966

1961	Rotherham U 2	Aston Villa 0	
	Webster, Kirkman		
	Aston Villa 3	Rotherham U 0*	
	O'Neill, Burrows, McParland		
1962	Rochdale 0	Norwich C..............................3	
	Lythgoe 2, Punton		
	Norwich C..............................1	Rochdale 0	
	Hill		
1963	Birmingham C..............................3	Aston Villa 1	
	Leek 2, Bloomfield	*Thomson*	
	Aston Villa 0	Birmingham C..............................0	
1964	Stoke C..............................1	Leicester C..............................1	
	Bebbington	*Gibson*	
	Leicester C..............................3	Stoke C..............................2	
	Stringfellow, Gibson, Riley	*Viollet, Kinnell*	
1965	Chelsea..............................3	Leicester C..............................2	
	Tambling, Venables (pen), McCreadie	*Appleton, Goodfellow*	
	Leicester C..............................0	Chelsea..............................0	
1966	West Ham U..............................2	WBA 1	
	Moore, Byrne	*Astle*	
	WBA 4	West Ham U..............................1	
	Kaye, Brown, Clark, Williams	*Peters*	
1967	QPR..............................3	WBA 2	
	Morgan R, Marsh, Lazarus	*Clark C 2*	
1968	Leeds U..............................1	Arsenal..............................0	
	Cooper		
1969	Swindon T..............................3	Arsenal..............................1*	
	Smart, Rogers 2	*Gould*	
1970	Manchester C..............................2	WBA 1*	
	Doyle, Pardoe	*Astle*	
1971	Tottenham H..............................2	Aston Villa 0	
	Chivers 2		
1972	Chelsea..............................1	Stoke C..............................2	
	Osgood	*Conroy, Eastham*	
1973	Tottenham H..............................1	Norwich C..............................0	
	Coates		
1974	Wolverhampton W 2	Manchester C 1	
	Hibbitt, Richards	*Bell*	
1975	Aston Villa 1	Norwich C..............................0	
	Graydon		
1976	Manchester C..............................2	Newcastle U 1	
	Barnes, Tueart	*Gowling*	
1977	Aston Villa 0	Everton 0	
Replay	Aston Villa 1	Everton 1*	
	Kenyon (og)	*Latchford*	

Replay	Aston Villa 3	Everton 2*	
	Little 2, Nicholl	*Latchford, Lyons*	
1978	Nottingham F 1	Liverpool 0*	
Replay	Nottingham F 1	Liverpool 0	
	Robertson (pen)		
1979	Nottingham F 3	Southampton 2	
	Birtles 2, Woodcock	*Peach, Holmes*	
1980	Wolverhampton W 1	Nottingham F 0	
	Gray		
1981	Liverpool 1	West Ham U 1*	
	Kennedy A	*Stewart (pen)*	
Replay	Liverpool 2	West Ham U 1	
	Dalglish, Hansen	*Goddard*	
1982	Liverpool 3	Tottenham H 1*	
	Whelan 2, Rush	*Archibald*	
1983	Liverpool 2	Manchester U 1*	
	Kennedy A, Whelan	*Whiteside*	
1984	Liverpool 0	Everton 0*	
Replay	Liverpool 1	Everton 0	
	Souness		
1985	Norwich C 1	Sunderland 0	
	Chisholm (og)		
1986	Oxford U 3	QPR 0	
	Hebberd, Houghton, Charles		
1987	Arsenal 2	Liverpool 1	
	Nicholas 2	*Rush*	
1988	Luton T 3	Arsenal 2	
	Stein B 2, Wilson	*Hayes, Smith*	
1989	Nottingham F 3	Luton T 1	
	Clough 2, Webb	*Harford*	
1990	Nottingham F 1	Oldham Ath 0	
	Jemson		
1991	Sheffield W 1	Manchester U 0	
	Sheridan		
1992	Manchester U 1	Nottingham F 0	
	McClair		
1993	Arsenal 2	Sheffield W 1	
	Merson, Morrow	*Harkes*	
1994	Aston Villa 3	Manchester U 1	
	Atkinson, Saunders 2 (1 pen)	*Hughes*	
1995	Liverpool 2	Bolton W 1	
	McManaman 2	*Thompson*	
1996	Aston Villa 3	Leeds U 0	
	Milosevic, Taylor, Yorke		
1997	Leicester C 1	Middlesbrough 1*	
	Heskey	*Ravanelli*	
Replay	Leicester C 1	Middlesbrough 0*	
	Claridge		
1998	Chelsea 2	Middlesbrough 0*	
	Sinclair, Di Matteo		

1999	Tottenham H	1	Leicester C	0
	Nielsen			
2000	Leicester C	2	Tranmere R	1
	Elliott 2		*Kelly*	
2001	Liverpool	1	Birmingham C	1
	Fowler		*Purse (pen)*	

Liverpool won 5-4 on penalties.

2002	Blackburn	2	Tottenham H	1
	Jansen, Cole		*Ziege*	
2003	Liverpool	2	Manchester U	0
	Gerrard, Owen			
2004	Middlesbrough	2	Bolton W	1
	Job, Zenden (pen)		*Davies*	
2005	Chelsea	3	Liverpool	2*
	Gerrard (og), Drogba, Kezman		*Riise, Nunez*	
2006	Manchester U	4	Wigan Ath	0
	Rooney 2, Saha, Ronaldo			

*After extra time

FOOTBALL LEAGUE TROPHY 2005–2006

NORTHERN SECTION FIRST ROUND

Barnsley	(1) 2	Doncaster R	(1) 5
Blackpool	(1) 4	Wrexham	(0) 3
Cambridge U	(0) 3	Chester C	(0) 0
Grimsby T	(0) 1	Morecambe	(1) 1

(aet; Morecambe won 4-3 on penalties.)

Halifax T	(2) 6	Bury	(0) 1
Kidderminster H	(1) 2	Darlington	(1) 1
Macclesfield T	(0) 2	Chesterfield	(0) 0
Mansfield T	(0) 0	Hereford U	(1) 1
Oldham Ath	(0) 1	Carlisle U	(1) 1

(aet; Carlisle U won 6-5 on penalties.)

Rochdale	(2) 3	Stockport Co	(1) 1
Rotherham U	(2) 3	Accrington S	(1) 3

(aet; Rotherham U won 3-2 on penalties.)

Scunthorpe U	(0) 1	Hartlepool U	(0) 0
Tranmere R	(1) 2	Lincoln C	(1) 1
Boston U	(1) 2	Huddersfield T	(0) 1

SOUTHERN SECTION FIRST ROUND

Barnet	(1) 3	Bristol C	(1) 2
Bournemouth	(1) 4	Aldershot T	(0) 1
Brentford	(1) 1	Oxford U	(1) 1

(aet; Oxford U won 4-3 on penalties.)

Gillingham	(0) 2	Crawley T	(0) 0
Leyton Orient	(1) 2	Yeovil T	(0) 0
Milton Keynes D	(1) 3	Exeter C	(0) 2
Northampton T	(3) 5	Notts Co	(1) 2
Peterborough U	(1) 2	Bristol R	(1) 1
Rushden & D	(1) 1	Southend U	(0) 0
Shrewsbury T	(0) 0	Cheltenham T	(1) 2
Swindon T	(1) 2	Stevenage B	(0) 0
Torquay U	(1) 1	Swansea C	(0) 3
Woking	(1) 3	Nottingham F	(2) 2
Wycombe W	(0) 2	Dagenham & R	(1) 1

NORTHERN SECTION SECOND ROUND

Cambridge U	(2) 3	Doncaster R	(1) 2
Carlisle U	(0) 2	Blackpool	(0) 1
Hereford U	(1) 2	Port Vale	(1) 1
Morecambe	(0) 0	Bradford C	(0) 1
Rotherham U	(1) 1	Macclesfield T	(0) 2
Tranmere R	(1) 3	Rochdale	(2) 2
Boston U	(0) 0	Kidderminster H	(3) 3
Halifax T	(0) 1	Scunthorpe U	(1) 3

SOUTHERN SECTION SECOND ROUND

Barnet	(0) 0	Milton Keynes D	(2) 3
Gillingham	(2) 2	Wycombe W	(2) 2

(aet; Wycombe W won 3-1 on penalties.)

Peterborough U	(1) 2	Swindon T	(0) 1
Swansea C	(1) 4	Rushden & D	(0) 0
Walsall	(0) 1	Bournemouth	(0) 2
Woking	(1) 1	Cheltenham T	(1) 2

(Abandoned due to fog.)

Colchester U	(0) 3	Northampton T	(1) 2

(aet.)

Oxford U	(1) 1	Leyton Orient	(0) 0
Woking	(1) 1	Cheltenham T	(0) 5
(aet.)			

NORTHERN QUARTER-FINALS

Macclesfield T	(3) 4	Cambridge U	(1) 2
Hereford U	(2) 2	Scunthorpe U	(0) 0
Kidderminster H	(1) 2	Bradford C	(0) 1
Tranmere R	(0) 0	Carlisle U	(0) 0
(aet; Carlisle U won 11-10 on penalties.)			

SOUTHERN QUARTER-FINALS

Swansea C	(0) 3	Peterborough U	(0) 1
(aet.)			
Cheltenham T	(1) 2	Oxford U	(0) 1
Milton Keynes D	(0) 1	Colchester U	(0) 2
Walsall	(2) 3	Wycombe W	(1) 2

NORTHERN SEMI-FINALS

| Carlisle U | (0) 1 | Kidderminster H | (0) 0 |
| Macclesfield T | (2) 2 | Hereford U | (0) 0 |

SOUTHERN SEMI-FINALS

Cheltenham T	(0) 0	Colchester U	(1) 1
Swansea C	(1) 2	Walsall	(0) 2
(aet; Swansea C won 6-5 on penalties.)			

NORTHERN FINAL FIRST LEG

| Carlisle U | (1) 2 | Macclesfield T | (1) 1 |

NORTHERN FINAL SECOND LEG

| Macclesfield T | (2) 3 | Carlisle U | (1) 2 |
| *(aet.)* | | | |

SOUTHERN FINAL FIRST LEG

| Swansea C | (1) 1 | Colchester U | (0) 0 |

SOUTHERN FINAL SECOND LEG

| Colchester U | (0) 1 | Swansea C | (0) 2 |

FOOTBALL LEAGUE TROPHY FINAL

Sunday, 2 April 2006

(at Millennium Stadium, Cardiff, attendance 42,028)

Carlisle U (1) 1   Swansea C (1) 2

Carlisle U: Westwood; Arnison (Grand), Aranalde, Billy, Gray, Livesey, Lumsdon, Murray A (Hackney), Holmes (Murray G), Hawley, Murphy.
Scorer: Murray A 40.

Swansea C: Gueret; Ricketts, Tate, O'Leary (Knight), Monk, Lowe, Britton, Tudur-Jones, Akinfenwa, Trundle, Robinson (Martinez).
Scorers: Trundle 3, Akinfenwa 81.

Referee: T. Leake (Lancashire).

FA CHARITY SHIELD WINNERS 1908–2005

1908	Manchester U v QPR	
	4-0 after 1-1 draw	
1909	Newcastle U v Northampton T	2-0
1910	Brighton v Aston Villa	1-0
1911	Manchester U v Swindon T	8-4
1912	Blackburn R v QPR	2-1
1913	Professionals v Amateurs	7-2
1920	Tottenham H v Burnley	2-0
1921	Huddersfield T v Liverpool	1-0
1922	Not played	
1923	Professionals v Amateurs	2-0
1924	Professionals v Amateurs	3-1
1925	Amateurs v Professionals	6-1
1926	Amateurs v Professionals	6-3
1927	Cardiff C v Corinthians	2-1
1928	Everton v Blackburn R	2-1
1929	Professionals v Amateurs	3-0
1930	Arsenal v Sheffield W	2-1
1931	Arsenal v WBA	1-0
1932	Everton v Newcastle U	5-3
1933	Arsenal v Everton	3-0
1934	Arsenal v Manchester C	4-0
1935	Sheffield W v Arsenal	1-0
1936	Sunderland v Arsenal	2-1
1937	Manchester C v Sunderland	2-0
1938	Arsenal v Preston NE	2-1
1948	Arsenal v Manchester U	4-3
1949	Portsmouth v Wolverhampton W	1-1*
1950	World Cup Team v	4-2
	Canadian Touring Team	
1951	Tottenham H v Newcastle U	2-1
1952	Manchester U v Newcastle U	4-2
1953	Arsenal v Blackpool	3-1
1954	Wolverhampton W v WBA	4-4*
1955	Chelsea v Newcastle U	3-0
1956	Manchester U v Manchester C	1-0
1957	Manchester U v Aston Villa	4-0
1958	Bolton W v Wolverhampton W	4-1
1959	Wolverhampton W v	3-1
	Nottingham F	
1960	Burnley v Wolverhampton W	2-2*
1961	Tottenham H v FA XI	3-2
1962	Tottenham H v Ipswich T	5-1

1963	Everton v Manchester U	4-0
1964	Liverpool v West Ham U	2-2*
1965	Manchester U v Liverpool	2-2*
1966	Liverpool v Everton	1-0
1967	Manchester U v Tottenham H	3-3*
1968	Manchester C v WBA	6-1
1969	Leeds U v Manchester C	2-1
1970	Everton v Chelsea	2-1
1971	Leicester C v Liverpool	1-0
1972	Manchester C v Aston Villa	1-0
1973	Burnley v Manchester C	1-0
1974	Liverpool† v Leeds U	1-1
1975	Derby Co v West Ham U	2-0
1976	Liverpool v Southampton	1-0
1977	Liverpool v Manchester U	0-0*
1978	Nottingham F v Ipswich T	5-0
1979	Liverpool v Arsenal	3-1
1980	Liverpool v West Ham U	1-0
1981	Aston Villa v Tottenham H	2-2*
1982	Liverpool v Tottenham H	1-0
1983	Manchester U v Liverpool	2-0
1984	Everton v Liverpool	1-0
1985	Everton v Manchester U	2-0
1986	Everton v Liverpool	1-1*
1987	Everton v Coventry C	1-0
1988	Liverpool v Wimbledon	2-1
1989	Liverpool v Arsenal	1-0
1990	Liverpool v Manchester U	1-1*
1991	Arsenal v Tottenham H	0-0*
1992	Leeds U v Liverpool	4-3
1993	Manchester U† v Arsenal	1-1
1994	Manchester U v Blackburn R	2-0
1995	Everton v Blackburn R	1-0
1996	Manchester U v Newcastle U	4-0
1997	Manchester U† v Chelsea	1-1
1998	Arsenal v Manchester U	3-0
1999	Arsenal v Manchester U	2-1
2000	Chelsea v Manchester U	2-0
2001	Liverpool v Manchester U	2-1
2002	Arsenal v Liverpool	1-0
2003	Manchester U† v Arsenal	1-1
2004	Arsenal v Manchester U	3-1
2005	Chelsea v Arsenal	2-1

*Each club retained shield for six months. †Won on penalties.

THE FA COMMUNITY SHIELD 2005

Chelsea (1) 2, Arsenal (0) 1

At Millennium Stadium, 7 August 2005, attendance 58,014

Chelsea: Cech; Paulo Ferreira, Del Horno, Makelele, Terry, Gallas, Duff (Cole J), Lampard (Geremi), Drogba (Crespo), Gudjohnsen (Tiago), Robben (Wright-Phillips).
Scorers: Drogba 8, 57.
Arsenal: Lehmann; Lauren (Hoyte), Cole, Flamini (Hleb), Toure, Senderos (Cygan), Ljungberg (Reyes), Fabregas, Henry, Bergkamp (Van Persie), Pires (Silva).
Scorer: Fabregas 65.
Referee: H. Webb (Yorkshire).

SCOTTISH LEAGUE REVIEW 2005–2006

Without doubt the two most talked about teams in Scotland during 2005–06 were Hearts and Gretna, both of whom benefited from heavy financial investment and were destined to oppose each other in the final of the Scottish Cup.

Hearts, too, made an impact in the Scottish Premier League, at one point threatening to win the title itself until caught by Celtic who went on to achieve their 40th championship.

It may be argued that a turmoil of events conspired to cause disruption which inevitably filtered down to the ranks and two managerial changes did not to restore stability on the pitch.

With just four matches completed, Hearts remained the only unbeaten team, Rangers having accounted for Celtic in the first Old Firm encounter 3-1 at Ibrox. After eight successive wins Hearts dropped their first points in a 2-2 draw at Falkirk.

Hearts' next fixture was at Parkhead and a 1-1 draw here at least kept up the momentum for the Tynecastle club. Alas before another fixture, the club parted company with manager George Burley.

And it was unlucky 13 when Hibs beat them in the Edinburgh derby leaving Celtic in front level on points with a better goal difference. By this time Rangers were in the toils and succumbed 3-0 at Parkhead.

After an interim period, Graham Rix was appointed manager of Hearts in early November and late in the month Celtic hit a hurdle when Dunfermline beat them on their own ground. Hearts' second defeat came in the middle of December 1-0 to Rangers when they finished with ten men.

However New Year's Day provided the killer punch. Hearts took a 2-0 lead against Celtic in eight minutes only to concede two sloppy goals by poor defending in the last few minutes as the gap grew to seven points. Hibs were a further seven away, Rangers already 17 behind Celtic.

In mid-March when the Celts were wrapping up the CIS Insurance Cup beating Dunfermline 3-0, Hearts could only draw 1-1 with Rangers, to leave them 24 points in the wake of Celtic who had a game in hand. Rix, too, left.

Decision day proved to be 5 April with Hearts visiting Celtic for their last faint hope of taking the title. A John Hartson goal after four minutes settled the issue. However, Hearts could at least look to the Scottish Cup, when three days earlier they had disposed Hibs 4-0 at Easter Road.

As with Hearts chairman Roman Romanov, Gretna had their sugar-daddy in Brooks Mileson. A touch fortunate not to have faced any Premier teams on their cup run, they nonetheless carried the Second Division title in style with an 18 point lead over Morton. Moreover in the Scottish Cup final they pushed Hearts all the way to a penalty shoot-out before being beaten.

In the end Rangers were only a point behind Hearts but had really saved their better performances for Europe and only going out on the away goals rule to Villarreal in the Champions League. But, they, too had a managerial change which took effect from the end of the season with Alex McLeish giving way to Paul Le Guen.

Another pleasant surprise might have been the fourth placing of Inverness Caley. But at the time of the split were five points adrift of the cut and since points gained in the last five matches are confined to the two sections their final resting place was seventh. This, in spite of winning their last five remaining fixtures.

So it was Hibs who were destined to finish fourth. Their high spot was in the Scottish Cup, too, when they trounced Rangers 3-0 at Ibrox. In fact, there were only two points separating Hibs, Kilmarnock and Aberdeen at the final reckoning.

Motherwell disappointed and were five points away from the top half. Again showing the disparity between the teams in the Premier League, Dundee United, Falkirk and Dunfermline were kept apart merely by goal difference on 33 points. The Fifers had vied with Livingston for cellar spot for half the campaign.

Restless as ever, the Scottish League implemented play-offs for the relegation and promotion from the bottom of Division 1 down. With St Mirren easing to a ten point lead to replace Livi, the issue at the foot concerned whether Stranraer could keep away from the last but one place until caught by South of Scotland neighbours Queen of the South, then losing in the play-offs to Division 2 Partick Thistle.

With Brechin doomed, the Jags went up at Morton and Peterhead's expense. Alloa came through the play-offs to stay in Division 2, with Dumbarton previously demoted. Thus no joy from Division 3 apart from champions Cowdenbeath, who only edged Berwick on goal difference, Stenhousemuir and Arbroath unable to take advantage of the lifeline offered.

SCOTTISH LEAGUE TABLES 2005–2006

Premier League	P	Home W	D	L	F	A	Away W	D	L	F	A	Total W	D	L	F	A	Gd	Pts
1 Celtic	38	14	4	1	41	15	14	3	2	52	22	28	7	3	93	37	56	91
2 Hearts	38	15	2	2	43	9	7	6	6	28	22	22	8	8	71	31	40	74
3 Rangers	38	13	4	2	38	11	8	5	5	29	26	21	10	7	67	37	30	73
4 Hibernian	38	11	1	7	39	24	6	4	9	22	32	17	5	16	61	56	5	56
5 Kilmarnock	38	11	3	5	39	29	4	7	8	24	35	15	10	13	63	64	-1	55
6 Aberdeen	38	8	9	3	30	17	5	6	7	16	23	13	15	10	46	40	6	54
7 Inverness CT	38	5	6	7	21	21	10	7	3	30	17	15	13	10	51	38	13	58
8 Motherwell	38	7	5	7	35	31	6	5	8	20	30	13	10	15	55	61	-6	49
9 Dundee U	38	5	8	6	22	28	2	4	13	19	38	7	12	19	41	66	-25	33
10 Falkirk	38	2	6	11	14	30	6	3	10	21	34	8	9	21	35	64	-29	33
11 Dunfermline Ath	38	3	5	11	17	39	5	4	10	16	29	8	9	21	33	68	-35	33
12 Livingston	38	3	4	12	15	33	1	2	16	10	46	4	6	28	25	79	-54	18

After 33 matches, the first six clubs play once against each other; bottom six likewise. Thus the finishing position of Inverness CT moves them from fourth to seventh place.

First Division	P	Home W	D	L	F	A	Away W	D	L	F	A	Total W	D	L	F	A	Gd	Pts
1 St Mirren	36	11	4	3	23	12	12	3	3	29	16	23	7	6	52	28	24	76
2 St Johnstone	36	8	9	1	30	14	10	3	5	29	20	18	12	6	59	34	25	66
3 Hamilton A	36	9	6	3	25	12	6	4	8	28	27	15	14	7	53	39	14	59
4 Ross Co	36	8	6	4	24	19	6	8	4	23	21	14	14	8	47	40	7	56
5 Clyde	36	9	5	4	30	18	6	5	7	24	24	15	10	11	54	42	12	55
6 Airdrie U	36	8	5	5	41	21	3	7	8	16	22	11	12	13	57	43	14	45
7 Dundee	36	6	5	7	26	25	3	11	4	17	25	9	16	11	43	50	-7	43
8 Queen of the S	36	5	7	6	17	19	2	5	11	14	35	7	12	17	31	54	-23	33
9 Stranraer	36	4	7	7	20	27	1	7	10	13	26	5	14	17	33	53	-20	29
10 Brechin C	36	1	7	10	18	36	1	4	13	10	38	2	11	23	28	74	-46	17

Second Division	P	Home W	D	L	F	A	Away W	D	L	F	A	Total W	D	L	F	A	Gd	Pts
1 Gretna	36	14	2	2	53	15	14	2	2	44	15	28	4	4	97	30	67	88
2 Morton	36	13	2	3	36	16	8	5	5	22	17	21	7	8	58	33	25	70
3 Peterhead	36	9	4	5	29	22	8	2	8	24	25	17	6	13	53	47	6	57
4 Partick Th	36	8	4	6	25	27	8	5	5	32	29	16	9	11	57	56	1	57
5 Stirling A	36	8	4	6	28	28	7	2	9	26	35	15	6	15	54	63	-9	51
6 Ayr U	36	5	5	8	23	26	5	7	6	33	35	10	12	14	56	61	-5	42
7 Raith R	36	5	5	8	25	28	6	4	8	19	26	11	9	16	44	54	-10	42
8 Forfar Ath	36	8	1	9	29	25	4	3	11	15	30	12	4	20	44	55	-11	40
9 Alloa Ath	36	3	5	10	15	37	5	3	10	21	40	8	8	20	36	77	-41	32
10 Dumbarton	36	5	3	10	26	26	2	2	14	14	37	7	5	24	40	63	-23	26

Third Division	P	Home W	D	L	F	A	Away W	D	L	F	A	Total W	D	L	F	A	Gd	Pts
1 Cowdenbeath	36	14	2	2	51	18	10	2	6	30	16	24	4	8	81	34	47	76
2 Berwick R	36	11	4	3	28	14	12	3	3	26	13	23	7	6	54	27	27	76
3 Stenhousemuir	36	13	1	4	45	17	10	3	5	33	21	23	4	9	78	38	40	73
4 Arbroath	36	12	2	4	35	18	4	5	9	22	29	16	7	13	57	47	10	55
5 Elgin C	36	6	5	7	28	30	9	2	7	27	28	15	7	14	55	58	-3	52
6 Queen's Park	36	6	7	5	29	24	7	5	6	18	18	13	12	11	47	42	5	51
7 East Fife	36	9	2	7	24	24	4	2	12	24	40	13	4	19	48	64	-16	43
8 Albion R	36	4	4	10	20	31	3	4	11	19	29	7	8	21	39	60	-21	29
9 Montrose	36	5	3	10	15	23	1	7	10	16	36	6	10	20	31	59	-28	28
10 East Stirling	36	5	4	9	14	30	1	1	16	14	59	6	5	25	28	89	-61	23

BANK OF SCOTLAND SCOTTISH LEAGUE—PREMIER LEAGUE

RESULTS 2005–2006

	Aberdeen	Celtic	Dundee U	Dunfermline Ath	Falkirk	Hearts	Hibernian	Inverness CT	Kilmarnock	Livingston	Motherwell	Rangers
Aberdeen	—	1-3 *2-2*	2-0	0-0	3-0	1-1	0-1 *4-0*	*0-0*	1-2	0-0	2-2	3-2
Celtic	2-0 *2-2*	—	3-3	0-1	1-0	1-1	1-0 *1-1*	2-1	2-2 *2-0*	3-0	2-2	2-0
Dundee U	3-0	2-4	—	2-1 *0-1*	3-1	1-0	3-2 *1-1*	1-1	4-2	2-0	5-0	3-0 *0-0*
Dunfermline Ath	1-1	0-4	2-1	—	0-1	1-1	1-0	1-1 *0-1*	0-0	2-0 *3-1*	1-1	0-0 *1-4*
Falkirk	0-2	1-8	1-1	1-1	—	2-2	1-2	2-4	0-1	2-0 *1-0*	0-3 *1-1*	3-3
Hearts	1-0	0-3	1-3	5-0	2-3	—	2-0 *2-1*	0-1	2-2	1-1 *1-0*	0-1 *1-1*	1-1
Hibernian	2-0 *1-0*	0-1	2-1	1-1	0-3 *2-0*	2-0	—	1-2	4-2	3-0	2-1 *3-0*	1-1
Inverness CT	1-2	1-2	1-1	3-1	1-1	0-1	2-2 *3-1*	—	2-1	7-0	0-2	1-2 *0-1*
Kilmarnock	4-2	0-1 *1-4*	2-1	3-2 *1-0*	1-1	2-4	1-2	1-2 2-2	—	3-0 *3-1*	4-1 *2-0*	0-1 *2-3*
Livingston	0-0	0-5 *0-2*	1-0 *3-1*	1-1	2-1	1-0	1-2	1-1 *0-1*	0-3	—	1-2 *0-1*	2-3 *2-2*
Motherwell	3-1	4-4 *1-3*	4-5 *1-1* *2-0*	5-0 *1-0*	5-1 *3-1*	2-3 *1-1*	1-3 *2-2* *0-3*	2-2 *0-2* *0-1*	2-2	1-0 *2-1*	—	0-1
Rangers	0-0 *1-0*	3-1 *0-1*	3-0	5-1 *1-0*	2-2	1-0 *2-0*	1-1	1-1	3-0 *4-0* *4-1*	2-0 *1-0*	—	—

BELL'S SCOTTISH LEAGUE—DIVISION ONE RESULTS 2005–2006

	Airdrie U	Brechin C	Clyde	Dundee	Hamilton A	Queen of the S	Ross Co	St Johnstone	St Mirren	Stranraer
Airdrie U	—	6-0 3-3	1-3 1-1	4-0 7-0	2-2 0-0	4-0 1-1	0-1 2-3	3-1 2-1	0-1 1-4	1-0 3-0
Brechin C	1-1 0-0	—	3-1	1-3 0-3	1-2 0-1	1-1 1-0	1-4 3-3	1-4 0-2	2-3 0-3	2-3 0-0
Clyde	1-0 3-1	2-1 5-1	—	1-1 3-3	1-1 2-2	3-0 3-1	1-0 2-0	0-1 2-3	1-2 0-1	1-1 1-1
Dundee	0-2 2-3	1-0 0-1	3-3 0-1	—	1-2 2-4	2-3 5-2	0-0 2-1	2-1 0-1	3-1 3-2	2-1 2-0
Hamilton A	1-1 3-0	3-0 2-0	1-1 2-0	1-1 0-0	—	0-2	0-0 2-3	1-2 1-3	4-0 3-1	1-0 1-1
Queen of the S	1-0 1-0	0-0 0-0	1-2 2-1	0-0 1-3	1-2 1-1	—	0-0	3-2 2-1	0-0 0-1	1-0 2-1
Ross Co	1-0 2-2	1-0 2-0	3-1 0-1	3-0 0-1	0-0 2-1	1-1 3-1	—	2-2	0-0 0-4	1-1 1-1
St Johnstone	0-1 2-2	3-1 3-0	0-0 1-0	0-0 2-1	5-1 1-1	4-0 2-1	1-1 1-1	—	0-2 1-2	3-2 0-0
St Mirren	1-1 3-0	1-0 3-2	2-1 2-1	0-0 1-1	2-1 0-2	2-0 1-0	2-0 0-1	0-0 0-1	—	3-1
Stranraer	1-0 1-1	1-1 2-0	1-2 0-5		1-2 5-4	0-0 1-0	2-3 2-2	1-1 0-2	0-0 1-2	—

BELL'S SCOTTISH LEAGUE—DIVISION TWO RESULTS 2005–2006

	Alloa Ath	Ayr U	Dumbarton	Forfar Ath	Gretna	Morton	Partick T	Peterhead	Raith R	Stirling A
Alloa Ath	—	0-4	1-4	1-1	0-3	0-3	1-6	4-1	1-2	2-4
Ayr U	1-1	—	1-0	0-1	0-3	0-0	2-1	0-2	1-1	0-0
Dumbarton	0-1	6-0	—	2-1	1-3	1-1	2-2	1-1	0-0	2-5
Forfar Ath	0-1	4-5	2-0	—	2-4	1-1	1-2	1-2	1-2	3-0
Gretna	3-1	1-2	2-0	0-0	—	0-2	1-2	1-0	0-1	2-0
Morton	4-0	1-0	2-3	5-1	3-1	—	2-3	2-3	5-2	3-2
Partick T	2-1	2-2	1-0	1-0	3-3	3-1	—	3-1	0-2	3-0
Peterhead	5-2	3-0	1-0	4-2	0-2	1-2	1-1	—	5-1	1-2
Raith R	4-1	2-1	3-1	1-1	0-2	1-1	1-2	3-0	—	1-0
Stirling A	4-3	1-0	3-2	0-2	0-5	1-1	1-2	3-1	2-2	—

BELL'S SCOTTISH LEAGUE—DIVISION THREE RESULTS 2005–2006

	Albion R	Arbroath	Berwick R	Cowdenbeath	East Fife	East Stirlingshire	Elgin C	Montrose	Queen's Park	Stenhousemuir
Albion R	—	2-2	0-2	0-3	2-4	4-2	0-2	1-1	1-1	0-2
Arbroath	1-2	—	0-1	1-3	3-1	2-0	1-2	1-1	1-0	1-2
Berwick R	1-0	0-2	—	0-3	1-0	7-2	2-0	2-1	1-1	1-1
Cowdenbeath	0-1	3-0	4-0	—	3-0	2-1	0-1	3-0	1-0	3-2
East Fife	2-1	2-1	0-2	1-0	—	3-2	3-1	1-1	1-0	0-2
East Stirlingshire	2-1	3-2	0-1	1-0	1-1	—	5-2	1-1	0-2	3-0
Elgin C	1-1	4-2	1-1	1-0	1-1	5-1	—	2-0	6-0	4-1
Montrose	1-0	1-1	0-4	2-1	4-1	5-0	2-1	—	1-0	1-1
Queen's Park	3-1	0-3	1-0	0-1	1-2	3-1	1-2	3-2	—	2-3
Stenhousemuir	2-0	3-1	1-2	1-1	2-1	1-2	0-2	4-0	0-4	—

ABERDEEN   PREMIER LEAGUE

Ground: Pittodrie Stadium, Aberdeen AB24 5QH (01224) 650400
Ground capacity: 21,421 (all seated). **Colours:** All red.
Manager: Jimmy Calderwood.
League Appearances: Anderson R 36; Byrne R 18(1); Clark C 30(1); Considine A
8(4); Craig S (2); Crawford S 27(3); Dempsey G 17(7); Diamond A 31(2); Donald
D (1); Esson R 18; Foster R 8(17); Griffin D 9(1); Hart M 4; Langfield J 20; Lovell
S 22(5); MacAulay K 3(2); Macfarlane N 2(4); Mackie D 11(17); Maguire C (2);
McNaughton K 34; Muirhead S 10(8); Nicholson B 32(1); Severin S 28; Smith J 35;
Snoyl F 9(3); Stewart J 2(15); Winter J 4(3).
Goals – League (46): Lovell 8, Smith 8, Anderson 6, Crawford 5, Mackie 4 (1 pen),
Clark 3, Severin 3, Stewart 3, Nicholson 2, Foster 1, Snoyl 1, Winter 1, own goal 1.
Scottish Cup (3): Crawford 2, Nicholson 1.
CIS Cup (5): Lovell 1, Nicholson 1, Smith 1, Winter 1, own goal 1.
Honours – Division 1: Champions – 1954-55, **Premier Division:** Champions – 1979-
80, 1983-84, 1984-85. **Scottish Cup winners** 1947, 1970, 1982, 1983, 1984, 1986, 1990.
League Cup winners 1956, 1977, 1986, 1990, 1996. **European Cup-Winners' Cup
winners** 1983.

AIRDRIE UNITED   DIV. 1

Ground: Shyberry Excelsior Stadium, Airdrie ML6 8QZ (01236) 622000
Ground capacity: 10,000 (all seated). **Colours:** White shirts with red diamond,
white shorts.
Manager: Sandy Stewart.
League Appearances: Barkey K 17(6); Coyle F 10(10); Docherty S 18(7); Dunn D
16(11); Hardie M 14(7); Hollis L 10; Holmes G 8(8); Lovering P 26(2); Marshall C
1(2); McCluskey S (1); McDougall S 19(12); McGowan N 34(1); McKenna S 31(1);
McKeown S 30(1); McLaren W 30(3); McManus A 30; McPhee B 25(7); Prunty B
31(1); Roberts M 2; Robertson S 26; Taylor S 3(4); Twigg G 15(9).
Goals – League (57): Prunty 15, McLaren 10, McPhee 9, McKeown 7 (5 pens),
Twigg 7 (1 pen), Hardie 4, Barkey 1, Coyle 1, Lovering 1, McDougall 1, McGowan
1.
Scottish Cup (5): Doherty 2, Hardie 1, McKeown 1, McLaren 1.
CIS Cup (0).
Challenge Cup (1): McPhee 1.
Honours – Second Division: Champions – 2003–04; **Division II:** Champions – 1902-
03, 1954-55, 1973-74. **Scottish Cup winners** 1924. **B&Q Cup winners** 1995. **Bell's
League Challenge winners** 2000-01, 2001-02.

ALBION ROVERS   DIV. 3

Ground: Cliftonhill Stadium, Main Street, Coatbridge ML5 3RB (01236) 606334
Ground capacity: 1249 (seated: 489). **Colours:** Primrose yellow shirts, red shorts,
red stockings.
Manager: Jim Chapman.
League Appearances: Aboubeaker M (3); Black D 11; Bonnar M 25(1); Chaplain
S 28(1); Chisholm I 18(10); Creer A 4; Donachy S 25(2); Donnelly C 32; Doyle J
10(5); Ewings J 18(1); Franch T 1(4); Friel S 35; Hardie C ; Houston S 1(1);
Lennon G 36; Lennox T 16(2); Love R (1); Mathie G 1(3); McGhee G 30; McG-
lynn G 13; Noble S 16(4); O'Neil K 4; Oné A 2; Quinn M 1(1); Quitongo J 1;
Reid A 1; Reid D 14(18); Selkirk A 4(7); Sichi L 9(7); Sim A 5(8); Stewart P 1; Wallace
G 21(1); Wilson L 3(5); Young C 10(11).

Goals – League (39): Chaplain 8, Wallace G 5, Donachy 4, Reid D 4, Young 4, Chisholm 3, Bonnar 2, Donnelly 2 (pens), Sim 2, Friel 1 (pen), Houston 1, McGhee 1, Noble 1, own goal 1.
Scottish Cup (2): Chisholm 1, Roberts 1.
CIS Cup (1): Chisholm 1.
Challenge Cup (0).
Honours – Division II: Champions – 1933-34. **Second Division:** Champions 1988-89.

ALLOA ATHLETIC   DIV. 2

Ground: Recreation Park, Alloa FK10 1RY (01259) 722695
Ground capacity: 3100. **Colours:** Gold shirts with black trim, black shorts with gold stripe.
Manager: Tom Hendrie.
League Appearances: Bolochoweckyj M 27(1); Brown A 16(1); Brown G 14(14); Evans J 8(2); Ferguson P 1(1); Forrest F 12(2); Grant J 8(1); Greenhill D 13(5); Greer A 13; Hamilton R 27(5); Hamilton S 5; Learmonth S 11(9); McColligan B 16; McGeown D 7(5); McGlynn G 14; McLeod P 9(3); Mortimer P 9(2); Nicolson I 16(5); Ovenstone J 32(1); Quitongo J 12(6); Sloan R 24(11); Stevenson A 11(1); Stevenson J 35; Stuart M (1); Swaney S 1; Thomson D 2(4); Townsley C 33; Walker R 20.
Goals – League (36): Stevenson J 9 (2 pens), Brown G 6, Sloan 6 (2 pens), Brown A 5, Hamilton R 2, Ovenstone 2, Bolochoweckyj 1, Forrest 1, Greenhill 1, McLeod 1, Thomson 1, own goal 1.
Scottish Cup (13): Hamilton R 3, Nicolson 3, Sloan 3, Bolochoweckyj 1, Brown A 1, Quitongo 1, Stevenson J 1.
CIS Cup (3): Stevenson J 2, Brown A 1.
Challenge Cup (0).
Honours – Division II: Champions – 1921-22. **Third Division:** Champions – 1997-98. **Bell's League Challenge winners** 1999-2000.

ARBROATH   DIV. 3

Ground: Gayfield Park, Arbroath DD11 1QB (01241) 872157
Ground capacity: 4020. **Colours:** Maroon shirts with white trim, white shorts.
Manager: John McGlashan.
League Appearances: Bishop J 17(7); Black R 24(7); Brazil A 17; Cairns M 3; Clarke P 13; Collier J 1; Cook S 14(4); Cormack P 3; Davidson H 12(2); Dobbins I 31; Henderson R (3); Inglis N 8; Jackson C 12(6); King M 2(2); McCulloch M 30(2); McGlashan J 1; McMullan K 31; Miller G 21(5); Peat M 25(1); Raeside R 17; Reilly A 10(12); Rennie S 20(2); Smith J (1); Smith N 6(6); Stein J 34; Swankie G 18; Taylor S 4(5); Voigt J 3(8); Warren G (4); Watson P 19(6).
Goals – League (57): Stein 9, Brazil 7 (2 pens), Swankie 7, Clarke 5, Raeside 4, Cook 3, McMullan 3, Bishop 2, Black 2, Dobbins 2, McCulloch 2, Rennie 2, Taylor 2, Watson 2, Davidson 1, Miller 1, Reilly 1, Smith N 1, Voigt 1.
Scottish Cup (1): Brazil 1.
CIS Cup (1): Brazil 1.
Challenge Cup (1): Brazil 1.
Honours – Nil.

AYR UNITED   DIV. 2

Ground: Somerset Park, Ayr KA8 9NB (01292) 263435
Ground capacity: 10,243 (1549 seated). **Colours:** White shirts with black trim, black shorts.
Manager: Robert Connor.

League Appearances: Anis J 4(1); Bailey J 2; Boyd S 3(2); Campbell M 16(3); Casey M 16(7); Cashmore I 3(13); Conway C 26(5); Essler A 3(3); Hyslop P 13(6); Joyce G 1(2); Logan R 33; Lowing D 11(1); Maisano J 1(2); McAnespie K 15; McGeown M 36; McKinstry J 27; McLaughlin B 21; Pettigrew C 1; Ramsay D 26(3); Reid A 15(14); Robertson C 34(2); Stirling J 1; Strain C 18(8); Tait T 3; Templeton P 1; Vareille J 27(1); Wardlaw G 19(14); Weaver P 21(5).
Goals – League (56): Vareille 14, Wardlaw 11, Robertson 8, Logan 6, Conway 4, Hyslop 2, McAnespie 2, Ramsay 2, Strain 2, Weaver 2, Boyd 1, Maisano 1, own goal 1.
Scottish Cup (4): Robertson 2, Wardlaw 2.
CIS Cup (5): Strain 2, Boyd 1, Vareille 1, Wardlaw 1.
Challenge Cup (0).
Honours – Division II: Champions – 1911-12, 1912-13, 1927-28, 1936-37, 1958-59, 1965-66. **Second Division:** Champions – 1987-88, 1996-97.

BERWICK RANGERS   DIV. 3

Ground: Shielfield Park, Berwick-on-Tweed TD15 2EF (01289) 307424
Ground capacity: 4131. **Colours:** Black with broad gold stripe, black shorts with white trim.
Manager: John Couglin.
League Appearances: Arthur R 12(2); Connelly G 12(2); Cowan M 30; Coyle C 13; Da Silva B 1(8); Gibson J (1); Gordon K 11(7); Greenhill G 14(11); Haynes K 30(3); Horn R 10(4); Hutchison G 35; Johnstone S ; Kane S ; Little I 31; Lucas S (1); Manson S 1(10); McGarty M 7(8); McGroarty C 33; McLeish K 34(2); McNicoll G 31; Murie D 36; O'Connor G 23; Paliczka S 9(5); Ramsay M (11); Shields J 12; Swanson D 11(16).
Goals – League (54): Haynes 15 (1 pen), Hutchison 9, McLeish 8 (4 pens), Little 6, McGroarty 4, Gordon 3, McNicoll 2, Arthur 1, Connelly 1, Cowan 1, Horn 1, Manson 1, Paliczka 1, Swanson 1.
Scottish Cup (0).
CIS Cup (4): Hutchison 2, McLeish 1, McNicoll 1.
Challenge Cup (3): Connelly 1, Hutchison 1, McLeish 1.
Honours – Second Division: Champions – 1978-79.

BRECHIN CITY   DIV. 2

Ground: Glebe Park, Brechin DD9 6BJ (01356) 622856
Ground capacity: 3980. **Colours:** Red with white trim.
Manager: Michael O'Neill.
League Appearances: Bollan G 17(1); Britton G 19(4); Burns A 14(6); Byers K 23(4); Callaghan S 19(10); Deas P 15(1); Devlin S 1(3); Ferguson S 6; Geddes C 3(5); Gibson G 5(3); Grainger D 10; Hamilton S 6(1); Hampshire S 28(3); Hannah D 7; Hillcoat J 3(1); Johnson G 19(4); King C 16(15); McEwan C 16(2); Mitchell A 26; Nelson C 33; Nicol K 1; Ritchie P 9(9); Smith D 18(14); Strachan R (1); Templeman C 3(7); Walker S 35; White D 27(4); Wilson S 3(1); Winter C 14(4).
Goals – League (28): Byers 6, Hampshire 4, Britton 3, Callaghan 3, Johnson 3, Devlin 2, Burns 1, Geddes 1, Hannah 1 (pen), Ritchie 1, Smith 1, Walker 1, White 1.
Scottish Cup (1): King 1.
CIS Cup (0).
Challenge Cup (3): Gibson 1, Hampshire 1, Ritchie 1.
Honours – Second Division: Champions – 1982-83, 1989-90, 2004-05. **Third Division:** Champions – 2001-02. **C Division:** Champions – 1953-54.

CELTIC   PREMIER LEAGUE

Ground: Celtic Park, Glasgow G40 3RE (0141) 556 2611
Ground capacity: 60,355 (all seated). **Colours:** Green and white hooped shirts, white shorts.
Manager: Gordon Strachan.
League Appearances: Agathe D (4); Balde D 28; Beattie C 7(6); Boruc A 34; Camara M 18; Dublin D 3(8); Hartson J 29(6); Keane R 10; Lawson P 1(2); Lennon N 32; Maloney S 27(9); Marshall D 4; McGeady A 11(9); McGlinchey M (1); McManus S 36; Nakamura S 30(3); Pearson S 2(16); Petrov S 36(1); Sutton C 7(1); Telfer P 36; Thompson A 11(6); Varga S 9(1); Virgo A 3(7); Wallace R 8(3); Wilson M 14(1); Zurawski M 22(2).
Goals – League (93): Hartson 18, Zurawski 14, Maloney 13 (2 pens), Petrov 10, McManus 7, Beattie 6, Nakamura 6, McGeady 4, Balde 2, Pearson 2, Sutton 2, Thompson 2, Dublin 1, Keane 1, Lennon 1, Telfer 1, Varga 1.
Scottish Cup (1): Zurawski 1.
CIS Cup (9): Maloney 3, Zurawski 3, Balde 1, Dublin 1, Hartson 1.
Honours – Division I: Champions – 1892-93, 1893-94, 1895-96, 1897-98, 1904-05, 1905-06, 1906-07, 1907-08, 1908-09, 1909-10, 1913-14, 1914-15, 1915-16, 1916-17, 1918-19, 1921-22, 1925-26, 1935-36, 1937-38, 1953-54, 1965-66, 1966-67, 1967-68, 1968-69, 1969-70, 1970-71, 1971-72, 1972-73, 1973-74. **Premier Division:** Champions – 1976-77, 1978-79, 1980-81, 1981-82, 1985-86, 1987-88, 1997-98. **Premier League:** 2000-01, 2001-02, 2003-04, 2005–06. **Scottish Cup winners** 1892, 1899, 1900, 1904, 1907, 1908, 1911, 1912, 1914, 1923, 1925, 1927, 1931, 1933, 1937, 1951, 1954, 1965, 1967, 1969, 1971, 1972, 1974, 1975, 1977, 1980, 1985, 1988, 1989, 1995, 2001, 2004, 2005. **League Cup winners** 1957, 1958, 1966, 1967, 1968, 1969, 1970, 1975, 1983, 1998, 2000, 2001, 2004, 2006. **European Cup winners** 1967.

CLYDE   DIV. 1

Ground: Broadwood Stadium, Cumbernauld G68 9NE (01236) 451511
Ground capacity: 8200. **Colours:** White shirts with red and black trim, black shorts.
Manager: Graham Roberts.
League Appearances: Arbuckle G 2(17); Bouadji R 9(4); Bradley K 1(7); Brawley W (3); Brighton T 34(2); Bryson C 30(3); Cherrie P 18(2); Dick A 2(6); Harris R 15(5); Higgins C 34; Hunter R 3(11); Imrie D 8(3); Jarvie P 18; Malone E 31; Masterton S 18(4); McDonald K 4(7); McGowan M 34(1); McGregor N 22; McHale P 16(1); McKenna S (1); McKeown C 34; Miller J 2(13); O'Donnell S 32(1); Williams A 29(3).
Goals – League (54): Williams 13, O'Donnell 11 (2 pens), Brighton 8, Hunter 4, McHale 3 (1 pen), Bouadji 2, Bryson 2, Imrie 2, McGowan M 2, Miller 2, McGregor N 1, McKeown 1, Malone 1, Masterton 1, own goal 1.
Scottish Cup (2): Bryson 1, Malone 1.
CIS Cup (6): Brighton 2, Arbuckle 1, Bryson 1, McGregor N 1, O'Donnell 1.
Challenge Cup (2): McGregor N 1, Williams 1.
Honours – Division II: Champions – 1904-05, 1951-52, 1956-57, 1961-62, 1972-73. **Second Division:** Champions – 1977-78, 1981-82, 1992-93, 1999-2000. **Scottish Cup winners** 1939, 1955, 1958.

COWDENBEATH   DIV. 2

Ground: Central Park, Cowdenbeath KY4 9EY (01383) 610166
Ground capacity: 5268. **Colours:** Royal blue with white cuffs and collar, white shorts.
Manager: Mixu Paatelainen.

League Appearances: Allison J (2); Baird S 1; Baxter M 25(2); Boyd S 1(1); Buchanan L 27(4); Carlin A 1; Downs R 7(2); Fusco G 22(8); Grant M 1; Gribben D 2(1); Guy G 24(3); Hay D 35; Hill D 15(10); Hughes C (1); Jackson A 13; Krobot L (9); Mauchlen I 13(5); McBride K 33; McBride P (6); McCallum R 13(3); McGregor D 7(8); McKenna D 17; Millar M 22(3); Oné A 10(1); Paatelainen Markus 24(1); Paatelainen Mikko 9; Ritchie I 24; Scullion P 7(4); Thomson D 6(4); Ward J 35; Wilson D 2(3).

Goals – League (81): Buchanan 17, McKenna 11 (1 pen), Oné 8, Mikko Paatelainen 7, McCallum 6, Markus Paatelainen 6, Ritchie 6, Ward 5, Jackson 4, Downs 3, Guy 3, Mauchlen 3 (1 pen), Hill 1, McBride P 1.

Scottish Cup (0).

CIS Cup (2): Gribben 1, Ward 1.

Challenge Cup (0).

Honours – Division II: Champions – 1913-14, 1914-15, 1938-39. **Third Division:** Champions – 2005-06.

DUMBARTON   DIV. 3

Ground: Strathclyde Homes Stadium, Dumbarton G82 1JJ (01389) 762569/767864.
Ground capacity: 2050. **Colours:** Gold shirts with black sleeves and black side panels, black shorts with three black side panels, black stockings.
Manager: Gerry McCabe.
League Appearances: Allan J 3(1); Bannerman S 16(7); Borris R 30; Boyle C 26; Brittain C 7(3); Connell G 16(11); Dempsie M 25; Dillon J 11(12); Ferguson S 11; Ferry D 10(7); Gaughan K 25(1); Gemmell J 14(12); Gentile C 19(3); Grindlay S 36; McDevitt G (1); McDonald K 7(5); McNaught D (3); McQuilken P 24(10); Rodgers A 27(6); Ronald P 2(3); Russell I 20(10); Smith J 33; Walker R 22; Winter C 12.
Goals – League (40): Rodgers 12 (3 pens), Russell 8 (2 pens), Gemmell 5, McQuilken 3, Boyle 2, Dillon 2, Smith 2, Borris 1, Connell 1, Gaughan 1, Gentile 1, Walker 1, own goal 1.
Scottish Cup (4): Rodgers 2, McQuilken 1, Russell 1.
CIS Cup (1): Rodgers 1.
Challenge Cup (1): Rodgers 1.
Honours – Division I: Champions – 1890-91 (Shared), 1891-92. **Division II:** Champions – 1910-11, 1971-72. **Second Division:** Champions – 1991-92. **Scottish Cup winners** 1883.

DUNDEE   DIV. 1

Ground: Dens Park, Dundee DD3 7JY (01382) 889966
Ground capacity: 11,760 (all seated). **Colours:** Navy shirts with white and red shoulder and sleeve flashes, white shorts with navy and red piping, navy stockings with two white hoops.
Manager: Alex Rae.
League Appearances: Allison M 1; Anderson I 12(1); Black D 1; Brady G 22(7); Britton G 1(1); Craig S 17(3); Deasley B 7(6); Dixon P 25(4); Ela Eyene J (2); Ferguson A 2(13); Fyfe G 1; Gates S 3(4); Hendry R 1; Hutchinson T 6(1); Jack K 14; Keane K 1; Kitamarike J (1); Law G 1(2); Lynch S 28(5); Macdonald C 25(2); Madaschi A 9; Mann R 35; Marshall C 9(4); McCluskey S 12(2); McDonald K 24(2); McManus T 18(5); McNally S 5; Murray S 16(2); O'Reilly C 4(11); Robb S 23(2); Robertson S 31(4); Smith B 36; Soutar D 6; Swankie G (2); Wilkie L 1(1).
Goals – League (43): Lynch 12 (3 pens), Craig 6, McManus 6, Mann 4, McDonald K 3, O'Reilly 3, Dixon 2, Ferguson 2, Anderson 1, Deasley 1, Marshall 1, Robertson 1, Wilkie 1`.
Scottish Cup (8): Lynch 3, Deasley 2, Craig 1, Mann 1, O'Reilly 1.

CIS Cup (1): Lynch 1.
Challenge Cup (3):Anderson 1, Lynch 1, Robertson 1.
Honours – Division I: Champions – 1961-62. **First Division:** Champions – 1978-79, 1991-92, 1997-98. **Division II:** Champions – 1946-47. **Scottish Cup winners** 1910. **League Cup winners** 1952, 1953, 1974. **B&Q (Centenary) Cup winners** 1991.

DUNDEE UNITED   PREMIER LEAGUE

Ground: Tannadice Park, Dundee DD3 7JW (01382) 833166
Ground capacity: 14,223. **Colours:** Tangerine shirts, tangerine shorts.
Manager: Craig Brewster.
League Appearances: Abbott S 2(1); Archibald A 33; Brebner G 26; Brewster C (1); Cameron G 2(2); Canero P 9(2); Crawford S 4; Duff S 24(5); Easton W (1); Fernandez D 29(1); Gardiner R 4; Goodwillie D (10); Kenneth G 12(4); Kerr M 35; Mair L 5(1); McCracken D 34; McInnes D 9(3); McIntyre J 18(7); Miller L 22(12); Mulgrew C 13; Ritchie P 20(1); Robertson D 6(5); Robson B 30(1); Samson C 8; Samuel C 23(12); Stillie D 30; Wilson M 20(1).
Goals – League (41): Miller 8, Samuel 7, Fernandez 5, Brebner 4, Canero 2, McCracken 2, McInnes 2, Mulgrew 2, Robson 2, Archibald 1, Goodwillie 1, Kenneth 1, Kerr 1, McIntyre 1, Robertson 1, own goal 1.
Scottish Cup (2): Fernandez 2.
CIS Cup (0).
Honours – Premier Division: Champions – 1982-83. **Division II:** Champions – 1924-25, 1928-29. **Scottish Cup winners** 1994. **League Cup winners** 1980, 1981.

DUNFERMLINE ATHLETIC   PREMIER LEAGUE

Ground: East End Park, Dunfermline KY12 7RB (01383) 724295
Ground capacity: 12,500. **Colours:** Black and white striped shirts, white shorts.
Director of Football: Jim Leishman.
League Appearances: Burchill M 24(7); Campbell A 1(4); Campbell I 14(3); Daquin F 2(7); Donnelly S 8(5); Dunn J ; Gunnlaursen G (1); Halliwell B 12; Horsted L 6(5); Hunt N 22(10); Labonte A 19(3); Makel L 20; Mason G 29; McCunnie J 18(4); McGregor A 26; Morrison S 3; Muirhead S 11(1); Phinn N 1(2); Ross G 21(2); Shields G 33; Simmons S 3(3); Skerla A 1(1); Tarachulski B 12(15); Thomson S 23(2); Tod A 26(4); Wilson C 5(9); Wilson S 31; Young Darren 20(1); Young Derek 13(5); Zambernardi Y 14(2).
Goals – League (33): Burchill 12 (2 pens), Hunt 4, Makel 2, Mason 2, Ross 2, Tod 2, Darren Young 2, Campbell I 1, Daquin 1, Donnelly 1, Shields 1, Wilson S 1, Derek Young 1, own goal 1.
Scottish Cup (3): Hunt 1, Mason 1, Derek Young 1.
CIS Cup (9): Burchill 3, Derek Young 3, McCunnie 1, Mason 1, Darren Young 1.
Honours – First Division: Champions – 1988-89, 1995-96. **Division II:** Champions – 1925-26. **Second Division:** Champions – 1985-86. **Scottish Cup winners** 1961, 1968.

EAST FIFE   DIV. 3

Ground: Bayview Park, Methil, Fife KY8 3RW (01333) 426323
Ground capacity: 2000 (all seated). **Colours:** Gold and black shirts, white shorts.
Manager: David Baikie.
League Appearances: Bain K 19(5); Beith G 20(3); Bradford J 22(9); Brash K 3; Campbell A 17; Condie C 1(2); Crawford R (1); Dodds J 30; Dodds K 4(1); Donaldson E 3(7); Doyle P 11; Fortune S 24(7); Gordon K 14; Graham R 1(3); Hampshire P 31(2); Johnston C (1); Kelly G 27(3); Lumsden C 25(4); Martin J 17(7); Mathie G 1; McDonald C 29; Mitchell J 3(4); Morrison S 6; Noble S 9(2); Paliczka S 8(12); Pelosi M 21(1); Port G 2(2); Samson C (1); Savage J 10(3); Smart C 26(2); Smith E 12; Taylor S (1).

Goals – League (48): Bradford 7, McDonald 7, Smart 7, Hampshire 5, Gordon 3, Kelly 3 (1 pen), Martin 3, Paliczka 3, Noble 2, Beith 1, Dodds K 1, Fortune 1, Lumsden 1, Mitchell 1, Pelosi 1 (pen), Savage 1, own goal 1.
Scottish Cup (0).
CIS Cup (0).
Challenge Cup (0).
Honours – Division II: Champions – 1947-48. Scottish Cup winners 1938. League Cup winners 1948, 1950, 1954.

EAST STIRLINGSHIRE DIV. 3

Ground: Firs Park, Falkirk FK2 7AY (01324) 623583
Ground capacity: 1880. Colours: Black shirts with white hoops, black shorts with white and red stripes.
Head Coach: Dennis Newall.
League Appearances: Blair S 13(7); Brand A 16(4); Carr M 1; Diack I 14; Dymock S 21(11); Gaughan P 17(4); Gillespie A 1(1); Gordon B 3; Graham A 14; Jackson D 33; Lejman K 1(3); Livingstone S 22(5); McKay J 8(3); McKenzie M 11; McWilliam G 5(1); Molloy M 11(1); Oates S 21(8); Owen A 12(1); Patrick A 9(4); Ross P 1; Smith J 23(2); Sobolewski M 7(6); Thomson A 1; Thywissen C 27(3); Tweedie P 8(1); Tyrrell M 27(2); Tyrrell P 24(1); Ure D 31(3); Walker J 5; Walsh G 9; Wilson E 1.
Goals – League (28): Diack 8 (1 pen), Dymock 6, Ure 4, Brand 2 (1 pen), , Thywissen 2, Graham 1, Livingstone 1, Patrick 1, Smith 1, Tweedie 1, Tyrrell P 1.
Scottish Cup (2): Dymock 1, Owen 1.
CIS Cup (1) Diack 1.
Challenge Cup (0).
Honours – Division II: Champions – 1931-32. C Division: Champions – 1947-48.

ELGIN CITY DIV. 3

Ground: Borough Briggs, Elgin IV30 1AP (01343) 551114
Ground capacity: 5000 (478 seated). Colours: Black and white vertical striped shirts, black shorts.
Manager: Brian Irvine.
League Appearances: Booth M 23(2); Bremner F 12(22); Cumming S 35; Dempsie A 27; Dickson H 27; Easton S 22(4); Gardiner C 23(8); Hind D 25(2); Jack M 1(4); Johnston M 31(1); Kaczan P 31(1); Lauchlan M 5(4); McIntosh S 2); McKenzie J 25(5); Melrose G (5); Muir A 15(6); Napier P 6(3); Nelson A 21; Ralph J 1(1); Reid P 2(2); Renton K 36; Scullion P 13; Shewan G 1(4); Stirling J 1; Tweedie G 2(4); Vigurs I 6(2); Wood G 5(7).
Goals – League (55): Johnston 20 (1 pen), Booth 9 (3 pens), Kaczan 5, Nelson 4, Gardiner 3, Dickson 2, McKenzie 2, Muir 2, Scullion 2, Bremner 1, Cumming 1, Napier 1, Tweedie 1, Vigurs I 1, Wood 1.
Scottish Cup (1): Gardiner 1.
CIS Cup (2): Dickson 1, Muir 1.
Challenge Cup (1) Booth 1.
Honours – Nil.

FALKIRK PREMIER LEAGUE

Ground: Brockville Park, Falkirk FK1 5AX (01324) 624121
Ground capacity: 6123. Colours: Navy blue shirts with white seams, navy shorts.
Head Coach: John Hughes.
League Appearances: Barr D (1); Churchill G (1); Craig L 10(6); Cregg P 14(2); Dodd K 8(1); Duffy D 19(2); Ferguson A 9; Glennon M 21; Gow A 30(4); Howard M 8; Hughes J 1; Ireland C 23; Latapy R 24(6); Lawrie A 27(2); Lecsinel J 8;

Lima V 21(7); MacSween I (1); McBreen D 21(12); McPherson C 12(6); McStay R 1(4); Milne K 32(1); Moutinho P 8(20); O'Donnell S 21(6); O'Neil J 3(4); Rodrigues T 31(1); Ross J 16(1); Scally N 13(5); Scobbie T 2(1); Thomson A (4); Thomson S 30(2); Twaddle M 5(1).
Goals – League (35): Duffy 9 (1 pen), Gow 6, McBreen 6, Latapy 2, Milne 2, Moutinho 2, Ross 2, Cregg 1, Ireland 1, O'Donnell 1, Thomson S 1, own goals 2.
Scottish Cup (5): Gow 3, McBreen 2.
CIS Cup (3): O'Donnell 2, Gow 1.
Honours – Division II: Champions – 1935-36, 1969-70, 1974-75. **First Division:** Champions – 1990-91, 1993-94, 2002-03, 2004-05. **Second Division:** Champions – 1979-80. **Scottish Cup winners** 1913, 1957. **League Challenge Cup winners** 1998, 2005.

FORFAR ATHLETIC   DIV. 2

Ground: Station Park, Forfar, Angus (01307) 463576
Ground capacity: 4640. **Colours:** Sky blue shirts with navy side panels and shoulder/sleeve bands, navy shorts with sky blue trims, sky blue stockings with navy band on top.
Manager: George Shaw.
League Appearances: Barr D 14(1); Bonar S 15(3); Brown M 2; Cameron M 19(4); Connelly C 4(6); Conway A 3(7); Cumming K (4); Donald B 22(3); Dubourdeau F 18; Dunn D 19(4); Ferrie N 1(1); Florence S 2(1); Forrest E 26(2); Gethins C 1; Gribben D 24(5); Jackson A 13; Keogh D 13(1); King D 21(1); Lombardi M 10(3); Lowing D 16(1); Lunan P 30; McClune D 24(6); Meldrum C 1; Montgomery R 10(1); Murdoch S 13; Peat M 1; Rattray A 26(1); Sellars B 31(1); Tosh P (8); Voigt J 1(12); Waddell R 16(2).
Goals – League (44): Gribben 10, Lunan 7, Jackson 5, Cameron 4, Sellars 4, Forrest 3, Bonar 2, Lombardi 2, Waddell 2, Connelly 1, Dunn 1, McClune 1, Voigt 1, own goal 1.
Scottish Cup (4): Gribben 2, Bonar 1, Cameron 1.
CIS Cup (1): Conway 1.
Challenge Cup (0).
Honours – Second Division: Champions – 1983-84. **Third Division:** Champions – 1994-95.

GRETNA   DIV. 1

Ground: Raydale Park, Gretna DG16 5AP (01461) 337602
Ground capacity: 2200. **Colours:** Black shirt with white hoops, black shorts with white trim.
Manager: Rowan Alexander.
League Appearances: Aitken A 5(2); Baldacchino R 19(2); Berkeley M 1(2); Bingham D 17(1); Birch M 25(2); Boyd M (1); Canning M 2(4); Collins D 7(3); Deuchar K 33(1); Grady J 29(3); Graham D 5(11); Innes C 29(2); Jenkins A 9(3); Main A 31; Mathieson D 5; McGuffie R 33(1); McQuilken J 10(15); Nicholls D 24(4); O'Neil J 11(4); Paterson S 3(1); Shields D 1(8); Skelton G 32(4); Tosh S 32(1); Townsley D 33.
Goals – League (97): Deuchar 18, Grady 16 (1 pen), McGuffie 13 (3 pens), Tosh 11, Innes 8, Skelton 6, Townsley 5, Bingham 3, Graham 3 (1 pen), Shields 3, McQuilken 2, O'Neil 2, Baldacchino 1, Berkeley 1, Birch 1, Jenkins 1, Nicholls 1, own goals 2.
Scottish Cup (21): Grady 8, Deuchar 5, McGuffie 2 (1 pen), Townsley 2, Bingham 1, Nicholls 1, Tosh 1, own goal 1.
CIS Cup (2): Deuchar 1, Grady 1.
Challenge Cup (2): Deuchar 1, Nicholls 1.
Honours – Second Division: Champions 2005–06. **Third Division:** Champions – 2004–05.

HAMILTON ACADEMICAL   DIV. 1

Ground: New Douglas Park, Cadzow Avenue, Hamilton ML3 0FT (01698) 368650
Ground capacity: 5396. **Colours:** Red and white hooped shirts, white shorts.
Manager: Billy Reid.
League Appearances: Agnew C 4(1); Anderson D 1(1); Anson S (1); Balmer S 15;
Bennett T 1; Carrigan B 20(5); Coult L (1); Elebert D 11(1); Ferguson B 24(5);
Fleming D 21(1); Galloway C 4(1); Gilhaney M 14(12); Hardy L 2(1); Hodge A
9(5); Jellema R 4; Jones G 8(5); Juanjo J 10(1); Keogh P 8(12); Mackenzie S 20;
McAlpine M (1); McArthur J 12(8); McCabe R (2); McEwan D 32; McJimpsey M
1(1); McLaughlin M 21(1); McLeod P 6(4); McMullan P 12(2); Neil A 32(1);
Robertson J 24(1); Sim A (1); Thomson S 29(3); Torres R 5(7); Tunbridge S 18(6);
Wake B 7(3); Wilson M 21.
Goals – League (53): Ferguson 7, Carrigan 6 (2 pens). Keogh 5, Wake 5, Gilhaney
4, Jones 3, McLeod 3, Tunbridge 3, Fleming 2 (1 pen), McLaughlin 2, Neil 2,
Robertson 2, Balmer 1, Elebert 1, Hardy 1, Juanjo 1, McArthur 1, Mackenzie 1,
McMullan 1, Thomson 1, Torres 1.
Scottish Cup (7): McLaughlin 2, Ferguson 1, McDonald 1, McManus 1, Neil 1, Torres 1.
CIS Cup (3): Tunbridge 2, Jones 1.
Challenge Cup (9): Ferguson 2, Keogh 2, Corrigan 1, Hardy 1, Neil 1, Thomson 1,
Tunbridge 1.
Honours – First Division: Champions – 1985-86, 1987-88. **Divison II:** Champions –
1903-04. **Division III:** Champions – 2000-01. **B&Q Cup winners** 1992, 1993.

HEART OF MIDLOTHIAN   PREMIER LEAGUE

Ground: Tynecastle Park, Gorgie Road, Edinburgh EH11 2NL (0131) 200 7200
Ground capacity: 17,402. **Colours:** Maroon shirts, white shorts.
Manager: Valdes Icanauskas.
League Appearances: Aguiar B 10; Banks S 2(1); Barasa N 1(3); Bednar R 19(3);
Berra C 10(2); Beslija M 2(1); Brellier J 28(2); Camazzola S 5(3); Cesnauskis D
15(10); Elliot C 17(11); Fyssas P 32; Gonçalves J 3(2); Gordon C 36; Hackett M
1(1); Hartley P 34; Hjalmar 1; Jankauskas E 24(1); Johnson L 1(3); MacFarlane
N 1(2); Makela J (2); McAllister J 8(9); McCann N 1; Mikoliunas S 16(7); Neilson
R 36(1); Petras M 4(1); Pospisil M 13(10); Pressley S 29; Simmons S 1(10); Skacel
R 33(2); Straceny L 1; Tall I 3(1); Wallace L 2(10); Webster A 30.
Goals – League (71): Skacel 16, Hartley 14 (2 pens), Jankauskas 8, Bednar 7,
Pospisil 7, Elliot 5, Pressley 5, Mikoliunas 3, Aguiar 1, Berra 1, Makela 1, Simmons
1, Webster 1, own goal 1.
Scottish Cup (12): Hartley 3 (1 pen), Jankauskas 2, Pressley 2, Cesnauskis 1, Elliot
1, McAllister 1, Pospisil 1, Skacel 1.
CIS Cup (2): Jankauskas 2.
Honours – Division I: Champions – 1894-95, 1896-97, 1957-58, 1959-60. **First Division:** Champions – 1979-80. **Scottish Cup winners** 1891, 1896, 1901, 1906, 1956,
1998, 2006. **League Cup winners** 1955, 1959, 1960, 1963.

HIBERNIAN   PREMIER LEAGUE

Ground: Easter Road Stadium, Edinburgh EH7 5QG (0131) 661 2159
Ground capacity: 17,400. **Colours:** Green shirts with white sleeves and collar, white
shorts with green stripe.
Manager: Tony Mowbray.
League Appearances: Benjelloun A 2(3); Beuzelin G 21; Brown Scott 16(3);
Brown Simon 7(1); Caldwell G 34; Campbell R (1); Dalglish P 4(7); Fletcher S
16(18); Glass S 23(5); Hogg C 21(2); Killen C 6(1); Kondé O 7(4); Konte A 1(12);

Lynch S (2); Malkowski Z 31(1); McCluskey J (3); McDonald K (2); Morrow S (8); Murphy D 30; Murray A 1; O'Connor G 24(2); Riordan D 32(4); Rudge H 4(2); Shields J 7; Shiels D 8(8); Smith G 19(1); Sproule I 18(14); Stewart M 24(1); Thomson K 28(3); Whittaker S 34.
Goals – League (61): Riordan 17 (1 pen), O'Connor 11 (1 pen), Fletcher 8, Beuzelin 5, Sproule 4, Killen 3, Shiels 2, Benjelloun 1, Scott Brown 1, Caldwell 1, Dalglish 1, Glass 1, Hogg 1, Murphy 1, Stewart 1, Whittaker 1, own goals 2.
Scottish Cup (14): O'Connor 3, Sproule 3, Scott Brown 2, Fletcher 2, Glass 1, Killen 1, Riordan 1, Stewart 1.
CIS Cup (2): Riordan 2.
Honours – Division I: Champions – 1902-03, 1947-48, 1950-51, 1951-52. **First Division:** Champions – 1980-81, 1998-99. **Division II:** Champions – 1893-94, 1894-95, 1932-33. **Scottish Cup winners** 1887, 1902. **League Cup winners** 1973, 1992.

INVERNESS CALEDONIAN THISTLE
PREMIER LEAGUE

Ground: Tulloch Caledonian Stadium, East Longman, Inverness IV1 1FF (01463) 715816
Ground capacity: 7400. **Colours:** Royal blue shirts with red and black stripes, royal blue shorts, royal blue stockings.
Manager: Charlie Christie.
League Appearances: Bayne G 8(9); Black I 24(2); Brewster C 16(1); Brown M 37; Dargo C 31(2); Dods D 37; Duncan R 28(2); Fox L 9(8); Fraser M 1; Golabek S 14(3); Hart R 11(20); Hastings R 26(1); Hislop S (3); Juanjo (2); Keogh L 5(3); McAllister R 2(12); McBain R 17(1); McCaffrey S 7(1); Morgan A 15(7); Munro S 32; Proctor D 12(5); Soane S (1); Sutherland A 1; Tokely R 34; Wilson B 33(1); Wyness D 18(9).
Goals – League (51): Dargo 17 (1 pen), Wyness 8, Brewster 6, Morgan 3, Proctor 3, Tokely 3, Wilson 3 (1 pen), Bayne 2, Dods 2, Black 1, Duncan 1, Fox 1, Hart 1.
Scottish Cup (6): Dargo 2 (1 pen), Wyness 2, McAllister 1, McBain 1.
CIS Cup (9): Wilson 2, Dargo 1, Duncan 1, Fox 1, Hart 1, McBain 1, Munro 1, Wyness 1.
Honours – First Division: Champions – 2003–04. **Third Division:** Champions – 1996-97. **Bell's League Challenge winners** 2004.

KILMARNOCK
PREMIER LEAGUE

Ground: Rugby Park, Kilmarnock KA1 2DP (01563) 525184
Ground capacity: 18,128. **Colours:** Blue and white striped shirts, blue shorts.
Manager: Jim Jefferies.
League Appearances: Boyd K 18(1); Campbell R (2); Combe A 32; Di Giacomo P 2(10); Dodds R 6(5); Ford S 32; Fowler J 38; Greer G 27; Hay G 35; Invincibile S 34(3); Johnston A 36(1); Leven P 4(2); Lilley D 8(3); Locke G 10(5); McDonald G 16(11); Murray S 1(14); Naismith S 32(4); Nish C 25(9); Smith G 6(1); Wales G 18(12); Wilson L 11(2); Wright F 27.
Goals – League (63): Boyd 15 (1 pen), Naismith 13 (2 pens), Wales 8, Invincibile 7, Nish 7, McDonald 3, Ford 2, Fowler 2, Greer 2, Johnston 2, Dodds 1, Lilley 1.
Scottish Cup (1): Nish 1.
CIS Cup (7): Boyd 2, DiGiacomo 1, Dodds 1, Invincibile 1, Wales 1, own goal1.
Honours – Division I: Champions – 1964-65. **Division II:** Champions – 1897-98, 1898-99. **Scottish Cup winners** 1920, 1929, 1997.

LIVINGSTON
DIV. 1

Ground: Almondvale Stadium, Alderton Road, Livingston EH54 7DN (01506) 417 000
Ground capacity: 10,024. **Colours:** Gold shirts, black shorts, white stockings.

Team Manager: John Robertson.
League Appearances: Adam S (2); Adams D 21(4); Barrett G 5; Barrett N 6(3); Boyd S 2(2); Brittain R 33(2); Dair J 21(1); Dalglish P 15(2); Dorado E 17(4); Dorrans G 4(4); Healy C 6(4); Hislop S 7(7); Houlahan W 14(2); Lambert P 8; Mackay D 38; McKenzie R 32; McLaughlin S 2(2); McNamee D 13(1); McPake J 5(10); Miller G 2(2); Morrow S 11; Pereira R 5(5); Pinxten H 26; Roy L 6; Scott M 8(11); Snodgrass R 12(15); Strong G 28(2); Tesovic D 2(2); Tierney P 25(6); Vincze G 11(6); Walker A 28(5); Weir S (1); Whelan N 5(2).
Goals – League (25): Brittain 4 (2 pens), Snodgrass 4, Dalglish 3, Pinxten 3, Healy 2, Morrow 2, Hislop 1, Mackay 1, Pereira 1, Strong 1, Vincze 1, Walker 1, Whelan 1.
Scottish Cup (2): Brittain 1, Dalglish 1.
CIS Cup (5): Dalglish 2, Dair 1, Mackay 1, Pereira 1.
Honours – First Division: Champions – 2000-01. **Second Division:** Champions – 1986-87, 1998-99. **Third Division:** Champions – 1995-96. **League Cup winners** 2004.

MONTROSE   DIV. 3

Ground: Links Park, Montrose DD10 8QD (01674) 673200
Ground capacity: 3292. **Colours:** Royal blue shirts and shorts.
Co-Managers: Ed Wolecki and David Robertson.
League Appearances: Brash K 8(3); Butter J 4(1); Cargill A 3(4); Corre G (4); Davidson H 15; Dodds K 12(7); Don K (3); Donachie B 23(3); Doyle P 16(6); Ferguson S 9(1); Fotheringham M 24(4); Fraser S 25(5); Hall E 22(2); Hanknson M 1; Hay G 14; Henslee R 33; Kelly D 8; Kerrigan S 19(3); Lombardi M (1); Martin W 6(4); McKenzie J 15(1); McLean D 3(2); McLeod I 6(3); McManus S 4(2); Middleton G 12(2); Rae C (1); Ralph J 1; Reid A 16; Reid P 1(4); Russell J 10(7); Smith E 20; Smith R 1; Stephen N 15; Watson C 16(10); Webster K 19(3); Wood A 15.
Goals – League (31): Henslee 10, Fotheringham 8 (1 pen), Kerrigan 2, Middleton 2, Russell 2, Webster 2, Davidson 1, Fraser 1, McLeod 1, Martin 1, Watson 1.
Scottish Cup (0).
CIS Cup (0).
Challenge Cup (1): Martin 1.
Honours – Second Division: Champions – 1984-85.

MORTON   DIV. 2

Ground: Cappielow Park, Greenock (01475) 723571
Ground capacity: 11,612. **Colours:** Royal blue and white hooped shirts, white shorts with royal blue panel down side.
Manager: Jim McInally.
League Appearances: Adam J 6(11); Black C 1; Finlayson K 30(5); Fulton M 1; Gilbride A 1; Gonet S 7; Graham B (1); Greacen S 26(1); Harding R 33(2); Keenan D 4(7); Lilley D 30(3); McAlister J 35; McGregor D 26(5); McGurn D 29; McLaren A 26(8); McLaughlin S 25(5); McLean K 1; McLeod D 1; McPake J 3(8); Millar C 35; Templeman C 9(10); Walker A 23(4); Walker J 9(26); Weatherson P 35.
Goals – League (58): Lilley 12, Weatherson 10, McLaren 7, Millar 5, Walker J 5, McAlister 4, Walker A 4, Greacen 2, McPake 2, Templeman 2, Finlayson 1, Harding 1, Macgregor 1, McLaughlin 1, own goal 1.
Scottish Cup (5): Lilley 2, Templeman 1,Walker J 1, Weatherson 1.
CIS Cup (1): Lilley 1.
Challenge Cup (7): Lilley 3, Walker J 2, McLaughlin 1, Templeman 1.
Honours – First Division: Champions – 1977-78, 1983-84, 1986-87. **Division II:** Champions – 1949-50, 1963-64, 1966-67. **Second Division:** Champions – 1994-95. **Third Division:** Champions 2002-03. **Scottish Cup winners** 1922.

MOTHERWELL   PREMIER LEAGUE

Ground: Fir Park, Motherwell ML1 2QN (01698) 333333
Ground capacity: 13,742. **Colours:** Amber shirts with claret hoop and trim, amber shorts, amber stockings with claret trim.
First Team Coach: Maurice Malpas.
League Appearances: Clarkson D 12(18); Coakley A (1); Corrigan M 27(2); Craigan S 36; Donnelly R 1(1); Fagan S 11(5); Fitzpatrick M 1(8); Foran R 29(3); Hamilton J 30(4); Hammell S 32(1); Keogh D (1); Kerr B 32(4); Kinniburgh W 17(4); Leitch S 1; Marshall G 1; McBride K 15(6); McCormack A 24; McDonald Scott 31(4); McDonald Steven (1); McGarry S 2(7); McLean B 27(2); Meldrum C 7(1); O'Donnell P 23(6); Paterson J 10(9); Quinn P 15(3); Reynolds M 1; Smith A 3(4); Smith D (1); Smith G 30; Thermeus A (1); Wright K (1).
Goals – League (55): Foran 11 (4 pens), McDonald Scott 11, Hamilton 10, Clarkson 4, Kerr 3, McLean 3, Craigan 2, Kinniburgh 2, McCormack 2, O'Donnell 2, Corrigan 1, Fagan 1, Fitzpatrick 1, McBride 1, Paterson 1.
Scottish Cup (0).
CIS Cup (6): Clarkson 1, Foran 1, Hamilton 1, Kerr 1, McDonald Scott 1 (pen), Smith D 1.
Honours – Division I: Champions – 1931-32. **First Division:** Champions – 1981-82, 1984-85. **Division II:** Champions – 1953-54, 1968-69. **Scottish Cup winners** 1952, 1991. **League Cup winners** 1951.

PARTICK THISTLE   DIV. 1

Ground: Firhill Stadium, Glasgow G20 7AL (0141) 579 1971
Ground capacity: 13,141. **Colours:** Red and yellow striped shirts, red shorts.
Manager: Dick Campbell.
League Appearances: Arthur K 24; Boyd S 7; Brady D 30(1); Craig D 14(4); Dodds W 2; Dorrans G 13(2); Fleming D 2; Gibson A 1(3); Gibson J 25(1); Gibson W 21(8); Gillies R 27(4); Hodge A 9(2); Kilgannon S 19(8); McConologue S 23(8); McCulloch S 27(2); McGoldrick J (2); Murray G 36; Nicholas S 6(16); Noble S ; Pronevych D 1(2); Quitongo J (2); Ritchie P 9(2); Roberts M 28(1); Santala J 14(2); Smyth M 26; Snowdon W 11(9); Stewart C 12; Strachan A 9(17).
Goals – League (57): Roberts 10 (2 pens), Santala 9, McConologue 8, McCulloch 8 (1 pen), Dorrans 5, Gibson W 5,.
Brady 2, Gibson J 2, Craig 1, Hodge 1, Kilgannon 1 (pen), Ritchie 1, Smyth 1, Snowdon 1, Strachan 1, own goal 1.
Scottish Cup (13): Roberts 7, Gillies 1, McConologue 1, McCulloch 1, Ritchie 1, Santala 1, Smyth 1.
CIS Cup (1): Gillies 1.
Challenge Cup (6): McConologue 2, Gibson a 1, Kilgannon 1, Roberts 1, Santala 1.
Honours – First Division: Champions – 1975-76, 2001-02. **Division II:** Champions – 1896-97, 1899-1900, 1970-71. **Second Division:** Champions 2000-01. **Scottish Cup winners** 1921. **League Cup winners** 1972.

PETERHEAD   DIV. 2

Ground: Balmoor Stadium, Peterhead AB42 1EU (01779) 478256
Ground capacity: 3250 (1000 seated). **Colours:** Royal blue with white shirts, royal blue shorts.
Manager: Iain Stewart.
League Appearances: Bavidge M 8(10); Buchan J 35(1); Cameron D 28(6); Duncan R (2); Gibson K 29(1); Good I 17(1); Hagen D 13(2); Hegarty C 17(2); Linn R 29(7); Mathers P 34; McCafferty J 2; Michie S 8(18); Nicol K 12; Perry M 36; Raeside R 6(1); Robertson C (2); Shand C 20(2); Sharp G 24(11); Stephen N 2(1); Stewart G 1; Tully C 28(3); Wood M 30(4); Youngson A 17(13).

Goals – League (53): Linn 11 (2 pens), Wood 6, Buchan 5, Gibson 5, Sharp 5, Bavidge 4, Cameron 4 (1 pen), Michie 4 (1 pen), Nicol 3, Shand 2, Good 1, Hegarty 1, Perry 1, Youngson 1.
Scottish Cup (3): Linn 1, Sharp 1, Wood 1.
CIS Cup (3): Linn 1, Michie 1 (pen), Youngson 1.
Challenge Cup (1): Bavidge 1.
Honours – Nil.

QUEEN OF THE SOUTH   DIV. 1

Ground: Palmerston Park, Dumfries DG2 9BA (01387) 254853
Ground capacity: 7412 (seated: 3509). **Colours:** Royal blue shirts with white sleeves, white shorts with blue piping.
Manager: Ian McCall.
League Appearances: Aitken A 12(1); Ardjogon T (1); Barnard R 16(1); Bowey S 24(5); Burns P 28(3); Carr C 6(5); Dillon S 4(3); English T 14(2); Gibson W 25(6); Hill S 7(1); Lovell S 26; Lyle D 18(10); McColligan B 10(1); McLaughlin B 9(4); McNiven D 8(8); McStay R 14; Mullen M 1(9); O'Connor S 2(2); O'Neill J 25(2); Paton E 32(3); Payne S 6(3); Pronevych D (2); Reid B 11(1); Robertson S 2(5); Scott C 20; Thomson A 8(5); Thomson J 33(1); Weir G 15; Wood G 20(7).
Goals – League (31): O'Neill 10 (5 pens), Burns 4, Thompson A 3, Lyle 2, Weir 2, Wood 2, Bowey 1, Lovell 1, McLaughlin 1, McNiven 1, Mullen 1, O'Connor 1, own goals 2.
Scottish Cup (1): Lyle 1.
CIS Cup (1): McNiven 1.
Challenge Cup (5): Burns 1, Lovell 1, Lyle 1, McLaughlin 1, McNiven 1.
Honours – Division II: Champions – 1950-51. **Second Division:** Champions – 2001-02. **Challenge Cup winners** 2003

QUEEN'S PARK   DIV. 3

Ground: Hampden Park, Glasgow G42 9BA (0141) 632 1275
Ground capacity: 52,000. **Colours:** Black and white hooped shirts, white shorts.
Coach: Billy Stark.
League Appearances: Agostini D 7(1); Bowers R 3(4); Cairney P 1(1); Cairns M 2(1); Canning S 3(3); Clark R 28(6); Crawford D 34; Dunlop M 28; Felvus B 11(13); Ferry M 35(1); Harvey P 18(6); Kettlewell S 29(2); McGinty A 8(1); Molloy S 10(7); Murray T 9(7); Paton P 22; Proctor K 7(5); Quinn A 26(4); Reilly S 31; Sinclair R 24; Trouten A 23(1); Weatherston D 29(4); Weir J 3(10); Whelan J 5(10).
Goals – League (47): Ferry 8, Weatherston 7, Reilly 6 (6 pens), Trouten 4 (1 pen), Felvus 3, Kettlewell 3, Canning 2, Clark 2, Harvey 2, Proctor 2, Quinn 2, Weir 2, Dunlop 1, Murray 1, Sinclair 1, own goal 1.
Scottish Cup (4): Weatherston 2, Felvus 1, Trouten 1.
CIS Cup (3): Ferry 1, Harvey 1, Weatherston 1.
Challenge Cup (0).
Honours – Division II: Champions – 1922-23. **B Division:** Champions – 1955-56. **Second Division:** Champions – 1980-81. **Third Division:** Champions – 1999-2000. **Scottish Cup winners** 1874, 1875, 1876, 1880, 1881, 1882, 1884, 1886, 1890, 1893.

RAITH ROVERS   DIV. 2

Ground: Stark's Park, Pratt Street, Kirkcaldy KY1 1SA (01592) 263514
Ground capacity: 10,104 (all seated). **Colours:** Navy blue shirts with white sleeves, white shorts with navy blue and red edges.
Manager: Gordon Dalziel.

League Appearances: Adam S 5(3); Annand E 7(8); Bagan D 1(9); Bonar S 10(2); Brown A 35; Campbell M 14; Clarke P 2(5); Crabbe S 17(6); Crilly M 28; Davidson I 25(4); Ellis L 33(2); Fairbairn B 24(12); Ferguson D 7(1); Hall S 1; Hilland P 5(2); Jablonski N 18(11); Jaconelli E 1(11); Leiper C 1; Lumsden T 36; Lyle W 28(2); McLeod C 25(4); McManus P 36; Silvestro C 31(2); Stirling J 1(1); Tulloch S 1(3); Wilson S 5(1).
Goals – League (44): McManus 15 (2 pens), Jablonski 5, Crilly 4, Ellis 3, Annand 2, Davidson 2, Fairbairn 2, Lumsden 2, McLeod 2, Adam 1, Campbell 1, Crabbe 1, Silvestro 1,own goals 3.
Scottish Cup (0).
CIS Cup (3): Annand 1, Jablonski 1, McManus 1.
Challenge Cup (6) : McManus 3, Crabbe 1, own goals 2.
Honours – First Division: Champions – 1992-93, 1994-95. **Second Division:** Champions – 2002-03. **Division II:** Champions – 1907-08, 1909-10 (Shared), 1937-38, 1948-49. **League Cup winners** 1995.

RANGERS   PREMIER LEAGUE

Ground: Ibrox Stadium, Glasgow G51 2XD (0870) 600 1972
Ground capacity: 50,444. **Colours:** Royal blue shirts with red and white trim, white shorts with blue and red trim.
Manager: Paul Le Guen
League Appearances: Adam C (1); Andrews M 21(2); Ashikodi M (1); Ball M 2; Bernard O 9; Boyd K 15(2); Buffel T 25(4); Burke C 25(2); Ferguson B 32; Hemdani B 18; Hutton A 17(2); Jeffers F 4(4); Klos S 2; Kyrgiakos S 28; Lovenkrands P 23(10); Lowing A 1(1); Malcolm R 11(3); McCormack R 2(6); Murray I 26(4); Namouchi H 6(1); Nieto F (3); Novo I 10(14); Pierre-Fanfan J 7; Prso D 29(3); Rae A 5(4); Rae G 4(4); Ricksen F 20(1); Rodriguez J 20(1); Ross M (1); Smith S 16(2); Thompson S 4(10); Waterreus R 36.
Goals – League (67): Boyd 17, Lovenkrands 14, Prso 9 (2 pens), Ferguson 6, Buffel 5, Andrews 3, Burke 3, Novo 2 (2 pens), Thompson 2, Kyrgiakos 1, McCormack 1, Nieto 1, Pierre-Fanfan 1, Rodriguez 1, own goal 1.
Scottish Cup (5): Boyd 3, Kyrgiakos 1, McCormack 1.
CIS Cup (5): Buffel 2, Nieto 2, Andrews 1.
Honours – Division I: Champions – 1890-91 (Shared), 1898-99, 1899-1900, 1900-01, 1901-02, 1910-11, 1911-12, 1912-13, 1917-18, 1919-20, 1920-21, 1922-23, 1923-24, 1924-25, 1926-27, 1927-28, 1928-29, 1929-30, 1930-31, 1932-33, 1933-34, 1934-35, 1936-37, 1938-39, 1946-47, 1948-49, 1949-50, 1952-53, 1955-56, 1956-57, 1958-59, 1960-61, 1962-63, 1963-64, 1974-75. **Premier Division:** Champions – 1975-76, 1977-78, 1986-87, 1988-89, 1989-90, 1990-91, 1991-92, 1992-93, 1993-94, 1994-95, 1995-96, 1996-97. **Premier League:** Champions – 1998-99, 1999-2000, 2002-03, 2004-05. **Scottish Cup winners** 1894, 1897, 1898, 1903, 1928, 1930, 1932, 1934, 1935, 1936, 1948, 1949, 1950, 1953, 1960, 1962, 1963, 1964, 1966, 1973, 1976, 1978, 1979, 1981, 1992, 1993, 1996, 1999, 2000, 2002, 2003. **League Cup winners** 1947, 1949, 1961, 1962, 1964, 1965, 1971, 1976, 1978, 1979, 1982, 1984, 1985, 1987, 1988, 1989, 1991, 1993, 1994, 1997, 1999, 2002, 2003, 2005. **European Cup-Winners' Cup winners** 1972.

ROSS COUNTY   DIV. 1

Ground: Victoria Park, Dingwall IV15 9QW (01349) 860860
Ground capacity: 6700. **Colours:** Navy blue with white and red pin stripe on collar and sleeves, white shorts with navy and red side stripe, navy stockings.
Manager: Scott Leitch
League Appearances: Anderson S 5(1); Burke A 25(3); Canning M 19; Cowan D 21; Cowie D 29(3); Djebi-Zadi L 36; Garden S 23(1); Gunn C (8); Higgins S 19(6); Hooks N 1; Lauchlan J 25(1); Macdonald N 8(2); Malin J 3(2); McCaldon I 10; McCulloch M 31; McGarry S 10(4); McKinlay K 14(13); McSwegan G 6(10); Niven

D 2(1); Nuckowski M 7(5); Rankin J 36; Taylor S 4(4); Tiernan F 17(3); Webb S 27; Winters D 18(15).
Goals – League (47): Rankin 12, Higgins 9, Winters 8 (2 pens), Burke 4, Cowie 4, Webb 2, Canning 1, Djebi-Zadi 1, McGarry 1, McKinlay 1, McSwegan 1, Nuckowski 1, Taylor 1, own goal 1.
Scottish Cup (6): Cowie 3, Burke 1, Higgins 1, McKinlay 1.
CIS Cup (5): Higgins 1, McGarry 1, Webb 1, Winters 1, own goal 1.
Challenge Cup (2): Rankin 1, Winters 1.
Honours – Third Division: Champions – 1998-99.

ST JOHNSTONE   DIV. 1

Ground: McDiarmid Park, Crieff Road, Perth PH1 2SJ (01738) 459090
Ground capacity: 10,673. **Colours:** Royal blue shirts with white trim, white shorts.
Manager: Owen Coyle.
League Appearances: Anderson S 19(4); Campbell M 3; Coyle O 5(10); Cuthbert K 23; Dobbie S 7(13); Doris S (3); Dyer W 1(2); Fotheringham K 2(3); Glennan M 12; Hardie M 1(2); Hardie W 9; Henry J 17(7); Jackson A (2); James K 31; Janczyk N 4(8); MacDonald P 2(7); McCallum N (3); McCann R 7(9); Mensing S 28(1); Milne S 25(4); Moon K (1); Paston M 1; Paterson S 3(1); Rutkiewicz K 31; Scotland J 31; Sheerin P 33(3); Sheridan D 32; Stanik G 35; Stevenson R 29(6); Winter J 5(3).
Goals – League (59): Scotland 15, Sheerin 10 (4 pens), Milne 8, James 6, Stevenson 5, Mensing 3, MacDonald 2 (1 pen), Rutkiewicz 2, Campbell 1, Dobbie 1, Glennan 1, Hardie 1, Stanik 1, own goals 3.
Scottish Cup (0).
CIS Cup (3): Dobbie 2, Milne 1.
Challenge Cup (12): Milne 4, Dobbie 2, Rutkiewicz 2, Janczyk 1, MacDonald 1, Mensing 1, Scotland 1.
Honours – First Division: Champions – 1982-83, 1989-90, 1996-97. **Division II:** Champions – 1923-24, 1959-60, 1962-63.

ST MIRREN   PREMIER LEAGUE

Ground: St Mirren Park, Paisley PA3 2EJ (0141) 889 2558, 840 1337
Ground capacity: 10,866 (all seated). **Colours:** Black and white striped shirts, white shorts with black trim.
Manager: Gus MacPherson.
League Appearances: Adam C 24(5); Anderson I 5(6); Baird J (2); Broadfoot K 25(2); Bullock A 12; Corcoran M 11(16); Hinchcliffe C 3; Kean S 29(6); Lappin S 33(2); Maxwell I 16(5); McGinty B (8); McGowne K 32; McKenna D (3); Mehmet W 10(19); Millen A 27(1); Molloy C 1(1); Murray H 27(2); Potter J 35; Reid A 15(9); Reilly M 11(3); Smith C 21(2); Sutton J 28(3); Van Zanten D 31(1).
Goals – League (52): Sutton 14 (2 pens), Kean 12 (4 pens), Adam 5, Anderson 3, Corcoran 3, Lappin 3, Van Zanten 3, Broadfoot 2, Mehmet 2, Baird 1, McGowne 1, Murray 1, Potter 1, own goal 1.
Scottish Cup (6): Adam 3, Maxwell 1, Potter 1, Sutton 1.
CIS Cup (1): McGowne 1.
Challenge Cup (8): Lappin 2, Sutton 2, Adam 1, Corcoran 1, Murray 1, Reid 1.
Honours – First Division: Champions – 1976-77, 1999-2000, 2005-06. **Division II:** Champions – 1967-68. **Scottish Cup winners** 1926, 1959, 1987.

STENHOUSEMUIR   DIV. 3

Ground: Ochilview Park, Stenhousemuir FK5 4QL (01324) 562992
Ground capacity: 2654. **Colours:** Maroon shirts with dark blue trim, white shorts.
Manager: Des McKeown.

League Appearances: Arbuckle A 2(1); Carroll F 10(3); Cassidy P 2(4); Collins L 8; Cramb C 25(2); Denham G 31; Diack I 11(4); Fahey C 6; Fallon S 9(2); Gibson A 9; Henderson R 25(1); McAlpine J 28(3); McBride J 32(1); McCulloch W 30; McGregor S 2; McGrillen P 26(5); McInally D 2(3); McKenzie M 1(5); McKeown J 19; Menzies C 18; Mercer J 24(6); Murphy P 23(3); Renwick M 26(3); Savage J 2(5); Sinclair T 21(7); Tait J 1(1); Templeton D 4(14).
Goals – League (78): Cramb 16 (1 pen), McGrillen 15 (4 pens), Diack 9, Mercer 8, Templeton 8, McBride 6 (3 pens), Sinclair 6, McAlpine 2, McKeown 2, Murphy 2, Carroll 1, Gibson 1, McInally 1, own goal 1.
Scottish Cup (4): Cramb 1, Mercer 1, Renwick 1, Sinclair 1.
CIS Cup (0).
Challenge Cup (8): Cramb 2, McGrillen 2, Carroll 1, Denham 1, Mercer 1, Savage 1.
Honours – League Challenge Cup: Winners – 1996.

STIRLING ALBION   DIV. 2

Ground: Forthbank Stadium, Springkerse Industrial Estate, Stirling FK7 7UJ (01786) 450399
Ground capacity: 3808. **Colours:** Red and white halved shirts, red shorts with white piping.
Manager: Allan Moore.
League Appearances: Aitken C 23(2); Bell A (1); Bell S 25(1); Boyack S 8(6); Christie S 1; Connolly P 35(1); Devine S 25(6); Dunn R 5(11); Forsyth R 31(3); Fraser J 28; Giacomi R 4; Graham A 30; Hay C 8(17); Hay P 26(2); Hogarth M 31; Hutchison S 1(2); McClare S 2(1); McNally M 29; McVicar N (5); Millar J 1(3); Nugent P 23; O'Brien D 29(6); Roycroft S 7(3); Scotland C 1; Taggart N (1); Turnbull D 4(4); Wilson D 19(11).
Goals – League (54): Connolly 14, Aitken 13 (4 pens), Hay C 5 (1 pen), O'Brien 5, Wilson 4, Bell S 2, Devine 2, Graham 2, Hay P 2, Dunn 1, Forsyth 1, Fraser 1, McVicar 1, Nugent 1.
Scottish Cup (3): Connolly 1, Forsyth 1, Hay C 1.
CIS Cup (3): Connolly 2, Boyack 1.
Challenge Cup (4): Aitken 1, Boyack 1, Fraser 1, Hay P 1.
Honours – Division II: Champions – 1952-53, 1957-58, 1960-61, 1964-65. **Second Division:** Champions – 1976-77, 1990-91, 1995-96.

STRANRAER   DIV. 2

Ground: Stair Park, Stranraer DG9 8BS (01776) 703271
Ground capacity: 5600. **Colours:** Blue shirts with white side panels, blue shorts with white side panels.
Manager: Gerry Britton.
League Appearances: Aitken S 16(7); Corr B 36; Dowie A 18(4); Gaughan K (1); Gilfillan B 14(1); Hamilton D 34(1); Harty I 3(2); Henderson M 34; Higgins C 26(6); Hinds L 24(7); Jenkins A 21; Keddie A 35; Maisano J 1(2); Marshall C 1(7); Martin W 5(9); McLean S 1(2); McPhee G 1; Moore M 28(3); Morrison A ; Payne S 13(2); Ross I 9(5); Sharp L 26(4); Shields D 3(8); Swift S 25(1); Walker P 11(12); Wingate D 11(4).
Goals – League (33): Hamilton 9 (2 pens), Moore 7, Swift 4, Henderson 3, Jenkins 2, Sharp 2, Hinds 1, Martin 1, Payne 1, Ross 1, Shields 1, Walker 1.
Scottish Cup (0).
CIS Cup (4): Hinds 2, Hamilton 1, Jenkins 1.
Challenge Cup (4): Hamilton 2, Jenkins 1, own goal 1.
Honours – Second Division: Champions – 1993-94, 1997-98. **Third Division:** Champions – 2003-04. **League Challenge Cup winners** 1997.

SCOTTISH LEAGUE HONOURS

*On goal average (ratio)/difference. †Held jointly after indecisive play-off.
‡Won on deciding match. ††Held jointly. ¶Two points deducted for fielding ineligible
player. Competition suspended 1940–45 during war; Regional Leagues operating.
‡‡Two points deducted for registration irregularities. §Not promoted after play-off.

PREMIER LEAGUE
Maximum points: 108

	First	Pts	Second	Pts	Third	Pts
1998–99	Rangers	77	Celtic	71	St Johnstone	57
1999–00	Rangers	90	Celtic	69	Hearts	54

Maximum points: 114

2000–01	Celtic	97	Rangers	82	Hibernian	66
2001–02	Celtic	103	Rangers	85	Livingston	58
2002–03	Rangers*	97	Celtic	97	Hearts	63
2003–04	Celtic	98	Rangers	81	Hearts	68
2004–05	Rangers	93	Celtic	92	Hibernian*	61
2005–06	Celtic	91	Hearts	74	Rangers	73

PREMIER DIVISION
Maximum points: 72

1975–76	Rangers	54	Celtic	48	Hibernian	43
1976–77	Celtic	55	Rangers	46	Aberdeen	43
1977–78	Rangers	55	Aberdeen	53	Dundee U	40
1978–79	Celtic	48	Rangers	45	Dundee U	44
1979–80	Aberdeen	48	Celtic	47	St Mirren	42
1980–81	Celtic	56	Aberdeen	49	Rangers*	44
1981–82	Celtic	55	Aberdeen	53	Rangers	43
1982–83	Dundee U	56	Celtic*	55	Aberdeen	55
1983–84	Aberdeen	57	Celtic	50	Dundee U	47
1984–85	Aberdeen	59	Celtic	52	Dundee U	47
1985–86	Celtic*	50	Hearts	50	Dundee U	47

Maximum points: 88

| 1986–87 | Rangers | 69 | Celtic | 63 | Dundee U | 60 |
| 1987–88 | Celtic | 72 | Hearts | 62 | Rangers | 60 |

Maximum points: 72

1988–89	Rangers	56	Aberdeen	50	Celtic	46
1989–90	Rangers	51	Aberdeen*	44	Hearts	44
1990–91	Rangers	55	Aberdeen	53	Celtic*	41

Maximum points: 88

1991–92	Rangers	72	Hearts	63	Celtic	62
1992–93	Rangers	73	Aberdeen	64	Celtic	60
1993–94	Rangers	58	Aberdeen	55	Motherwell	54

Maximum points: 108

1994–95	Rangers	69	Motherwell	54	Hibernian	53
1995–96	Rangers	87	Celtic	83	Aberdeen*	55
1996–97	Rangers	80	Celtic	75	Dundee U	60
1997–98	Celtic	74	Rangers	72	Hearts	67

DIVISION 1
Maximum points: 52

| 1975–76 | Partick Th | 41 | Kilmarnock | 35 | Montrose | 30 |

			Maximum points: 78			
1976–77	St Mirren	62	Clydebank	58	Dundee	51
1977–78	Morton*	58	Hearts	58	Dundee	57
1978–79	Dundee	55	Kilmarnock*	54	Clydebank	54
1979–80	Hearts	53	Airdrieonians	51	Ayr U*	44
1980–81	Hibernian	57	Dundee	52	St Johnstone	51
1981–82	Motherwell	61	Kilmarnock	51	Hearts	50
1982–83	St Johnstone	55	Hearts	54	Clydebank	50
1983–84	Morton	54	Dumbarton	51	Partick Th	46
1984–85	Motherwell	50	Clydebank	48	Falkirk	45
1985–86	Hamilton A	56	Falkirk	45	Kilmarnock	44

			Maximum points: 88			
1986–87	Morton	57	Dunfermline Ath	56	Dumbarton	53
1987–88	Hamilton A	56	Meadowbank Th	52	Clydebank	49

			Maximum points: 78			
1988–89	Dunfermline Ath	54	Falkirk	52	Clydebank	48
1989–90	St Johnstone	58	Airdrieonians	54	Clydebank	44
1990–91	Falkirk	54	Airdrieonians	53	Dundee	52

			Maximum points: 88			
1991–92	Dundee	58	Partick Th*	57	Hamilton A	57
1992–93	Raith R	65	Kilmarnock	54	Dunfermline Ath	52
1993–94	Falkirk	66	Dunfermline Ath	65	Airdrieonians	54

			Maximum points: 108			
1994–95	Raith R	69	Dunfermline Ath*	68	Dundee	68
1995–96	Dunfermline Ath	71	Dundee U*	67	Morton	67
1996–97	St Johnstone	80	Airdrieonians	60	Dundee*	58
1997–98	Dundee	70	Falkirk	65	Raith R*	60
1998–99	Hibernian	89	Falkirk	66	Ayr U	62
1999–00	St Mirren	76	Dunfermline Ath	71	Falkirk	68
2000–01	Livingston	76	Ayr U	69	Falkirk	56
2001–02	Partick Th	66	Airdrieonians	56	Ayr U	52
2002–03	Falkirk	81	Clyde	72	St Johnstone	67
2003–04	Inverness CT	70	Clyde	69	St Johnstone	57
2004–05	Falkirk	75	St Mirren*	60	Clyde	60
2005–06	St Mirren	76	St Johnstone	66	Hamilton A	59

DIVISION 2

			Maximum points: 52			
1975–76	Clydebank*	40	Raith R	40	Alloa Ath	35

			Maximum points: 78			
1976–77	Stirling A	55	Alloa Ath	51	Dunfermline Ath	50
1977–78	Clyde*	53	Raith R	53	Dunfermline Ath	48
1978–79	Berwick R	54	Dunfermline Ath	52	Falkirk	50
1979–80	Falkirk	50	East Stirling	49	Forfar Ath	46
1980–81	Queen's Park	50	Queen of the S	46	Cowdenbeath	45
1981–82	Clyde	59	Alloa Ath*	50	Arbroath	50
1982–83	Brechin C	55	Meadowbank Th	54	Arbroath	49
1983–84	Forfar Ath	63	East Fife	47	Berwick R	43
1984–85	Montrose	53	Alloa Ath	50	Dunfermline Ath	49
1985–86	Dunfermline Ath	57	Queen of the S	55	Meadowbank Th	49
1986–87	Meadowbank Th	55	Raith R*	52	Stirling A*	52
1987–88	Ayr U	61	St Johnstone	59	Queen's Park	51
1988–89	Albion R	50	Alloa Ath	45	Brechin C	43

	First		Second		Third	
1989–90	Brechin C	49	Kilmarnock	48	Stirling A	47
1990–91	Stirling A	54	Montrose	46	Cowdenbeath	45
1991–92	Dumbarton	52	Cowdenbeath	51	Alloa Ath	50
1992–93	Clyde	54	Brechin C*	53	Stranraer	53
1993–94	Stranraer	56	Berwick R	48	Stenhousemuir*	47

Maximum points: 108

1994–95	Morton	64	Dumbarton	60	Stirling A	58
1995–96	Stirling A	81	East Fife	67	Berwick R	60
1996–97	Ayr U	77	Hamilton A	74	Livingston	64
1997–98	Stranraer	61	Clydebank	60	Livingston	59
1998–99	Livingston	77	Inverness CT	72	Clyde	59
1999–00	Clyde	65	Alloa Ath	64	Ross County	62
2000–01	Partick Th	75	Arbroath	58	Berwick R*	54
2001–02	Queen of the S	67	Alloa Ath	59	Forfar Ath	53
2002–03	Raith R	59	Brechin C	55	Airdrie U	54
2003–04	Airdrie U	70	Hamilton A	62	Dumbarton	60
2004–05	Brechin C	72	Stranraer	63	Morton	62
2005–06	Gretna	88	Morton§	70	Peterhead*§	57

DIVISION 3

Maximum points: 108

1994–95	Forfar Ath	80	Montrose	67	Ross Co	60
1995–96	Livingston	72	Brechin C	63	Caledonian T	57
1996–97	Inverness CT	76	Forfar Ath*	67	Ross Co	67
1997–98	Alloa Ath	76	Arbroath	68	Ross Co*	67
1998–99	Ross Co	77	Stenhousemuir	64	Brechin C	59
1999–00	Queen's Park	69	Berwick R	66	Forfar Ath	61
2000–01	Hamilton A*	76	Cowdenbeath	76	Brechin C	72
2001–02	Brechin C	73	Dumbarton	61	Albion R	59
2002–03	Morton	72	East Fife	71	Albion R	70
2003–04	Stranraer	79	Stirling A	77	Gretna	68
2004–05	Gretna	98	Peterhead	78	Cowdenbeath	51
2005–06	Cowdenbeath*	76	Berwick R§	76	Stenhousemuir§	73

DIVISION 1 to 1974–75

Maximum points: a 36; b 44; c 40; d 52; e 60; f 68; g 76; h 84.

	First	Pts	Second	Pts	Third	Pts
1890–91a	Dumbarton††	29	Rangers††	29	Celtic	21
1891–92b	Dumbarton	37	Celtic	35	Hearts	34
1892–93a	Celtic	29	Rangers	28	St Mirren	20
1893–94a	Celtic	29	Hearts	26	St Bernard's	23
1894–95a	Hearts	31	Celtic	26	Rangers	22
1895–96a	Celtic	30	Rangers	26	Hibernian	24
1896–97a	Hearts	28	Hibernian	26	Rangers	25
1897–98a	Celtic	33	Rangers	29	Hibernian	22
1898–99a	Rangers	36	Hearts	26	Celtic	24
1899–1900a	Rangers	32	Celtic	25	Hibernian	24
1900–01c	Rangers	35	Celtic	29	Hibernian	25
1901–02a	Rangers	28	Celtic	26	Hearts	22
1902–03b	Hibernian	37	Dundee	31	Rangers	29
1903–04d	Third Lanark	43	Hearts	39	Celtic*	38
1904–05d	Celtic‡	41	Rangers	41	Third Lanark	35
1905–06e	Celtic	49	Hearts	43	Airdrieonians	38
1906–07f	Celtic	55	Dundee	48	Rangers	45
1907–08f	Celtic	55	Falkirk	51	Rangers	50

205

Season	Team	Pts	Team	Pts	Team	Pts
1908–09f	Celtic	51	Dundee	50	Clyde	48
1909–10f	Celtic	54	Falkirk	52	Rangers	46
1910–11f	Rangers	52	Aberdeen	48	Falkirk	44
1911–12f	Rangers	51	Celtic	45	Clyde	42
1912–13f	Rangers	53	Celtic	49	Hearts*	41
1913–14g	Celtic	65	Rangers	59	Hearts*	54
1914–15g	Celtic	65	Hearts	61	Rangers	50
1915–16g	Celtic	67	Rangers	56	Morton	51
1916–17g	Celtic	64	Morton	54	Rangers	53
1917–18f	Rangers	56	Celtic	55	Kilmarnock*	43
1918–19f	Celtic	58	Rangers	57	Morton	47
1919–20h	Rangers	71	Celtic	68	Motherwell	57
1920–21h	Rangers	76	Celtic	66	Hearts	50
1921–22h	Celtic	67	Rangers	66	Raith R	51
1922–23g	Rangers	55	Airdrieonians	50	Celtic	46
1923–24g	Rangers	59	Airdrieonians	50	Celtic	46
1924–25g	Rangers	60	Airdrieonians	57	Hibernian	52
1925–26g	Celtic	58	Airdrieonians*	50	Hearts	50
1926–27g	Rangers	56	Motherwell	51	Celtic	49
1927–28g	Rangers	60	Celtic*	55	Motherwell	55
1928–29g	Rangers	67	Celtic	51	Motherwell	50
1929–30g	Rangers	60	Motherwell	55	Aberdeen	53
1930–31g	Rangers	60	Celtic	58	Motherwell	56
1931–32g	Motherwell	66	Rangers	61	Celtic	48
1932–33g	Rangers	62	Motherwell	59	Hearts	50
1933–34g	Rangers	66	Motherwell	62	Celtic	47
1934–35g	Rangers	55	Celtic	52	Hearts	50
1935–36g	Celtic	66	Rangers*	61	Aberdeen	61
1936–37g	Rangers	61	Aberdeen	54	Celtic	52
1937–38g	Celtic	61	Hearts	58	Rangers	49
1938–39g	Rangers	59	Celtic	48	Aberdeen	46
1946–47e	Rangers	46	Hibernian	44	Aberdeen	39
1947–48e	Hibernian	48	Rangers	46	Partick Th	36
1948–49e	Rangers	46	Dundee	45	Hibernian	39
1949–50e	Rangers	50	Hibernian	49	Hearts	43
1950–51e	Hibernian	48	Rangers*	38	Dundee	38
1951–52e	Hibernian	45	Rangers	41	East Fife	37
1952–53e	Rangers*	43	Hibernian	43	East Fife	39
1953–54e	Celtic	43	Hearts	38	Partick Th	35
1954–55e	Aberdeen	49	Celtic	46	Rangers	41
1955–56f	Rangers	52	Aberdeen	46	Hearts*	45
1956–57f	Rangers	55	Hearts	53	Kilmarnock	42
1957–58f	Hearts	62	Rangers	49	Celtic	46
1958–59f	Rangers	50	Hearts	48	Motherwell	44
1959–60f	Hearts	54	Kilmarnock	50	Rangers*	42
1960–61f	Rangers	51	Kilmarnock	50	Third Lanark	42
1961–62f	Dundee	54	Rangers	51	Celtic	46
1962–63f	Rangers	57	Kilmarnock	48	Partick Th	46
1963–64f	Rangers	55	Kilmarnock	49	Celtic*	47
1964–65f	Kilmarnock*	50	Hearts	50	Dunfermline Ath	49
1965–66f	Celtic	57	Rangers	55	Kilmarnock	45
1966–67f	Celtic	58	Rangers	55	Clyde	46
1967–68f	Celtic	63	Rangers	61	Hibernian	45
1968–69f	Celtic	54	Rangers	49	DunfermlineAth	45
1969–70f	Celtic	57	Rangers	45	Hibernian	44

1970–71*f*	Celtic	56	Aberdeen	54	St Johnstone	44
1971–72*f*	Celtic	60	Aberdeen	50	Rangers	44
1972–73*f*	Celtic	57	Rangers	56	Hibernian	45
1973–74*f*	Celtic	53	Hibernian	49	Rangers	48
1974–75*f*	Rangers	56	Hibernian	49	Celtic	45

DIVISION 2 to 1974–75

Maximum points: a 76; b 72; c 68; d 52; e 60; f 36; g 44.

Year						
1893–94*f*	Hibernian	29	Cowlairs	27	Clyde	24
1894–95*f*	Hibernian	30	Motherwell	22	Port Glasgow	20
1895–96*f*	Abercorn	27	Leith Ath	23	Renton	21
1896–97*f*	Partick Th	31	Leith Ath	27	Kilmarnock*	21
1897–98*f*	Kilmarnock	29	Port Glasgow	25	Morton	22
1898–99*f*	Kilmarnock	32	Leith Ath	27	Port Glasgow	25
1899–1900*f*	Partick Th	29	Morton	28	Port Glasgow	20
1900–01*f*	St Bernard's	25	Airdrieonians	23	Abercorn	21
1901–02*g*	Port Glasgow	32	Partick Th	31	Motherwell	26
1902–03*g*	Airdrieonians	35	Motherwell	28	Ayr U*	27
1903–04*g*	Hamilton A	37	Clyde	28	Ayr U	28
1904–05*g*	Clyde	32	Falkirk	28	Hamilton A	27
1905–06*g*	Leith Ath	34	Clyde	31	Albion R	27
1906–07*g*	St Bernard's	32	Vale of Leven*	27	Arthurlie	27
1907–08*g*	Raith R	30	Dumbarton‡‡	27	Ayr U	27
1908–09*g*	Abercorn	31	Raith R*	28	Vale of Leven	28
1909–10*g*	Leith Ath‡	33	Raith R	33	St Bernard's	27
1910–11*g*	Dumbarton	31	Ayr U	27	Albion R	25
1911–12*g*	Ayr U	35	Abercorn	27	Dumbarton	23
1912–13*d*	Ayr U	34	Dunfermline Ath	33	East Stirling	32
1913–14*g*	Cowdenbeath	31	Albion R	27	Dunfermline Ath*	26
1914–15*d*	Cowdenbeath*	37	St Bernard's*	37	Leith Ath	37
1921–22*a*	Alloa Ath	60	Cowdenbeath	47	Armadale	45
1922–23*a*	Queen's Park	57	Clydebank ¶	50	St Johnstone ¶	45
1923–24*a*	St Johnstone	56	Cowdenbeath	55	Bathgate	44
1924–25*a*	Dundee U	50	Clydebank	48	Clyde	47
1925–26*a*	Dunfermline Ath	59	Clyde	53	Ayr U	52
1926–27*a*	Bo'ness	56	Raith R	49	Clydebank	45
1927–28*a*	Ayr U	54	Third Lanark	45	King's Park	44
1928–29*b*	Dundee U	51	Morton	50	Arbroath	47
1929–30*a*	Leith Ath*	57	East Fife	57	Albion R	54
1930–31*a*	Third Lanark	61	Dundee U	50	Dunfermline Ath	47
1931–32*a*	East Stirling*	55	St Johnstone	55	Raith R*	46
1932–33*c*	Hibernian	54	Queen of the S	49	Dunfermline Ath	47
1933–34*c*	Albion R	45	Dunfermline Ath*	44	Arbroath	44
1934–35*c*	Third Lanark	52	Arbroath	50	St Bernard's	47
1935–36*c*	Falkirk	59	St Mirren	52	Morton	48
1936–37*c*	Ayr U	54	Morton	51	St Bernard's	48
1937–38*c*	Raith R	59	Albion R	48	Airdrieonians	47
1938–39*c*	Cowdenbeath	60	Alloa Ath*	48	East Fife	48
1946–47*d*	Dundee	45	Airdrieonians	42	East Fife	31
1947–48*e*	East Fife	53	Albion R	42	Hamilton A	40
1948–49*e*	Raith R*	42	Stirling A	42	Airdrieonians*	41
1949–50*e*	Morton	47	Airdrieonians	44	Dunfermline Ath*	36
1950–51*e*	Queen of the S*	45	Stirling A	45	Ayr U*	36
1951–52*e*	Clyde	44	Falkirk	43	Ayr U	39
1952–53*e*	Stirling A	44	Hamilton A	43	Queen's Park	37

1953–54e	Motherwell	45	Kilmarnock	42	Third Lanark*	36
1954–55e	Airdrieonians	46	Dunfermline Ath	42	Hamilton A	39
1955–56b	Queen's Park	54	Ayr U	51	St Johnstone	49
1956–57b	Clyde	64	Third Lanark	51	Cowdenbeath	45
1957–58b	Stirling A	55	Dunfermline Ath	53	Arbroath	47
1958–59b	Ayr U	60	Arbroath	51	Stenhousemuir	46
1959–60b	St Johnstone	53	Dundee U	50	Queen of the S	49
1960–61b	Stirling A	55	Falkirk	54	Stenhousemuir	50
1961–62b	Clyde	54	Queen of the S	53	Morton	44
1962–63b	St Johnstone	55	East Stirling	49	Morton	48
1963–64b	Morton	67	Clyde	53	Arbroath	46
1964–65b	Stirling A	59	Hamilton A	50	Queen of the S	45
1965–66b	Ayr U	53	Airdrieonians	50	Queen of the S	47
1966–67a	Morton	69	Raith R	58	Arbroath	57
1967–68b	St Mirren	62	Arbroath	53	East Fife	49
1968–69b	Motherwell	64	Ayr U	53	East Fife*	48
1969–70b	Falkirk	56	Cowdenbeath	55	Queen of the S	50
1970–71b	Partick Th	56	East Fife	51	Arbroath	46
1971–72b	Dumbarton*	52	Arbroath	52	Stirling A	50
1972–73b	Clyde	56	Dumfermline Ath	52	Raith R*	47
1973–74b	Airdrieonians	60	Kilmarnock	58	Hamilton A	55
1974–75a	Falkirk	54	Queen of the S*	53	Montrose	53

Elected to Division 1: 1894 Clyde; 1895 Hibernian; 1896 Abercorn; 1897 Partick Th; 1899 Kilmarnock; 1900 Morton and Partick Th; 1902 Port Glasgow and Partick Th; 1903 Airdrieonians and Motherwell; 1905 Falkirk and Aberdeen; 1906 Clyde and Hamilton A; 1910 Raith R; 1913 Ayr U and Dumbarton.

SCOTTISH LEAGUE PLAY-OFFS 2005–2006

SCOTTISH DIVISION 1 SEMI-FINAL FIRST LEG

Morton	(0) 0	Peterhead	(0) 0
Stranraer	(1) 1	Partick T	(0) 3

SCOTTISH DIVISION 1 SEMI-FINAL SECOND LEG

Partick T	(0) 1	Stranraer	(0) 2
Peterhead	(1) 1	Morton	(0) 0

SCOTTISH DIVISION 1 FINAL FIRST LEG

Partick T	(1) 1	Peterhead	(0) 2

SCOTTISH DIVISION 1 FINAL SECOND LEG

Peterhead	(1) 1	Partick T	(1) 2

(aet; Partick T won 4-2 on penalties.)

SCOTTISH DIVISION 2 SEMI-FINAL FIRST LEG

Arbroath	(1) 1	Alloa Ath	(0) 1
Stenhousemuir	(0) 0	Berwick R	(0) 1

SCOTTISH DIVISION 2 SEMI-FINAL SECOND LEG

Alloa Ath	(0) 1	Arbroath	(0) 0
Berwick R	(0) 0	Stenhousemuir	(0) 0

SCOTTISH DIVISION 2 FINAL FIRST LEG

Alloa Ath	(2) 4	Berwick R	(0) 0

SCOTTISH DIVISION 2 FINAL SECOND LEG

Berwick R	(0) 2	Alloa Ath	(1) 1

RELEGATED CLUBS

From Premier League

1998–99 Dunfermline Ath
1999–00 *No relegated team*
2000–01 St Mirren
2001–02 St Johnstone

2002–03 *No relegated team*
2003–04 Partick Th
2004–05 Dundee
2005–06 Livingston

From Premier Division

1974–75 *No relegation due to League reorganisation*
1975–76 Dundee, St Johnstone
1976–77 Hearts, Kilmarnock
1977–78 Ayr U, Clydebank
1978–79 Hearts, Motherwell
1979–80 Dundee, Hibernian
1980–81 Kilmarnock, Hearts
1981–82 Partick Th, Airdrieonians
1982–83 Morton, Kilmarnock
1983–84 St Johnstone, Motherwell
1984–85 Dumbarton, Morton
1985–86 *No relegation due to League reorganisation*

1986–87 Clydebank, Hamilton A
1987–88 Falkirk, Dunfermline Ath, Morton
1988–89 Hamilton A
1989–90 Dundee
1990–91 None
1991–92 St Mirren, Dunfermline Ath
1992–93 Falkirk, Airdrieonians
1993–94 *See footnote*
1994–95 Dundee U
1995–96 Partick Th, Falkirk
1996–97 Raith R
1997–98 Hibernian

From Division 1

1974–75 *No relegation due to League reorganisation*
1975–76 Dunfermline Ath, Clyde
1976–77 Raith R, Falkirk
1977–78 Alloa Ath, East Fife
1978–79 Montrose, Queen of the S
1979–80 Arbroath, Clyde
1980–81 Stirling A, Berwick R
1981–82 East Stirling, Queen of the S
1982–83 Dunfermline Ath, Queen's Park
1983–84 Raith R, Alloa Ath
1984–85 Meadowbank Th, St Johnstone
1985–86 Ayr U, Alloa Ath
1986–87 Brechin C, Montrose
1987–88 East Fife, Dumbarton
1988–89 Kilmarnock, Queen of the S
1989–90 Albion R, Alloa Ath

1990–91 Clyde, Brechin C
1991–92 Montrose, Forfar Ath
1992–93 Meadowbank Th, Cowdenbeath
1993–94 *See footnote*
1994–95 Ayr U, Stranraer
1995–96 Hamilton A, Dumbarton
1996–97 Clydebank, East Fife
1997–98 Partick Th, Stirling A
1998–99 Hamilton A, Stranraer
1999–00 Clydebank
2000–01 Morton, Alloa Ath
2001–02 Raith R
2002–03 Alloa Ath, Arbroath
2003–04 Ayr U, Brechin C
2004–05 Partick Th, Raith R
2005–06 Stranraer, Brechin C

From Division 2

1994–95 Meadowbank Th, Brechin C
1995–96 Forfar Ath, Montrose
1996–97 Dumbarton, Berwick R
1997–98 Stenhousemuir, Brechin C
1998–99 East Fife, Forfar Ath
1999–00 Hamilton A**

2000–01 Queen's Park, Stirling A
2001–02 Morton
2002–03 Stranraer, Cowdenbeath
2003–04 East Fife, Stenhousemuir
2004–05 Arbroath, Berwick R
2005–06 Dumbarton

From Division 1 1973–74

1921–22 *Queen's Park, Dumbarton, Clydebank
1922–23 Albion R, Alloa Ath
1923–24 Clyde, Clydebank
1924–25 Third Lanark, Ayr U
1925–26 Raith R, Clydebank
1926–27 Morton, Dundee U
1927–28 Dunfermline Ath, Bo'ness
1928–29 Third Lanark, Raith R
1929–30 St Johnstone, Dundee U
1930–31 Hibernian, East Fife
1931–32 Dundee U, Leith Ath
1932–33 Morton, East Stirling
1933–34 Third Lanark, Cowdenbeath
1934–35 St Mirren, Falkirk
1935–36 Airdrieonians, Ayr U
1936–37 Dunfermline Ath, Albion R
1937–38 Dundee, Morton
1938–39 Queen's Park, Raith R
1946–47 Kilmarnock, Hamilton A
1947–48 Airdrieonians, Queen's Park
1948–49 Morton, Albion R
1949–50 Queen of the S, Stirling A

1950–51 Clyde, Falkirk
1951–52 Morton, Stirling A
1952–53 Motherwell, Third Lanark
1953–54 Airdrieonians, Hamilton A
1954–55 *No clubs relegated*
1955–56 Stirling A, Clyde
1956–57 Dunfermline Ath, Ayr U
1957–58 East Fife, Queen's Park
1958–59 Queen of the S, Falkirk
1959–60 Arbroath, Stirling A
1960–61 Ayr U, Clyde
1961–62 St Johnstone, Stirling A
1962–63 Clyde, Raith R
1963–64 Queen of the S, East Stirling
1964–65 Airdrieonians, Third Lanark
1965–66 Morton, Hamilton A
1966–67 St Mirren, Ayr U
1967–68 Motherwell, Stirling A
1968–69 Falkirk, Arbroath
1969–70 Raith R, Partick Th
1970–71 St Mirren, Cowdenbeath
1971–72 Clyde, Dunfermline Ath
1972–73 Kilmarnock, Airdrieonians
1973–74 East Fife, Falkirk

*Season 1921–22 – only 1 club promoted, 3 clubs relegated.
**15 pts deducted for failing to field a team.*

Scottish League championship wins: Rangers 51, Celtic 40, Aberdeen 4, Hearts 4, Hibernian 4, Dumbarton 2, Dundee 1, Dundee U 1, Kilmarnock 1, Motherwell 1, Third Lanark 1.

The Scottish Football League was reconstructed into three divisions at the end of the 1974–75 season, so the usual relegation statistics do not apply. Further reorganization took place at the end of the 1985–86 season. From 1986–87, the Premier and First Division had 12 teams each. The Second Division remained at 14. From 1988–89, the Premier Division reverted to 10 teams, and the First Division to 14 teams but in 1991–92 the Premier and First Division reverted to 12. At the end of the 1997–98 season, the top nine clubs in Premier Division broke away from the Scottish League to form a new competition, the Scottish Premier League, with the club promoted from Division One. At the end of the 1999–2000 season two teams were added to the Scottish League. There was no relegation from the Premier League but two promoted from the First Division and three from each of the Second and Third Divisions. One team was relegated from the First Division and one from the Second Division, leaving 12 teams in each division. In season 2002–03, Falkirk were not promoted to the Premier League due to the failure of their ground to meet League standards. Inverness CT were promoted after a previous refusal in 2003–04 because of ground sharing. At the end of 2005–06 the Scottish League introduced play-offs for the team finishing second from the bottom of Division 1 against the winners of the second, third and fourth finishing teams in Division 2 and with a similar procedure for Division 2 and Division 3.

PAST SCOTTISH LEAGUE CUP FINALS

Year	Winner			Loser		
1946–47	Rangers		4	Aberdeen		0
1947–48	East Fife	0	4	Falkirk	0*	1
1948–49	Rangers		2	Raith Rovers		0
1949–50	East Fife		3	Dunfermline		0
1950–51	Motherwell		3	Hibernian		0
1951–52	Dundee		3	Rangers		2
1952–53	Dundee		2	Kilmarnock		0
1953–54	East Fife		3	Partick Th		2
1954–55	Hearts		4	Motherwell		2
1955–56	Aberdeen		2	St Mirren		1
1956–57	Celtic	0	3	Partick Th	0	0
1957–58	Celtic		7	Rangers		1
1958–59	Hearts		5	Partick Th		1
1959–60	Hearts		2	Third Lanark		1
1960–61	Rangers		2	Kilmarnock		0
1961–62	Rangers	1	3	Hearts	1	1
1962–63	Hearts		1	Kilmarnock		0
1963–64	Rangers		5	Morton		0
1964–65	Rangers		2	Celtic		1
1965–66	Celtic		2	Rangers		1
1966–67	Celtic		1	Rangers		0
1967–68	Celtic		5	Dundee		3
1968–69	Celtic		6	Hibernian		2
1969–70	Celtic		1	St Johnstone		0
1970–71	Rangers		1	Celtic		0
1971–72	Partick Th		4	Celtic		1
1972–73	Hibernian		2	Celtic		1
1973–74	Dundee		1	Celtic		0
1974–75	Celtic		6	Hibernian		3
1975–76	Rangers		1	Celtic		0
1976–77	Aberdeen		2	Celtic		1
1977–78	Rangers		2	Celtic		1*
1978–79	Rangers		2	Aberdeen		1
1979–80	Aberdeen	0	0	Dundee U	0*	3
1980–81	Dundee		0	Dundee U		3
1981–82	Rangers		2	Dundee U		1
1982–83	Celtic		2	Rangers		1
1983–84	Rangers		3	Celtic		2
1984–85	Rangers		1	Dundee U		0
1985–86	Aberdeen		3	Hibernian		0
1986–87	Rangers		2	Celtic		1
1987–88	Rangers†		3	Aberdeen		3*
1988–89	Aberdeen		2	Rangers		3*
1989–90	Aberdeen		2	Rangers		1
1990–91	Rangers		2	Celtic		1
1991–92	Hibernian		2	Dunfermline Ath		0
1992–93	Rangers		2	Aberdeen		1*
1993–94	Rangers		2	Hibernian		1
1994–95	Raith R†		2	Celtic		2*
1995–96	Aberdeen		2	Dundee		0
1996–97	Rangers		4	Hearts		3
1997–98	Celtic		3	Dundee U		0
1998–99	Rangers		2	St Johnstone		1
1999–2000	Celtic		2	Aberdeen		0
2000–01	Celtic		3	Kilmarnock		0
2001–02	Rangers		4	Ayr U		0
2002–03	Rangers		2	Celtic		1
2003–04	Livingston		2	Hibernian		0
2004–05	Rangers		5	Motherwell		1
2005–06	Celtic		3	Dunfermline Ath		0

†Won on penalties *After extra time

CIS SCOTTISH LEAGUE CUP 2005–2006

FIRST ROUND

Alloa Ath	(1) 2	Arbroath	(1) 1
(aet)			
Berwick R	(0) 4	Elgin C	(2) 2
Brechin C	(0) 0	Partick T	(0) 0
(aet; Partick T won 3-1 on penalties.)			
Cowdenbeath	(1) 2	St Johnstone	(2) 3
East Fife	(0) 0	Stranraer	(0) 1
East Stirling	(0) 1	Queen's Park	(3) 3
Forfar Ath	(0) 1	Ross Co	(1) 4
(aet)			
Hamilton A	(0) 2	Dumbarton	(1) 1
Montrose	(0) 0	Clyde	(1) 1
Morton	(0) 1	Ayr U	(2) 2
Raith R	(1) 2	Airdrie U	(0) 0
Stenhousemuir	(0) 0	Peterhead	(1) 1
Albion R	(0) 1	Gretna	(1) 2
Stirling Albion	(2) 2	Queen of the S	(1) 1

SECOND ROUND

Aberdeen	(1) 3	Berwick R	(0) 0
Falkirk	(2) 2	Partick T	(1) 1
Gretna	(0) 0	Dunfermline	(1) 1
Inverness CT	(4) 6	Alloa Ath	(1) 1
Kilmarnock	(1) 4	Stirling Albion	(1) 1
Motherwell	(1) 2	Hamilton A	(1) 1
Peterhead	(2) 2	Clyde	(1) 3
Queen's Park	(0) 0	Hearts	(2) 2
Raith R	(1) 1	Livingston	(0) 2
Ross Co	(1) 1	Ayr U	(2) 2
St Johnstone	(0) 0	St Mirren	(1) 1
Stranraer	(2) 3	Dundee	(0) 1

THIRD ROUND

Inverness CT	(2) 2	Dundee U	(0) 0
Kilmarnock	(0) 3	Dunfermline Ath	(3) 4
Rangers	(1) 5	Clyde	(0) 2
(aet)			
St Mirren	(0) 0	Motherwell	(0) 2
(aet)			
Stranraer	(0) 0	Aberdeen	(0) 2
Ayr U	(0) 1	Hibernian	(2) 2
Celtic	(0) 2	Falkirk	(0) 1
Livingston	(0) 1	Hearts	(0) 0

QUARTER-FINALS

Dunfermline Ath	(0) 3	Hibernian	(0) 0
Livingston	(1) 2	Inverness CT	(1) 1
(aet)			
Motherwell	(1) 1	Aberdeen	(0) 0
Celtic	(1) 2	Rangers	(0) 0

SEMI-FINALS

Dunfermline Ath	(1) 1	Livingston	(0) 0
Motherwell	(1) 1	Celtic	(1) 2

FINAL

Celtic	(1) 3	Dunfermline Ath	(0) 0

BELL'S LEAGUE CHALLENGE 2005–2006

FIRST ROUND

Arbroath	(0) 1	Stranraer	(0) 3
Ayr U	(0) 0	Stirling Albion	(0) 1
(aet)			
Brechin C	(1) 3	Clyde	(1) 2
(aet)			
East Fife	(0) 0	Stenhousemuir	(2) 4
Morton	(1) 3	Gretna	(0) 2
(aet)			
Partick T	(1) 2	Cowdenbeath	(0) 0
Peterhead	(1) 1	Berwick R	(0) 2
(aet)			
Queen of the S	(1) 4	Albion R	(0) 0
Queen's Park	(0) 0	Hamilton A	(0) 3
Raith R	(1) 3	Elgin C	(1) 1
(aet)			
Ross Co	(1) 2	Montrose	(1) 1
St Johnstone	(0) 2	Alloa Ath	(0) 0
St Mirren	(0) 1	Forfar Ath	(0) 0
(aet)			
Dundee	(2) 2	East Stirling	(0) 0

SECOND ROUND

Brechin C	(0) 0	Morton	(2) 2
Dundee	(1) 1	Airdrie U	(0) 1
(aet; Dundee won 3-2 on penalties.)			
Partick T	(0) 4	St Johnstone	(0) 4
(aet; St Johnstone won 4-3 on penalties.)			
Raith R	(0) 2	Dumbarton	(0) 1
(aet)			
Ross Co	(0) 0	Hamilton A	(1) 1
Queen of the S	(0) 1	St Mirren	(1) 2
Stirling Albion	(1) 2	Berwick R	(0) 1
Stranraer	(1) 1	Stenhousemuir	(1) 2

QUARTER-FINALS

Hamilton A	(1) 2	Dundee	(0) 0
St Johnstone	(3) 5	Raith R	(1) 1
St Mirren	(3) 3	Stenhousemuir	(2) 2
Stirling Albion	(1) 1	Morton	(1) 2

SEMI-FINALS

St Johnstone	(1) 1	Hamilton A	(1) 2
St Mirren	(0) 0	Morton	(0) 0
(aet; St Mirren won 4-2 on penalties.)			

FINAL

St Mirren	(1) 2	Hamilton A	(0) 1

TENNENT'S SCOTTISH CUP 2005–2006

FIRST ROUND

Partick T	(1) 1	Albion R	(0) 1
Preston Ath	(0) 2	Gretna	(3) 6
Cowdenbeath	(0) 0	Morton	(1) 3
Dumbarton	(3) 4	Forres Mechanics	(1) 1
Spartans	(0) 1	Berwick R	(0) 0
Stirling Albion	(2) 2	Elgin C	(0) 1
Alloa Ath	(3) 9	Selkirk	(0) 0
Stenhousemuir	(2) 3	East Stirling	(1) 2

FIRST ROUND REPLAY

Albion R	(0) 1	Partick T	(1) 3

SECOND ROUND

Alloa Ath	(1) 1	Montrose	(0) 0
Arbroath	(1) 1	Dumbarton	(0) 0
Ayr U	(0) 3	Morton	(0) 2
East Fife	(0) 0	Peterhead	(2) 3
Gretna	(3) 6	Cove R	(1) 1
Lossiemouth	(0) 0	Spartans	(1) 5
Queen's Park	(1) 2	Raith R	(0) 0
Stenhousemuir	(1) 1	Partick T	(2) 4
Stirling Albion	(0) 1	Inverurie	(0) 0
Threave R	(0) 0	Forfar Ath	(3) 4

THIRD ROUND

Alloa Ath	(0) 1	Livingston	(0) 1
Dundee U	(2) 2	Aberdeen	(0) 3
Dunfermline Ath	(2) 3	Airdrie U	(1) 4
Falkirk	(1) 2	Brechin C	(1) 1
Hearts	(1) 2	Kilmarnock	(0) 1
Hibernian	(2) 6	Arbroath	(0) 0
Inverness CT	(0) 1	Ayr U	(0) 1
Queen of the S	(0) 1	Hamilton A	(0) 1
Rangers	(1) 5	Peterhead	(0) 0
Ross Co	(2) 5	Forfar Ath	(0) 0
Spartans	(1) 3	Queen's Park	(1) 2
St Johnstone	(0) 0	Gretna	(1) 1
St Mirren	(1) 3	Motherwell	(0) 0
Stirling Albion	(0) 0	Partick T	(1) 1
Clyde	(2) 2	Celtic	(0) 1
Dundee	(0) 2	Stranraer	(0) 0

THIRD ROUND REPLAYS

Livingston	(1) 1	Alloa Ath	(0) 2
Ayr U	(0) 0	Inverness CT	(1) 2
Hamilton A	(0) 1	Queen of the S	(0) 0
(aet)			

FOURTH ROUND

Airdrie U	(0) 1	Dundee	(1) 1
Clyde	(0) 0	Gretna	(0) 0
Falkirk	(0) 1	Ross Co	(1) 1
Hamilton A	(0) 0	Alloa Ath	(0) 0

Hearts	(3) 3	Aberdeen	(0) 0
Inverness CT	(0) 2	Partick T	(1) 2
Rangers	(0) 0	Hibernian	(0) 3
Spartans	(0) 0	St Mirren	(0) 0

FOURTH ROUND REPLAYS

Alloa Ath	(0) 0	Hamilton A	(2) 3
Dundee	(1) 2	Airdrie U	(0) 0
Gretna	(1) 4	Clyde	(0) 0
Ross Co	(0) 0	Falkirk	(0) 1
St Mirren	(2) 3	Spartans	(0) 0
Partick T	(1) 1	Inverness CT	(1) 1

(aet; Partick T won 4-2 on penalties.)

QUARTER-FINALS

Falkirk	(0) 1	Hibernian	(1) 5
Gretna	(0) 1	St Mirren	(0) 0
Hamilton A	(0) 0	Dundee	(0) 0
Hearts	(1) 2	Partick T	(0) 1

QUARTER-FINAL REPLAY

| Dundee | (0) 3 | Hamilton A | (0) 2 |

(aet)

SEMI-FINALS

| Gretna | (1) 3 | Dundee | (0) 0 |
| Hibernian | (0) 0 | Hearts | (1) 4 |

FINAL

| Hearts | (1) 1 | Gretna | (0) 1 |

(aet; Hearts won 4-2 on penalties.)

PAST LEAGUE CHALLENGE FINALS

1990–91	Dundee	3	Ayr U	2
1991–92	Hamilton A	1	Ayr U	0
1992–93	Hamilton A	3	Morton	2
1993–94	St Mirren	9	Falkirk	3
1994–95	Airdrieonians	3	Dundee	2
1995–96	Stenhousemuir	0	Dundee U	0
	(Stenhousemuir won 5-4 on penalties)			
1996–97	Stranraer	1	St Johnstone	0
1997–98	Falkirk	1	Qeeen of the South	0
1998–99	no competition			
1999–2000	Alloa Ath	4	Inverness CT	4
	(Alloa Ath won 5-4 on penalties)			
2000–01	Airdrieonians	2	Livingston	2
	(Airdrieonians won 3-2 on penalties)			
2001–02	Airdrieonians	2	Alloa Ath	1
2002–03	Queen of the S	2	Brechin C	0
2003–04	Inverness CT	2	Airdrie U	0
2004–05	Falkirk	2	Ross Co	1
2005–06	St Mirren	2	Hamilton A	1

PAST SCOTTISH CUP FINALS

Year					
1874	Queen's Park	2	Clydesdale	0
1875	Queen's Park	3	Renton	0
1876	Queen's Park	1 2	Third Lanark	1 0
1877	Vale of Leven	0 1 3	Rangers	0 1 2
1878	Vale of Leven	1	Third Lanark	0
1879	Vale of Leven	1	Rangers	1
1880	*Vale of Leven awarded cup, Rangers did not appear for replay*			
1880	Queen's Park	3	Thornlibank	0
1881	Queen's Park	2 3	Dumbarton	1 1
1881	*Replayed because of protest*			
1882	Queen's Park	2 4	Dumbarton	2 1
1883	Dumbarton	2 2	Vale of Leven	2 1
1884	*Queen's Park awarded cup when Vale of Leven did not appear for the final*			
1885	Renton	0 3	Vale of Leven	0 1
1886	Queen's Park	3	Renton	1
1887	Hibernian	2	Dumbarton	1
1888	Renton	6	Cambuslang	1
1889	Third Lanark	3 2	Celtic	0 1
1889	*Replayed because of protest*			
1890	Queen's Park	1 2	Vale of Leven	1 1
1891	Hearts	1	Dumbarton	0
1892	Celtic	1 5	Queen's Park	0 1
1892	*Replayed because of protest*			
1893	Queen's Park	2	Celtic	1
1894	Rangers	3	Celtic	1
1895	St Bernards	3	Renton	1
1896	Hearts	3	Hibernian	1
1897	Rangers	5	Dumbarton	1
1898	Rangers	2	Kilmarnock	0
1899	Celtic	2	Rangers	0
1900	Celtic	4	Queen's Park	3
1901	Hearts	4	Celtic	3
1902	Hibernian	1	Celtic	0
1903	Rangers	1 0 2	Hearts	1 0 0
1904	Celtic	3	Rangers	2
1905	Third Lanark	0 3	Rangers	0 1
1906	Hearts	1	Third Lanark	0
1907	Celtic	3	St Mirren	0
1908	Celtic	5	St Mirren	1
1909	*After two drawn games between Celtic and Rangers, 2.2, 1.1, there was a riot and the cup was withheld*			
1910	Dundee	2 0 2	Clyde	2 0 1
1911	Celtic	0 2	Hamilton Acad	0 0
1912	Celtic	2	Clyde	0
1913	Falkirk	2	Raith R	0
1914	Celtic	0 4	Hibernian	0 1
1920	Kilmarnock	3	Albion R	2
1921	Partick Th	1	Rangers	0
1922	Morton	1	Rangers	0
1923	Celtic	1	Hibernian	0
1924	Airdrieonians	2	Hibernian	0
1925	Celtic	2	Dundee	1
1926	St Mirren	2	Celtic	0

Year				
1927	Celtic	3	East Fife	1
1928	Rangers	4	Celtic	0
1929	Kilmarnock	2	Rangers	0
1930	Rangers	0 2	Partick Th	0 1
1931	Celtic	2 4	Motherwell	2 2
1932	Rangers	1 3	Kilmarnock	1 0
1933	Celtic	1	Motherwell	0
1934	Rangers	5	St Mirren	0
1935	Rangers	2	Hamilton Acad	1
1936	Rangers	1	Third Lanark	0
1937	Celtic	2	Aberdeen	1
1938	East Fife	1 4	Kilmarnock	1 2
1939	Clyde	4	Motherwell	0
1947	Aberdeen	2	Hibernian	1
1948	Rangers	1 1	Morton	1 0
1949	Rangers	4	Clyde	1
1950	Rangers	3	East Fife	0
1951	Celtic	1	Motherwell	0
1952	Motherwell	4	Dundee	0
1953	Rangers	1 1	Aberdeen	1 0
1954	Celtic	2	Aberdeen	1
1955	Clyde	1 1	Celtic	1 0
1956	Hearts	3	Celtic	1
1957	Falkirk	1 2	Kilmarnock	1 1
1958	Clyde	1	Hibernian	0
1959	St Mirren	3	Aberdeen	1
1960	Rangers	2	Kilmarnock	0
1961	Dunfermline Ath	0 2	Celtic	0 0
1962	Rangers	2	St Mirren	0
1963	Rangers	1 3	Celtic	1 0
1964	Rangers	3	Dundee	1
1965	Celtic	3	Dunfermline Ath	2
1966	Rangers	0 1	Celtic	0 0
1967	Celtic	2	Aberdeen	0
1968	Dunfermline Ath	3	Hearts	1
1969	Celtic	4	Rangers	0
1970	Aberdeen	3	Celtic	1
1971	Celtic	1 2	Rangers	1 1
1972	Celtic	6	Hibernian	1
1973	Rangers	3	Celtic	2
1974	Celtic	3	Dundee U	0
1975	Celtic	3	Airdrieonians	1
1976	Rangers	3	Hearts	1
1977	Celtic	1	Rangers	0
1978	Rangers	2	Aberdeen	1
1979	Rangers	0 0 3	Hibernian	0 0 2
1980	Celtic	1	Rangers	0
1981	Rangers	0 4	Dundee U	0 1
1982	Aberdeen	4	Rangers	1 (aet)
1983	Aberdeen	1	Rangers	0 (aet)
1984	Aberdeen	2	Celtic	1 (aet)
1985	Celtic	2	Dundee U	1
1986	Aberdeen	3	Hearts	0
1987	St Mirren	1	Dundee U	0 (aet)
1988	Celtic	2	Dundee U	1

| 1989 | Celtic | 1 | Rangers | 0 |
| 1990 | Aberdeen† | 0 | Celtic | 0 |

(Aberdeen won 9-8 on penalties)

1991	Motherwell	4	Dundee U	3 (aet)
1992	Rangers	2	Airdrieonians	1
1993	Rangers	2	Aberdeen	1
1994	Dundee U	1	Rangers	0
1995	Celtic	1	Airdrieonians	0
1996	Rangers	5	Hearts	1
1997	Kilmarnock	1	Falkirk	0
1998	Hearts	2	Rangers	1
1999	Rangers	1	Celtic	0
2000	Rangers	4	Aberdeen	0
2001	Celtic	3	Hibernian	0
2002	Rangers	3	Celtic	2
2003	Rangers	1	Dundee	0
2004	Celtic	3	Dunfermline Ath	1
2005	Celtic	1	Dundee U	0
2006	Hearts†	1	Gretna	1 (aet)

(Hearts won 4-2 on penalties)

†won on penalties

SCOTS-ADS HIGHLAND LEAGUE 2005–2006

	P	W	D	L	F	A	GD	Pts
Deveronvale	28	20	4	4	77	29	48	64
Inverurie Loco Works	28	19	3	6	72	26	46	60
Buckie Thistle	28	16	8	4	48	23	25	56
Forres Mechanics	28	17	3	8	76	37	39	54
Keith	28	16	4	8	63	41	22	52
Huntly	28	15	6	7	66	41	25	51
Fraserburgh	28	13	6	9	68	45	23	45
Cove Rangers	28	12	6	10	55	46	9	42
Clachnacuddin	28	12	5	11	56	57	–1	41
Nairn County	28	12	4	12	57	46	11	40
Rothes	28	9	1	18	48	75	–27	28
Wick Academy	28	7	4	17	41	67	–26	25
Lossiemouth	28	7	4	17	40	97	–57	25
Brora Rangers	28	4	1	23	31	82	–51	13
Fort William	28	1	1	26	18	104	–86	4

WELSH LEAGUE 2005–2006

VAUXHALL MASTERFIT RETAILERS WELSH PREMIER LEAGUE

		Home					Away					Total						
	P	W	D	L	F	A	W	D	L	F	A	W	D	L	F	A	Gd	Pts
1 TNS	34	15	2	0	47	5	12	3	2	40	12	27	5	2	87	17	70	86
2 Llanelli	34	9	4	4	30	14	12	1	4	34	14	21	5	8	64	28	36	68
3 Rhyl	34	10	5	2	34	13	8	5	4	31	17	18	10	6	65	30	35	64
4 Carmarthen T	34	8	5	4	35	17	9	1	7	27	25	17	6	11	62	42	20	57
5 Port Talbot T	34	7	7	3	20	12	8	4	5	27	18	15	11	8	47	30	17	56
6 Welshpool T	34	10	4	3	37	23	5	5	7	22	25	15	9	10	59	48	11	54
7 Aberystwyth T	34	8	6	3	32	19	6	4	7	27	29	14	10	10	59	48	11	52
8 Haverfordwest Co	34	4	9	4	25	18	8	5	4	24	18	12	14	8	49	36	13	50
9 Bangor City	34	6	0	11	26	30	8	3	6	25	24	14	3	17	51	54	–3	45
10 Caersws	34	6	4	7	21	30	5	8	4	23	26	11	12	11	44	56	–12	45
11 Porthmadog	34	7	5	5	38	25	5	3	9	19	34	12	8	14	57	59	–2	44
12 Connah's Quay No	34	7	2	8	15	17	3	6	8	21	29	10	8	16	36	46	–10	38
13 Caernarfon T	34	4	5	8	23	26	5	5	7	24	29	9	10	15	47	55	–8	37
14 Newtown	34	4	2	11	23	33	6	4	7	19	28	10	6	18	42	61	–19	36
15 Newi Cefn Druids	34	5	8	4	27	24	2	3	12	15	34	7	11	16	42	58	–16	32
16 Airbus UK	34	4	2	11	17	30	4	6	7	18	30	8	8	18	35	60	–25	32
17 Cwmbran T*	34	4	3	10	23	38	4	5	8	19	35	8	8	18	42	73	–31	19
18 Cardiff Grange Q	34	3	1	13	14	50	1	3	13	9	60	4	4	26	23	110	–87	15

Cwmbran T deducted 13 points for fielding two ineligible players.

NORTHERN IRELAND LEAGUE 2005–2006

IRISH PREMIER LEAGUE

	P	W	D	L	F	A	GD	Pts
Linfield	30	23	6	1	88	23	65	75
Glentoran	30	19	6	5	60	28	32	63
Portadown	30	16	6	8	56	36	20	54
Dungannon Swifts	30	13	10	7	61	41	20	49
Cliftonville	30	13	8	9	45	35	10	47
Newry City	30	12	9	9	45	35	10	45
Ballymena United	30	13	6	11	42	48	–6	45
Lisburn Distillery	30	12	8	10	44	38	6	44
Coleraine	30	11	4	15	40	57	–17	37
Limavady United	30	9	9	12	42	49	–7	36
Loughgall	30	9	9	7	14	33	38	–5	34
Larne	30	7	9	14	42	63	–21	30
Glenavon	30	7	9	14	35	59	–24	30
Armagh City	30	9	3	18	38	69	–31	30
Institute+	30	6	8	16	37	58	–21	26
Ards*	30	6	2	22	31	62	–31	20

Ards 0, Glenavon 3; result annulled and Ards awarded 1-0 victory, Glenavon fielded an ineligible player.
relegated; †relegated after play-off.

EUROPEAN REVIEW 2005-2006

Two English teams, one in each European final yet nothing to show for their outstanding endeavours in reaching this stage. Middlesbrough had shown courage and determination before the final crucial defeat. Arsenal suffered the early dismissal of their goalkeeper and despite heroic efforts holding on to a precious goal lead, also had to admit ultimate defeat.

Naturally the beginning of both the Champions League and UEFA Cup painted a different canvas. And for all their breathtaking achievement the previous season, Liverpool had to start at the first qualifying stage. Actually it was touch and go whether they would be allowed in at all!

As fate would have it, the Welsh club TNS who had offered to play the champions, found themselves drawn against them and duly lost both legs 3-0. Liverpool then summarily disposed of Kaunas at which point Celtic found themselves rudely beaten 5-0 by Artmedia, the Bratislava club. Celtic did pull four goals back at home.

The third qualifying round included Manchester United, Everton and Rangers. Everton went out to Villarreal, but naturally had a chance in the UEFA Cup, meanwhile their neighbours Liverpool won in Sofia against CSKA, only to hang on in the Merseyside return.

Enter groupies Arsenal and Chelsea who were in the same section as Liverpool. Arsenal impressively topped Group B dropping just two points, but Manchester United were eliminated at the bottom of Group D won by Villarreal.

Liverpool and Chelsea played out two goalless draws in their meetings, while Rangers in a group headed by Internazionale managed a creditable second place.

Shocks in the opening knockout round, with Benfica taking a slender home leg over Liverpool, Arsenal winning 2-1 in Madrid against Real and Chelsea losing similarly at Stamford Bridge to Barcelona. Rangers were held by Villarreal.

Chelsea managed a draw away but only at the death, Rangers drew away and sneaked through on away goals while Arsenal's defence kept Real out at Highbury. However Benfica hit two at Anfield, leaving just the Gunners from the home country.

In the quarter-finals, Arsenal took a more than useful 2-0 lead over Juventus; Benfica and Barcelona were goalless, Internazionale edging Villarreal 2-1 and AC Milan holding Lyon in France.

Villarreal on away goals, AC Milan and Barcelona rather more comfortably joined Arsenal in the last four after the Londoners had held Juventus 0-0 in Turin. Then semifinal time saw Barca winning a 1-0 lead over AC Milan, and Arsenal leading Villarreal by the same slender margin. With both second legs scoreless the dream final of Arsenal and Barcelona became a reality.

Surely Thierry Henry and Ronaldinho would be outstanding on the day. Alas, neither played to their ability. When Arsenal had Lehmann sent off for pulling Samuel Eto'o down in the penalty area it looked daunting for the Gunners.

Not a bit of it. They took the lead, albeit from a dubious free-kick floated in by Henry and powerfully headed home by Sol Campbell. Barcelona laboured long to break the gallant rearguard lined up in opposition. Even more controversy over the Eto'o equaliser concerning offside. But little doubt about Belletti's winner. In between Henry had missed a one-on-one with the goalkeeper and Ronaldinho was wide and not too handsome with three free-kicks.

Middlesbrough were not the sole English entries in the UEFA Cup, Bolton Wanderers making their debut in Europe also joined them. Everton soon crashed out trailing 5-1 to Dinamo Bucharest in the first leg, retrieving one goal from the return.

Bolton did better with wins against Lokomotiv Plovdiv while Boro eased past Xanthi. Kept apart for the group games, both made encouraging starts and Boro topped their section and though Bolton were unbeaten they drew three of their four, significantly once with Sevilla who were to play the ultimate role with Boro.

The eliminations restarted and Bolton were held at home by Marseille, while Boro won in Stuttgart. An own goal consigned Bolton to defeat in the second leg and the Germans shocked Boro with victory at the Riverside, leaving the Teessiders to scrape through on away goals.

Middlesbrough took a narrow lead over Roma and were able to survive themselves on an away goal in Italy only to slump 2-0 at Basle in the quarter-finals. Worse followed at home when the Swiss led to leave Boro trailing 3-0 on aggregate. Then came the fight back and four goals!

In the semis they lost in Bucharest to Steaua – were two down at home before again amazingly pulling out another four goals! Then came the definitive anti-climax with Sevilla scoring three of their four in the last 12 minutes.

UEFA CHAMPIONS LEAGUE 2005–2006

FIRST QUALIFYING ROUND FIRST LEG

Dinamo Minsk	(0) 1	Anorthosis	(1) 1
Kairat	(1) 2	Artmedia	(0) 0
Levadia	(1) 1	Dinamo Tbilisi	(0) 0
Neftchi	(1) 2	Hafnarfjordur	(0) 0
Rabotnicki	(1) 6	Skonto Riga	(0) 0
Sliema Wanderers	(0) 1	Serif	(2) 4
F91 Dudelange	(0) 0	Zrinjski	(1) 1
Glentoran	(0) 1	Shelbourne	(0) 2
HB Torshavn	(1) 2	Kaunas	(3) 4
HIT Gorica	(0) 2	Dinamo Tirana	(0) 0
Haka	(1) 1	Pyunik	(0) 0
Liverpool	(2) 3	TNS	(0) 0

FIRST QUALIFYING ROUND SECOND LEG

Dinamo Tbilisi	(0) 2	Levadia	(0) 0
Kaunas	(1) 4	HB Torshavn	(0) 0
TNS	(0) 0	Liverpool	(1) 3
Anorthosis	(0) 1	Dinamo Minsk	(0) 0
Artmedia	(1) 4	Kairat	(0) 1
(aet.)			
Dinamo Tirana	(2) 3	HIT Gorica	(0) 0
Hafnarfjordur	(0) 1	Neftchi	(0) 2
Pyunik	(2) 2	Haka	(1) 2
Serif	(0) 2	Sliema Wanderers	(0) 0
Shelbourne	(2) 4	Glentoran	(1) 1
Skonto Riga	(0) 1	Rabotnicki	(0) 0
Zrinjski	(0) 0	F91 Dudelange	(0) 4
(aet.)			

SECOND QUALIFYING ROUND FIRST LEG

Anderlecht	(4) 5	Neftchi	(0) 0
Anorthosis	(1) 3	Trabzonspor	(0) 1
Dinamo Tbilisi	(0) 0	Brondby	(0) 2
Dynamo Kiev	(2) 2	Thun	(1) 2
Kaunas	(1) 1	Liverpool	(2) 3
Valerenga	(0) 1	Haka	(0) 0
Artmedia	(1) 5	Celtic	(0) 0
Debrecen	(2) 3	Hajduk Split	(0) 0
Dinamo Tirana	(0) 0	CSKA Sofia	(0) 2
F91 Dudelange	(1) 1	Rapid Vienna	(4) 6
Malmo	(1) 3	Maccabi Haifa	(2) 2
Partizan Belgrade	(0) 1	Serif	(0) 0
Rabotnicki	(1) 1	Lokomotiv Moskow	(0) 1
Shelbourne	(0) 0	Steaua	(0) 0

SECOND QUALIFYING ROUND SECOND LEG

Celtic	(2) 4	Artmedia	(0) 0
Liverpool	(0) 2	Kaunas	(0) 0
Brondby	(2) 3	Dinamo Tbilisi	(0) 1
CSKA Sofia	(1) 2	Dinamo Tirana	(0) 0
Hajduk Split	(0) 0	Debrecen	(3) 5
Haka	(1) 1	Valerenga	(2) 4
Lokomotiv Moscow	(0) 2	Rabotnicki	(0) 0
Maccabi Haifa	(1) 2	Malmo	(1) 2
Neftchi	(1) 1	Anderlecht	(0) 0
Rapid Vienna	(0) 3	F91 Dudelange	(2) 2
Serif	(0) 0	Partizan Belgrade	(0) 1
Steaua	(2) 4	Shelbourne	(1) 1
Thun	(0) 1	Dynamo Kiev	(0) 0
Trabzonspor	(1) 1	Anorthosis	(0) 0

THIRD QUALIFYING ROUND FIRST LEG

Anorthosis	(0) 1	Rangers	(0) 2
Betis	(0) 1	Monaco	(0) 0
Everton	(1) 1	Villarreal	(2) 2
Manchester United	(1) 3	Debrecen	(0) 0
Valarenga	(0) 1	FC Brugge	(0) 0
Wisla	(1) 3	Panathinaikos	(1) 1
Anderlecht	(2) 2	Slavia Prague	(1) 1
Artmedia	(0) 0	Partizan Belgrade	(0) 0
Basle	(1) 2	Werder Bremen	(0) 1
Brondby	(1) 2	Ajax	(1) 2
CSKA Sofia	(1) 1	Liverpool	(2) 3
Malmo	(0) 0	Thun	(1) 1
Rapid Vienna	(0) 1	Lokomotiv Moscow	(1) 1
Shakhtar Donetsk	(0) 0	Internazionale	(0) 2
Sporting Lisbon	(0) 0	Udinese	(1) 1
Steaua	(1) 1	Rosenborg	(0) 1

THIRD QUALIFYING ROUND SECOND LEG

Liverpool	(0) 0	CSKA Sofia	(1) 1
Lokomotiv Moscow	(0) 0	Rapid Vienna	(0) 1
Monaco	(1) 2	Betis	(1) 2
Panathinaikos	(0) 4	Wisla	(0) 1
(aet.)			
Partizan Belgrade	(0) 0	Artmedia	(0) 0
(aet; Artmedia won 4-3 on penalties.)			
Rosenborg	(1) 3	Steaua	(0) 2
Thun	(2) 3	Malmo	(0) 0
Udinese	(2) 3	Sporting Lisbon	(1) 2
Ajax	(0) 3	Brondby	(1) 1
Debrecen	(0) 0	Manchester United	(1) 3
FC Brugge	(0) 1	Valarenga	(0) 0
(aet; FC Brugge won 4-3 on penalties.)			
Internazionale	(1) 1	Shakhtar Donetsk	(1) 1
(Behind closed doors.)			
Rangers	(1) 2	Anorthosis	(0) 0
Slavia Prague	(0) 0	Anderlecht	(0) 2
Villarreal	(1) 2	Everton	(0) 1
Werder Bremen	(0) 3	Basle	(0) 0

GROUP A

FC Brugge	(0) 1	Juventus	(0) 2
Rapid Vienna	(0) 0	Bayern Munich	(0) 1
Bayern Munich	(1) 1	FC Brugge	(0) 0
Juventus	(1) 3	Rapid Vienna	(0) 0
Bayern Munich	(2) 2	Juventus	(0) 1
Rapid Vienna	(0) 0	FC Brugge	(0) 1
FC Brugge	(2) 3	Rapid Vienna	(1) 2
Juventus	(0) 2	Bayern Munich	(0) 1
Bayern Munich	(1) 4	Rapid Vienna	(0) 0
Juventus	(0) 1	FC Brugge	(0) 0
FC Brugge	(1) 1	Bayern Munich	(1) 1
Rapid Vienna	(0) 1	Juventus	(3) 3

Group A Final Table	P	W	D	L	F	A	Pts
Juventus	6	5	0	1	12	5	15
Bayern Munich	6	4	1	1	10	4	13
FC Brugge	6	2	1	3	6	7	7
Rapid Vienna	6	0	0	6	3	15	0

GROUP B

Arsenal	(0) 2	Thun	(0) 1
Sparta Prague	(0) 1	Ajax	(0) 1
Ajax	(0) 1	Arsenal	(1) 2

Thun	(0) 1	Sparta Prague	(0) 0
Ajax	(1) 2	Thun	(0) 0
Sparta Prague	(0) 0	Arsenal	(1) 2
Arsenal	(1) 3	Sparta Prague	(0) 0
Thun	(0) 2	Ajax	(1) 4
Ajax	(0) 2	Sparta Prague	(0) 1
Thun	(0) 0	Arsenal	(0) 1
Arsenal	(0) 0	Ajax	(0) 0
Sparta Prague	(0) 0	Thun	(0) 0

Group B Final Table	P	W	D	L	F	A	Pts
Arsenal	6	5	1	0	10	2	16
Ajax	6	3	2	1	10	6	11
Thun	6	1	1	4	4	9	4
Sparta Prague	6	0	2	4	2	9	2

GROUP C

Udinese	(1) 3	Panathinaikos	(0) 0
Werder Bremen	(0) 0	Barcelona	(1) 2
Barcelona	(3) 4	Udinese	(1) 1
Panathinaikos	(2) 2	Werder Bremen	(1) 1
Panathinaikos	(0) 0	Barcelona	(0) 0
Udinese	(0) 1	Werder Bremen	(0) 1
Barcelona	(4) 5	Panathinaikos	(0) 0
Werder Bremen	(2) 4	Udinese	(0) 3
Barcelona	(2) 3	Werder Bremen	(1) 1
Panathinaikos	(1) 1	Udinese	(0) 2
Udinese	(0) 0	Barcelona	(0) 2
Werder Bremen	(3) 5	Panathinaikos	(0) 1

Group C Final Table	P	W	D	L	F	A	Pts
Barcelona	6	5	1	0	16	2	16
Werder Bremen	6	2	1	3	12	12	7
Udinese	6	2	1	3	10	12	7
Panathinaikos	6	1	1	4	4	16	4

GROUP D

Benfica	(0) 1	Lille	(0) 0
Villarreal	(0) 0	Manchester United	(0) 0
Lille	(0) 0	Villarreal	(0) 0
(Played in Paris.)			
Manchester United	(1) 2	Benfica	(0) 1
Manchester United	(0) 0	Lille	(0) 0
Villarreal	(0) 1	Benfica	(0) 1
Benfica	(0) 0	Villarreal	(0) 1
Lille	(1) 1	Manchester United	(0) 0
(Played in Paris.)			
Lille	(0) 0	Benfica	(0) 0
(Played in Paris.)			
Manchester United	(0) 0	Villarreal	(0) 0
Benfica	(2) 2	Manchester United	(1) 1
Villarreal	(0) 1	Lille	(0) 0

Group D Final Table	P	W	D	L	F	A	Pts
Villarreal	6	2	4	0	3	1	10
Benfica	6	2	2	2	5	5	8
Lille	6	1	3	2	1	2	6
Manchester United	6	1	3	2	3	4	6

GROUP E

AC Milan	(1) 3	Fenerbahce	(0) 1
PSV Eindhoven	(1) 1	Schalke	(0) 0
Fenerbahce	(1) 3	PSV Eindhoven	(0) 0
Schalke	(1) 2	AC Milan	(1) 2
AC Milan	(0) 0	PSV Eindhoven	(0) 1
Fenerbahce	(1) 3	Schalke	(0) 3

PSV Eindhoven	(1) 1	AC Milan	(0) 0
Schalke	(1) 2	Fenerbahce	(0) 0
Fenerbahce	(0) 0	AC Milan	(1) 4
Schalke	(1) 3	PSV Eindhoven	(0) 0
AC Milan	(1) 3	Schalke	(1) 2
PSV Eindhoven	(1) 2	Fenerbahce	(0) 0

Group E Final Table	P	W	D	L	F	A	Pts
AC Milan	6	3	2	1	12	6	11
PSV Eindhoven	6	3	1	2	4	6	10
Schalke	6	2	2	2	12	9	8
Fenerbahce	6	1	1	4	7	14	4

GROUP F

Lyon	(3) 3	Real Madrid	(0) 0
Olympiakos	(1) 1	Rosenborg	(1) 3
Real Madrid	(1) 2	Olympiakos	(0) 1
Rosenborg	(0) 0	Lyon	(1) 1
Lyon	(1) 2	Olympiakos	(0) 1
Real Madrid	(0) 4	Rosenborg	(1) 1
Olympiakos	(1) 1	Lyon	(2) 4
Rosenborg	(0) 0	Real Madrid	(2) 2
Real Madrid	(1) 1	Lyon	(0) 1
Rosenborg	(0) 1	Olympiakos	(0) 1
Lyon	(1) 2	Rosenborg	(0) 1
Olympiakos	(0) 2	Real Madrid	(1) 1

Group F Final Table	P	W	D	L	F	A	Pts
Lyon	6	5	1	0	13	4	16
Real Madrid	6	3	1	2	10	8	10
Rosenborg	6	1	1	4	6	11	4
Olympiakos	6	1	1	4	7	13	4

GROUP G

Betis	(0) 0	Liverpool	(2) 2
Chelsea	(1) 1	Anderlecht	(0) 0
Anderlecht	(0) 0	Betis	(0) 1
Liverpool	(0) 0	Chelsea	(0) 0
Anderlecht	(0) 0	Liverpool	(1) 1
Chelsea	(2) 4	Betis	(0) 0
Betis	(1) 1	Chelsea	(0) 0
Liverpool	(1) 3	Anderlecht	(0) 0
Anderlecht	(0) 0	Chelsea	(2) 2
Liverpool	(0) 0	Betis	(0) 0
Betis	(0) 0	Anderlecht	(1) 1
Chelsea	(0) 0	Liverpool	(0) 0

Group G Final Table	P	W	D	L	F	A	Pts
Liverpool	6	3	3	0	6	1	12
Chelsea	6	3	2	1	7	1	11
Betis	6	2	1	3	3	7	7
Anderlecht	6	1	0	5	1	8	3

GROUP H

Artmedia	(0) 0	Internazionale	(1) 1
Rangers	(1) 3	Porto	(0) 2
Internazionale	(0) 1	Rangers	(0) 0
(Behind closed doors.)			
Porto	(2) 2	Artmedia	(1) 3
Porto	(2) 2	Internazionale	(0) 0
Rangers	(0) 0	Artmedia	(0) 0
Artmedia	(1) 2	Rangers	(2) 2
Internazionale	(0) 2	Porto	(1) 1
(Behind closed doors.)			
Internazionale	(2) 4	Artmedia	(0) 0
(Behind closed doors.)			

Porto	(0) 1		Rangers	(0) 1
Artmedia	(0) 0		Porto	(0) 0
Rangers	(1) 1		Internazionale	(1) 1

Group H Final Table	P	W	D	L	F	A	Pts
Internazionale	6	4	1	1	9	4	13
Rangers	6	1	4	1	7	7	7
Artmedia	6	1	3	2	5	9	6
Porto	6	1	2	3	8	9	5

KNOCK-OUT ROUND FIRST LEG

Bayern Munich	(1) 1		AC Milan	(0) 1
Benfica	(0) 1		Liverpool	(0) 0
PSV Eindhoven	(0) 0		Lyon	(0) 1
Real Madrid	(0) 0		Arsenal	(0) 1
Ajax	(2) 2		Internazionale	(0) 2
Chelsea	(0) 1		Barcelona	(0) 2
Rangers	(1) 2		Villarreal	(2) 2
Werder Bremen	(1) 3		Juventus	(0) 2

KNOCK-OUT ROUND SECOND LEG

Barcelona	(0) 1		Chelsea	(0) 1
Juventus	(0) 2		Werder Bremen	(1) 1
Villarreal	(0) 1		Rangers	(1) 1
AC Milan	(2) 4		Bayern Munich	(1) 1
Arsenal	(0) 0		Real Madrid	(0) 0
Liverpool	(0) 0		Benfica	(1) 2
Lyon	(2) 4		PSV Eindhoven	(0) 0
Internazionale	(0) 0		Ajax	(0) 0

QUARTER-FINALS FIRST LEG

Arsenal	(1) 2		Juventus	(0) 0
Benfica	(0) 0		Barcelona	(0) 0
Internazionale	(1) 2		Villarreal	(1) 1
Lyon	(0) 0		AC Milan	(0) 0

QUARTER-FINALS SECOND LEG

AC Milan	(1) 3		Lyon	(1) 1
Villarreal	(0) 1		Internazionale	(0) 0
Barcelona	(1) 2		Benfica	(0) 0
Juventus	(0) 0		Arsenal	(0) 0

SEMI-FINALS FIRST LEG

| AC Milan | (0) 0 | | Barcelona | (0) 1 |
| Arsenal | (1) 1 | | Villarreal | (0) 0 |

SEMI-FINALS SECOND LEG

| Villarreal | (0) 0 | | Arsenal | (0) 0 |
| Barcelona | (0) 0 | | AC Milan | (0) 0 |

UEFA CHAMPIONS LEAGUE FINAL 2006

Wednesday, 17 May 2006

Barcelona (0) 2 *(Eto'o 76, Belletti 81)*   **Arsenal (1) 1** *(Campbell 37)*

(at Stade de France, Paris, 79,500)

Barcelona: Valdes; Oleguer (Belletti 71), Van Bronckhorst, Marquez, Puyol, Edmilson (Iniesta 46), Giuly, Deco, Eto'o, Ronaldinho, Van Bommel (Larsson 61).

Arsenal: Lehmann■; Eboue, Cole, Silva, Toure, Campbell, Hleb (Reyes 85), Fabregas (Flamini 74), Henry, Ljungberg, Pires (Almunia 18).

Referee: T. Hauge (Norway).

■ *Denotes player sent off.*

INTERTOTO CUP 2005

FIRST ROUND, FIRST LEG
Beitar Jerusalem 4, Sileks 3; Bohemians 1, Gent 0; Cluj-Napoca 3, Vetra 2; Tiligul 0, Pogon 3; Dinamo Tirana 2, Varteks 1; Slaven 1, Drava 0; Olympiakos (Cy) 0, Gloria 5,; Skala 0, Tampere U 2; Trans 0, Lokeren 2; Valletta 0, Buducnost 5; Vasas 0, Dubnica 0; Victoria 1, IFK Gothenburg 2; Ararat 1, Neuchatel Xamax 3; Smederevo 0, Pobeda 1; Karvan 1, Lech 2; Venecia 1, Sturm Graz 1; Neman 0, Zlin 1; FC Inter 0, IA Akranes 0; Bangor C 1, Dinaburg 2; Zalgiris 1, Lisburn 0; Lombard 2, WIT Georgia 1

FIRST ROUND, SECOND LEG
Buducnost 2, Valletta 2; Sileks 1, Beitar Jerusalem 2; Gent 3, Bohemians 1; IFK Gothenburg 5, Victoria 1; Lech 2, Karvan 0; Lisburn 0, Zalgiris 1; Lokeren 0, Trans 1; Neuchatel Xamax 6, Ararat 0; Drava 0, Slaven 1; Pogon 6, Tiligul 2; Sturm Graz 5, Venecia 0; Varteks 4, Dinamo Tirana 1; Dinaburg 2, Bangor C 0; Pobeda 2, Smederevo 0; Zlin 0, Neman 0; Vetra 1, Cluj-Napoca 4; Gloria 11, Olympiakos (Cy) 0; IA Akranes 0, FC Inter 4; Tampere U 1, Skala 0; WIT Georgia 0, Lombard 1; Dubnica 2, Vasas 0

SECOND ROUND, FIRST LEG
Ankara 0, Dubnica 4; Cluj-Napoca 1, Athletic Bilbao 0; La Coruna 3, Buducnost 0; Gent 1, Zlin 0; Hamburg 4, Pobeda 1; Slovan Liberec 5, Beitar Jerusalem 1; Lokeren 1, Young Boys 4; Slaven 3, Drava 0; Sigma Olomouc 1, Pogon 0; St Etienne 1, Neuchatel Xamax 1; Varteks 4, FC Inter 3; Wolfsburg 2, Sturm Graz 2; Lens 2, Lech 1; Lombard 2, IFK Gothenburg 3; Tampere U 1, Charleroi 2; Zalgiris 2, Dinaburg 0

SECOND ROUND, SECOND LEG
Athletic Bilbao 0, Cluj-Napoca 1; Buducnost 2, La Coruna 1; Charleroi 1, Tampere U 0; Dinaburg 2, Zalgiris 1; IFK Gothenburg 1, Lombard 0; Pogon 0, Sigma Olomouc 0; Sturm Graz 1, Wolfsburg 3; Dubnica 0, Ankara 1; Beitar Jerusalem 1, Slovan Liberec 1; FC Inter 2, Varteks 2; Pobeda 1, Hamburg 4; Zlin 0, Gent 0; Gloria 0, Slaven 1; Lech 0, Lens 1; Neuchatel Xamax 1, St Etienne 2; Young Boys 2, Lokeren 1

THIRD ROUND, FIRST LEG
Aigaleo 1, Zalgiris 3; Borussia Dortmund 1, Sigma Olomouc 1; La Coruna 1, Slaven 0; Roda JC 0, Slovan Liberec 0; Uniao Leiria 0, Hamburg 1; Varteks 1, Lens 1; Young Boys 2, Marseille 3; Gent 0,

Valencia 0; Cluj-Napoca 1, St Etienne 1; IFK Gothenburg 0, Wolfsburg 2; Lazio 3, Tampere U 0; Dubnica 1, Newcastle U 3

THIRD ROUND, SECOND LEG
Zalgiris 2, Aigaleo 3; Hamburg 2, Uniao Leiria 0; Lens 4, Varteks 1; Slovan Liberec 1, Roda JC 1; Marseille 2, Young Boys 1; Slaven 0, La Coruna 3; Newcastle U 2, Dubnica 0; Sigma Olomouc 0, Borussia Dortmund 0; Tampere U 1, Lazio 1; Valencia 2, Gent 0; Wolfsburg 2, IFK Gothenburg 0; St Etienne 2, Cluj-Napoca 2

SEMI-FINAL, FIRST LEG
La Coruna 2, Newcastle U 1; Lazio 1, Marseille 1; Sigma Olomouc 0, Hamburg 1; Wolfsburg 0, Lens 0; Zalgiris 1, Cluj-Napoca 2; Valencia 4, Roda JC 0

SEMI-FINAL, SECOND LEG
Cluj-Napoca 5, Zalgiris 1; Hamburg 3, Sigma Olomouc 0; Lens 4, Wolfsburg 0; Marseille 3, Lazio 0; Newcastle U 1, La Coruna 2; Roda JC 0, Valencia 0

FINAL FIRST LEG
Cluj-Napoca 1, Lens 1; Hamburg 1, Valencia 0; La Coruna 2, Marseille 0

FINAL SECOND-LEG
Lens 3, Cluj-Napoca 1; Marseille 5, La Coruna 1; Valencia 0, Hamburg 0
Winners qualify for the UEFA Cup.

Dubnica (1) 1 *(Tesak 42)*
Newcastle U (2) 3 *(Chopra 4, Shearer 6, Milner 70)*
Newcastle: Harper; Taylor, Babayaro, Faye, Elliott, Boumsong, Milner, Butt, Shearer, Chopra (Brittain 58), N'Zogbia.

Newcastle U (0) 2 *(Shearer 72, 90)*
Dubnica (0) 0   25,135
Newcastle U: Given; Carr, Babayaro, Faye, Taylor, Boumsong, Jenas, Bowyer, Shearer, Milner, N'Zogbia (Brittain 60).

La Coruna (1) 2 *(Ruben Castro 11, Andrade 58)*
Newcastle U (0) 1 *(Bowyer 47)*
Newcastle U: Given; Carr, Babayaro, Faye, Taylor, Boumsong, Milner (Chopra 71), Butt, Shearer, Bowyer, N'Zogbia.

Newcastle U (1) 1 *(Milner 39)*
La Coruna (1) 2 *(Andrade 45, Munitis 48)* 35,000
Newcastle U: Given; Carr, Elliott, Faye (Ameobi 53), Taylor, Boumsong, Milner (N'Zogbia 72), Bowyer, Shearer, Parker, Emre (Brittain 90).

UEFA CUP 2005–2006

■ *Denotes player sent off.*
* *Winner after extra time.* †*Winner after extra time and penalties*

QUALIFYING STAGE

First Qualifying Round, First Leg

Allianssi	(2) 3	Petange	(0) 0
Torpedo Kutaisi	(0) 0	BATE Borisov	(1) 1
Banants	(0) 2	Lokomotivi Tbilisi	(1) 3
Baskimi	(0) 0	Zepce	(0) 0
Birkirkara	(0) 0	Apoel	(0) 2
Domagnano	(0) 0	Domzale	(1) 5
Elbasan	(1) 1	Vardar	(0) 1
Esbjerg	(0) 1	Flora	(0) 2
Etzella	(0) 0	Keflavik	(1) 4
Otaci	(1) 3	Khazar	(1) 1
Vaduz	(0) 2	Dacia	(0) 0
Ferencvaros	(0) 0	MTZ-RIPO	(1) 2
Omonia	(1) 3	Hibernians	(0) 0
Vestmann	(1) 1	B36	(1) 1
Teuta	(2) 3	Siroki	(0) 1
Karat	(0) 1	Zilina	(0) 0
Mainz	(2) 4	Mika	(0) 0
Runavik	(0) 0	Metalurgs	(1) 3
VMK	(1) 1	MyPa	(0) 1
Sant Julia	(0) 0	Rapid Bucharest	(2) 5
Ekranas	(0) 0	Cork City	(1) 2
Linfield	(1) 1	Ventspils	(0) 0
Longford Town	(1) 2	Carmarthen	(0) 0
Portadown	(0) 1	Viking	(0) 2
Rhyl	(1) 2	Atlantas	(0) 1

First Qualifying Round, Second Leg

Apoel	(1) 4	Birkirkara	(0) 0
B36	(1) 2	Vestmann	(1) 1
BATE Borisov	(5) 5	Torpedo Kutaisi	(0) 0
Dacia	(0) 1	Vaduz	(0) 0
Domzale	(1) 3	Domagnano	(0) 0
Flora	(0) 0	Esbjerg	(4) 6
Hibernians	(0) 0	Omonia	(1) 3
Keflavik	(0) 2	Etzella	(0) 0
Khazar	(0) 1	Otaci	(2) 2
Lokomotivi Tbilisi	(0) 0	Banants	(1) 2
Metalurgs	(2) 3	Runavik	(0) 0
Mika	(0) 0	Mainz	(0) 0
MTZ-RIPO	(0) 1	Ferencvaros	(1) 2
MyPa	(0) 1	VMK	(0) 0
Petange	(0) 1	Allianssi	(0) 1
Rapid Bucharest	(4) 5	Sant Julia	(0) 0
Siroki	(2) 3	Teuta	(0) 0
Vardar	(0) 0	Elbasan	(0) 0
Zepce	(0) 1	Baskimi	(0) 1
Zilina	(2) 3	Karat	(0) 1
Atlantas	(1) 3	Rhyl	(1) 2
Carmarthen	(1) 5	Longford Town	(1) 1
Cork City	(0) 0	Ekranes	(0) 1
Viking	(0) 1	Portadown	(0) 0
Ventspils	(1) 2	Linfield	(1) 1

Second Qualifying Round, First Leg

Apoel	(0) 1	Maccabi Tel Aviv	(0) 0
Ashdod	(2) 2	Domzale	(2) 2
Banants	(2) 2	Dnepr	(0) 4

Baskimi	(0) 0	Maccabi Petah Tikva	(3) 5
OFK Belgrade	(2) 2	Lokomotiv Plovdiv	(0) 1
Brann	(0) 0	Allianssi	(0) 0
Dinamo Bucharest	(3) 3	Omonia	(1) 1
Esbjerg	(0) 0	Tromso	(1) 1
Grasshoppers	(0) 1	Wisla Plock	(0) 0
Groclin	(0) 4	Bystrica	(0) 1
Inter Zapresic	(1) 1	Red Star Belgrade	(1) 3
Krylia	(1) 2	BATE Borisov	(0) 0
Legia	(0) 0	Zurich	(0) 1
Litets	(0) 1	Rijeka	(0) 0
Mainz	(1) 2	Keflavik	(0) 0
Matav	(0) 0	Metalurg Donetsk	(0) 3
Metalurgs	(1) 2	Genk	(0) 3
Midtjylland	(1) 2	B36	(0) 1
MTZ-RIPO	(0) 1	Teplice	(1) 1
Otaci	(0) 0	Graz	(0) 2
Pasching	(1) 2	Zenit	(1) 2
Publikum	(0) 1	Levski	(0) 0
Rapid Bucharest	(1) 3	Vardar	(0) 0
Vaduz	(0) 0	Besiktas	(1) 1
Zeta	(0) 0	Siroki	(0) 1
Zilina	(1) 1	FK Austria	(0) 2
FC Copenhagen	(0) 2	Carmarthen	(0) 0
Djurgaarden	(0) 1	Cork City	(1) 1
Halmstad	(1) 1	Linfield	(0) 1
MyPa	(0) 0	Dundee United	(0) 0
Rhyl	(0) 0	Viking	(1) 1

Second Qualifying Round, Second Leg

Allianssi	(0) 0	Brann	(0) 2
FK Austria	(0) 2	Zilina	(2) 2
B36	(1) 2	Midtjylland	(2) 2
BATE Borisov	(0) 0	Krylia	(1) 2
Besiktas	(1) 5	Vaduz	(1) 1
Bystrica	(0) 0	Groclin	(0) 0
Dnepr	(3) 4	Banants	(0) 0
Domzale	(0) 1	Ashdod	(0) 1
Genk	(3) 3	Metalurgs	(0) 0
Graz	(1) 1	Otaci	(0) 0
Keflavik	(0) 0	Mainz	(1) 2
Levski	(1) 3	Publikum	(0) 0
Lokomotiv Plovdiv	(0) 1	OFK Belgrade	(0) 0
Maccabi Petah Tikva	(3) 6	Baskimi	(0) 0
Maccabi Tel Aviv*	(0) 2	Apoel	(0) 2
Metalurg Donetsk	(0) 2	Matav	(0) 1
Omonia	(2) 2	Dinamo Bucharest	(0) 1
Red Star Belgrade	(3) 4	Inter Zapresic	(0) 0
Rijeka	(0) 2	Litets	(1) 1
Siroki	(3) 4	Zeta	(2) 2
Teplice	(0) 2	MTZ-RIPO	(0) 1
Tromso†	(0) 0	Esbjerg	(1) 1
Vardar	(1) 1	Rapid Bucharest	(0) 1
Wisla Plock	(3) 3	Grasshoppers	(1) 2
Zenit	(1) 1	Pasching	(0) 0
Zurich	(2) 4	Legia	(1) 1
Carmarthen	(0) 0	FC Copenhagen	(2) 2
Cork City	(0) 0	Djurgaarden	(0) 0
Dundee United	(2) 2	MyPa	(0) 2
Linfield	(0) 2	Halmstad	(3) 4
Viking	(2) 2	Rhyl	(1) 1

First Round, First Leg

Apoel	(0) 0	Hertha Berlin	(0) 1
Auxerre	(0) 2	Levski	(1) 1
Banik Ostrava	(2) 2	Heerenveen	(0) 0

Basle	(1) 5	Siroki	(0) 0
Beerschott	(0) 0	Marseille	(0) 0
Besiktas	(0) 0	Malmo	(0) 1
Brann	(1) 1	Lokomotiv Moscow	(0) 2
Brondby	(1) 2	Zurich	(0) 0
CSKA Moscow	(1) 3	Midtjylland	(1) 1
(Behind closed doors.)			
Feyenoord	(1) 1	Rapid Bucharest	(0) 1
Grasshoppers	(1) 1	MyPa	(1) 1
Graz	(0) 0	Strasbourg	(2) 2
Guimaraes	(1) 3	Wisla	(0) 0
Halmstad	(1) 1	Sporting Lisbon	(1) 2
Hamburg	(1) 1	FC Copenhagen	(1) 1
Krylia	(2) 5	AZ	(1) 3
Lens	(1) 1	Groclin	(1) 1
Leverkusen	(0) 0	CSKA Sofia	(1) 1
Litets	(0) 2	Genk	(0) 2
Maccabi Petah Tikva	(0) 0	Partizan Belgrade	(1) 2
Monaco	(1) 2	Willem II	(0) 0
PAOK Salonika	(1) 1	Metalurg Donetsk	(0) 1
Palermo	(2) 2	Anorthosis	(0) 1
Red Star Belgrade	(0) 0	Braga	(0) 0
Rennes	(1) 3	Osasuna	(0) 1
Roma	(4) 5	Aris Salonika	(1) 1
Setubal	(0) 1	Sampdoria	(1) 1
Sevilla	(0) 0	Mainz	(0) 0
Shakhtar Donetsk	(3) 4	Debrecen	(0) 1
Stuttgart	(1) 2	Domzale	(0) 0
Teplice	(0) 1	Espanyol	(0) 1
Tromso	(0) 1	Galatasaray	(0) 0
Valerenga	(0) 0	Steaua	(2) 3
Viking	(0) 1	FK Austria	(0) 0
Zenit	(0) 0	AEK Athens	(0) 0
Bolton Wanderers	(0) 2	Lokomotiv Plovdiv	(1) 1
Dinamo Bucharest	(1) 5	Everton	(1) 1
Hibernian	(0) 0	Dnepr	(0) 0
Middlesbrough	(1) 2	Xanthi	(0) 0
Slavia Prague	(0) 2	Cork City	(0) 0

First Round, Second Leg

AEK Athens	(0) 0	Zenit	(0) 1
AZ	(1) 3	Krylia	(1) 1
Anorthosis	(0) 0	Palermo	(1) 4
Aris Salonika	(0) 0	Roma	(0) 0
FK Austria	(1) 2	Viking	(1) 1
Braga	(0) 1	Red Star Belgrade	(1) 1
FC Copenhagen	(0) 0	Hamburg	(0) 1
CSKA Sofia	(0) 1	Leverkusen	(0) 0
Debrecen	(0) 0	Shakhtar Donetsk	(2) 2
Domzale	(1) 1	Stuttgart	(0) 0
Espanyol	(0) 2	Teplice	(0) 0
Galatasaray	(0) 1	Tromso	(1) 1
Genk	(0) 0	Litets	(0) 0
Groclin	(0) 2	Lens	(2) 4
Heerenveen	(2) 5	Banik Ostrava	(0) 0
Hertha Berlin	(2) 3	Apoel	(0) 1
Levski	(1) 1	Auxerre	(0) 0
Lokomotiv Moscow	(0) 3	Brann	(1) 2
Mainz	(0) 0	Sevilla	(2) 2
(Played in Frankfurt.)			
Malmo	(0) 1	Besiktas	(2) 4
Marseille	(0) 0	Beerschot	(0) 0
Metalurg Donetsk	(1) 2	PAOK Salonika	(2) 2
Midtjylland	(1) 1	CSKA Moscow	(0) 3
MyPa	(0) 0	Grasshoppers	(0) 3

Osasuna	(0) 0	Rennes	(0) 0
Partizan Belgrade	(2) 2	Maccabi Petah Tikvah	(3) 5
Rapid Bucharest	(1) 1	Feyenoord	(0) 0
Sampdoria	(1) 1	Setubal	(0) 0
Siroki	(0) 0	Basle	(1) 1
Sporting Lisbon	(1) 2	Halmstad	(1) 2
Steaua	(2) 3	Valerenga	(0) 1
Strasbourg	(2) 5	Graz	(0) 0
Willem II	(0) 1	Monaco	(0) 3
Wisla	(0) 0	Guimaraes	(0) 1
Zurich	(1) 2	Brondby	(0) 1
Cork City	(0) 1	Slavia Prague	(1) 2
Dnepr	(3) 5	Hibernian	(1) 1
Everton	(1) 1	Dinamo Bucharest	(0) 0
Lokomotiv Plovdiv	(0) 1	Bolton Wanderers	(0) 2
Xanthi	(0) 0	Middlesbrough	(0) 0

GROUP STAGE

GROUP A

CSKA Sofia	(0) 0	Hamburg	(0) 1
Viking	(1) 1	Monaco	(0) 0
Hamburg	(1) 2	Viking	(0) 0
Slavia Prague	(2) 4	CSKA Sofia	(1) 2
Monaco	(1) 2	Hamburg	(0) 0
Viking	(1) 2	Slavia Prague	(0) 2
CSKA Sofia	(1) 2	Viking	(0) 0
Slavia Prague	(0) 0	Monaco	(1) 2
Hamburg	(1) 2	Slavia Prague	(0) 0
Monaco	(0) 2	CSKA Sofia	(0) 1

Group A Final Table	P	W	D	L	F	A	Pts
Monaco	4	3	0	1	6	2	9
Hamburg	4	3	0	1	5	2	9
Slavia Prague	4	1	1	2	6	8	4
Viking	4	1	1	2	3	6	4
CSKA Sofia	4	1	0	3	5	7	3

GROUP B

Lokomotiv Moscow	(0) 0	Espanyol	(0) 1
Maccabi Petah Tikva	(1) 1	Palermo	(1) 2
Brondby	(0) 2	Maccabi Petah Tikva	(0) 0
Palermo	(0) 0	Lokomotiv Moscow	(0) 0
Lokomotiv Moscow	(0) 4	Brondby	(2) 2
Espanyol	(0) 1	Palermo	(1) 1
Brondby	(0) 1	Espanyol	(1) 1
Maccabi Petah Tikva	(0) 0	Lokomotiv Moscow	(1) 4
Espanyol	(0) 1	Maccabi Petah Tikva	(0) 0
Palermo	(2) 3	Brondby	(0) 0

Group B Final Table	P	W	D	L	F	A	Pts
Palermo	4	2	2	0	6	2	8
Espanyol	4	2	2	0	4	2	8
Lokomotiv Moscow	4	2	1	1	8	3	7
Brondby	4	1	1	2	5	8	4
Maccabi Petah Tikva	4	0	0	4	1	9	0

GROUP C

Halmstad	(0) 0	Hertha Berlin	(0) 1
(Played in Gothenburg.)			
Steaua	(3) 4	Lens	(0) 0
Lens	(2) 5	Halmstad	(0) 0
Sampdoria	(0) 0	Steaua	(0) 0
Halmstad	(1) 1	Sampdoria	(1) 3
Hertha Berlin	(0) 0	Lens	(0) 0
Sampdoria	(0) 0	Hertha Berlin	(0) 0
Steaua	(1) 3	Halmstad	(0) 0

| Hertha Berlin | (0) 0 | Steaua | (0) 0 |
| Lens | (1) 2 | Sampdoria | (1) 1 |

	Group C Final Table	P	W	D	L	F	A	Pts
	Steaua	4	2	2	0	7	0	8
	Lens	4	2	1	1	7	5	7
	Hertha Berlin	4	1	3	0	1	0	6
	Sampdoria	4	1	2	1	4	3	5
	Halmstad	4	0	0	4	1	12	0

GROUP D

Dnepr	(0) 1	AZ	(1) 2
Grasshoppers	(0) 0	Middlesbrough	(1) 1
Litets	(1) 2	Grasshoppers	(0) 0
Middlesbrough	(1) 3	Dnepr	(0) 0
AZ	(0) 0	Middlesbrough	(0) 0
Dnepr	(0) 0	Litets	(0) 2
Grasshoppers	(0) 2	Dnepr	(1) 3
Litets	(0) 0	AZ	(1) 2
AZ	(0) 1	Grasshoppers	(0) 0
Middlesbrough	(0) 2	Litets	(0) 0

	Group D Final Table	P	W	D	L	F	A	Pts
	Middlesbrough	4	3	1	0	6	0	10
	AZ	4	3	1	0	5	1	10
	Litets	4	2	0	2	4	5	6
	Dnepr	4	1	0	3	4	9	3
	Grasshoppers	4	0	0	4	3	7	0

GROUP E

Basle	(0) 0	Strasbourg	(2) 2
Tromso	(1) 1	Roma	(1) 2
Red Star Belgrade	(1) 1	Basle	(1) 2
(Behind closed doors.)			
Strasbourg	(1) 2	Tromso	(0) 0
Roma	(0) 1	Strasbourg	(0) 1
Tromso	(2) 3	Red Star Belgrade	(1) 1
Basle	(1) 4	Tromso	(3) 3
Red Star Belgrade	(1) 3	Roma	(1) 1
Roma	(2) 3	Basle	(0) 1
Strasbourg	(0) 2	Red Star Belgrade	(1) 2

	Group E Final Table	P	W	D	L	F	A	Pts
	Strasbourg	4	2	2	0	7	3	8
	Roma	4	2	1	1	7	6	7
	Basle	4	2	0	2	7	9	6
	Red Star Belgrade	4	1	1	2	7	8	4
	Tromso	4	1	0	3	7	9	3

GROUP F

CSKA Moscow	(0) 1	Marseille	(2) 2
Dinamo Bucharest	(0) 0	Heerenveen	(0) 0
Heerenveen	(0) 0	CSKA Moscow	(0) 0
Levski	(0) 1	Dinamo Bucharest	(0) 0
CSKA Moscow	(0) 2	Levski	(0) 1
Marseille	(0) 1	Heerenveen	(0) 0
Dinamo Bucharest	(0) 1	CSKA Moscow	(0) 0
Levski	(0) 1	Marseille	(0) 0
Heerenveen	(0) 2	Levski	(0) 1
Marseille	(2) 2	Dinamo Bucharest	(0) 1

	Group F Final Table	P	W	D	L	F	A	Pts
	Marseille	4	3	0	1	5	3	9
	Levski	4	2	0	2	4	4	6
	Heerenveen	4	1	2	1	2	2	5
	CSKA Moscow	4	1	1	2	3	4	4
	Dinamo Bucharest	4	1	1	2	2	3	4

GROUP G

Rennes	(0) 0	Stuttgart	(0) 2
Shakhtar Donetsk	(0) 1	PAOK Salonika	(0) 0
Rapid Bucharest	(1) 2	Rennes	(0) 0
Stuttgart	(0) 0	Shakhtar Donetsk	(1) 2
PAOK Salonika	(0) 1	Stuttgart	(0) 2
Shakhtar Donetsk	(0) 0	Rapid Bucharest	(0) 1
Rapid Bucharest	(1) 1	PAOK Salonika	(0) 0
Rennes	(0) 0	Shakhtar Donetsk	(1) 1
PAOK Salonika	(2) 5	Rennes	(0) 1
Stuttgart	(2) 2	Rapid Bucharest	(0) 1

Group G Final Table	P	W	D	L	F	A	Pts
Rapid Bucharest	4	3	0	1	5	2	9
Shakhtar Donetsk	4	3	0	1	4	1	9
Stuttgart	4	3	0	1	6	4	9
PAOK Salonika	4	1	0	3	6	5	3
Rennes	4	0	0	4	1	10	0

GROUP H

Besiktas	(1) 1	Bolton Wanderers	(1) 1
Zenit	(1) 2	Guimaraes	(0) 1
Bolton Wanderers	(1) 1	Zenit	(0) 0
Sevilla	(0) 3	Besiktas	(0) 0
Guimaraes	(0) 1	Bolton Wanderers	(0) 1
Zenit	(1) 2	Sevilla	(0) 1
Besiktas	(1) 1	Zenit	(1) 1
Sevilla	(3) 3	Guimaraes	(1) 1
Bolton Wanderers	(0) 1	Sevilla	(0) 1
Guimaraes	(1) 1	Besiktas	(2) 3

Group H Final Table	P	W	D	L	F	A	Pts
Sevilla	4	2	1	1	8	4	7
Zenit	4	2	1	1	5	4	7
Bolton Wanderers	4	1	3	0	4	3	6
Besiktas	4	1	2	1	5	6	5
Guimaraes	4	0	1	3	4	9	1

KNOCKOUT STAGE

THIRD ROUND FIRST LEG

Artmedia	(0) 0	Levski	(1) 1
Basle	(0) 1	Monaco	(0) 0
Betis	(0) 2	AZ	(0) 0
Bolton Wanderers	(0) 0	Marseille	(0) 0
FC Brugge	(0) 1	Roma	(1) 2
Heerenveen	(1) 1	Steaua	(1) 3
Hertha Berlin	(0) 0	Rapid Bucharest	(0) 0
Lille	(1) 3	Shakhtar Donetsk	(0) 2
Litets	(0) 0	Strasbourg	(1) 2
Lokomotiv Moscow	(0) 0	Sevilla	(0) 1
Rosenborg	(0) 0	Zenit	(2) 2
Schalke	(0) 2	Espanyol	(1) 1
Udinese	(1) 3	Lens	(0) 0
Slavia Prague	(1) 2	Palermo	(0) 1
Stuttgart	(0) 1	Middlesbrough	(1) 2

THIRD ROUND SECOND LEG

AZ	(2) 2	Betis*	(0) 1
Espanyol	(0) 0	Schalke	(0) 3
Hamburg	(2) 2	Thun	(0) 0
Lens	(0) 1	Udinese	(0) 0
Levski	(2) 2	Artmedia	(0) 0
Marseille	(1) 2	Bolton Wanderers	(1) 1
Middlesbrough	(0) 0	Stuttgart	(1) 1
Monaco	(1) 1	Basle	(0) 1

232

Palermo	(0) 1	Slavia Prague		(0) 0
Rapid Bucharest	(0) 2	Hertha Berlin		(0) 0
Roma	(0) 2	FC Brugge		(0) 1
Sevilla	(1) 2	Lokomotiv Moscow		(0) 0
Shakhtar Donetsk	(0) 0	Lille		(0) 0
Steaua	(0) 0	Heerenveen		(0) 1
Strasbourg	(0) 0	Litets		(0) 0
Zenit	(0) 2	Rosenborg		(1) 1

FOURTH ROUND FIRST LEG

Basle	(1) 2	Strasbourg	(0) 0
Lille	(1) 1	Sevilla	(0) 0
Marseille	(0) 0	Zenit	(0) 1
Middlesbrough	(1) 1	Roma	(0) 0
Palermo	(1) 1	Schalke	(0) 0
Rapid Bucharest	(1) 2	Hamburg	(0) 0
Steaua	(0) 0	Betis	(0) 0
Udinese	(0) 0	Levski	(0) 0

FOURTH ROUND SECOND LEG

Hamburg	(2) 3	Rapid Bucharest	(0) 1
Roma	(1) 2	Middlesbrough	(1) 1
Sevilla	(2) 2	Lille	(0) 0
Betis	(0) 0	Steaua	(0) 3
Levski	(0) 2	Udinese	(1) 1
Schalke	(1) 3	Palermo	(0) 0
Strasbourg	(1) 2	Basle	(2) 2
Zenit	(0) 1	Marseille	(0) 1

QUARTER-FINALS FIRST LEG

Basle	(2) 2	Middlesbrough	(0) 0
Levski	(1) 1	Schalke	(0) 3
Rapid Bucharest	(0) 1	Steaua	(1) 1
Sevilla	(1) 4	Zenit	(1) 1

QUARTER-FINALS SECOND LEG

Middlesbrough	(1) 4	Basle	(1) 1
Schalke	(0) 1	Levski	(1) 1
Steaua	(0) 0	Rapid Bucharest	(0) 0
Zenit	(0) 1	Sevilla	(0) 1

SEMI-FINALS FIRST LEG

Schalke	(0) 0	Sevilla	(0) 0
Steaua	(1) 1	Middlesbrough	(0) 0

SEMI-FINALS SECOND LEG

Middlesbrough	(1) 4	Steaua	(2) 2
Sevilla*	(0) 1	Schalke	(0) 0

UEFA CUP FINAL 2006

Wednesday, 10 May 2005

(in Eindhoven, 31,000)

Middlesbrough (0) 0   Sevilla (1) 4 *(Luis Fabiano 26, Maresca 78, 84, Kanoute 89)*

Middlesbrough: Schwarzer; Parnaby, Queudrue (Yakubu 70), Boateng, Riggott, Southgate, Morrison (Maccarone 46), Rochemback, Hasselbaink, Viduka (Cattermole 85), Downing.

Sevilla: Palop; Daniel Alves, Javi Navarro, Escude, David, Jesus Navas, Marti, Maresca, Adriano Correia (Puerta 85), Luis Fabiano (Renato 73), Saviola (Kanoute 46).

Referee: H. Fandel (Germany).

PAST EUROPEAN CUP FINALS

Year	Winner	Score	Runner-up	Score
1956	Real Madrid	4	Stade de Rheims	3
1957	Real Madrid	2	Fiorentina	0
1958	Real Madrid	3	AC Milan	2*
1959	Real Madrid	2	Stade de Rheims	0
1960	Real Madrid	7	Eintracht Frankfurt	3
1961	Benfica	3	Barcelona	2
1962	Benfica	5	Real Madrid	3
1963	AC Milan	2	Benfica	1
1964	Internazionale	3	Real Madrid	1
1965	Internazionale	1	SL Benfica	0
1966	Real Madrid	2	Partizan Belgrade	1
1967	Celtic	2	Internazionale	1
1968	Manchester U	4	Benfica	1*
1969	AC Milan	4	Ajax	1
1970	Feyenoord	2	Celtic	1*
1971	Ajax	2	Panathinaikos	0
1972	Ajax	2	Internazionale	0
1973	Ajax	1	Juventus	0
1974	Bayern Munich	1 4	Atletico Madrid	1 0
1975	Bayern Munich	2	Leeds U	0
1976	Bayern Munich	1	St Etienne	0
1977	Liverpool	3	Borussia Moenchengladbach	1
1978	Liverpool	1	FC Brugge	0
1979	Nottingham F	1	Malmö	0
1980	Nottingham F	1	Hamburg	0
1981	Liverpool	1	Real Madrid	0
1982	Aston Villa	1	Bayern Munich	0
1983	Hamburg	1	Juventus	0
1984	Liverpool†	1	Roma	1
1985	Juventus	1	Liverpool	0
1986	Steaua Bucharest†	0	Barcelona	0
1987	Porto	2	Bayern Munich	1
1988	PSV Eindhoven†	0	Benfica	0
1989	AC Milan	4	Steaua Bucharest	0
1990	AC Milan	1	Benfica	0
1991	Red Star Belgrade†	0	Marseille	0
1992	Barcelona	1	Sampdoria	0

PAST UEFA CHAMPIONS LEAGUE FINALS

Year	Winner	Score	Runner-up	Score
1993	Marseille	1	AC Milan	0
(Marseille subsequently stripped of title)				
1994	AC Milan	4	Barcelona	0
1995	Ajax	1	AC Milan	0
1996	Juventus†	1	Ajax	1
1997	Borussia Dortmund	3	Juventus	1
1998	Real Madrid	1	Juventus	0
1999	Manchester U	2	Bayern Munich	1
2000	Real Madrid	3	Valencia	0
2001	Bayern Munich†	1	Valencia	1
2002	Real Madrid	2	Leverkusen	1
2003	AC Milan†	0	Juventus	0
2004	Porto	3	Monaco	0
2005	Liverpool†	3	AC Milan	3
2006	Barcelona	2	Arsenal	1

† aet; won on penalties.   * aet.

234

PAST UEFA CUP FINALS

Year	Winner	Score		Runner-up	Score	
1972	Tottenham H	2	1	Wolverhampton W	1	1
1973	Liverpool	3	0	Borussia Moenchengladbach	0	2
1974	Feyenoord	2	2	Tottenham H	2	0
1975	Borussia Moenchengladbach	0	5	Twente Enschede	0	1
1976	Liverpool	3	1	FC Brugge	2	1
1977	Juventus**	1	1	Athletic Bilbao	0	2
1978	PSV Eindhoven	0	3	SEC Bastia	0	0
1979	Borussia Moenchengladbach	..1	1	Red Star Belgrade	1	0
1980	Borussia Moenchengladbach	..3	0	Eintracht Frankfurt**	2	1
1981	Ipswich T	3	2	AZ 67 Alkmaar	0	4
1982	IFK Gothenburg	1	3	SV Hamburg	0	0
1983	Anderlecht	1	1	Benfica	0	1
1984	Tottenham H†	1	1	RSC Anderlecht	1	1
1985	Real Madrid	3	0	Videoton	0	1
1986	Real Madrid	5	0	Cologne	1	2
1987	IFK Gothenburg	1	1	Dundee U	0	1
1988	Bayer Leverkusen†	0	3	Espanol	0·3	
1989	Napoli	2	3	Stuttgart	1	3
1990	Juventus	3	0	Fiorentina	1	0
1991	Internazionale	2	0	AS Roma	0	1
1992	Ajax**	0	2	Torino	0	2
1993	Juventus	3	3	Borussia Dortmund	1	0
1994	Internazionale	1	1	Salzburg	0	0
1995	Parma	1	1	Juventus	0	1
1996	Bayern Munich	2	3	Bordeaux	0	1
1997	Schalke*†	1	0	Internazionale	0	1
1998	Internazionale	3		Lazio	0	
1999	Parma	3		Marseille	0	
2000	Galatasaray†	0		Arsenal	0	
2001	Liverpool§	5		Alaves	4	
2002	Feyenoord	3		Borussia Dortmund	2	
2003	Porto*	3		Celtic	2	
2004	Valencia	2		Marseille	0	
2005	CSKA Moscow	3		Sporting Lisbon	1	
2006	Sevilla	4		Middlesbrough	0	

*After extra time **Won on away goals †Won on penalties §Won on sudden death.

UEFA CHAMPIONS LEAGUE 2006–2007

PARTICIPATING CLUBS
FC Barcelona (holders); Real Madrid CF; Valencia CF; CA Osasuna; Chelsea FC; Manchester United FC; Liverpool FC; Arsenal FC; Juventus; AC Milan; FC Internazionale Milano; ACF Fiorentina; Olympique Lyonnais; FC Girondins de Bordeaux; LOSC Lille Métropole; FC Bayern München; Werder Bremen; Hamburger SV; FC Porto; Sporting Clube de Portugal; SL Benfica; PSV Eindhoven; AFC Ajax; Olympiacos CFP; AEK Athens FC; RSC Anderlecht; R. Standard de Liège; Celtic FC; Heart of Midlothian FC; Galatasaray SK; Fenerbahçe SK; FC Slovan Liberec; FK Mladá Boleslav; PFC CSKA Moskva; FC Spartak Moskva; FK Austria Wien; SV Austria Salzburg; FC Shakhtar Donetsk; FC Dynamo Kyiv; Maccabi Haifa FC; FK Crvena Zvezda; Legia Warszawa; FC Zürich; Vålerenga IF; PFC Levski Sofia; NK Dinamo Zagreb; FC København; Debreceni VSC; FC Steaua Bucuresti; Djurgårdens IF; MFK Ružomberok; NK Gorica; Apollon Limassol FC; NK Široki Brijeg; FHK Liepajas Metalurgs; Myllykosken Pallo-47; FC Sheriff; FC Sioni Bolnisi; FK Ekranas; FH Hafnarfjördur; FK Rabotnicki; Cork City FC; FC Shakhtyor Soligorsk; FC Pyunik; Birkirkara FC; KS Elbasani; FC TVMK Tallinn; Linfield FC; The New Saints FC; F91 Dudelange; FK Baku; B36 Tórshavn; FK Aktobe.

UEFA CUP 2006–2007

PARTICIPATING CLUBS
Sevilla FC (holders); RCD Espanyol*; RC Celta de Vigo; Tottenham Hotspur FC;
Blackburn Rovers FC; West Ham United FC**; AS Roma; S.S. Lazio; AC Chievo
Verona; Paris Saint-Germain FC; RC Lens; AS Nancy-Lorraine***; FC Schalke 04;
Bayer 04 Leverkusen; Eintracht Frankfurt**; SC Braga; CD Nacional; Vitória FC**;
FC Groningen; AZ Alkmaar; Feyenoord; SC Heerenveen; Panathinaikos FC; Iraklis
FC; Skoda Xanthi FC; Atromitos FC; SV Zulte-Waregem*; Club Brugge KV;
KSV Roeselare*****; Rangers FC; Gretna FC; Beşiktaş JK; Trabzonspor; AC Sparta
Praha*; SK Slavia Praha; FC Lokomotiv Moskva; FC Rubin Kazan; SV Pasching;
SV Mattersburg; FC Chornomorets Odesa; FC Metalurh Zaporizhya**; Hapoel Tel-
Aviv FC*; Beitar Jerusalem FC; Bnei Yehuda Tel-Aviv FC; FK Partizan; FK Hajduk
Kula; OFK Beograd**; Wisła Płock*; Wisła Kraków; Zagebie Lubin; FC Sion*;
FC Basel 1893; BSC Young Boys; Molde FK*; IK Start; SFK Lyn Oslo;
SK Brann*****; PFC CSKA Sofia*; PFC Litex Lovech; PFC Lokomotiv Sofia;
HNK Rijeka*; NK Varteks; Randers FC*; Brøndby IF; FC Fehérvár*; Újpesti TE;
AFC Rapid Bucuresti*; FC Dinamo 1948 Bucuresti; IFK Göteborg; Åtvidabergs
FF**; Gefle IF*****; FC Artmedia; FC Spartak Trnava; FC Koper*; NK Domžale;
APOEL FC*; AC Omonia; NK Orašje*; FK Sarajevo; FK Ventspils*; Skonto FC*;
FC Haka*; HJK Helsinki; CSF Zimbru Chisinau; FC Nistru Otaci**; FC Ameri Tbil-
isi*; FC WIT Georgia; FBK Kaunas*; FK Suduva; IValur Reykjavík*; ÍA Akranes;
FK Makedonija GP Skopje*; FK Vardar; Drogheda United FC*; Derry City FC; FC
BATE Borisov*; FC Dinamo Minsk; FC Vaduz****; FC MIKA*; FC Banants; Hiber-
nians FC*; Sliema Wanderers FC; KF Tirana*; KS Dinamo Tirana; FC Levadia
Tallinn; FC Flora**; Glentoran FC; Portadown FC; Rhyl FC*; Llanelli FC;
AS Jeunesse Esch; FC Etzella Ettlebrück; FK Karabakh*; FK Karvan Evlakh; GÍ
Gøta*; Skála Ítróttarfelag; FC Tobol Kostanay; FC Kairat Almaty; FC Rànger's;
S.S. Murata; TBC, 11 Teams as winners of UEFA Intertoto Cup.

*domestic cup winners, **losing domestic cup finalists, ***domestic league cup
winners, ****national domestic title winners, *****Fair Play winners.

PAST EUROPEAN CHAMPIONSHIP FINALS

Year	Winners		Runners-up		Venue	Attendance
1960	USSR	2	Yugoslavia	1	Paris	17,966
1964	Spain	2	USSR	1	Madrid	120,000
1968	Italy	2	Yugoslavia	0	Rome	60,000
	(After 1-1 draw)					75,000
1972	West Germany	3	USSR	0	Brussels	43,437
1976	Czechoslovakia	2	West Germany	2	Belgrade	45,000
	(Czechoslovakia won on penalties)					
1980	West Germany	2	Belgium	1	Rome	47,864
1984	France	2	Spain	0	Paris	48,000
1988	Holland	2	USSR	0	Munich	72,308
1992	Denmark	2	Germany	0	Gothenburg	37,800
1996	Germany	2	Czech Republic	1	Wembley	73,611
	(Germany won on sudden death)					
2000	France	2	Italy	1	Rotterdam	50,000
	(France won on sudden death)					
2004	Greece	1	Portugal	0	Lisbon	62,865

EUROPEAN CHAMPIONSHIPS 2008

Top two from each group qualify for finals; Austria and Switzerland qualify as co-hosts.
Final Tournament June 7 to 29 2008. ;

GROUP A

16.08.06	Belgium v Kazakhstan
02.09.06	Poland v Finland; Serbia & Montenegro v Azerbaijan
06.09.06	Armenia v Belgium; Azerbaijan v Kazakhstan; Finland v Portugal; Poland v Serbia & Montenegro
07.10.06	Armenia v Finland; Kazakhstan v Poland; Portugal v Azerbaijan; Serbia & Montenegro v Belgium
11.10.06	Belgium v Azerbaijan; Kazakhstan v Finland; Poland v Portugal; Serbia & Montenegro v Armenia
15.11.06	Belgium v Poland; Finland v Armenia; Portugal v Kazakhstan
24.03.07	Kazakhstan v Serbia & Montenegro; Poland v Azerbaijan; Portugal v Belgium
28.03.07	Azerbaijan v Finland; Poland v Armenia; Serbia & Montenegro v Portugal
02.06.07	Azerbaijan v Poland; Belgium v Portugal; Finland v Serbia & Montenegro; Kazakhstan v Armenia
06.06.07	Armenia v Poland; Finland v Belgium; Kazakhstan v Azerbaijan
22.08.07	Armenia v Portugal; Belgium v Serbia & Montenegro; Finland v Kazakhstan
08.09.07	Azerbaijan v Armenia; Portugal v Poland; Serbia & Montengro v Finland
12.09.07	Armenia v Azerbaijan; Finland v Poland; Kazakhstan v Belgium
21.09.07	Portugal v Serbia & Montenegro
13.10.07	Armenia v Serbia & Montenegro; Azerbaijan v Portugal; Belgium v Finland; Poland v Kazakhstan
17.10.07	Azerbaijan v Serbia & Montenegro; Belgium v Armenia; Kazakhstan v Poland
17.11.07	Finland v Azerbaijan; Poland v Belgium; Portugal v Armenia; Serbia & Montenegro v Kazakhstan
21.11.07	Armenia v Kazakhstan; Azerbaijan v Belgium; Portugal v Finland; Serbia & Montenegro v Poland

Group B

16.08.06	Faeroes v Georgia
02.09.06	Georgia v France; Italy v Lithuania; Scotland v Faeroes
06.09.06	France v Italy; Lithuania v Scotland; Ukraine v Georgia
07.10.06	Faeroes v Lithuania; Italy v Ukraine; Scotland v France
11.10.06	France v Faeroes; Georgia v Italy; Ukraine v Scotland
24.03.07	Lithuania v France; Scotland v Georgia
28.03.07	Georgia v Faeroes; Italy v Scotland; Ukraine v Lithuania
02.06.07	France v Ukraine; Lithuania v Georgia; Faeroes v Italy
06.06.07	Faeroes v Scotland; France v Georgia; Lithuania v Italy
22.08.07	Faeroes v Ukraine
08.09.07	Georgia v Ukraine; Italy v France; Scotland v Lithuania
12.09.07	France v Scotland; Lithuania v Faeroes; Ukraine v Italy
13.10.07	Faeroes v France; Italy v Georgia; Scotland v Ukraine
17.10.07	France v Lithuania; Scotland v Georgia; Ukraine v Faeroes; Lithuania v Ukraine; Scotland v Italy
21.11.07	Georgia v Lithuania; Italy v Faeroes; Ukraine v France

Group C

02.09.06	Hungary v Norway; Malta v Bosnia; Moldova v Greece
06.09.06	Bosnia v Hungary; Norway v Moldova; Turkey v Malta
07.10.06	Greece v Norway; Hungary v Turkey; Moldova v Bosnia
11.10.06	Bosnia v Greece; Malta v Hungary; Turkey v Moldova
24.03.07	Greece v Turkey; Moldova v Malta; Norway v Bosnia
28.03.07	Hungary v Moldova; Malta v Greece; Turkey v Norway
02.06.07	Bosnia v Turkey; Greece v Hungary; Norway v Malta
06.06.07	Greece v Moldova; Bosnia v Malta; Norway v Hungary
08.09.07	Hungary v Bosnia; Malta v Turkey; Moldova v Norway
12.09.07	Bosnia v Moldova; Norway v Greece; Turkey v Hungary
13.10.07	Greece v Bosnia; Hungary v Malta; Moldova v Turkey
17.10.07	Bosnia v Norway; Malta v Moldova; Turkey v Greece
17.11.07	Greece v Malta; Moldova v Hungary; Norway v Turkey
21.11.07	Hungary v Greece; Malta v Norway; Turkey v Bosnia

Group D

02.09.06	Czech Republic v Wales; Germany v Republic of Ireland; Slovakia v Cyprus
06.09.06	San Marino v Germany; Slovakia v Czech Republic

07.10.06	Cyprus v Republic of Ireland; Czech Republic v San Marino; Wales v Slovakia
11.10.06	Republic of Ireland v Czech Republic; Slovakia v Germany; Wales v Cyprus
15.11.06	Cyprus v Germany; Republic of Ireland v San Marino
07.02.07	San Marino v Republic of Ireland
24.03.07	Cyprus v Slovakia; Czech Republic v Germany; Republic of Ireland v Wales
28.03.07	Czech Republic v Cyprus; Republic of Ireland v Slovakia; Wales v San Marino
02.06.07	Germany v San Marino; Wales v Czech Republic
06.06.07	Germany v Slovakia
22.08.07	San Marino v Cyprus
08.09.07	San Marino v Czech Republic; Slovakia v Republic of Ireland; Wales v Germany
12.09.07	Cyprus v San Marino; Czech Republic v Republic of Ireland; Slovakia v Wales
13.10.07	Cyprus v Wales; Republic of Ireland v Germany; Slovakia v San Marino
17.10.07	Germany v Czech Republic; Republic of Ireland v Cyprus; San Marino v Wales
17.11.07	Czech Republic v Slovakia; Czech Republic v Slovakia; Germany v Cyprus; Wales v Republic of Ireland
21.11.07	Cyprus v Czech Republic; Germany v Wales; San Marino v Slovakia

Group E

16.08.06	Estonia v Macedonia
02.09.06	England v Andorra; Estonia v Israel
06.09.06	Israel v Andorra; Macedonia v England; Russia v Croatia
07.10.06	Croatia v Andorra; England v Macedonia; Russia v Israel
11.10.06	Andorra v Macedonia; Croatia v England; Russia v Estonia
15.11.06	Israel v Croatia; Macedonia v Russia
24.03.07	Croatia v Macedonia; Estonia v Russia; Israel v England
28.03.07	Andorra v England; Israel v Estonia
02.06.07	Estonia v Croatia; Macedonia v Israel; Russia v Andorra
06.06.07	Andorra v Israel; Croatia v Russia; Estonia v England
22.08.07	Estonia v Andorra
08.09.07	Croatia v Estonia; England v Israel; Russia v Macedonia
12.09.07	Andorra v Croatia; England v Russia; Macedonia v Estonia
13.10.07	England v Estonia
17.10.07	Croatia v Russia; Macedonia v Andorra; Russia v England
17.11.07	Andorra v Israel; Israel v Russia; Macedonia v Croatia
21.11.07	Andorra v Russia; England v Croatia; Israel v Macedonia

Group F

02.09.06	Latvia v Sweden; Northern Ireland v Iceland; Spain v Liechtenstein
06.09.06	Iceland v Denmark; Northern Ireland v Spain; Sweden v Liechtenstein
07.10.06	Denmark v Northern Ireland; Latvia v Iceland; Sweden v Spain
11.10.06	Iceland v Sweden; Liechtenstein v Denmark; Northern Ireland v Latvia
24.03.07	Liechtenstein v Northern Ireland; Spain v Denmark
28.03.07	Liechtenstein v Latvia; Northern Ireland v Sweden; Spain v Iceland
02.06.07	Denmark v Sweden; Iceland v Liechtenstein; Latvia v Spain
06.06.07	Latvia v Denmark; Liechtenstein v Spain; Sweden v Iceland
22.08.07	Northern Ireland v Liechtenstein
08.09.07	Iceland v Spain; Latvia v Northern Ireland; Sweden v Denmark
12.09.07	Denmark v Liechtenstein; Iceland v Northern Ireland; Spain v Latvia
13.10.07	Denmark v Spain; Iceland v Latvia; Liechtenstein v Sweden
17.10.07	Denmark v Latvia; Liechtenstein v Iceland; Sweden v Northern Ireland
17.11.07	Latvia v Liechtenstein; Northern Ireland v Denmark; Spain v Sweden
21.11.07	Denmark v Iceland; Spain v Northern Ireland; Sweden v Latvia

Group G

02.09.06	Belarus v Albania; Luxembourg v Holland; Romania v Bulgaria
06.09.06	Albania v Romania; Bulgaria v Slovenia; Holland v Belarus
07.10.06	Bulgaria v Holland; Romania v Belarus; Slovenia v Luxembourg
11.10.06	Belarus v Slovenia; Luxembourg v Bulgaria; Holland v Albania
24.03.07	Albania v Slovenia; Luxembourg v Belarus; Holland v Romania
28.03.07	Bulgaria v Albania; Romania v Luxembourg; Slovenia v Holland
02.06.07	Albania v Luxembourg; Belarus v Bulgaria; Slovenia v Romania
06.06.07	Bulgaria v Belarus; Luxembourg v Albania; Romania v Slovenia
08.09.07	Belarus v Romania; Luxembourg v Slovenia; Holland v Bulgaria
12.09.07	Albania v Holland; Bulgaria v Luxembourg; Slovenia v Belarus
13.10.07	Belarus v Luxembourg; Romania v Holland; Slovenia v Albania
17.10.07	Albania v Bulgaria; Luxembourg v Romania; Holland v Slovenia
17.11.07	Albania v Belarus; Bulgaria v Romania; Holland v Luxembourg
21.11.07	Belarus v Holland; Romania v Albania; Slovenia v Bulgaria

WORLD CUP 2006 QUALIFYING RESULTS

EUROPE

* *Qualify with best second-placed record.*
† *Qualify for play-offs.*
■ *Denotes player sent off.*

GROUP 1

Skopje, 17 August 2005, 7000

Macedonia (0) 0

Finland (2) 3 *(Eremenko Jr 8, 45, Roiha 87)*

Macedonia: Madzovski; Sedloski, Petrov, Sumulikoski, Popov G, Vasoski (Popov R 66), Noveski, Mitreski A, Maznov, Nuhiji (Grozdanovski 62), Pandev (Nalimi 31).
Finland: Jaaskelainen; Tihinen, Hyypia, Pasanen, Heikkinen, Tainio, Kallio, Lagerblom (Litmanen 79), Eremenko Jr (Saarinen 85), Forssell (Roiha 62), Kuqi.
Referee: Messias (England).

Constanta, 17 August 2005, 8200

Romania (2) 2 *(Mutu 29, 41)*

Andorra (0) 0

Romania: Lobont; Contra, Chivu, Tamas, Rat (Pascovici 79), Dica, Petre F (Balan 72), Munteanu D (Tararache 46), Mutu, Niculescu C, Cocis.
Andorra: Koldo; Lima, Sivera, Escura (Javi Sanchez 46), Sonejee, Pujol, Ayala, Bernaus, Silva, Riera (Moreno 79), Rodriguez (Garcia 90).
Referee: Jakov (Israel).

La Vella, 3 September 2005, 1000

Andorra (0) 0

Finland (0) 0

Andorra: Koldo; Escura, Sivera, Lima I, Lima A, Jimenez, Juli Sanchez, Javi Sanchez (Riera 73), Ruiz (Fernandez 88), Sonejee, Pujol (Garcia 84).
Finland: Kaven; Kallio, Hyypia, Tihinen, Kopteff (Lagerblom 46), Saarinen, Kuivasto, Eremenko Jr (Riihilahti 64), Tainio, Forssell (Sjolund 75), Kuqi.
Referee: Vereecke (Belgium).

Erevan, 3 September 2005, 6000

Armenia (0) 0

Holland (0) 1 *(Van Nistelrooy 63)*

Armenia: Berezovski; Hovsepian, Dokhoyan, Arzumanian, Tadevosian, Khachatrian, Aleksanian K, Mkhitarian, Melikian (Aleksanian V 84), Manucharian (Ara Hakobian 17), Aram Hakobian (Aram Voskanian 80).
Holland: Van der Sar; Kromkamp (Vennegoor of Hesselink 63), Boulahrouz, Opdam, Van Bronckhorst, Landzaat (Sneijder 51), Maduro, Cocu, Kuijt, Van Nistelrooy, Van Persie (Van der Vaart 75).
Referee: Dougal (Scotland).

Constanza, 3 September 2005, 7000

Romania (1) 2 *(Mutu 28, 56)*

Czech Republic (0) 0

Romania: Lobont; Contra, Tamas, Chivu, Rat, Petre F (Badoi 52), Petre O, Munteanu D (Codrea 70), Cocis, Mazilu, Mutu (Bucur 87).
Czech Republic: Cech; Grygera, Bolf (Sivok 58), Ujfalusi, Jankulovsi (Pospech 14), Smicer, Poborsky, Polak, Heinz (Jun 72), Koller, Baros.
Referee: Hauge (Norway).

Olomouc, 7 September 2005, 12,015

Czech Republic (0) 4 *(Heinz 47, Polak 52, 76, Baros 58)*

Armenia (0) 1 *(Ara Hakobian 86)*

Czech Republic: Blazek; Grygera, Polak, Galasek, Poborsky, Koller, Skacel (Smicer 46), Baros (Jun 80), Heinz, Ujfalusi, Rozehnal (Sivok 70).
Armenia: Berezovski; Hovsepian, Dokhoyan, Arzumanian, Tadevosian (Melikian 64), Aleksanian V, Khachatrian (Tigranian 71), Aleksanian K, Mkrtchian, Ara Hakobian, Aram Hakobian (Petrosian 57).
Referee: Hansson (Sweden).

Tampere, 7 September 2005, 8000

Finland (3) 5 *(Forssell 11, 13, 62, Tihinen 42, Eremenko Jr 55)*

Macedonia (0) 1 *(Maznov 49)*

Finland: Kaven; Pasanen, Saarinen (Nyman 53), Hyypia, Tihinen, Heikkinen, Tainio (Johansson 82), Riihilahti (Kopteff 72), Kallio, Eremenko Jr, Forssell.
Macedonia: Jovcev; Bozinovski, Lazarevski, Mitreski A, Noveski, Mustafi, Popov R, Sumulikoski (Popov G 46), Grozdanovski (Ignatov 58), Pandev, Maznov.
Referee: Jakobsson (Iceland).

Eindhoven, 7 September 2005, 35,000

Holland (3) 4 *(Van der Vaart 23, Lima T 27 (og), Van Nistelrooy 42, 89)*

Andorra (0) 0

Holland: Van der Sar; Lucius (Vennegoor of Hesselink 67), De Cler, Cocu■, Boulahrouz, Opdam, Sneijder (Maduro 78), Van der Vaart, Van Nistelrooy, Robben, Van Persie.
Andorra: Koldo; Javi Sanchez, Fernandez, Lima T, Sivera, Sonejee, Jimenez (Juli Sanchez 76), Ayala, Bernaus, Ruiz (Escura 30), Silva (Riera 54).
Referee: Hanacsek (Hungary).

Prague, 8 October 2005, 17,478

Czech Republic (0) 0

Holland (2) 2 *(Van der Vaart 30, Opdam 37)*

Czech Republic: Cech; Grygera, Jiranek (Smicer 44), Ujfalusi, Rozehnal, Polak (Heinz 57), Rosicky, Poborsky, Galasek, Baros, Stajner (Jarolim 77).
Holland: Van der Sar; Kromkamp (De Jong 84), Boulahrouz (Vlaar 57), Opdam, Van Bronckhorst, Maduro, Landzaat, Van der Vaart, Van Nistelrooy, Kuijt, Robben (Van Persie 77).
Referee: Sars (France).

Helsinki, 8 October 2005, 10,117

Finland (0) 0

Romania (1) 1 *(Mutu 41 (pen))*

Finland: Jaaskelainen; Kallio, Hyypia, Kuivasto, Lagerblom, Saarinen (Kopteff 76), Heikkinen, Nyman (Johansson 63), Tainio, Forssell (Sjolund 74), Eremenko Jr.
Romania: Lobont; Contra (Badoi 54), Tamas, Iencsi, Rat, Petre F, Petre O, Cocis, Munteanu D, Mutu (Rosu 81), Mazilu (Niculae 90).
Referee: Guenov (Bulgaria).

La Valle, 12 October 2005, 250

Andorra (0) 0

Armenia (1) 3 *(Sonejee 39 (og), Aram Hakobian 52, Ara Hakobian 62)*

Andorra: Koldo; Ayala, Lima A, Lima I, Javi Sanchez, Riera (Jimenez 82), Ruiz, Sivera (Juli Sanchez 18), Sonejee, Bernaus, Vieira (Clemente 56).

Armenia: Kasparov; Aleksanian V (Melkonian 77), Aleksanian K, Arzumanian, Dokhoyan, Khachatrian, Tadevosian, Melikian, Mkhitarian (Art Voskanian 82), Ara Hakobian, Aram Hakobian (Aram Voskanian 80).
Referee: Stokes (Republic of Ireland).

Helsinki, 12 October 2005, 11,234

Finland (0) 0

Czech Republic (1) 3 *(Jun 6, Rosicky 51, Heinz 58)*

Finland: Jaaskelainen; Saarinen (Kopteff 12), Hyypia, Kuivasto, Kolkka, Kallio, Heikkinen, Lagerblom (Nyman 60), Tainio, Sjolund (Forssell 61), Johansson.
Czech Republic: Cech; Grygera, Rozehnal, Ujfalusi, Mares, Poborsky, Galasek, Rosicky (Stajner 86), Heinz, Smicer (Polak 60), Jun (Kovac 73).
Referee: Gonzalez (Spain).

Amsterdam, 12 October 2005, 50,000

Holland (0) 0

Macedonia (0) 0

Holland: Van der Sar; De Jong, Boulahrouz, Opdam, Van Bronckhorst, Landzaat (Sneijder 46), Maduro (Davids 64), Van der Vaart, Kuijt, Van Nistelrooy, Van Persie (Babel 85).
Macedonia: Milosevski; Noveski, Popov G (Sumulikoski 54), Mitreski I, Sedloski, Vasoski, Meglehski, Tasevski (Stojkov 71), Masev, Naumoski (Hristov 90), Pandev.
Referee: Farina (Italy).

Group 1 Final table	P	W	D	L	F	A	Pts
Holland	12	10	2	0	27	3	32
†Czech Republic	12	9	0	3	35	12	27
Romania	12	8	1	3	20	10	25
Finland	12	5	1	6	21	19	16
Macedonia	12	2	3	7	11	24	9
Armenia	12	2	1	9	9	25	7
Andorra	12	1	2	9	4	34	5

GROUP 2

Almaty, 17 August 2005, 9000

Kazakhstan (1) 1 *(Kenzhekhanov 20)*

Georgia (0) 2 *(Demetradze 51, 84)*

Kazakhstan: Lorya; Irismetov, Familtsev, Zhumaskaliyev, Kuchma, Azovsky M, Baizhanov, Travin, Kenzhekhanov (Nizovtsev 60), Larin (Chichulin 85), Khokhlov.
Georgia: Lomaia; Kaladze, Khizanishvili, Mentesheshvili (Mujiri 66), Tskitishvili, Gakhokidze, Kobiashvili, Kankava, Aladashvili (Ganugrava 90), Iashvili, Demetradze.
Referee: Stredak (Slovakia).

Tirana, 3 September 2005, 2000

Albania (0) 2 *(Myrtaj 54, Bogdani 56)*

Kazakhstan (0) 1 *(Nizovtsev 64)*

Albania: Lika; Hasi, Murati, Beqiri E, Cana, Lala, Skela, Haxhi (Agolli 46), Jupi, Myrtaj (Kaplani 90), Bogdani (Bushi 85).
Kazakhstan: Loriya; Irismetov, Smakov, Travin, Kuchma, Baltiev, Larin, Kenzhekhanov, Baizhanov (Nizovtsev 55), Zhumaskaliev (Karpovich 61), Khokhlov.
Referee: Slupik (Poland).

Tbilisi, 3 September 2005, 10,000

Georgia (0) 1 *(Gakhokidze 89)*

Ukraine (1) 1 *(Rotan 44)*

Georgia: Lomaia; Tskitishvili, Khizanishvili, Odikadze, Kaladze, Gakhokidze, Kankava, Kobiashvili (Gogua 75), Mentesheshvili (Mujiri 75), Asatiani M (Ashvetia 86), Demetradze.
Ukraine: Shovkovskyi; Fedorov, Nesmachni, Yezerski, Rusol, Shychenko (Rebrov 66), Gusin, Tymoschuk, Rotan, Shevchenko, Voronin (Nazarenko 73).
Referee: Ovrebo (Norway).

Istanbul, 3 September 2005, 30,000

Turkey (0) 2 *(Okan B 48, Tumer 81)*

Denmark (1) 2 *(Jensen C 41, Larsen 90)*

Turkey: Volkan; Hamit Altintop, Alpay, Ibrahim, Umit O, Hasan Sas (Okan B 46), Selcuk, Basturk (Huseyin 46), Tumer (Tolga 85), Hakan Sukur, Fatih.
Denmark: Sorensen; Priske (Gravgaard 46), Helveg, Agger, Jensen N (Larsen S 85), Poulsen, Jensen C, Gravesen, Rommedahl, Tomasson, Jorgensen (Gronkjaer 79).
Referee: Gonzalez (Spain).

Copenhagen, 7 September 2005, 27,177

Denmark (3) 6 *(Jensen C 9, Poulsen 30, Agger 42, Tomasson 54, Larsen 79, 83)*

Georgia (1) 1 *(Demetradze 36 (pen))*

Denmark: Sorensen; Helveg, Jensen N, Gravesen, Gravgaard, Agger, Poulsen (Kahlenberg 62), Jensen C (Larsen S 63), Tomasson (Perez 67), Jorgensen, Rommedahl.
Georgia: Lomaia; Kaladze, Khizanishvili■, Asatiani M, Gakhokidze, Odikadze (Ganugrava 62), Kobiashvili (Salukvadze 81), Demetradze (Mujiri 67), Mentesheshvili, Gogua, Tskitishvili.
Referee: Bozinovski (Macedonia).

Almaty, 7 September 2005, 15,000

Kazakhstan (0) 1 *(Zhumaskaliev 53)*

Greece (0) 2 *(Giannakopoulos 79, Liberopoulos 90)*

Kazakhstan: Loriya; Familtsev (Travin 74), Avdeyev, Smakov, Azovsky M (Larin 52), Kuchma, Karpovich■, Khokhlov, Zhumaskaliev (Baltiev 81), Litvinenko, Rodionov■.
Greece: Nikopolidis; Fyssas (Gekas 76), Kapsis, Seitaridis, Basinas, Giannakopoulos, Karagounis, Katsouranis (Kafes 60), Zagorakis, Charisteas, Vryzas (Liberopoulos 55).
Referee: Tudor (Romania).

Kiev, 7 September 2005, 60,000

Ukraine (0) 0

Turkey (0) 1 *(Tumer 55)*

Ukraine: Shovkovskyi; Fedorov, Vaschuk, Rusol, Nesmachni, Tymoschuk, Gusev, Rotan (Venhlinsky 68), Shelayev (Rebrov 79), Voronin (Gusin 84), Bielik.
Turkey: Volkan; Hamit Altintop, Alpay, Ibrahim, Umit D, Okan (Serhat 90), Selcuk, Gokdeniz (Huseyin 46), Tumer, Fatih (Hasan Sas 83), Hakan Sukur.
Referee: Sars (France).

Copenhagen, 8 October 2005, 42,099

Denmark (1) 1 *(Gravgaard 39)*

Greece (0) 0

Denmark: Sorensen; Poulsen, Gravgaard, Nielsen P, Jensen N, Priske, Gravesen, Jensen C (Larsen S 85), Tomasson, Jorgensen, Rommedahl (Gronkjaer 71).

Greece: Nikopolidis; Seitaridis, Basinas (Salpingidis 46), Zagorakis, Giannakopoulos, Vryzas (Gekas 76), Kapsis, Karagounis, Katsouranis, Kyrgiakos, Liberopoulos (Kafes 51).
Referee: De Bleeckere (Belgium).

Tbilisi, 8 October 2005, 10,000

Georgia (0) 0

Kazakhstan (0) 0

Georgia: Revishvili; Mjavanadze, Asatiani M, Salukvadze, Kaladze, Ganugrava, Kankava, Kobiashvili, Mujiri, Ashvetia (Tsinamdzgvrishvili 86), Demetradze.
Kazakhstan: Loriya; Mukanov, Kuchma (Familtsev 50), Smakov, Irismetov, Larin (Khokhlov 51), Azovsky M, Travin, Nizovtsev, Zhumaskaliev, Litvinenko (Kenzhekhanov 64).
Referee: Hyytia (Finland).

Dnepr, 8 October 2005, 26,000

Ukraine (1) 2 *(Shevchenko 45, Rotan 86)*

Albania (0) 2 *(Bogdani 75, 82)*

Ukraine: Shovkovskyi; Fedorov, Tymoschuk, Shelayev, Rusol, Rotan, Gusev, Voronin, Nazarenko (Vorobei 70), Shevchenko (Bielik 58), Shevchuk.
Albania: Lika; Beqiri E, Dallku, Cana, Hasi (Murati 84), Aliaj, Skela, Lala, Tare (Kapllani 70), Bogdani, Haxhi.
Referee: Verbist (Belgium).

Tirana, 12 October 2005, 13,200

Albania (0) 0

Turkey (0) 1 *(Tumer 57)*

Albania: Lika; Hasi, Dallku (Jupi 63), Beqiri E, Cana, Lala, Skela, Haxhi (Murati 50), Aliaj, Tare (Kapllani 73), Bogdani.
Turkey: Volkan; Hamit Altintop, Alpay, Ibrahim, Umit D, Okan B (Nihat 46), Huseyin, Basturk, Selcuk (Emre B 46), Tumer, Halil Altintop (Necati 90).
Referee: Ibanez (Spain).

Athens, 12 October 2005, 25,000

Greece (1) 1 *(Papadopoulos 17)*

Georgia (0) 0

Greece: Nikopolidis; Seitaridis, Dellas (Anatolakis 64), Goumas, Kapsis, Katsouranis, Zagorakis (Kafes 54), Basinas, Mantzios (Vryzas 46), Salpingidis, Papadopoulos.
Georgia: Revishvili; Mjavanadze, Khizanishvili, Salukvadze (Tsinamdzghvrishvili 46), Kaladze, Ganugrava, Kankava, Mujiri, Kobiashvili, Gogua, Demetradze (Gakhokidze 86).
Referee: Trefoloni (Italy).

Almaty, 12 October 2005, 17,000

Kazakhstan (0) 1 *(Kuchma 86)*

Denmark (0) 2 *(Gravgaard 46, Tomasson 49)*

Kazakhstan: Novikov; Avdeyev▪, Familtsev (Larin 56), Irismetov (Travin 66), Khokhlov, Kuchma, Litvinenko (Kenzhekhanov 51), Mukanov, Smakov, Zhumaskaliev, Karpovich.
Denmark: Sorensen (Christiansen 46); Priske, Gravgaard, Nielsen P, Jensen N (Helveg 88), Rommedahl (Kahlenberg 46), Poulsen, Jensen D, Jorgensen, Tomasson, Larsen S.
Referee: Trivkovic (Croatia).

243

Group 2 Final table

	P	W	D	L	F	A	Pts
Ukraine	12	7	4	1	18	7	25
†Turkey	12	6	5	1	23	9	23
Denmark	12	6	4	2	24	12	22
Greece	12	6	3	3	15	9	21
Albania	12	4	1	7	11	20	13
Georgia	12	2	4	6	14	25	10
Kazakhstan	12	0	1	11	6	29	1

GROUP 3

Riga, 17 August 2005, 9500

Latvia (1) 1 *(Astafjevs 6)*

Russia (1) 1 *(Arshavin 26)*

Latvia: Kolinko; Smirnovs, Stepanovs, Korablovs, Zirnis, Astafjevs, Bleidelis, Rubins, Laizans, Verpakovskis, Rimkus (Prohorenkovs 77).
Russia: Akinfeev; Evseev, Ignachevitch, Berezutski A, Sennikov, Arshavin, Karyaka (Bystrov 59), Khokhlov (Semshov 67), Kerzhakov, Aldonin, Bilyaletdinov (Kirichenko 83).
Referee: Poll (England).

Vaduz, 17 August 2005, 1150

Liechtenstein (0) 0

Slovakia (0) 0

Liechtenstein: Jehle; Michael Stocklasa (Ritzberger 89), Telser, Vogt (Frick D 80), Martin Stocklasa, Beck T, Wolfinger, Buchel R, Rohrer (Alabor 87), Buchel M, Beck R.
Slovakia: Contofalsky; Karhan, Kratochvil, Zabavnik, Had, Kisel, Mintal, Hlinka (Sninsky 46), Gresko (Slovak 56), Vittek, Jakubko (Reiter 46).
Referee: Layec (France).

Tallinn, 3 September 2005, 3000

Estonia (1) 2 *(Oper 11, Smirnov 70)*

Latvia (0) 1 *(Laizans 90)*

Estonia: Kotenko; Piiroja, Stepanov, Jaager, Kruglov, Leetma, Dmitrijev, Viikmae (Neemelo 57), Terehhov, Smirnov (Teever 78), Oper.
Latvia: Kolinko; Stepanovs, Smirnovs, Zirnis (Morozs 86), Korablovs, Laizans, Astafjevs, Bleidelis, Rubins, Verpakovskis (Solonicins 81), Rimkus (Prohorenkovs 75).
Referee: Mallenco (Spain).

Faro, 3 September 2005, 26,340

Portugal (3) 6 *(Jorge Andrade 22, Ricardo Carvalho 30, Pauleta 36, 56, Simao Sabrosa 78, 84)*

Luxembourg (0) 0

Portugal: Ricardo; Paulo Ferreira, Ricardo Carvalho, Jorge Andrade, Nuno Valente, Costinha, Deco (Helder Postiga 66), Maniche (Joao Moutinho 46), Figo, Pauleta, Ronaldo (Simao Sabrosa 60).
Luxembourg: Oberweis; Federspiel, Heinz, Strasser, Lang (Schnell 39), Reiter, Pace (Sagramola 61), Collette, Leweck A, Hoffmann, Remy (Sabotic 66).
Referee: Van Egmond (Holland).

Moscow, 3 September 2005, 18,123

Russia (1) 2 *(Kerzhakov 27, 66)*

Liechtenstein (0) 0

Russia: Akinfeev; Berezutski A, Ignachevitch, Berezutsky V, Anyukov, Smertin, Izmailov, Arshavin (Titov 74), Bilyaletdinov, Kerzhakov (Kirichenko 82), Pavluchenko (Aldonin 65).

Liechtenstein: Jehle; D'Elia, Buchel M (Fischer 68), Telser, Michael Stocklasa, Martin Stocklasa, Buchel R, Burgmeier, Vogt (Rohrer 46), Frick M, Beck T (Frick D 85).
Referee: Hyytia (Finland).

Riga, 7 September 2005, 8800

Latvia (0) 1 *(Laizans 74)*

Slovakia (1) 1 *(Vittek 35)*

Latvia: Kolinko; Korablovs (Zavoronkovs 24), Isakovs, Zakresevskis, Zirnis, Astafjevs, Bleidelis, Laizans, Rubins, Rimkus (Morozs 71), Verpakovskis.
Slovakia: Contofalsky; Had, Kratochvil, Skrtel, Valachovic (Varga 86), Zabavnik, Gresko, Karhan, Holosko (Kisel 77), Mintal (Hlinka 65), Vittek.
Referee: Plautz (Austria).

Vaduz, 7 September 2005, 1000

Liechtenstein (1) 3 *(Frick M 38, Fischer 77, Beck T 90)*

Luxembourg (0) 0

Liechtenstein: Jehle; Michael Stocklasa, Telser, Buchel M (Rohrer 76), Martin Stocklasa, Beck T, Buchel R (Beck R 83), Burgmeier, D'Elia, Fischer, Frick M (Frick D 89).
Luxembourg: Oberweis; Federspiel, Hoffmann, Strasser, Remy (Sabotic 63), Collette (Pace 80), Leweck C, Schnell, Reiter, Joachim■, Sagramola (Da Luz 69).
Referee: Skomina (Slovenia).

Moscow, 7 September 2005, 28,800

Russia (0) 0

Portugal (0) 0

Russia: Akinfeev; Berezutski A, Ignachevitch, Berezutski V, Sennikov, Bilyaletdinov, Aldonin, Izmailov (Semak 74), Smertin■, Arshavin (Anyukov 87), Kerzhakov.
Portugal: Ricardo; Paulo Ferreira, Jorge Andrade, Nuno Valente, Ricardo Carvalho, Costinha, Maniche (Joao Moutinho 83), Deco (Simao Sabrosa 76), Figo, Pauleta (Helder Postiga 68), Ronaldo.
Referee: Merk (Germany).

Aveiro, 8 October 2005, 30,000

Portugal (0) 2 *(Pauleta 49, Nuno Gomes 86)*

Liechtenstein (1) 1 *(Fischer 33)*

Portugal: Ricardo; Jorge Andrade, Nuno Valente, Paulo Ferreira, Ricardo Carvalho, Figo, Maniche (Tiago 72), Petit, Simao Sabrosa (Hugo Viana 75), Pauleta, Ronaldo (Nuno Gomes 84).
Liechtenstein: Jehle; Hasler, Martin Stocklasa, Telser, Michael Stocklasa, Beck T (Frick D 88), Buchel R, Burgmeier, D'Elia, Frick M (Rohrer 52), Fischer (Beck R 57).
Referee: Gilewski (Poland).

Moscow, 8 October 2005, 25,000

Russia (2) 5 *(Izmailov 7, Kerzhakov 18, Pavluchenko 65, Kirichenko 75, 90)*

Luxembourg (0) 1 *(Reiter 52 (pen))*

Russia: Akinfeev; Anyukov, Berezutski A, Sennikov, Berezutski V, Gusev, Izmailov (Semak 55), Loskov, Semshov, Arshavin (Pavluchenko 61), Kerzhakov (Kirichenko 68).
Luxembourg: Gillet; Hoffmann, Reiter, Schnell, Leweck A, Peters, Remy, Collette (Sabotic 77), Leweck C (Federspiel 76), Mannon (Da Luz 86), Mutsch.
Referee: Tudor (Romania).

Bratislava, 8 October 2005, 12,837

Slovakia (0) 1 *(Hlinka 76)*

Estonia (0) 0

Slovakia: Contofalsky; Had (Reiter 71), Kratochvil, Skrtel, Zabavnik, Hlinka, Hodur (Sapara 80), Kisel, Nemeth, Sestak (Holosko 46), Vittek.
Estonia: Kotenko; Jaager, Kruglov, Piiroja, Stepanov, Dmitrijev, Leetma (Rahn 86), Smirnov, Terehhov, Oper, Viikmae (Neemelo 37).
Referee: Allaerts (Belgium).

Luxembourg, 12 October 2005, 1000

Luxembourg (0) 0

Estonia (1) 2 *(Oper 7, 79 (pen))*

Luxembourg: Gillet; Kintziger, Leweck A, Hoffmann, Collette, Peters, Mutsch (Federspiel 73), Reiter, Remy, Leweck C (Da Luz 78), Mannon (Kitenge 57).
Estonia: Kotenko; Dmitrijev, Jaager, Piiroja, Klavan, Kruglov, Viikmae, Terehhov (Smirnov 63), Rahn (Reim 63), Oper, Neemelo.
Referee: Dereli (Turkey).

Oporto, 12 October 2005, 36,860

Portugal (2) 3 *(Pauleta 18, 20, Hugo Viana 85)*

Latvia (0) 0

Portugal: Quim; Miguel, Fernando Meira, Jorge Andrade, Caneira, Maniche, Tiago, Deco, Figo (Hugo Viana 80), Pauleta (Helder Postiga 56), Ronaldo (Nuno Gomes 46).
Latvia: Kolinko; Stepanovs, Astafjevs, Zakresevskis, Morozs, Isakovs, Zirnis, Solonicins (Visnakovs 52), Rimkus (Kalnins 56), Verpakovskis (Korablovs 73), Rubins.
Referee: Frofdfeldt (Sweden).

Bratislava, 12 October 2005, 30,000

Slovakia (0) 0

Russia (0) 0

Slovakia: Contofalsky; Kratochvil, Skrtel, Valachovic, Zabavnik, Hodur (Holosko 56), Karhan (Kisel 67), Hlinka, Had, Vittek, Nemeth (Durica 82).
Russia: Akinfeev; Berezutski A, Sennikov, Berezutski V, Bilyaletdinov (Semak 58), Arshavin, Anyukov (Pavluchenko 83), Smertin, Loskov, Kerzhakov (Kirichenko 67), Izmailov.
Referee: Rosetti (Italy).

Group 3 Final table	P	W	D	L	F	A	Pts
Portugal	12	9	3	0	35	5	30
†Slovakia	12	6	5	1	24	8	23
Russia	12	6	5	1	23	12	23
Estonia	12	5	2	5	16	17	17
Latvia	12	4	3	5	18	21	15
Liechtenstein	12	2	2	8	13	23	8
Luxembourg	12	0	0	12	5	48	0

GROUP 4

Toftir, 17 August 2005, 1500

Faeroes (0) 0

Cyprus (1) 3 *(Konstantinou M 39, 86 (pen), Krassas 90)*

Faeroes: Knudsen; Hansen, Johannesen O, Jacobsen JR, Danielsen, Olsen (Horg 14), Borg, Jacobsen R, Jorgensen, Flotum, Jonsson (Jacobsen C 46).

Cyprus: Morfis; Louka, Michael, Garpozis (Okkarides 63), Krassas, Charalambides, Theodotou (Charalambous 80), Makridis, Lufteris■, Okkas, Konstantinou M (Yiasoumi 87).
Referee: Johannesson (Sweden).

Lens, 3 September 2005, 40,126

France (2) 3 *(Cisse 13, 76, Olsen 19 (og))*

Faeroes (0) 0

France: Coupet; Sagnol, Thuram (Squillaci 76), Boumsong, Gallas, Makelele, Vieira, Zidane (Dhorasoo 58), Malouda, Cisse, Henry (Wiltord 67).
Faeroes: Mikkelsen; Horg (Jacobsen C 56), Johannesen O, Jacobsen JR, Olsen, Borg, Jorgensen (Lakjuni 76), Hojsted, Benjaminsen, Flotum, Jonsson (Jacobsen R 67).
Referee: Jara (Czech Republic).

Basle, 3 September 2005, 30,000

Switzerland (1) 1 *(Frei 5)*

Israel (1) 1 *(Keisi 20)*

Switzerland: Zuberbuhler; Degen P, Senderos, Muller, Magnin (Spycher 89), Gygax, Vogel, Barnetta, Yakin H (Cabanas 65), Frei, Vonlanthen (Lustrinelli 82).
Israel: Davidovitch; Saban, Harazi, Benado, Ben Haim, Nimni (Zandberg 71), Badir, Keisi, Tal, Benayoun (Suan 90), Katan (Golan 65).
Referee: Rosetti (Italy).

Nicosia, 7 September 2005, 3500

Cyprus (1) 1 *(Aloneftis 35)*

Switzerland (1) 3 *(Frei 15, Senderos 70, Gygax 84)*

Cyprus: Morfis; Elia, Okkarides (Lambrou 46), Louka, Aloneftis, Krassias (Nikolaou 64), Okkas, Charalambides, Konstantinou M, Michael (Yiasoumi 82), Charalambous.
Switzerland: Zuberbuhler; Degen P, Muller, Senderos, Spycher, Gygax, Vogel, Barnetta (Huggel 89), Wicky, Frei (Yakin H 73), Vonlanthen (Lustrinelli 81).
Referee: Ivanov (Russia).

Torshavn, 7 September 2005, 2240

Faeroes (0) 0

Israel (0) 2 *(Nimni 55, Katan 80)*

Faeroes: Mikkelsen; Horg, Johannesen O, Jacobsen JR, Olsen, Benjaminsen, Hojsted (Flotum 61), Borg (Lakjuni 69), Jacobsen R, Jorgensen (Samuelsen 85), Jacobsen C.
Israel: Davidovitch; Benado, Harazi, Ben Haim, Benayoun, Keissi, Nimni, Suan, Badir, Balili (Tal 66), Katan (Biton 86).
Referee: Vink (Holland).

Dublin, 7 September 2005, 36,000

Republic of Ireland (0) 0

France (0) 1 *(Henry 67)*

Republic of Ireland: Given; Carr, O'Shea, Roy Keane, Cunningham, Dunne, Reid A, Kilbane (Doherty 79), Robbie Keane, Morrison (Harte 79), Duff.
France: Coupet; Sagnol (Givet 89), Thuram, Gallas, Boumsong, Makelele, Wiltord, Vieira, Dhorasoo, Henry (Cisse 75), Zidane (Malouda 69).
Referee: Fandel (Germany).

Nicosia, 8 October 2005, 13,546

Cyprus (0) 0

Republic of Ireland (1) 1 *(Elliott 6)*

Cyprus: Panayiotou N; Elia (Maragos 74), Lambrou, Louka, Makridis, Michael, Konstantinou M (Krassas 30), Charalambides, Aloneftis, Okkas (Yiasoumi 70), Garpozis.
Republic of Ireland: Given; Carr, O'Shea, Kavanagh, Dunne, Cunningham, Finnan (Holland 46), Kilbane, Robbie Keane (Connolly 88), Elliott, Duff (Reid S 61).
Referee: Kassai (Hungary).

Tel Aviv, 8 October 2005, 21,500

Israel (1) 2 *(Benayoun 1, Zandberg 89)*

Faeroes (0) 1 *(Samuelsen 90)*

Israel: Davidovitch; Harazi, Benado, Keisi, Ben Haim, Badir, Suan (Zandberg 46), Nimni, Benayoun, Katan (Balili 73), Golan (Arbeitman 66).
Faeroes: Mikkelsen; Horg, Johannesen O, Jacobsen JR, Hansen (Danielsen 15), Benjaminsen, Flotum (Frederiksberg 66), Jacobsen C (Samuelsen 80), Hojsted, Jacobsen R, Jorgensen.
Referee: Brugger (Austria).

Berne, 8 October 2005, 31,400

Switzerland (0) 1 *(Magnin 79)*

France (0) 1 *(Cisse 52)*

Switzerland: Zuberbuhler; Degen P, Magnin, Muller, Senderos, Barnetta (Behrami 90), Cabanas, Vogel, Wicky (Lustrinelli 83), Frei, Vonlanthen (Gygax 60).
France: Coupet; Thuram, Gallas, Makelele, Reveillere, Boumsong, Malouda (Govou 90), Vieira, Dhorasoo (Cisse 46), Wiltord, Zidane.
Referee: Hauge (Norway).

Saint-Denis, 12 October 2005, 80,000

France (3) 4 *(Zidane 29, Wiltord 31, Dhorasoo 43, Giuly 84)*

Cyprus (0) 0

France: Coupet; Sagnol, Thuram, Boumsong, Gallas, Dhorasoo, Zidane, Vieira (Diarra 25), Govou (Jurietti 90), Cisse, Wiltord (Giuly 59).
Cyprus: Morfis; Elia, Lambrou, Louka, Garpozis (Maragos 46), Charalambides, Charalambous, Makridis (Nicolaou 81), Krassas, Yiasoumi (Filaniotis 63), Alòneftis.
Referee: Stark (Germany).

Dublin, 12 October 2005, 36,000

Republic of Ireland (0) 0

Switzerland (0) 0

Republic of Ireland: Given; Carr, Harte, O'Shea, Dunne, Cunningham, Holland, Reid A (Reid S 80), Morrison (Doherty 87), Robbie Keane (Elliott 68), Kilbane.
Switzerland: Zuberbuhler; Degen P, Muller, Senderos, Magnin, Barnetta (Gygax 89), Vogel, Cabanas, Wicky, Vonlanthen (Streller 53), Frei.
Referee: Merk (Germany).

Group 4 Final table	P	W	D	L	F	A	Pts
France	10	5	5	0	14	2	20
†Switzerland	10	4	6	0	18	7	18
Israel	10	4	6	0	15	10	18
Republic of Ireland	10	4	5	1	12	5	17
Cyprus	10	1	1	8	8	20	4
Faeroes	10	0	1	9	4	27	1

GROUP 5

Chisinau, 3 September 2005, 5000

Moldova (1) 2 *(Rogaciov 15, 49)*

Belarus (0) 0

Moldova: Hmaruc; Rebeja, Olexici, Catinsus, Priganiuc, Covalciuc (Frunza 86), Ivanov, Savinov, Rogaciov (Popovici 55), Boret (Bordian 46), Dadu.
Belarus: Zhevnov; Shtanyuk, Kulchi, Yaskovic, Omelyanchuk, Belkevich, Gurenko, Hleb A, Kalachev (Bulyga 56), Korytko (Hleb V 69), Kutuzov.
Referee: Duhamel (France).

Glasgow, 3 September 2005, 50,185

Scotland (1) 1 *(Miller 13)*

Italy (0) 1 *(Grosso 76)*

Scotland: Gordon; Alexander G, McNamara, Dailly, Weir, Webster, Hartley, Ferguson B, Miller (Beattie 77), Quashie (McCann 67), Fletcher.
Italy: Peruzzi; Zaccardo (Grosso 46), Nesta, Cannavaro, Zambrotta, Gattuso, Pirlo, Totti, De Rossi (Camoranesi 60), Iaquinta (Toni 71), Vieri.
Referee: Lubos (Slovakia).

Celje, 3 September 2005, 9000

Slovenia (1) 2 *(Cimirotic 3, Zlogar 83)*

Norway (2) 3 *(Carew 1, Lundekvam 24, Pedersen M 90)*

Slovenia: Mavric B; Knavs, Mavric M, Cesar, Ceh, Zlogar, Komac, Acimovic (Lavric 56), Filekovic (Koren 60), Cimirotic, Rodic.
Norway: Myhre; Hoiland, Lundekvam, Hagen, Bergdolmo, Solli (Andresen 66), Hestad, Grindheim, Pedersen M, Iversen (Braaten 11) (Arst 82), Carew.
Referee: Cantalejo (Spain).

Minsk, 7 September 2005, 38,000

Belarus (1) 1 *(Kutuzov 4)*

Italy (3) 4 *(Toni 6, 14, 55, Camoranesi 45)*

Belarus: Zhevnov; Yaskovic (Tarlovsky 33), Omelyanchuk, Shtanyuk, Lavrik, Kulchi (Korytko 80), Kovba, Belkevich, Hleb A, Bulyga, Kutuzov (Hleb V 76).
Italy: Peruzzi; Zaccardo, Nesta, Cannavaro, Grosso, Camoranesi (Barzagli 83), Pirlo, Gattuso, Totti, Gilardino (Barone 57), Toni (Iaquinta 67).
Referee: Temmink (Holland).

Chisinau, 7 September 2005, 7000

Moldova (1) 1 *(Rogaciov 34)*

Slovenia (0) 2 *(Lavric 47, Mavric M 57)*

Moldova: Hmaruc; Olexici, Savinov, Rebeja, Catinsus, Priganiuc, Covalciuc (Epureanu 89), Ivanov, Rogaciov (Popovici 90), Bordian, Dadu (Frunza 83).
Slovenia: Handanovic; Filekovic (Lavric 46), Mavric M, Cesar, Knavs, Koren, Ceh, Zlogar, Cimirotic (Pecnik 46), Rodic (Sukalo 89), Seslar.
Referee: Baskakov (Russia).

Oslo, 7 September 2005, 24,904

Norway (0) 1 *(Arst 89)*

Scotland (2) 2 *(Miller 21, 31)*

Norway: Myhre; Bergdolmo, Riise, Grindheim, Lundekvam, Riseth, Solli (Hestad 46), Andresen, Carew, Ostenstad (Arst 46), Valencia (Braaten 46).
Scotland: Gordon; Alexander G, Webster, Ferguson B, Weir, Pressley, Fletcher, McNamara, Hartley, Miller (McCann 40), McFadden (Beattie 72).
Referee: Hamer (Luxembourg).

249

Palermo, 8 October 2005, 19,611

Italy (0) 1 *(Zaccardo 77)*

Slovenia (0) 0

Italy: Peruzzi; Zambrotta, Nesta, Cannavaro, Grosso, Camoranesi, Pirlo (De Rossi 81), Gattuso, Toni (Vieri 88), Gilardino (Zaccardo 59), Totti.
Slovenia: Mavric B; Mavric M, Knavs, Cesar, Filekovic, Komac, Zlogar, Koren, Acimovic, Rodic (Siljak 87), Pokorn (Cimirotic 46).
Referee: Poulat (France).

Oslo, 8 October 2005, 23,409

Norway (0) 1 *(Rushfeldt 49)*

Moldova (0) 0

Norway: Myhre; Bergdolmo, Hagen, Hangeland, Grindheim, Hestad, Pedersen M, Riise, Iversen (Helstad 90), Johnsen M (Solli 63), Rushfeldt (Braaten 82).
Moldova: Hmaruc; Bordian (Boret 68), Catinsus, Lascencov, Olexici, Priganiuc, Savinov, Covalciuc, Ivanov (Gatcan 82), Dadu (Popovici 73), Rogaciov.
Referee: Bennett (South Africa).

Glasgow, 8 October 2005, 51,105

Scotland (0) 0

Belarus (1) 1 *(Kutuzov 6)*

Scotland: Gordon; Alexander G, Murray (Maloney 46), Ferguson, Pressley, Weir, Fletcher, Dailly, McCulloch, Miller, Hartley.
Belarus: Khomutovsky; Kulchi, Korytko, Ostrovski, Tarlovsky, Kovba, Bulyga (Sascheka 89), Lavrik, Hleb A, Kalachev, Kutuzov.
Referee: Szabo (Hungary).

Minsk, 12 October 2005, 16,000

Belarus (0) 0

Norway (0) 1 *(Helstad 72)*

Belarus: Khomutovsky; Kulchi, Ostrovski, Shtanyuk, Kalachev, Tarlovsky, Kovba (Kirilchik 58), Omelyanchuk, Sashcheka (Loshankov 64), Bulyga, Kutuzov.
Norway: Myhre; Hoiland, Hagen (Borgersen 81), Hangeland, Riise, Stromstad, Grindheim, Solli (Gashi 73), Pedersen M, Rushfeldt (Helstad 46), Iversen.
Referee: Plautz (Austria).

Lecce, 12 October 2005, 28,167

Italy (0) 2 *(Vieri 71, Gilardino 85)*

Moldova (0) 1 *(Gatcan 76)*

Italy: De Sanctis; Zaccardo, Bonera (Blasi 46), Materazzi, Grosso (Zambrotta 62), Diana, De Rossi, Barone, Iaquinta (Gilardino 68), Vieri, Del Piero.
Moldova: Pascenco; Lascencov, Catinsus, Priganiuc, Savinov, Olexici, Gatcan, Boret, Covalciuc, Rogaciov (Miterev 87), Dadu.
Referee: Benquerenca (Portugal).

Celje, 12 October 2005, 10,000

Slovenia (0) 0

Scotland (1) 3 *(Fletcher 4, McFadden 47, Hartley 84)*

Slovenia: Handanovic; Mavric M (Pecnik 25) (Ilic 62), Knavs, Cesar, Komac, Koren, Zlogar, Ceh, Acimovic, Cimirotic, Rodic (Siljak 53).
Scotland: Gordon; Alexander G, Murray, Dailly, Pressley (O'Connor 46), Weir, Fletcher, Quashie (Caldwell S 72), McFadden, Miller (Caldwell G 46), Hartley.
Referee: Temmink (Holland).

Group 5 Final table

	P	W	D	L	F	A	Pts
Italy	10	7	2	1	17	8	23
†Norway	10	5	3	2	12	7	18
Scotland	10	3	4	3	9	7	13
Slovenia	10	3	3	4	10	13	12
Belarus	10	2	4	4	12	14	10
Moldova	10	1	2	7	5	16	5

GROUP 6

Belfast, 3 September 2005, 11,909

Northern Ireland (0) 2 *(Elliott 60, Feeney 85 (pen))*

Azerbaijan (0) 0

Northern Ireland: Taylor; Baird, Capaldi, Davis, Hughes A, Craigan, Gillespie, Johnson, Quinn (Feeney 72), Healy (Jones S 79), Elliott (Robinson 89).
Azerbaijan: Kramarenko; Hajiyev, Sadygov, Amirbekov, Tagizade (Nabiyev 84), Kerimov, Kurbanov M (Ponomarev 65), Kuliyev E, Imamaliev, Muzika, Aliyev (Chukurov 74).
Referee: Stanisic (Serbia & Montenegro).

Chorzow, 3 September 2005, 45,000

Poland (2) 3 *(Smolarek 13, Kosowski 22, Michal Zewlakow 68)*

Austria (0) 2 *(Linz 61, 80)*

Poland: Boruc; Baszczynski (Michal Zewlakow 88), Bak, Klos, Rzasa, Sobolewski (Mila 73), Szymkowiak (Radomski 83), Kosowski, Zurawski, Rasiak, Smolarek.
Austria: Schranz; Hieblinger, Pogatetz, Standfest, Ehmann, Kuhbauer, Aufhauser, Stranzl, Ivanschitz, Schopp (Kiesenebner 81), Mayrleb (Linz 46) (Kuljic 84).
Referee: De Santis (Italy).

Cardiff, 3 September 2005, 70,715

Wales (0) 0

England (0) 1 *(Cole J 54)*

Wales: Coyne; Page (Collins J 65), Duffy, Robinson (Koumas 55), Gabbidon, Partridge, Davies S (Earnshaw 69), Fletcher, Hartson, Giggs, Ricketts.
England: Robinson; Young, Cole A, Gerrard (Richardson 84), Ferdinand, Carragher, Wright-Phillips (Defoe 68), Beckham, Rooney, Lampard, Cole J (Hargreaves 76).
Referee: Ivanov (Russia).

Baku, 7 September 2005, 5012

Azerbaijan (0) 0

Austria (0) 0

Azerbaijan: Kramarenko; Amirbekov, Hajiyev, Muzika (Bakhshiyev 78), Akhmedov, Kuliyev E, Kuliyev K, Tagizade (Nabiyev 88), Chukurov, Kerimov, Kurbanov G (Aliyev 90).
Austria: Schranz; Ibertsberger, Stranzl (Hieblinger 50), Pogatetz, Gercaliv (Kovacevic 83), Morz, Mayrleb (Kuljic 62), Kuhbauer, Linz, Ivanschitz, Amerhauser.
Referee: Verbist (Belgium).

Belfast, 7 September 2005, 14,000

Northern Ireland (0) 1 *(Healy 74)*

England (0) 0

Northern Ireland: Taylor; Baird, Capaldi, Davis, Hughes A, Craigan, Gillespie, Johnson, Quinn (Feeney 79), Healy (Sproule 88), Elliott (Duff 90).
England: Robinson; Young, Cole A, Beckham, Ferdinand, Carragher, Lampard (Hargreaves 80), Gerrard (Defoe 75), Owen, Rooney, Wright-Phillips (Cole J 54).
Referee: Busacca (Switzerland).

Warsaw, 7 September 2005, 13,500

Poland (0) 1 *(Zurawski 54 (pen))*

Wales (0) 0

Poland: Boruc; Baszczynski, Jop, Bak, Rzasa, Smolarek (Michal Zewlakow 86), Sobolewski, Szymkowiak, Kosowski (Radomski 79), Zurawski, Rasiak (Frankowski 65).
Wales: Coyne; Edwards (Duffy 45), Ricketts, Fletcher, Gabbidon, Collins J, Davies S, Koumas (Davies C 68), Earnshaw (Ledley 80), Giggs, Partridge.
Referee: Larsen (Denmark).

Old Trafford, 8 October 2005, 64,822

England (1) 1 *(Lampard 25 (pen))*

Austria (0) 0

England: Robinson; Young, Carragher, Gerrard, Terry, Campbell (Ferdinand 65), Beckham■, Lampard, Crouch, Owen (Richardson 81), Cole J (King 62).
Austria: Macho; Dober, Scharner, Stranzl, Ibertsberger (Lasnik 80), Schopp (Kuljic 64), Aufhauser, Kiesenebner, Weissenberger (Sariyar 46), Ivanschitz, Linz.
Referee: Cantalejo (Spain).

Belfast, 8 October 2005, 14,000

Northern Ireland (0) 2 *(Gillespie 46, Davis 50)*

Wales (2) 3 *(Davies S 27, Robinson 38, Giggs 61)*

Northern Ireland: Taylor; Duff (Jones S 82), Capaldi, Davis, Murdock, Craigan, Gillespie, Johnson, Quinn, Healy, Elliott (Brunt 65).
Wales: Jones P; Delaney, Ricketts (Collins D 87), Fletcher, Partridge, Collins J (Duffy 52), Davies S, Robinson, Hartson, Earnshaw (Vaughan 77), Giggs.
Referee: Bossen (Holland).

Vienna, 12 October 2005, 20,000

Austria (1) 2 *(Aufhauser 44, 90)*

Northern Ireland (0) 0

Austria: Macho; Dober (Ibertsberger 46), Scharner, Pogatetz■, Stranzl, Schopp (Standfest 55), Kiesenebner, Aufhauser, Ivanschitz, Wallner (Gercaliv 77), Linz.
Northern Ireland: Taylor; Duff, Baird, Davis, Murdock, Craigan, Gillespie, Johnson■, Healy, Quinn (Feeney 56), Brunt (Elliott 76).
Referee: Briakos (Greece).

Old Trafford, 12 October 2005, 65,467

England (1) 2 *(Owen 44, Lampard 80)*

Poland (1) 1 *(Frankowski 45)*

England: Robinson; Young, Carragher, King, Terry, Ferdinand, Wright-Phillips (Crouch 66), Lampard, Rooney, Owen (Jenas 83), Cole J (Smith 86).
Poland: Boruc; Baszczynski, Jop, Bak, Kosowski, Sobolewski (Radomski 78), Lewandowski M, Michal Zewlakow, Smolarek (Krzynowek 46), Zurawski (Frankowski 38), Rasiak.
Referee: Nielsen (Denmark).

Cardiff, 12 October 2005, 50,000

Wales (1) 2 *(Giggs 3, 51)*

Azerbaijan (0) 0

Wales: Jones P; Duffy, Collins D (Ricketts 54), Fletcher (Crofts 69), Gabbidon, Vaughan, Davies S, Robinson, Hartson, Giggs (Cotterill 73), Collins J.
Azerbaijan: Kramarenko; Chukurov (Poladov 69), Agayev, Sadygov, Amirbekov (Bakhshiyev 80), Kerimov, Kuliyev V, Muzika, Ismailov, Imamaliev, Tagizade.
Referee: Hansson (Sweden).

Group 6 Final table

	P	W	D	L	F	A	Pts
England	10	8	1	1	17	5	25
*Poland	10	8	0	2	27	9	24
Austria	10	4	3	3	15	12	15
Northern Ireland	10	2	3	5	10	18	9
Wales	10	2	2	6	10	15	8
Azerbaijan	10	0	3	7	1	21	3

GROUP 7

Zenica, 3 September 2005, 15,000

Bosnia (0) 1 *(Barbarez 62)*

Belgium (0) 0

Bosnia: Hasagic; Spahic, Berberovic, Papac, Music, Bartolovic (Jakirovic 88), Grujic, Bajramovic, Milenkovic (Hrgovic 77), Barbarez, Bolic (Misimovic 72).
Belgium: Proto; Vanden Borre (Daerden 78), Kompany, Van Buyten, Deschacht, Mpenza M, Vanderhaeghe, Simons, Van Damme (Garaerts 78), Buffel (Vandenbergh 68), Pieroni.
Referee: Benquerenca (Portugal).

Belgrade, 3 September 2005, 25,000

Serbia-Montenegro (1) 2 *(Kezman 18, Ilic 75)*

Lithuania (0) 0

Serbia-Montenegro: Jevric; Gavrancic, Vidic, Krstajic, Dragutinovic, Duljaj, Stankovic, Djordjevic P, Ilic (Vukic 82), Kezman (Zigic 74), Milosevic (Koroman 59).
Lithuania: Karcemarskas; Semberas, Dziaukstas (Zutautas 80), Paulauskas, Skerla, Skarbalius, Cesnauskis E, Jankauskas, Savenas (Preiksaitis 70), Mikoliunas (Radzinevicius 66), Cesnauskis D.
Referee: Nielsen (Denmark).

Antwerp, 7 September 2005, 8000

Belgium (3) 8 *(Simons 34 (pen), Daerden 39, 67, Buffel 44, Mpenza M 52, 71, Vandenbergh 53, Van Buyten 83)*

San Marino (0) 0

Belgium: Proto; Deschacht, Kompany (Daerden 12), Simons, Van Buyten, Vanden Borre (Hoefkens 69), Goor, Vanderhaeghe (Bisconti 69), Buffel, Mpenza M, Vandenbergh.
San Marino: Ceccoli; Valentini C[a], Andreini, Crescentini (Nanni L 76), Della Valle, Bacciocchi, Maiani (Selva R 61), Domeniconi, Gasperoni A, Selva A, Moretti M (Ciacci 70).
Referee: Stokes (Republic of Ireland).

Vilnius, 7 September 2005, 4000

Lithuania (0) 0

Bosnia (1) 1 *(Barbarez 28)*

Lithuania: Karcemarskas; Semberas, Dziaukstas, Stankevicius, Cesnauskis D (Mikoliunas 66), Zvirgzdauskas, Skarbalius (Savenas 46), Cesnauskis E[a], Jankauskas, Danilevicius, Poskus.
Bosnia: Hasagic; Milenkovic, Bajic, Papac, Berberovic, Grlic, Bajramovic, Music (Jakirovic 64), Beslija (Bartolovic 59), Barbarez, Bolic (Misimovic 87).
Referee: Kassai (Hungary).

Madrid, 7 September 2005, 55,000

Spain (1) 1 *(Raul 18)*

Serbia-Montenegro (0) 1 *(Kezman 68)*

Spain: Casillas; Michel Salgado, Del Horno, Marchena, Xabi Alonso, Puyol, Vicente (Luque 74), Xavi, Raul, Fernando Torres (Tamudo 53), Joaquin (Luis Garcia 66).
Serbia-Montenegro: Jevric; Djordjevic P, Dragutinovic, Gavrancic, Krstajic, Vidic, Duljaj■, Koroman (Maric 84), Ilic (Zigic 46) (Kovacevic N 90), Stankovic, Kezman.
Referee: Farina (Italy).

Brussels, 8 October 2005, 40,000

Belgium (0) 0

Spain (0) 2 *(Fernando Torres 56, 59)*

Belgium: Proto; Deschacht, Hoefkens, Simons, Van Buyten, Vanden Borre (Deflandre 61), Goor, Vanderhaeghe, Buffel (Walasiak 61), Mpenza M (Pieroni 74), Mpenza E.
Spain: Casillas; Michel Salgado, Antonio Lopez, Marchena, Puyol, Albelda, Xavi, Joaquin (Villa 52), Vicente (Reyes 52), Fernando Torres (Baraja 68), Raul.
Referee: Michel (Slovakia).

Zenica, 8 October 2005, 7000

Bosnia (0) 3 *(Bolic 48, 75, 85)*

San Marino (0) 0

Bosnia: Hasagic; Spahic, Music, Bajic, Konjic, Grlic, Grujic, Barbarez, Salihamidzic, Bolic, Bartolovic.
San Marino: Ceccoli; Andreini, Vannucci, Crescentini (Palazzi 71), Della Valle, Nanni L, Domeniconi (Moretti M 90), Gasperoni A, Selva A, Manuel Marani (Montagna 80), Michele Marani.
Referee: Hamer (Luxembourg).

Vilnius, 8 October 2005, 3000

Lithuania (0) 0

Serbia-Montenegro (1) 2 *(Kezman 42, Vukic 88)*

Lithuania: Karcemarskas; Stankevicius, Dziaukstas, Paulauskas (Laurisas 77), Skerla, Preiksaitis, Savenas, Cesnauskis D, Jankauskas, Mikoliunas (Morinas 60), Danilevicius (Radzinevicius 88).
Serbia-Montenegro: Jevric; Vidic, Gavrancic, Nadj, Kezman, Stankovic (Mladenovic 10), Djordjevic P, Vukic, Lukovic, Zigic (Ljuboja 56), Krstajic.
Referee: Wegereef (Holland).

Vilnius, 12 October 2005, 2000

Lithuania (1) 1 *(Deschacht 38 (og))*

Belgium (1) 1 *(Garaerts 20)*

Lithuania: Karcemarskas; Zutautas, Skerla, Dziaukstas, Paulauskas, Preiksaitis, Semberas■, Stankevicius (Radzinevicius 90), Morinas (Mikoliunas 83), Danilevicius, Savenas.
Belgium: Proto; Deflandre, Hoefkens (Maertens 46), Simons, Deschacht, Walasiak, Vanderhaeghe, Garaerts (Vanden Borre 46), Goor, Mpenza M, Mpenza E.
Referee: Riley (England).

Serravalle, 12 October 2005, 3400

San Marino (0) 0

Spain (3) 6 *(Antonio Lopez 1, Fernando Torres 10, 76 (pen), 88, Sergio Ramos 30, 49)*

San Marino: Gasperoni F; Andreini (Palazzi 84), Bacciocchi, Nanni L, Della Valle, Vannucci, Gasperoni A, Domeniconi, Manuel Marani (Nanni F 87), Michele Marani, Montagna (Masi 71).

254

Spain: Casillas; Sergio Ramos, Juanito, Pablo, Antonio Lopez, De La Pena, Albelda, Raul (Mista 73), Reyes (Vicente 68), Fernando Torres, Villa (Baraja 58).
Referee: Meyer (Germany).

Belgrade, 12 October 2005, 55,000

Serbia-Montenegro (1) 1 *(Kezman 7)*

Bosnia (0) 0

Serbia-Montenegro: Jevric; Gavrancic, Vidic■, Krstajic, Koroman, Nadj (Ilic 72), Duljaj, Djordjevic P, Vukic (Mladenovic 66), Kezman (Lukovic 87), Zigic.
Bosnia: Hasagic; Berberovic, Music (Beslija 65), Spahic, Bajramovic, Milenkovic, Salihamidzic, Barbarez, Grlic (Bartolovic 46), Jakirovic, Bolic (Misimovic 70).
Referee: Vassaras (Greece).

Group 7 Final table	P	W	D	L	F	A	Pts
Serbia-Montenegro	10	6	4	0	16	1	22
†Spain	10	5	5	0	19	3	20
Bosnia	10	4	4	2	12	9	16
Belgium	10	3	3	4	16	11	12
Lithuania	10	2	4	4	8	9	10
San Marino	10	0	0	10	2	40	0

GROUP 8

Budapest, 3 September 2005, 10,000

Hungary (1) 4 *(Torghelle 35, Wellman 57 (og), Takacs 65, Rajczi 85)*

Malta (0) 0

Hungary: Kiraly; Bodnar, Juhasz, Vanczak, Halmosi, Boor (Huszti 58), Gera (Buzsaky 76), Takacs, Hajnal, Kenesei (Rajczi 69), Torghelle.
Malta: Haber; Pullicino, Wellman, Said, Scicluna (Zahra 54), Mattocks, Briffa, Woods, Grima (Sammut 68), Anonam, Cohen (Ciantar 85).
Referee: Godulyan (Ukraine).

Reykjavik, 3 September 2005, 5000

Iceland (1) 1 *(Gudjohnsen E 24)*

Croatia (1) 3 *(Balaban 56, 61, Srna 82)*

Iceland: Arason; Sigurdsson K, Helgason (Arnason 79), Hreidarsson, Sigurdsson I (Vidarsson 43), Steinsson, Gunnarsson B, Gislason, Einarsson, Gudjohnsen E, Helguson (Thorvaldsson 24).
Croatia: Pletikosa; Srna, Kovac R, Simunic, Simic, Tudor, Kovac N, Kranjcar, Babic (Bosnjak 82), Balaban, Prso.
Referee: Stark (Germany).

Stockholm, 3 September 2005, 33,883

Sweden (0) 3 *(Ljungberg 60, Mellberg 75, Ibrahimovic 90)*

Bulgaria (0) 0

Sweden: Isaksson; Ostlund, Mellberg, Lucic, Edman, Wilhelmsson (Jonson M 80), Linderoth, Kallstrom (Alexandersson N 72), Ljungberg (Andersson D 90), Ibrahimovic, Larsson.
Bulgaria: Ivankov; Kishishev, Iliev V, Topuzakov, Petkov I, Georgiev■, Yankov (Iliev G 77), Petrov S, Petrov M, Lazarov (Kamburov 77), Ivanov G (Gargorov 58).
Referee: De Bleeckere (Belgium).

Sofia, 7 September 2005, 4836

Bulgaria (1) 3 *(Berbatov 21, Iliev G 69, Petrov M 86)*

Iceland (2) 2 *(Steinsson 9, Hreidarsson 16)*

Bulgaria: Ivankov; Iliev V, Petkov I, Kishishev, Topuzakov, Gargorov (Karaslavov 90), Yankov (Iliev G 46), Berbatov, Lazarov (Genkov 77), Petrov M, Petrov S.
Iceland: Arason; Sigurdsson K, Hreidarsson, Sigurdsson I, Gunnarsson B, Gislason, Helgason, Arnason (Vidarsson 75), Steinsson, Helguson, Gudjohnsen E.
Referee: Demirlek (Turkey).

Budapest, 7 September 2005, 30,000

Hungary (0) 0

Sweden (0) 1 *(Ibrahimovic 90)*

Hungary: Kiraly; Bodnar, Juhasz (Gyepes 46), Eger, Vanczak, Boor (Halmosi 87), Takacs, Hajnal (Kerekez 90), Huszti, Gera, Torghelle.
Sweden: Isaksson; Andersson C, Lucic, Ostlund, Mellberg, Alexandersson N, Linderoth, Wilhelmsson, Ibrahimovic (Allback 90), Larsson (Jonson M 82), Ljungberg.
Referee: Poll (England).

Ta'Qali, 7 September 2005, 4000

Malta (0) 1 *(Wellman 74)*

Croatia (1) 1 *(Kranjcar 19)*

Malta: Haber; Wellman, Scicluna (Sammut 46), Said, Pullicino, Agius G, Briffa, Anonam, Woods, Mattocks (Ciantar 73), Cohen (Grima 89).
Croatia: Pletikosa; Simunic, Tokic, Simic (Klasnic 80), Seric (Leko J 67), Babic, Kovac N, Srna, Kranjcar, Prso, Balaban (Bosnjak 68).
Referee: Briakos (Greece).

Sofia, 8 October 2005, 4652

Bulgaria (1) 2 *(Berbatov 30, Lazarov 55)*

Hungary (0) 0

Bulgaria: Ivankov; Iliev V, Topuzakov, Venkov, Iliev G, Kishishev, Lazarov (Georgiev 61), Petrov S (Kamburov 73), Yankov (Gargorov 68), Berbatov, Petrov M.
Hungary: Kiraly; Bodnar, Gyepes, Stark, Vanczak, Buzsaky (Kovacs 75), Hajnal, Halmosi (Kerekes 46), Huszti, Balog Z, Torghelle■.
Referee: Delevic (Serbia-Montenegro).

Zagreb, 8 October 2005, 15,000

Croatia (0) 1 *(Srna 56 (pen))*

Sweden (0) 0

Croatia: Butina; Srna, Simunic, Kovac R, Tudor, Tomas, Kranjcar, Babic, Prso (Simic 90), Kovac N, Klasnic (Bosnjak 70).
Sweden: Isaksson; Ostlund, Mellberg, Lucic, Edman, Linderoth (Wilhelmsson 66), Alexandersson N, Anders Svensson (Kallstrom 71), Ljungberg, Jonson M (Elmander 64), Larsson.
Referee: De Santis (Italy).

Budapest, 12 October 2005, 11,000

Hungary (0) 0

Croatia (0) 0

Hungary: Kiraly; Bodnar, Stark, Gyepes, Vanczak, Korsos G, Boor, Huszti, Baranyos (Buzsaky 76), Hajnal, Kovacs.
Croatia: Srna, Kovac R, Tudor, Vranjes, Babic, Tokic, Tomas, Leko I (Leko J 63), Klasnic (Bosnjak 63) (Simic 90), Balaban.
Referee: Larsen (Denmark).

Valletta, 12 October 2005, 6000

Malta (0) 1 *(Barbara 78)*

Bulgaria (0) 1 *(Yankov 66)*

Malta: Haber; Ciantar, Azzopardi (Zahra 65), Said, Dimech, Briffa, Wellman, Pullicino, Woods (Barbara 70), Mallia, Cohen (Grima 88).
Bulgaria: Kolev; Iliev V, Tupyzakov, Venkov, Gargarov, Iliev G, Kishishev (Kamburov 87), Yankov, Petrov M (Lazarov 46), Berbatov, Bojinov (Georgiev 60).
Referee: Godulyan (Ukraine).

Stockholm, 12 October 2005, 33,716

Sweden (2) 3 *(Ibrahimovic 29, Larsson 42, Kallstrom 90)*

Iceland (1) 1 *(Arnason 25)*

Sweden: Isaksson; Ostlund, Mellberg, Lucic, Edman, Wilhelmsson (Alexandersson N 66), Linderoth, Anders Svensson (Kallstrom 74), Ljungberg, Ibrahimovic (Allback 74), Larsson.
Iceland: Arason; Sigurdsson K, Helgason, Jonsson, Sigurdsson I, Steinsson, Gunnarsson G (Vidarsson 84), Thorvaldsson (Sigurdsson H 74), Gislason, Arnason (Einarsson 70), Helguson.
Referee: Ivanov (Russia).

Group 8 Final table	P	W	D	L	F	A	Pts
Croatia	10	7	3	0	21	5	24
*Sweden	10	8	0	2	30	4	24
Bulgaria	10	4	3	3	17	17	15
Hungary	10	4	2	4	13	14	14
Iceland	10	1	1	8	14	27	4
Malta	10	0	3	7	4	32	3

SOUTH AMERICA

Final table	P	W	D	L	F	A	Pts
Brazil	18	9	7	2	35	17	34
Argentina	18	10	4	4	29	17	34
Ecuador	18	8	4	6	23	19	28
Paraguay	18	8	4	6	23	23	28
Uruguay	18	6	7	5	23	28	25
Colombia	18	6	6	6	24	16	24
Chile	18	5	7	6	18	22	22
Peru	18	4	6	8	20	28	18
Venezuela	18	5	3	10	20	28	18
Bolivia	18	4	2	12	20	37	14

Top four qualified for finals; Uruguay played Australia (Oceania winner) for place in finals.

ASIA

Top two in each group qualified for finals: Saudi Arabia, South Korea, Iran, Japan.

CONCACAF

USA, Mexico and Costa Rica qualified for finals; Trinidad & Tobago played Bahrain (fifth-placed Asian team) for place in finals.

AFRICA

Group winners qualify for finals: Togo, Ghana, Ivory Coast, Angola, Tunisia.

WORLD CUP 2006 PLAY-OFFS

PLAY-OFFS FIRST LEG

Oslo, 12 November 2005, 24,264

Norway (0) 0

Czech Republic (1) 1 *(Smicer 31)*

Norway: Myhre; Bergdolmo, Hagen, Hangeland, Riise, Solli (Braaten 46), Hestad, Grindheim (Stromstad 85), Pedersen M, Carew, Iversen (Aarst 77).
Czech Republic: Cech; Grygera, Jankulovski, Rozehnal, Ujfalusi, Galasek, Nedved, Poborsky, Rosicky (Jarosik 86), Smicer (Heinz 77), Baros (Polak 60).
Referee: Bussacca (Switzerland).

Madrid, 12 November 2005, 54,851

Spain (2) 5 *(Luis Garcia 10, 18, 74, Fernando Torres 65 (pen), Morientes 79)*

Slovakia (0) 1 *(Nemeth 49)*

Spain: Casillas; Michel Salgado, Del Horno, Puyol, Pablo, Albelda (Xabi Alonso 66), Xavi, Luis Garcia (Morientes 76), Fernando Torres, Reyes (Vicente 56), Raul.
Slovakia: Contofalsky; Petras, Skrtel, Kratochvil, Had■, Zabavnik, Karhan (Janocko 73), Hlinka, Hodur (Gresko 67), Holosko (Nemeth 46), Vittek.
Referee: De Sanctis (Italy).

Berne, 12 November 2005, 31,130

Switzerland (1) 2 *(Senderos 41, Behrami 86)*

Turkey (0) 0

Switzerland: Zuberbuhler; Magnin, Muller, Senderos, Degen P, Vogel, Barnetta (Behrami 83), Cabanas, Gygax, Streller (Vonlanthen 77), Frei.
Turkey: Volkan; Serkan, Alpay, Ibrahim, Umit O (Halil Altintop 77), Huseyin, Tuncay (Ergun 83), Selcuk, Tumer, Nihat (Okan B 46), Hakan Sukur.
Referee: Michel (Slovakia).

Montevideo, 12 November 2005, 75,000

Uruguay (1) 1 *(Rodriguez D 35)*

Australia (0) 0

Uruguay: Carini; Diogo, Diego Lopez (Rodriguez G 62), Montero, Rodriguez D, Perez, Pablo Garcia, Recoba, Zalayeta (Estoyanoff 62), Morales, Forlan (Dario Silva 17).
Australia: Schwarzer; Neill, Vidmar, Popovic, Grella, Emerton, Culina, Chipperfield, Kewell, Thompson (Bresciano 52), Viduka (Aloisi 79).
Referee: Larsen (Denmark).

PLAY-OFFS SECOND LEG

Sydney, 16 November 2005, 82,698

Australia (1) 1 *(Bresciano 35)*

Uruguay (0) 0

Australia: Schwarzer; Neill, Chipperfield, Cahill, Vidmar, Emerton (Skoko 110), Viduka, Grella, Bresciano (Aloisi 96), Culina, Popovic (Kewell 31).
Uruguay: Carini; Lugano, Rodriguez G, Pablo Garcia, Rodriguez D, Montero (Sosa 81), Varela, Diogo, Morales, Recoba (Zalayeta 72), Regueiro (Estoyanoff 97).
aet; Australia won 4-2 on penalties.
Referee: Cantalejo (Spain).

Prague, 16 November 2005, 17,464

Czech Republic (1) 1 *(Rosicky 35)*

Norway (0) 0

Czech Republic: Cech; Grygera, Ujfalusi, Rozehnal, Poborsky, Smicer (Stajner 75), Rosicky (Kovac 67), Nedved, Polak, Baros (Plasil 90), Jankulovski.
Norway: Myhre; Hoiland, Hagen, Hangeland, Riise (Johnsen M 88), Helstad (Arst 57), Hestad, Stromstad, Pedersen M, Carew, Iversen (Solli 46).
Referee: Poll (England).

Bratislava, 16 November 2005, 23,567

Slovakia (0) 1 *(Holosko 50)*

Spain (0) 1 *(Villa 70)*

Slovakia: Contofalsky; Skrtel, Kratochvil, Gresko (Cech 78), Durica, Zabavnik, Hlinka, Krajcik, Vittek, Hodur (Holosko 46), Nemeth (Fodrek 83).
Spain: Casillas; Michel Salgado, Antonio Lopez, Puyol, Baraja, Xavi (Sergio Ramos 74), Vicente, Raul (Morientes 65), Fernando Torres (Villa 61), Xabi Alonso, Pablo.
Referee: Merk (Germany).

Istanbul, 16 November 2005, 40,000

Turkey (2) 4 *(Tuncay 22, 36, 89, Necati 52 (pen))*

Switzerland (1) 2 *(Frei 2 (pen), Streller 84)*

Turkey: Volkan; Tolga, Necati (Fatih 81), Alpay, Emre B (Basturk 82), Ergun, Selcuk, Serhat (Tumer 70), Hakan Sukur, Hamit Altintop, Tuncay.
Switzerland: Zuberbuhler; Senderos, Degen P (Behrami 46), Spycher, Muller, Barnetta, Wicky, Cabanas, Vogel, Gygax (Streller 33) (Huggel 86), Frei.
Referee: De Bleeckere (Belgium).

PAST WORLD CUP FINALS

Year	Winners		Runners-up		Venue	Att.	Referee
1930	Uruguay	4	Argentina	2	Montevideo	90,000	Langenus (B)
1934	Italy*	2	Czechoslovakia	1	Rome	50,000	Eklind (Se)
1938	Italy	4	Hungary	2	Paris	45,000	Capdeville (F)
1950	Uruguay	2	Brazil	1	Rio de Janeiro	199,854	Reader (E)
1954	West Germany	3	Hungary	2	Berne	60,000	Ling (E)
1958	Brazil	5	Sweden	2	Stockholm	49,737	Guigue (F)
1962	Brazil	3	Czechoslovakia	1	Santiago	68,679	Latychev (USSR)
1966	England*	4	West Germany	2	Wembley	93,802	Dienst (Sw)
1970	Brazil	4	Italy	1	Mexico City	107,412	Glockner (EG)
1974	West Germany	2	Holland	1	Munich	77,833	Taylor (E)
1978	Argentina*	3	Holland	1	Buenos Aires	77,000	Gonella (I)
1982	Italy	3	West Germany	1	Madrid	90,080	Coelho (Br)
1986	Argentina	3	West Germany	2	Mexico City	114,580	Filho (Br)
1990	West Germany	1	Argentina	0	Rome	73,603	Mendez (Mex)
1994	Brazil* *(Brazil won 3-2 on penalties aet)*	0	Italy	0	Los Angeles	94,194	Puhl (H)
1998	France	3	Brazil	0	St-Denis	75,000	Belqola (Mor)
2002	Brazil	2	Germany	0	Yokohama	69,029	Collina (I)

*After extra time.

WORLD CUP 2006 REVIEW

Any moral judgement on the team who deserved to win the 2006 World Cup final was negated when Zinedine Zidane was sent off for head-butting Italy's Marco Materazzi albeit after alleged racist remarks aimed at him. France disqualified themselves from a moral point of view at this juncture whatever the provocation. Having said that for any team to win any competition by penalty kicks continues to make a mockery of the spirit of the game.

Back to the real action and Italy certainly had the better of the first half, conceding a penalty awarded when Florent Malouda went to ground from Materazzi, the Italian defender trying desperately to avoid any collision. Up came Zidane to fool Gianluigi Buffon in the Italian goal with the cheekiest of chips which hit the underside of the bar and dropped down on the right side for France. Just seven minutes had been played and already Thierry Henry had received attention after running into Fabio Cannavaro.

Italy equalised when Materazzi climbed higher than anyone to power a header through goalkeeper Fabien Barthez and two defenders on the line, following an inch-perfect cross from Andrea Pirlo. Subsequently after a smart defence-splitting move Toni had a shot brilliantly blocked by Thuram and then struck the bar with a header from another excellent corner. The first half certainly saw Italy enjoying more of the ball.

The second half was a different story as France began to control affairs in midfield with the Italians stretched to contain their thoroughness. While Italy were forced back deep into their own half, Toni was left upfield, an isolated figure having to attempt a holding operation with the ball in the hope of support.

Marcello Lippi the Italian coach realised his midfield were losing it and made two changes. Unfortunately it did not improve matters and Henry was proving a handful for the Italian defence at the point of the French attack.

Patrick Vieira pulled up sharply with a twinge and had to be replaced by Alou Diarra. Both teams were feeling the effects of the tournament and another sultry evening, but France seemed the more likely scorers. Extra time produced a good deal of fear as ever, Henry went off with injury and then came the Zidane incident.

So it was penalties and while the Italians converted their handful, David Trezeguet had the misfortune to strike the bar with his effort. So Italy were World Cup champions for the fourth time in their history.

Despite his fall from grace Zidane was awarded the Golden Ball as the outstanding player in the tournament. Is this FIFA's way of condoning the assault or just to ignore it? As an example to the youth of today, it is shameful.

In a tournament in which goals were scarce, Miroslav Klose of Germany was top scorer with just five goals. Brazil and Spain shared the Fair Play Award, Italy's Gianluigi Buffon took the Lev Yashin trophy as the best goalkeeper. Ronaldo the portly Brazilian striker managed to establish a World Cup record with his 15th goal in finals, overtaking Gerd Muller of West Germany as it was when he was active.

The FIFA crackdown on tackling merely served to produce more diving than ever before, but naturally a host of yellow and red cards which set a record for the competition. For the first time in its history, a match produced 16 yellow cards and four dismissals when Portugal beat Holland which finished as a nine-a-side affair.

It did nothing to create more openings or produce more goals. The total of 147 at 2.30 goals per game is the second worst since 1990 – in Italy – worrying for if nothing else what FIFA might decide to do in the future. A non-contact sport is surely not far away.

Extra time is a waste of it. Scrap the extra period and simply play on until someone scores a goal.

The group system of matches invariably produces meaningless matches either between two teams who have already qualified or a couple who have already booked their passage home. Attendances were good, 3,354,646 for an average of 52,416, third best in history behind USA (1994) and Brazil (1950).

African countries performed better than expected, Ghana and Ivory Coast the pick of them. The South Americans fared less well except for Argentina who arguably played the best of the football but were badly served by poor substitution judgements.

Germany, the hosts, scored more goals and were involved in the best game of an average tournament when beaten by Italy.

WORLD CUP 2006 FINALS

GROUP A

Munich, 9 June 2006, 59,416
Germany (2) 4 *(Lahm 6, Klose 17, 61, Frings 87)*
Costa Rica (1) 2 *(Wanchope 12, 73)*
Germany: Lehmann; Friedrich, Mertesacker, Metzelder, Lahm, Frings, Schneider (Odonkor 90), Borowski (Kehl 72), Klose (Neuville 79), Podolski, Schweinsteiger.
Costa Rica: Porras; Umana, Sequeira, Marin, Martinez (Drummond 66), Fonseca, Gonzalez L, Solis (Bolanos 78), Gomez (Azofeifa 90), Wanchope, Centeno.
Referee: Elizondo (Argentina).

Gelsenkirchen, 9 June 2006, 48,426
Poland (0) 0
Ecuador (1) 2 *(Tenorio C 24, Delgado 80)*
Poland: Boruc; Baszczynski, Michal Zewlakow, Radomski, Bak, Jop, Sobolewski (Jelen 68), Smolarek, Zurawski (Brozek 84), Szymkowiak, Krzynowek (Kosowski 78).
Ecuador: Mora; De la Cruz, Reasco, Tenorio E, Hurtado I (Guagua 69), Espinoza G, Castillo, Valencia, Delgado (Urrutia 83), Tenorio C (Kaviedes 65), Mendez.
Referee: Kamikawa (Japan).

Dortmund, 14 June 2006, 65,000
Germany (0) 1 *(Neuville 90)*
Poland (0) 0
Germany: Lehmann; Friedrich (Odonkor 63), Lahm, Frings, Mertesacker, Metzelder, Schneider, Ballack, Klose, Podolski (Neuville 70), Schweinsteiger.
Poland: Boruc; Baszczynski, Michal Zewlakow (Dudka 83), Sobolewski■, Bosacki, Bak, Jelen (Brozek 90), Radomski, Zurawski, Smolarek, Krzynowek (Lewandowski M 77).
Referee: Cantalejo (Spain).

Hamburg, 15 June 2006, 50,000
Ecuador (1) 3 *(Tenorio C 8, Delgado 54, Kaviedes 90)*
Costa Rica (0) 0
Ecuador: Mora; De la Cruz, Reasco, Tenorio E, Hurtado I, Espinoza G (Guagua 69), Valencia (Urrutia 73), Castillo, Delgado, Tenorio C (Kaviedes 46), Mendez.
Costa Rica: Porras; Sequeira, Fonseca (Saborio 29), Marin, Umana, Gonzalez L (Hernandez 56), Wallace, Solis, Wanchope, Gomez, Centeno (Bernard 84).
Referee: Codjia (Benin).

Hanover, 20 June 2006, 43,000
Costa Rica (1) 1 *(Gomez 24)*
Poland (1) 2 *(Bosacki 33, 66)*
Costa Rica: Porras; Umana, Drummond (Wallace 70), Marin, Badilla, Solis, Gonzalez L, Bolanos (Saborio 78), Wanchope, Centeno, Gomez (Hernandez 82).
Poland: Boruc; Baszczynski, Michal Zewlakow, Radomski (Lewandowski M 64), Bak, Bosacki, Smolarek (Rasiak 85), Szymkowiak, Jelen, Zurawski (Brozek 46), Krzynowek.
Referee: Maidin (Singapore).

Berlin, 20 June 2006, 72,000
Ecuador (0) 0
Germany (2) 3 *(Klose 4, 44, Podolski 57)*
Ecuador: Mora; De la Cruz, Ambrosi, Tenorio E, Guagua, Espinoza G, Valencia (Lara 63), Ayovi M (Urrutia 68), Borja (Benitez 46), Kaviedes, Mendez.
Germany: Lehmann; Friedrich, Lahm, Frings (Borowski 66), Mertesacker, Huth, Schneider (Asamoah 73), Ballack, Podolski, Klose (Neuville 66), Schweinsteiger.
Referee: Ivanov (Russia).

GROUP A FINAL TABLE	P	W	D	L	F	A	Pts
Germany	3	3	0	0	8	2	9
Ecuador	3	2	0	1	5	3	6
Poland	3	1	0	2	2	4	3
Costa Rica	3	0	0	3	3	9	0

GROUP B
Frankfurt, 10 June 2006, 43,324
England (1) 1 *(Gamarra 3 (og))*
Paraguay (0) 0
England: Robinson; Neville G, Cole A, Gerrard, Ferdinand, Terry, Beckham, Lampard, Crouch, Owen (Downing 56), Cole J (Hargreaves 83).
Paraguay: Villar (Bobadilla 8); Caniza, Toledo (Nunez 82), Toro Acuna, Caceres JC, Gamarra, Bonet (Cuevas 68), Paredes, Santa Cruz, Valdez, Riveros.
Referee: Moreno (Mexico).

Dortmund, 10 June 2006, 60,285
Trinidad & Tobago (0) 0
Sweden (0) 0
Trinidad & Tobago: Hislop; Gray, John A■, Birchall, Lawrence, Sancho, Yorke, Theobald (Whitley 67), John S, Samuel (Glen 53), Edwards.
Sweden: Shaaban; Alexandersson N, Edman, Linderoth (Kallstrom 78), Mellberg, Lucic, Wilhelmsson (Jonson M 79), Ljungberg, Ibrahimovic, Larsson, Anders Svensson (Allback 62).
Referee: Maidin (Singapore).

Nuremberg, 15 June 2006, 41,000
England (0) 2 *(Crouch 83, Gerrard 90)*
Trinidad & Tobago (0) 0
England: Robinson; Carragher (Lennon 58), Cole A, Gerrard, Ferdinand, Terry, Beckham, Lampard, Crouch, Owen (Rooney 58), Cole J (Downing 75).
Trinidad & Tobago: Hislop; Edwards, Gray, Yorke, Lawrence, Sancho, Birchall, Whitley, John S, Jones (Glen 70), Theobald (Wise 85).
Referee: Kamikawa (Japan).

Berlin, 15 June 2006, 72,000
Sweden (0) 1 *(Ljungberg 89)*
Paraguay (0) 0
Sweden: Isaksson; Alexandersson N, Edman, Linderoth, Mellberg, Lucic, Wilhelmsson (Jonson M 88), Kallstrom (Elmander 86), Ibrahimovic (Allback 46), Larsson, Ljungberg.
Paraguay: Bobadilla; Caniza, Nunez, Toro Acuna, Caceres JC, Gamarra, Bonet (Barreto 81), Paredes, Santa Cruz (Lopez 63), Valdez, Riveros (Dos Santos 62).
Referee: Michel (Slovakia).

Kaiserslautern, 20 June 2006, 46,000
Paraguay (1) 2 *(Sancho 25 (og), Cuevas 86)*
Trinidad & Tobago (0) 0
Paraguay: Bobadilla; Caniza (Da Silva 89), Nunez, Toro Acuna, Caceres JC (Manzur 77), Gamarra, Barreto, Dos Santos, Valdez (Cuevas 66), Santa Cruz, Paredes.
Trinidad & Tobago: Jack; Edwards, John A (Jones 31), Yorke, Lawrence, Sancho, Birchall, Whitley (Latapy 67), John S, Glen (Wise 41), Theobald.
Referee: Rosetti (Italy).

Cologne, 20 June 2006, 45,000
Sweden (0) 2 *(Allback 50, Larsson 90)*
England (1) 2 *(Cole J 34, Gerrard 85)*
Sweden: Isaksson; Alexandersson N, Edman, Linderoth (Andersson D 90), Mellberg, Lucic, Jonson M (Wilhelmsson 54), Kallstrom, Allback (Elmander 75), Larsson, Ljungberg.
England: Robinson; Carragher, Cole A, Hargreaves, Ferdinand, Terry (Campbell 56), Beckham, Lampard, Owen (Crouch 4), Rooney (Gerrard 69), Cole J.
Referee: Busacca (Switzerland).

GROUP B FINAL TABLE	P	W	D	L	F	A	Pts
England	3	2	1	0	5	2	7
Sweden	3	1	2	0	3	2	5
Paraguay	3	1	0	2	2	2	3
Trinidad & Tobago	3	0	1	2	0	4	1

GROUP C

Hamburg, 10 June 2006, 45,442

Argentina (2) 2 *(Crespo 24, Saviola 38)*

Ivory Coast (0) 1 *(Drogba 82)*

Argentina: Abbondanzieri; Burdisso, Sorin, Maxi Rodriguez, Ayala, Heinze, Cambiasso, Mascherano, Saviola (Gonzalez L 76), Crespo (Palacio 64), Riquelme (Aimar 90).
Ivory Coast: Tizie; Eboue, Boka, Toure Y, Toure K, Meite, Zokora, Keita (Kone A 77), Kalou (Dindane 56), Drogba, Akale (Kone B 62).
Referee: De Bleeckere (Belgium).

Leipzig, 11 June 2006, 37,216

Serbia & Montenegro (0) 0

Holland (1) 1 *(Robben 18)*

Serbia & Montenegro: Jevric; Djordjevic N (Koroman 43), Dragutinovic, Duljaj, Gavrancic, Krstajic, Stankovic, Nadj, Milosevic (Zigic 46), Kezman (Ljuboja 67), Djordjevic P.
Holland: Van der Sar; Heitinga, Van Bronckhorst, Van Bommel (Landzaat 60), Ooijer, Mathijsen (Boulahrouz 86), Sneijder, Cocu, Van Nistelrooy (Kuijt 69), Van Persie, Robben.
Referee: Merk (Germany).

Gelsenkirchen, 16 June 2006, 52,000

Argentina (3) 6 *(Maxi Rodriguez 6, 41, Cambiasso 31, Crespo 79, Tevez 84, Messi 89)*

Serbia & Montenegro (0) 0

Argentina: Abbondanzieri; Burdisso, Sorin, Mascherano, Ayala, Heinze, Gonzalez L (Cambiasso 17), Maxi Rodriguez (Messi 75), Crespo, Saviola (Tevez 59), Riquelme.
Serbia & Montenegro: Jevric; Duljaj, Krstajic, Nadj (Ergic 46), Dudic, Gavrancic, Koroman (Ljuboja 50), Djordjevic P, Milosevic (Vukic 70), Kezman■, Stankovic.
Referee: Rosetti (Italy).

Stuttgart, 16 June 2006, 52,000

Holland (2) 2 *(Van Persie 23, Van Nistelrooy 26)*

Ivory Coast (1) 1 *(Kone B 38)*

Holland: Van der Sar; Heitinga (Boulahrouz 46), Van Bronckhorst, Sneijder (Van der Vaart 50), Ooijer, Mathijsen, Van Persie, Van Bommel, Van Nistelrooy (Landzaat 73), Cocu, Robben.
Ivory Coast: Tizie; Eboue, Boka, Zokora, Toure K, Meite, Toure Y, Kone B (Dindane 62), Drogba, Kone A (Akale 73), Romaric (Yapi Yapo 62).
Referee: Acosta (Colombia).

Frankfurt, 21 June 2006, 48,000

Holland (0) 0

Argentina (0) 0

Holland: Van der Sar; Jaliens, De Cler, Sneijder (Maduro 86), Boulahrouz, Ooijer, Van Persie (Landzaat 67), Van der Vaart, Cocu, Van Nistelrooy (Babel 56), Kuijt.
Argentina: Abbondanzieri; Burdisso (Coloccini 24), Cufre, Mascherano, Ayala, Milito, Messi (Cruz 70), Maxi Rodriguez, Riquelme (Aimar 80), Cambiasso, Tevez.
Referee: Cantalejo (Spain).

Munich, 21 June 2006, 66,000

Ivory Coast (1) 3 *(Dindane 37 (pen), 67, Kalou B 85 (pen))*

Serbia & Montenegro (2) 2 *(Zigic 10, Ilic 20)*

Ivory Coast: Barry; Eboue, Boka, Zokora, Kouassi, Domoraud■, Keita (Kalou B 73), Toure Y, Dindane, Kone A, Akale (Kone B 60).
Serbia & Montenegro: Jevric; Djordjevic N, Dudic, Duljaj, Gavrancic, Krstajic (Nadj■ 16), Stankovic, Ergic, Zigic (Milosevic 67), Ilic, Djordjevic P.
Referee: Moreno (Mexico).

GROUP C FINAL TABLE	P	W	D	L	F	A	Pts
Argentina	3	2	1	0	8	1	7
Holland	3	2	1	0	3	1	7
Ivory Coast	3	1	0	2	5	6	3
Serbia & Montenegro	3	0	0	3	2	10	0

GROUP D

Cologne, 11 June 2006, 45,000

Angola (0) 0

Portugal (1) 1 *(Pauleta 4)*

Angola: Joao Ricardo; Loco, Delgado, Figueiredo (Miloy 80), Jamba, Kali, Andre Makanga, Mateus, Akwa (Mantorras 60), Ze Kalanga (Edson 70), Mendonca.
Portugal: Ricardo; Miguel, Nuno Valente, Petit (Maniche 72), Fernando Meira, Ricardo Carvalho, Ronaldo (Costinha 60), Figo, Pauleta, Tiago (Hugo Viana 82), Simao Sabrosa.
Referee: Larrionda (Uruguay).

Nuremberg, 11 June 2006, 36,898

Mexico (1) 3 *(Bravo 28, 76, Zinha 79)*

Iran (1) 1 *(Golmohammadi 36)*

Mexico: Sanchez O; Marquez, Salcido, Pardo, Osorio, Torrado (Perez L 46), Mendez, Bravo, Borgetti (Fonseca 52), Franco (Zinha 46), Pineda.
Iran: Mirzapour; Kaabi, Nosrati (Borhani 81), Teymourian, Golmohammadi, Rezaei, Mahdavikia, Nekounam, Daei, Hashemian, Karimi (Madanchi 63).
Referee: Rosetti (Italy).

Hanover, 16 June 2006, 43,000

Mexico (0) 0

Angola (0) 0

Mexico: Sanchez O; Marquez, Mendez, Osorio, Salcido, Pardo, Torrado, Zinha (Arellano 52), Bravo, Franco (Fonseca 74), Pineda (Morales 78).
Angola: Joao Ricardo; Loco, Delgado, Figueiredo (Rui Marques 73), Jamba, Kali, Andre Makanga■, Ze Kalanga (Miloy 83), Mendonca, Akwa, Mateus (Mantorras 68).
Referee: Maidin (Singapore).

Frankfurt, 17 June 2006, 48,000

Portugal (0) 1 *(Deco 63, Ronaldo 80 (pen))*

Iran (0) 0

Portugal: Ricardo; Miguel, Nuno Valente, Maniche (Petit 67), Fernando Meira, Ricardo Carvalho, Figo (Simao Sabrosa 88), Deco (Tiago 80), Pauleta, Costinha, Ronaldo.
Iran: Mirzapour; Kaabi, Nosrati, Teymourian, Golmohammadi (Bakhtiarizadeh 88), Rezaei, Mahdavikia, Karimi (Zandi 65), Hashemian, Nekounam, Madanchi (Khatibi 66).
Referee: Poulet (France).

Liepzig, 21 June 2006, 38,000

Iran (0) 1 *(Bakhtiarizadeh 75)*

Angola (0) 1 *(Flavio 60)*

Iran: Mirzapour; Kaabi (Borhani 67), Nosrati (Shojaei 13), Teymourian, Rezaei, Bakhtiarizadeh, Mahdavikia, Zandi, Hashemian (Khatibi 39), Daei, Madanchi.
Angola: Joao Ricardo; Loco, Delgado, Figueiredo (Rui Marques 73), Jamba, Kali, Ze Kalanga, Miloy, Akwa (Flavio 51), Mendonca, Mateus (Love 23).
Referee: Shield (Australia).

Gelsenkirchen, 21 June 2006, 52,000

Portugal (2) 2 *(Maniche 6, Simao Sabrosa 24 (pen))*

Mexico (1) 1 *(Fonseca 29)*

Portugal: Ricardo; Miguel (Paulo Ferreira 61), Caneira, Petit, Fernando Meira, Ricardo Carvalho, Figo (Boa Morte 80), Tiago, Helder Postiga (Nuno Gomes 69), Simao Sabrosa, Maniche.
Mexico: Sanchez O; Mendez (Franco 80), Marquez, Rodriguez (Zinha 46), Osorio, Salcido, Pardo, Perez L■, Fonseca, Bravo, Pineda (Castro 69).
Referee: Michel (Slovakia).

GROUP D FINAL TABLE	P	W	D	L	F	A	Pts
Portugal	3	3	0	0	5	1	9
Mexico	3	1	1	1	4	3	4
Angola	3	0	2	1	1	2	2
Iran	3	0	1	2	2	6	1

GROUP E

Hanover, 12 June 2006, 43,000

Italy (1) 2 *(Pirlo 40, Iaquinta 83)*

Ghana (0) 0

Italy: Buffon; Zaccardo, Grosso, De Rossi, Nesta, Cannavaro, Perrotta, Pirlo, Toni (Del Piero 82), Totti (Camoranesi 56), Gilardino (Iaquinta 64).
Ghana: Kingston; Pantsil, Pappoe (Shilla Illiasu 46), Muntari, Mensah, Kuffour, Appiah, Essien, Amoah (Pimpong 68), Gyan (Tachie-Mensah 89), Addo E.
Referee: Simon (Brazil).

Gelsenkirchen, 12 June 2006, 48,426

USA (0) 0

Czech Republic (2) 3 *(Koller 5, Rosicky 36, 76)*

USA: Keller; Cherundolo (O'Brien 46), Lewis, Mastroeni (Johnson 46), Pope, Onyewu, Beasley, Reyna, McBride (Wolff 77), Donovan, Convey.
Czech Republic: Cech; Grygera, Jankulovski, Galasek, Rozehnal, Ujfalusi, Poborsky (Polak 83), Nedved, Koller (Lokvenc 45), Rosicky (Stajner 86), Plasil.
Referee: Demarqui (Paraguay).

Cologne, 17 June 2006, 45,000

Czech Republic (0) 0

Ghana (1) 2 *(Gyan 2, Muntari 82)*

Czech Republic: Cech; Grygera, Jankulovski, Galasek (Polak 46), Rozehnal, Ujfalusi■, Poborsky (Stajner 56), Nedved, Lokvenc, Rosicky, Plasil (Sionko 68).
Ghana: Kingston; Pantsil, Mohamed, Essien, Mensah, Shilla Illiasu, Addo O (Boateng 46), Appiah, Amoah (Addo E 80), Gyan (Pimpong 85), Muntari.
Referee: Elizondo (Argentina).

Kaiserslautern, 17 June 2006, 46,000

Italy (1) 1 *(Gilardino 22)*

USA (1) 1 *(Zaccardo 27 (og))*

Italy: Buffon; Zaccardo (Del Piero 54), Zambrotta, De Rossi■, Nesta, Cannavaro, Pirlo, Perrotta, Toni (Iaquinta 61), Totti (Gattuso 35), Gilardino.
USA: Keller; Cherundolo, Bocanegra, Mastroeni■, Pope■, Onyewu, Dempsey (Beasley 62), Reyna, McBride, Donovan, Convey (Conrad 52).
Referee: Larrionda (Uruguay).

Hamburg, 22 June 2006, 50,000

Czech Republic (0) 0

Italy (1) 2 *(Materazzi 26, Inzaghi 87)*

Czech Republic: Cech; Grygera, Jankulovski, Polak■, Kovac R (Heinz 78), Rozehnal, Poborsky (Stajner 46), Nedved, Baros (Jarolim 64), Rosicky, Plasil.
Italy: Buffon; Zambrotta, Grosso, Gattuso, Nesta (Materazzi 17), Cannavaro, Pirlo, Camoranesi (Barone 74), Gilardino (Inzaghi 61), Totti, Perrotta.
Referee: Telez (Mexico).

Nuremberg, 22 June 2006, 41,000

Ghana (2) 2 *(Draman 22, Appiah 45 (pen))*

USA (1) 1 *(Dempsey 43)*

Ghana: Kingston; Pantsil, Mohamed, Essien, Mensah, Shilla Illiasu, Boateng (Addo O 46), Appiah, Amoah (Addo E 59), Pimpong, Draman (Tachie-Mensah 80).
USA: Keller; Cherundolo (Johnson 61), Bocanegra, Reyna (Olsen 40), Onyewu, Conrad, Dempsey, Donovan, McBride, Beasley, Lewis (Convey 74).
Referee: Merk (Germany).

GROUP E FINAL TABLE	P	W	D	L	F	A	Pts
Italy	3	2	1	0	5	1	7
Ghana	3	2	0	1	4	3	6
Czech Republic	3	1	0	2	3	4	3
USA	3	0	1	2	2	6	1

GROUP F

Kaiserslautern, 12 June 2006, 46,000

Australia (0) 3 *(Cahill 84, 89, Aloisi 90)*

Japan (1) 1 *(Nakamura 26)*

Australia: Schwarzer; Moore (Kennedy 61), Neill, Chipperfield, Grella, Wilkshire (Aloisi 75), Culina, Emerton, Viduka, Kewell, Bresciano (Cahill 53).

Japan: Kawaguchi; Komano, Santos, Nakata, Miyamoto, Nakazawa, Fukunishi, Tsuboi (Moniwa 56) (Oguro 90), Yanagisawa (Ono 79), Takahara, Nakamura.

Referee: El Fatah (Egypt).

Berlin, 13 June 2006, 72,000

Brazil (1) 1 *(Kaka 44)*

Croatia (0) 0

Brazil: Dida; Cafu, Roberto Carlos, Emerson, Lucio, Juan, Ze Roberto, Kaka, Adriano, Ronaldo (Robinho 69), Ronaldinho.

Croatia: Pletikosa; Srna, Babic, Simic, Kovac R, Simunic, Tudor, Kranjcar, Klasnic (Olic 56), Prso, Kovac N (Leko J 41).

Referee: Tellez (Mexico).

Munich, 18 June 2006, 66,000

Brazil (0) 2 *(Adriano 49, Fred 89)*

Australia (0) 0

Brazil: Dida; Cafu, Roberto Carlos, Emerson (Gilberto Silva 72), Juan, Lucio, Ze Roberto, Kaka, Ronaldo (Robinho 72), Adriano (Fred 88), Ronaldinho.

Australia: Schwarzer; Emerton, Chipperfield, Moore (Aloisi 69), Neill, Popovic (Bresciano 41), Culina, Grella, Viduka, Cahill (Kewell 56), Sterjovski.

Referee: Merk (Germany).

Nuremberg, 18 June 2006, 41,000

Japan (0) 0

Croatia (0) 0

Japan: Kawaguchi; Kaji, Santos, Fukunishi (Inamoto 46), Miyamoto, Nakazawa, Nakamura, Nakata H, Yanagisawa (Tamada 62), Takahara (Oguro 85), Ogasawara.

Croatia: Pletikosa; Simic, Tudor (Olic 70), Kovac R, Simunic, Kovac N, Srna (Bosnjak 87), Kranjcar (Modric 78), Klasnic, Prso, Babic.

Referee: De Bleeckere (Belgium).

Stuttgart, 22 June 2006, 52,000

Croatia (1) 2 *(Srna 2, Kovac N 56)*

Australia (1) 2 *(Moore 38 (pen), Kewell 79)*

Croatia: Pletikosa; Simic■, Babic, Kovac N, Tomas, Simunic■, Srna, Tudor, Prso, Olic (Modric 74), Kranjcar (Leko J 65).

Australia: Kalac; Emerton■, Chipperfield (Kennedy 75), Grella (Aloisi 63), Neill, Moore, Sterjovski (Bresciano 71), Culina, Viduka, Cahill, Kewell.

Referee: Poll (England).

Dortmund, 22 June 2006, 65,000

Japan (1) 1 *(Tamada 34)*

Brazil (1) 4 *(Ronaldo 45, 81, Juninho Pernambucano 53, Gilberto 59)*

Japan: Kawaguchi; Kaji, Santos, Nakata H, Tsuboi, Nakazawa, Nakamura, Inamoto, Maki (Takahara 60) (Oguro 66), Tamada, Ogasawara (Nakata K 56).

Brazil: Dida (Rogerio Ceni 82); Cicinho, Gilberto, Gilberto Silva, Lucio, Juan, Kaka (Ze Roberto 71), Juninho Pernambucano, Ronaldo, Robinho, Ronaldinho (Ricardinho 71).

Referee: Poulat (France).

GROUP F FINAL TABLE	P	W	D	L	F	A	Pts
Brazil	3	3	0	0	7	1	9
Australia	3	1	1	1	5	5	4
Croatia	3	0	2	1	2	3	2
Japan	3	0	1	2	2	7	1

GROUP G

Stuttgart, 13 June 2006, 56,000
France (0) 0
Switzerland (0) 0
France: Barthez; Sagnol, Abidal, Makelele, Thuram, Gallas, Wiltord (Dhorasoo 84), Vieira, Henry, Zidane, Ribery (Saha 70).
Switzerland: Zuberbuhler; Degen P, Magnin, Vogel, Muller (Djourou 75), Senderos, Barnetta, Wicky (Margairaz 82), Frei, Streller (Gygax 56), Cabanas.
Referee: Ivanov (Russia).

Frankfurt, 13 June 2006, 48,000
South Korea (0) 2 *(Lee C-S 54, Ahn 72)*
Togo (1) 1 *(Kader 31)*
South Korea: Lee W-J; Song C-G, Lee Y-P, Choi J-C, Kim Y-C, Kim J-K (Ahn 46), Ho Lee, Park J-S, Lee C-S, Cho J-J (Kim S-S 83), Lee E-Y (Kim N-I 68).
Togo: Agassa; Tchangai, Assemoassa (Forson 62), Romao, Abalo■, Nibombe, Senaya (Toure 55), Mamam, Adebayor, Kader, Salifou M (Aziawonou 86).
Referee: Poll (England).

Leipzig, 18 June 2006, 43,000
France (1) 1 *(Henry 9)*
South Korea (0) 1 *(Park J-S 81)*
France: Barthez; Sagnol, Abidal, Makelele, Thuram, Gallas, Wiltord (Ribery 60), Vieira, Henry, Zidane (Trezeguet 90), Malouda (Dhorasoo 88).
South Korea: Lee W-J; Lee Y-P, Kim D-J, Kim N-I, Choi J-C, Kim Y-C, Lee C-S (Ahn 72), Ho Lee (Kim S-S 69), Cho J-J, Lee E-Y (Seol K-H 46), Park J-S.
Referee: Tellez (Mexico).

Dortmund, 19 June 2006, 65,000
Togo (0) 0
Switzerland (1) 2 *(Frei 16, Barnetta 88)*
Togo: Agassa; Toure, Forson, Agboh (Salifou M 25), Tchangai, Nibombe, Dossevi (Senaya 69), Romao, Adebayor, Kader, Mamam (Malm 87).
Switzerland: Zuberbuhler; Degen P, Magnin, Vogel, Muller, Senderos, Barnetta, Cabanas (Streller 77), Gygax (Yakin 46), Frei (Lustrinelli 87), Wicky.
Referee: Demarqui (Paraguay).

Hanover, 23 June 2006, 43,000
Switzerland (1) 2 *(Senderos 23, Frei 77)*
South Korea (0) 0
Switzerland: Zuberbuhler; Degen P, Spycher, Vogel, Muller, Senderos (Djourou 54), Barnetta, Cabanas, Yakin (Margairaz 72), Frei, Wicky (Behrami 88).
South Korea: Lee W-J; Lee Y-P (Ahn 64), Kim D-J, Kim N-I, Choi J-C, Kim J-K, Park J-S, Ho Lee, Lee C-S, Cho J-J, Park C-J (Seol K-H 67).
Referee: Elizondo (Argentina).

Cologne, 23 June 2006, 45,000
Togo (0) 0
France (0) 2 *(Vieira 55, Henry 61)*
Togo: Agassa; Tchangai, Forson, Aziawonou, Abalo, Nibombe, Senaya, Mamam (Olufade 59), Adebayor (Dossevi 75), Kader, Salifou M.
France: Barthez; Sagnol, Silvestre, Makelele, Thuram, Gallas, Ribery (Gouvou 77), Vieira (Diarra 81), Trezeguet, Henry, Malouda (Wiltord 74).
Referee: Larrionda (Uruguay).

GROUP G FINAL TABLE	P	W	D	L	F	A	Pts
Switzerland	3	2	1	0	4	0	7
France	3	1	2	0	3	1	5
South Korea	3	1	1	1	3	4	4
Togo	3	0	0	3	1	6	0

GROUP H

Leipzig, 14 June 2006, 43,000

Spain (2) 4 *(Xabi Alonso 13, Villa 17, 48 (pen), Fernando Torres 81)*

Ukraine (0) 0

Spain: Casillas; Sergio Ramos, Pernia, Xabi Alonso (Albelda 55), Pablo, Puyol, Marcos Senna, Luis Garcia (Fabregas 77), Fernando Torres, Villa (Raul 55), Xavi.
Ukraine: Shovkovskyi; Yezerskiy, Nesmachni, Tymoschuk, Rusol, Vashchuk■, Gusev (Vorobei 46), Gusin (Shelayev 46), Voronin, Shevchenko, Rotan (Rebrov 64).
Referee: Busacca (Switzerland).

Munich, 14 June 2006, 66,000

Tunisia (1) 2 *(Jaziri 23, Jaidi 90)*

Saudi Arabia (0) 2 *(Al-Kahtani 57, Al-Jaber 84)*

Tunisia: Boumnijel; Trabelsi, Jemmali, Mnari, Haggui, Jaidi, Bouazizi (Nafti 55), Namouchi, Jaziri, Chikhaoui (Essediri 82), Chedli (Ghodhbane 69).
Saudi Arabia: Zaid; Dokhy, Sulimani, Aziz, Fallatah, Al-Montashari, Al-Ghamdi, Noor (Ameen 75), Al-Temyat (Mouath 67), Al-Kahtani (Al-Jaber 82), Khariri.
Referee: Shield (Australia).

Hamburg, 19 June 2006, 50,000

Saudi Arabia (0) 0

Ukraine (2) 4 *(Rusol 4, Rebrov 36, Shevchenko 46, Kalinichenko 84)*

Saudi Arabia: Zaid; Dokhy (Al-Khathran 55), Sulimani, Aziz, Al-Montashari, Fallatah, Al-Ghamdi, Noor (Al-Jaber 77), Ameen (Mouath 55), Al-Kahtani, Khariri.
Ukraine: Shovkovskyi; Gusev, Nesmachni, Tymoschuk, Sviderskiy, Rusol, Rebrov (Rotan 71), Shelayev, Voronin (Gusin 79), Shevchenko (Milevski 86), Kalinichenko.
Referee: Poll (England).

Stuttgart, 19 June 2006, 52,000

Spain (0) 3 *(Raul 71, Fernando Torres 76, 90 (pen))*

Tunisia (1) 1 *(Mnari 8)*

Spain: Casillas; Sergio Ramos, Pernia, Xabi Alonso, Puyol, Pablo, Marcos Senna (Fabregas 46), Luis Garcia (Raul 46), Fernando Torres, Villa (Joaquin 46), Xavi.
Tunisia: Boumnijel; Trabelsi, Ayari (Yahia A 57), Nafti, Haggui, Jaidi, Bouazizi (Ghodhbane 57), Namouchi, Jaziri, Mnari, Chedli (Guemamdia 80).
Referee: Simon (Brazil).

Kaiserslautern, 23 June 2006, 46,000

Saudi Arabia (0) 0

Spain (1) 1 *(Juanito 36)*

Saudi Arabia: Zaid; Dokhy, Al-Khathran, Khariri, Fallatah, Al-Montashari, Noor, Aziz (Al-Temyat 13), Al-Harthi, Al-Jaber (Mouath 68), Sulimani (Massad 81).
Spain: Canizares; Michel Salgado, Antonio Lopez, Albelda, Juanito, Marchena, Joaquin, Fabregas (Xavi 66), Reyes (Fernando Torres 69), Raul (Villa 46), Iniesta.
Referee: Codjia (Benin).

Berlin, 23 June 2006, 72,000

Ukraine (0) 1 *(Shevchenko 70 (pen))*

Tunisia (0) 0

Ukraine: Shovkovskyi; Gusev, Nesmachni, Tymoschuk, Sviderskiy, Rusol, Rebrov (Vorobei 55), Shelayev, Voronin, Shevchenko (Milevski 88), Kalinichenko (Gusin 75).
Tunisia: Boumnijel; Trabelsi, Ayari, Nafti (Ghodhbane 90), Haggui, Jaidi, Bouazizi (Ben Saada 80), Namouchi, Jaziri■, Mnari, Chedli (Santos 79).
Referee: Demarqui (Paraguay).

GROUP H FINAL TABLE	P	W	D	L	F	A	Pts
Spain	3	3	0	0	8	1	9
Ukraine	3	2	0	1	5	4	6
Tunisia	3	0	1	2	3	6	1
Saudi Arabia	3	0	1	2	2	7	1

SECOND ROUND

Liepzig, 24 June 2006, 43,000

Argentina (1) 2 *(Borgetti 9 (og), Maxi Rodriguez 98)*

Mexico (1) 1 *(Marquez 5)*

Argentina: Abbondanzieri; Scaloni, Sorin, Mascherano, Ayala, Heinze, Maxi Rodriguez, Cambiasso (Aimar 76), Crespo (Tevez 75), Saviola (Messi 84), Riquelme.

Mexico: Sanchez O; Mendez, Guardado (Pineda 67), Marquez, Osorio, Salcido, Castro, Pardo (Torrado 38), Borgetti, Fonseca, Morales (Zinha 74).

(aet.)

Referee: Busacca (Switzerland).

Munich, 24 June 2006, 66,000

Germany (2) 2 *(Podolski 4, 12)*

Sweden (0) 0

Germany: Lehmann; Friedrich, Lahm, Frings (Kehl 85), Mertesacker, Metzelder, Schneider, Ballack, Podolski (Neuville 74), Klose, Schweinsteiger (Borowski 72).

Sweden: Isaksson; Alexandersson N, Edman, Linderoth, Mellberg, Lucic■, Jonson M (Wilhelmsson 53), Kallstrom (Hansson 39), Ibrahimovic (Allback 72), Larsson, Ljungberg.

Referee: Simon (Brazil).

Stuttgart, 25 June 2006, 52,000

England (0) 1 *(Beckham 60)*

Ecuador (0) 0

England: Robinson; Hargreaves, Cole A, Carrick, Ferdinand, Terry, Beckham (Lennon 87), Lampard, Rooney, Gerrard (Downing 90), Cole J (Carragher 77).

Ecuador: Mora; De la Cruz, Reasco, Castillo, Hurtado I, Espinoza G, Valencia, Tenorio E (Lara 69), Delgado, Tenorio C (Kaviedes 71), Mendez.

Referee: De Bleeckere (Belgium).

Nuremberg, 25 June 2006, 41,000

Portugal (1) 1 *(Maniche 23)*

Holland (0) 0

Portugal: Ricardo; Miguel, Nuno Valente, Costinha■, Fernando Meira, Ricardo Carvalho, Deco■, Figo (Tiago 84), Pauleta (Petit 46), Maniche, Ronaldo (Simao Sabrosa 34).

Holland: Van der Sar; Boulahrouz■, Van Bronckhorst■, Sneijder, Ooijer, Mathijsen (Van der Vaart 56), Van Persie, Van Bommel (Heitinga 67), Kuijt, Cocu (Vennegoor of Hesselink 84), Robben.

Referee: Ivanov (Russia).

Kaiserslautern, 26 June 2006, 46,000

Italy (0) 1 *(Totti 90 (pen))*

Australia (0) 0

Italy: Buffon; Zambrotta, Grosso, Gattuso, Cannavaro, Materazzi■, Perrotta, Pirlo, Toni (Barzagli 56), Del Piero (Totti 75), Gilardino (Iaquinta 46).

Australia: Schwarzer; Culina, Wilkshire, Moore, Neill, Chipperfield, Grella, Sterjovski (Aloisi 81), Bresciano, Viduka, Cahill.

Referee: Cantalejo (Spain).

Cologne, 26 June 2006, 45,000

Switzerland (0) 0

Ukraine (0) 0

Switzerland: Zuberbuhler; Degen P, Magnin, Vogel, Djourou (Grichting 34), Muller, Wicky, Cabanas, Yakin (Streller 64), Frei (Lustrinelli 117), Barnetta.

Ukraine: Shovkovskyi; Gusev, Nesmachni, Tymoschuk, Gusin, Vashchuk, Vorobei (Rebrov 94), Shelayev, Voronin (Milevski 111), Shevchenko, Kalinichenko (Rotan 75).

aet; Ukraine won 3-0 on penalties: Shevchenko saved; Streller saved; Milevski scored; Barnetta hit bar; Rebrov scored; Cabanas saved; Gusev scored.

Referee: Tellez (Mexico).

Dortmund, 27 June 2006, 65,000
Brazil (2) 3 *(Ronaldo 5, Adriano 45, Ze Roberto 84)*
Ghana (0) 0
Brazil: Dida; Cafu, Roberto Carlos, Ze Roberto, Lucio, Juan, Emerson (Gilberto Silva 46), Kaka (Ricardinho 83), Ronaldo, Adriano (Juninho Pernambucano 61), Ronaldinho.
Ghana: Kingston; Pantsil, Pappoe, Addo E (Boateng 60), Mensah, Shilla Illiasu, Draman, Appiah, Amoah (Tachie-Mensah 70), Gyan■, Muntari.
Referee: Michel (Slovakia).

Hanover, 27 June 2006, 43,000
Spain (1) 1 *(Villa 28 (pen))*
France (1) 3 *(Ribery 41, Vieira 83, Zidane 90)*
Spain: Casillas; Sergio Ramos, Pernia, Xabi Alonso, Pablo, Puyol, Xavi (Marcos Senna 72), Fabregas, Fernando Torres, Villa (Joaquin 54), Raul (Luis Garcia 54).
France: Barthez; Sagnol, Abidal, Makelele, Thuram, Gallas, Ribery, Vieira, Henry (Wiltord 88), Zidane, Malouda (Govou 74).
Referee: Rosetti (Italy).

QUARTER-FINALS

Berlin, 30 June 2006, 72,000
Germany (0) 1 *(Klose 80)*
Argentina (0) 1 *(Ayala 49)*
Germany: Lehmann; Friedrich, Lahm, Frings, Mertesacker, Metzelder, Schneider (Odonkor 62), Ballack, Podolski, Klose (Neuville 86), Schweinsteiger (Borowski 74).
Argentina: Abbondanzieri (Leo Franco 71); Coloccini, Sorin, Mascherano, Ayala, Heinze, Maxi Rodriguez, Gonzalez L, Crespo (Cruz 79), Riquelme (Cambiasso 72), Tevez.
aet; Germany won 4-2 on penalties: Neuville scored; Cruz scored; Ballack scored; Ayala saved; Podolski scored; Maxi Rodriguez saved; Borowski scored; Cambiasso saved. Unused sub Cufre■.
Referee: Michel (Slovakia).

Hamburg, 30 June 2006, 50,000
Italy (1) 3 *(Zambrotta 6, Toni 59, 69)*
Ukraine (0) 0
Italy: Buffon; Zambrotta, Grosso, Gattuso (Zaccardo 77), Cannavaro, Barzagli, Camoranesi (Oddo 68), Pirlo (Barone 68), Toni, Totti, Perrotta.
Ukraine: Shovkovskyi; Gusev, Nesmachni, Rusol (Vashchuk 45), Gusin, Sviderskiy (Vorobei 20), Tymoschuk, Shelayev, Milevski (Byelik 72), Shevchenko, Kalinichenko.
Referee: De Bleeckere (Belgium).

Frankfurt, 1 July 2006, 48,000
Brazil (0) 0
France (0) 1 *(Henry 57)*
Brazil: Dida (Cicinho 76), Roberto Carlos, Gilberto Silva, Lucio, Juan, Ze Roberto, Juninho Pernambucano (Adriano 63), Ronaldo, Kaka (Robinho 79), Ronaldinho.
France: Barthez; Sagnol, Abidal, Makelele, Thuram, Gallas, Ribery (Govou 77), Vieira, Henry (Saha 86), Zidane, Malouda (Wiltord 81).
Referee: Cantalejo (Spain).

Gelsenkirchen, 1 July 2006, 52,000
England (0) 0
Portugal (0) 0
England: Robinson; Neville G, Cole A, Hargreaves, Ferdinand, Terry, Beckham (Lennon 52) (Carragher 119), Lampard, Rooney■, Gerrard, Cole J (Crouch 65).
Portugal: Ricardo; Miguel, Nuno Valente, Petit, Fernando Meira, Ricardo Carvalho, Figo (Helder Postiga 86), Maniche, Pauleta (Simao Sabrosa 63), Tiago (Hugo Viana 75), Ronaldo.
aet; Portugal won 3-1 on penalties: Simao Sabrosa scored; Lampard saved; Hugo Viana hit post; Hargreaves scored; Petit missed; Gerrard saved; Helder Postiga scored; Carragher scored ordered retaken saved; Ronaldo scored.
Referee: Elizondo (Argentina).

SEMI-FINALS

Dortmund, 4 July 2006, 65,000

Germany (0) 0

Italy (0) 2 *(Grosso 119, Del Piero 120)*

Germany: Lehmann; Friedrich, Lahm, Kehl, Mertesacker, Metzelder, Schneider (Odonkor 83), Ballack, Podolski, Klose (Neuville 111), Borowski (Schweinsteiger 73).
Italy: Buffon; Zambrotta, Grosso, Gattuso, Materazzi, Cannavaro, Camoranesi (Iaquinta 91), Pirlo, Toni (Gilardino 74), Totti, Perrotta (Del Piero 104).
(aet.)
Referee: Tellez (Mexico).

Munich, 5 July 2006, 66,000

Portugal (0) 0

France (1) 1 *(Zidane 33 (pen))*

Portugal: Ricardo; Miguel (Paulo Ferreira 62), Nuno Valente, Costinha (Helder Postiga 75), Fernando Meira, Ricardo Carvalho, Figo, Deco, Pauleta (Simao Sabrosa 68), Maniche, Ronaldo.
France: Barthez; Sagnol, Abidal, Makelele, Thuram, Gallas, Ribery (Govou 72), Vieira, Henry (Saha 85), Zidane, Malouda (Wiltord 69).
Referee: Larrionda (Uruguay).

MATCH FOR THIRD PLACE

Stuttgart, 8 July 2006, 52,000

Germany (0) 3 *(Schweinsteiger 56, 78, Petit 61 (og))*

Portugal (0) 1 *(Nuno Gomes 88)*

Germany: Kahn; Lahm, Jansen, Frings, Nowotny, Metzelder, Schneider, Kehl, Podolski (Hanke 71), Klose (Neuville 65), Schweinsteiger (Hitzlsperger 79).
Portugal: Ricardo; Paulo Ferreira, Nuno Valente (Nuno Gomes 69), Costinha (Petit 46), Fernando Meira, Ricardo Costa, Ronaldo, Deco, Pauleta (Figo 77), Maniche, Simao Sabrosa.
Referee: Kamikawa (Japan).

THE WORLD CUP FINAL 2006

Berlin, 9 July 2006, 69,000

Italy (1) 1 *(Materazzi 19)*   **France (1) 1** *(Zidane 7 (pen))*

Italy: Buffon; Zambrotta, Grosso, Gattuso, Cannavaro, Materazzi, Pirlo, Camoranesi (Del Piero 86), Toni, Totti (De Rossi 61), Perrotta (Iaquinta 61).

France: Barthez; Sagnol, Abidal, Makelele, Thuram, Gallas, Ribery (Trezeguet 100), Vieira (Diarra 56), Henry (Wiltord 107), Zidane▪, Malouda.

aet; Italy won 5-3 on penalties: Pirlo scored; Wiltord scored; Materazzi scored; Trezeguet hit bar; De Rossi scored; Abidal scored; Del Piero scored; Sagnol scored; Grosso scored.

Referee: Elizondo (Argentina).

271

FIFA CLUB WORLD CHAMPIONSHIP 2005–06

Quarter-Finals

Al Ittihad (0) 1 *(Noor 78)*, **Al Ahly (0) 0**
att: 28,281 in Tokyo.

Sydney FC (0) 0, Deportivo Saprissa (0) 1 *(Bolanos 47)*
att: 28,538 in Toyota.

Semi-Finals

Al Ittihad (1) 2 *(Noor 33, Al Montashari 68)*
Sao Paulo (1) 3 *(Amoroso 16, 47, Rogerio Ceni 57 (pen))*
att: 31,510 in Tokyo.

Deportivo Saprissa (0) 0, Liverpool (2) 3 *(Crouch 3, 58, Gerrard 32)*
Liverpool: Reina; Josemi, Traore, Xabi Alonso (Hamann 79), Carragher, Hyypia (Luis Garcia 72), Sissoko, Gerrard (Sinama-Pongolle 64), Crouch, Cisse, Riise.
att: 43,902 in Yokohama.

Match for 5th Place

Al Ahly (1) 1 *(Motab 45)*, **Sydney FC (1) 2** *(Yorke 35, Carney 66)*
att: 15,951 in Tokyo.

Match for 3rd Place

Al Ittihad (1) 2 *(Kallon 28, Job 53 (pen))*
Deportivo Saprissa (1) 3 *(Saborio 13, 85 (pen), Gomez 89)*
in Yokohama.

Final

Sao Paulo (1) 1 *(Mineiro 27)*
Liverpool (0) 0
Sao Paulo: Rogerio Ceni; Cicinho, Fabao, Edcarlos, Lugano, Junior, Mineiro, Josue, Danilo, Amoroso, Aloisio (Grafite 75).
Liverpool: Reina; Finnan, Warnock (Riise 79), Xabi Alonso, Carragher, Hyypia, Sissoko (Sinama Pongolle 79), Gerrard, Luis Garcia, Morientes (Crouch 85), Kewell.
att: 66,821 in Yokohama.

WORLD CLUB CHAMPIONSHIP

Played annually up to 1974 and intermittently since then between the winners of the European Cup and the winners of the South American Champions Cup — known as the Copa Libertadores. In 1980 the winners were decided by one match arranged in Tokyo in February 1981 which remained the venue until 2004, after which the match was superseded by the FIFA World Club Championship. AC Milan replaced Marseille who had been stripped of their European Cup title in 1993.

1960 Real Madrid beat Penarol 0-0, 5-1	1971 Nacional beat Panathinaikos* 1-1, 2-1
1961 Penarol beat Benfica 0-1, 5-0, 2-1	1972 Ajax beat Independiente 1-1, 3-0
1962 Santos beat Benfica 3-2, 5-2	1973 Independiente beat Juventus* 1-0
1963 Santos beat AC Milan 2-4, 4-2, 1-0	1974 Atlético Madrid* beat Independiente 0-1, 2-0
1964 Inter-Milan beat Independiente 0-1, 2-0, 1-0	1975 Independiente and Bayern Munich could not agree dates; no matches.
1965 Inter-Milan beat Independiente 3-0, 0-0	1976 Bayern Munich beat Cruzeiro 2-0, 0-0
1966 Penarol beat Real Madrid 2-0, 2-0	1977 Boca Juniors beat Borussia Moenchengladbach* 2-2, 3-0
1967 Racing Club beat Celtic 0-1, 2-1, 1-0	1978 Not contested
1968 Estudiantes beat Manchester United 1-0, 1-1	1979 Olimpia beat Malmö* 1-0, 2-1
1969 AC Milan beat Estudiantes 3-0, 1-2	1980 Nacional beat Nottingham Forest 1-0
1970 Feyenoord beat Estudiantes 2-2, 1-0	1981 Flamengo beat Liverpool 3-0

1982	Penarol beat Aston Villa 2-0	1993	Sao Paulo beat AC Milan 3-2
1983	Gremio Porto Alegre beat SV Hamburg 2-1	1994	Velez Sarsfield beat AC Milan 2-0
1984	Independiente beat Liverpool 1-0	1995	Ajax beat Gremio Porto Alegre 4-3 on penalties after 0-0 draw
1985	Juventus beat Argentinos Juniors 4-2 on penalties after a 2-2 draw	1996	Juventus beat River Plate 1-0
1986	River Plate beat Steaua Bucharest 1-0	1997	Borussia Dortmund beat Cruzeiro 2-0
1987	FC Porto beat Penarol 2-1 after extra time	1998	Real Madrid beat Vasco da Gama 2-1
		1999	Manchester U beat Palmeiras 1-0
1988	Nacional (Uru) beat PSV Eindhoven 7-6 on penalties after 1-1 draw	2000	Boca Juniors beat Real Madrid 2-1
		2001	Bayern Munich beat Boca Juniors 1-0 after extra time
1989	AC Milan beat Atletico Nacional (Col) 1-0 after extra time	2002	Real Madrid beat Olimpia 2-0
1990	AC Milan beat Olimpia 3-0	2003	Boca Juniors beat AC Milan 3-1 on penalties after 1-1 draw
1991	Red Star Belgrade beat Colo Colo 3-0	2004	Porto beat Once Caldas 8-7 on penalties afer 0-0 draw
1992	Sao Paulo beat Barcelona 2-1		

European Cup runners-up; winners declined to take part.

EUROPEAN SUPER CUP

Played annually between the winners of the European Champions' Cup and the European Cup-Winners' Cup (UEFA Cup from 2000). AC Milan replaced Marseille in 1993–94.

Previous Matches

1972	Ajax beat Rangers 3-1, 3-2	1989	AC Milan beat Barcelona 1-1, 1-0
1973	Ajax beat AC Milan 0-1, 6-0	1990	AC Milan beat Sampdoria 1-1, 2-0
1974	Not contested	1991	Manchester U beat Red Star Belgrade 1-0
1975	Dynamo Kiev beat Bayern Munich 1-0, 2-0	1992	Barcelona beat Werder Bremen 1-1, 2-1
1976	Anderlecht beat Bayern Munich 4-1, 1-2	1993	Parma beat AC Milan 0-1, 2-0
1977	Liverpool beat Hamburg 1-1, 6-0	1994	AC Milan beat Arsenal 0-0, 2-0
1978	Anderlecht beat Liverpool 3-1, 1-2	1995	Ajax beat Zaragoza 1-1, 4-0
1979	Nottingham F beat Barcelona 1-0, 1-1	1996	Juventus beat Paris St Germain 6-1, 3-1
1980	Valencia beat Nottingham F 1-0, 1-2	1997	Barcelona beat Borussia Dortmund 2-0, 1-1
1981	Not contested	1998	Chelsea beat Real Madrid 1-0
1982	Aston Villa beat Barcelona 0-1, 3-0	1999	Lazio beat Manchester U 1-0
1983	Aberdeen beat Hamburg 0-0, 2-0	2000	Galatasaray beat Real Madrid 2-1 *(aet; Galatasaray won on sudden death.)*
1984	Juventus beat Liverpool 2-0		
1985	Juventus v Everton not contested due to UEFA ban on English clubs	2001	Liverpool beat Bayern Munich 3-2
		2002	Real Madrid beat Feyenoord 3-1
1986	Steaua Bucharest beat Dynamo Kiev 1-0	2003	AC Milan beat Porto 1-0
		2004	Valencia beat Porto 2-1
1987	FC Porto beat Ajax 1-0, 1-0	2005	Liverpool beat CSKA Moscow 3-1
1988	KV Mechelen beat PSV Eindhoven 3-0, 0-1		

EUROPEAN SUPER CUP 2005–06

26 August 2005, in Monaco

Liverpool (0) 3 *(Cisse 82, 102, Luis Garcia 109)*

CSKA Moscow (1) 1 *(Daniel Carvalho 28)* 16,000

Liverpool: Reina; Josemi, Riise (Cisse 79), Hamann, Carragher, Hyypia, Finnan (Sinama-Pongolle 54), Xabi Alonso (Sissoko 70), Luis Garcia, Morientes, Zenden.

CSKA Moscow: Akinfeev; Odiah Chidi, Zhirkov (Semberas 65), Berezoutski V, Ignashevich, Berezoutski A, Rahmic, Krasic (Dudu 84), Vagner Love, Daniel Carvalho, Aldonin.

Referee: R. Timmink (Holland).

OTHER BRITISH AND IRISH INTERNATIONAL MATCHES 2005–2006

■ *Denotes player sent off.*

Graz, 17 August 2005, 13,800

Austria (0) 2 *(Ibertsberger 83, Standfest 87)*

Scotland (2) 2 *(Miller 3, O'Connor 39)*

Austria: Payer (Schranz 46); Gercaliu, Dospel (Standfest 54), Pogatetz, Ehmann, Aufhauser, Schopp (Ibertsberger 68), Kuhbauer (Saumel 77), Mayrleb (Kuljic 66), Ivanschitz, Vastic (Akagunduz 66).

Scotland: Gordon; McNamara, Alexander G, Caldwell S, Pressley (Anderson 46), Webster, Dailly, O'Neil (Severin 46), O'Connor, Miller (Riordan 46), Quashie (Hughes R 73).

Referee: Selcuk (Turkey).

Glasgow, 12 November 2005, 26,708

Scotland (1) 1 *(Webster 37)*

USA (1) 1 *(Wolff 9 (pen))*

Scotland: Gordon; Alexander G, Webster, Dailly (Caldwell G 46), Weir, Pressley (Caldwell S 46), Fletcher, Quashie (Maloney 74), O'Connor (Brown 74), Hartley, McCann (McFadden 54).

USA: Keller; Spector, Bocanegra (Conrad 79), Cherundolo, Berhalter, Gaven (Quaranta 46), Carroll, Zavagnin (Olsen 46), Beasley (Pearce 76), Ching, Wolff (Rolfe 58).

Referee: A. Mallenco (Spain).

Glasgow, 1 March 2006, 20,952

Scotland (0) 1 *(Miller 55)*

Switzerland (2) 3 *(Barnetta 21, Gygax 41, Cabanas 69)*

Scotland: Gordon (Alexander N 49); Dailly, Alexander G, Ferguson (Teale 50), Weir (Caldwell S 56), Webster, Fletcher, Caldwell G, McFadden, Miller, Quashie.

Switzerland: Zuberbuhler (Coltorti 50); Degn, Senderos (Lustrinelli 73), Grichting, Behrami (Djourou 50), Barnetta, Vogel (Dzemaili 80), Cabanas, Wicky (Vonlanthen 50), Streller (Smiljanic 74), Gygax.

Referee: B. Coue (France).

Kobe, 11 May 2006, 5780

Bulgaria (1) 1 *(Todorov Y 26)*

Scotland (2) 5 *(Boyd 12, 43, McFadden 69, Burke 76, 88)*

Bulgaria: Kolev (Mihailov 71); Kirilov, Topuzakov, Karaslavov (Yanev 55), Wagner, Todorov Y, Telkiyski, Angelov, Domovchisky (Iliev 71), Petrov M, Todorov S (Genkov 71).

Scotland: Alexander N; Weir, Naysmith, Murty (McNamee 82), Anderson, Caldwell G, Fletcher, Severin (Rae 69), McCulloch (Murray 78), Teale (Burke 74), Boyd (McFadden 52).

Referee: T. Kamikawa (Japan).

Saitama, 13 May 2006, 58,648

Japan (0) 0

Scotland (0) 0

Japan: Kawaguchi; Miyamoto, Santos, Nakazawa (Tsuboi 50), Kaji, Fukunishi, Ogasawara, Ono, Endo (Sato 72), Kubo (Maki 62), Tamada.
Scotland: Alexander N; Weir, Naysmith (Murray 46), Murty (McNamee 79), Anderson, Caldwell G, Fletcher, Severin (Rae 46), McCulloch (Miller L 69), Teale (Burke 59), McFadden (Boyd 59).
Scotland won the Kirin Cup.
Referee: E. Gonzalez (Spain).

Copenhagen, 17 August 2005, 41,438

Denmark (0) 4 *(Rommedahl 60, Tomasson 63, Gravgaard 67, Larsen S 90)*

England (0) 1 *(Rooney 87)*

Denmark: Sorensen; Agger, Nielsen P (Gravgaard 46), Jensen N, Priske, Poulsen (Jensen D 87), Gravesen, Gronkjaer (Rommedahl 46), Jensen C (Perez 75), Tomasson (Larsen S 64), Jorgensen (Kahlenberg 46).
England: Robinson (James 46); Neville G (Johnson 46), Cole A, Gerrard (Jenas 84), Ferdinand, Terry (Carragher 46), Beckham, Lampard (Hargreaves 64), Rooney, Defoe (Owen 46), Cole J.
Referee: T. Ovrebo (Norway).

Geneva, 12 November 2005, 29,000

Argentina (1) 2 *(Crespo 34, Samuel 53)*

England (1) 3 *(Rooney 39, Owen 86, 90)*

Argentina: Abbondanzieri; Ayala (Coloccini 74), Sorin, Zanetti, Demichelis, Samuel, Riquelme (Gonzalez L 84), Rodriguez M, Cambiasso, Tevez (Cruz 80), Crespo (Saviola 70).
England: Robinson; Young (Crouch 80), Bridge (Konchesky 46), Ferdinand, Terry, King (Cole J 57), Beckham, Lampard, Rooney, Owen, Gerrard.
Referee: P. Lueuba (Switzerland).

Liverpool, 1 March 2006, 40,013

England (0) 2 *(Crouch 75, Cole J 90)*

Uruguay (1) 1 *(Pouso 26)*

England: Robinson; Neville, Bridge (Carragher 30), Gerrard (Jenas 46), Terry (King 46), Ferdinand, Beckham (Wright-Phillips 64), Carrick, Bent D (Defoe 82), Rooney (Crouch 64), Cole J.
Uruguay: Carini (Viera 46); Diogo, Lugano, Godin, Lima, Pouso, Perez (Gonzalez 88), Varela (Valdez 90), Vargas (Pereira 76), Regueiro (Martinez 83), Forlan (Medina 86).
Referee: S. Farina (Italy).

Reading, 25 May 2006, 22,032

England B (1) 1 *(Jenas 34)*

Belarus (0) 2 *(Kutuzov 50, Kornilenko 81)*

England: James (Green 46) (Carson 50); Hargreaves, Cole A, Carrick, Carragher, Campbell, Lennon, Jenas (Cole J 62), Crouch (Dawson 79), Owen (Walcott 62), Downing (Defoe 79).
Belarus: Zhevnov (Khomutovski 46); Kulchi, Lentsevich, Omelyanchuk■, Shtanyuk, Korytsko, Yurevich (Shagoiko 61), Bulyga (Kornilenko 46), Romaschenko (Kashevsky 74), Kalachev (Pankovets 80), Kutuzov (Kontsevoy 64).
Referee: D. McKeown (Ireland).

Old Trafford, 30 May 2006, 56,323

England (0) 3 *(Gerrard 47, Terry 51, Crouch 84)*

Hungary (0) 1 *(Dardai 55)*

England: Robinson; Neville G (Hargreaves 46), Cole A, Carragher, Ferdinand, Terry (Campbell 76), Beckham, Lampard, Gerrard (Crouch 65), Owen (Walcott 65), Cole J.

Hungary: Kiraly; Feher C, Komlosi (Vanczak 8), Halmosi, Eger, Molnar (Vadocz 82), Huszti, Dardai, Gera, Toth B (Torghelle 62), Szabics (Polonkai 73).

Referee: P. Vink (Holland).

Old Trafford, 3 June 2006, 70,373

England (4) 6 *(Lampard 11, Taylor 17 (og), Crouch 29, 65, 89, Owen 32)*

Jamaica (0) 0

England: Robinson (James 46); Carragher, Cole A (Bridge 33), Gerrard, Ferdinand, Terry (Campbell 35), Beckham (Lennon 66), Lampard (Carrick 66), Crouch, Owen, Cole J.

Jamaica: Ricketts; Reid, Davis, Stewart, Daley, Hue (Johnson 85), Taylor (Crawford 46), Euell (Stephenson 78), Campbell-Ryce, Shelton (Burton 47), Fuller (Bennett 76).

Referee: K. Plautz (Austria).

Ta'Qali, 17 August 2005, 1850

Malta (1) 1 *(Woods 35)*

Northern Ireland (1) 1 *(Healy 9)*

Malta: Haber; Pullicino (Ciantar 62), Said, Dimech (Scicluna 62), Wellman, Woods■, Agius G (Mallia 74), Briffa, Mattocks, Anonam, Cohen (Sammut 86).

Northern Ireland: Taylor; Gillespie■, Hughes A, Davis (Mulryne 88), Murdock, Craigan, Johnson, Whitley (Jones S 59), Quinn (Feeney 69), Healy, Elliott (Brunt 59).

Referee: M. Riley (England).

Belfast, 15 November 2005, 20,000

Northern Ireland (0) 1 *(Feeney 54)*

Portugal (1) 1 *(Craigan 41 (og))*

Northern Ireland: Taylor; Gillespie (Shiels 86), Capaldi, Davis, Murdock, Craigan, Jones S (McAuley 46), Elliott (McCann 46), Quinn (Thompson 77), Feeney (Sproule 86), Brunt.

Portugal: Paulo Santos; Paulo Ferreira, Costinha (Alves 67), Petit, Ricardo Carvalho, Meira, Jorge Ribeiro, Ronaldo (Helder Postiga 69), Pauleta (Nuno Gomes 46), Boa Morte (Caneira 62), Tiago (Frechaut 76).

Referee: H. Webb (England).

Belfast, 1 March 2006, 14,000

Northern Ireland (1) 1 *(Sproule 2)*

Estonia (0) 0

Northern Ireland: Taylor; Duff, Capaldi, Davis (Elliott 68), Craigan (McLean 46), McAuley, Sproule (Jones 46), Baird, Quinn (Thompson 59), Healy (Feeney 59), Brunt (McCann 68).

Estonia: Poom; Jaager, Stepanov, Piiroja, Rooba U, Rahn (Reim 78), Teever (Kuresoo 73), Dmitrijev, Neemelo, Lindpere (Oper 54), Sidorenkov (Ahjupera 84).

Referee: P. Vink (Holland).

New Jersey, 21 May 2006, 4152

Northern Ireland (0) 0

Uruguay (1) 1 *(Estoyanoff 33)*

Northern Ireland: Ingham; Duff (Webb 82), Capaldi, Murdock (McAuley 82), Craigan, Davis, Jones S (Thompson 59), Clingan (Hughes M 82), Sproule, Quinn (Lafferty 75), Hughes J (Shiels 75).
Uruguay: Carini; Valdez, Godin, Scotti, Garcia, Lopez, Estoyanoff (Surraco 82), Perez, Abreu, Giacomazzi, Vargas.

Chicago, 27 May 2006, 15,000

Romania (2) 2 *(Balan 7, Niculae 13)*

Northern Ireland (0) 0

Romania: Coman; Goian (Iencsi 56), Maftei, Pulhac (Stoica 88), Radoi (Soava 46), Badoi, Balan (Vasile-Cocis 46), Bostina, Nicolita (Oprita 65), Niculae (Mutu 46), Buga.
Northern Ireland: Blayney; Duff, Capaldi (Hughes J 57), McAuley (Murdock 82), Craigan (Webb 71), Davis, Shiels (Jones S 66), Clingan, Sproule (Hughes M 57), Quinn■, Thompson (Lafferty 66).
Referee: M. Kennedy (USA).

Dublin, 17 August 2005, 44,000

Republic of Ireland (1) 1 *(Reid A 32)*

Italy (2) 2 *(Pirlo 10, Gilardino 31)*

Republic of Ireland: Given; Finnan (Carr 57), O'Shea (Miller 78), Holland (Harte 39), Cunningham, Dunne (O'Brien A 46), Reid A (Elliott 74), Reid S, Morrison, Kilbane, Duff.
Italy: Roma; Zaccardo, Zambrotta, Pirlo (Barone 76), Nesta (Materazzi 46), Cannavaro (Barzagli 63), Gattuso, De Rossi (Grosso 46), Del Piero (Iaquinta 46), Vieri, Gilardino (Diana 46).
Referee: Paulo Costa (Portugal).

Dublin, 1 March 2006, 34,000

Republic of Ireland (1) 3 *(Duff 35, Robbie Keane 47, Miller 70)*

Sweden (0) 0

Republic of Ireland: Given (Henderson 48); O'Brien J (Miller 61), Harte (Kilbane 61), O'Shea (Ireland 48), O'Brien A, Dunne, Elliott (Kavanagh 48), Reid S, Robbie Keane, Doyle (Morrison 68), Duff.
Sweden: Isaksson; Ostlund (Andersson C 74), Mellberg, Hansson, Edman, Linderoth (Andersson D 69), Elmander (Jonson 60), Kallstrom (Svensson A 60), Wilhelmsson, Ibrahimovic (Rosenberg 37), Larsson (Allback 78).
Referee: D. Ledentu (France).

Dublin, 24 May 2006, 41,200

Republic of Ireland (0) 0

Chile (0) 1 *(Iturra 49)*

Republic of Ireland: Given (Henderson 54); Kelly (Reid A 84), Dunne, Breen (Harte 53), Kilbane, Miller (Kavanagh 54), Reid S, O'Shea (McGeady 54), Doyle (Byrne 72), Robbie Keane, Duff.
Chile: Bravo; Jara, Vargas, Contreras, Olarra, Jimenez, Acuna, Iturra, Gonzalez M (Zenteno 90), Navia (Sanchez 76), Suazo (Galaz 81).
Referee: M. Ingvarsson (Sweden).

Swansea, 17 August 2005, 10,016

Wales (0) 0

Slovenia (0) 0

Wales: Coyne; Duffy (Edwards 73), Ricketts, Page, Gabbidon, Partridge (Roberts G 89), Robinson (Davies C 85), Vaughan (Parry 68), Hartson, Earnshaw (Williams G 62), Fletcher.
Slovenia: Mavric B (Handanovic 63); Cesar, Filekovic, Mavric M (Sukalo 46), Knavs, Acimovic (Cimirotic 46), Zlogar, Ceh, Pokorn (Ilic 56), Lavric (Rodic 46), Komac (Pecnik 87).
Referee: I. Stokes (Republic of Ireland).

Limassol, 16 November 2005, 1000

Cyprus (1) 1 *(Michael 42 (pen))*

Wales (0) 0

Cyprus: Morfis (Georgallides 71); Okkarides, Lambrou (Louka 79), Michael, Charalambidis, Elia (Theofilou 70), Garpozis, Krassas, Makrides, Okkas, Yiasoumi (Alecou 76).
Wales: Price; Duffy (Edwards 76), Collins D (Williams G 46), Gabbidon, Page, Fletcher, Ricketts, Robinson, Hartson, Bellamy, Vaughan (Earnshaw 66).
Referee: H. Jacov (Israel).

Cardiff, 1 March 2006, 12,324

Wales (0) 0

Paraguay (0) 0

Wales: Jones P (Price 66); Edwards, Ricketts, Gabbidon, Collins J, Nyatanga, Fletcher (Robinson 75), Bellamy (Earnshaw 78), Koumas (Ledley 70), Davies S (Crofts 76), Giggs (Cotterill 86).
Paraguay: Villar; Caceres J, Toledo, Caniza, Da Silva, Paredes, Ramirez (Cabanas 77), Barreto, Dos Santos (Riveros 67), Acuna, Haedo Valdez (Cardozo 71).
Referee: D. McDonald (Scotland).

Bilbao, 21 May 2006, 15,000

Basque Country (0) 0

Wales (0) 1 *(Giggs 76)*

Basque Country: Lafuente (Riesgo 46); Edu Alonso, Lopez Rekarte (Garrido 46), Campo (Sarriegi 46), Labaka, Punal, Preto, Guerrero (Munoz 46), Etxeberria, Alonso (Llorente 63), Gabilondo.
Wales: Jones P; Ledley, Nyatanga, Gabbidon, Collins J, Robinson (Cotterill 73), Fletcher, Bellamy (Crofts 56), Earnshaw, Davies S, Giggs.
Referee: E. Gonzalez (Spain).

Graz, 27 May 2006, 8000

Trinidad & Tobago (1) 1 *(John S 32)*

Wales (1) 2 *(Earnshaw 38, 87)*

Trinidad & Tobago: Jack; John A, Andrews, Lawrence (Samuell 35), Birchall, Gray, Edwards, John S, Jones (Latapy 62), Theobald (Whitley 77), Yorke.
Wales: Brown (Garner 46); Robinson, Ledley, Gabbidon, Collins J, Partridge (Nyatanga 46), Fletcher (Crofts 46), Earnshaw, Cotterill (Davies C 46), Davies S (Aaron Davies 78), Vaughan (Bale 55).
Referee: S. Messner (Austria).

ENGLAND UNDER-21 TEAMS 2005–2006

■*Denotes player sent off.*

Herning, 16 August 2005, 4012

Denmark (0) 0 *Rasmuşsen M*■
England (0) 1 *(Ambrose 90)*

England: Carson (Camp 46); Hunt, Ridgewell (Whittingham 46), Reo-Coker (Soares 46), Dawson (Ferdinand 46), Davenport, Milner, Richardson, Cole C, Ashton (Stead 46), Downing (Ambrose 46).

Wrexham, 2 September 2005, 4109
Wales (0) 0
England (2) 4 *(Stead 5, Whittingham 27, 89, Dawson 68)*

Wales: Hennessey; Beevers, Gilbert, Birchall, Anthony, Nyatanga (Adam Davies 56), Crofts, Davies C (Fleetwood 72), Aaron Davies, Cotterill, Tudor Jones.
England: Carson; Johnson, Dawson, Reo-Coker, Ferdinand, Ridgewell (Hunt 57), Milner, Ambrose, Cole C (Welsh 60), Stead (Nugent 60), Whittingham.

Mainz, 6 September 2005, 7000
Germany (1) 1 *(Kiessling 17)*
England (1) 1 *(Taylor S 42)*

England: Carson; Hunt (Baines 46), Taylor S, Dawson, Ferdinand, O'Neil, Welsh (Nugent 78), Reo-Coker, Cole C, Milner, Whittingham (Soares 46).

Leeds, 7 October 2005, 28,030
England (1) 1 *(Cole C 18)*
Austria (0) 2 *(Janko 56, 76)*

England: Carson; Taylor S, Baines, Dawson, Ferdinand (Taylor R 71), Huddlestone, Milner, Soares (Moore 61), Cole C (Jerome 87), Thomas, Lennon.

Hillsborough, 11 October 2005, 23,110
England (3) 4 *(Cole C 18, Thomas 21, Taylor S 37, 88)*
Poland (1) 1 *(Kukut 39)*

England: Carson; Taylor R (Onuoha 85), Whittingham, Taylor S, Ferdinand, Huddlestone, Reo-Coker, O'Neil, Cole C (Stead 87), Lennon, Thomas (Milner 65).

Tottenham, 11 November 2005, 34,494
England (0) 1 *(Ambrose 88)*
France (0) 1 *(Le Tallec 47)*

England: Carson; Taylor R, Whittingham, Dawson, Ferdinand, Huddlestone, Milner (Ashton 79), Ambrose, Cole C, Bent, Richardson.

Nancy, 15 November 2005, 13,045
France (0) 2 *(Ribery 58, Briand 85 (pen))*
England (0) 1 *(Bent 55)*

England: Carson; Taylor R, Onuoha (Whittingham 79), Huddlestone, Dawson, Ferdinand, Ambrose (Ashton 66), O'Neil, Bent, Cole C (Jerome 89), Richardson.

Reading, 28 February 2006, 15,022
England (1) 3 *(Whittingham 24, Bentley 54, 60)*
Norway (0) 1 *(Steenslid 52)*

England: Carson (Camp 46); Johnson (Hoyte 65), Whittingham (Taylor 65), Ridgewell (Davies 46), Ferdinand, Huddlestone, Reo-Coker (Soares 46), Bentley (Welsh 73), Nugent (Lita 46), Milner (Jerome 46), Routledge (McLeod 73).

POST-WAR INTERNATIONAL APPEARANCES

As at July 2006 *(Season of first cap given)*

ENGLAND

A'Court, A. (5) 1957/8 Liverpool
Adams, T. A. (66) 1986/7 Arsenal
Allen, C. (5) 1983/4 QPR, Tottenham H
Allen, R. (5) 1951/2 WBA
Allen, T. (3) 1959/60 Stoke C
Anderson, S. (2) 1961/2 Sunderland
Anderson, V. (30) 1978/9 Nottingham F, Arsenal, Manchester U
Anderton, D. R. (30) 1993/4 Tottenham H
Angus, J. (1) 1960/1 Burnley
Armfield, J. (43) 1958/9 Blackpool
Armstrong, D. (3) 1979/80 Middlesbrough, Southampton
Armstrong, K. (1) 1954/5 Chelsea
Astall, G. (2) 1955/6 Birmingham C
Astle, J. (5) 1968/9 WBA
Aston, J. (17) 1948/9 Manchester U
Atyeo, J. (6) 1955/6 Bristol C

Bailey, G. R. (2) 1984/5 Manchester U
Bailey, M. (2) 1963/4 Charlton
Baily, E. (9) 1949/50 Tottenham H
Baker, J. (8) 1959/60 Hibernian, Arsenal
Ball, A. (72) 1964/5 Blackpool, Everton, Arsenal
Ball, M. J. (1) 2000/01 Everton
Banks, G. (73) 1962/3 Leicester C, Stoke C
Banks, T. (6) 1957/8 Bolton W
Bardsley, D. (2) 1992/3 QPR
Barham, M. (2) 1982/3 Norwich C
Barlow, R. (1) 1954/5 WBA
Barmby, N. J. (23) 1994/5 Tottenham H, Middlesbrough, Everton, Liverpool
Barnes, J. (79) 1982/3 Watford, Liverpool
Barnes, P. (22) 1977/8 Manchester C, WBA, Leeds U
Barrass, M. (3) 1951/2 Bolton W
Barrett, E. D. (3) 1990/1 Oldham Ath, Aston Villa
Barry, G. (8) 1999/00 Aston Villa
Barton, W. D. (3) 1994/5 Wimbledon, Newcastle U
Batty, D. (42) 1990/1 Leeds U, Blackburn R, Newcastle U, Leeds U
Baynham, R. (3) 1955/6 Luton T
Beardsley, P. A. (59) 1985/6 Newcastle U, Liverpool, Newcastle U
Beasant, D. J. (2) 1989/90 Chelsea

Beattie, J. S. (5) 2002/03 Southampton
Beattie, T. K. (9) 1974/5 Ipswich T
Beckham, D. R. J. (94) 1996/7 Manchester U, Real Madrid
Bell, C. (48) 1967/8 Manchester C
Bent D. A. (1) 2005/06 Charlton Ath
Bentley, R. (12) 1948/9 Chelsea
Berry, J. (4) 1952/3 Manchester U
Birtles, G. (3) 1979/80 Nottingham F
Blissett, L. (14) 1982/3 Watford, AC Milan
Blockley, J. (1) 1972/3 Arsenal
Blunstone, F. (5) 1954/5 Chelsea
Bonetti, P. (7) 1965/6 Chelsea
Bould, S. A. (2) 1993/4 Arsenal
Bowles, S. (5) 1973/4 QPR
Bowyer, L. D. (1) 2002/03 Leeds U
Boyer, P. (1) 1975/6 Norwich C
Brabrook, P. (3) 1957/8 Chelsea
Bracewell, P. W. (3) 1984/5 Everton
Bradford, G. (1) 1955/6 Bristol R
Bradley, W. (3) 1958/9 Manchester U
Bridge, W. M. (23) 2001/02 Southampton, Chelsea
Bridges, B. (4) 1964/5 Chelsea
Broadbent, P. (7) 1957/8 Wolverhampton W
Broadis, I. (14) 1951/2 Manchester C, Newcastle U
Brooking, T. (47) 1973/4 West Ham U
Brooks, J. (3) 1956/7 Tottenham H
Brown, A. (1) 1970/1 WBA
Brown, K. (1) 1959/60 West Ham U
Brown, W. M. (9) 1998/9 Manchester U
Bull, S. G. (13) 1988/9 Wolverhampton W
Butcher, T. (77) 1979/80 Ipswich T, Rangers
Butt, N. (39) 1996/7 Manchester U, Newcastle U
Byrne, G. (2) 1962/3 Liverpool
Byrne, J. (11) 1961/2 Crystal P, West Ham U
Byrne, R. (33) 1953/4 Manchester U

Callaghan, I. (4) 1965/6 Liverpool
Campbell, S. (69) 1995/6 Tottenham H, Arsenal
Carragher, J. L. (29) 1998/9 Liverpool
Carrick, M. (7) 2000/01 West Ham U, Tottenham H
Carter, H. (7) 1946/7 Derby Co
Chamberlain, M. (8) 1982/3 Stoke C

Channon, M. (46) 1972/3 Southampton, Manchester C
Charles, G. A. (2) 1990/1 Nottingham F
Charlton, J. (35) 1964/5 Leeds U
Charlton, R. (106) 1957/8 Manchester U
Charnley, R. (1) 1962/3 Blackpool
Cherry, T. (27) 1975/6 Leeds U
Chilton, A. (2) 1950/1 Manchester U
Chivers, M. (24) 1970/1 Tottenham H
Clamp, E. (4) 1957/8 Wolverhampton W
Clapton, D. (1) 1958/9 Arsenal
Clarke, A. (19) 1969/70 Leeds U
Clarke, H. (1) 1953/4 Tottenham H
Clayton, R. (35) 1955/6 Blackburn R
Clemence, R (61) 1972/3 Liverpool, Tottenham H
Clement, D. (5) 1975/6 QPR
Clough, B. (2) 1959/60 Middlesbrough
Clough, N. H. (14) 1988/9 Nottingham F
Coates, R. (4) 1969/70 Burnley, Tottenham H
Cockburn, H. (13) 1946/7 Manchester U
Cohen, G. (37) 1963/4 Fulham
Cole, Andy (15) 1994/5 Manchester U
Cole, Ashley (51) 2000/01 Arsenal
Cole, J. J. (37) 2000/01 West Ham U, Chelsea
Collymore, S. V. (3) 1994/5 Nottingham F, Aston Villa
Compton, L. (2) 1950/1 Arsenal
Connelly, J. (20) 1959/60 Burnley, Manchester U
Cooper, C. T. (2) 1994/5 Nottingham F
Cooper, T. (20) 1968/9 Leeds U
Coppell, S. (42) 1977/8 Manchester U
Corrigan, J. (9) 1975/6 Manchester C
Cottee, A. R. (7) 1986/7 West Ham U, Everton
Cowans, G. (10) 1982/3 Aston Villa, Bari, Aston Villa
Crawford, R. (2) 1961/2 Ipswich T
Crouch, P. J. (7) 2004/05 Southampton, Liverpool
Crowe, C. (1) 1962/3 Wolverhampton W
Cunningham, L. (6) 1978/9 WBA, Real Madrid
Curle, K. (3) 1991/2 Manchester C
Currie, A. (17) 1971/2 Sheffield U, Leeds U

Daley, A. M. (7) 1991/2 Aston Villa
Davenport, P. (1) 1984/5 Nottingham F
Deane, B. C. (3) 1990/1 Sheffield U
Deeley, N. (2) 1958/9 Wolverhampton W

Defoe, J. C. (16) 2003/04 Tottenham H
Devonshire, A. (8) 1979/80 West Ham U
Dickinson, J. (48) 1948/9 Portsmouth
Ditchburn, E. (6) 1948/9 Tottenham H
Dixon, K. M. (8) 1984/5 Chelsea
Dixon, L. M. (22) 1989/90 Arsenal
Dobson, M. (5) 1973/4 Burnley, Everton
Dorigo, A. R. (15) 1989/90 Chelsea, Leeds U
Douglas, B. (36) 1957/8 Blackburn R
Downing S. (4) 2004/05 Middlesbrough
Doyle, M. (5) 1975/6 Manchester C
Dublin, D. (4) 1997/8 Coventry C, Aston Villa
Dunn, D. J. I. (1) 2002/03 Blackburn R
Duxbury, M. (10) 1983/4 Manchester U
Dyer, K. C. (28) 1999/00 Newcastle U

Eastham, G. (19) 1962/3 Arsenal
Eckersley, W. (17) 1949/50 Blackburn R
Edwards, D. (18) 1954/5 Manchester U
Ehiogu, U. (4) 1995/6 Aston Villa, Middlesbrough
Ellerington, W. (2) 1948/9 Southampton
Elliott, W. H. (5) 1951/2 Burnley

Fantham, J. (1) 1961/2 Sheffield W
Fashanu, J. (2) 1988/9 Wimbledon
Fenwick, T. (20) 1983/4 QPR, Tottenham H
Ferdinand, L. (17) 1992/3 QPR, Newcastle U, Tottenham H
Ferdinand, R. G. (52) 1997/8 West Ham U, Leeds U, Manchester U
Finney, T. (76) 1946/7 Preston NE
Flowers, R. (49) 1954/5 Wolverhampton W
Flowers, T. (11) 1992/3 Southampton, Blackburn R
Foster, S. (3) 1981/2 Brighton
Foulkes, W. (1) 1954/5 Manchester U
Fowler, R. B. (26) 1995/6 Liverpool, Leeds U
Francis, G. (12) 1974/5 QPR
Francis, T. (52) 1976/7 Birmingham C, Nottingham F, Manchester C, Sampdoria
Franklin, N. (27) 1946/7 Stoke C
Froggatt, J. (13) 1949/50 Portsmouth
Froggatt, R. (4) 1952/3 Sheffield W

Gardner, A. (1) 2003/04 Tottenham H
Garrett, T. (3) 1951/2 Blackpool
Gascoigne, P. J. (57) 1988/9 Tottenham H, Lazio, Rangers, Middlesbrough
Gates, E. (2) 1980/1 Ipswich T

George, F. C. (1) 1976/7 Derby Co
Gerrard, S. G. (47) 1999/00 Liverpool
Gidman, J. (1) 1976/7 Aston Villa
Gillard, I. (3) 1974/5 QPR
Goddard, P. (1) 1981/2 West Ham U
Grainger, C. (7) 1955/6 Sheffield U,
   Sunderland
Gray, A. A. (1) 1991/2 Crystal P
Gray, M. (3) 1998/9 Sunderland
Greaves, J. (57) 1958/9 Chelsea,
   Tottenham H
Green, R. P. (1) 2004/05 Norwich C
Greenhoff, B. (18) 1975/6 Manchester
   U, Leeds U
Gregory, J. (6) 1982/3 QPR
Guppy, S. (1) 1999/00 Leicester C

Hagan, J. (1) 1948/9 Sheffield U
Haines, J. (1) 1948/9 WBA
Hall, J. (17) 1955/6 Birmingham C
Hancocks, J. (3) 1948/9
   Wolverhampton W
Hardwick, G. (13) 1946/7
   Middlesbrough
Harford, M. G. (2) 1987/8 Luton T
Hargreaves, O. (34) 2001/02 Bayern
   Munich
Harris, G. (1) 1965/6 Burnley
Harris, P. (2) 1949/50 Portsmouth
Harvey, C. (1) 1970/1 Everton
Hassall, H. (5) 1950/1 Huddersfield T,
   Bolton W
Hateley, M. (32) 1983/4 Portsmouth,
   AC Milan, Monaco, Rangers
Haynes, J. (56) 1954/5 Fulham
Hector, K. (2) 1973/4 Derby Co
Hellawell, M. (2) 1962/3 Birmingham C
Hendrie, L. A. (1) 1998/9 Aston Villa
Henry, R. (1) 1962/3 Tottenham H
Heskey, E. W. (43) 1998/9 Leicester C,
   Liverpool, Birmingham C
Hill, F. (2) 1962/3 Bolton W
Hill, G. (6) 1975/6 Manchester U
Hill, R. (3) 1982/3 Luton T
Hinchcliffe, A. G. (7) 1996/7 Everton,
   Sheffield W
Hinton, A. (3) 1962/3 Wolverhampton
   W, Nottingham F
Hirst, D. E. (3) 1990/1 Sheffield W
Hitchens, G. (7) 1960/1 Aston Villa,
   Internazionale
Hoddle, G. (53) 1979/80 Tottenham H,
   Monaco
Hodge, S. B. (24) 1985/6 Aston Villa,
   Tottenham H, Nottingham F
Hodgkinson, A. (5) 1956/7 Sheffield U
Holden, D. (5) 1958/9 Bolton W
Holliday, E. (3) 1959/60 Middlesbrough
Hollins, J. (1) 1966/7 Chelsea
Hopkinson, E. (14) 1957/8 Bolton W

Howe, D. (23) 1957/8 WBA
Howe, J. (3) 1947/8 Derby Co
Howey, S. N. (4) 1994/5 Newcastle U
Hudson, A. (2) 1974/5 Stoke C
Hughes, E. (62) 1969/70 Liverpool,
   Wolverhampton W
Hughes, L. (3) 1949/50 Liverpool
Hunt, R. (34) 1961/2 Liverpool
Hunt, S. (2) 1983/4 WBA
Hunter, N. (28) 1965/6 Leeds U
Hurst, G. (49) 1965/6 West Ham U

Ince, P. (53) 1992/3 Manchester U,
   Internazionale, Liverpool,
   Middlesbrough

James, D. B. (34) 1996/7 Liverpool,
   Aston Villa, West Ham U,
   Manchester C
Jeffers, F. (1) 2002/03 Arsenal
Jenas, J. A. (15) 2002/03 Newcastle U,
   Tottenham H
Jezzard, B. (2) 1953/4 Fulham
Johnson, A. (2) 2004/05 Crystal P
Johnson, D. (8) 1974/5 Ipswich T,
   Liverpool
Johnson, G. M. C. (5) 2003/04 Chelsea
Johnson, S. A. M. (1) 2000/01 Derby
   Co
Johnston, H. (10) 1946/7 Blackpool
Jones, M. (3) 1964/5 Sheffield U, Leeds
   U
Jones, R. (8) 1991/2 Liverpool
Jones, W. H. (2) 1949/50 Liverpool

Kay, A. (1) 1962/3 Everton
Keegan, K. (63) 1972/3 Liverpool, SV
   Hamburg, Southampton
Kennedy, A. (2) 1983/4 Liverpool
Kennedy, R. (17) 1975/6 Liverpool
Keown, M. R. (43) 1991/2 Everton,
   Arsenal
Kevan, D. (14) 1956/7 WBA
Kidd, B. (2) 1969/70 Manchester U
King, L. B. (16) 2001/02 Tottenham H
Knight, Z. (2) 2004/05 Fulham
Knowles, C. (4) 1967/8 Tottenham H
Konchesky, P. M. (2) 2002/03 Charlton
   Ath, West Ham U

Labone, B. (26) 1962/3 Everton
Lampard, F. J. (45) 1999/00 West Ham
   U, Chelsea
Lampard, F. R. G. (2) 1972/3 West
   Ham U
Langley, J. (3) 1957/8 Fulham
Langton, R. (11) 1946/7 Blackburn R,
   Preston NE, Bolton W
Latchford, R. (12) 1977/8 Everton
Lawler, C. (4) 1970/1 Liverpool

Lawton, T. (15) 1946/7 Chelsea, Notts Co

Lee, F. (27) 1968/9 Manchester C

Lee, J. (1) 1950/1 Derby C

Lee, R. M. (21) 1994/5 Newcastle U

Lee, S. (14) 1982/3 Liverpool

Lennon, A. J. (4) 2005/06 Tottenham H

Le Saux, G. P. (36) 1993/4 Blackburn R, Chelsea

Le Tissier, M. P. (8) 1993/4 Southampton

Lindsay, A. (4) 1973/4 Liverpool

Lineker, G. (80) 1983/4 Leicester C, Everton, Barcelona, Tottenham H

Little, B. (1) 1974/5 Aston Villa

Lloyd, L. (4) 1970/1 Liverpool, Nottingham F

Lofthouse, N. (33) 1950/1 Bolton W

Lowe, E. (3) 1946/7 Aston Villa

Mabbutt, G. (16) 1982/3 Tottenham H

Macdonald, M. (14) 1971/2 Newcastle U

Madeley, P. (24) 1970/1 Leeds U

Mannion, W. (26) 1946/7 Middlesbrough

Mariner, P. (35) 1976/7 Ipswich T, Arsenal

Marsh, R. (9) 1971/2 QPR, Manchester C

Martin, A. (17) 1980/1 West Ham U

Martyn, A. N. (23) 1991/2 Crystal P, Leeds U

Marwood, B. (1) 1988/9 Arsenal

Matthews, R. (5) 1955/6 Coventry C

Matthews, S. (37) 1946/7 Stoke C, Blackpool

McCann, G. P. (1) 2000/01 Sunderland

McDermott, T. (25) 1977/8 Liverpool

McDonald, C. (8) 1957/8 Burnley

McFarland, R. (28) 1970/1 Derby C

McGarry, W. (4) 1953/4 Huddersfield T

McGuinness, W. (2) 1958/9 Manchester U

McMahon, S. (17) 1987/8 Liverpool

McManaman, S. (37) 1994/5 Liverpool, Real Madrid

McNab, R. (4) 1968/9 Arsenal

McNeil, M. (9) 1960/1 Middlesbrough

Meadows, J. (1) 1954/5 Manchester C

Medley, L. (6) 1950/1 Tottenham H

Melia, J. (2) 1962/3 Liverpool

Merrick, G. (23) 1951/2 Birmingham C

Merson, P. C. (21) 1991/2 Arsenal, Middlesbrough, Aston Villa

Metcalfe, V. (2) 1950/1 Huddersfield T

Milburn, J. (13) 1948/9 Newcastle U

Miller, B. (1) 1960/1 Burnley

Mills, D. J. (19) 2000/01 Leeds U

Mills, M. (42) 1972/3 Ipswich T

Milne, G. (14) 1962/3 Liverpool

Milton, C. A. (1) 1951/2 Arsenal

Moore, R. (108) 1961/2 West Ham U

Morley, A. (6) 1981/2 Aston Villa

Morris, J. (3) 1948/9 Derby Co

Mortensen, S. (25) 1946/7 Blackpool

Mozley, B. (3) 1949/50 Derby Co

Mullen, J. (12) 1946/7 Wolverhampton W

Mullery, A. (35) 1964/5 Tottenham H

Murphy, D. B. (9) 2001/02 Liverpool

Neal, P. (50) 1975/6 Liverpool

Neville, G. A. (81) 1994/5 Manchester U

Neville, P. J. (52) 1995/6 Manchester U

Newton, K. (27) 1965/6 Blackburn R, Everton

Nicholls, J. (2) 1953/4 WBA

Nicholson, W. (1) 1950/1 Tottenham H

Nish, D. (5) 1972/3 Derby Co

Norman, M. (23) 1961/2 Tottenham H

O'Grady, M. (2) 1962/3 Huddersfield T, Leeds U

Osgood, P. (4) 1969/70 Chelsea

Osman, R. (11) 1979/80 Ipswich T

Owen, M. J. (80) 1997/8 Liverpool, Real Madrid, Newcastle U

Owen, S. (3) 1953/4 Luton T

Paine, T. (19) 1962/3 Southampton

Pallister, G. (22) 1987/8 Middlesbrough, Manchester U

Palmer, C. L. (18) 1991/2 Sheffield W

Parker, P. A. (19) 1988/9 QPR, Manchester U

Parker, S. M. (2) 2003/04 Charlton Ath, Chelsea

Parkes, P. (1) 1973/4 QPR

Parlour, R. (10) 1998/9 Arsenal

Parry, R. (2) 1959/60 Bolton W

Peacock, A. (6) 1961/2 Middlesbrough, Leeds U

Pearce, S. (78) 1986/7 Nottingham F, West Ham U

Pearson, Stan (8) 1947/8 Manchester U

Pearson, Stuart (15) 1975/6 Manchester U

Pegg, D. (1) 1956/7 Manchester U

Pejic, M. (4) 1973/4 Stoke C

Perry, W. (3) 1955/6 Blackpool

Perryman, S. (1) 1981/2 Tottenham H

Peters, M. (67) 1965/6 West Ham U, Tottenham H

Phelan, M. C. (1) 1989/90 Manchester U

Phillips, K. (8) 1998/9 Sunderland

Phillips, L. (3) 1951/2 Portsmouth

Pickering, F. (3) 1963/4 Everton

Pickering, N. (1) 1982/3 Sunderland
Pilkington, B. (1) 1954/5 Burnley
Platt, D. (62) 1989/90 Aston Villa, Bari, Juventus, Sampdoria, Arsenal
Pointer, R. (3) 1961/2 Burnley
Powell, C. G. (5) 2000/01 Charlton Ath
Pye, J. (1) 1949/50 Wolverhampton W

Quixall, A. (5) 1953/4 Sheffield W

Radford, J. (2) 1968/9 Arsenal
Ramsey, A. (32) 1948/9 Southampton, Tottenham H
Reaney, P. (3) 1968/9 Leeds U
Redknapp, J. F. (17) 1995/6 Liverpool
Reeves, K. (2) 1979/80 Norwich C, Manchester C
Regis, C. (5) 1981/2 WBA, Coventry C
Reid, P. (13) 1984/5 Everton
Revie, D. (6) 1954/5 Manchester C
Richards, J. (1) 1972/3 Wolverhampton W
Richardson, K. (1) 1993/4 Aston Villa
Richardon, K. E. (4) 2004/05 Manchester U
Rickaby, S. (1) 1953/4 WBA
Ricketts, M. B. (1) 2001/02 Bolton W
Rimmer, J. (1) 1975/6 Arsenal
Ripley, S. E. (2) 1993/4 Blackburn R
Rix, G. (17) 1980/1 Arsenal
Robb, G. (1) 1953/4 Tottenham H
Roberts, G. (6) 1982/3 Tottenham H
Robinson, P. W. (26) 2002/03 Leeds U, Tottenham H
Robson, B. (90) 1979/80 WBA, Manchester U
Robson, R. (20) 1957/8 WBA
Rocastle, D. (14) 1988/9 Arsenal
Rooney, W. (33) 2002/03 Everton. Manchester U
Rowley, J. (6) 1948/9 Manchester U
Royle, J. (6) 1970/1 Everton, Manchester C
Ruddock, N. (1) 1994/5 Liverpool

Sadler, D. (4) 1967/8 Manchester U
Salako, J. A. (5) 1990/1 Crystal P
Sansom, K. (86) 1978/9 Crystal P, Arsenal
Scales, J. R. (3) 1994/5 Liverpool
Scholes, P. (66) 1996/7 Manchester U
Scott, L. (17) 1946/7 Arsenal
Seaman, D. A. (75) 1988/9 QPR, Arsenal
Sewell, J. (6) 1951/2 Sheffield W
Shackleton, L. (5) 1948/9 Sunderland
Sharpe, L. S. (8) 1990/1 Manchester U
Shaw, G. (5) 1958/9 Sheffield U
Shearer, A. (63) 1991/2 Southampton, Blackburn R, Newcastle U

Shellito, K. (1) 1962/3 Chelsea
Sheringham, E. (51) 1992/3 Tottenham H, Manchester U, Tottenham H
Sherwood, T. A. (3) 1998/9 Tottenham H
Shilton, P. (125) 1970/1 Leicester C, Stoke C, Nottingham F, Southampton, Derby Co
Shimwell, E. (1) 1948/9 Blackpool
Sillett, P. (3) 1954/5 Chelsea
Sinclair, T. (12) 2001/02 West Ham U, Manchester C
Sinton, A. (12) 1991/2 QPR, Sheffield W
Slater, W. (12) 1954/5 Wolverhampton W
Smith, A. (16) 2000/01 Leeds U, Manchester U
Smith, A. M. (13) 1988/9 Arsenal
Smith, L. (6) 1950/1 Arsenal
Smith, R. (15) 1960/1 Tottenham H
Smith, Tom (1) 1970/1 Liverpool
Smith, Trevor (2) 1959/60 Birmingham C
Southgate, G. (57) 1995/6 Aston Villa, Middlesbrough
Spink, N. (1) 1982/3 Aston Villa
Springett, R. (33) 1959/60 Sheffield W
Staniforth, R. (8) 1953/4 Huddersfield T
Statham, D. (3) 1982/3 WBA
Stein, B. (1) 1983/4 Luton T
Stepney, A. (1) 1967/8 Manchester U
Sterland, M. (1) 1988/9 Sheffield W
Steven, T. M. (36) 1984/5 Everton, Rangers, Marseille
Stevens, G. A. (7) 1984/5 Tottenham H
Stevens, M. G. (46) 1984/5 Everton, Rangers
Stewart, P. A. (3) 1991/2 Tottenham H
Stiles, N. (28) 1964/5 Manchester U
Stone, S. B. (9) 1995/6 Nottingham F
Storey-Moore, I. (1) 1969/70 Nottingham F
Storey, P. (19) 1970/1 Arsenal
Streten, B. (1) 1949/50 Luton T
Summerbee, M. (8) 1967/8 Manchester C
Sunderland, A. (1) 1979/80 Arsenal
Sutton, C. R. (1) 1997/8 Blackburn R
Swan, P. (19) 1959/60 Sheffield W
Swift, F. (19) 1946/7 Manchester C

Talbot, B. (6) 1976/7 Ipswich T, Arsenal
Tambling, R. (3) 1962/3 Chelsea
Taylor, E. (1) 1953/4 Blackpool
Taylor, J. (2) 1950/1 Fulham
Taylor, P. H. (3) 1947/8 Liverpool
Taylor, P. J. (4) 1975/6 Crystal P

Taylor, T. (19) 1952/3 Manchester U
Temple, D. (1) 1964/5 Everton
Terry, J. G. (29) 2002/03 Chelsea
Thomas, Danny (2) 1982/3 Coventry C
Thomas, Dave (8) 1974/5 QPR
Thomas, G. R. (9) 1990/1 Crystal P
Thomas, M. L. (2) 1988/9 Arsenal
Thompson, A. (1) 2003/04 Celtic
Thompson, P. (16) 1963/4 Liverpool
Thompson, P. B. (42) 1975/6 Liverpool
Thompson, T. (2) 1951/2 Aston Villa,
  Preston NE
Thomson, R. (8) 1963/4
  Wolverhampton W
Todd, C. (27) 1971/2 Derby Co
Towers, T. (3) 1975/6 Sunderland
Tueart, D. (6) 1974/5 Manchester C

Ufton, D. (1) 1953/4 Charlton Ath
Unsworth, D. G. (1) 1994/5 Everton
Upson, M. J. (7) 2002/03 Birmingham
  C

Vassell, D. (22) 2001/02 Aston Villa
Venables, T. (2) 1964/5 Chelsea
Venison, B. (2) 1994/5 Newcastle U
Viljoen, C. (2) 1974/5 Ipswich T
Viollet, D. (2) 1959/60 Manchester U

Waddle, C. R. (62) 1984/5 Newcastle U,
  Tottenham H, Marseille
Waiters, A. (5) 1963/4 Blackpool
Walcott, T. J. (1) 2005/06 Arsenal
Walker, D. S. (59) 1988/9 Nottingham
  F, Sampdoria, Sheffield W
Walker, I. M. (4) 1995/6 Tottenham H,
  Leicester C
Wallace, D. L. (1) 1985/6 Southampton
Walsh, P. (5) 1982/3 Luton T
Walters, K. M. (1) 1990/1 Rangers
Ward, P. (1) 1979/80 Brighton
Ward, T. (2) 1947/8 Derby C
Watson, D. (12) 1983/4 Norwich C,
  Everton
Watson, D. V. (65) 1973/4 Sunderland,
  Manchester C, Werder Bremen,
  Southampton, Stoke C

NORTHERN IRELAND

Aherne, T. (4) 1946/7 Belfast Celtic,
  Luton T
Anderson, T. (22) 1972/3 Manchester
  U, Swindon T, Peterborough U
Armstrong, G. (63) 1976/7 Tottenham
  H, Watford, Real Mallorca, WBA,
  Chesterfield

Baird, C. P. (20) 2002/03 Southampton
Barr, H. (3) 1961/2 Linfield, Coventry C

Watson, W. (4) 1949/50 Sunderland
Webb, N. (26) 1987/8 Nottingham F,
  Manchester U
Weller, K. (4) 1973/4 Leicester C
West, G. (3) 1968/9 Everton
Wheeler, J. (1) 1954/5 Bolton W
White, D. (1) 1992/3 Manchester C
Whitworth, S. (7) 1974/5 Leicester C
Whymark, T. (1) 1977/8 Ipswich T
Wignall, F. (2) 1964/5 Nottingham F
Wilcox, J. M. (3) 1995/6 Blackburn R,
  Leeds U
Wilkins, R. (84) 1975/6 Chelsea,
  Manchester U, AC Milan
Williams, B. (24) 1948/9
  Wolverhampton W
Williams, S. (6) 1982/3 Southampton
Willis, A. (1) 1951/2 Tottenham H
Wilshaw, D. (12) 1953/4
  Wolverhampton W
Wilson, R. (63) 1959/60 Huddersfield T,
  Everton
Winterburn, N. (2) 1989/90 Arsenal
Wise, D. F. (21) 1990/1 Chelsea
Withe, P. (11) 1980/1 Aston Villa
Wood, R. (3) 1954/5 Manchester U
Woodcock, A. (42) 1977/8 Nottingham
  F, FC Cologne, Arsenal
Woodgate, J. S. (5) 1998/9 Leeds U,
  Newcastle U
Woods, C. C. E. (43) 1984/5 Norwich C,
  Rangers, Sheffield W
Worthington, F. (8) 1973/4 Leicester C
Wright, I. E. (33) 1990/1 Crystal P,
  Arsenal, West Ham U
Wright, M. (45) 1983/4 Southampton,
  Derby C, Liverpool
Wright, R. I. (2) 1999/00 Ipswich T,
  Arsenal
Wright, T. (11) 1967/8 Everton
Wright, W. (105) 1946/7
  Wolverhampton W
Wright-Phillips, S. C. (8) 2004/05
  Manchester C, Chelsea
Young, G. (1) 1964/5 Sheffield W
Young, L. P. (7) 2004/05 Charlton Ath

Best, G. (37) 1963/4 Manchester U,
  Fulham
Bingham, W. (56) 1950/1 Sunderland,
  Luton T, Everton, Port Vale
Black, K. (30) 1987/8 Luton T,
  Nottingham F
Blair, R. (5) 1974/5 Oldham Ath
Blanchflower, D. (54) 1949/50 Barnsley,
  Aston Villa, Tottenham H

285

Blanchflower, J. (12) 1953/4 Manchester U
Blayney, A. (1) 2005/06 Doncaster R
Bowler, G. (3) 1949/50 Hull C
Braithwaite, R. (10) 1961/2 Linfield, Middlesbrough
Brennan, R. (5) 1948/9 Luton T, Birmingham C, Fulham
Briggs, R. (2) 1961/2 Manchester U, Swansea
Brotherston, N. (27) 1979/80 Blackburn R
Bruce, W. (2) 1960/1 Glentoran
Brunt, C. (7) 2004/05 Sheffield W

Campbell, A. (2) 1962/3 Crusaders
Campbell, D. A. (10) 1985/6 Nottingham F, Charlton Ath
Campbell, J. (2) 1950/1 Fulham
Campbell, R. M. (2) 1981/2 Bradford C
Campbell, W. (6) 1967/8 Dundee
Capaldi, A. C. (18) 2003/04 Plymouth Arg
Carey, J. (7) 1946/7 Manchester U
Carroll, R. E. (17) 1996/7 Wigan Ath, Manchester U
Casey, T. (12) 1954/5 Newcastle U, Portsmouth
Caskey, A. (8) 1978/9 Derby C, Tulsa Roughnecks
Cassidy, T. (24) 1970/1 Newcastle U, Burnley
Caughey, M. (2) 1985/6 Linfield
Clarke, C. J. (38) 1985/6 Bournemouth, Southampton, Portsmouth
Cleary, J. (5) 1981/2 Glentoran
Clements, D. (48) 1964/5 Coventry C, Sheffield W, Everton, New York Cosmos
Clingan, S. G. (2) 2005/06 Nottingham F
Clyde, M.G. (3) 2004/05 Wolverhampon W
Cochrane, D. (10) 1946/7 Leeds U
Cochrane, T. (26) 1975/6 Coleraine, Burnley, Middlesbrough, Gillingham
Connell, T. E. (1) 1977/8 Coleraine
Coote, A. (6) 1998/9 Norwich C
Cowan, J. (1) 1969/70 Newcastle U
Coyle, F. (4) 1955/6 Coleraine, Nottingham F
Coyle, L. (1) 1988/9 Derry C
Coyle, R. (5) 1972/3 Sheffield W
Craig, D. (25) 1966/7 Newcastle U
Craigan, S. (21) 2002/03 Partick T, Motherwell
Crossan, E. (3) 1949/50 Blackburn R
Crossan, J. (24) 1959/60 Sparta Rotterdam, Sunderland, Manchester C, Middlesbrough

Cunningham, W. (30) 1950/1 St Mirren, Leicester C, Dunfermline Ath
Cush, W. (26) 1950/1 Glentoran, Leeds U, Portadown

D'Arcy, S. (5) 1951/2 Chelsea, Brentford
Davis, S. (13) 2004/05 Aston Villa
Davison, A. J. (3) 1995/6 Bolton W, Bradford C, Grimsby T
Dennison, R. (18) 1987/8 Wolverhampton W
Devine, J. (1) 1989/90 Glentoran
Dickson, D. (4) 1969/70 Coleraine
Dickson, T. (1) 1956/7 Linfield
Dickson, W. (12) 1950/1 Chelsea, Arsenal
Doherty, L. (2) 1984/5 Linfield
Doherty, P. (6) 1946/7 Derby Co, Huddersfield T, Doncaster R
Doherty, T. E. (9) 2002/03 Bristol C
Donaghy, M. (91) 1979/80 Luton T, Manchester U, Chelsea
Dougan, D. (43) 1957/8 Portsmouth, Blackburn R, Aston Villa, Leicester C, Wolverhampton W
Douglas, J. P. (1) 1946/7 Belfast Celtic
Dowd, H. (3) 1973/4 Glenavon, Sheffield W
Dowie, I. (59) 1989/90 Luton T, West Ham U, Southampton, Crystal P, West Ham U, QPR
Duff, M. J. (10) 2001/02 Cheltenham T, Burnley
Dunlop, G. (4) 1984/5 Linfield

Eglington, T. (6) 1946/7 Everton
Elder, A. (40) 1959/60 Burnley, Stoke C
Elliott, S. (34) 2000/01 Motherwell, Hull C

Farrell, P. (7) 1946/7 Everton
Feeney, J. (2) 1946/7 Linfield, Swansea T
Feeney, W. (1) 1975/6 Glentoran
Feeney, W. J. (11) 2001/02 Bournemouth, Luton T
Ferguson, G. (5) 1998/9 Linfield
Ferguson, W. (2) 1965/6 Linfield
Ferris, R. (3) 1949/50 Birmingham C
Fettis, A. (25) 1991/2 Hull C, Nottingham F, Blackburn R
Finney, T. (14) 1974/5 Sunderland, Cambridge U
Fleming, J. G. (31) 1986/7 Nottingham F, Manchester C, Barnsley
Forde, T. (4) 1958/9 Ards
Gallogly, C. (2) 1950/1 Huddersfield T
Garton, R. (1) 1968/9 Oxford U

Gillespie, K. R. (68) 1994/5 Manchester U, Newcastle U, Blackburn R, Leicester C, Sheffield U
Gorman, W. (4) 1946/7 Brentford
Graham, W. (14) 1950/1 Doncaster R
Gray, P. (26) 1992/3 Luton T, Sunderland, Nancy, Luton T, Burnley, Oxford U
Gregg, H. (25) 1953/4 Doncaster R, Manchester U
Griffin, D. J. (29) 1995/6 St Johnstone, Dundee U, Stockport Co

Hamill, R. (1) 1998/9 Glentoran
Hamilton, B. (50) 1968/9 Linfield, Ipswich T, Everton, Millwall, Swindon T
Hamilton, G. (5) 2002/03 Portadown
Hamilton, W. (41) 1977/8 QPR, Burnley, Oxford U
Harkin, T. (5) 1967/8 Southport, Shrewsbury T
Harvey, M. (34) 1960/1 Sunderland
Hatton, S. (2) 1962/3 Linfield
Healy, D. J. (49) 1999/00 Manchester U, Preston NE, Leeds U
Healy, P. J. (4) 1981/2 Coleraine, Glentoran
Hegan, D. (7) 1969/70 WBA, Wolverhampton W
Hill, C. F. (27) 1989/90 Sheffield U, Leicester C, Trelleborg, Northampton T
Hill, J. (7) 1958/9 Norwich C, Everton
Hinton, E. (7) 1946/7 Fulham, Millwall
Holmes, S. P. (1) 2001/02 Wrexham
Horlock, K. (32) 1994/5 Swindon T, Manchester C
Hughes, A. W. (46) 1997/8 Newcastle U, Aston Villa
Hughes, J, (2) 2005/06 Lincoln C
Hughes, M. A. (2) 2005/06 Oldham Ath
Hughes, M. E. (71) 1991/2 Manchester C, Strasbourg, West Ham U, Wimbledon, Crystal P
Hughes, P. (3) 1986/7 Bury
Hughes, W. (1) 1950/1 Bolton W
Humphries, W. (14) 1961/2 Ards, Coventry C, Swansea T
Hunter, A. (53) 1969/70 Blackburn R, Ipswich T
Hunter, B. V. (15) 1994/5 Wrexham, Reading
Hunter, V. (2) 1961/2 Coleraine

Ingham, M.G. (2) 2004/05 Sunderland, Wrexham
Irvine, R. (8) 1961/2 Linfield, Stoke C
Irvine, W. (23) 1962/3 Burnley, Preston NE, Brighton & HA

Jackson, T. (35) 1968/9 Everton, Nottingham F, Manchester U
Jamison, A. (1) 1975/6 Glentoran
Jenkins, I. (6) 1996/7 Chester C, Dundee U
Jennings, P. (119) 1963/4 Watford, Tottenham H, Arsenal, Tottenham H
Johnson, D. M. (42) 1998/9 Blackburn R, Birmingham C
Johnston, W. (2) 1961/2 Glenavon, Oldham Ath
Jones, J. (3) 1955/6 Glenavon
Jones, S. G. (24) 2002/03 Crewe Alex

Keane, T. (1) 1948/9 Swansea T
Kee, P. V. (9) 1989/90 Oxford U, Ards
Keith, R. (23) 1957/8 Newcastle U
Kelly, H. (4) 1949/50 Fulham, Southampton
Kelly, P. (1) 1949/50 Barnsley
Kennedy, P. H. (20) 1998/9 Watford, Wigan Ath
Kirk, A. R. (8) 1999/00 Heart of Midlothian, Boston U, Northampton T

Lafferty, K. (2) 2005/06 Burnley
Lawther, I. (4) 1959/60 Sunderland, Blackburn R
Lennon, N. F. (40) 1993/4 Crewe Alex, Leicester C, Celtic
Lockhart, N. (8) 1946/7 Linfield, Coventry C, Aston Villa
Lomas, S. M. (45) 1993/4 Manchester C, West Ham U
Lutton, B. (6) 1969/70 Wolverhampton W, West Ham U

Magill, E. (26) 1961/2 Arsenal, Brighton & HA
Magilton, J. (52) 1990/1 Oxford U, Southampton, Sheffield W, Ipswich T
Mannus, A. (1) 2003/04 Linfield
Martin, C. (6) 1946/7 Glentoran, Leeds U, Aston Villa
McAdams, W. (15) 1953/4 Manchester C, Bolton W, Leeds U
McAlinden, J. (2) 1946/7 Portsmouth, Southend U
McAuley, G. (5) 2004/05 Lincoln C
McBride, S. (4) 1990/1 Glenavon
McCabe, J. (6) 1948/9 Leeds U
McCann, G. S. (11) 2001/02 West Ham U, Cheltenham T
McCarthy, J. D. (18) 1995/6 Port Vale, Birmingham C
McCartney, G. (20) 2001/02 Sunderland
McCavana, T. (3) 1954/5 Coleraine
McCleary, J. W. (1) 1954/5 Cliftonville

McClelland, J. (6) 1960/1 Arsenal, Fulham
McClelland, J. (53) 1979/80 Mansfield T, Rangers, Watford, Leeds U
McCourt, F. (6) 1951/2 Manchester C
McCourt, P. J. (1) 2001/02 Rochdale
McCoy, R. (1) 1986/7 Coleraine
McCreery, D. (67) 1975/6 Manchester U, QPR, Tulsa Roughnecks, Newcastle U, Heart of Midlothian
McCrory, S. (1) 1957/8 Southend U
McCullough, W. (10) 1960/1 Arsenal, Millwall
McCurdy, C. (1) 1979/80 Linfield
McDonald, A. (52) 1985/6 QPR
McElhinney, G. (6) 1983/4 Bolton W
McEvilly, L. R. (1) 2001/02 Rochdale
McFaul, I. (6) 1966/7 Linfield, Newcastle U
McGarry, J. K. (3) 1950/1 Cliftonville
McGaughey, M. (1) 1984/5 Linfield
McGibbon, P. C. G. (7) 1994/5 Manchester U, Wigan Ath
McGrath, R. (21) 1973/4 Tottenham H, Manchester U
McIlroy, J. (55) 1951/2 Burnley, Stoke C
McIlroy, S. B. (88) 1971/2 Manchester U, Stoke C, Manchester C
McKeag, W. (2) 1967/8 Glentoran
McKenna, J. (7) 1949/50 Huddersfield T
McKenzie, R. (1) 1966/7 Airdrieonians
McKinney, W. (1) 1965/6 Falkirk
McKnight, A. (10) 1987/8 Celtic, West Ham U
McLaughlin, J. (12) 1961/2 Shrewsbury T, Swansea T
McLean, B. S. (1) 2005/06 Rangers
McMahon, G. J. (17) 1994/5 Tottenham H, Stoke C
McMichael, A. (39) 1949/50 Newcastle U
McMillan, S. (2) 1962/3 Manchester U
McMordie, E. (21) 1968/9 Middlesbrough
McMorran, E. (15) 1946/7 Belfast Celtic, Barnsley, Doncaster R
McNally, B. A. (5) 1985/6 Shrewsbury T
McParland, P. (34) 1953/4 Aston Villa, Wolverhampton W
McVeigh, P. (20) 1998/9 Tottenham H, Norwich C
Montgomery, F. J. (1) 1954/5 Coleraine
Moore, C. (1) 1948/9 Glentoran
Moreland, V. (6) 1978/9 Derby Co
Morgan, S. (18) 1971/2 Port Vale, Aston Villa, Brighton & HA, Sparta Rotterdam

Morrow, S. J. (39) 1989/90 Arsenal, QPR
Mullan, G. (4) 1982/3 Glentoran
Mulryne, P. P. (27) 1996/7 Manchester U, Norwich C, Cardiff C
Murdock, C. J. (34) 1999/00 Preston NE, Hibernian, Crewe Alex, Rotherham U

Napier, R. (1) 1965/6 Bolton W
Neill, T. (59) 1960/1 Arsenal, Hull C
Nelson, S. (51) 1969/70 Arsenal, Brighton & HA
Nicholl, C. (51) 1974/5 Aston Villa, Southampton, Grimsby T
Nicholl, J. M. (73) 1975/6 Manchester U, Toronto Blizzard, Sunderland, Rangers, WBA
Nicholson, J. (41) 1960/1 Manchester U, Huddersfield T
Nolan, I. R. (18) 1996/7 Sheffield W, Bradford C, Wigan Ath

O'Boyle, G. (13) 1993/4 Dunfermline Ath, St Johnstone
O'Doherty, A. (2) 1969/70 Coleraine
O'Driscoll, J. (3) 1948/9 Swansea T
O'Kane, L. (20) 1969/70 Nottingham F
O'Neill, C. (3) 1988/9 Motherwell
O'Neill, H. M. (64) 1971/2 Distillery, Nottingham F, Norwich C, Manchester C, Norwich C, Notts Co
O'Neill, J. (1) 1961/2 Sunderland
O'Neill, J. P. (39) 1979/80 Leicester C
O'Neill, M. A. (31) 1987/8 Newcastle U, Dundee U, Hibernian, Coventry C

Parke, J. (13) 1963/4 Linfield, Hibernian, Sunderland
Patterson, D. J. (17) 1993/4 Crystal P, Luton T, Dundee U
Peacock, R. (31) 1951/2 Celtic, Coleraine
Penney, S. (17) 1984/5 Brighton & HA
Platt, J. A. (23) 1975/6 Middlesbrough, Ballymena U, Coleraine

Quinn, J. M. (46) 1984/5 Blackburn R, Swindon T, Leicester, Bradford C, West Ham U, Bournemouth, Reading
Quinn, S. J. (46) 1995/6 Blackpool, WBA, Willem II, Sheffield W, Peterborough U

Rafferty, P. (1) 1979/80 Linfield
Ramsey, P. (14) 1983/4 Leicester C
Rice, P. (49) 1968/9 Arsenal

288

Robinson, S. (6) 1996/7 Bournemouth, Luton T
Rogan, A. (18) 1987/8 Celtic, Sunderland, Millwall
Ross, E. (1) 1968/9 Newcastle U
Rowland, K. (19) 1994/5 West Ham U, QPR
Russell, A. (1) 1946/7 Linfield
Ryan, R. (1) 1949/50 WBA

Sanchez, L. P. (3) 1986/7 Wimbledon
Scott, J. (2) 1957/8 Grimsby T
Scott, P. (10) 1974/5 Everton, York C, Aldershot
Sharkey, P. (1) 1975/6 Ipswich T
Shields, J. (1) 1956/7 Southampton
Shiels, D. (3) 2005/06 Hibernian
Simpson, W. (12) 1950/1 Rangers
Sloan, D. (2) 1968/9 Oxford
Sloan, T. (3) 1978/9 Manchester U
Sloan, W. (1) 1946/7 Arsenal
Smith, A. W. (18) 2002/03 Glentoran, Preston NE
Smyth, S. (9) 1947/8 Wolverhampton W, Stoke C
Smyth, W. (4) 1948/9 Distillery
Sonner, D. J. (13) 1997/8 Ipswich T, Sheffield W, Birmingham C, Nottingham F, Peterborough U
Spence, D. (29) 1974/5 Bury, Blackpool, Southend U
Sproule, I. (5) 2005/06 Hibernian
Stevenson, A. (3) 1946/7 Everton
Stewart, A. (7) 1966/7 Glentoran, Derby
Stewart, D. (1) 1977/8 Hull C
Stewart, I. (31) 1981/2 QPR, Newcastle U
Stewart, T. (1) 1960/1 Linfield

Taggart, G. P. (51) 1989/90 Barnsley, Bolton W, Leicester C

SCOTLAND

Aird, J. (4) 1953/4 Burnley
Aitken, G. G. (8) 1948/9 East Fife, Sunderland
Aitken, R. (57) 1979/80 Celtic, Newcastle U, St Mirren
Albiston, A. (14) 1981/2 Manchester U
Alexander, G. (23) 2001/02 Preston NE
Alexander, N. (3) 2005/06 Cardiff C
Allan, T. (2) 1973/4 Dundee
Anderson, J. (1) 1953/4 Leicester C
Anderson, R. (9) 2002/03 Aberdeen
Archibald, S. (27) 1979/80 Aberdeen, Tottenham H, Barcelona
Auld, B. (3) 1958/9 Celtic

Taylor, M. S. (52) 1998/9 Fulham, Birmingham C
Thompson, P. (4) 2005/06 Linfield
Todd, S. (11) 1965/6 Burnley, Sheffield W
Toner, C. (2) 2002/03 Leyton Orient
Trainor, D. (1) 1966/7 Crusaders
Tully, C. (10) 1948/9 Celtic

Uprichard, N. (18) 1951/2 Swindon T, Portsmouth

Vernon, J. (17) 1946/7 Belfast Celtic, WBA

Walker, J. (1) 1954/5 Doncaster R
Walsh, D. (9) 1946/7 WBA
Walsh, W. (5) 1947/8 Manchester C
Watson, P. (1) 1970/1 Distillery
Webb, S. M. (2) 2005/06 Ross Co
Welsh, S. (4) 1965/6 Carlisle U
Whiteside, N. (38) 1981/2 Manchester U, Everton
Whitley, Jeff (20) 1996/7 Manchester C, Sunderland, Cardiff C
Whitley, Jim (3) 1997/8 Manchester C
Williams, M. S. (36) 1998/9 Chesterfield, Watford, Wimbledon, Stoke C, Wimbledon, Milton Keynes D
Williams, P. (1) 1990/1 WBA
Wilson, D. J. (24) 1986/7 Brighton & HA, Luton, Sheffield W
Wilson, K. J. (42) 1986/7 Ipswich T, Chelsea, Notts C, Walsall
Wilson, S. (12) 1961/2 Glenavon, Falkirk, Dundee
Wood, T. J. (1) 1995/6 Walsall
Worthington, N. (66) 1983/4 Sheffield W, Leeds U, Stoke C
Wright, T. J. (31) 1988/9 Newcastle U, Nottingham F, Manchester C

Baird, H. (1) 1955/6 Airdrieonians
Baird, S. (7) 1956/7 Rangers
Bannon, E. (11) 1979/80 Dundee U
Bauld, W. (3) 1949/50 Heart of Midlothian
Baxter, J. (34) 1960/1 Rangers, Sunderland
Beattie, C. (2) 2005/06 Celtic
Bell, W. (2) 1965/6 Leeds U
Bernard, P. R. (2) 1994/5 Oldham Ath
Bett, J. (25) 1981/2 Rangers, Lokeren, Aberdeen
Black, E. (2) 1987/8 Metz
Black, I. (1) 1947/8 Southampton

289

Blacklaw, A. (3) 1962/3 Burnley
Blackley, J. (7) 1973/4 Hibernian
Blair, J. (1) 1946/7 Blackpool
Blyth, J. (2) 1977/8 Coventry C
Bone, J. (2) 1971/2 Norwich C
Booth, S. (21) 1992/3 Aberdeen,
Borussia Dortmund, Twente
Bowman, D. (6) 1991/2 Dundee U
Boyd, K. (2) 2005/06 Rangers
Boyd, T. (72) 1990/1 Motherwell,
Chelsea, Celtic
Brand, R. (8) 1960/1 Rangers
Brazil, A. (13) 1979/80 Ipswich T,
Tottenham H
Bremner, D. (1) 1975/6 Hibernian
Bremner, W. (54) 1964/5 Leeds U
Brennan, F. (7) 1946/7 Newcastle U
Brogan, J. (4) 1970/1 Celtic
Brown, A. (14) 1949/50 East Fife,
Blackpool
Brown, H. (3) 1946/7 Partick Th
Brown, J. (1) 1974/5 Sheffield U
Brown, R. (3) 1946/7 Rangers
Brown, S. (1) 2005/06 Hibernian
Brown, W. (28) 1957/8 Dundee,
Tottenham H
Brownlie, J. (7) 1970/1 Hibernian
Buchan, M. (34) 1971/2 Aberdeen,
Manchester U
Buckley, P. (3) 1953/4 Aberdeen
Burchill, M. J. (6) 1999/00 Celtic
Burke, C. (2) 2005/06 Rangers
Burley, C. W. (46) 1994/5 Chelsea,
Celtic, Derby Co
Burley, G. (11) 1978/9 Ipswich T
Burns, F. (1) 1969/70 Manchester U
Burns, K. (20) 1973/4 Birmingham C,
Nottingham F
Burns, T. (8) 1980/1 Celtic

Calderwood, C. (36) 1994/5 Tottenham
H, Aston Villa
Caldow, E. (40) 1956/7 Rangers
Caldwell, G. (20) 2001/02 Newcastle U,
Hibernian
Caldwell, S. (9) 2000/01 Newcastle U,
Sunderland
Callaghan, W. (2) 1969/70 Dunfermline
Cameron, C. (28) 1998/9 Heart of
Midlothian, Wolverhampton W
Campbell, R. (5) 1946/7 Falkirk,
Chelsea
Campbell, W. (5) 1946/7 Morton
Canero, P. (1) 2003/04 Leicester C
Carr, W. (6) 1969/70 Coventry C
Chalmers, S. (5) 1964/5 Celtic
Clark, J. (4) 1965/6 Celtic
Clark, R. (17) 1967/8 Aberdeen
Clarke, S. (6) 1987/8 Chelsea

Collins, J. (58) 1987/8 Hibernian,
Celtic, Monaco, Everton
Collins, R. (31) 1950/1 Celtic, Everton,
Leeds U
Colquhoun, E. (9) 1971/2 Sheffield U
Colquhoun, J. (2) 1987/8 Heart of
Midlothian
Combe, R. (3) 1947/8 Hibernian
Conn, A. (1) 1955/6 Heart of
Midlothian
Conn, A. (2) 1974/5 Tottenham H
Connachan, E. (2) 1961/2 Dunfermline
Ath
Connelly, G. (2) 1973/4 Celtic
Connolly, J. (1) 1972/3 Everton
Connor, R. (4) 1985/6 Dundee,
Aberdeen
Cooke, C. (16) 1965/6 Dundee, Chelsea
Cooper, D. (22) 1979/80 Rangers,
Motherwell
Cormack, P. (9) 1965/6 Hibernian,
Nottingham F
Cowan, J. (25) 1947/8 Morton
Cowie, D. (20) 1952/3 Dundee
Cox, C. (1) 1947/8 Heart of Midlothian
Cox, S. (24) 1947/8 Rangers
Craig, J. (1) 1976/7 Celtic
Craig, J. P. (1) 1967/8 Celtic
Craig, T. (1) 1975/6 Newcastle U
Crainey, S. (6) 2001/02 Celtic,
Southampton
Crawford, S. (25) 1994/5 Raith R,
Dunfermline Ath, Plymouth Arg
Crerand, P. (16) 1960/1 Celtic,
Manchester U
Cropley, A. (2) 1971/2 Hibernian
Cruickshank, J. (6) 1963/4 Heart of
Midlothian
Cullen, M. (1) 1955/6 Luton T
Cumming, J. (9) 1954/5 Heart of
Midlothian
Cummings, W. (1) 2001/02 Chelsea
Cunningham, W. (8) 1953/4 Preston NE
Curran, H. (5) 1969/70 Wolverhampton
W

Dailly, C. (61) 1996/7 Derby Co,
Blackburn R, West Ham U
Dalglish, K. (102) 1971/2 Celtic,
Liverpool
Davidson, C. I. (17) 1998/9 Blackburn
R, Leicester C
Davidson, J. (8) 1953/4 Partick Th
Dawson, A. (5) 1979/80 Rangers
Deans, D. (2) 1974/5 Celtic
Delaney, J. (4) 1946/7 Manchester U
Devlin, P. J. (10) 2002/03 Birmingham
C
Dick, J. (1) 1958/9 West Ham U

290

Dickov, P. (10) 2000/01 Mancheser C,
Leicester C, Blackburn R
Dickson, W. (5) 1969/70 Kilmarnock
Dobie, R. S. (6) 2001/02 WBA
Docherty, T. (25) 1951/2 Preston NE,
Arsenal
Dodds, D. (2) 1983/4 Dundee U
Dodds, W. (26) 1996/7 Aberdeen,
Dundee U, Rangers
Donachie, W. (35) 1971/2 Manchester
C
Donnelly, S. (10) 1996/7 Celtic
Dougall, C. (1) 1946/7 Birmingham C
Dougan, R. (1) 1949/50 Heart of
Midlothian
Douglas, R. (19) 2001/02 Celtic,
Leicester C
Doyle, J. (1) 1975/6 Ayr U
Duncan, A. (6) 1974/5 Hibernian
Duncan, D. (3) 1947/8 East Fife
Duncanson, J. (1) 1946/7 Rangers
Durie, G. S. (43) 1987/8 Chelsea,
Tottenham H, Rangers
Durrant, I. (20) 1987/8 Rangers,
Kilmarnock

Elliott, M. S. (18) 1997/8 Leicester C
Evans, A. (4) 1981/2 Aston Villa
Evans, R. (48) 1948/9 Celtic, Chelsea
Ewing, T. (2) 1957/8 Partick Th

Farm, G. (10) 1952/3 Blackpool
Ferguson, B. (33) 1998/9 Rangers,
Blackburn R, Rangers
Ferguson, Derek (2) 1987/8 Rangers
Ferguson, Duncan (7) 1991/2 Dundee
U, Everton
Ferguson, I. (9) 1988/9 Rangers
Ferguson, R. (7) 1965/6 Kilmarnock
Fernie, W. (12) 1953/4 Celtic
Flavell, R. (2) 1946/7 Airdrieonians
Fleck, R. (4) 1989/90 Norwich C
Fleming, C. (1) 1953/4 East Fife
Fletcher, D. B. (23) 2003/04
Manchester U
Forbes, A. (14) 1946/7 Sheffield U,
Arsenal
Ford, D. (3) 1973/4 Heart of Midlothian
Forrest, J. (1) 1957/8 Motherwell
Forrest, J. (5) 1965/6 Rangers,
Aberdeen
Forsyth, A. (10) 1971/2 Partick Th,
Manchester U
Forsyth, C. (4) 1963/4 Kilmarnock
Forsyth, T. (22) 1970/1 Motherwell,
Rangers
Fraser, D. (2) 1967/8 WBA
Fraser, W. (2) 1954/5 Sunderland
Freedman, D. A. (2) 2001/02 Crystal P

Gabriel, J. (2) 1960/1 Everton
Gallacher, K. W. (53) 1987/8 Dundee
U, Coventry C, Blackburn R,
Newcastle U
Gallacher, P. (8) 2001/02 Dundee U
Gallagher, P. (1) 2003/04 Blackburn R
Galloway, M. (1) 1991/2 Celtic
Gardiner, W. (1) 1957/8 Motherwell
Gemmell, T. (2) 1954/5 St Mirren
Gemmell, T. (18) 1965/6 Celtic
Gemmill, A. (43) 1970/1 Derby Co,
Nottingham F, Birmingham C
Gemmill, S. (26) 1994/5 Nottingham F,
Everton
Gibson, D. (7) 1962/3 Leicester C
Gillespie, G. T. (13) 1987/8 Liverpool
Gilzean, A. (22) 1963/4 Dundee,
Tottenham H
Glass, S. (1) 1998/9 Newcastle U
Glavin, R. (1) 1976/7 Celtic
Glen, A. (2) 1955/6 Aberdeen
Goram, A. L. (43) 1985/6 Oldham Ath,
Hibernian, Rangers
Gordon, C. S. (15) 2003/04 Heart of
Midlothian
Gough, C. R. (61) 1982/3 Dundee U,
Tottenham H, Rangers
Gould, J. (2) 1999/00 Celtic
Govan, J. (6) 1947/8 Hibernian
Graham, A. (11) 1977/8 Leeds U
Graham, G. (12) 1971/2 Arsenal,
Manchester U
Grant, J. (2) 1958/9 Hibernian
Grant, P. (2) 1988/9 Celtic
Gray, A. (20) 1975/6 Aston Villa,
Wolverhampton W, Everton
Gray, A. D. (2) 2002/03 Bradford C
Gray, E. (12) 1968/9 Leeds U
Gray F. (32) 1975/6 Leeds U,
Nottingham F, Leeds U
Green, A. (6) 1970/1 Blackpool,
Newcastle U
Greig, J. (44) 1963/4 Rangers
Gunn, B. (6) 1989/90 Norwich C

Haddock, H. (6) 1954/5 Clyde
Haffey, F. (2) 1959/60 Celtic
Hamilton, A. (24) 1961/2 Dundee
Hamilton, G. (5) 1946/7 Aberdeen
Hamilton, W. (1) 1964/5 Hibernian
Hammell, S. (1) 2004/05 Motherwell
Hansen, A. (26) 1978/9 Liverpool
Hansen, J. (2) 1971/2 Partick Th
Harper, J. (4) 1972/3 Aberdeen,
Hibernian, Aberdeen
Hartford, A. (50) 1971/2 WBA,
Manchester C, Everton, Manchester
C
Hartley, P. J. (7) 2004/05 Heart of
Midlothian

Harvey, D. (16) 1972/3 Leeds U
Haughney, M. (1) 1953/4 Celtic
Hay, D. (27) 1969/70 Celtic
Hegarty, P. (8) 1978/9 Dundee U
Henderson, J. (7) 1952/3 Portsmouth, Arsenal
Henderson, W. (29) 1962/3 Rangers
Hendry, E. C. J. (51) 1992/3 Blackburn R, Rangers, Coventry C, Bolton W
Herd, D. (5) 1958/9 Arsenal
Herd, G. (5) 1957/8 Clyde
Herriot, J. (8) 1968/9 Birmingham C
Hewie, J. (19) 1955/6 Charlton Ath
Holt, D. D. (5) 1962/3 Heart of Midlothian
Holt, G. J. (10) 2000/01 Kilmarnock, Norwich C
Holton, J. (15) 1972/3 Manchester U
Hope, R. (2) 1967/8 WBA
Hopkin, D. (7) 1996/7 Crystal P, Leeds U
Houliston, W. (3) 1948/9 Queen of the South
Houston, S. (1) 1975/6 Manchester U
Howie, H. (1) 1948/9 Hibernian
Hughes, J. (8) 1964/5 Celtic
Hughes, R. D. (5) 2003/04 Portsmouth
Hughes, W. (1) 1974/5 Sunderland
Humphries, W. (1) 1951/2 Motherwell
Hunter, A. (4) 1971/2 Kilmarnock, Celtic
Hunter, W. (3) 1959/60 Motherwell
Husband, J. (1) 1946/7 Partick Th
Hutchison, D. (26) 1998/9 Everton, Sunderland, West Ham U
Hutchison, T. (17) 1973/4 Coventry C

Imlach, S. (4) 1957/8 Nottingham F
Irvine, B. (9) 1990/1 Aberdeen

Jackson, C. (8) 1974/5 Rangers
Jackson, D. (28) 1994/5 Hibernian, Celtic
Jardine, A. (38) 1970/1 Rangers
Jarvie, A. (3) 1970/1 Airdrieonians
Jess, E. (18) 1992/3 Aberdeen, Coventry C, Aberdeen
Johnston, A. (18) 1998/9 Sunderland, Rangers, Middlesbrough
Johnston, M. (38) 1983/4 Watford, Celtic, Nantes, Rangers
Johnston, L. (2) 1947/8 Clyde
Johnston, W. (22) 1965/6 Rangers, WBA
Johnstone, D. (14) 1972/3 Rangers
Johnstone, J. (23) 1964/5 Celtic
Johnstone, R. (17) 1950/1 Hibernian, Manchester C
Jordan, J. (52) 1972/3 Leeds U, Manchester U, AC Milan

Kelly, H. (1) 1951/2 Blackpool
Kelly, J. (2) 1948/9 Barnsley
Kennedy, Jim (6) 1963/4 Celtic
Kennedy, John (1) 2003/04 Celtic
Kennedy, S. (5) 1974/5 Rangers
Kennedy, S. (8) 1977/8 Aberdeen
Kerr, A. (2) 1954/5 Partick Th
Kerr, B. (3) 2002/03 Newcastle U
Kyle, K. (9) 2001/02 Sunderland
Lambert, P. (40) 1994/5 Motherwell, Borussia Dortmund, Celtic
Law, D. (55) 1958/9 Huddersfield T, Manchester C, Torino, Manchester U, Manchester C
Lawrence, T. (3) 1962/3 Liverpool
Leggat, G. (18) 1955/6 Aberdeen, Fulham
Leighton, J. (91) 1982/3 Aberdeen, Manchester U, Hibernian, Aberdeen
Lennox, R. (10) 1966/7 Celtic
Leslie, L. (5) 1960/1 Airdrieonians
Levein, C. (16) 1989/90 Heart of Midlothian
Liddell, W. (28) 1946/7 Liverpool
Linwood, A. (1) 1949/50 Clyde
Little, R. J. (1) 1952/3 Rangers
Logie, J. (1) 1952/3 Arsenal
Long, H. (1) 1946/7 Clyde
Lorimer, P. (21) 1969/70 Leeds U

Macari, L. (24) 1971/2 Celtic, Manchester U
Macaulay, A. (7) 1946/7 Brentford, Arsenal
MacDougall, E. (7) 1974/5 Norwich C
Mackay, D. (22) 1956/7 Heart of Midlothian, Tottenham H
Mackay, G. (4) 1987/8 Heart of Midlothian
Mackay, M. (5) 2003/04 Norwich C
Maloney, S. R. (2) 2005/06 Celtic
Malpas, M. (55) 1983/4 Dundee U
Marshall, D. J. (2) 2004/05 Celtic
Marshall, G. (1) 1991/2 Celtic
Martin, B. (2) 1994/5 Motherwell
Martin, F. (6) 1953/4 Aberdeen
Martin, N. (3) 1964/5 Hibernian, Sunderland
Martis, J. (1) 1960/1 Motherwell
Mason, J. (7) 1948/9 Third Lanark
Masson, D. (17) 1975/6 QPR, Derby C
Mathers, D. (1) 1953/4 Partick Th
Matteo, D. (6) 2000/01 Leeds U
McAllister, B. (3) 1996/7 Wimbledon
McAllister, G. (57) 1989/90 Leicester C, Leeds U, Coventry C
McAllister, J. R. (1) 2003/04 Livingston
McAvennie, F. (5) 1985/6 West Ham U, Celtic
McBride, J. (2) 1966/7 Celtic

292

McCall, S. M. (40) 1989/90 Everton, Rangers

McCalliog, J. (5) 1966/7 Sheffield W, Wolverhampton W

McCann, N. D. (26) 1998/9 Heart of Midlothian, Rangers, Southampton

McCann, R. (5) 1958/9 Motherwell

McClair, B. (30) 1986/7 Celtic, Manchester U

McCloy, P. (4) 1972/3 Rangers

McCoist, A. (61) 1985/6 Rangers, Kilmarnock

McColl, I. (14) 1949/50 Rangers

McCreadie, E. (23) 1964/5 Chelsea

McCulloch, L. (7) 2004/05 Wigan Ath

MacDonald, A. (1) 1975/6 Rangers

McDonald, J. (1) 1955/6 Sunderland

McFadden, J. (27) 2001/02 Motherwell, Everton

McFarlane, W. (1) 1946/7 Heart of Midlothian

McGarr, E. (2) 1969/70 Aberdeen

McGarvey, F. (7) 1978/9 Liverpool, Celtic

McGhee, M. (4) 1982/3 Aberdeen

McGinlay, J. (13) 1993/4 Bolton W

McGrain, D. (62) 1972/3 Celtic

McGrory, J. (3) 1964/5 Kilmarnock

McInally, A. (8) 1988/9 Aston Villa, Bayern Munich

McInally, J. (10) 1986/7 Dundee U

McInnes, D. (2) 2002/03 WBA

MacKay, D. (14) 1958/9 Celtic

McKean, R. (1) 1975/6 Rangers

MacKenzie, J. (9) 1953/4 Partick Th

McKimmie, S. (40) 1988/9 Aberdeen

McKinlay, T. (22) 1995/6 Celtic

McKinlay, W. (29) 1993/4 Dundee U, Blackburn R

McKinnon, Rob (3) 1993/4 Motherwell

McKinnon, Ronnie (28) 1965/6 Rangers

McLaren, Alan (24) 1991/2 Heart of Midlothian, Rangers

McLaren, Andy (4) 1946/7 Preston NE

McLaren, Andy (1) 2000/01 Kilmarnock

McLean, G. (1) 1967/8 Dundee

McLean, T. (6) 1968/9 Kilmarnock

McLeish, A. (77) 1979/80 Aberdeen

McLeod, J. (4) 1960/1 Hibernian

MacLeod, M. (20) 1984/5 Celtic, Borussia Dortmund, Hibernian

McLintock, F. (9) 1962/3 Leicester C, Arsenal

McMillan, I. (6) 1951/2 Airdrieonians, Rangers

McNamara, J. (33) 1996/7 Celtic, Wolverhampton W

McNamee, D. (4) 2003/04 Livingston

McNaught, W. (5) 1950/1 Raith R

McNaughton, K. (3) 2001/02 Aberdeen

McNeill, W. (29) 1960/1 Celtic

McPhail, J. (5) 1949/50 Celtic

McPherson, D. (27) 1988/9 Heart of Midlothian, Rangers

McQueen, G. (30) 1973/4 Leeds U, Manchester U

McStay, P. (76) 1983/4 Celtic

McSwegan, G. (2) 1999/00 Heart of Midlothian

Millar, J. (2) 1962/3 Rangers

Miller, C. (1) 2000/01 Dundee U

Miller, K. (26) 2000/01 Rangers, Wolverhampton W

Miller, L. (1) 2005/06 Dundee U

Miller, W. (6) 1946/7 Celtic

Miller, W. (65) 1974/5 Aberdeen

Mitchell, R. (2) 1950/1 Newcastle U

Mochan, N. (3) 1953/4 Celtic

Moir, W. (1) 1949/50 Bolton W

Moncur, R. (16) 1967/8 Newcastle U

Morgan, W. (21) 1967/8 Burnley, Manchester U

Morris, H. (1) 1949/50 East Fife

Mudie, J. (17) 1956/7 Blackpool

Mulhall, G. (3) 1959/60 Aberdeen, Sunderland

Munro, F. (9) 1970/1 Wolverhampton W

Munro, I. (7) 1978/9 St Mirren

Murdoch, R. (12) 1965/6 Celtic

Murray, I. (6) 2002/03 Hibernian, Rangers

Murray, J. (5) 1957/8 Heart of Midlothian

Murray, S. (1) 1971/2 Aberdeen

Murty, G. S. (3) 2003/04 Reading

Narey, D. (35) 1976/7 Dundee U

Naysmith, G. A. (30) 1999/00 Heart of Midlothian, Everton

Nevin, P. K. F. (28) 1985/6 Chelsea, Everton, Tranmere R

Nicholas, C. (20) 1982/3 Celtic, Arsenal, Aberdeen

Nicholson, B. (3) 2000/01 Dunfermline Ath

Nicol, S. (27) 1984/5 Liverpool

O'Connor, G. (7) 2001/02 Hibernian

O'Donnell, P. (1) 1993/4 Motherwell

O'Hare, J. (13) 1969/70 Derby Co

O'Neil, B. (7) 1995/6 Celtic, Wolfsburg, Derby Co, Preston NE

O'Neil, J. (1) 2000/01 Hibernian

Ormond, W. (6) 1953/4 Hibernian

Orr, T. (2) 1951/2 Morton

Parker, A. (15) 1954/5 Falkirk, Everton

Parlane, D. (12) 1972/3 Rangers
Paton, A. (2) 1951/2 Motherwell
Pearson, S. P. (6) 2003/04 Motherwell, Celtic
Pearson, T. (2) 1946/7 Newcastle U
Penman, A. (1) 1965/6 Dundee
Pettigrew, W. (5) 1975/6 Motherwell
Plenderleith, J. (1) 1960/1 Manchester C
Pressley, S. J. (28) 1999/00 Heart of Midlothian
Provan, David (10) 1979/80 Celtic
Provan, Davie (5) 1963/4 Rangers

Quashie, N. F. (12) 2003/04 Portsmouth, Southampton, WBA
Quinn, P. (4) 1960/1 Motherwell

Rae, G. (11) 2000/01 Dundee, Rangers
Redpath, W. (9) 1948/9 Motherwell
Reilly, L. (38) 1948/9 Hibernian
Ring, T. (12) 1952/3 Clyde
Rioch, B. (24) 1974/5 Derby Co, Everton, Derby Co
Riordan, D. G. (1) 2005/06 Hibernian
Ritchie, P. S. (7) 1998/9 Heart of Midlothian, Bolton W, Walsall
Ritchie, W. (1) 1961/2 Rangers
Robb, D. (5) 1970/1 Aberdeen
Robertson, A. (5) 1954/5 Clyde
Robertson, D. (3) 1991/2 Rangers
Robertson, H. (1) 1961/2 Dundee
Robertson, J. (16) 1990/1 Heart of Midlothian
Robertson, J. G. (1) 1964/5 Tottenham H
Robertson, J. N. (28) 1977/8 Nottingham F, Derby Co
Robinson, B. (4) 1973/4 Dundee
Ross, M. (13) 2001/02 Rangers
Rough, A. (53) 1975/6 Partick Th, Hibernian
Rougvie, D. (1) 1983/4 Aberdeen
Rutherford, E. (1) 1947/8 Rangers

St John, I. (21) 1958/9 Motherwell, Liverpool
Schaedler, E. (1) 1973/4 Hibernian
Scott, A. (16) 1956/7 Rangers, Everton
Scott, Jimmy (1) 1965/6 Hibernian
Scott, Jocky (2) 1970/1 Dundee
Scoular, J. (9) 1950/1 Portsmouth
Severin, S. D. (13) 2001/02 Heart of Midlothian, Aberdeen
Sharp, G. M. (12) 1984/5 Everton
Shaw, D. (8) 1946/7 Hibernian
Shaw, J. (4) 1946/7 Rangers
Shearer, D. (7) 1993/4 Aberdeen
Shearer, R. (4) 1960/1 Rangers
Simpson, N. (4) 1982/3 Aberdeen
Simpson, R. (5) 1966/7 Celtic

Sinclair, J. (1) 1965/6 Leicester C
Smith, D. (2) 1965/6 Aberdeen, Rangers
Smith, E. (2) 1958/9 Celtic
Smith, G. (18) 1946/7 Hibernian
Smith, H. G. (3) 1987/8 Heart of Midlothian
Smith, J. (4) 1967/8 Aberdeen, Newcastle U
Smith, J. (2) 2002/03 Celtic
Souness, G. (54) 1974/5 Middlesbrough, Liverpool, Sampdoria
Speedie, D. R. (10) 1984/5 Chelsea, Coventry C
Spencer, J. (14) 1994/5 Chelsea, QPR
Stanton, P. (16) 1965/6 Hibernian
Steel, W. (30) 1946/7 Morton, Derby C, Dundee
Stein, C. (21) 1968/9 Rangers, Coventry C
Stephen, J. (2) 1946/7 Bradford PA
Stewart, D. (1) 1977/8 Leeds U
Stewart, J. (2) 1976/7 Kilmarnock, Middlesbrough
Stewart, M. J. (3) 2001/02 Manchester U
Stewart, R. (10) 1980/1 West Ham U
Stockdale, R. K. (5) 2001/02 Middlesbrough
Strachan, G. (50) 1979/80 Aberdeen, Manchester U, Leeds U
Sturrock, P. (20) 1980/1 Dundee U
Sullivan, N. (28) 1996/7 Wimbledon, Tottenham H

Teale, G. (3) 2005/06 Wigan Ath
Telfer, P. N. (1) 1999/00 Coventry C
Telfer, W. (1) 1953/4 St Mirren
Thompson, S. (16) 2001/02 Dundee U, Rangers
Thomson, W. (7) 1979/80 St Mirren
Thornton, W. (7) 1946/7 Rangers
Toner, W. (2) 1958/9 Kilmarnock
Turnbull, E. (8) 1947/8 Hibernian

Ure, I. (11) 1961/2 Dundee, Arsenal

Waddell, W. (17) 1946/7 Rangers
Walker, A. (3) 1987/8 Celtic
Walker, J. N. (2) 1992/3 Heart of Midlothian, Partick Th
Wallace, I. A. (3) 1977/8 Coventry C
Wallace, W. S. B. (7) 1964/5 Heart of Midlothian, Celtic
Wardhaugh, J. (2) 1954/5 Heart of Midlothian
Wark, J. (29) 1978/9 Ipswich T, Liverpool

Watson, J. (2) 1947/8 Motherwell, Huddersfield T
Watson, R. (1) 1970/1 Motherwell
Webster, A. (22) 2002/03 Heart of Midlothian
Weir, A. (6) 1958/9 Motherwell
Weir, D. G. (48) 1996/7 Heart of Midlothian, Everton
Weir, P. (6) 1979/80 St Mirren, Aberdeen
White, J. (22) 1958/9 Falkirk, Tottenham H
Whyte, D. (12) 1987/8 Celtic, Middlesbrough, Aberdeen
Wilkie, L. (11) 2001/02 Dundee
Williams, G. (5) 2001/02 Nottingham F
Wilson, A. (1) 1953/4 Portsmouth
Wilson, D. (22) 1960/1 Rangers

Wilson, I. A. (5) 1986/7 Leicester C, Everton
Wilson, P. (1) 1974/5 Celtic
Wilson, R. (2) 1971/2 Arsenal
Winters, R. (1) 1998/9 Aberdeen
Wood, G. (4) 1978/9 Everton, Arsenal
Woodburn, W. (24) 1946/7 Rangers
Wright, K. (1) 1991/2 Hibernian
Wright, S. (2) 1992/3 Aberdeen
Wright, T. (3) 1952/3 Sunderland
Yeats, R. (2) 1964/5 Liverpool
Yorston, H. (1) 1954/5 Aberdeen
Young, A. (8) 1959/60 Heart of Midlothian, Everton
Young, G. (53) 1946/7 Rangers
Younger, T. (24) 1954/5 Hibernian, Liverpool

WALES

Aizlewood, M. (39) 1985/6 Charlton Ath, Leeds U, Bradford C, Bristol C, Cardiff C
Allchurch, I. (68) 1950/1 Swansea T, Newcastle U, Cardiff C, Swansea T
Allchurch, L. (11) 1954/5 Swansea T, Sheffield U
Allen, B. (2) 1950/1 Coventry C
Allen, M. (14) 1985/6 Watford, Norwich C, Millwall, Newcastle U

Baker, C. (7) 1957/8 Cardiff C
Baker, W. (1) 1947/8 Cardiff C
Bale, G. (1) 2005/06 Southampton
Barnard, D. S. (22) 1997/8 Barnsley, Grimsby T
Barnes, W. (22) 1947/8 Arsenal
Bellamy, C. D. (35) 1997/8 Norwich C, Coventry C, Newcastle U, Blackburn R
Berry, G. (5) 1978/9 Wolverhampton W, Stoke C
Blackmore, C. G. (39) 1984/5 Manchester U, Middlesbrough
Blake, N. (29) 1993/4 Sheffield U, Bolton W, Blackburn R, Wolverhampton W
Bodin, P. J. (23) 1989/90 Swindon T, Crystal P, Swindon T
Bowen, D. (19) 1954/5 Arsenal
Bowen, J. P. (2) 1993/4 Swansea C, Birmingham C
Bowen, M. R. (41) 1985/6 Tottenham H, Norwich C, West Ham U
Boyle, T. (2) 1980/1 Crystal P
Brown, J. R. (1) 2005/06 Gillingham
Browning, M. T. (5) 1995/6 Bristol R, Huddersfield T

Burgess, R. (32) 1946/7 Tottenham H
Burton, O. (9) 1962/3 Norwich C, Newcastle U

Cartwright, L. (7) 1973/4 Coventry C, Wrexham
Charles, J. (38) 1949/50 Leeds U, Juventus, Leeds U, Cardiff C
Charles, J. M. (19) 1980/1 Swansea C, QPR, Oxford U
Charles, M. (31) 1954/5 Swansea T, Arsenal, Cardiff C
Clarke, R. (22) 1948/9 Manchester C
Coleman, C. (32) 1991/2 Crystal P, Blackburn R, Fulham
Collins, D. L. (3) 2004/05 Sunderland
Collins, J. M. (13) 2003/04 Cardiff C, West Ham U
Cornforth, J. M. (2) 1994/5 Swansea C
Cotterill, D. R. G. B. (3) 2005/06 Bristol C
Coyne, D. (11) 1995/6 Tranmere R, Grimsby T, Leicester C, Burnley
Crofts, A. L. (3) 2005/06 Gillingham
Crossley, M. G. (8) 1996/7 Nottingham F, Middlesbrough, Fulham
Crowe, V. (16) 1958/9 Aston Villa
Curtis, A. (35) 1975/6 Swansea C, Leeds U, Swansea C, Southampton, Cardiff C

Daniel, R. (21) 1950/1 Arsenal, Sunderland
Davies, A. (13) 1982/3 Manchester U, Newcastle U, Swansea C, Bradford C
Davies, A. R. (1) 2005/06 Yeovil T
Davies, C. (1) 1971/2 Charlton Ath

Davies, C. M. (3) 2005/06 Oxford U, Verona
Davies, D. (52) 1974/5 Everton, Wrexham, Swansea C
Davies, G. (16) 1979/80 Fulham, Manchester C
Davies, R. Wyn (34) 1963/4 Bolton W, Newcastle U, Manchester C, Manchester U, Blackpool
Davies, Reg (6) 1952/3 Newcastle U
Davies, Ron (29) 1963/4 Norwich C, Southampton, Portsmouth
Davies, S. (30) 2000/01 Tottenham H, Everton
Davies, S. I. (1) 1995/6 Manchester U
Davis, G. (3) 1977/8 Wrexham
Deacy, N. (12) 1976/7 PSV Eindhoven, Beringen
Delaney, M. A. (34) 1999/00 Aston Villa
Derrett, S. (4) 1968/9 Cardiff C
Dibble, A. (3) 1985/6 Luton T, Manchester C
Duffy, R. M. (6) 2005/06 Portsmouth
Durban, A. (27) 1965/6 Derby C
Dwyer, P. (10) 1977/8 Cardiff C

Earnshaw, R. (26) 2001/02 Cardiff C, WBA, Norwich C
Edwards, C. N. H. (1) 1995/6 Swansea C
Edwards, G. (12) 1946/7 Birmingham C, Cardiff C
Edwards, I. (4) 1977/8 Chester, Wrexham
Edwards, R. O. (11) 2002/03 Aston Villa, Wolverhampton W
Edwards, R. W. (4) 1997/8 Bristol C
Edwards, T. (2) 1956/7 Charlton Ath
Emanuel, J. (2) 1972/3 Bristol C
England, M. (44) 1961/2 Blackburn R, Tottenham H
Evans, B. (7) 1971/2 Swansea C, Hereford U
Evans, I. (13) 1975/6 Crystal P
Evans, P. S. (2) 2001/02 Brentford, Bradford C
Evans, R. (1) 1963/4 Swansea T

Felgate, D. (1) 1983/4 Lincoln C
Fletcher, C. N. (15) 2003/04 Bournemouth, West Ham U
Flynn, B. (66) 1974/5 Burnley, Leeds U, Burnley
Ford, T. (38) 1946/7 Swansea T, Aston Villa, Sunderland, Cardiff C
Foulkes, W. (11) 1951/2 Newcastle U
Freestone, R. (1) 1999/00 Swansea C

Gabbidon, D. L. (26) 2001/02 Cardiff C, West Ham U

Garner, G. (1) 2005/06 Leyton Orient
Giggs, R. J. (56) 1991/2 Manchester U
Giles, D. (12) 1979/80 Swansea C, Crystal P
Godfrey, B. (3) 1963/4 Preston NE
Goss, J. (9) 1990/1 Norwich C
Green, C. (15) 1964/5 Birmingham C
Green, R. M. (2) 1997/8 Wolverhampton W
Griffiths, A. (17) 1970/1 Wrexham
Griffiths, H. (1) 1952/3 Swansea T
Griffiths, M. (11) 1946/7 Leicester C

Hall, G. D. (9) 1987/8 Chelsea
Harrington, A. (11) 1955/6 Cardiff C
Harris, C. (24) 1975/6 Leeds U
Harris, W. (6) 1953/4 Middlesbrough
Hartson, J. (51) 1994/5 Arsenal, West Ham U, Wimbledon, Coventry C, Celtic
Haworth, S. O. (5) 1996/7 Cardiff C, Coventry C
Hennessey, T. (39) 1961/2 Birmingham C, Nottingham F, Derby Co
Hewitt, R. (5) 1957/8 Cardiff C
Hill, M. (2) 1971/2 Ipswich T
Hockey, T. (9) 1971/2 Sheffield U, Norwich C, Aston Villa
Hodges, G. (18) 1983/4 Wimbledon, Newcastle U, Watford, Sheffield U
Holden, A. (1) 1983/4 Chester C
Hole, B. (30) 1962/3 Cardiff C, Blackburn R, Aston Villa, Swansea C
Hollins, D. (11) 1961/2 Newcastle U
Hopkins, J. (16) 1982/3 Fulham, Crystal P
Hopkins, M. (34) 1955/6 Tottenham H
Horne, B. (59) 1987/8 Portsmouth, Southampton, Everton, Birmingham C
Howells, R. (2) 1953/4 Cardiff C
Hughes, C. M. (8) 1991/2 Luton T, Wimbledon
Hughes, I. (4) 1950/1 Luton T
Hughes, L. M. (72) 1983/4 Manchester U, Barcelona, Manchester U, Chelsea, Southampton
Hughes, W. (3) 1946/7 Birmingham C
Hughes, W. A. (5) 1948/9 Blackburn R
Humphreys, J. (1) 1946/7 Everton

Jackett, K. (31) 1982/3 Watford
James, G. (9) 1965/6 Blackpool
James, L. (54) 1971/2 Burnley, Derby C, QPR, Burnley, Swansea C, Sunderland
James, R. M. (47) 1978/9 Swansea C, Stoke C, QPR, Leicester C, Swansea C

Jarvis, A. (3) 1966/7 Hull C
Jenkins, S. R. (16) 1995/6 Swansea C, Huddersfield T
Johnson, A. J. (15) 1998/9 Nottingham F, WBA
Johnson, M. (1) 1963/4 Swansea T
Jones, A. (6) 1986/7 Port Vale, Charlton Ath
Jones, Barrie (15) 1962/3 Swansea T, Plymouth Argyle, Cardiff C
Jones, Bryn (4) 1946/7 Arsenal
Jones, C. (59) 1953/4 Swansea T, Tottenham H, Fulham
Jones, D. (8) 1975/6 Norwich C
Jones, E. (4) 1947/8 Swansea T, Tottenham H
Jones, J. (72) 1975/6 Liverpool, Wrexham, Chelsea, Huddersfield T
Jones, K. (1) 1949/50 Aston Villa
Jones, M. G. (13) 1999/00 Leeds U, Leicester C
Jones, P. L. (2) 1996/7 Liverpool, Tranmere R
Jones, P. S. (46) 1996/7 Stockport Co, Southampton, Wolverhampton W, QPR
Jones, R. (1) 1993/4 Sheffield W
Jones, T. G. (13) 1946/7 Everton
Jones, V. P. (9) 1994/5 Wimbledon
Jones, W. (1) 1970/1 Bristol R

Kelsey, J. (41) 1953/4 Arsenal
King, J. (1) 1954/5 Swansea T
Kinsey, N. (7) 1950/1 Norwich C, Birmingham C
Knill, A. R. (1) 1988/9 Swansea C
Koumas, J. (17) 2000/01 Tranmere R, WBA
Krzywicki, R. (8) 1969/70 WBA, Huddersfield T

Lambert, R. (5) 1946/7 Liverpool
Law, B. J. (1) 1989/90 QPR
Lea, C. (2) 1964/5 Ipswich T
Ledley, J. C. (3) 2005/06 Cardiff C
Leek, K. (13) 1960/1 Leicester C, Newcastle U, Birmingham C, Northampton T
Legg, A. (6) 1995/6 Birmingham C, Cardiff C
Lever, A. (1) 1952/3 Leicester C
Lewis, D. (1) 1982/3 Swansea C
Llewellyn, C. M. (4) 1997/8 Norwich C, Wrexham
Lloyd, B. (3) 1975/6 Wrexham
Lovell, S. (6) 1981/2 Crystal P, Millwall
Lowndes, S. (10) 1982/3 Newport Co, Millwall, Barnsley
Lowrie, G. (4) 1947/8 Coventry C, Newcastle U

Lucas, M. (4) 1961/2 Leyton Orient
Lucas, W. (7) 1948/9 Swansea T

Maguire, G. T. (7) 1989/90 Portsmouth
Mahoney, J. (51) 1967/8 Stoke C, Middlesbrough, Swansea C
Mardon, P. J. (1) 1995/6 WBA
Margetson, M. W. (1) 2003/04 Cardiff C
Marriott, A. (5) 1995/6 Wrexham
Marustik, C. (6) 1981/2 Swansea C
Medwin, T. (30) 1952/3 Swansea T, Tottenham H
Melville, A. K. (65) 1989/90 Swansea C, Oxford U, Sunderland, Fulham, West Ham U
Mielczarek, R. (1) 1970/1 Rotherham U
Millington, A. (21) 1962/3 WBA, Crystal P, Peterborough U, Swansea C
Moore, G. (21) 1959/60 Cardiff C, Chelsea, Manchester U, Northampton T, Charlton Ath
Morris, W. (5) 1946/7 Burnley

Nardiello, D. (2) 1977/8 Coventry C
Neilson, A. B. (5) 1991/2 Newcastle U, Southampton
Nicholas, P. (73) 1978/9 Crystal P, Arsenal, Crystal P, Luton T, Aberdeen, Chelsea, Watford
Niedzwiecki, E. A. (2) 1984/5 Chelsea
Nogan, L. M. (2) 1991/2 Watford, Reading
Norman, A. J. (5) 1985/6 Hull C
Nurse, M. T. G. (12) 1959/60 Swansea T, Middlesbrough
Nyatanga, L. J. (2) 2005/06 Derby Co

O'Sullivan, P. (3) 1972/3 Brighton & HA
Oster, J. M. (13) 1997/8 Everton, Sunderland

Page, M. (28) 1970/1 Birmingham C
Page, R. J. (41) 1996/7 Watford, Sheffield U, Cardiff C, Coventry C
Palmer, D. (3) 1956/7 Swansea T
Parry, J. (1) 1950/1 Swansea T
Parry, P. I. (6) 2003/04 Cardiff C
Partridge, D. W. (7) 2004/05 Motherwell, Bristol C
Pascoe, C. (10) 1983/4 Swansea C, Sunderland
Paul, R. (33) 1948/9 Swansea T, Manchester C
Pembridge, M. A. (54) 1991/2 Luton T, Derby C, Sheffield W, Benfica, Everton, Fulham
Perry, J. (1) 1993/4 Cardiff C

Phillips, D. (62) 1983/4 Plymouth Argyle, Manchester C, Coventry C, Norwich C, Nottingham F
Phillips, J. (4) 1972/3 Chelsea
Phillips, L. (58) 1970/1 Cardff C, Aston Villa, Swansea C, Charlton Ath
Pipe, D. R. (1) 2002/03 Coventry C
Pontin, K. (2) 1979/80 Cardiff C
Powell, A. (8) 1946/7 Leeds U, Everton, Birmingham C
Powell, D. (11) 1967/8 Wrexham, Sheffield U
Powell, I. (8) 1946/7 QPR, Aston Villa
Price, L. P. (2) 2005/06 Ipswich T
Price, P. (25) 1979/80 Luton T, Tottenham H
Pring, K. (3) 1965/6 Rotherham U
Pritchard, H. K. (1) 1984/5 Bristol C

Rankmore, F. (l) 1965/6 Peterborough U
Ratcliffe, K. (59) 1980/1 Everton, Cardiff C
Ready, K. (5) 1996/7 QPR
Reece, G. (29) 1965/6 Sheffield U, Cardiff C
Reed, W. (2) 1954/5 Ipswich T
Rees, A. (1) 1983/4 Birmingham C
Rees, J. M. (1) 1991/2 Luton T
Rees, R. (39) 1964/5 Coventry C, WBA, Nottingham F
Rees, W. (4) 1948/9 Cardiff C, Tottenham H
Richards, S. (1) 1946/7 Cardiff C
Ricketts, S. (10) 2004/05 Swansea C
Roberts, A. M. (2) 1992/3 QPR
Roberts, D. (17) 1972/3 Oxford U, Hull C
Roberts, G. W. (9) 1999/00 Tranmere R
Roberts, I. W. (15) 1989/90 Watford, Huddersfield T, Leicester C, Norwich C
Roberts, J. G. (22) 1970/1 Arsenal, Birmingham C
Roberts, J. H. (1) 1948/9 Bolton W
Roberts, N. W. (4) 1999/00 Wrexham, Wigan Ath
Roberts, P. (4) 1973/4 Portsmouth
Roberts, S. W. (1) 2004/05 Wrexham
Robinson, C. P. (29) 1999/00 Wolverhampton W, Portsmouth, Sunderland, Norwich C
Robinson, J. R. C. (30) 1995/6 Charlton Ath
Rodrigues, P. (40) 1964/5 Cardiff C, Leicester C, Sheffield W
Rouse, V. (1) 1958/9 Crystal P
Rowley, T. (1) 1958/9 Tranmere R
Rush, I. (73) 1979/80 Liverpool, Juventus, Liverpool

Saunders, D. (75) 1985/6 Brighton & HA, Oxford U, Derby C, Liverpool, Aston Villa, Galatasaray, Nottingham F, Sheffield U, Benfica, Bradford C
Savage, R. W. (39) 1995/6 Crewe Alexandra, Leicester C, Birmingham C
Sayer, P. (7) 1976/7 Cardiff C
Scrine, F. (2) 1949/50 Swansea T
Sear, C. (1) 1962/3 Manchester C
Sherwood, A. (41) 1946/7 Cardiff C, Newport C
Shortt, W. (12) 1946/7 Plymouth Argyle
Showers, D. (2) 1974/5 Cardiff C
Sidlow, C. (7) 1946/7 Liverpool
Slatter, N. (22) 1982/3 Bristol R, Oxford U
Smallman, D. (7) 1973/4 Wrexham, Everton
Southall, N. (92) 1981/2 Everton
Speed, G. A. (85) 1989/90 Leeds U, Everton, Newcastle U, Bolton W
Sprake, G. (37) 1963/4 Leeds U, Birmingham C
Stansfield, F. (1) 1948/9 Cardiff C
Stevenson, B. (15) 1977/8 Leeds U, Birmingham C
Stevenson, N. (4) 1981/2 Swansea C
Stitfall, R. (2) 1952/3 Cardiff C
Sullivan, D. (17) 1952/3 Cardiff C
Symons, C. J. (37) 1991/2 Portsmouth, Manchester C, Fulham, Crystal P

Tapscott, D. (14) 1953/4 Arsenal, Cardiff C
Taylor, G. K. (15) 1995/6 Crystal P, Sheffield U, Burnley, Nottingham F
Thatcher, B. D. (7) 2003/04 Leicester C, Manchester C
Thomas, D. (2) 1956/7 Swansea T
Thomas, M. (51) 1976/7 Wrexham, Manchester U, Everton, Brighton & HA, Stoke C, Chelsea, WBA
Thomas, M. R. (1) 1986/7 Newcastle U
Thomas, R. (50) 1966/7 Swindon T, Derby C, Cardiff C
Thomas, S. (4) 1947/8 Fulham
Toshack, J. (40) 1968/9 Cardiff C, Liverpool, Swansea C
Trollope, P. J. (9) 1996/7 Derby Co, Fulham, Coventry C, Northampton T

Van Den Hauwe, P. W. R. (13) 1984/5 Everton
Vaughan, D. O. (7) 2002/03 Crewe Alex
Vaughan, N. (10) 1982/3 Newport Co, Cardiff C

Vearncombe, G. (2) 1957/8 Cardiff C
Vernon, R. (32) 1956/7 Blackburn R, Everton, Stoke C
Villars, A. (3) 1973/4 Cardiff C

Walley, T. (1) 1970/1 Watford
Walsh, I. (18) 1979/80 Crystal P, Swansea C
Ward, D. (2) 1958/9 Bristol R, Cardiff C
Ward, D. (5) 1999/00 Notts Co, Nottingham F
Webster, C. (4) 1956/7 Manchester U
Weston, R. D. (7) 1999/00 Arsenal, Cardiff C
Williams, A. (13) 1993/4 Reading, Wolverhampton W, Reading
Williams, A. P. (2) 1997/8 Southampton
Williams, D. G. 1987/8 13, Derby Co, Ipswich T

Williams, D. M. (5) 1985/6 Norwich C
Williams, G. (1) 1950/1 Cardiff C
Williams, G. E. (26) 1959/60 WBA
Williams, G. G. (5) 1960/1 Swansea T
Williams, G. J. (2) 2005/06 Ipswich T
Williams, H. (4) 1948/9 Newport Co, Leeds U
Williams, Herbert (3) 1964/5 Swansea T
Williams, S. (43) 1953/4 WBA, Southampton
Witcomb, D. (3) 1946/7 WBA, Sheffield W
Woosnam, P. (17) 1958/9 Leyton Orient, West Ham U, Aston Villa

Yorath, T. (59) 1969/70 Leeds U, Coventry C, Tottenham H, Vancouver Whitecaps
Young, E. (21) 1989/90 Wimbledon, Crystal P, Wolverhampton W

REPUBLIC OF IRELAND

Aherne, T. (16) 1945/6 Belfast Celtic, Luton T
Aldridge, J. W. (69) 1985/6 Oxford U, Liverpool, Real Sociedad, Tranmere R
Ambrose, P. (5) 1954/5 Shamrock R
Anderson, P. (16) 1979/80 Preston NE, Newcastle U

Babb, P. (35) 1993/4 Coventry C, Liverpool, Sunderland
Bailham, E. (1) 1963/4 Shamrock R
Barber, E. (2) 1965/6 Shelbourne, Birmingham C
Barrett, G. (6) 2002/03 Arsenal, Coventry C
Beglin, J. (15) 1983/4 Liverpool
Bonner, P. (80) 1980/1 Celtic
Braddish, S. (1) 1977/8 Dundalk
Brady, T. R. (6) 1963/4 QPR
Brady, W. L. (72) 1974/5 Arsenal, Juventus, Sampdoria, Internazionale, Ascoli, West Ham U
Branagan, K. G. (1) 1996/7 Bolton W
Breen, G. (63) 1995/6 Birmingham C, Coventry C, West Ham U, Sunderland
Breen, T. (3) 1946/7 Shamrock R
Brennan, F. (1) 1964/5 Drumcondra
Brennan, S. A. (19) 1964/5 Manchester U, Waterford
Browne, W. (3) 1963/4 Bohemians
Buckley, L. (2) 1983/4 Shamrock R, Waregem
Burke, F. (1) 1951/2 Cork Ath
Butler, P. J. (1) 1999/00 Sunderland

Butler, T. (2) 2002/03 Sunderland
Byrne, A. B. (14) 1969/70 Southampton
Byrne, J. (23) 1984/5 QPR, Le Havre, Brighton & HA, Sunderland, Millwall
Byrne, J. (2) 2003/04 Shelbourne
Byrne, P. (8) 1983/4 Shamrock R

Campbell, A. (3) 1984/5 Santander
Campbell, N. (11) 1970/1 St Patrick's Ath, Fortuna Cologne
Cantwell, N. (36) 1953/4 West Ham U, Manchester U
Carey, B. P. (3) 1991/2 Manchester U, Leicester C
Carey, J. J. (21) 1945/6 Manchester U
Carolan, J. (2) 1959/60 Manchester U
Carr, S. (41) 1998/9 Tottenham H, Newcastle U
Carroll, B. (2) 1948/9 Shelbourne
Carroll, T. R. (17) 1967/8 Ipswich T, Birmingham C
Carsley, L. K. (29) 1997/8 Derby Co, Blackburn R, Coventry C, Everton
Cascarino, A. G. (88) 1985/6 Gillingham, Millwall, Aston Villa, Celtic, Chelsea, Marseille, Nancy
Chandler, J. (2) 1979/80 Leeds U
Clarke, C. R. (2) 2003/04 Stoke C
Clarke, J. (1) 1977/8 Drogheda United
Clarke, K. (2) 1947/8 Drumcondra
Clarke, M. (1) 1949/50 Shamrock R
Clinton, T. J. (3) 1950/1 Everton
Coad, P. (11) 1946/7 Shamrock R
Coffey, T. (1) 1949/50 Drumcondra
Colfer, M. D. (2) 1949/50 Shelbourne

Colgan, N, (8) 2001/02 Hibernian
Conmy, O. M. (5) 1964/5 Peterborough U
Connolly, D. J. (41) 1995/6 Watford, Feyenoord, Wolverhampton W, Excelsior, Wimbledon, West Ham U, Wigan Ath
Conroy, G. A. (27) 1969/70 Stoke C
Conway, J. P. (20) 1966/7 Fulham, Manchester C
Corr, P. J. (4) 1948/9 Everton
Courtney, E. (1) 1945/6 Cork U
Coyle, O. (1) 1993/4 Bolton W
Coyne, T. (22) 1991/2 Celtic, Tranmere R, Motherwell
Crowe, G. (2) 2002/03 Bohemians
Cummins, G. P. (19) 1953/4 Luton T
Cuneen, T. (1) 1950/1 Limerick
Cunningham, K. (72) 1995/6 Wimbledon, Birmingham C
Curtis, D. P. (17) 1956/7 Shelbourne, Bristol C, Ipswich T, Exeter C
Cusack, S. (1) 1952/3 Limerick

Daish, L. S. (5) 1991/2 Cambridge U, Coventry C
Daly, G. A. (48) 1972/3 Manchester U, Derby C, Coventry C, Birmingham C, Shrewsbury T
Daly, M. (2) 1977/8 Wolverhampton W
Daly, P. (1) 1949/50 Shamrock R
Deacy, E. (4) 1981/2 Aston Villa
Delap, R. J. (11) 1997/8 Derby Co, Southampton
De Mange, K. J. P. P. (2) 1986/7 Liverpool, Hull C
Dempsey, J. T. (19) 1966/7 Fulham, Chelsea
Dennehy, J. (11) 1971/2 Cork Hibernian, Nottingham F, Walsall
Desmond, P. (4) 1949/50 Middlesbrough
Devine, J. (13) 1979/80 Arsenal, Norwich C
Doherty, G. M. T. (34) 1999/00 Luton T, Tottenham H, Norwich C
Donovan, D. C. (5) 1954/5 Everton
Donovan, T. (1) 1979/80 Aston Villa
Douglas, J. (2) 2003/04 Blackburn R
Doyle, C. (1) 1958/9 Shelbourne
Doyle, K. E. (2) 2005/06 Reading
Doyle, M. P. (1) 2003/04 Coventry C
Duff, D. A. (59) 1997/8 Blackburn R, Chelsea
Duffy, B. (1) 1949/50 Shamrock R
Dunne, A. P. (33) 1961/2 Manchester U, Bolton W
Dunne, J. C. (1) 1970/1 Fulham
Dunne, P. A. J. (5) 1964/5 Manchester U

Dunne, R. P. (29) 1999/00 Everton, Manchester C
Dunne, S. (15) 1952/3 Luton T
Dunne, T. (3) 1955/6 St Patrick's Ath
Dunning, P. (2) 1970/1 Shelbourne
Dunphy, E. M. (23) 1965/6 York C, Millwall
Dwyer, N. M. (14) 1959/60 West Ham U, Swansea T

Eccles, P. (1) 1985/6 Shamrock R
Eglington, T. J. (24) 1945/6 Shamrock R, Everton
Elliott, S. W. (7) 2004/05 Sunderland
Evans, M. J. (1) 1997/8 Southampton

Fagan, E. (1) 1972/3 Shamrock R
Fagan, F. (8) 1954/5 Manchester C, Derby C
Fairclough, M. (2) 1981/2 Dundalk
Fallon, S. (8) 1950/1 Celtic
Farrell, P. D. (28) 1945/6 Shamrock R, Everton
Farrelly, G. (6) 1995/6 Aston Villa, Everton, Bolton W
Finnan, S. (38) 1999/00 Fulham, Liverpool
Finucane, A. (11) 1966/7 Limerick
Fitzgerald, F. J. (2) 1954/5 Waterford
Fitzgerald, P. J. (5) 1960/1 Leeds U, Chester
Fitzpatrick, K. (1) 1969/70 Limerick
Fitzsimons, A. G. (26) 1949/50 Middlesbrough, Lincoln C
Fleming, C. (10) 1995/6 Middlesbrough
Fogarty, A. (11) 1959/60 Sunderland, Hartlepool U
Foley, D. J. (6) 1999/00 Watford
Foley, T. C. (9) 1963/4 Northampton T
Fullam, J. 1960/1 Preston NE, Shamrock R

Gallagher, C. (2) 1966/7 Celtic
Gallagher, M. (1) 1953/4 Hibernian
Galvin, A. (29) 1982/3 Tottenham H, Sheffield W, Swindon T
Gannon, E. (14) 1948/9 Notts Co, Sheffield W, Shelbourne K
Gannon, M. (1) 1971/2 Shelbourne
Gavin, J. T. (7) 1949/50 Norwich C, Tottenham H, Norwich C
Gibbons, A. (4) 1951/2 St Patrick's Ath
Gilbert, R. (1) 1965/6 Shamrock R
Giles, C. (1) 1950/1 Doncaster R
Giles, M. J. (59) 1959/60 Manchester U, Leeds U, WBA, Shamrock R
Given, S. J. J. (76) 1995/6 Blackburn R, Newcastle U

300

Givens, D. J. (56) 1968/9 Manchester U, Luton T, QPR, Birmingham C, Neuchatel Xamax
Glynn, D. (2) 1951/2 Drumcondra
Godwin, T. F. (13) 1948/9 Shamrock R, Leicester C, Bournemouth
Goodman, J. (4) 1996/7 Wimbledon
Goodwin, J. (1) 2002/03 Stockport Co
Gorman, W. C. (2) 1946/7 Brentford
Grealish, A. (45) 1975/6 Orient, Luton T, Brighton & HA, WBA
Gregg, E. (8) 1977/8 Bohemians
Grimes, A. A. (18) 1977/8 Manchester U, Coventry C, Luton T

Hale, A. (13) 1961/2 Aston Villa, Doncaster R, Waterford
Hamilton, T. (2) 1958/9 Shamrock R
Hand, E. K. (20) 1968/9 Portsmouth
Harte, I. P. (63) 1995/6 Leeds U, Levante
Hartnett, J. B. (2) 1948/9 Middlesbrough
Haverty, J. (32) 1955/6 Arsenal, Blackburn R, Millwall, Celtic, Bristol R, Shelbourne
Hayes, A. W. P. (1) 1978/9 Southampton
Hayes, W. E. (2) 1946/7 Huddersfield T
Hayes, W. J. (1) 1948/9 Limerick
Healey, R. (2) 1976/7 Cardiff C
Healy, C. (13) 2001/02 Celtic, Sunderland
Heighway, S. D. (34) 1970/1 Liverpool, Minnesota Kicks
Henderson, B. (2) 1947/8 Drumcondra
Henderson, W. C. P. (2) 2005/06 Brighton & HA
Hennessy, J. (5) 1964/5 Shelbourne, St Patrick's Ath
Herrick, J. (3) 1971/2 Cork Hibernians, Shamrock R
Higgins, J. (1) 1950/1 Birmingham C
Holland, M. R. (49) 1999/00 Ipswich T, Charlton Ath
Holmes, J. (30) 1970/1 Coventry C, Tottenham H, Vancouver Whitecaps
Houghton, R. J. (73) 1985/6 Oxford U, Liverpool, Aston Villa, Crystal P, Reading
Howlett, G. (1) 1983/4 Brighton & HA
Hughton, C. (53) 1979/80 Tottenham H, West Ham U
Hurley, C. J. (40) 1956/7 Millwall, Sunderland, Bolton W

Ireland S. J. (1) 2005/06 Manchester C
Irwin, D. J. (56) 1990/1 Manchester U

Kavanagh, G. A. (15) 1997/8 Stoke C, Cardiff C, Wigan Ath
Keane, R. D. (66) 1997/8 Wolverhampton W, Coventry C, Internazionale, Leeds U, Tottenham H
Keane, R. M. (67) 1990/1 Nottingham F, Manchester U
Keane, T. R. (4) 1948/9 Swansea T
Kearin, M. (1) 1971/2 Shamrock R
Kearns, F. T. (1) 1953/4 West Ham U
Kearns, M. (18) 1969/70 Oxford U, Walsall, Wolverhampton W
Kelly, A. T. (34) 1992/3 Sheffield U, Blackburn R
Kelly, D. T. (26) 1987/8 Walsall, West Ham U, Leicester C, Newcastle U, Wolverhampton W, Sunderland, Tranmere R
Kelly, G. (52) 1993/4 Leeds U
Kelly, J. A. (48) 1956/7 Drumcondra, Preston NE
Kelly, J. P. V. (5) 1960/1 Wolverhampton W
Kelly, M. J. (4) 1987/8 Portsmouth
Kelly, N. (1) 1953/4 Nottingham F
Kelly, S. M. (1) 2005/06 Tottenham H
Kenna, J. (27) 1994/5 Blackburn R
Kennedy, M. (34) 1995/6 Liverpool, Wimbledon, Manchester C, Wolverhampton W
Kennedy, M. F. (2) 1985/6 Portsmouth
Kenny, P. (5) 2003/04 Sheffield U
Keogh, J. (1) 1965/6 Shamrock R
Keogh, S. (1) 1958/9 Shamrock R
Kernaghan, A. N. (22) 1992/3 Middlesbrough, Manchester C
Kiely, D. L. (8) 1999/00 Charlton Ath
Kiernan, F. W. (5) 1950/1 Shamrock R, Southampton
Kilbane, K. D. (70) 1997/8 WBA, Sunderland, Everton
Kinnear, J. P. (26) 1966/7 Tottenham H, Brighton & HA
Kinsella, M. A. (48) 1997/8 Charlton Ath, Aston Villa, WBA

Langan, D. (26) 1977/8 Derby Co, Birmingham C, Oxford U
Lawler, J. F. (8) 1952/3 Fulham
Lawlor, J. C. (3) 1948/9 Drumcondra, Doncaster R
Lawlor, M. (5) 1970/1 Shamrock R
Lawrenson, M. (39) 1976/7 Preston NE, Brighton & HA, Liverpool
Lee, A. L. (8) 2002/03 Rotherham U, Cardiff C
Leech, M. (8) 1968/9 Shamrock R
Lowry, D. (1) 1961/2 St Patrick's Ath

McAlinden, J. (2) 1945/6 Portsmouth

McAteer, J. W. (52) 1993/4 Bolton W, Liverpool, Blackburn R, Sunderland

McCann, J. (1) 1956/7 Shamrock R

McCarthy, M. (57) 1983/4 Manchester C, Celtic, Lyon, Millwall

McConville, T. (6) 1971/2 Dundalk, Waterford

McDonagh, Jim (25) 1980/1 Everton, Bolton W, Notts C

McDonagh, Jacko (3) 1983/4 Shamrock R

McEvoy, M. A. (17) 1960/1 Blackburn R

McGeady, A. (4) 2003/04 Celtic

McGee, P. (15) 1977/8 QPR, Preston NE

McGoldrick, E. J. (15) 1991/2 Crystal P, Arsenal

McGowan, D. (3) 1948/9 West Ham U

McGowan, J. (1) 1946/7 Cork U

McGrath, M. (22) 1957/8 Blackburn R, Bradford Park Avenue

McGrath, P. (83) 1984/5 Manchester U, Aston Villa, Derby C

McLoughlin, A. F. (42) 1989/90 Swindon T, Southampton, Portsmouth

McMillan, W. (2) 1945/6 Belfast Celtic

McNally, J. B. (3) 1958/9 Luton T

McPhail, S. (10) 1999/00 Leeds U

Macken, A. (1) 1976/7 Derby Co

Macken, J. P. (1) 2004/05 Manchester C

Mackey, G. (3) 1956/7 Shamrock R

Mahon, A. J. (2) 1999/00 Tranmere R

Malone, G. (1) 1948/9 Shelbourne

Mancini, T. J. (5) 1973/4 QPR, Arsenal

Martin, C. J. (30) 1945/6 Glentoran, Leeds U, Aston Villa

Martin, M. P. (52) 1971/2 Bohemians, Manchester U, WBA, Newcastle U

Maybury, A. (10) 1997/8 Leeds U, Heart of Midlothian, Leicester C

Meagan, M. K. (17) 1960/1 Everton, Huddersfield T, Drogheda

Miller, L. W. P. (12) 2003/04 Celtic, Manchester U

Milligan, M. J. (1) 1991/2 Oldham Ath

Mooney, J. (2) 1964/5 Shamrock R

Moore, A. (8) 1995/6 Middlesbrough

Moran, K. (71) 1979/80 Manchester U, Sporting Gijon, Blackburn R

Moroney, T. (12) 1947/8 West Ham U, Evergreen U

Morris, C. B. (35) 1987/8 Celtic, Middlesbrough

Morrison, C. H. (34) 2001/02 Crystal P, Birmingham C, Crystal P

Moulson, G. B. (3) 1947/8 Lincoln C

Mucklan, C. (1) 1977/8 Drogheda

Mulligan, P. M. (50) 1968/9 Shamrock R, Chelsea, Crystal P, WBA, Shamrock R

Munroe, L. (1) 1953/4 Shamrock R

Murphy, A. (1) 1955/6 Clyde

Murphy, B. (1) 1985/6 Bohemians

Murphy, Jerry (1) 1979/80 Crystal P

Murphy, Joe (1) 2003/04 WBA

Murray, T. (1) 1949/50 Dundalk

Newman, W. (1) 1968/9 Shelbourne

Nolan, R. (10) 1956/7 Shamrock R

O'Brien, A. J. (23) 2000/01 Newcastle U, Portsmouth

O'Brien, F. (3) 1979/80 Philadelphia Fury

O'Brien, J. M. (1) 2005/06 Bolton W

O'Brien, L. (16) 1985/6 Shamrock R, Manchester U, Newcastle U, Tranmere R

O'Brien, R. (5) 1975/6 Notts Co

O'Byrne, L. B. (1) 1948/9 Shamrock R

O'Callaghan, B. R. (6) 1978/9 Stoke C

O'Callaghan, K. (21) 1980/1 Ipswich T, Portsmouth

O'Connell, A. (2) 1966/7 Dundalk, Bohemians

O'Connor, T. (4) 1949/50 Shamrock R

O'Connor, T. (7) 1967/8 Fulham, Dundalk, Bohemians

O'Driscoll, J. F. (3) 1948/9 Swansea T

O'Driscoll, S. (3) 1981/2 Fulham

O'Farrell, F. (9) 1951/2 West Ham U, Preston NE

O'Flanagan, K. P. (3) 1946/7 Arsenal

O'Flanagan, M. (1) 1946/7 Bohemians

O'Hanlon, K. G. (1) 1987/8 Rotherham U

O'Keefe, E. (5) 1980/1 Everton, Port Vale

O'Leary, D. (68) 1976/7 Arsenal

O'Leary, P. (7) 1979/80 Shamrock R

O'Neill, F. S. (20) 1961/2 Shamrock R

O'Neill, J. (17) 1951/2 Everton

O'Neill, J. (1) 1960/1 Preston NE

O'Neill, K. P. (13) 1995/6 Norwich C, Middlesbrough

O'Regan, K. (4) 1983/4 Brighton & HA

O'Reilly, J. (2) 1945/6 Cork U

O'Shea, J. F. (30) 2001/02 Manchester U

Peyton, G. (33) 1976/7 Fulham, Bournemouth, Everton

Peyton, N. (6) 1956/7 Shamrock R, Leeds U

Phelan, T. (42) 1991/2 Wimbledon, Manchester C, Chelsea, Everton, Fulham

302

Quinn, A. (6) 2002/03 Sheffield W, Sheffield U
Quinn, B. S. (4) 1999/00 Coventry C
Quinn, N. J. (91) 1985/6 Arsenal, Manchester C, Sunderland

Reid, A. M. (22) 2003/04 Nottingham F, Tottenham H
Reid, S. J. (16) 2001/02 Millwall, Blackburn R
Richardson, D. J. (3) 1971/2 Shamrock R, Gillingham
Ringstead, A. (20) 1950/1 Sheffield U
Robinson, M. (24) 1980/1 Brighton & HA, Liverpool, QPR
Roche, P. J. (8) 1971/2 Shelbourne, Manchester U
Rogers, E. (19) 1967/8 Blackburn R, Charlton Ath
Rowlands, M. C. (3) 2003/04 QPR
Ryan, G. (18) 1977/8 Derby Co, Brighton & HA
Ryan, R. A. (16) 1949/50 WBA, Derby C

Sadlier, R. T. (1) 2001/02 Millwall
Savage, D. P. T. (5) 1995/6 Millwall
Saward, P. (18) 1953/4 Millwall, Aston Villa, Huddersfield T
Scannell, T. (1) 1953/4 Southend U
Scully, P. J. (1) 1988/9 Arsenal
Sheedy, K. (46) 1983/4 Everton, Newcastle U
Sheridan, J. J. (34) 1987/8 Leeds U, Sheffield W
Slaven, B. (7) 1989/90 Middlesbrough
Sloan, J. W. (2) 1945/6 Arsenal
Smyth, M. (1) 1968/9 Shamrock R
Stapleton, F. (71) 1976/7 Arsenal, Manchester U, Ajax, Le Havre, Blackburn R

Staunton, S. (102) 1988/9 Liverpool, Aston Villa, Liverpool, Aston Villa
Stevenson, A. E. (6) 1946/7 Everton
Strahan, F. (5) 1963/4 Shelbourne
Swan, M. M. G. (1) 1959/60 Drumcondra
Synott, N. (3) 1977/8 Shamrock R

Taylor, T. (1) 1958/9 Waterford
Thomas, P. (2) 1973/4 Waterford
Thompson, J. (1) 2003/04 Nottingham F
Townsend, A. D. (70) 1988/9 Norwich C, Chelsea, Aston Villa, Middlesbrough
Traynor, T. J. (8) 1953/4 Southampton
Treacy, R. C. P. (42) 1965/6 WBA, Charlton Ath, Swindon T, Preston NE, WBA, Shamrock R
Tuohy, L. (8) 1955/6 Shamrock R, Newcastle U, Shamrock R
Turner, P. (2) 1962/3 Celtic

Vernon, J. (2) 1945/6 Belfast Celtic

Waddock, G. (21) 1979/80 QPR, Millwall
Walsh, D. J. (20) 1945/6 Linfield, WBA, Aston Villa
Walsh, J. (1) 1981/2 Limerick
Walsh, M. (21) 1975/6 Blackpool, Everton, QPR, Porto
Walsh, M. (4) 1981/2 Everton
Walsh, W. (9) 1946/7 Manchester C
Waters, J. (2) 1976/7 Grimsby T
Whelan, R. (2) 1963/4 St Patrick's Ath
Whelan, R. (53) 1980/1 Liverpool, Southend U
Whelan, W. (4) 1955/6 Manchester U
Whittaker, R. (1) 1958/9 Chelsea

REPUBLIC OF IRELAND LEAGUE 2005

	P	W	D	L	F	A	Pts
Cork City	33	22	8	3	53	18	74
Derry City	33	22	6	5	56	25	72
Shelbourne	33	20	7	6	62	25	67
Drogheda United	33	12	12	9	40	33	48
Longford Town	33	12	9	12	29	32	45
Bohemians	33	13	6	14	42	47	45
Bray Wanderers	33	11	6	16	40	57	39
Waterford United	33	9	7	17	30	49	34
UCD	33	7	12	14	28	44	33
St Patrick's Ath	33	7	11	15	26	36	32
Shamrock Rovers†	33	9	8	16	33	52	27
Finn Harps*	33	5	6	22	30	51	21

Shamrock Rovers deducted 8 points for financial irregularities.
*relegated; †relegated after play-off.

BRITISH ISLES INTERNATIONAL GOALSCORERS SINCE 1946

ENGLAND

Name	Goals	Name	Goals	Name	Goals
A'Court, A.	1	Defoe, J. C.	1	Lampard, F.J.	11
Adams, T.A.	5	Dixon, L.M.	1	Langton, R.	1
Allen, R.	2	Dixon, K.M.	4	Latchford, R.D.	5
Anderson, V.	2	Douglas, B.	11	Lawler, C.	1
Anderton, D.R.	7			Lawton, T.	16
Astall, G.	1	Eastham, G.	2	Lee, F.	10
Atyeo, P.J.W.	5	Edwards, D.	5	Lee, J.	1
		Ehiogu, U.	1	Lee, R.M.	2
Baily, E.F.	5	Elliott, W.H.	3	Lee, S.	2
Baker, J.H.	3			Le Saux, G.P.	1
Ball, A.J.	8	Ferdinand, L.	5	Lineker, G.	48
Barnes, J.	11	Ferdinand, R.G.	1	Lofthouse, N.	30
Barnes, P.S.	4	Finney, T.	30		
Barmby, N.J.	4	Flowers, R.	10	Mabbutt, G.	1
Beardsley, P.A.	9	Fowler, R.B.	7	McDermott, T.	3
Beattie, J.K.	1	Francis, G.C.J.	3	Macdonald, M.	6
Beckham, D.R.J.	17	Francis, T.	12	McManaman, S.	3
Bell, C.	9	Froggatt, J.	2	Mannion, W.J.	11
Bentley, R.T.F.	9	Froggatt, R.	2	Mariner, P.	13
Blissett, L.	3			Marsh, R.W.	1
Bowles, S.	1	Gascoigne, P.J.	10	Matthews, S.	3
Bradford, G.R.W.	1	Gerrard, S.G.	9	Medley, L.D.	1
Bradley, W.	2	Goddard, P.	1	Melia, J.	1
Bridge, W. M.	1	Grainger, C.	3	Merson, P.C.	3
Bridges, B.J.	1	Greaves, J.	44	Milburn, J.E.T.	10
Broadbent, P.F.	2			Moore, R.F.	2
Broadis, I.A.	8	Haines, J.T.W.	2	Morris, J.	3
Brooking, T.D.	5	Hancocks, J.	2	Mortensen, S.H.	23
Brooks, J.	2	Hassall, H.W.	4	Mullen, J.	6
Bull, S.G.	4	Hateley, M.	9	Mullery, A.P.	1
Butcher, T.	3	Haynes, J.N.	18	Murphy, D. B.	1
Byrne, J.J.	8	Heskey, E.W.	5		
		Hirst, D.E.	1	Neal, P.G.	5
Campbell, S. J.	1	Hitchens, G.A.	5	Nicholls, J.	1
Carter, H.S.	5	Hoddle, G.	8	Nicholson, W.E.	1
Chamberlain, M.	1	Hughes, E.W.	1		
Channon, M.R.	21	Hunt, R.	18	O'Grady, M.	3
Charlton, J.	6	Hunter, N.	2	Owen, M.J.	36
Charlton, R.	49	Hurst, G.C.	24	Own goals	19
Chivers, M.	13				
Clarke, A.J.	10	Ince P.E.C.	2	Paine, T.L.	7
Cole, A.	1			Palmer, C.L.	1
Cole, J.J.	6	Jeffers, F.	1	Parry, R.A.	1
Connelly, J.M.	7	Johnson, D.E.	6	Peacock, A.	3
Coppell, S.J.	7			Pearce, S.	5
Cowans, G.	2	Kay, A.H.	1	Pearson, J.S.	5
Crawford, R.	1	Keegan, J.K.	21	Pearson, S.C.	5
Crouch, P.J.	6	Kennedy, R.	3	Perry, W.	2
Currie, A.W.	3	Keown, M.R.	2	Peters, M.	20
		Kevan, D.T.	8	Pickering, F.	5
		Kidd, B.	1	Platt, D.	27
		King, L.B.	1	Pointer, R.	2

304

Ramsay, A.E.	3			Gemmell, T.K	
Redknapp, J.F.	1	Baird, S.	2	*(Celtic)*	1
Revie, D.G.	4	Bannon, E.	1	Gemmill, A.	8
Richardson, K.E.	2	Bauld, W.	2	Gemmill, S.	1
Robson, B.	26	Baxter, J.C.	3	Gibson, D.W.	3
Robson, R.	4	Bett, J.	1	Gilzean, A.J.	12
Rooney, W.	11	Bone, J.	1	Gough, C.R.	6
Rowley, J.F.	6	Booth, S.	6	Graham, A.	2
Royle, J.	2	Boyd, K.	2	Graham, G.	3
		Boyd, T.	1	Gray, A.	7
Sansom, K.	1	Brand, R.	8	Gray, E.	3
Scholes, P.	14	Brazil, A.	1	Gray, F.	1
Sewell, J.	3	Bremner, W.J.	3	Greig, J.	3
Shackleton, L.F.	1	Brown, A.D.	6		
Shearer, A.	30	Buckley, P.	1	Hamilton, G.	4
Sheringham, E.P.	11	Burke, C.	2	Harper, J.M.	2
Smith, A.	1	Burley, C.W.	3	Hartford, R.A.	4
Smith, A.M.	2	Burns, K.	1	Hartley, P.J.	1
Smith, R.	13			Henderson, J.G.	1
Southgate, G.	2	Caldwell, G.	1	Henderson, W.	5
Steven, T.M.	4	Calderwood, C.	1	Hendry, E.C.J.	3
Stiles, N.P.	1	Caldow, E.	4	Herd, D.G.	3
Stone, S.B.	2	Cameron, C.	2	Herd, G.	1
Summerbee, M.G.	1	Campbell, R.	1	Hewie, J.D.	2
		Chalmers, S.	3	Holt, G.J.	1
Tambling, R.V.	1	Collins, J.	12	Holton, J.A.	2
Taylor, P.J.	2	Collins, R.V.	10	Hopkin, D.	2
Taylor, T.	16	Combe, J.R.	1	Houliston, W.	2
Terry, J.G.	1	Conn, A.	1	Howie, H.	1
Thompson, P.B.	1	Cooper, D.	6	Hughes, J.	1
Tueart, D.	2	Craig, J.	1	Hunter, W.	1
		Crawford, S.	4	Hutchison, D.	6
Vassell, D.	6	Curran, H.P.	1	Hutchison, T.	1
Viollet, D.S.	1				
		Dailly, C.	5	Jackson, C.	1
Waddle, C.R.	6	Dalglish, K.	30	Jackson, D.	4
Wallace, D.L.	1	Davidson, J.A.	1	Jardine, A.	1
Walsh, P.	1	Dickov, P.	1	Jess, E.	2
Watson, D.V.	4	Dobie, R. S.	1	Johnston, A.	2
Webb, N.	4	Docherty, T.H.	1	Johnston, L.H.	1
Weller, K.	1	Dodds, D.	1	Johnston, M.	14
Wignall, F.	2	Dodds, W.	7	Johnstone, D.	2
Wilkins, R.G.	3	Duncan, D.M.	1	Johnstone, J.	4
Wilshaw, D.J.	10	Durie, G.S.	7	Johnstone, R.	10
Wise, D.F.	1			Jordan, J.	11
Withe, P.	1	Elliott, M.S.	1		
Woodcock, T.	16			Kyle, K.	1
Worthington, F.S.	2	Ferguson, B.	2		
Wright, I.E.	9	Fernie, W.	1	Lambert, P.	1
Wright, M.	1	Flavell, R.	2	Law, D.	30
Wright, W.A.	3	Fleming, C.	2	Leggat, G.	8
Wright-Phillips, S.C.	1	Fletcher, D.	3	Lennox, R.	3
		Freedman, D.A.	1	Liddell, W.	6
SCOTLAND				Linwood, A.B.	1
Aitken, R.	1	Gallacher, K.W.	9	Lorimer, P.	4
Archibald, S.	4	Gemmell, T.K			
		(St Mirren)	1	Macari, L.	5

McAllister, G.	5	Reilly, L.	22	Davies, R.T.	9
MacDougall, E.J.	3	Ring, T.	2	Davies, R.W.	6
MacKay, D.C.	4	Rioch, B.D.	6	Davies, Simon	5
Mackay, G.	1	Ritchie, P.S.	1	Deacy, N.	4
MacKenzie, J.A.	1	Robertson, A.	2	Durban, A.	2
MacLeod, M.	1	Robertson, J.	3	Dwyer, P.	2
McAvennie, F.	1	Robertson, J.N.	8		
McCall, S.M.	1			Earnshaw, R.	11
McCalliog, J.	1	St John, I.	9	Edwards, G.	2
McCann, N.	3	Scott, A.S.	5	Edwards, R.I.	4
McClair, B.	2	Sharp, G.	1	England, H.M.	4
McCoist, A.	19	Shearer, D.	2	Evans, I.	1
McFadden, J.	8	Smith, G.	4		
McGhee, M.	2	Souness, G.J.	4	Flynn, B.	7
McGinlay, J.	3	Steel, W.	12	Ford, T.	23
McInally, A.	3	Stein, C.	10	Foulkes, W.J.	1
McKimmie, S.I.	1	Stewart, R.	1		
McKinlay, W.	1	Strachan, G.	5	Giggs, R.J.	11
McKinnon, R.	1	Sturrock, P.	3	Giles, D.	2
McLaren, A.	4			Godfrey, B.C.	2
McLean, T.	1	Thompson, S.	3	Griffiths, A.T.	6
McLintock, F.	1	Thornton, W.	1	Griffiths, M.W.	2
McMillan, I.L.	2				
McNeill, W.	3	Waddell, W.	6	Harris, C.S.	1
McPhail, J.	3	Wallace, I.A.	1	Hartson, J.	14
McQueen, G.	5	Wark, J.	7	Hewitt, R.	1
McStay, P.	9	Webster, A.	1	Hockey, T.	1
McSwegan, G.J.	1	Weir, A.	1	Hodges, G.	2
Mason, J.	4	Weir, D.	1	Horne, B.	2
Masson, D.S.	1	White, J.A.	3	Hughes, L.M.	16
Miller, K.	7	Wilkie, L.	1		
Miller, W.	1	Wilson, D.	9	James, L.	10
Mitchell, R.C.	1			James, R.	7
Morgan, W.	1	Young, A.	2	Jones, A.	1
Morris, H.	3			Jones, B.S.	2
Mudie, J.K.	9	**WALES**		Jones, Cliff	16
Mulhall, G.	1	Allchurch, I.J.	23	Jones, D.E.	1
Murdoch, R.	5	Allen, M.	3	Jones, J.P.	1
Murray, J.	1				
		Barnes, W.	1	Koumas, J.	1
Narey, D.	1	Bellamy, C.D.	9	Kryzwicki, R.I.	1
Naysmith, G.A.	1	Blackmore, C.G.	1		
Nevin, P.K.F.	5	Blake, N.A.	4	Leek, K.	5
Nicholas, C.	5	Bodin, P.J.	3	Lovell, S.	1
		Bowen, D.I.	3	Lowrie, G.	2
O'Connor, G.	1	Bowen, M.	2		
O'Hare, J.	5	Boyle, T.	1	Mahoney, J.F.	1
Ormond, W.E.	2	Burgess, W.A.R.	1	Medwin, T.C.	6
Orr, T.	1			Melville, A.K.	3
Own goals	10	Charles, J.	1	Moore, G.	1
		Charles, M.	6		
Parlane, D.	1	Charles, W.J.	15	Nicholas, P.	2
Pettigrew, W.	2	Clarke, R.J.	5		
Provan, D.	1	Coleman, C.	4	O'Sullivan, P.A.	1
		Curtis, A.	6	Own goals	5
Quashie, N.F.	1				
Quinn, J.	7	Davies, G.	2	Palmer, D.	1
Quinn, P.	1			Parry, P.I.	1

Paul, R.	1	
Pembridge, M.A.	6	
Phillips, D.	2	
Powell, A.	1	
Powell, D.	1	
Price, P.	1	
Reece, G.I.	2	
Rees, R.R.	3	
Roberts, P.S.	1	
Robinson, C.P.	1	
Robinson, J.R.C.	3	
Rush, I.	28	
Saunders, D.	22	
Savage R.W.	2	
Slatter, N.	2	
Smallman, D.P.	1	
Speed, G.A.	7	
Symons, C.J.	2	
Tapscott, D.R.	4	
Taylor, G.J.	1	
Thomas, M.	4	
Toshack, J.B.	12	
Vernon, T.R.	8	
Walsh, I.	7	
Williams, A.	1	
Williams, G.E.	1	
Williams, G.G.	1	
Woosnam, A.P.	3	
Yorath, T.C.	2	
Young, E.	1	

NORTHERN IRELAND

Anderson, T.	4	
Armstrong, G.	12	
Barr, H.H.	1	
Best, G.	9	
Bingham, W.L.	10	
Black, K.	1	
Blanchflower, D.	2	
Blanchflower, J.	1	
Brennan, R.A.	1	
Brotherston, N.	3	
Campbell, W.G.	1	
Casey, T.	2	
Caskey, W.	1	
Cassidy, T.	1	
Clarke, C.J.	13	
Clements, D.	2	
Cochrane, T.	1	
Crossan, E.	1	
Crossan, J.A.	10	
Cush, W.W.	5	
Davis, S.	1	
D'Arcy, S.D.	1	
Doherty, I.	1	
Doherty, P.D.	2	
Dougan, A.D.	8	
Dowie, I.	12	
Elder, A.R.	1	
Elliott, S.	4	
Feeney, W.J.	2	
Ferguson, W.	1	
Ferris, R.O.	1	
Finney, T.	2	
Gillespie, K.R.	2	
Gray, P.	6	
Griffin, D.J.	1	
Hamilton, B.	4	
Hamilton, W.	5	
Harkin, J.T.	2	
Harvey, M.	3	
Healy, D.J.	19	
Hill, C.F.	1	
Humphries, W.	1	
Hughes, M.E.	5	
Hunter, A.	1	
Hunter, B.V.	1	
Irvine, W.J.	8	
Johnston, W.C.	1	
Jones, J.	1	
Jones, S.	1	
Lennon, N.F.	2	
Lockhart, N.	3	
Lomas, S.M.	3	
Magilton, J.	5	
McAdams, W.J.	7	
McCartney, G.	1	
McClelland, J.	1	
McCrory, S.	1	
McCurdy, C.	1	
McDonald, A.	3	
McGarry, J.K.	1	
McGrath, R.C.	4	
McIlroy, J.	10	
McIlroy, S.B.	5	
McLaughlin, J.C.	6	
McMahon, G.J.	2	
McMordie, A.S.	3	
McMorran, E.J.	4	
McParland, P.J.	10	
Moreland, V.	1	
Morgan, S.	3	
Morrow, S.J.	1	
Mulryne, P.P.	3	
Murdoch, C.J.	1	
Neill, W.J.T.	2	
Nelson, S.	1	
Nicholl, C.J.	3	
Nicholl, J.M.	1	
Nicholson, J.J.	6	
O'Boyle, G.	1	
O'Kane, W.J.	1	
O'Neill, J.	2	
O'Neill, M.A.	4	
O'Neill, M.H.	8	
Own goals	17	
Patterson, D.J.	1	
Peacock, R.	2	
Penney, S.	2	
Quinn, J.M.	12	
Quinn, S.J.	4	
Rowland, K.	1	
Simpson, W.J.	5	
Smyth, S.	5	
Spence, D.W.	3	
Sproule, I.	1	
Stewart, I.	2	
Taggart, G.P.	7	
Tully, C.P.	3	
Walker, J.	1	
Walsh, D.J.	5	
Welsh, E.	1	
Whiteside, N.	9	
Whitley, Jeff	2	
Williams, M.S.	1	
Wilson, D.J.	1	
Wilson, K.J.	6	
Wilson, S.J.	7	

EIRE

Aldridge, J.	19	
Ambrose, P.	1	
Anderson, J.	1	
Barrett, G.	2	

Brady, L.	9	Grealish, T.	8	Moroney, T.	1
Breen, G.	6	Grimes, A.A.	1	Morrison, C.H.	9
Byrne, J.	4			Mulligan, P.	1
		Hale, A.	2		
Cantwell, J.	14	Hand, E.	2	O'Brien, A.J.	1
Carey, J.	3	Harte, I.P.	11	O'Callaghan, K.	1
Carroll, T.	1	Haverty, J.	3	O'Connor, T.	2
Cascarino, A.	19	Healy, C.	1	O'Farrell, F.	2
Coad, P.	3	Holland, M.R.	5	O'Keefe, E.	1
Connolly, D.J.	9	Holmes, J.	1	O'Leary, D.A.	1
Conroy, T.	2	Houghton, R.	6	O'Neill, F.	1
Conway, J.	3	Hughton, C.	1	O'Neill, K.P.	4
Coyne, T.	6	Hurley, C.	2	O'Reilly, J.	1
Cummins, G.	5			O'Shea, J.F.	1
Curtis, D.	8	Irwin, D.	4	Own goals	10
Daly, G.	13	Kavanagh, G.A.	1	Quinn, N.	21
Dempsey, J.	1	Keane, R.D.	26		
Dennehy, M.	2	Keane, R.M.	9	Reid, A.M.	3
Doherty, G.M.T.	4	Kelly, D.	9	Reid, S.J.	2
Duff, D.A.	7	Kelly, G.	2	Ringstead, A.	7
Duffy, B.	1	Kennedy, M.	4	Robinson, M.	4
Dunne, R.P.	4	Kernaghan, A.	1	Rogers, E.	5
		Kilbane, K.D.	5	Ryan, G.	1
Eglinton, T.	2	Kinsella, M.A.	3	Ryan, R.	3
Elliott, S.W.	1				
		Lawrenson, M.	5	Sheedy, K.	9
Fagan, F.	5	Leech, M.	2	Sheridan, J.	5
Fallon, S.	2			Slaven, B.	1
Farrell, P.	3	McAteer, J.W.	3	Sloan, J.	1
Finnan, S.	1	McCann, J.	1	Stapleton, F.	20
Fitzgerald, J.	1	McCarthy, M.	2	Staunton, S.	7
Fitzgerald, P.	2	McEvoy, A.	6	Strahan, F.	1
Fitzsimons, A.	7	McGee, P.	4		
Fogarty, A.	3	McGrath, P.	8	Townsend, A.D.	7
Foley, D.	2	McLoughlin, A.	2	Treacy, R.	5
Fullam, J.	1	McPhail, S.	1	Tuohy, L.	4
		Mancini, T.	1		
Galvin, A.	1	Martin, C.	6	Waddock, G.	3
Gavin, J.	2	Martin, M.	4	Walsh, D.	5
Giles, J.	5	Miller, L.W.P.	1	Walsh, M.	3
Givens, D.	19	Mooney, J.	1	Waters, J.	1
Glynn, D.	1	Moran, K.	6	Whelan, R.	3

UEFA UNDER-21 CHAMPIONSHIP 2004–06

GROUP 1
Romania 1, Finland 0
Macedonia 4, Armenia 0
Romania 5, Macedonia 1
Holland 0, Czech Republic 0
Armenia 0, Finland 1
Czech Republic 4, Romania 1
Finland 0, Armenia 1
Macedonia 0, Holland 2
Holland 4, Finland 1
Armenia 0, Czech Republic 4
Armenia 1, Romania 5
Macedonia 2, Czech Republic 2
Romania 2, Holland 0
Czech Republic 3, Finland 0
Holland 0, Armenia 0
Macedonia 1, Romania 0
Holland 2, Romania 0
Armenia 0, Macedonia 0
Czech Republic 2, Macedonia 0
Finland 1, Holland 2
Romania 2, Armenia 0

GROUP 2
Albania 1, Greece 1
Denmark 3, Ukraine 2
Turkey 0, Georgia 0
Kazakhstan 0, Ukraine 1
Georgia 2, Albania 1
Greece 2, Turkey 1
Albania 1, Denmark 2
Ukraine 1, Greece 0
Turkey 1, Kazakhstan 0
Kazakhstan 0, Albania 1
Ukraine 6, Georgia 0
Denmark 1, Turkey 1
Greece 5, Kazakhstan 0
Georgia 2, Denmark 4
Turkey 1, Ukraine 0
Albania 1, Ukraine 1
Greece 0, Denmark 1
Denmark 5, Kazakhstan 1
Georgia 1, Greece 1
Turkey 4, Albania 0
Georgia 0, Turkey 2
Greece 2, Albania 0
Ukraine 0, Denmark 1
Albania 0, Georgia 1
Ukraine 2, Kazakhstan 1
Turkey 0, Greece 2
Kazakhstan 2, Turkey 1
Denmark 7, Albania 0
Greece 0, Ukraine 1

GROUP 3
Slovakia 1, Luxembourg 0
Estonia 0, Luxembourg 0
Latvia 1, Portugal 2

Russia 4, Slovakia 0
Luxembourg 1, Latvia 2
Portugal 3, Estonia 0
Luxembourg 0, Russia 4
Slovakia 3, Latvia 1
Latvia 0, Estonia 0
Portugal 2, Russia 0
Russia 3, Estonia 0
Luxembourg 1, Portugal 6
Estonia 0, Slovakia 2
Latvia 2, Luxembourg 1
Slovakia 0, Portugal 1
Estonia 1, Russia 5
Portugal 2, Slovakia 1
Russia 1, Latvia 1
Luxembourg 0, Slovakia 2
Estonia 0, Portugal 5

GROUP 4
France 1, Israel 0
Republic of Ireland 3, Cyprus 0
Israel 1, Cyprus 0
Switzerland 4, Republic of Ireland 2
Israel 1, Switzerland 1
France 1, Republic of Ireland 0
Cyprus 0, France 1
Cyprus 0, Israel 1
Israel 3, Republic of Ireland 1
France 1, Switzerland 1
Israel 3, France 2
Switzerland 3, Cyprus 0
Republic of Ireland 2, Israel 2

GROUP 5
Italy 2, Norway 0
Slovenia 1, Moldova 0
Norway 2, Belarus 3
Scotland 1, Slovenia 1
Moldova 0, Italy 1
Belarus 2, Moldova 3
Scotland 0, Norway 2
Slovenia 0, Italy 3
Moldova 0, Scotland 0
Norway 0, Slovenia 0
Italy 2, Belarus 1
Italy 2, Scotland 0
Moldova 1, Norway 3
Slovenia 1, Belarus 4
Belarus 1, Slovenia 2
Scotland 0, Moldova 0
Norway 1, Italy 0
Belarus 3, Scotland 2

GROUP 6
Azerbaijan 0, Wales 1
Austria 0, England 2
Austria 3, Azerbaijan 0
Poland 1, England 3
Austria 0, Poland 3

England 2, Wales 0
Azerbaijan 0, Germany 2
Wales 2, Poland 2
Germany 2, Austria 0
Azerbaijan 0, England 0
Germany 1, Poland 1
Wales 0, Germany 4
Wales 1, Austria 0
Poland 3, Azerbaijan 0
England 2, Germany 2
Austria 2, Wales 0
England 2, Azerbaijan 0
Azerbaijan 1, Poland 1

GROUP 7

Belgium 3, Lithuania 0
San Marino 0, Serbia & Montenegro 5
Bosnia 0, Spain 2
Lithuania 2, San Marino 0
Bosnia 1, Serbia & Montenegro 3
Spain 2, Belgium 0
Serbia & Montenegro 9, San Marino 0
Lithuania 1, Spain 1
Belgium 4, Serbia & Montenegro 0
San Marino 1, Lithuania 2
Spain 14, San Marino 0
Belgium 2, Bosnia 1
Serbia & Montenegro 1, Spain 0
Bosnia 2, Lithuania 0
San Marino 0, Belgium 4
Serbia & Montenegro 1, Belgium 1
San Marino 1, Bosnia 4
Spain 2, Lithuania 0
Spain 4, Bosnia 2

GROUP 8

Iceland 3, Bulgaria 1
Croatia 1, Hungary 0

Malta 0, Sweden 1
Hungary 1, Iceland 0
Sweden 0, Croatia 2
Croatia 1, Bulgaria 0
Malta 1, Iceland 0
Sweden 2, Hungary 1
Iceland 3, Sweden 1
Bulgaria 2, Malta 1
Malta 0, Hungary 2
Bulgaria 1, Sweden 2
Croatia 2, Iceland 1
Hungary 1, Bulgaria 0
Croatia 1, Malta 0
Bulgaria 2, Croatia 1
Iceland 0, Hungary 1
Sweden 6, Malta 0
Iceland 0, Malta 0

PLAY-OFFS, FIRST LEG

Czech Republic 0, Germany 2
England 1, France 1
Hungary 1, Italy 1
Russia 0, Denmark 1
Serbia & Montenegro 3, Croatia 1
Slovenia 0, Holland 0
Switzerland 1, Portugal 1
Ukraine 2, Belgium 3

PLAY-OFFS, SECOND LEG

Belgium 1, Ukraine 3
Croatia 1, Serbia & Montenegro 2
Denmark 3, Russia 1
France 2, England 1
Germany 1, Czech Republic 0
Holland 2, Slovenia 0
Italy 1, Hungary 0
Portugal 2, Switzerland 1

Final Tournament (in Portugal)

GROUP A

Germany 0, Portugal 1
France 2, Serbia & Montenegro 0
France 3, Germany 0
Portugal 0, Serbia & Montenegro 2
Serbia & Montenegro 0, Germany 1
Portugal 0, France 1

GROUP B

Holland 1, Italy 0

Denmark 1, Ukraine 2
Denmark 1, Holland 1
Italy 1, Ukraine 0
Ukraine 2, Holland 1
Italy 3, Denmark 3

SEMI-FINALS

France 2, Holland 3
Ukraine 0, Serbia & Montenegro 0
Ukraine won 5-4 on penalties.

FINAL

Holland (2) 3 *(Huntelaar 11, 43 (pen), Hofs 90)*   **Ukraine 0 (0)**

Holland: Vermeer; Tiendalli, Vlaar, Luirink, Emanuelson, Aissati (Zomer 78), De Zeeuw, Schaars, Hofs, Huntelaar, Castelen (De Ridder 69).
Ukraine: Pyatov; Yarmash, Chygrynskiy, Yatsenko, Romanchuk■, Mikhalik, Godin (Feschuk 46), Cheberyachko, Maksymov, Milevskiy, Fomin (Aliyev 46).

■ *Denotes player sent off.*

NATIONWIDE CONFERENCE 2005–2006

		Home					Away					Total						
	P	W	D	L	F	A	W	D	L	F	A	W	D	L	F	A	Gd	Pts
1 Accrington S	42	16	3	2	38	17	12	4	5	38	28	28	7	7	76	45	31	91
2 Hereford U	42	11	7	3	30	14	11	7	3	29	19	22	14	6	59	33	26	80
3 Grays Ath	42	7	9	5	46	32	14	4	3	48	23	21	13	8	94	55	39	76
4 Halifax T	42	14	6	1	31	11	7	6	8	24	29	21	12	9	55	40	15	75
5 Morecambe	42	15	4	2	44	17	7	4	10	24	24	22	8	12	68	41	27	74
6 Stevenage B	42	15	3	3	38	15	4	9	8	24	32	19	12	11	62	47	15	69
7 Exeter C	42	11	3	7	41	22	7	6	8	24	26	18	9	15	65	48	17	63
8 York C	42	10	5	6	36	26	7	7	7	27	22	17	12	13	63	48	15	63
9 Burton Alb	42	8	7	6	23	21	8	5	8	27	31	16	12	14	50	52	–2	60
10 Dagenham & R	42	8	4	9	31	32	8	6	7	32	27	16	10	16	63	59	4	58
11 Woking	42	8	7	6	30	20	6	7	8	28	27	14	14	14	58	47	11	56
12 Cambridge U	42	11	6	4	35	25	4	4	13	16	32	15	10	17	51	57	–6	55
13 Aldershot T	42	10	4	7	30	30	6	2	13	31	44	16	6	20	61	74	–13	54
14 Canvey Is*	42	6	8	7	23	27	7	4	10	24	31	13	12	17	47	58	–11	51
15 Kidderminster H	42	8	5	8	21	27	5	6	10	18	28	13	11	18	39	55	–16	50
16 Gravesend & N	42	8	4	9	25	25	5	6	10	20	32	13	10	19	45	57	–12	49
17 Crawley T	42	9	4	8	27	22	3	7	11	21	33	12	11	19	48	55	–7	47
18 Southport	42	7	3	11	24	38	3	7	11	12	30	10	10	22	36	68	–32	40
19 Forest Green R	42	7	7	7	30	27	1	7	13	19	35	8	14	20	49	62	–13	38
20 Tamworth	42	4	10	7	17	23	4	4	13	15	40	8	14	20	32	63	–31	38
21 Scarborough§	42	4	7	10	24	30	5	3	13	16	36	9	10	23	40	66	–26	37
22 Altrincham†	42	7	5	9	25	30	3	6	12	15	41	10	11	21	40	71	–31	23

Canvey Is resigned from Football Conference and will play 2006-07 season in Ryman Premier League.
†Altrincham deducted 18 points for breach of rule.
§Scarborough relegated for financial reasons.

Leading Goalscorers 2005–06

	League	P-offs	FA Cup	LDV	Trophy	Total
Andy Bishop (York C)	23	0	2	0	1	26
Justin Richards (Woking)	21	0	0	1	0	22
Danny Carlton (Morecambe)	17	0	1	0	0	18
Colin Little (Altrincham)	17	0	0	0	0	17
Clayton Donaldson (York C)	16	0	1	0	0	17
Chris Moore (Dagenham & R)	15	0	2	0	3	20
Michael Kightly (Grays Ath)	14	1	1	0	2	18
Paul Mullin (Accrington S)	14	0	0	0	3	17
Glenn Poole (Grays Ath)	13	0	1	0	4	18
Lee Phillips (Exeter C)	13	0	0	1	3	17
Ian Craney (Accrington S)	13	0	0	0	3	16
Gary Roberts (Accrington S)	13	0	2	0	0	15
Daryl Clare (Burton Albion)	13	0	0	0	0	13

(Includes 11 League goals for Crawley T).

NATIONWIDE CONFERENCE RESULTS 2005–2006

	Accrington S	Aldershot T	Altrincham	Burton Alb	Cambridge U	Canvey Island	Crawley T	Dagenham & R	Exeter C	Forest Green R	Gravesend & N	Grays Ath	Halifax T	Hereford U	Kidderminster H	Morecambe	Scarborough	Southport	Stevenage B	Tamworth	Woking	York C
Accrington S	—	1-0	1-0	2-1	1-1	1-0	4-2	1-0	1-2	1-2	1-1	2-3	1-1	1-0	1-0	2-0	1-0	2-0	1-1	2-1	2-1	2-1
Aldershot T	3-2	—	0-2	2-1	1-3	0-2	3-2	0-5	1-1	2-1	0-1	0-3	3-1	0-1	1-0	2-0	0-1	4-0	1-1	0-2	0-4	2-1
Altrincham	0-1	5-1	—	1-0	1-0	1-2	1-3	0-5	1-1	0-1	1-1	0-3	2-1	1-0	1-1	2-0	1-1	1-1	3-1	1-1	0-1	0-0
Burton Alb	1-1	1-0	1-0	—	1-1	1-2	3-1	2-2	2-1	1-0	0-0	1-1	1-2	1-0	1-0	2-0	0-4	1-0	3-1	1-1	1-1	0-0
Cambridge U	1-0	1-3	2-0	2-0	—	1-1	1-0	4-0	1-0	1-0	0-0	2-3	4-0	2-2	2-0	1-0	3-0	2-1	1-1	1-0	1-1	0-0
Canvey Island	1-0	2-2	1-2	1-2	1-1	—	2-2	1-2	1-0	1-2	1-2	1-0	1-1	1-0	0-1	0-2	0-1	0-1	1-1	0-1	1-1	0-1
Crawley T	4-2	3-2	1-3	1-1	1-0	0-3	—	4-0	2-2	1-1	1-0	2-1	2-1	0-1	1-1	3-0	1-2	1-1	3-2	2-0	0-1	1-1
Dagenham & R	1-0	3-1	1-2	4-0	3-1	2-2	4-0	—	3-1	2-0	0-0	3-1	2-0	1-0	1-1	0-0	5-0	3-1	0-2	3-0	1-3	0-2
Exeter C	1-1	4-0	2-4	1-2	1-0	2-2	1-0	3-1	—	0-0	2-2	1-2	4-2	0-2	0-0	3-1	5-1	2-1	0-2	2-1	1-3	1-3
Forest Green R	1-3	2-5	2-0	2-3	4-0	1-1	2-0	0-0	0-0	—	2-0	1-3	2-2	2-2	1-0	1-0	5-1	1-2	0-2	3-0	0-3	2-1
Gravesend & N	1-3	0-3	1-1	0-0	5-3	1-2	1-0	0-2	3-0	2-0	—	6-1	4-0	2-2	1-2	1-0	1-0	2-1	1-1	0-1	2-2	1-0
Grays Ath	2-1	2-1	2-1	1-0	3-0	1-0	2-1	0-4	0-3	0-1	2-1	—	1-0	2-2	2-2	1-2	0-3	2-1	1-1	0-1	0-2	0-0
Halifax T	1-1	2-1	1-0	2-0	1-0	3-1	2-1	0-2	4-0	1-0	1-0	1-3	—	2-2	2-2	0-0	0-1	4-0	3-2	3-1	4-0	2-2
Hereford U	1-0	2-1	1-0	1-0	0-1	2-0	2-1	1-0	2-0	5-1	6-1	1-3	1-0	—	2-2	1-0	2-1	1-1	0-2	2-1	0-1	2-2
Kidderminster H	2-2	2-1	2-0	1-0	1-0	1-0	0-1	1-1	3-0	1-2	1-1	0-5	0-1	0-1	—	1-0	2-1	2-1	1-1	0-1	2-2	1-1
Morecambe	3-2	5-2	3-1	2-3	0-1	2-0	3-0	1-0	3-1	0-1	1-2	1-3	4-0	1-0	1-0	—	4-1	2-1	4-1	0-1	4-0	0-3
Scarborough	2-2	2-2	1-2	3-0	0-1	2-0	1-2	0-1	0-3	3-2	0-2	2-7	2-0	1-4	0-1	1-0	—	2-1	3-2	0-1	2-2	2-0
Southport	2-2	2-2	1-1	0-1	1-2	1-0	3-0	0-1	2-2	3-1	3-1	0-5	2-0	0-0	1-4	1-0	2-0	—	1-1	1-0	1-1	0-1
Stevenage B	3-1	2-1	3-0	2-3	1-1	1-0	2-1	0-0	2-0	0-0	3-1	1-2	1-2	0-0	2-2	1-0	2-0	4-1	—	1-0	3-2	2-1
Tamworth	3-1	1-2	1-1	2-1	0-1	1-0	2-1	2-1	0-3	2-1	0-1	1-2	1-2	1-1	0-1	0-0	2-0	0-1	3-1	—	1-1	2-1
Woking	0-1	1-2	1-1	0-0	1-0	1-0	0-0	1-3	1-0	2-1	1-0	2-2	1-0	1-1	4-0	3-1	1-1	1-1	1-0	1-1	—	2-1
York C	2-4	3-2	0-1	1-0	1-0	2-1	1-1	3-1	4-2	5-1	1-0	0-2	0-2	2-2	2-1	1-1	3-1	0-0	0-1	2-1	2-0	—

APPEARANCES AND GOALSCORERS 2005-2006

ACCRINGTON STANLEY
Goals: *League (76):* Mullin 14, Craney 13 (1 pen), Roberts 13, Brown D 8 (1 pen), Jagielka 6, Todd 6, Mangan 5, Boco 4, Cavanagh 4 (3 pens), Welch 1, Williams 1, own goal 1.
FA Cup (3): Roberts 2, Welch 1.
Football League Trophy (3): Brown D 1, Mangan 1, Williams 1.
FA Trophy (8): Craney 3, Mullin 3, Boko 1, Brown D 1.
League Appearances: Alcock, 1; Barry, 26; Boco, 24+6; Bossu, 1; Boyd, 4+2; Brown, D. 26+9; Brown, P. 1+2; Butler, 3; Cavanagh, 19+5; Cook, 1+3; Craney, 38+1; Dibble, 1; Edwards, 27; Elliott, 23; Flynn, 12; Jagielka, 22+8; Jones, 2; Mangan, 5+33; Mullin, 40+1; Navarro, 0+3; O'Neill, 0+3; Proctor, 3+3; Randolph, 14; Richardson, 33; Roberts, 40+2; Todd, 13+1; Tretton, 6+1; Ventre, 10+2; Welch, 32+1; Williams, 35+1.

ALDERSHOT TOWN
Goals: *League (61):* Sills 10 (1 pen), Barnard 8 (5 pens), Williams 7, Crittenden N 6, Griffiths 6, Dixon 4, Holloway 3, Somner 3, Heald 2, Hudson 2, Jinadu 2, McPhee 2 (1 pen), Coleman 1, Guyett 1, Matthews 1, Sulaiman 1, Tinnion 1, own goal 1.
FA Cup (4): Brough 1, Deen 1, Heald 1, Sills 1.
Football League Trophy (1): Heald 1.
FA Trophy (1): Barnard 1 (pen).
League Appearances: Ahmad, 2+5; Barnard, 24+2; Boucaud, 8+1; Brayley, 2+3; Brough, 12+3; Bull, 42; Coleman, 3; Cozic, 2; Crittenden, N. 38+3; Crockford, 3+3; Deen, 9+3; Dixon, 10; Elphick, 2+1; Gearing, 0+4; Gordon, 0+1; Griffiths, 15+2; Guyett, 13; Hamilton, 27+3; Heald, 28; Holloway, 25+4; Hudson, 9+3; Jinadu, 10+3; Kitson, 0+1; Lee, 2; Matthews, 2+5; McPhee, 12+2; Mustafa, 5+3; Nurse, 1; Reed, 4+1; Scott, 16+11; Sills, 20+1; Simpemba, 10; Somner, 29+2; Sulaiman, 10+13; Tinnion, 7; Turner, 3+1; Vincent, 3; Walker, 0+1; Watson, 24+2; Weait, 0+1; Williams, 24+1; Winfield, 6+6.

ALTRINCHAM
Goals: *League (40):* Little 17 (2 pens), Potts 4, Robinson 4, Thornley 4, Aspinall 2 (2 pens), Murphy 2, Peyton 2, Band 1, Lugsden 1, Olsen 1, Talbot 1, own goal 1.
FA Cup (1): own goal 1.
FA Trophy (0).
League Appearances: Adams, 31+1; Aspinall, 20+3; Band, 39; Bushell, 7; Butler, 1; Chalmers, 13+16; Coburn, 42; Hawes, 14; Hendley, 0+4; Hilton, 3+1; James, 2+1; Little, 41+1; Lugsden, 1+26; Maddox, 27+2; McFadden, 1+5; McKenzie, 3+4; Melling, 3+2; Munroe, 13+8; Murphy, 22+1; Norton, 3+3; Olsen, 5+4; Owen, 32; Peyton, 23+1; Potts, 19+16; Robinson, 8+6; Rose, 11+5; Scott, 27+1; Talbot, 20+3; Thornley, 21+3; Williams, G. 6+6; Wilson, 4+1.

BURTON ALBION
Goals: *League (50):* Shaw 11, Webster 8 (2 pens), Harrad 7, Hall 4, Taylor K 4, Anderson 3, Gilroy 3, Clare 2, Moore 2, Todd 2, Bell 1, Ducros 1, Stride 1, own goal 1.
FA Cup (7): Gilroy 2, Harrad 2, Shaw 2, Stride 1.
FA Trophy (0).
League Appearances: Anderson, 8+12; Austin, 28+2; Bacon, 4+1; Bell, 6; Brayford, 0+1; Clare, 7+1; Clough, 4+3; Corbett, 38+2; Crane, 12; Deeney, 30; Ducros, 23+7; Gilroy, 31+2; Graves, 1+3; Hall, 27+10; Harrad, 32+7; Henshaw, 16+12; Moore, 2+13; Rowett, 15+2; Sedgemore, 9; Shaw, 35+6; Stride, 38+3; Taylor, K. 16+2; Tinson, 41; Todd, 10+11; Webster, 33+1.

CAMBRIDGE UNITED
Goals: *League (51):* Onibuje 9, Westcarr 8 (1 pen), Bridges 5, Pitt 5, Duncan 3, Hanlon 3, Peters 3, Woolaston 3, Guy 2, Morrison 2, Smith 2, Angel 1, Atkins 1, Brady 1, Chick 1, Quinton 1, own goal 1.
FA Cup (1): Peters 1.
Football League Trophy (8): Bridges 2, Onibuje 2, Atkins 1, Hanlon 1, Morrison 1, Smith 1.
FA Trophy (2): Bridges 1, Morrison 1.
League Appearances: Angel, 6+2; Atkins, 1+8; Behcet, 7; Bloomer, 8; Brady, 19; Bridges, 33+2; Bunce, 5+8; Chick, 6+1; Coldicott, 4; Daniels, 1+2; Davies, 8+4; Duffy, 5+4; Duncan, 31+1; Fuller, 1; Gleeson, 23+1; Guy, 12; Hanlon, 22+3; Harkness, 7; Heeroo, 8+1; Howie, 33; Jaszczun, 16; Medine, 2+3; Morrison, 21+1; Nicholls, 3+1; Nolan, 3+7; Okai, 6+7; Onibuje, 25+9; Peters, 34+1; Pitt, 29+1; Porter, 3+5; Quinton, 11+6; Robbins, 3+1; Robinson, 3+1; Smith, 21+5; Turner, 6+3; Westcarr, 23+8; Woolaston, 13.

CANVEY ISLAND
Goals: *League (47):* Boylan 12 (2 pens), Hallett 9, Ibe 6, Minton 6, Sedgemore 3, Clarke 2, Tait 2, Chenery 1, Duffy 1, Gregory 1 (pen), Kennedy 1, Noto 1, Sterling 1, own goal 1.
FA Cup (2): Ibe 2.
FA Trophy (4): Hallett 2, Boylan 1, Clarke 1.

313

League Appearances: Bimson, 20+2; Boylan, 20+5; Bunce, 2; Chenery, 36+1; Clarke, 32+4; Conroy, 8+2; Dolan, 4+1; Duffy, 29+1; Gregory, 5+10; Hallett, 18+14; Harrison, 0+1; Ibe, 21+14; Keeling, 20+11; Kennedy, 38; Lowes, 0+1; McGhee, 17+3; McKinney, 19; Minton, 38+2; Noto, 15+12; Potter, 23; Sedgemore, 34+1; Sterling, 20+4; Tait, 10+16; Theobald, 3; Ward, 30+2.

CRAWLEY TOWN

Goals: *League (48):* Clare 11 (4 pens), Burton 7, Coleman 4, Bostwick 3, Cade 3, Wormull 3, Armstrong 2, Giles 2, Scully 2, Brown 1, Clay 1, Douglas 1, Ekoku 1, Jenkins 1, Judge 1, Lindegaard 1, Opinel 1, Whitman 1, Woozley 1, own goal 1.
FA Cup (0).
FA Trophy (5): Burton 2, Giles 1, Scully 1, Wormull 1.
League Appearances: Armstrong, 29+1; Blackburn, 24+11; Bostwick, 5+3; Brown, 23; Burton, 29+7; Cade, 15+4; Clare, 25; Clay, 8+3; Coleman, 6+3; Davidson, 0+2; Donovan, 1; Douglas, 2+5; Ekoku, 8+19; El-Abd, 1; Elam, 4+1; Giles, 22+6; Gordon, 3+2; Hodgson, 4; Jenkins, 14+9; Judge, 39; Keehan, 1+1; Kember, 4+1; Lindegaard, 10; Macleod, 1; Marshall, 3+3; Mendy, 21; Opinel, 19+4; Proffit, 0+2; Scully, 20; Simpemba, 26; Smith, 38; Ward, 4; Whitman, 3+2; Woozley, 29+1; Wormull, 21+2.

DAGENHAM & REDBRIDGE

Goals: *League (63):* Moore 15 (2 pens), Mackail-Smith 11, Kandol 6, Akurang 5, Southam 5 (1 pen), Bruce 4, Goodwin 4, Cole 3, Griffiths 3, Leberl 3, Saunders 2, Benson 1, Foster 1.
FA Cup (4): Kandol 2, Moore 2.
Football League Trophy (1): Benson 1.
FA Trophy (10): Mackail-Smith 3, Moore 3, Southam 2, Saunders 1, own goal 1.
League Appearances: Akurang, 12+6; Batt, 0+2; Benson, 13+13; Blackett, 39; Bruce, 26; Clark, 2; Cole, 20+2; Foster, 37; Goodwin, 22; Griffiths, 42; Kandol, 10+2; Leberl, 10+1; Lettejallon, 4+4; Mackail-Smith, 36+3; Marwa, 10+2; Moore, 33+7; Roberts, 42; Saunders, 15+7; Southam, 42; Uddin, 38; Vickers, 9+13.

EXETER CITY

Goals: *League (65):* Phillips 13 (2 pens), Challinor 12, Farrell 8, Jones B 7 (5 pens), Flack 5, Todd 4, Buckle 3, Mackie 3, Scully 3, Afful 1, Carlisle 1, Edwards 1, Gill 1, Moxey 1, Seaborne 1, Watkins 1.
FA Cup (0).
Football League Trophy (2): Phillips 1, Taylor 1.
FA Trophy (11): Phillips 3, Jones B 2,

Challinor 1, Flack 1, Mackie 1, Robinson 1, Todd 1, own goal 1.
League Appearances: Afful, 4+6; Buckle, 24+4; Bye, 0+1; Carlisle, 4+2; Challinor, 40+2; Clay, 1+2; Cronin, 28+2; Edwards, 8+6; Farrell, 26+12; Flack, 11+26; Friend, 1; Gaia, 14+3; Gill, 13+3; Hiley, 13+1; Jones, B. 36+1; Jones, P. 37; Mackie, 13+11; Moxey, 12+9; Phillips, 34+3; Rice, 5; Robinson, 0+1; Sawyer, 26+4; Scully, 10+3; Seaborne, 4; Taylor, 29+6; Todd, 41; Vinnicombe, 1+2; Watkins, 0+5; Woodards, 27.

FOREST GREEN ROVERS

Goals: *League (49):* Wanless 10 (4 pens), Madjo 9, Alsop 5, Meechan 5, Teixeira 5, Sall 4, Brough 3 (3 pens), Abbey 2, Rendell 2, Richardson 2, Harding 1, Hayes 1.
FA Cup (2): Beswetherick 1, Meechan 1.
FA Trophy (5): Gadsby 1, Harding 1, Hayes 1, Madjo 1, Wanless 1.
League Appearances: Abbey, 18+8; Alsop, 20+3; Anthony, 1; Beesley, 11+5; Beswetherick, 11+4; Brough, 13+1; Byron, 3; Clarke, 42; Coleman, 2; Dove, 1+4; Gadsby, 20+8; Garner, 16+4; Gosling, 3+6; Graham, 24+3; Haldane, 3+4; Harding, 9; Harley, 1; Harrison, 0+1; Hayes, 4; Howell, 6+1; Jones, 9+1; Madjo, 18+6; McConnell, 2+2; Meechan, 41; Rendell, 8+10; Richardson, 25; Rogers, 5+5; Sall, 24+2; Searle, 37; Simpson, 31+2; Stonehouse, 2+2; Taylor, 10; Teixeira, 12+15; Wanless, 30; Whittington, 0+1.

GRAVESEND & NORTHFLEET

Goals: *League (45):* MacDonald 12 (2 pens), Jackson 5, Johnson Bradley 5 (1 pen), Drury 4 (1 pen), Graham-Smith 3, Sodje 3, McCarthy 2, Saunders 2, Slatter 2, Smith 2, Bowry 1, Coleman 1, Grant 1, Moore 1, Rawle 1.
FA Cup (0).
FA Trophy (3): MacDonald 2, Smith 1.
League Appearances: Bowry, 35; Coleman, 6; Darvill, 0+2; Drury, 30+2; Fuller, 4+9; Glozier, 6+4; Gooding, 24+4; Graham-Smith, 39; Grant, 5+2; Guy, 0+1; Hawkins, 4+1; Hodgson, 1+4; Holloway, 32+1; Jackson, 26+3; Johnson, Bradley 21+4; Johnson, Brett 4; Kerr, 5+1; MacDonald, 20; McCarthy, 30; McKimm, 6+4; McShane, 5; Moore, 10+18; Mott, 0+1; Omoyinmi, 5+7; Protheroe, 15+1; Rawle, 9+2; Saunders, 24+2; Skinner, 19+3; Slatter, 37+2; Smith, 18+4; Sodje, 8+6; Surey, 1+9; Tann, 1; Watkins, 12+1.

GRAYS ATHLETIC

Goals: *League (94):* Kightly 14, Poole 13, Slabber 11 (1 pen), McLean 10, Oli 9, Thirgood 9 (6 pens), Hooper 8, Martin 7

(1 pen), Battersby 3, Stuart 3, De Bolla 2, Angus 1, Matthews 1, own goals 3.

FA Cup (5): Kightly 1, McLean 1, Poole 1, Slabber 1, own goal 1.

FA Trophy (12): Poole 4, Kightly 2, McLean 2, Nutter 1, Oli 1, Slabber 1, Stuart 1.

Play-Offs (4): Oli 2, Knightly 1, Nutter 1.

League Appearances: Angus, 11; Battersby, 13+1; Bayes, 25; Brayley, 0+4; Brennan, 6+2; Bruce, 9+3; De Bolla, 5+3; Edwards, 4+1; Eyre, 17; Hanson, 18+1; Hooper, 16+22; Johnson, 4+1; Kightly, 27+8; Koo-Boothe, 2; Martin, 31+3; Matthews, 8+3; Mawer, 16+2; McLean, 28+2; Nutter, 40; Olayinka, 6+9; Oli, 26+8; Poole, 31+6; Sambrook, 23+2; Slabber, 18+10; Stuart, 34; Thirgood, 40; Williams, 0+1; Williamson, 4+9.

HALIFAX TOWN

Goals: *League (55):* Grant 12, Killeen 9, Senior 6, Sugden 6, Forrest 5, Midgley 4 (3 pens), Foster 3 (1 pen), Quinn 3, Bushell 2, Mansaram 2, Brabin 1, Thompson 1, Young 1.

FA Cup (3): Senior 3.

Football League Trophy (7): Mansaram 2, Doughty 1, Haslam 1, Killeen 1, Midgley 1 (pen), own goal 1.

FA Trophy (1): Forrest 1.

Play-Offs (7): Foster 2 (1 pen), Killeen 2, Bushell 1, Grant 1, Sugden 1.

League Appearances: Atherton, 12+2; Bowler, 5+14; Brabin, 4; Bushell, 7+7; Butler, 3; Doughty, 31+1; Dunbavin, 14; Forrest, 32+4; Foster, 35+1; Grant, 30+10; Haslam, 40; Howell, 5+1; Ingram, 18+2; Jacobs, 8+3; Kennedy, 15; Killeen, 32+4; Legzdins, 10; Leister, 2+7; Mansaram, 1+2; Midgley, 14+10; Prendergast, 6; Quinn, 37; Senior, 10+20; Smickle, 11+1; Sugden, 12+10; Thompson, 37+4; Toulson, 1+1; Wright, 10+1; Yates, 0+3; Young, 24+6.

HEREFORD UNITED

Goals: *League (59):* Williams 10, Carey-Bertram 8, Ipoua 7, Stansfield 6, Fleetwood 5, Mkandawire 5, Purdie 4 (1 pen), Jeannin 3, Beckwith 2, Ferrell 2, Bailey 1, Green 1, James 1 (pen), King 1, Nicolau 1, Pitman 1, Stanley 1.

FA Cup (2): Barry 1, Stanley 1.

Football League Trophy (5): Mkandawire 2, Carey-Bertram 1, Stansfield 1, own goal 1.

FA Trophy (8): Purdie 2 (1 pen), Stansfield 2, Ipoua 1, Pitman 1, Stanley 1, Williams 1.

Play-Offs (4): Ipoua 2, Williams 2, Green 1, Mkandawire 1, Purdie 1 (pen).

League Appearances: Bailey, 5; Beckwith, 29+3; Blewitt, 10+1; Brady, 18+2; Brown, 33; Carey-Bertram, 18+14; Coldicott, 4+1; Evans, 2+5; Ferrell, 30+1; Fleetwood,

13+4; Green, 25+2; Gwynne, 0+1; Ipoua 13+6; James, 20+3; Jeannin, 37; King, 5; Mawson, 9; Mkandawire, 36+3; Nicolau, 10; Pitman, 14+8; Purdie, 33+7; Stanley, 35+3; Stansfield, 17+6; Taylor, 8+2; Travis, 15+3; Williams, 23+8.

KIDDERMINSTER HARRIERS

Goals: *League (39):* Christie 10 (1 pen), Atieno 5 (2 pens), Reynolds 4, Jackson 3, Fleming 2, Hatswell 2, Mullins 2, Russell 2, Sheldon 2, Blackwood 1, Harkness 1, Heslop 1, Pugh 1, Thompson 1, White 1, own goal 1.

FA Cup (0).

Football League Trophy (7): Christie 3, Blackwood 1, Hatswell 1, Penn 1, Sheldon 1 (pen).

FA Trophy (4): Blackwood 1, Christie 1, Heslop 1, Thompson 1.

League Appearances: Atieno, 13+9; Blackwood, 24+6; Burgess, 34; Burton, 1+3; Byrne, 0+2; Christie, 23+1; Danby, 27; Evans, 13; Fleming, 37+1; Flynn, 5; Francis, 3+3; Graves, 3+2; Hanley, 0+1; Harkness, 13+1; Hatswell, 42; Heslop, 15+7; Howarth, 0+1; Hurren, 10+3; Jackson, 26; Lewis, 15; McGrath, 1+3; Mullins, 25; Newby, 5+2; O'Connor, 12; Osborne, 3; Penn, 22; Pugh, 5+2; Rea, 7; Reynolds, 8; Russell, 23+8; Sedgemore, 11; Sheldon, 24+10; Smith, 0+3; Thompson, 16+16; Walker, 1+1; White, 5; Wilson, 8+14.

MORECAMBE

Goals: *League (68):* Carlton 17, Curtis 11, Twiss 11, Thompson 9, Barlow 5, Bentley 4, O'Connor 3, Hunter 2, Blackburn 1, Brannan 1, Kelly 1, Perkins 1, own goals 2.

FA Cup (3): Carlton 1, O'Connor 1, Walmsley 1.

Football League Trophy (1): Lloyd 1.

FA Trophy (4): Twiss 2, Bentley 1, Curtis 1.

Play-Offs (3): Bentley 1, Curtis 1 (pen), Twiss 1.

League Appearances: Barlow, 10+6; Bentley, 40; Blackburn, 35+3; Brannan, 23+2; Carlton, 27+13; Curtis, 37+3; Dodgson, 0+4; Drench, 24+1; Hardiker, 15+2; Heard, 4+2; Howard, 28; Hunter, 21+2; Kelly, 16+7; Kempson, 30+2; Lloyd, 0+5; McLachlan, 7+1; O'Connor, 4+10; Perkins, 34+2; Rigoglioso, 0+7; Robinson, 18; Ruffer, 0+3; Stringfellow, 0+6; Thompson, 39+1; Twiss, 40+2; Walmsley, 10+7.

SCARBOROUGH

Goals: *League (40):* Coulson 7, McNiven 6, Wake 5, Fowler 3, Hackworth 3, Quayle 3, Redfearn 3 (2 pens), Hughes 2, Nicholson 2, Speight 2, Clark 1 (pen), Foot 1, Weaver 1, own goal 1.

FA Cup (0).

FA Trophy (0).

League Appearances: Atkinson, 20+2; Baker, S. 34+1; Baker, T. 1; Beadle, 5+3; Bertos, 1; Bishop, 23+1; Blott, 0+3; Blunt, 4+1; Carl, 1+1; Clark, 20; Cook, 11; Coulson, 11+22; Dunbavin, 14; Eccles, 4+4; Elebert, 11+1; Foot, 14+6; Fowler, 24+1; Hackworth, 36+3; Harper, 4; Hughes, 22+2; Ingram, 14+1; Jarvis, 0+1; Kell, 2; Lyth, 21+9; McClare, 6+9; McNiven, 16+2; Nicholson, 38+1; Palmer, 2+2; Parton, 1+1; Pounder, 7+2; Quayle, 15+4; Redfearn, 17+4; Rix, 1; Speight, 5+3; Wake, 7+6; Walker, 28; Weaver, 22; Yates, 0+1.

SOUTHPORT

Goals: *League (36):* Daly 12, Baker 7 (1 pen), Robinson 7 (2 pens), Blakeman 3, Leadbetter 3, Pickford 2, Rogan 1, own goal 1.
FA Cup (2): Lane 1, Leadbitter 1.
FA Trophy (0).
League Appearances: Aggrey, 3; Bailey, 1+1; Baker, 33+3; Blakeman, 15+1; Booth, 5+18; Brabin, 12+2; Brass, 5; Brooks, 0+1; Daly, 34+2; Davis, 32+2; Dickinson, 40; Evans, 0+1; Fearns, 5+4; Field, 0+2; Fitzgerald, 31+5; Fitzhenry, 14+2; Jackson, 2+6; Kilbane, 12+2; Krief, 11; Lane, 37; Leadbetter, 20+7; Lynch, 6+9; McGinn, 13+14; Morley, 31+1; Pickford, 34; Powell, 13+10; Price, 3+3; Rigoglioso, 1; Roberts, 18; Robinson, 26+6; Rogan, 3+8; Speare, 0+1; Stringfellow, 0+1.

STEVENAGE BOROUGH

Goals: *League (62):* Stamp 12 (4 pens), Boyd 10, Nurse 9, Elding 7, Maamria 3 (3 pens), Louis 6, Goodliffe 2, Laker 2, Berquez 1, Bulman 1, Gregory 1, Miller 1, Williams D 1, own goals 2.
FA Cup (6): Boyd 2, Elding 2, Laker 1, Stamp 1.
Football League Trophy (0).
FA Trophy (0).
League Appearances: Berquez, 17+13; Boyd, 42; Brough, 5+1; Bulman, 39; Duffy, 0+1; Elding, 16+1; Goodliffe, 14+2; Gore, 1; Gregory, 20+9; Henry, 32; Hocking, 15+2; Julian, 41; Laker, 21+2; Lewis, 0+1; Louis, 12+10; Maamria, 25+5; Miller, 14+1; Nurse, 33+6; Obinna, 1+8; Oliver, 12; Perpetuini, 12+7; Quinn, 24+2; Stamp, 29+5; Sullivan, 0+1; Warner, 28+6; Weatherstone, 6+13; Williams, D. 3+14.

TAMWORTH

Goals: *League (32):* Heggs 5, Williams 5 (1 pen), Edwards 4 (1 pen), Cooper 2, Alsop 1, Bampton 1, Brown 1, Davidson 1, Folkes 1, Hollis 1, Jackson 1, Johnson 1, Mansaram 1, Melton 1, Neilson 1, Redmile 1, Storer 1 (pen), Ward 1, Whitman 1, own goal 1.
FA Cup (8): Edwards 3, Jackson 1, Redmile 1, Robinson 1, Storer 1, Wood 1.

FA Trophy (3): Anaclet 1, Davidson 1, Ward 1.
League Appearances: Alsop, 7+2; Anaclet, 8; Bampton, 24; Bevan, 10; Bowles, 15; Breedon, 1; Brown, 15; Campbell, 2+1; Cooper, 9+6; Davidson, 14+4; Dormand, 14; Douglas, 0+1; Dryden, 0+1; Edwards, 8; Folkes, 11+4; Francis, 3+8; Gayle, 2+1; Heggs, 18+9; Hollis, 5+2; Jackson, 11+13; Johnson, 6+1; Lake, 0+1; Mansaram, 4+2; McAuley, 7+1; McConnell, 2; Melton, 7; Merson, 1; Motteram, 1+1; Neilson, 1+2; Redmile, 37; Reid, 2; Rickards, 4+3; Robinson, 2+1; Roma, 15; Smith, 36+1; Stamps, 26+3; Starosta, 3+1; Storer, 20+7; Summerbee, 4; Taylor, 11+14; Touhy, 12+3; Turner, 16+7; Ward, 34+1; Whitman, 14+5; Williams, 8; Wright, 1.

WOKING

Goals: *League (58):* Richards 21 (5 pens), McAllister 8, Ferguson 7, Murray 6, Selley 4 (2 pens), Evans 3, Watson 3, MacDonald 2, Cockerill L 1, Rawle 1, Sharpling 1, own goal 1.
FA Cup (6): Ferguson 2, Evans 1, Jackson 1, McAllister 1, Oliver 1.
Football League Trophy (4): Rawle 2, Blackman 1, Richards 1.
FA Trophy (16): McAllister 4, Ferguson 3, Evans 2, Hutchinson 2, Murray 1, Rawle 1, Selley 1 (pen), Sharpling 1, Smith 1.
League Appearances: Aggrey, 5; Blackman, 11+6; Buari, 2+4; Cockerill, L 10+6; Cockerill, S. 0+3; Davies, 1+1; El-Salahi, 17+5; Evans, 31+3; Ferguson, 35+2; Hutchinson, 19+1; Jackson, 33+2; Jalal, 41; MacDonald, 27+3; McAllister, 33+6; Murray, 39; Nethercott, 32+1; Oliver, 13; Oyedele, 6+5; Rawle, 4+13; Reed, 4+2; Richards, 35+3; Selley, 18+5; Sharpling, 5+3; Smith, 27+5; Watson, 14+1.

YORK CITY

Goals: *League (63):* Bishop A 23 (4 pens), Donaldson 16, Convery 6, Dudgeon 6, O'Neill 5, McGurk 2, Stewart 2, Bishop N 1, Dunning 1, Thomas 1.
FA Cup (4): Bishop A 2 (1 pen), Convery 1, Donaldson 1.
FA Trophy (1): Bishop A 1.
League Appearances: Andrews, 9; Barwick, 3; Bertos, 3+3; Bishop, A. 35+5; Bishop, N. 14; Convery, 38+4; Craddock, 4; Donaldson, 42; Dudgeon, 30+1; Dunning, 41; Horwood, 4; Hotte, 16+4; Kamara, 0+2; Mallon, 1+4; Mansaram, 4+1; McGurk, 36; Merris, 18+7; N'Toya, 2+1; O'Neill, 25+12; Palmer, 0+3; Panther, 36+1; Peat, 20+3; Porter, 41; Price, 21+1; Rhodes, 0+1; Stewart, 2+19; Stockdale, 1+1; Thomas, 12+2; Webster, 0+3; Yalcin, 4+7.

CONFERENCE NATIONAL PLAY-OFFS 2005–2006

CONFERENCE FIRST LEG

Halifax T	(3) 3	Grays Ath	(0) 2
Morecambe	(1) 1	Hereford U	(0) 1

CONFERENCE SECOND LEG

Grays Ath	(0) 2	Halifax T	(1) 2
Hereford U	(2) 3	Morecambe	(1) 2

(aet.)

CONFERENCE FINAL Saturday, 20 May 2006 *(at Leicester)*

Halifax T (1) 2 *(Killeen 27, Grant 73)*

Hereford U (1) 3 *(Williams 34, Ipoua 80, Green 108)*   15,499

Halifax T: Kennedy; Haslam, Doughty (Senior), Atherton, Young (Bushell), Quinn, Thompson, Foster, Killeen, Sugden (Grant), Forrest.
Hereford U: Brown; Green, Jeannin, Mkandawire, Purdie, Beckwith, Travis, Stanley (Pitman), Stansfield (Fleetwood), Williams (Ipoua), Ferrell.
Referee: D. Whitestone (Northamptonshire).
(aet.)

ATTENDANCES BY CLUB 2005–2006

	Aggregate 2005–06	Average 2005–06	Highest Attendance 2005–06
Exeter City	79,590	3,790	6,682 v Grays Athletic
York City	60,281	2,871	4,921 v Scarborough
Hereford United	58,655	2,793	4,497 v Accrington Stanley
Cambridge United	54,739	2,607	3,697 v Stevenage Borough
Aldershot Town	48,172	2,294	3,136 v Exeter City
Stevenage Borough	45,746	2,178	3,463 v Cambridge United
Woking	40,943	1,950	3,244 v Aldershot Town
Accrington Stanley	39,791	1,895	3,320 v Scarborough
Morecambe	37,383	1,780	2,788 v Southport
Kidderminster Harriers	37,275	1,775	3,241 v Hereford United
Halifax Town	36,732	1,749	2,688 v Accrington Stanley
Burton Albion	36,212	1,724	2,680 v Tamworth
Scarborough	33,686	1,604	4,057 v York City
Crawley Town	32,192	1,533	2,454 v Exeter City
Grays Athletic	30,325	1,444	2,910 v Canvey Island
Tamworth	26,182	1,247	2,151 v Burton Albion
Southport	26,124	1,244	1,807 v Morecambe
Dagenham & Redbridge	26,110	1,243	2,017 v Grays Athletic
Gravesend & Northfleet	22,934	1,092	1,616 v Accrington Stanley
Altrincham	22,006	1,048	1,447 v Morecambe
Forest Green Rovers	20,517	977	1,957 v Hereford United
Canvey Island	16,938	807	1,458 v Dagenham & Redbridge

CONFERENCE SECOND DIVISION NORTH 2005-2006

FINAL LEAGUE TABLE

			Home					Away					Total					
	P	W	D	L	F	A	W	D	L	F	A	W	D	L	F	A	Gd	Pts
1 Northwich Victoria	42	16	3	2	53	16	13	2	6	44	33	29	5	8	97	49	48	92
2 Stafford Rangers	42	12	5	4	36	17	13	5	3	32	17	25	10	7	68	34	34	85
3 Nuneaton Borough	42	13	7	1	43	21	9	4	8	25	22	22	11	9	68	43	25	77
4 Droylsden	42	15	3	3	52	24	5	9	7	28	32	20	12	10	80	56	24	72
5 Harrogate Town	42	14	4	3	35	16	8	1	12	31	40	22	5	15	66	56	10	71
6 Kettering Town	42	14	2	5	38	18	5	8	8	25	31	19	10	13	63	49	14	67
7 Stalybridge Celtic	42	15	3	3	51	23	4	6	11	23	31	19	9	14	74	54	20	66
8 Worcester City	42	7	8	6	27	20	9	6	6	31	26	16	14	12	58	46	12	62
9 Moor Green	42	5	10	7	28	33	10	6	4	39	31	15	16	11	67	64	3	61
10 Hinckley United	42	7	7	7	31	28	7	9	5	29	27	14	16	12	60	55	5	58
11 Hyde United	42	7	6	8	39	37	8	5	8	29	24	15	11	16	68	61	7	56
12 Hucknall Town	42	9	6	6	33	25	5	7	9	23	29	14	13	15	56	54	2	55
13 Workington	42	7	6	8	29	29	7	7	7	31	33	14	13	15	60	62	-2	55
14 Barrow	42	9	6	6	39	33	3	5	13	23	34	12	11	19	62	67	-5	47
15 Lancaster City	42	7	8	6	29	26	5	3	13	23	40	12	11	19	52	66	-14	47
16 Gainsborough T	42	6	8	7	26	30	5	5	11	19	35	11	13	18	45	65	-20	46
17 Alfreton Town	42	9	5	6	29	27	1	10	11	17	31	10	15	17	46	58	-12	45
18 Vauxhall Motors	42	6	3	12	28	37	6	4	11	22	34	12	7	23	50	71	-21	43
19 Worksop Town	42	7	8	6	27	31	3	3	15	19	40	10	11	21	46	71	-25	41
20 Leigh RMI	42	7	6	8	20	25	2	7	12	25	54	9	14	20	45	79	-34	40
21 Redditch United	42	6	5	10	29	34	3	7	11	23	44	9	12	21	52	78	-26	39
22 Hednesford	42	3	7	11	16	37	4	7	10	26	50	7	14	21	42	87	-45	35

NATIONWIDE CONFERENCE NORTH LEADING GOALSCORER

	League	FA Cup	Trophy	Total
Jon Allan (Northwich Victoria)	24	1	6	31

CONFERENCE SECOND DIVISION NORTH PLAY-OFFS
SEMI-FINALS

Nuneaton Borough 0, Droylsden 1
Stafford Rangers 1, Harrogate Town 0

FINAL

Droylsden 1, Stafford Rangers 1
Stafford Rangers won 5-3 on penalties.

CONFERENCE SECOND DIVISION NORTH RESULTS 2005–2006

	Alfreton T	Barrow	Droylsden	Gainsborough T	Harrogate T	Hednesford T	Hinckley U	Hucknall T	Hyde U	Kettering T	Lancaster C	Leigh RMI	Moor Green	Northwich Vic	Nuneaton B	Reddicth U	Stafford R	Stalybridge C	Vauxhall M	Worcester C	Workington	Worksop T
Alfreton T	—	2-1	1-3	1-2	4-1	3-2	1-1	1-1	2-0	1-1	0-2	1-1	1-1	1-2	1-0	2-1	2-1	2-1	2-0	1-0	1-3	2-1
Barrow	2-1	—	2-0	3-1	3-1	3-1	2-5	3-2	1-0	0-1	1-4	4-1	2-2	2-4	0-3	2-1	1-1	4-2	2-0	0-2	6-1	1-0
Droylsden	1-0	2-2	—	2-0	0-2	3-1	1-3	2-1	2-0	3-1	6-1	3-1	1-4	4-3	2-1	2-1	2-1	1-0	1-0	1-0	2-3	3-1
Gainsborough T	2-2	3-1	2-0	—	0-2	2-3	1-2	3-2	0-3	0-2	1-0	3-0	3-0	0-2	1-2	2-2	1-2	1-0	1-1	0-1	1-1	3-1
Harrogate T	2-2	1-1	1-1	1-1	—	2-3	1-2	3-2	0-1	1-1	0-1	3-0	1-2	0-2	1-2	1-1	0-1	0-0	0-1	0-1	0-1	2-0
Hednesford T	1-0	1-1	2-1	1-0	1-3	—	3-4	2-3	2-1	1-1	3-3	1-3	1-2	1-4	2-0	1-1	0-1	1-1	0-1	0-4	0-0	2-0
Hinckley U	1-0	1-1	2-0	4-1	1-1	1-2	—	3-1	1-1	1-1	0-0	5-1	2-2	0-0	0-1	1-1	0-1	1-1	1-2	1-1	1-0	2-1
Hucknall T	1-0	2-2	2-2	0-1	2-3	4-0	0-2	—	1-3	3-0	2-4	2-3	2-2	3-2	0-0	4-0	0-2	2-1	2-3	1-2	1-0	0-0
Hyde U	1-0	1-3	1-0	1-2	0-1	1-2	2-2	3-1	—	3-0	0-2	3-3	0-3	3-1	3-0	4-0	1-3	1-3	1-0	1-0	1-1	0-0
Kettering T	1-0	1-3	2-2	1-2	1-1	1-2	0-2	0-0	3-2	—	2-0	4-0	3-3	2-0	3-1	2-1	0-1	4-1	1-0	2-1	0-1	1-0
Lancaster C	1-0	1-3	1-0	2-3	4-1	1-0	1-1	0-0	0-1	0-1	—	4-1	1-1	1-3	1-0	2-1	0-1	0-1	2-1	0-1	0-1	1-0
Leigh RMI	2-2	0-1	1-3	1-1	3-1	2-2	2-0	2-1	1-2	0-2	4-1	—	1-1	1-2	0-4	5-1	3-1	2-2	1-1	1-4	1-4	0-1
Moor Green	0-0	0-1	0-1	1-1	2-0	0-0	2-1	2-4	1-0	4-1	1-2	2-2	—	1-2	2-0	2-1	0-1	2-1	3-2	0-1	4-1	1-0
Northwich Vic	0-1	1-1	1-1	2-3	3-1	8-0	1-1	2-1	1-2	2-1	0-2	3-1	2-2	—	0-2	3-0	0-1	1-0	3-0	0-0	4-1	4-1
Nuneaton B	1-1	2-0	2-0	1-0	4-0	3-2	2-1	2-1	1-1	2-1	3-1	1-2	1-2	1-2	—	1-2	2-3	1-0	3-0	1-1	3-1	3-1
Reddicth U	1-0	2-1	1-1	1-0	3-2	4-0	1-2	2-1	1-0	2-0	2-1	6-1	1-2	2-1	2-0	—	2-1	1-1	2-1	2-2	3-6	0-3
Stafford R	1-0	2-2	0-1	3-0	3-1	3-0	2-1	2-1	1-2	1-3	0-1	3-1	1-2	3-3	2-0	3-0	—	1-4	0-1	1-0	2-2	4-2
Stalybridge C	3-0	4-1	2-1	1-0	4-0	3-1	0-0	2-1	0-2	2-0	1-0	1-0	3-3	0-3	1-2	1-2	2-3	—	0-0	1-1	2-1	2-1
Vauxhall M	3-1	0-1	1-0	1-1	2-0	0-1	0-0	2-3	2-1	2-0	3-1	4-1	0-1	0-1	0-2	2-2	1-3	4-2	—	1-0	1-1	5-2
Worcester C	2-2	3-1	1-0	1-0	0-1	6-2	1-1	0-1	1-0	2-0	2-0	0-0	4-1	5-2	1-1	2-2	1-0	0-1	0-0	—	1-1	1-1
Workington	2-0	0-1	2-1	3-0	2-4	2-0	0-0	2-3	1-1	3-2	0-1	1-4	0-1	1-2	0-2	2-1	2-2	1-2	1-1	2-2	—	1-2
Worksop T	1-1	1-0	2-1	1-2	1-0	3-3	3-0	2-1	1-1	1-0	6-1	0-1	0-2	4-1	0-4	0-3	4-2	2-1	5-2	0-3	1-2	—

CONFERENCE SECOND DIVISION SOUTH 2005–2006

FINAL LEAGUE TABLE

	P	W	D	L	F	A	W	D	L	F	A	W	D	L	F	A	Gd	Pts
		Home					*Away*					*Total*						
1 Weymouth	42	17	3	1	47	13	13	1	7	33	21	30	4	8	80	34	46	94
2 St Albans City	42	17	1	3	54	19	10	4	7	40	28	27	5	10	94	47	47	86
3 Farnborough	42	12	4	5	33	17	11	5	5	32	24	23	9	10	65	41	24	78
4 Lewes	42	12	4	5	38	27	9	6	6	40	30	21	10	11	78	57	21	73
5 Histon	42	12	4	5	41	30	9	4	8	29	26	21	8	13	70	56	14	71
6 Havant & W	42	12	5	4	29	17	9	5	7	35	31	21	10	11	64	48	16	70
7 Cambridge City	42	10	4	7	35	23	10	6	5	43	23	20	10	12	78	46	32	67
8 Eastleigh	42	12	1	8	33	28	9	2	10	32	30	21	3	18	65	58	7	66
9 Welling United	42	11	8	2	32	20	5	9	7	27	24	16	17	9	59	44	15	65
10 Thurrock	42	9	2	10	33	31	7	8	6	27	29	16	16	16	60	60	0	58
11 Dorchester Town	42	7	5	9	32	41	9	2	10	28	32	16	7	19	60	73	–13	55
12 Bognor Regis T	42	7	8	6	31	23	5	5	11	23	32	12	13	17	54	55	–1	49
13 Sutton United	42	9	7	5	28	25	4	3	14	20	36	13	10	19	48	61	–13	49
14 Weston-Super-Mare	42	5	4	12	25	46	9	3	9	31	42	14	7	21	56	88	–32	49
15 Bishop's Stortford	42	8	5	8	35	33	3	10	8	20	30	11	15	16	55	63	–8	48
16 Yeading	42	3	5	13	18	38	10	3	8	29	24	13	8	21	47	62	–15	47
17 Eastbourne Bor	42	4	12	5	24	24	6	4	11	27	36	10	16	16	51	60	–9	46
18 Newport County	42	7	3	11	28	34	5	5	11	22	30	12	8	22	50	67	–17	44
19 Basingstoke T	42	6	5	10	21	37	6	3	12	26	35	12	8	22	47	72	–25	44
20 Hayes	42	8	1	12	26	28	3	8	10	21	32	11	9	22	47	60	–13	42
21 Carshalton Ath	42	4	10	7	21	27	4	6	11	21	41	8	16	18	42	68	–26	40
22 Maidenhead U	42	3	5	13	25	49	5	4	12	24	50	8	9	25	49	99	–50	33

NATIONWIDE CONFERENCE SOUTH LEADING GOALSCORER

	League	FA Cup	Trophy	Total
Paul Booth (Cambridge City)	24	6	2	32

CONFERENCE SECOND DIVISION SOUTH PLAY-OFFS
SEMI-FINALS

Farnborough Town 0, Histon 3
(Lewes declined to play in the play-offs).

FINAL

St Albans City 2, Histon 0

CONFERENCE SECOND DIVISION SOUTH RESULTS 2005–2006

	Basingstoke T	Bishop's Stortford	Bognor Regis T	Cambridge C	Carshalton Ath	Dorchester T	Eastbourne B	Eastleigh	Farnborough T	Havant & W	Hayes	Histon	Lewes	Maidenhead U	Newport Co	St Albans C	Sutton U	Thurrock	Welling U	Weston-S-Mare	Weymouth	Yeading
Basingstoke T	—	1-1	2-3	1-1	0-2	1-1	2-2	2-3	1-0	2-1	1-0	2-0	2-0	0-1	1-0	2-0	2-0	0-3	2-2	3-1	1-0	1-1
Bishop's Stortford	1-1	—	1-0	2-0	2-1	1-0	3-0	0-1	2-2	1-0	2-2	2-1	1-0	3-0	1-2	2-0	0-3	2-0	1-1	3-1	0-2	2-1
Bognor Regis T	2-1	2-2	—	4-2	0-2	0-1	2-3	1-0	1-0	1-2	0-1	0-0	1-1	1-0	1-2	1-0	1-3	1-0	1-3	2-1	0-2	0-2
Cambridge C	1-0	1-1	4-2	—	1-0	2-3	2-3	1-1	2-1	0-5	1-1	3-1	0-2	2-2	0-2	1-1	1-1	6-0	0-0	1-1	1-3	0-2
Carshalton Ath	1-2	2-0	0-0	0-2	—	4-1	2-3	0-1	0-3	2-2	0-0	3-1	0-2	4-1	2-4	0-2	0-0	0-0	0-0	1-1	2-1	2-2
Dorchester T	1-2	1-3	1-1	0-2	2-0	—	3-0	0-1	2-0	2-6	0-0	0-3	1-2	4-1	2-0	2-1	1-0	0-0	0-3	1-2	2-0	4-0
Eastbourne B	2-3	0-1	2-1	2-3	2-3	2-1	—	1-0	2-3	4-1	2-1	1-1	2-2	3-3	2-0	0-0	0-5	0-0	1-3	4-1	0-2	2-1
Eastleigh	1-0	0-1	1-0	3-0	0-1	3-0	2-3	—	2-0	2-6	0-0	0-3	2-0	3-1	2-1	1-4	0-5	3-0	1-3	5-0	0-1	0-3
Farnborough T	1-0	3-0	1-0	1-1	1-1	1-1	2-0	0-1	—	1-2	0-0	0-1	0-0	1-2	3-2	0-0	1-0	3-0	1-3	3-2	1-0	1-0
Havant & W	1-2	2-2	2-1	1-1	1-2	0-2	4-1	1-0	1-2	—	2-3	2-1	2-3	2-1	2-1	2-0	1-0	0-0	4-1	4-1	1-2	1-0
Hayes	2-0	2-0	0-3	1-1	0-0	0-0	2-1	0-0	0-0	2-3	—	1-1	2-3	2-1	2-1	1-0	1-0	1-3	1-1	2-2	2-3	3-0
Histon	1-2	3-2	2-2	3-1	3-1	0-3	1-1	0-2	0-1	2-1	2-3	—	0-3	3-1	3-2	0-0	2-0	0-0	1-1	3-1	1-1	0-1
Lewes	2-0	2-1	2-0	0-2	0-2	1-2	2-2	2-0	0-0	2-3	2-2	3-0	—	4-1	2-0	0-1	1-3	1-1	4-1	4-1	1-5	0-4
Maidenhead U	0-0	1-0	3-2	2-2	4-1	4-1	3-3	3-1	1-2	2-1	2-1	3-1	2-2	—	2-0	0-1	3-0	1-3	2-1	8-1	2-2	1-2
Newport Co	0-0	1-0	1-0	0-2	2-4	2-0	2-0	2-1	3-2	2-1	2-1	3-2	2-0	3-0	—	1-3	1-0	2-0	2-0	1-1	0-3	1-3
St Albans C	3-1	3-0	1-0	1-1	0-2	2-1	0-0	1-4	0-0	2-0	1-0	0-0	0-1	0-1	1-3	—	4-0	1-3	4-1	4-1	4-0	5-2
Sutton U	0-1	2-0	1-3	1-1	0-0	1-0	0-5	0-5	1-0	1-0	1-0	2-0	1-3	3-0	1-0	4-0	—	0-0	1-0	1-0	0-3	0-0
Thurrock	4-1	0-1	1-0	6-0	0-0	0-0	0-0	3-0	3-0	0-0	1-3	0-0	1-1	1-3	0-1	1-3	0-0	—	1-1	3-4	3-2	1-1
Welling U	3-2	2-1	1-2	0-0	0-0	0-3	1-3	1-3	1-3	4-1	1-1	1-1	4-1	2-4	4-2	3-1	5-3	1-1	—	1-0	1-2	0-1
Weston-S-Mare	4-3	0-1	2-1	1-1	1-1	1-2	4-1	5-0	3-2	4-1	2-2	3-1	4-1	2-2	4-0	3-2	2-3	2-0	1-0	—	1-3	1-0
Weymouth	0-1	3-1	0-2	1-1	2-1	2-0	0-2	0-1	1-0	1-2	2-3	1-1	0-3	2-2	1-2	3-2	3-1	2-0	2-1	2-1	—	1-1
Yeading	0-4	0-0	0-2	0-2	2-2	4-0	2-1	0-3	1-0	1-0	3-0	0-1	1-0	1-2	1-3	2-2	0-2	1-1	1-0	1-2	0-1	—

UNIBOND LEAGUE 2005–2006

Premier Division		Home					Away					Total				
	P	W	D	L	F	A	W	D	L	F	A	W	D	L	F	A	Gd Pts
1 Blyth Spartans	42	13	6	2	37	16	13	5	3	42	16	26	11	5	79	32	47 89
2 Frickley Athletic	42	13	5	3	35	17	13	3	5	37	19	26	8	8	72	36	36 86
3 Marine	42	12	6	3	33	12	11	6	4	28	13	23	12	7	61	25	36 81
4 Farsley Celtic	42	12	4	5	47	22	11	6	4	37	12	23	10	9	84	34	50 79
5 North Ferriby Utd	42	12	4	5	39	24	9	6	6	38	30	21	10	11	77	54	23 73
6 Whitby Town	42	13	4	4	39	23	5	6	10	21	36	18	10	14	60	59	1 64
7 Burscough	42	8	5	8	33	31	11	1	9	31	33	19	6	17	64	64	0 63
8 Witton Albion	42	7	5	9	30	22	10	4	7	37	31	17	9	16	68	55	14 60
9 Matlock Town	42	8	5	8	24	26	8	6	7	34	28	16	11	15	60	55	4 59
10 AFC Telford Utd	42	10	7	4	33	27	4	10	7	21	25	14	17	11	54	52	2 59
11 Ossett Town	42	11	3	7	36	30	6	4	11	21	31	17	7	18	57	61	−4 58
12 Leek Town	42	5	10	6	21	24	9	4	8	29	29	14	14	14	50	53	−3 56
13 Prescot Cables	42	7	6	8	23	26	8	2	11	26	34	15	8	19	49	60	−11 53
14 Guiseley	42	8	3	10	23	33	6	6	9	22	25	14	9	19	45	58	−13 51
15 Ashton United	42	8	5	8	42	31	5	5	11	20	32	13	10	19	62	63	−1 49
16 Ilkeston Town	42	10	5	6	26	16	2	8	11	22	35	12	13	17	48	51	−3 49
17 Gateshead	42	8	4	9	31	41	4	6	11	21	36	12	10	20	52	77	−25 46
18 Radcliffe Borough	42	8	2	11	36	30	4	6	11	18	32	12	8	22	54	62	−8 44
19 Lincoln United	42	3	8	10	21	31	7	6	8	23	33	10	14	18	44	64	−20 44
20 Wakefield Emley	42	6	5	10	17	26	5	4	12	21	43	11	9	22	38	69	−31 42
21 Bradford Park Av	42	6	5	10	33	36	4	4	13	31	50	10	9	23	64	86	−22 39
22 Runcorn AFC H	42	4	6	11	21	51	2	5	14	15	57	6	11	25	36	108	−72 29

Farsley Celetic promoted to Conference North as Play-Off winners.
Lincoln United not relegated as they had a superior record to the club in the Isthmian League.

SOUTHERN LEAGUE 2005–2006

Premier Division		Home					Away					Total				
	P	W	D	L	F	A	W	D	L	W	D	L	F	A	GD	Pts
1 Salisbury City	42	16	2	3	14	3	4	30	5	7	83	27	56	95		
2 Bath City	42	12	4	5	13	4	4	25	8	9	66	33	33	83		
3 King's Lynn	42	14	3	4	11	4	6	25	7	10	73	41	32	82		
4 Chippenham Town	42	14	5	2	8	6	7	22	11	9	69	45	24	77		
5 Bedford Town	42	12	6	3	10	4	7	22	10	10	69	53	16	76		
6 Yate Town	42	15	3	3	6	2	13	21	5	16	78	74	4	68		
7 Banbury United	42	11	5	5	6	9	17	11	14	66	61	5	62			
8 Halesowen Town	42	9	7	5	6	8	7	15	15	12	54	45	9	60		
9 Merthyr Tydfil	42	9	4	8	8	5	8	17	9	16	62	58	4	60		
10 Mangotsfield United	42	6	6	9	9	7	5	15	13	14	67	67	0	58		
11 Grantham Town	42	6	8	7	9	3	9	15	11	16	49	49	0	56		
12 Tiverton Town	42	9	5	7	5	5	11	14	10	18	69	65	4	52		
13 Gloucester City	42	9	5	7	5	5	11	14	10	18	57	60	−3	52		
14 Hitchin Town	42	9	6	6	4	6	11	13	12	17	59	76	−17	51		
15 Rugby Town	42	8	4	9	5	7	9	13	11	18	58	66	−8	50		
16 Cheshunt	42	8	4	9	5	5	11	13	9	20	57	70	−13	48		
17 Team Bath	42	7	2	12	7	4	10	14	6	22	55	68	−13	48		
18 Cirencester Town	42	8	3	12	8	1	12	14	4	24	49	68	−19	46		
19 Northwood	42	7	5	9	5	1	15	12	6	24	53	88	−35	42		
20 Evesham United	42	5	7	9	4	7	10	9	14	19	46	58	−12	41		
21 Aylesbury United	42	7	4	10	2	8	11	9	12	21	43	69	−26	39		
22 Chesham United	42	4	6	11	5	3	13	9	9	24	43	84	−41	36		

RYMAN LEAGUE 2005–2006

Premier Division							Home					Away					Total					
	P	W	D	L	F	A	W	D	L	F	A	W	D	L	F	A	Gd	Pts
1 Braintree Town	42	18	3	0	45	12	10	7	4	29	20	28	10	4	74	32	+42	94
2 Heybridge Swifts	42	14	3	4	32	16	14	0	7	38	30	28	3	11	70	46	+24	87
3 Fisher Athletic	42	10	6	5	36	24	16	1	4	48	22	26	7	9	84	46	+38	85
4 AFC Wimbledon	42	9	8	4	33	23	13	3	5	34	13	22	11	9	67	36	+31	77
5 Hampton & Richmond Borough	42	12	1	8	36	27	12	2	7	37	27	24	3	15	73	54	+19	75
6 Staines Town	42	9	4	8	31	26	11	6	4	43	30	20	10	12	74	56	+18	70
7 Billericay Town	42	10	5	6	38	28	9	7	5	31	17	19	12	11	69	45	+24	69
8 Worthing	42	12	4	5	41	26	7	6	8	30	34	19	10	13	71	60	+11	67
9 Walton & Hersham	42	11	3	7	28	23	8	4	9	27	27	19	7	16	55	50	+5	64
10 Chelmsford City	42	10	5	6	32	27	8	5	8	25	35	18	10	14	57	62	-5	64
11 Bromley	42	9	8	4	34	24	7	6	8	23	25	16	14	12	57	49	+8	62
12 East Thurrock U	42	10	2	9	33	34	8	3	10	27	26	18	5	19	60	60	+0	59
13 Folkestone Invicta	42	11	4	6	28	19	5	6	10	19	32	16	10	16	47	51	-4	58
14 Margate	42	5	10	6	24	27	6	7	8	25	28	11	17	14	49	55	-6	50
15 Leyton	42	6	2	13	28	30	7	7	7	30	31	13	9	20	58	61	-3	48
16 Harrow Borough	42	7	7	7	32	31	6	2	13	24	42	13	9	20	56	73	-17	48
17 Slough Town	42	6	4	11	29	38	7	4	10	34	37	13	8	21	63	75	-12	47
18 Wealdstone	42	5	2	14	37	48	8	3	10	31	34	13	5	24	68	82	-14	44
19 Hendon	42	4	8	9	22	26	5	4	12	22	38	9	12	21	44	64	-20	39
20 Maldon Town	42	4	3	14	21	40	4	8	9	20	33	8	11	23	41	73	-32	35
21 Windsor & Eton	42	5	4	12	16	32	3	4	14	21	43	8	8	26	37	75	-38	32
22 Redbridge	42	3	2	16	17	48	0	3	18	11	49	3	5	34	28	97	-69	14

CUP FINALS 2005–2006

UNIBOND LEAGUE

CHALLENGE CUP FINAL
Farsley Celtic 1, Stocksbridge Park Steels 0

PRESIDENT'S CUP FINAL
Ilkeston Town 0, Bradford Park Avenue 1

CHAIRMAN'S CUP FINAL
Blyth Spartans 2, Ossett Town 0

PREMIER DIVISION PLAY-OFF FINAL
Farsley Celtic 2, North Ferriby United 1

UNIBOND LEAGUE FIRST DIVISION PLAY-OFF FINAL
Kendal Town 2, Gresley Rovers 1

SOUTHERN LEAGUE

ERREA SOUTHERN LEAGUE CUP FINAL
First Leg
Hitchin Town 1, Bromsgrove Rovers 0

Second Leg
Bromsgrove Rovers 1, Hitchin Town 2

SOUTHERN LEAGUE PREMIER DIVISION PLAY-OFF FINAL
Chippenham Town 2, Bedford Town 3

SOUTHERN LEAGUE DIVISION ONE EAST PLAY-OFF FINAL
Stamford 2, Wivenhoe Town 1

SOUTHERN LEAGUE DIVISION ONE WEST PLAY-OFF FINAL
Brackley Town 2, Hemel Hempstead Town 3

RYMAN LEAGUE

WESTVIEW LEAGUE CUP FINAL
Billericay Town 0, Fisher Athletic 4

ASSOCIATE MEMBERS TROPHY FINAL
Brook House 3, Hertford Town 1

RYMAN LEAGUE PLAY-OFFS
Premier Division Play-Off Final
Fisher Athletic 3, Hampton & Richmond Borough 0

Division One Play-Off Final
Tonbridge Angels 3, Dover Athletic 2

PONTIN'S HOLIDAYS LEAGUE 2005–2006

DIVISON ONE CENTRAL

	P	W	D	L	F	A	GD	Pts
Sheffield W	18	10	5	3	26	13	13	35
Huddersfield T	18	10	4	4	24	16	8	34
Oldham Ath	18	9	5	4	29	17	12	32
Sheffield U A	18	9	3	6	42	28	14	30
Nottingham F	18	6	5	7	34	27	7	23
Stoke C	18	7	2	9	22	30	–8	23
Barnsley	18	6	4	8	26	33	–7	22
Walsall	18	6	3	9	29	41	–12	21
Rotherham U	18	3	8	7	26	30	–4	17
Bradford C	18	3	3	12	19	42	–23	12

DIVISON ONE WEST

	P	W	D	L	F	A	GD	Pts
Carlisle U	18	11	4	3	39	16	23	37
Bury	18	9	4	5	31	25	6	31
Preston NE	18	7	8	3	32	22	10	29
Tranmere R	18	7	7	4	30	26	4	28
Blackpool	18	8	1	9	31	31	0	25
Shrewsbury T	18	6	6	6	23	25	–2	24
Rochdale	18	7	1	10	23	35	–12	22
Chester C	18	4	6	8	21	30	–9	18
Burnley*	18	5	5	8	26	31	–5	17
Wrexham	18	3	4	11	22	37	–15	13

Burnley deducted three points.

DIVISON ONE EAST

	P	W	D	L	F	A	GD	Pts
Doncaster R	18	11	3	4	34	16	18	36
Sheffield U B	18	10	1	7	39	27	12	31
Hull C	18	8	7	3	28	24	4	31
Lincoln C	18	7	6	5	29	28	1	27
Darlington	18	8	3	7	24	38	–14	27
Scarborough	18	7	5	6	31	26	5	26
York C	18	8	2	8	26	23	3	26
Hartlepool U	18	7	4	7	33	24	9	25
Scunthorpe U	18	4	4	10	16	26	–10	16
Grimsby T	18	0	5	13	17	45	–28	5

PONTIN'S HOLIDAYS COMBINATION 2005–2006

CENTRAL DIVISION

	P	W	D	L	F	A	GD	Pts
Reading	16	12	2	2	48	10	38	38
Millwall	16	10	2	4	37	21	16	32
Brighton & HA	16	9	2	5	40	21	19	29
Gillingham	16	8	3	5	25	25	0	27
QPR	16	5	6	5	30	26	4	21
Wycombe W	16	6	1	9	27	26	1	19
Aldershot T	16	5	1	10	24	42	–18	16
Crawley T	16	4	0	12	23	39	–16	12
Woking	16	3	3	10	12	56	–44	12

WALES AND WEST DIVISION

	P	W	D	L	F	A	GD	Pts
Cheltenham T	16	13	2	1	36	17	16	41
Cardiff C	16	9	4	3	28	14	14	31
Swindon T	16	7	4	5	36	25	11	25
Bristol C	16	7	4	5	27	20	7	25
Yeovil T	16	5	4	7	33	26	7	19
Bristol R	16	5	3	8	29	26	3	18
Plymouth Arg	16	4	6	6	23	24	–1	18
AFC Bournemouth	16	5	2	9	30	37	–7	17
Swansea C	16	2	1	13	20	70	–50	7

EAST DIVISION

	P	W	D	L	F	A	GD	Pts
Luton T	16	12	2	2	44	19	25	38
Northampton T	16	10	3	3	34	13	21	33
Colchester U	16	10	3	3	33	21	12	32
Milton Keynes D	16	7	5	4	27	18	9	26
Southend U	16	6	2	8	20	25	–5	20
Leyton Orient	16	5	1	10	20	31	–11	16
Barnet	16	5	1	10	25	40	–15	16
Stevenage B	16	5	1	10	15	30	–15	16
Oxford U	16	1	5	10	13	33	–20	8

FA ACADEMY UNDER-18 LEAGUE 2005–06

GROUP A	P	W	D	L	F	A	GD	Pts
Southampton	28	17	5	6	72	35	37	56
Chelsea	28	17	5	6	45	21	24	56
West Ham U	28	13	6	9	51	41	10	45
Arsenal	28	11	5	12	47	47	0	38
Norwich C	28	10	6	12	31	34	–3	36
Fulham	28	9	5	14	30	46	–16	32
Ipswich T	28	8	7	13	53	64	–11	31
Crystal Palace	28	8	6	14	54	59	–5	30
Charlton Ath	28	8	4	16	36	52	–16	28
Millwall	28	6	8	14	30	52	–22	26

GROUP B	P	W	D	L	F	A	GD	Pts
Aston Villa	28	17	5	6	63	33	30	56
Leicester C	28	17	3	8	54	41	13	54
Bristol C	28	12	8	8	47	37	10	44
Coventry C	28	12	8	8	40	40	0	44
Watford	28	11	9	8	41	41	0	42
Tottenham H	28	11	5	12	45	49	–4	38
Cardiff C	28	10	5	13	36	41	–5	35
Milton Keynes D	28	10	5	13	37	48	–11	35
Reading	28	9	6	13	43	41	2	33
Birmingham C	28	8	8	12	33	45	–12	32

GROUP C	P	W	D	L	F	A	GD	Pts
Blackburn R	28	17	3	8	51	36	15	54
Manchester U	28	16	4	8	56	30	26	52
Manchester C	28	14	7	7	50	37	13	49
Everton	28	14	7	7	33	24	9	49
Liverpool	28	13	5	10	47	35	12	44
Stoke C	28	10	8	10	42	37	5	38
Bolton W	28	9	11	8	31	35	–4	38
Crewe Alex	28	9	8	11	38	42	–4	35
WBA	28	6	9	13	39	52	–13	27
Wolverhampton W	28	6	8	14	25	39	–14	26

GROUP D	P	W	D	L	F	A	GD	Pts
Derby Co	28	16	7	5	49	26	23	55
Leeds U	28	16	5	7	51	26	25	53
Newcastle U	28	12	5	11	37	37	0	41
Nottingham F	28	9	7	12	32	34	–2	34
Sunderland	28	10	4	14	31	37	–6	34
Sheffield U	28	8	8	12	32	40	–8	32
Middlesbrough	28	8	6	14	30	48	–18	30
Barnsley	28	7	7	14	22	42	–20	28
Sheffield W	28	7	4	17	29	55	–26	25
Huddersfield T	28	5	6	17	26	60	–34	21

FA PREMIER RESERVE LEAGUES 2005–06

NORTH SECTION

	P	W	D	L	F	A	GD	Pts
Manchester U	28	19	2	7	68	32	36	59
Aston Villa	28	16	8	4	59	26	33	56
Manchester C	28	15	8	5	47	37	10	53
Middlesbrough	28	15	7	6	50	27	23	52
Newcastle U	28	12	8	8	45	40	5	44
Liverpool	28	13	5	10	31	31	0	44
Sunderland	28	11	7	10	40	41	–1	40
Everton	28	10	8	10	31	35	–4	38
Leeds U	28	9	11	8	27	31	–4	38
Blackburn R	28	8	7	13	38	46	–8	31
Birmingham C	28	7	9	12	32	36	–4	30
Wolverhampton W	28	6	8	14	28	37	–9	26
Bolton W	28	6	6	16	25	46	–21	24
WBA	28	6	6	16	26	55	–29	24
Wigan Ath	28	5	4	19	24	51	–27	19

Leading Goalscorers

Rossi G (Manchester U)	26	Finnigan C (Newcastle U)	9
Chopra M (Newcastle U)	14	Nicholson S (WBA)	8
Miller I (Manchester C)	13	Johnson J (Blackburn R)	7
Agbonlahor G (Aston Villa)	11	Peter S (Blackburn R)	7
Wright-Phillips B (Manchester C)	11	Calliste R (Liverpool)	7
Graham D (Middlesbrough)	11	Murphy D (Sunderland)	7
Williams S (Aston Villa)	10	Johansson A (Wigan Ath)	7
Craddock T (Middlesbrough)	10	Whittingham P (Aston Villa)	6
Anichebe V (Everton)	9	De Vita R (Blackburn R)	6
Campbell F (Manchester U)	9	Smith J (Bolton W)	6
Ebanks-Blake S (Manchester U)	9	Johnson A (Middlesbrough)	6

SOUTH SECTION

	P	W	D	L	F	A	GD	Pts
Tottenham H	26	20	3	3	57	13	44	63
Southampton	26	17	3	7	50	26	24	51
Arsenal	26	14	7	5	60	34	26	49
Charlton Ath	26	13	4	9	37	30	7	43
Coventry C	26	13	1	12	30	36	–6	40
Chelsea	26	10	9	7	34	24	10	39
Crystal Palace	26	11	5	10	44	41	3	38
Fulham	26	11	3	12	26	32	–6	36
Ipswich T	26	10	1	15	44	54	–10	31
West Ham U	26	7	8	11	37	38	–1	29
Leicester C	26	7	7	12	38	57	–19	28
Watford	26	8	3	15	25	51	–26	27
Portsmouth	26	6	4	16	35	54	–19	22
Norwich C	26	4	6	16	19	46	–27	18

Leading Goalscorers

Barnard L (Tottenham H)	20	Bowditch D (Ipswich T)	7
Bendtner N (Arsenal)	19	Dodds L (Leicester C)	7
Lupoli A (Arsenal)	17	O'Grady C (Leicester C)	7
McGoldrick D (Southampton)	12	Simpson J (Arsenal)	6
Reid C (Coventry C)	10	Hollands D (Chelsea)	6
Lisbie K (Charlton Ath)	8	Smith J (Chelsea)	6
Andrews W (Crystal Palace)	7	Hall R (Crystal Palace)	6
Grabban L (Crystal Palace)	7	Grant J (Watford)	6

WOMEN'S FOOTBALL 2005–2006

PREMIER LEAGUE
NATIONAL DIVISION

	P	W	D	L	F	A	GD	Pts
Arsenal	18	16	2	0	83	20	63	50
Everton	18	14	2	2	46	20	26	44
Charlton Athletic	18	12	3	3	41	13	28	39
Doncaster Rovers Belles	18	7	2	9	32	34	–2	23
Bristol Academy	18	4	8	6	19	29	–10	20
Birmingham City	18	6	2	10	24	40	–16	20
Leeds United	18	4	6	8	27	36	–9	18
Fulham	18	4	2	12	24	45	–21	14
Sunderland	18	3	4	11	22	57	–35	13
Chelsea	18	3	3	12	22	46	–24	12

NORTHERN DIVISION

	P	W	D	L	F	A	GD	Pts
Blackburn Rovers	22	20	2	0	55	12	43	62
Liverpool	22	15	3	4	39	17	22	48
Tranmere Rovers	22	13	4	5	41	29	12	43
Lincoln City	22	11	3	8	40	31	9	36
Nottingham Forest	22	8	6	8	33	30	3	30
Wolverhampton Wanderers	22	6	10	6	29	33	–4	28
Aston Villa	22	8	2	12	33	38	–5	26
Newcastle United	22	6	7	9	32	33	–1	25
Stockport County	22	5	7	10	24	31	–7	22
Curzon Ashton	22	4	6	12	27	64	–37	18
Manchester City	22	3	7	12	19	31	–12	16
Middlesbrough	22	3	3	16	18	41	–23	12

SOUTHERN DIVISION

	P	W	D	L	F	A	GD	Pts
Cardiff City	22	14	7	1	53	17	36	49
Bristol City	22	16	1	5	51	30	21	49
Watford	22	14	5	3	59	28	31	47
Portsmouth	22	12	4	6	58	39	19	40
Millwall Lionesses	22	11	5	6	51	31	20	38
West Ham United	22	8	4	10	31	33	–2	28
AFC Wimbledon	22	8	3	11	39	52	–13	27
Reading Royals	22	7	2	13	34	42	–8	23
Crystal Palace	22	7	1	14	38	52	–14	22
Southampton Saints	22	6	0	16	30	70	–40	18
Brighton & Hove Albion	22	4	5	13	33	53	–20	17
Langford	22	4	5	13	30	60	–30	17

THE FA WOMEN'S CUP FINAL 2005–2006

Monday, 1 May 2006
(at Upton Park)

Arsenal 5 *(Ward 3 (og), Fleeting 34, Yankey 35, Smith 73 (pen), Sanderson 77)*
Leeds United 0   13,452

Arsenal: Byrne; Scott (Daniels 84), Champ, Ludlow (Grant 73), White, Phillip (McArthur 78), Asante, Smith, Fleeting, Yankey, Sanderson.

Leeds United: Fay; Cook (Walton 52), Culvin, Emmanuel, Haigh, Ward, Clarke, Burke, Walker (Panesar 85), Preston (Owen 85), Smith.

Referee: P. Crossley (Kent).

ENGLAND WOMEN'S INTERNATIONAL MATCHES 2005–2006

1 September 2005 (in Amsterdam)
Austria 1 *(Celouch 20)*
England 4 *(Williams 23 (pen), Smith K 35, Barr 55, Smith S 90)*   1700
England: Brown; Scott (Stoney 61), White, Phillip, Unitt, Carny, Chapman, Williams, Potter (Smith S 46), Smith K (Westwood 67), Barr.

27 October 2005 (in Tapolca)
Hungary 0
England 13 *(Smith K 3, Aluko 2, Scott 2, Williams 2, Yankey, Chapman, Handley, Potter).*
England: Brown (Chamberlain 72); Stoney, Phillip, Johnson, Unitt, Scott, Chapman, Williams, Yankey (Potter 40), Smith K, Aluko (Handley 63).

17 November 2005 (in Zwollen)
Holland 0
England 1 *(Williams 55 (pen))*   2319
England: Brown; Stoney, White, Phillip, Unitt, Carney (Potter 59), Exley (Asante 81), Williams, Yankey, Smith K, Aluko (Barr 46).

7 February 2006 (in Larnaca)
Sweden 0
England 0
England: Brown; Phillip, Stoney, Unitt, Asante (Potter 86), Chapman, Exley, Williams, Aluko (Barr 74), Carney (Handley 66), Yankey (Smith S 66).

9 February 2006 (in Achna)
Sweden 1 *(Aronsson 5)*
England 1 *(Unitt 64)*
England: Brown; Johnson, Unitt, Asante, Chapman, Phillip, Carney, Williams, Barr (Stoney 63), Smith K (Aluko 82), Potter.

9 March 2006 (in Norwich)
England 1 *(Carney 79)*
Iceland 0   9616
England: Brown (Chamberlain 46); Stoney (Johnson 46), Unitt, Asante, Chapman, Phillip, Carney, Williams, Aluko (Scott 60), Smith K, Yankey (Potter 67).

26 March 2006 (at Blackburn)
England 0
France 0   12,164
England: Brown; Stoney, Unitt, Asante (Exley 88), Chapman, Phillip, Carney, Williams, Aluko (Scott 75), Smith K, Yankey.

20 April 2006 (at Gillingham)
England 4 *(Spieler 36 (og), Williams 85, Smith S 87, Handley 90)*
Austria 0   8068
England: Brown; Johnson, Unitt, Chapman, White, Phillip, Carney, Williams, Barr (Handley 59), Smith K, Yankey (Smith S 84).

11 May 2006 (at Southampton)
England 2 *(Exley 41, Scott 90)*
Hungary 0   8817
England: Brown; Johnson (Stoney 69), Unitt, Asante, White, Phillip, Carney (Scott 57), Potter, Handley (Sanderson 54), Exley, Smith S.

THE FA TROPHY 2005–2006

FINAL (at Upton Park) – Sunday, 14 May 2006

Grays Athletic (2) 2 *(Oli 41, Poole 45)*

Woking (0) 0   13,800

Grays Athletic: Bayes; Sambrook, Nutter, Thurgood, Stuart, Hanson, Kightly (Williamson 90), Martin, McLean, Oli, Poole.
Woking: Jalal; Jackson, Hutchinson, Murray, Nethercott (Cockerill L 60), MacDonald, Smith (Watson 60), Ferguson, Richards, McAllister, Evans (Blackman 83).
Referee: H. Webb (Sheffield & Hallamshire).

THE FA VASE 2005–2006

FINAL (at St Andrews, Birmingham City FC) – Saturday, 6 May 2006

Hillingdon Borough (0) 1 *(Nelson 90)*

Nantwich Town (2) 3 *(Kinsey 14, 68, Scheuber 30)*   3286

Hillingdon Borough: Harris; Brown, Rundell (Fenton 80), Tilbury, Phillips, Kidson, Hibbs, Duncan (Nelson 47), Lawrence, Wharton (Lyons 37), Craft.
Nantwich Town: Hackney; Taylor A, Taylor P, Donnelly, Smith, Davis, Beasley, Scheuber (Parkinson 72), Blake (Scarlett 85), Kinsey (Marrow 72), Griggs.
Referee: P. Armstrong (Berkshire).

THE FA YOUTH CUP 2005–2006

FINAL (First Leg) – Thursday, 13 April 2005

Liverpool (2) 3 *(Threlfall 18, Flynn 32, Roque 84)*

Manchester City (0) 0   12,744

Liverpool: Roberts; Darby, Hobbs, Antwii, Threlfall, Barnett, Flynn (Spearing 88), Barratt, Hamill (Roque 77), Anderson, Lindfield.
Manchester City: Matthewson; Obeng, Logan, Williamson, Breen, Marshall, Williams, Johnson, Etuhu, Sturridge, Moore (Evans 81).

FINAL (Second Leg) – Friday, 21 April 2005

Manchester City (1) 2 *(Sturridge 32, 56)*

Liverpool (0) 0   10,601

Manchester City: Matthewson; Obeng, Logan, Richards, Breen, Evans, Marshall, Johnson, Moore, Etuhu, Sturridge.
Liverpool: Roberts; Darby, Threlfall, Hobbs, Antwii, Barnett (Roque 46), Barratt, Flynn, Lindfield, Anderson, Hamill (Spearing 59).

THE FA SUNDAY CUP 2005–2006

FINAL (at Liverpool FC)
Hetton Lyons Cricket Club 5 *(Brightwell 3, Pearson, Johnston)*
St Joseph's (Luton) 3 *(Hayes 2, Fontanelle)*

THE FA COUNTY YOUTH CUP 2005–2006

FINAL (at Darlington FC)

Durham (0) 2 *(Forrest 60, Brown 73)*

Bedfordshire (1) 3 *(Cunnington 11 (pen), Grieve 84, Lewis 85)*

Durham: Lawson; Burns, Davidson, Basham■, Brown, Hall■, Forrest, Magnay, Pennock (Hunter 77), Thackray (McRow 46), Coe.
Bedfordshire: Tompkins; Lewis, Moulds, Grieve, Lynch, Walsh (Thrower 46), Hall, Darvall, Cunnington, Howson (Funge 74), Douglas (Woodley 86).

■ *Denotes player sent off.*

SOUTH AMERICAN CHAMPIONSHIP

(Copa America)

1916	Uruguay	1939	Peru	1967	Uruguay
1917	Uruguay	1941	Argentina	1975	Peru
1919	Brazil	1942	Uruguay	1979	Paraguay
1920	Uruguay	1945	Argentina	1983	Uruguay
1921	Argentina	1946	Argentina	1987	Uruguay
1922	Brazil	1947	Argentina	1989	Brazil
1923	Uruguay	1949	Brazil	1991	Argentina
1924	Uruguay	1953	Paraguay	1993	Argentina
1925	Argentina	1955	Argentina	1995	Uruguay
1926	Uruguay	1956	Uruguay	1997	Brazil
1927	Argentina	1957	Argentina	1999	Brazil
1929	Argentina	1959	Argentina	2001	Colombia
1935	Uruguay	1959	Uruguay	2004	Brazil
1937	Argentina	1963	Bolivia		

SOUTH AMERICAN CUP

(Copa Libertadores)

1960	Penarol (Uruguay)	1983	Gremio Porto Alegre (Brazil)
1961	Penarol	1984	Independiente
1962	Santos (Brazil)	1985	Argentinos Juniors (Argentina)
1963	Santos	1986	River Plate (Argentina)
1964	Independiente (Argentina)	1987	Penarol
1965	Independiente	1988	Nacional (Uruguay)
1966	Penarol	1989	Nacional (Colombia)
1967	Racing Club (Argentina)	1990	Olimpia
1968	Estudiantes (Argentina)	1991	Colo Colo (Chile)
1969	Estudiantes	1992	São Paulo (Brazil)
1970	Estudiantes	1993	São Paulo
1971	Nacional (Uruguay)	1994	Velez Sarsfield (Argentina)
1972	Independiente	1995	Gremio Porto Alegre
1973	Independiente	1996	River Plate
1974	Independiente	1997	Cruzeiro
1975	Independiente	1998	Vasco da Gama
1976	Cruzeiro (Brazil)	1999	Palmeiras
1977	Boca Juniors (Argentina)	2000	Boca Juniors
1978	Boca Juniors	2001	Boca Juniors
1979	Olimpia (Paraguay)	2002	Olimpia
1980	Nacional	2003	Boca Juniors
1981	Flamengo (Brazil)	2004	Once Caldas
1982	Penarol	2005	São Paulo (Brazil)

AFRICAN NATIONS CUP

(Final Tournament in Egypt}

GROUP A
Morocco 0, Ivory Coast 1
Egypt 3, Libya 0
Egypt 0, Morocco 0
Libya 1, Ivory Coast 2
Egypt 3, Ivory Coast 1
Libya 0, Morocco 0

GROUP B
Cameroon 3, Angola 1
Togo 0, DR Congo 2
Angola 0, DR Congo 0
Cameroon 2, Togo 0
Angola 3, Togo 2
Cameroon 2, DR Congo 0

GROUP C
South Africa 0, Guinea 2
Tunisia 4, Zambia 1
Tunisia 2, South Africa 0
Zambia 1, Guinea 2
Tunisia 0, Guinea 3
Zambia 1, South Africa 0

GROUP D
Nigeria 1, Ghana 0
Zimbabwe 0, Senegal 2

Ghana 1, Senegal 0
Nigeria 2, Zimbabwe 0
Ghana 1, Zimbabwe 2
Nigeria 2, Senegal 1

QUARTER-FINALS
Guinea 2, Senegal 3
Egypt 4, DR Congo 1
Cameroon 1, Ivory Coast 1
aet; Ivory Coast won 12-11 on penalties.
Nigeria 1, Tunisia 1
aet; Nigeria won 7-6 on penalties.

SEMI-FINALS
Egypt 2, Senegal 1
Nigeria 0, Ivory Coast 1

MATCH FOR THIRD PLACE
Nigeria 1, Senegal 0

FINAL
Egypt 0, Ivory Coast 0
aet; Egypt won 4-2 on penalties.

ASIA

ARAB CHAMPIONS LEAGUE FINAL
ENPPI (Cairo) 1, Raja Casablanca 2
Raja Casablanca 1, ENPPI 0.

AFC CHALLENGE CUP
Sri Lanka 0, Tajikistan 4

NATIONAL LIST OF REFEREES FOR SEASON 2006–2007

Armstrong, P (Paul) – Berkshire
Atkinson, M (Martin) – Yorkshire
Bates, A (Tony) – Staffordshire
Beeby, RJ (Richard) – Northamptonshire
Bennett, SG (Steve) – Kent
Booth, RJ (Russell) – Nottinghamshire
Boyeson, C (Carl) – Yorkshire
Bratt, SJ (Steve) – West Midlands
Clattenburg, M (Mark) – Tyne & Wear
Cowburn, MG (Mark) – Lancashire
Crossley, PT (Phil) – Kent
Deadman, D (Darren) – Cambridgeshire
Dean, ML (Mike) – Wirral
Desmond, RP (Bob) – Wiltshire
Dorr, SJ (Steve) – Worcestershire
Dowd, P (Phil) – Staffordshire
Drysdale, D (Darren) – Lincolnshire
D'Urso, AP (Andy) – Essex
Foster, D (David) – Tyne & Wear
Foy, CJ (Chris) – Merseyside
Friend, KA (Kevin) – Leicestershire
Gallagher, DJ (Dermot) – Oxfordshire
Graham, F (Fred) – Essex
Hall, AR (Andy) – West Midlands
Halsey, MR (Mark) – Lancashire
Haywood, M (Mark) – Yorkshire
Hegley, GK (Grant) – Hertfordshire
Hill, KD (Keith) – Hertfordshire
Ilderton, EL (Eddie) – Tyne & Wear
Jones, MJ (Michael) – Cheshire
Joslin, PJ (Phil) – Nottinghamshire
Kettle, TM (Trevor) – Rutland
Knight, B (Barry) – Kent
Laws, G (Graham) – Tyne & Wear
Lee, R (Ray) – Essex
Lewis, RL (Rob) – Shropshire
McDermid, D (Danny) – London
Marriner, AM (Andre) – West Midlands
Mason, LS (Lee) – Lancashire

Mathieson, SW (Scott) – Cheshire
Melin, PW (Paul) – Surrey
Miller, NS (Nigel) – Co. Durham
Miller, P (Pat) – Bedfordshire
Moss, J (Jon) – Yorkshire
Oliver, CW (Clive) – Northumberland
Olivier, RJ (Ray) – West Midlands
Parkes, TA (Trevor) – West Midlands
Penn, AM (Andy) – West Midlands
Penton, C (Clive) – Sussex
Pike, MS (Mike) – Cumbria
Poll, G (Graham) – Hertfordshire
Probert, LW (Lee) – Gloucestershire
Prosser, PJ (Phil) – Yorkshire
Rennie, UD (Uriah) – Yorkshire
Riley, MA (Mike) – Yorkshire
Robinson, JP (Paul) – Yorkshire
Russell, MP (Mike) – Hertfordshire
Salisbury, G (Graham) – Lancashire
Shoebridge, RL (Rob) – Derbyshire
Singh, J (Jarnail) – Middlesex
Stroud, KP (Keith) – Hampshire
Styles, R (Rob) – Hampshire
Sutton, GJ (Gary) – Lincolnshire
Swarbrick, ND (Neil) – Lancashire
Tanner SJ, (Steve) – Somerset
Taylor, A (Anthony) – Cheshire
Taylor, P (Paul) – Hertfordshire
Thorpe, M (Mike) – Norfolk
Walton, P (Peter) – Northamptonshire
Webb, HM (Howard) – Yorkshire
Webster, CH (Colin) – Tyne & Wear
Whitestone, D (Dean) – Northampton-
shire
Wiley, AG (Alan) – Staffordshire
Williamson IG, (Iain) – Berkshire
Woolmer, KA (Andy) – Northampton-
shire
Wright, KK (Kevin) – Cambridgeshire

USEFUL ADDRESSES

The Football Association: The Secretary, 25 Soho Square, London W1D 4FA. *0207 745 4545*

Scotland: D. Taylor, Hampden Park, Glasgow G42 9AY. *0141 616 6000*

Northern Ireland (Irish FA): Chief Executive: Howard J. C. Wells, 20 Windsor Avenue, Belfast BT9 6EG. *028 9066 9458*

Wales: D. Collins, 3 Westgate Street, Cardiff, South Glamorgan CF10 1DP. *029 2037 2325*

Republic of Ireland (FA of Ireland): B. Menton, 80 Merrion Square South, Dublin 2. *00353 16766864*

International Federation (FIFA): Secretary, PO Box 85 8030 Zurich, Switzerland. *00 411 384 9595. Fax: 00 411 384 9696*

Union of European Football Associations: Secretary, Route de Geneve 46, Case Postale, CH-1260 Nyon, Switzerland. *0041 22 994 4444. Fax: 0041 22 994 4488*

The Premier League: M. Foster, 11 Connaught Place, London W2 2ET. *0207 298 1600*

The Football League: Secretary, The Football League, Unit 5, Edward VII Quay, Navigation Way, Preston, Lancashire PR2 2YF. *0870 442 0 1888. Fax 0870 442 0 1188*

Scottish Premier League: R. Mitchell, Hampden Park, Somerville Drive, Glasgow G42 9BA. *0141 646 6962*

The Scottish League: The Secretary, Hampden Park, Glasgow G42 9AY. *0141 616 6000*

The Irish League: Secretary, 96 University Street, Belfast BT7 1HE. *028 9024 2888*

Football League of Ireland: D. Crowther, 80 Merrion Square, Dublin 2. *00353 167 65120*

Conference National: Riverside House, 14b High Street, Crayford DA1 4HG. *01322 411021*

Northern Premier: R. D. Bayley, 22 Woburn Drive, Hale, Altrincham, Cheshire WA15 8LZ. *0161 980 7007*

Isthmian League: N. Robinson, Triumph House, Station Approach, Sanderstead Road, South Croydon, Surrey CR2 0PL. *020 8409 1978*

Southern League: D. J. Strudwick, 8 College Yard, Worcester WR1 2LA. *01905 330444*

English Schools FA: Mike Spinks, 1/2 Eastgate Street, Stafford ST16 2NQ. *01785 251142*

The Football Supporters Federation: Chairman: Ian D. Todd MBE, 8 Wyke Close, Wyke Gardens, Isleworth, Middlesex TW7 5PE. *020 8847 2905 (and fax). Mobile: 0961 558908.* National Secretary: Mark Agate, 'The Stadium', 14 Coombe Close, Lordswood, Chatham, Kent ME5 8NU. *01634 319461 (and fax)*

Professional Footballers' Association: G. Taylor, 2 Oxford Court, Bishopsgate, Off Lower Mosley Street, Manchester 3 3WQ. *0161 236 0575*

Referees' Association: A. Smith, 1 Westhill Road, Coundon, Coventry CV6 2AD. *024 7660 1701*

Women's Football Alliance: The Football Association, 25 Soho Square, London W1D 4FA. *0207 745 4545*

The Football Programme Directory: David Stacey, 'The Beeches', 66 Southend Road, Wickford, Essex SS11 8EN. *01268 732041 (and fax)*

England Football Supporters Association: Publicity Officer, David Stacey, 66 Southend Road, Wickford, Essex SS11 8EN. *01268 732041 (and fax)*

World Cup (1966) Association: Hon. Secretary: David Duncan, 96 Glenlea Road, Eltham, London SE9 1DZ.

The Football Foundation Ltd: 25 Soho Square, London W1D 4FF. *0207 534 4210. Fax 0207 287 0459*

ENGLISH LEAGUE FIXTURES 2006–2007

*Sky Sports; †PremPlus pay per view

Saturday, 5 August 2006
**Coca-Cola Football League
Championship**
Barnsley v Cardiff C
Birmingham C v Colchester U
Burnley v QPR
Ipswich T v Crystal Palace
Leeds U v Norwich C
Luton T v Leicester C* (12.30)
Plymouth Arg v Wolverhampton W
Preston NE v Sheffield W
Southend U v Stoke C
WBA v Hull C

Sunday, 6 August 2006
**Coca-Cola Football League
Championship**
Coventry C v Sunderland* (1.30)
Derby Co v Southampton* (4.00)

Coca-Cola Football League One
Bournemouth v Chesterfield
Brentford v Blackpool
Bristol C v Scunthorpe U
Carlisle U v Doncaster R
Crewe Alex v Northampton T
Gillingham v Huddersfield T
Millwall v Yeovil T
Nottingham F v Bradford C
Port Vale v Leyton Orient
Rotherham U v Brighton & HA
Swansea C v Cheltenham T
Tranmere R v Oldham Ath

Coca-Cola Football League Two
Barnet v Torquay U
Chester C v Accrington S
Darlington v Macclesfield T
Grimsby T v Boston U
Hartlepool U v Swindon T
Lincoln C v Notts Co
Milton Keynes Dons v Bury
Peterborough U v Bristol R
Rochdale v Walsall
Shrewsbury T v Mansfield T
Stockport Co v Hereford U
Wycombe W v Wrexham

Tuesday, 8 August 2006
**Coca-Cola Football League
Championship**
Cardiff C v WBA
Colchester U v Plymouth Arg
Crystal Palace v Southend U
Hull C v Barnsley
Leicester C v Burnley
Norwich C v Preston NE
QPR v Leeds U
Sheffield W v Luton T
Stoke C v Derby Co
Sunderland v Birmingham C
Wolverhampton W v Ipswich T

Coca-Cola Football League One
Blackpool v Nottingham F
Bradford C v Bristol C
Brighton & HA v Gillingham
Cheltenham T v Tranmere R
Doncaster R v Crewe Alex
Huddersfield T v Rotherham U
Leyton Orient v Millwall
Northampton T v Brentford
Oldham Ath v Port Vale
Scunthorpe U v Swansea C
Yeovil T v Bournemouth

Coca-Cola Football League Two
Accrington S v Darlington
Bristol R v Wycombe W
Bury v Chester C
Hereford U v Lincoln C
Macclesfield T v Hartlepool U
Mansfield T v Milton Keynes Dons
Notts Co v Shrewsbury T
Swindon T v Barnet
Torquay U v Rochdale
Walsall v Stockport Co
Wrexham v Grimsby T

Wednesday, 9 August 2006
**Coca-Cola Football League
Championship**
Southampton v Coventry C

Coca-Cola Football League One
Chesterfield v Carlisle U

Coca-Cola Football League Two
Boston U v Peterborough U

Friday, 11 August 2006
Coca-Cola Football League Championship
Wolverhampton W v Preston NE* (7.45)

Saturday, 12 August 2006
Coca-Cola Football League Championship
Cardiff C v Coventry C
Colchester U v Barnsley
Hull C v Derby Co* (5.30)
Leicester C v Ipswich T
Norwich C v Luton T
QPR v Southend U
Sheffield W v Burnley
Southampton v WBA
Stoke C v Birmingham C* (12.30)
Sunderland v Plymouth Arg

Sunday, 13 August 2006
Coca-Cola Football League Championship
Crystal Palace v Leeds U* (12.00)

Coca-Cola Football League One
Blackpool v Rotherham U
Bradford C v Gillingham
Brighton & HA v Brentford
Cheltenham T v Port Vale
Chesterfield v Millwall
Doncaster R v Tranmere R
Huddersfield T v Bristol C
Leyton Orient v Bournemouth
Northampton T v Nottingham F
Oldham Ath v Swansea C
Scunthorpe U v Crewe Alex
Yeovil T v Carlisle U

Coca-Cola Football League Two
Accrington S v Barnet
Boston U v Darlington
Bristol R v Grimsby T
Bury v Shrewsbury T
Hereford U v Chester C
Macclesfield T v Milton Keynes Dons
Mansfield T v Stockport Co
Notts Co v Wycombe W
Swindon T v Rochdale
Torquay U v Lincoln C
Walsall v Hartlepool U
Wrexham v Peterborough U

Friday, 18 August 2006
Coca-Cola Football League Championship
Coventry C v Leicester C (7.45)

Saturday, 19 August 2006
Barclays Premiership
Arsenal v Aston Villa
Bolton W v Tottenham H† (5.15)
Everton v Watford
Newcastle U v Wigan Ath
Portsmouth v Blackburn R
Reading v Middlesbrough
Sheffield U v Liverpool* (12.45)
West Ham U v Charlton Ath

Coca-Cola Football League Championship
Barnsley v Southampton
Birmingham C v Crystal Palace
Burnley v Wolverhampton W
Derby Co v Norwich C
Ipswich T v Hull C
Leeds U v Cardiff C
Luton T v Stoke C
Plymouth Arg v Sheffield W
Preston NE v QPR
Southend U v Sunderland
WBA v Colchester U

Coca-Cola Football League One
Bournemouth v Cheltenham T
Brentford v Huddersfield T
Bristol C v Blackpool
Carlisle U v Leyton Orient
Crewe Alex v Bradford C
Gillingham v Northampton T
Millwall v Oldham Ath
Nottingham F v Brighton & HA
Port Vale v Chesterfield
Rotherham U v Scunthorpe U
Swansea C v Doncaster R
Tranmere R v Yeovil T

Coca-Cola Football League Two
Barnet v Hereford U
Chester C v Wrexham
Darlington v Swindon T
Grimsby T v Mansfield T
Hartlepool U v Torquay U
Lincoln C v Walsall
Milton Keynes Dons v Bristol R
Peterborough U v Macclesfield T
Rochdale v Notts Co
Shrewsbury T v Boston U
Stockport Co v Accrington S
Wycombe W v Bury

Sunday, 20 August 2006
Barclays Premiership
Chelsea v Manchester C* (4.00)
Manchester U v Fulham† (1.30)

Tuesday, 22 August 2006
Barclays Premiership
Charlton Ath v Manchester U
Middlesbrough v Chelsea
Tottenham H v Sheffield U
Watford v West Ham U
Wigan Ath v Arsenal

Wednesday, 23 August 2006
Barclays Premiership
Aston Villa v Reading
Blackburn R v Everton
Fulham v Bolton W
Manchester C v Portsmouth

Friday, 25 August 2006
Coca-Cola Football League
Championship
QPR v Ipswich T* (7.45)

Saturday, 26 August 2006
Barclays Premiership
Aston Villa v Newcastle U
Charlton Ath v Bolton W
Fulham v Sheffield U
Liverpool v West Ham U† (12.45)
Manchester C v Arsenal† (5.15)
Tottenham H v Everton
Watford v Manchester U
Wigan Ath v Reading

Coca-Cola Football League
Championship
Cardiff C v Birmingham C
Colchester U v Derby Co
Crystal Palace v Burnley
Hull C v Coventry C
Leicester C v Southend U
Norwich C v Barnsley
Southampton v Preston NE
Stoke C v Plymouth Arg
Wolverhampton W v Luton T

Coca-Cola Football League One
Blackpool v Gillingham
Bradford C v Rotherham U
Brighton & HA v Crewe Alex
Cheltenham T v Millwall
Chesterfield v Tranmere R
Doncaster R v Bournemouth
Huddersfield T v Nottingham F
Leyton Orient v Swansea C
Oldham Ath v Carlisle U

Scunthorpe U v Brentford
Yeovil T v Port Vale

Coca-Cola Football League Two
Accrington S v Rochdale
Boston U v Milton Keynes Dons
Bristol R v Shrewsbury T
Bury v Grimsby T
Hereford U v Hartlepool U
Macclesfield T v Wycombe W
Mansfield T v Lincoln C
Notts Co v Peterborough U
Swindon T v Stockport Co
Torquay U v Chester C
Walsall v Darlington
Wrexham v Barnet

Sunday, 27 August 2006
Barclays Premiership
Blackburn R v Chelsea* (4.00)

Coca-Cola Football League
Championship
Sheffield W v Leeds U* (1.15)

Monday, 28 August 2006
Barclays Premiership
Middlesbrough v Portsmouth* (8.00)

Coca-Cola Football League
Championship
Sunderland v WBA* (3.00)

Tuesday, 29 August 2006
Northampton T v Bristol C* (7.45)

Saturday, 2 September 2006
Coca-Cola Football League One
Bournemouth v Oldham Ath
Brentford v Bradford C
Bristol C v Brighton & HA
Carlisle U v Cheltenham T
Crewe Alex v Huddersfield T* (12.15)
Gillingham v Scunthorpe U
Millwall v Blackpool
Nottingham F v Chesterfield
Rotherham U v Northampton T
Swansea C v Yeovil T
Tranmere R v Leyton Orient

Coca-Cola Football League Two
Barnet v Walsall
Chester C v Swindon T
Darlington v Torquay U
Grimsby T v Macclesfield T
Hartlepool U v Boston U
Lincoln C v Accrington S
Milton Keynes Dons v Notts Co
Peterborough U v Bury

Rochdale v Hereford U
Shrewsbury T v Wrexham
Stockport Co v Bristol R
Wycombe W v Mansfield T

Sunday, 3 September 2006
Coca-Cola Football League One
Port Vale v Doncaster R* (4.00)

Saturday, 9 September 2006
Barclays Premiership
Arsenal v Middlesbrough
Bolton W v Watford
Chelsea v Charlton Ath
Everton v Liverpool† (12.45)
Manchester U v Tottenham H† (5.15)
Newcastle U v Fulham
Portsmouth v Wigan Ath
Sheffield U v Blackburn R

Coca-Cola Football League
Championship
Barnsley v Stoke C
Birmingham C v Hull C
Burnley v Colchester U
Coventry C v Norwich C
Derby Co v Sunderland
Ipswich T v Southampton
Luton T v Crystal Palace
Plymouth Arg v QPR
Preston NE v Cardiff C
Southend U v Sheffield W
WBA v Leicester C

Coca-Cola Football League One
Bournemouth v Crewe Alex
Carlisle U v Northampton T
Cheltenham T v Huddersfield T
Chesterfield v Rotherham U
Doncaster R v Gillingham
Leyton Orient v Brentford
Millwall v Brighton & HA
Oldham Ath v Scunthorpe U
Port Vale v Blackpool
Swansea C v Bradford C
Tranmere R v Bristol C
Yeovil T v Nottingham F

Coca-Cola Football League Two
Boston U v Stockport Co
Bristol R v Rochdale
Bury v Torquay U
Grimsby T v Walsall
Macclesfield T v Barnet
Mansfield T v Hereford U
Milton Keynes Dons v Hartlepool U
Notts Co v Accrington S
Peterborough U v Darlington
Shrewsbury T v Lincoln C

Wrexham v Swindon T
Wycombe W v Chester C

Sunday, 10 September 2006
Barclays Premiership
West Ham U v Aston Villa* (4.00)

Coca-Cola Football League
Championship
Leeds U v Wolverhampton W* (1.15)

Monday, 11 September 2006
Barclays Premiership
Reading v Manchester C* (8.00)

Tuesday, 12 September 2006
Coca-Cola Football League
Championship
Burnley v Barnsley
Crystal Palace v Southampton
Ipswich T v Coventry C
Leeds U v Sunderland
Leicester C v Hull C
Luton T v Colchester U
Plymouth Arg v Cardiff C
Preston NE v WBA
QPR v Birmingham C
Sheffield W v Stoke C
Southend U v Norwich C
Wolverhampton W v Derby Co

Coca-Cola Football League One
Blackpool v Chesterfield
Bradford C v Carlisle U
Brentford v Swansea C
Brighton & HA v Bournemouth
Bristol C v Leyton Orient
Crewe Alex v Cheltenham T
Gillingham v Millwall
Huddersfield T v Doncaster R
Northampton T v Yeovil T
Nottingham F v Oldham Ath
Rotherham U v Tranmere R
Scunthorpe U v Port Vale

Coca-Cola Football League Two
Accrington S v Wrexham
Barnet v Boston U
Chester C v Notts Co
Darlington v Bury
Hartlepool U v Mansfield T
Hereford U v Wycombe W
Lincoln C v Macclesfield T
Rochdale v Grimsby T
Stockport Co v Shrewsbury T
Swindon T v Milton Keynes Dons
Torquay U v Bristol R
Walsall v Peterborough U

Friday, 15 September 2006
Coca-Cola Football League Championship
Hull C v Sheffield W* (7.45)

Saturday, 16 September 2006
Barclays Premiership
Blackburn R v Manchester C
Bolton W v Middlesbrough
Charlton Ath v Portsmouth† (12.45)
Everton v Wigan Ath
Sheffield U v Reading
Tottenham H v Fulham
Watford v Aston Villa† (5.15)

Coca-Cola Football League Championship
Barnsley v Wolverhampton W
Birmingham C v Ipswich T
Cardiff C v Luton T
Colchester U v QPR
Coventry C v Leeds U
Derby Co v Preston NE
Norwich C v Crystal Palace
Southampton v Plymouth Arg
Stoke C v Burnley
Sunderland v Leicester C
WBA v Southend U

Coca-Cola Football League One
Blackpool v Oldham Ath
Bradford C v Port Vale
Brentford v Bournemouth
Brighton & HA v Leyton Orient
Bristol C v Chesterfield
Crewe Alex v Millwall
Gillingham v Swansea C
Huddersfield T v Yeovil T
Northampton T v Tranmere R
Nottingham F v Carlisle U
Rotherham U v Doncaster R
Scunthorpe U v Cheltenham T

Coca-Cola Football League Two
Accrington S v Boston U
Barnet v Notts Co
Chester C v Grimsby T
Darlington v Bristol R
Hartlepool U v Shrewsbury T
Hereford U v Bury
Lincoln C v Milton Keynes Dons
Rochdale v Wycombe W
Stockport Co v Wrexham
Swindon T v Peterborough U
Torquay U v Mansfield T
Walsall v Macclesfield T

Sunday, 17 September 2006
Barclays Premiership
Chelsea v Liverpool* (1.30)
Manchester U v Arsenal* (4.00)
West Ham U v Newcastle U (3.00)

Wednesday, 20 September 2006
Barclays Premiership
Liverpool v Newcastle U (8.00)

Friday, 22 September 2006
Coca-Cola Football League Championship
Preston NE v Barnsley* (7.45)

Saturday, 23 September 2006
Barclays Premiership
Arsenal v Sheffield U
Aston Villa v Charlton Ath
Fulham v Chelsea
Liverpool v Tottenham H* (12.45)
Manchester C v West Ham U
Middlesbrough v Blackburn R
Reading v Manchester U† (5.15)
Wigan Ath v Watford

Coca-Cola Football League Championship
Burnley v Southampton
Crystal Palace v Coventry C
Ipswich T v Sunderland
Leeds U v Birmingham C
Leicester C v Colchester U
Luton T v WBA
Plymouth Arg v Norwich C
QPR v Hull C
Sheffield W v Derby Co
Wolverhampton W v Stoke C

Coca-Cola Football League One
Bournemouth v Scunthorpe U
Carlisle U v Brighton & HA
Cheltenham T v Bradford C
Chesterfield v Brentford
Doncaster R v Blackpool
Leyton Orient v Rotherham U
Millwall v Northampton T
Oldham Ath v Gillingham
Port Vale v Bristol C
Swansea C v Huddersfield T
Tranmere R v Nottingham F
Yeovil T v Crewe Alex

Coca-Cola Football League Two
Boston U v Rochdale
Bristol R v Walsall
Bury v Barnet
Grimsby T v Stockport Co
Macclesfield T v Torquay U
Mansfield T v Accrington S

Milton Keynes Dons v Chester C
Notts Co v Swindon T
Peterborough U v Hartlepool U
Shrewsbury T v Darlington
Wrexham v Hereford U
Wycombe W v Lincoln C

Sunday, 24 September 2006
Barclays Premiership
Newcastle U v Everton* (4.00)

**Coca-Cola Football League
Championship**
Southend U v Cardiff C* (1.15)

Monday, 25 September 2006
Barclays Premiership
Portsmouth v Bolton W* (8.00)

Tuesday, 26 September 2006
Coca-Cola Football League One
Bournemouth v Bristol C
Carlisle U v Blackpool
Cheltenham T v Northampton T
Doncaster R v Bradford C
Leyton Orient v Gillingham
Millwall v Brentford
Oldham Ath v Rotherham U
Port Vale v Nottingham F
Swansea C v Crewe Alex
Tranmere R v Huddersfield T
Yeovil T v Brighton & HA

Coca-Cola Football League Two
Bristol R v Hereford U
Bury v Accrington S
Grimsby T v Hartlepool U
Macclesfield T v Chester C
Mansfield T v Darlington
Milton Keynes Dons v Torquay U
Notts Co v Stockport Co
Peterborough U v Barnet
Shrewsbury T v Walsall
Wrexham v Rochdale
Wycombe W v Swindon T

Wednesday, 27 September 2006
Coca-Cola Football League One
Chesterfield v Scunthorpe U

Coca-Cola Football League Two
Boston U v Lincoln C

Friday, 29 September 2006
**Coca-Cola Football League
Championship**
Colchester U v Ipswich T* (7.45)

Saturday, 30 September 2006
Barclays Premiership
Blackburn R v Wigan Ath
Bolton W v Liverpool* (12.45)
Charlton Ath v Arsenal
Chelsea v Aston Villa
Everton v Manchester C
Manchester U v Newcastle U
Sheffield U v Middlesbrough† (5.15)
West Ham U v Reading

**Coca-Cola Football League
Championship**
Barnsley v Luton T
Birmingham C v Leicester C
Cardiff C v Wolverhampton W
Coventry C v Plymouth Arg
Derby Co v Southend U
Hull C v Crystal Palace
Southampton v QPR
Stoke C v Preston NE
Sunderland v Sheffield W
WBA v Leeds U

Coca-Cola Football League One
Blackpool v Leyton Orient
Bradford C v Tranmere R
Brentford v Yeovil T
Brighton & HA v Chesterfield
Bristol C v Oldham Ath
Crewe Alex v Carlisle U
Gillingham v Cheltenham T
Huddersfield T v Bournemouth
Northampton T v Port Vale
Nottingham F v Swansea C
Rotherham U v Millwall
Scunthorpe U v Doncaster R

Coca-Cola Football League Two
Accrington S v Wycombe W
Barnet v Milton Keynes Dons
Chester C v Bristol R
Darlington v Grimsby T
Hartlepool U v Wrexham
Hereford U v Macclesfield T
Lincoln C v Bury
Rochdale v Shrewsbury T
Stockport Co v Peterborough U
Swindon T v Boston U
Torquay U v Notts Co
Walsall v Mansfield T

Sunday, 1 October 2006
Barclays Premiership
Tottenham H v Portsmouth* (4.00)

**Coca-Cola Football League
Championship**
Norwich C v Burnley* (1.15)

Monday, 2 October 2006
Barclays Premiership
Watford v Fulham* (8.00)

Saturday, 7 October 2006
Coca-Cola Football League One
Bournemouth v Northampton T
Bradford C v Huddersfield T
Brentford v Bristol C
Carlisle U v Millwall
Crewe Alex v Gillingham
Doncaster R v Oldham Ath
Leyton Orient v Chesterfield
Nottingham F v Scunthorpe U* (12.15)
Port Vale v Rotherham U
Swansea C v Tranmere R
Yeovil T v Cheltenham T

Coca-Cola Football League Two
Accrington S v Swindon T
Bristol R v Boston U
Bury v Wrexham
Chester C v Walsall
Darlington v Rochdale
Lincoln C v Hartlepool U
Mansfield T v Notts Co
Milton Keynes Dons v Peterborough U
Shrewsbury T v Macclesfield T
Stockport Co v Barnet
Wycombe W v Torquay U

Sunday, 8 October 2006
Coca-Cola Football League One
Brighton & HA v Blackpool* (1.30)

Coca-Cola Football League Two
Grimsby T v Hereford U* (4.00)

Saturday, 14 October 2006
Barclays Premiership
Arsenal v Watford
Aston Villa v Tottenham H
Liverpool v Blackburn R
Manchester C v Sheffield U
Middlesbrough v Everton
Portsmouth v West Ham U
Reading v Chelsea† (5.15)
Wigan Ath v Manchester U* (12.45)

Coca-Cola Football League Championship
Burnley v Hull C
Crystal Palace v Cardiff C
Ipswich T v WBA
Leeds U v Stoke C
Leicester C v Southampton
Luton T v Birmingham C
Preston NE v Sunderland
QPR v Norwich C

Sheffield W v Barnsley
Southend U v Coventry C
Wolverhampton W v Colchester U

Coca-Cola Football League One
Blackpool v Yeovil T
Bristol C v Crewe Alex
Cheltenham T v Doncaster R
Chesterfield v Swansea C
Gillingham v Nottingham F
Huddersfield T v Carlisle U
Millwall v Bournemouth
Northampton T v Bradford C
Oldham Ath v Leyton Orient
Rotherham U v Brentford
Scunthorpe U v Brighton & HA
Tranmere R v Port Vale

Coca-Cola Football League Two
Barnet v Lincoln C
Boston U v Mansfield T
Hartlepool U v Stockport Co
Hereford U v Darlington
Macclesfield T v Bury
Notts Co v Bristol R
Peterborough U v Shrewsbury T
Rochdale v Chester C
Swindon T v Grimsby T
Torquay U v Accrington S
Walsall v Wycombe W
Wrexham v Milton Keynes Dons

Sunday, 15 October 2006
Barclays Premiership
Newcastle U v Bolton W* (4.00)

Coca-Cola Football League Championship
Plymouth Arg v Derby Co* (1.15)

Monday, 16 October 2006
Barclays Premiership
Fulham v Charlton Ath* (8.00)

Tuesday, 17 October 2006
Coca-Cola Football League Championship
Barnsley v Plymouth Arg
Birmingham C v Norwich C
Burnley v Southend U
Cardiff C v Southampton
Colchester U v Sheffield W
Crystal Palace v WBA
Hull C v Luton T
Ipswich T v Preston NE
Leeds U v Leicester C
QPR v Derby Co
Stoke C v Sunderland
Wolverhampton W v Coventry C

Saturday, 21 October 2006
Barclays Premiership
Aston Villa v Fulham† (5.15)
Blackburn R v Bolton W
Charlton Ath v Watford
Chelsea v Portsmouth
Everton v Sheffield U
Middlesbrough v Newcastle U
Tottenham H v West Ham U
Wigan Ath v Manchester C† (12.45)

**Coca-Cola Football League
Championship**
Coventry C v Colchester U
Derby Co v Birmingham C
Leicester C v Crystal Palace
Luton T v Leeds U
Norwich C v Cardiff C
Plymouth Arg v Burnley
Preston NE v Hull C
Sheffield W v QPR
Southampton v Stoke C
Southend U v Ipswich T
Sunderland v Barnsley
WBA v Wolverhampton W

Coca-Cola Football League One
Bournemouth v Rotherham U
Bradford C v Scunthorpe U
Brentford v Gillingham
Brighton & HA v Northampton T
Carlisle U v Tranmere R
Crewe Alex v Blackpool
Doncaster R v Chesterfield
Leyton Orient v Cheltenham T
Nottingham F v Bristol C
Port Vale v Huddersfield T
Swansea C v Millwall
Yeovil T v Oldham Ath

Coca-Cola Football League Two
Accrington S v Walsall
Bristol R v Macclesfield T
Bury v Boston U
Chester C v Hartlepool U
Darlington v Barnet
Grimsby T v Notts Co
Lincoln C v Rochdale
Mansfield T v Wrexham
Milton Keynes Dons v Hereford U
Shrewsbury T v Swindon T
Stockport Co v Torquay U
Wycombe W v Peterborough U

Sunday, 22 October 2006
Barclays Premiership
Manchester U v Liverpool* (1.00)
Reading v Arsenal* (4.00)

Friday, 27 October 2006
**Coca-Cola Football League
Championship**
Burnley v Preston NE* (7.45)

Saturday, 28 October 2006
Barclays Premiership
Arsenal v Everton
Bolton W v Manchester U
Fulham v Wigan Ath
Liverpool v Aston Villa
Newcastle U v Charlton Ath† (5.15)
Portsmouth v Reading
Sheffield U v Chelsea† (12.45)
Watford v Tottenham H

**Coca-Cola Football League
Championship**
Barnsley v Coventry C
Birmingham C v WBA
Cardiff C v Derby Co
Colchester U v Southampton
Crystal Palace v Plymouth Arg
Hull C v Sunderland
Leeds U v Southend U
QPR v Leicester C
Stoke C v Norwich C
Wolverhampton W v Sheffield W

Coca-Cola Football League One
Blackpool v Bradford C
Bristol C v Doncaster R
Cheltenham T v Nottingham F
Chesterfield v Yeovil T
Gillingham v Carlisle U
Huddersfield T v Brighton & HA
Millwall v Port Vale
Northampton T v Swansea C
Oldham Ath v Brentford
Rotherham U v Crewe Alex
Scunthorpe U v Leyton Orient
Tranmere R v Bournemouth

Coca-Cola Football League Two
Barnet v Chester C
Boston U v Wycombe W
Hartlepool U v Darlington
Hereford U v Accrington S
Macclesfield T v Mansfield T
Notts Co v Bury
Peterborough U v Grimsby T
Rochdale v Stockport Co
Swindon T v Lincoln C
Torquay U v Shrewsbury T
Walsall v Milton Keynes Dons
Wrexham v Bristol R

Sunday, 29 October 2006
Barclays Premiership
West Ham U v Blackburn R* (4.00)

Coca-Cola Football League
Championship
Ipswich T v Luton T* (1.15)

Monday, 30 October 2006
Barclays Premiership
Manchester C v Middlesbrough* (8.00)

Tuesday, 31 October 2006
Coca-Cola Football League
Championship
Coventry C v Birmingham C
Leicester C v Stoke C
Luton T v Burnley
Norwich C v Colchester U
Plymouth Arg v Ipswich T
Preston NE v Leeds U
Sheffield W v Crystal Palace
Southend U v Hull C
Sunderland v Cardiff C
WBA v QPR

Wednesday, 1 November 2006
Coca-Cola Football League
Championship
Derby Co v Barnsley
Southampton v Wolverhampton W

Saturday, 4 November 2006
Barclays Premiership
Aston Villa v Blackburn R
Bolton W v Wigan Ath
Charlton Ath v Manchester C
Fulham v Everton* (12.45)
Liverpool v Reading
Manchester U v Portsmouth
Newcastle U v Sheffield U† (5.15)
Watford v Middlesbrough

Coca-Cola Football League
Championship
Barnsley v Leeds U
Burnley v Ipswich T
Colchester U v Cardiff C
Derby Co v WBA
Norwich C v Sunderland
Plymouth Arg v Birmingham C
Preston NE v Luton T
QPR v Crystal Palace
Sheffield W v Leicester C
Southampton v Hull C
Stoke C v Coventry C
Wolverhampton W v Southend U

Coca-Cola Football League One
Bradford C v Brighton & HA
Carlisle U v Rotherham U
Cheltenham T v Oldham Ath
Crewe Alex v Port Vale
Doncaster R v Leyton Orient
Gillingham v Chesterfield
Huddersfield T v Scunthorpe U
Northampton T v Blackpool
Nottingham F v Brentford
Swansea C v Bournemouth
Tranmere R v Millwall
Yeovil T v Bristol C

Coca-Cola Football League Two
Boston U v Notts Co
Bristol R v Mansfield T
Darlington v Chester C
Grimsby T v Milton Keynes Dons
Hartlepool U v Barnet
Peterborough U v Accrington S
Rochdale v Bury
Shrewsbury T v Wycombe W
Stockport Co v Lincoln C
Swindon T v Hereford U
Walsall v Torquay U
Wrexham v Macclesfield T

Sunday, 5 November 2006
Barclays Premiership
Tottenham H v Chelsea* (4.00)
West Ham U v Arsenal* (1.30)

Saturday, 11 November 2006
Barclays Premiership
Blackburn R v Manchester U† (5.15)
Chelsea v Watford
Everton v Aston Villa
Manchester C v Newcastle U* (12.45)
Middlesbrough v West Ham U
Portsmouth v Fulham
Sheffield U v Bolton W
Wigan Ath v Charlton Ath

Coca-Cola Football League
Championship
Birmingham C v Barnsley
Cardiff C v Burnley
Coventry C v Derby Co
Crystal Palace v Stoke C
Hull C v Wolverhampton W
Ipswich T v Sheffield W
Leeds U v Colchester U
Leicester C v Plymouth Arg
Luton T v QPR
Southend U v Preston NE
Sunderland v Southampton
WBA v Norwich C

Sunday, 12 November 2006
Barclays Premiership
Arsenal v Liverpool* (4.00)
Reading v Tottenham H* (1.30)

Saturday, 18 November 2006
Barclays Premiership
Arsenal v Newcastle U
Chelsea v West Ham U
Everton v Bolton W
Manchester C v Fulham† (12.45)
Middlesbrough v Liverpool (5.15)
Portsmouth v Watford
Reading v Charlton Ath
Sheffield U v Manchester U

Coca-Cola Football League
Championship
Birmingham C v Wolverhampton W
Cardiff C v QPR
Coventry C v Sheffield W
Crystal Palace v Barnsley
Hull C v Stoke C
Ipswich T v Norwich C
Leeds U v Southampton
Leicester C v Preston NE
Luton T v Derby Co
Southend U v Plymouth Arg
Sunderland v Colchester U
WBA v Burnley

Coca-Cola Football League One
Blackpool v Huddersfield T
Bournemouth v Carlisle U
Brentford v Crewe Alex
Brighton & HA v Tranmere R
Bristol C v Gillingham
Chesterfield v Cheltenham T
Leyton Orient v Yeovil T
Millwall v Doncaster R
Oldham Ath v Bradford C
Port Vale v Swansea C
Rotherham U v Nottingham F
Scunthorpe U v Northampton T

Coca-Cola Football League Two
Accrington S v Hartlepool U
Barnet v Rochdale
Bury v Bristol R
Chester C v Stockport Co
Hereford U v Walsall
Lincoln C v Darlington
Macclesfield T v Boston U
Mansfield T v Peterborough U
Milton Keynes Dons v Shrewsbury T
Notts Co v Wrexham
Torquay U v Swindon T
Wycombe W v Grimsby T

Sunday, 19 November 2006
Barclays Premiership
Blackburn R v Tottenham H* (4.00)
Wigan Ath v Aston Villa* (1.30)

Saturday, 25 November 2006
Barclays Premiership
Aston Villa v Middlesbrough
Bolton W v Arsenal† (5.15)
Charlton Ath v Everton† (12.45)
Fulham v Reading
Liverpool v Manchester C
Tottenham H v Wigan Ath
Watford v Blackburn R
West Ham U v Sheffield U

Coca-Cola Football League
Championship
Barnsley v Ipswich T
Burnley v Birmingham C
Colchester U v Southend U
Derby Co v Leicester C
Norwich C v Hull C
Plymouth Arg v Leeds U
Preston NE v Crystal Palace
QPR v Coventry C
Sheffield W v Cardiff C
Southampton v Luton T
Stoke C v WBA
Wolverhampton W v Sunderland

Coca-Cola Football League One
Bradford C v Bournemouth
Carlisle U v Port Vale
Cheltenham T v Brentford
Crewe Alex v Chesterfield
Doncaster R v Brighton & HA
Gillingham v Rotherham U
Huddersfield T v Oldham Ath
Northampton T v Leyton Orient
Nottingham F v Millwall
Swansea C v Bristol C
Tranmere R v Blackpool
Yeovil T v Scunthorpe U

Coca-Cola Football League Two
Boston U v Hereford U
Bristol R v Barnet
Darlington v Milton Keynes Dons
Grimsby T v Accrington S
Hartlepool U v Wycombe W
Peterborough U v Torquay U
Rochdale v Mansfield T
Shrewsbury T v Chester C
Stockport Co v Macclesfield T
Swindon T v Bury
Walsall v Notts Co
Wrexham v Lincoln C

Sunday, 26 November 2006
Barclays Premiership
Newcastle U v Portsmouth* (1.30)
Manchester U v Chelsea* (4.00)

Tuesday, 28 November 2006
Barclays Premiership
Watford v Sheffield U* (8.00)

Coca-Cola Football League
Championship
Barnsley v Southend U
Burnley v Leeds U
Colchester U v Hull C
Norwich C v Leicester C
Plymouth Arg v Luton T
Preston NE v Coventry C
QPR v Sunderland
Sheffield W v WBA
Stoke C v Cardiff C
Wolverhampton W v Crystal Palace

Wednesday, 29 November 2006
Barclays Premiership
Bolton W v Chelsea* (8.00)
Aston Villa v Manchester C
Fulham v Arsenal
Liverpool v Portsmouth
Manchester U v Everton

Coca-Cola Football League
Championship
Derby Co v Ipswich T
Southampton v Birmingham C

Saturday, 2 December 2006
Barclays Premiership
Arsenal v Tottenham H† (12.45)
Blackburn R v Fulham
Chelsea v Newcastle U
Middlesbrough v Manchester U† (5.15)
Portsmouth v Aston Villa
Reading v Bolton W
Sheffield U v Charlton Ath
Wigan Ath v Liverpool

Coca-Cola Football League
Championship
Birmingham C v Plymouth Arg
Cardiff C v Colchester U
Coventry C v Stoke C
Crystal Palace v QPR
Hull C v Southampton
Ipswich T v Burnley
Leeds U v Barnsley
Leicester C v Sheffield W
Luton T v Preston NE
Southend U v Wolverhampton W
Sunderland v Norwich C
WBA v Derby Co

Sunday, 3 December 2006
Barclays Premiership
Everton v West Ham U* (4.00)

Monday, 4 December 2006
Barclays Premiership
Manchester C v Watford* (8.00)

Tuesday, 5 December 2006
Barclays Premiership
Charlton Ath v Blackburn R
Tottenham H v Middlesbrough

Coca-Cola Football League One
Blackpool v Cheltenham T
Bournemouth v Nottingham F
Brentford v Doncaster R
Brighton & HA v Swansea C
Bristol C v Carlisle U
Leyton Orient v Bradford C
Millwall v Huddersfield T
Oldham Ath v Crewe Alex
Port Vale v Gillingham
Rotherham U v Yeovil T
Scunthorpe U v Tranmere R

Coca-Cola Football League Two
Accrington S v Shrewsbury T
Barnet v Grimsby T
Bury v Walsall
Chester C v Boston U
Hereford U v Peterborough U
Lincoln C v Bristol R
Macclesfield T v Rochdale
Mansfield T v Swindon T
Milton Keynes Dons v Stockport Co
Notts Co v Hartlepool U
Torquay U v Wrexham
Wycombe W v Darlington

Wednesday, 6 December 2006
Barclays Premiership
Newcastle U v Reading
West Ham U v Wigan Ath

Coca-Cola Football League One
Chesterfield v Northampton T

Saturday, 9 December 2006
Barclays Premiership
Blackburn R v Newcastle U
Bolton W v West Ham U† (5.15)
Liverpool v Fulham
Manchester U v Manchester C† (12.45)
Middlesbrough v Wigan Ath
Portsmouth v Everton
Tottenham H v Charlton Ath
Watford v Reading

**Coca-Cola Football League
Championship**
Barnsley v WBA
Birmingham C v Preston NE
Cardiff C v Ipswich T
Coventry C v Burnley
Crystal Palace v Colchester U
Leeds U v Derby Co
Norwich C v Sheffield W
Plymouth Arg v Hull C
Southend U v Southampton
Stoke C v QPR
Sunderland v Luton T
Wolverhampton W v Leicester C

Coca-Cola Football League One
Blackpool v Swansea C
Bournemouth v Port Vale
Brentford v Tranmere R
Brighton & HA v Cheltenham T
Carlisle U v Scunthorpe U
Chesterfield v Oldham Ath
Crewe Alex v Nottingham F
Leyton Orient v Huddersfield T
Millwall v Bradford C
Northampton T v Doncaster R
Rotherham U v Bristol C
Yeovil T v Gillingham

Coca-Cola Football League Two
Accrington S v Milton Keynes Dons
Boston U v Wrexham
Bristol R v Hartlepool U
Chester C v Lincoln C
Grimsby T v Shrewsbury T
Hereford U v Torquay U
Mansfield T v Bury
Notts Co v Macclesfield T
Rochdale v Peterborough U
Stockport Co v Darlington
Walsall v Swindon T
Wycombe W v Barnet

**Saturday, 10 December 2006
Barclays Premiership**
Chelsea v Arsenal* (4.00)

**Monday, 11 December 2006
Barclays Premiership**
Sheffield U v Aston Villa* (8.00)

**Saturday, 16 December 2006
Barclays Premiership**
Arsenal v Portsmouth
Aston Villa v Bolton W
Charlton Ath v Liverpool† (12.45)
Fulham v Middlesbrough
Manchester C v Tottenham H† (5.15)
Newcastle U v Watford

Reading v Blackburn R
Wigan Ath v Sheffield U

**Coca-Cola Football League
Championship**
Burnley v Sunderland
Colchester U v Stoke C
Derby Co v Crystal Palace
Hull C v Cardiff C
Ipswich T v Leeds U
Leicester C v Barnsley
Luton T v Southend U
Preston NE v Plymouth Arg
QPR v Wolverhampton W
Sheffield W v Birmingham C
Southampton v Norwich C
WBA v Coventry C

Coca-Cola Football League One
Bradford C v Chesterfield
Bristol C v Millwall
Cheltenham T v Rotherham U
Doncaster R v Yeovil T
Gillingham v Bournemouth
Huddersfield T v Northampton T
Nottingham F v Leyton Orient
Oldham Ath v Brighton & HA
Port Vale v Brentford
Scunthorpe U v Blackpool
Swansea C v Carlisle U
Tranmere R v Crewe Alex

Coca-Cola Football League Two
Barnet v Mansfield T
Bury v Stockport Co
Darlington v Notts Co
Hartlepool U v Rochdale
Lincoln C v Grimsby T
Macclesfield T v Accrington S
Milton Keynes Dons v Wycombe W
Peterborough U v Chester C
Shrewsbury T v Hereford U
Swindon T v Bristol R
Torquay U v Boston U
Wrexham v Walsall

**Sunday, 17 December 2006
Barclays Premiership**
Everton v Chelsea* (1.30)
West Ham U v Manchester U* (4.00)

**Saturday, 23 December 2006
Barclays Premiership**
Arsenal v Blackburn R
Aston Villa v Manchester U
Fulham v West Ham U* (12.45)
Liverpool v Watford
Manchester C v Bolton W
Middlesbrough v Charlton Ath

Newcastle U v Tottenham H
Portsmouth v Sheffield U
Reading v Everton
Wigan Ath v Chelsea† (5.15)

**Coca-Cola Football League
Championship**
Burnley v Derby Co
Crystal Palace v Sunderland
Ipswich T v Stoke C
Leeds U v Hull C
Leicester C v Cardiff C
Luton T v Coventry C
Plymouth Arg v WBA
Preston NE v Colchester U
QPR v Barnsley
Sheffield W v Southampton
Southend U v Birmingham C
Wolverhampton W v Norwich C

Coca-Cola Football League One
Bournemouth v Blackpool
Carlisle U v Brentford
Cheltenham T v Bristol C
Chesterfield v Huddersfield T
Doncaster R v Nottingham F
Leyton Orient v Crewe Alex
Millwall v Scunthorpe U
Oldham Ath v Northampton T
Port Vale v Brighton & HA
Swansea C v Rotherham U
Tranmere R v Gillingham
Yeovil T v Bradford C

Coca-Cola Football League Two
Boston U v Walsall
Bristol R v Accrington S
Bury v Hartlepool U
Grimsby T v Torquay U
Macclesfield T v Swindon T
Mansfield T v Chester C
Milton Keynes Dons v Rochdale
Notts Co v Hereford U
Peterborough U v Lincoln C
Shrewsbury T v Barnet
Wrexham v Darlington
Wycombe W v Stockport Co

Tuesday, 26 December 2006
Barclays Premiership
Blackburn R v Liverpool† (3.00)
Bolton W v Newcastle U
Chelsea v Reading* (1.00)
Everton v Middlesbrough
Manchester U v Wigan Ath
Sheffield U v Manchester C
Tottenham H v Aston Villa
Watford v Arsenal* (5.30)
West Ham U v Portsmouth

**Coca-Cola Football League
Championship**
Barnsley v Burnley
Birmingham C v QPR
Cardiff C v Plymouth Arg
Colchester U v Luton T
Coventry C v Ipswich T
Derby Co v Wolverhampton W
Hull C v Leicester C
Norwich C v Southend U
Southampton v Crystal Palace
Stoke C v Sheffield W
Sunderland v Leeds U
WBA v Preston NE

Coca-Cola Football League One
Blackpool v Carlisle U
Bradford C v Doncaster R
Brentford v Millwall
Brighton & HA v Yeovil T
Bristol C v Bournemouth
Crewe Alex v Swansea C
Gillingham v Leyton Orient
Huddersfield T v Tranmere R
Northampton T v Cheltenham T
Nottingham F v Port Vale
Rotherham U v Oldham Ath
Scunthorpe U v Chesterfield

Coca-Cola Football League Two
Accrington S v Bury
Barnet v Peterborough U
Chester C v Macclesfield S
Darlington v Mansfield T
Hartlepool U v Grimsby T
Hereford U v Bristol R
Lincoln C v Boston U
Rochdale v Wrexham
Stockport Co v Notts Co
Swindon T v Wycombe W
Torquay U v Milton Keynes Dons
Walsall v Shrewsbury T

Wednesday, 27 December 2006
Barclays Premiership
Charlton Ath v Fulham* (8.00)

Saturday, 30 December 2006
Barclays Premiership
Blackburn R v Middlesbrough
Bolton W v Portsmouth
Charlton Ath v Aston Villa
Chelsea v Fulham
Everton v Newcastle U
Manchester U v Reading
Sheffield U v Arsenal
Tottenham H v Liverpool
Watford v Wigan Ath
West Ham U v Manchester C

Coca-Cola Football League Championship
Barnsley v Sheffield W
Birmingham C v Luton T
Cardiff C v Crystal Palace
Colchester U v Wolverhampton W
Coventry C v Southend U
Derby Co v Plymouth Arg
Hull C v Burnley
Norwich C v QPR
Southampton v Leicester C
Stoke C v Leeds U
Sunderland v Preston NE
WBA v Ipswich T

Coca-Cola Football League One
Blackpool v Doncaster R
Bradford C v Cheltenham T
Brentford v Chesterfield
Brighton & HA v Carlisle U
Bristol C v Port Vale
Crewe Alex v Yeovil T
Gillingham v Oldham Ath
Huddersfield T v Swansea C
Northampton T v Millwall
Nottingham F v Tranmere R
Rotherham U v Leyton Orient
Scunthorpe U v Bournemouth

Coca-Cola Football League Two
Accrington S v Mansfield T
Barnet v Bury
Chester C v Milton Keynes Dons
Darlington v Shrewsbury T
Hartlepool U v Peterborough U
Hereford U v Wrexham
Lincoln C v Wycombe W
Rochdale v Boston U
Stockport Co v Grimsby T
Swindon T v Notts Co
Torquay U v Macclesfield T
Walsall v Bristol R

Monday, 1 January 2007
Barclays Premiership
Arsenal v Charlton Ath
Aston Villa v Chelsea
Fulham v Watford
Liverpool v Bolton W
Manchester C v Everton
Middlesbrough v Sheffield U
Newcastle U v Manchester U
Portsmouth v Tottenham H
Reading v West Ham U
Wigan Ath v Blackburn R

Coca-Cola Football League Championship
Burnley v Stoke C

Crystal Palace v Norwich C
Ipswich T v Birmingham C
Leeds U v Coventry C
Leicester C v Sunderland
Luton T v Cardiff C
Plymouth Arg v Southampton
Preston NE v Derby Co
QPR v Colchester U
Sheffield W v Hull C
Southend U v WBA
Wolverhampton W v Barnsley

Coca-Cola Football League One
Bournemouth v Brighton & HA
Carlisle U v Bradford C
Cheltenham T v Crewe Alex
Chesterfield v Blackpool
Doncaster R v Huddersfield T
Leyton Orient v Bristol C
Millwall v Gillingham
Oldham Ath v Nottingham F
Port Vale v Scunthorpe U
Swansea C v Brentford
Tranmere R v Rotherham U
Yeovil T v Northampton T

Coca-Cola Football League Two
Boston U v Barnet
Bristol R v Torquay U
Bury v Darlington
Grimsby T v Rochdale
Macclesfield T v Lincoln C
Mansfield T v Hartlepool U
Milton Keynes Dons v Swindon T
Notts Co v Chester C
Peterborough U v Walsall
Shrewsbury T v Stockport Co
Wrexham v Accrington S
Wycombe W v Hereford U

Saturday, 6 January 2007
Coca-Cola Football League One
Bournemouth v Brentford
Carlisle U v Nottingham F
Cheltenham T v Scunthorpe U
Chesterfield v Bristol C
Doncaster R v Rotherham U
Leyton Orient v Brighton & HA
Millwall v Crewe Alex
Oldham Ath v Blackpool
Port Vale v Bradford C
Swansea C v Gillingham
Tranmere R v Northampton T
Yeovil T v Huddersfield T

Coca-Cola Football League Two
Boston U v Accrington S
Bristol R v Darlington
Bury v Hereford U

348

Grimsby T v Chester C
Macclesfield T v Walsall
Mansfield T v Torquay U
Milton Keynes Dons v Lincoln C
Notts Co v Barnet
Peterborough U v Swindon T
Shrewsbury T v Hartlepool U
Wrexham v Stockport Co
Wycombe W v Rochdale

Saturday, 13 January 2007
Barclays Premiership
Blackburn R v Arsenal
Bolton W v Manchester C
Charlton Ath v Middlesbrough
Chelsea v Wigan Ath
Everton v Reading
Manchester U v Aston Villa
Sheffield U v Portsmouth
Tottenham H v Newcastle U
Watford v Liverpool
West Ham U v Fulham

Coca-Cola Football League Championship
Barnsley v Preston NE
Birmingham C v Leeds U
Cardiff C v Southend U
Colchester U v Leicester C
Coventry C v Crystal Palace
Derby Co v Sheffield W
Hull C v QPR
Norwich C v Plymouth Arg
Southampton v Burnley
Stoke C v Wolverhampton W
Sunderland v Ipswich T
WBA v Luton T

Coca-Cola Football League One
Blackpool v Port Vale
Bradford C v Swansea C
Brentford v Leyton Orient
Brighton & HA v Millwall
Bristol C v Tranmere R
Crewe Alex v Bournemouth
Gillingham v Doncaster R
Huddersfield T v Cheltenham T
Northampton T v Carlisle U
Nottingham F v Yeovil T
Rotherham U v Chesterfield
Scunthorpe U v Oldham Ath

Coca-Cola Football League Two
Accrington S v Notts Co
Barnet v Macclesfield T
Chester C v Wycombe W
Darlington v Peterborough U
Hartlepool U v Milton Keynes Dons
Hereford U v Mansfield T

Lincoln C v Shrewsbury T
Rochdale v Bristol R
Stockport Co v Boston U
Swindon T v Wrexham
Torquay U v Bury
Walsall v Grimsby T

Saturday, 20 January 2007
Barclays Premiership
Arsenal v Manchester U
Aston Villa v Watford
Fulham v Tottenham H
Liverpool v Chelsea
Manchester C v Blackburn R
Middlesbrough v Bolton W
Newcastle U v West Ham U
Portsmouth v Charlton Ath
Reading v Sheffield U
Wigan Ath v Everton

Coca-Cola Football League Championship
Burnley v Norwich C
Crystal Palace v Hull C
Ipswich T v Colchester U
Leeds U v WBA
Leicester C v Birmingham C
Luton T v Barnsley
Plymouth Arg v Coventry C
Preston NE v Stoke C
QPR v Southampton
Sheffield W v Sunderland
Southend U v Derby Co
Wolverhampton W v Cardiff C

Coca-Cola Football League One
Bournemouth v Huddersfield T
Carlisle U v Crewe Alex
Cheltenham T v Gillingham
Chesterfield v Brighton & HA
Doncaster R v Scunthorpe U
Leyton Orient v Blackpool
Millwall v Rotherham U
Oldham Ath v Bristol C
Port Vale v Northampton T
Swansea C v Nottingham F
Tranmere R v Bradford C
Yeovil T v Brentford

Coca-Cola Football League Two
Boston U v Swindon T
Bristol R v Chester C
Bury v Lincoln C
Grimsby T v Darlington
Macclesfield T v Hereford U
Mansfield T v Walsall
Milton Keynes Dons v Barnet
Notts Co v Torquay U
Peterborough U v Stockport Co

Shrewsbury T v Rochdale
Wrexham v Hartlepool U
Wycombe W v Accrington S

Saturday, 27 January 2007
Coca-Cola Football League One
Blackpool v Bournemouth
Bradford C v Yeovil T
Brentford v Carlisle U
Brighton & HA v Port Vale
Bristol C v Cheltenham T
Crewe Alex v Leyton Orient
Gillingham v Tranmere R
Huddersfield T v Chesterfield
Northampton T v Oldham Ath
Nottingham F v Doncaster R
Rotherham U v Swansea C
Scunthorpe U v Millwall

Coca-Cola Football League Two
Accrington S v Bristol R
Barnet v Shrewsbury T
Chester C v Mansfield T
Darlington v Wrexham
Hartlepool U v Bury
Hereford U v Notts Co
Lincoln C v Peterborough U
Rochdale v Milton Keynes Dons
Stockport Co v Wycombe W
Swindon T v Macclesfield T
Torquay U v Grimsby T
Walsall v Boston U

Tuesday, 30 January 2007
Barclays Premiership
Arsenal v Manchester C
Bolton W v Charlton Ath
Portsmouth v Middlesbrough
Reading v Wigan Ath
Sheffield U v Fulham

Coca-Cola Football League
Championship
Barnsley v QPR
Birmingham C v Southend U
Cardiff C v Leicester C
Colchester U v Preston NE
Coventry C v Luton T
Hull C v Leeds U
Norwich C v Wolverhampton W
Stoke C v Ipswich T
Sunderland v Crystal Palace
WBA v Plymouth Arg

Wednesday, 31 January 2007
Barclays Premiership
Chelsea v Blackburn R
Everton v Tottenham H
Manchester U v Watford

Newcastle U v Aston Villa
West Ham U v Liverpool

Coca-Cola Football League
Championship
Derby Co v Burnley
Southampton v Sheffield W

Saturday, 3 February 2007
Barclays Premiership
Aston Villa v West Ham U
Blackburn R v Sheffield U
Charlton Ath v Chelsea
Fulham v Newcastle U
Liverpool v Everton
Manchester C v Reading
Middlesbrough v Arsenal
Tottenham H v Manchester U
Watford v Bolton W
Wigan Ath v Portsmouth

Coca-Cola Football League
Championship
Cardiff C v Barnsley
Colchester U v Birmingham C
Crystal Palace v Ipswich T
Hull C v WBA
Leicester C v Luton T
Norwich C v Leeds U
QPR v Burnley
Sheffield W v Preston NE
Southampton v Derby Co
Stoke C v Southend U
Sunderland v Coventry C
Wolverhampton W v Plymouth Arg

Coca-Cola Football League One
Blackpool v Brentford
Bradford C v Nottingham F
Brighton & HA v Rotherham U
Cheltenham T v Swansea C
Chesterfield v Bournemouth
Doncaster R v Carlisle U
Huddersfield T v Gillingham
Leyton Orient v Port Vale
Northampton T v Crewe Alex
Oldham Ath v Tranmere R
Scunthorpe U v Bristol C
Yeovil T v Millwall

Coca-Cola Football League Two
Accrington S v Chester C
Boston U v Grimsby T
Bristol R v Peterborough U
Bury v Milton Keynes Dons
Hereford U v Stockport Co
Macclesfield T v Darlington
Mansfield T v Shrewsbury T
Notts Co v Lincoln C
Swindon T v Hartlepool U

Torquay U v Barnet
Walsall v Rochdale
Wrexham v Wycombe W

Saturday, 10 February 2007
Barclays Premiership
Arsenal v Wigan Ath
Bolton W v Fulham
Chelsea v Middlesbrough
Everton v Blackburn R
Manchester U v Charlton Ath
Newcastle U v Liverpool
Portsmouth v Manchester C
Reading v Aston Villa
Sheffield U v Tottenham H
West Ham U v Watford

Coca-Cola Football League Championship
Barnsley v Colchester U
Birmingham C v Stoke C
Burnley v Sheffield W
Coventry C v Cardiff C
Derby Co v Hull C
Ipswich T v Leicester C
Leeds U v Crystal Palace
Luton T v Norwich C
Plymouth Arg v Sunderland
Preston NE v Wolverhampton W
Southend U v QPR
WBA v Southampton

Coca-Cola Football League One
Bournemouth v Leyton Orient
Brentford v Brighton & HA
Bristol C v Huddersfield T
Carlisle U v Yeovil T
Crewe Alex v Scunthorpe U
Gillingham v Bradford C
Millwall v Chesterfield
Nottingham F v Northampton T
Port Vale v Cheltenham T
Rotherham U v Blackpool
Swansea C v Oldham Ath
Tranmere R v Doncaster R

Coca-Cola Football League Two
Barnet v Accrington S
Chester C v Hereford U
Darlington v Boston U
Grimsby T v Bristol R
Hartlepool U v Walsall
Lincoln C v Torquay U
Milton Keynes Dons v Macclesfield T
Peterborough U v Wrexham
Rochdale v Swindon T
Shrewsbury T v Bury
Stockport Co v Mansfield T
Wycombe W v Notts Co

Saturday, 17 February 2007
Coca-Cola Football League Championship
Cardiff C v Leeds U
Colchester U v WBA
Crystal Palace v Birmingham C
Hull C v Ipswich T
Leicester C v Coventry C
Norwich C v Derby Co
QPR v Preston NE
Sheffield W v Plymouth Arg
Southampton v Barnsley
Stoke C v Luton T
Sunderland v Southend U
Wolverhampton W v Burnley

Coca-Cola Football League One
Blackpool v Bristol C
Bradford C v Crewe Alex
Brighton & HA v Nottingham F
Cheltenham T v Bournemouth
Chesterfield v Port Vale
Doncaster R v Swansea C
Huddersfield T v Brentford
Leyton Orient v Carlisle U
Northampton T v Gillingham
Oldham Ath v Millwall
Scunthorpe U v Rotherham U
Yeovil T v Tranmere R

Coca-Cola Football League Two
Accrington S v Stockport Co
Boston U v Shrewsbury T
Bristol R v Milton Keynes Dons
Bury v Wycombe W
Hereford U v Barnet
Macclesfield T v Peterborough U
Mansfield T v Grimsby T
Notts Co v Rochdale
Swindon T v Darlington
Torquay U v Hartlepool U
Walsall v Lincoln C
Wrexham v Chester C

Tuesday, 20 February 2007
Coca-Cola Football League Championship
Barnsley v Hull C
Birmingham C v Sunderland
Burnley v Leicester C
Coventry C v Southampton
Ipswich T v Wolverhampton W
Leeds U v QPR
Luton T v Sheffield W
Plymouth Arg v Colchester U
Preston NE v Norwich C
Southend U v Crystal Palace
WBA v Cardiff C

351

Coca-Cola Football League One
Bournemouth v Yeovil T
Brentford v Northampton T
Bristol C v Bradford C
Carlisle U v Chesterfield
Crewe Alex v Doncaster R
Gillingham v Brighton & HA
Millwall v Leyton Orient
Nottingham F v Blackpool
Port Vale v Oldham Ath
Rotherham U v Huddersfield T
Swansea C v Scunthorpe U
Tranmere R v Cheltenham T

Coca-Cola Football League Two
Barnet v Swindon T
Chester C v Bury
Darlington v Accrington S
Grimsby T v Wrexham
Hartlepool U v Macclesfield T
Lincoln C v Hereford U
Milton Keynes Dons v Mansfield T
Peterborough U v Boston U
Rochdale v Torquay U
Shrewsbury T v Notts Co
Stockport Co v Walsall
Wycombe W v Bristol R

Wednesday, 21 February 2007
Coca-Cola Football League
Championship
Derby Co v Stoke C

Saturday, 24 February 2007
Barclays Premiership
Aston Villa v Arsenal
Blackburn R v Portsmouth
Charlton Ath v West Ham U
Fulham v Manchester U
Liverpool v Sheffield U
Manchester C v Chelsea
Middlesbrough v Reading
Tottenham H v Bolton W
Watford v Everton
Wigan Ath v Newcastle U

Coca-Cola Football League
Championship
Cardiff C v Preston NE
Colchester U v Burnley
Crystal Palace v Luton T
Hull C v Birmingham C
Leicester C v WBA
Norwich C v Coventry C
QPR v Plymouth Arg
Sheffield W v Southend U
Southampton v Ipswich T
Stoke C v Barnsley

Sunderland v Derby Co
Wolverhampton W v Leeds U

Coca-Cola Football League One
Blackpool v Millwall
Bradford C v Brentford
Brighton & HA v Bristol C
Cheltenham T v Carlisle U
Chesterfield v Nottingham F
Doncaster R v Port Vale
Huddersfield T v Crewe Alex
Leyton Orient v Tranmere R
Northampton T v Rotherham U
Oldham Ath v Bournemouth
Scunthorpe U v Gillingham
Yeovil T v Swansea C

Coca-Cola Football League Two
Accrington S v Lincoln C
Boston U v Hartlepool U
Bristol R v Stockport Co
Bury v Peterborough U
Hereford U v Rochdale
Macclesfield T v Grimsby T
Mansfield T v Wycombe W
Notts Co v Milton Keynes Dons
Swindon T v Chester C
Torquay U v Darlington
Walsall v Barnet
Wrexham v Shrewsbury T

Saturday, 3 March 2007
Barclays Premiership
Arsenal v Reading
Bolton W v Blackburn R
Fulham v Aston Villa
Liverpool v Manchester U
Manchester C v Wigan Ath
Newcastle U v Middlesbrough
Portsmouth v Chelsea
Sheffield U v Everton
Watford v Charlton Ath
West Ham U v Tottenham H

Coca-Cola Football League
Championship
Barnsley v Norwich C
Birmingham C v Cardiff C
Burnley v Crystal Palace
Coventry C v Hull C
Derby Co v Colchester U
Ipswich T v QPR
Leeds U v Sheffield W
Luton T v Wolverhampton W
Plymouth Arg v Stoke C
Preston NE v Southampton
Southend U v Leicester C
WBA v Sunderland

Coca-Cola Football League One
Bournemouth v Doncaster R
Brentford v Scunthorpe U
Bristol C v Northampton T
Carlisle U v Oldham Ath
Crewe Alex v Brighton & HA
Gillingham v Blackpool
Millwall v Cheltenham T
Nottingham F v Huddersfield T
Port Vale v Yeovil T
Rotherham U v Bradford C
Swansea C v Leyton Orient
Tranmere R v Chesterfield

Coca-Cola Football League Two
Barnet v Wrexham
Chester C v Torquay U
Darlington v Walsall
Grimsby T v Bury
Hartlepool U v Hereford U
Lincoln C v Mansfield T
Milton Keynes Dons v Boston U
Peterborough U v Notts Co
Rochdale v Accrington S
Shrewsbury T v Bristol R
Stockport Co v Swindon T
Wycombe W v Macclesfield T

Saturday, 10 March 2007
Coca-Cola Football League Championship
Barnsley v Sunderland
Birmingham C v Derby Co
Burnley v Plymouth Arg
Cardiff C v Norwich C
Colchester U v Coventry C
Crystal Palace v Leicester C
Hull C v Preston NE
Ipswich T v Southend U
Leeds U v Luton T
QPR v Sheffield W
Stoke C v Southampton
Wolverhampton W v WBA

Coca-Cola Football League One
Blackpool v Brighton & HA
Bristol C v Brentford
Cheltenham T v Yeovil T
Chesterfield v Leyton Orient
Gillingham v Crewe Alex
Huddersfield T v Bradford C
Millwall v Carlisle U
Northampton T v Bournemouth
Oldham Ath v Doncaster R
Rotherham U v Port Vale
Scunthorpe U v Nottingham F
Tranmere R v Swansea C

Coca-Cola Football League Two
Barnet v Stockport Co
Boston U v Bristol R
Hartlepool U v Lincoln C
Hereford U v Grimsby T
Macclesfield T v Shrewsbury T
Notts Co v Mansfield T
Peterborough U v Milton Keynes Dons
Rochdale v Darlington
Swindon T v Accrington S
Torquay U v Wycombe W
Walsall v Chester C
Wrexham v Bury

Tuesday, 13 March 2007
Coca-Cola Football League Championship
Coventry C v Wolverhampton W
Leicester C v Leeds U
Luton T v Hull C
Norwich C v Birmingham C
Plymouth Arg v Barnsley
Preston NE v Ipswich T
Sheffield W v Colchester U
Southend U v Burnley
Sunderland v Stoke C
WBA v Crystal Palace

Wednesday, 14 March 2007
Coca-Cola Football League Championship
Derby Co v QPR
Southampton v Cardiff C

Saturday, 17 March 2007
Barclays Premiership
Aston Villa v Liverpool
Blackburn R v West Ham U
Charlton Ath v Newcastle U
Chelsea v Sheffield U
Everton v Arsenal
Manchester U v Bolton W
Middlesbrough v Manchester C
Reading v Portsmouth
Tottenham H v Watford
Wigan Ath v Fulham

Coca-Cola Football League Championship
Coventry C v Barnsley
Derby Co v Cardiff C
Leicester C v QPR
Luton T v Ipswich T
Norwich C v Stoke C
Plymouth Arg v Crystal Palace
Preston NE v Burnley
Sheffield W v Wolverhampton W
Southampton v Colchester U
Southend U v Leeds U

Sunderland v Hull C
WBA v Birmingham C

Coca-Cola Football League One
Bournemouth v Millwall
Bradford C v Northampton T
Brentford v Rotherham U
Brighton & HA v Scunthorpe U
Carlisle U v Huddersfield T
Crewe Alex v Bristol C
Doncaster R v Cheltenham T
Leyton Orient v Oldham Ath
Nottingham F v Gillingham
Port Vale v Tranmere R
Swansea C v Chesterfield
Yeovil T v Blackpool

Coca-Cola Football League Two
Accrington S v Torquay U
Bristol R v Notts Co
Bury v Macclesfield T
Chester C v Rochdale
Darlington v Hereford U
Grimsby T v Swindon T
Lincoln C v Barnet
Mansfield T v Boston U
Milton Keynes Dons v Wrexham
Shrewsbury T v Peterborough U
Stockport Co v Hartlepool U
Wycombe W v Walsall

Saturday, 24 March 2007
Coca-Cola Football League One
Bournemouth v Tranmere R
Bradford C v Blackpool
Brentford v Oldham Ath
Brighton & HA v Huddersfield T
Carlisle U v Gillingham
Crewe Alex v Rotherham U
Doncaster R v Bristol C
Leyton Orient v Scunthorpe U
Nottingham F v Cheltenham T
Port Vale v Millwall
Swansea C v Northampton T
Yeovil T v Chesterfield

Coca-Cola Football League Two
Accrington S v Hereford U
Bristol R v Wrexham
Bury v Notts Co
Chester C v Barnet
Darlington v Hartlepool U
Grimsby T v Peterborough U
Lincoln C v Swindon T
Mansfield T v Macclesfield T
Milton Keynes Dons v Walsall
Shrewsbury T v Torquay U
Stockport Co v Rochdale
Wycombe W v Boston U

Saturday, 31 March 2007
Barclays Premiership
Aston Villa v Everton
Bolton W v Sheffield U
Charlton Ath v Wigan Ath
Fulham v Portsmouth
Liverpool v Arsenal
Manchester U v Blackburn R
Newcastle U v Manchester C
Tottenham H v Reading
Watford v Chelsea
West Ham U v Middlesbrough

Coca-Cola Football League Championship
Barnsley v Derby Co
Birmingham C v Coventry C
Burnley v Luton T
Cardiff C v Sunderland
Colchester U v Norwich C
Crystal Palace v Sheffield W
Hull C v Southend U
Ipswich T v Plymouth Arg
Leeds U v Preston NE
QPR v WBA
Stoke C v Leicester C
Wolverhampton W v Southampton

Coca-Cola Football League One
Blackpool v Crewe Alex
Bristol C v Nottingham F
Cheltenham T v Leyton Orient
Chesterfield v Doncaster R
Gillingham v Brentford
Huddersfield T v Port Vale
Millwall v Swansea C
Northampton T v Brighton & HA
Oldham Ath v Yeovil T
Rotherham U v Bournemouth
Scunthorpe U v Bradford C
Tranmere R v Carlisle U

Coca-Cola Football League Two
Barnet v Darlington
Boston U v Bury
Hartlepool U v Chester C
Hereford U v Milton Keynes Dons
Macclesfield T v Bristol R
Notts Co v Grimsby T
Peterborough U v Wycombe W
Rochdale v Lincoln C
Swindon T v Shrewsbury T
Torquay U v Stockport Co
Walsall v Accrington S
Wrexham v Mansfield T

Saturday, 7 April 2007
Barclays Premiership
Arsenal v West Ham U

Blackburn R v Aston Villa
Chelsea v Tottenham H
Everton v Fulham
Manchester C v Charlton Ath
Middlesbrough v Watford
Portsmouth v Manchester U
Reading v Liverpool
Sheffield U v Newcastle U
Wigan Ath v Bolton W

Coca-Cola Football League Championship
Birmingham C v Burnley
Cardiff C v Sheffield W
Coventry C v QPR
Crystal Palace v Preston NE
Hull C v Norwich C
Ipswich T v Barnsley
Leeds U v Plymouth Arg
Leicester C v Derby Co
Luton T v Southampton
Southend U v Colchester U
Sunderland v Wolverhampton W
WBA v Stoke C

Coca-Cola Football League One
Blackpool v Tranmere R
Bournemouth v Bradford C
Brentford v Cheltenham T
Brighton & HA v Doncaster R
Bristol C v Swansea C
Chesterfield v Crewe Alex
Leyton Orient v Northampton T
Millwall v Nottingham F
Oldham Ath v Huddersfield T
Port Vale v Carlisle U
Rotherham U v Gillingham
Scunthorpe U v Yeovil T

Coca-Cola Football League Two
Accrington S v Peterborough U
Barnet v Hartlepool U
Bury v Rochdale
Chester C v Darlington
Hereford U v Swindon T
Lincoln C v Stockport Co
Macclesfield T v Wrexham
Mansfield T v Bristol R
Milton Keynes Dons v Grimsby T
Notts Co v Boston U
Torquay U v Walsall
Wycombe W v Shrewsbury T

Monday, 9 April 2007
Barclays Premiership
Aston Villa v Wigan Ath
Bolton W v Everton
Charlton Ath v Reading
Fulham v Manchester C

Liverpool v Middlesbrough
Manchester U v Sheffield U
Newcastle U v Arsenal
Tottenham H v Blackburn R
Watford v Portsmouth
West Ham U v Chelsea

Coca-Cola Football League Championship
Barnsley v Birmingham C
Burnley v Cardiff C
Colchester U v Leeds U
Derby Co v Coventry C
Norwich C v WBA
Plymouth Arg v Leicester C
Preston NE v Southend U
QPR v Luton T
Sheffield W v Ipswich T
Southampton v Sunderland
Stoke C v Crystal Palace
Wolverhampton W v Hull C

Coca-Cola Football League One
Bradford C v Oldham Ath
Carlisle U v Bournemouth
Cheltenham T v Chesterfield
Crewe Alex v Brentford
Doncaster R v Millwall
Gillingham v Bristol C
Huddersfield T v Blackpool
Northampton T v Scunthorpe U
Nottingham F v Rotherham U
Swansea C v Port Vale
Tranmere R v Brighton & HA
Yeovil T v Leyton Orient

Coca-Cola Football League Two
Boston U v Macclesfield T
Bristol R v Bury
Darlington v Lincoln C
Grimsby T v Wycombe W
Hartlepool U v Accrington S
Peterborough U v Mansfield T
Rochdale v Barnet
Shrewsbury T v Milton Keynes Dons
Stockport Co v Chester C
Swindon T v Torquay U
Walsall v Hereford U
Wrexham v Notts Co

Saturday, 14 April 2007
Barclays Premiership
Arsenal v Bolton W
Blackburn R v Watford
Chelsea v Manchester U
Everton v Charlton Ath
Manchester C v Liverpool
Middlesbrough v Aston Villa
Portsmouth v Newcastle U

Reading v Fulham
Sheffield U v West Ham U
Wigan Ath v Tottenham H

**Coca-Cola Football League
Championship**
Birmingham C v Southampton
Cardiff C v Stoke C
Coventry C v Preston NE
Crystal Palace v Wolverhampton W
Hull C v Colchester U
Ipswich T v Derby Co
Leeds U v Burnley
Leicester C v Norwich C
Luton T v Plymouth Arg
Southend U v Barnsley
Sunderland v QPR
WBA v Sheffield W

Coca-Cola Football League One
Blackpool v Northampton T
Bournemouth v Swansea C
Brentford v Nottingham F
Brighton & HA v Bradford C
Bristol C v Yeovil T
Chesterfield v Gillingham
Leyton Orient v Doncaster R
Millwall v Tranmere R
Oldham Ath v Cheltenham T
Port Vale v Crewe Alex
Rotherham U v Carlisle U
Scunthorpe U v Huddersfield T

Coca-Cola Football League Two
Accrington S v Grimsby T
Barnet v Bristol R
Bury v Swindon T
Chester C v Shrewsbury T
Hereford U v Boston U
Lincoln C v Wrexham
Macclesfield T v Stockport Co
Mansfield T v Rochdale
Milton Keynes Dons v Darlington
Notts Co v Walsall
Torquay U v Peterborough U
Wycombe W v Hartlepool U

Saturday, 21 April 2007
Barclays Premiership
Aston Villa v Portsmouth
Bolton W v Reading
Charlton Ath v Sheffield U
Fulham v Blackburn R
Liverpool v Wigan Ath
Manchester U v Middlesbrough
Newcastle U v Chelsea
Tottenham H v Arsenal
Watford v Manchester C
West Ham U v Everton

**Coca-Cola Football League
Championship**
Barnsley v Crystal Palace
Burnley v WBA
Colchester U v Sunderland
Derby Co v Luton T
Norwich C v Ipswich T
Plymouth Arg v Southend U
Preston NE v Leicester C
QPR v Cardiff C
Sheffield W v Coventry C
Southampton v Leeds U
Stoke C v Hull C
Wolverhampton W v Birmingham C

Coca-Cola Football League One
Bradford C v Leyton Orient
Carlisle U v Bristol C
Cheltenham T v Blackpool
Crewe Alex v Oldham Ath
Doncaster R v Brentford
Gillingham v Port Vale
Huddersfield T v Millwall
Northampton T v Chesterfield
Nottingham F v Bournemouth
Swansea C v Brighton & HA
Tranmere R v Scunthorpe U
Yeovil T v Rotherham U

Coca-Cola Football League Two
Boston U v Chester C
Bristol R v Lincoln C
Darlington v Wycombe W
Grimsby T v Barnet
Hartlepool U v Notts Co
Peterborough U v Hereford U
Rochdale v Macclesfield T
Shrewsbury T v Accrington S
Stockport Co v Milton Keynes Dons
Swindon T v Mansfield T
Walsall v Bury
Wrexham v Torquay U

Saturday, 28 April 2007
Barclays Premiership
Arsenal v Fulham
Blackburn R v Charlton Ath
Chelsea v Bolton W
Everton v Manchester U
Manchester C v Aston Villa
Middlesbrough v Tottenham H
Portsmouth v Liverpool
Reading v Newcastle U
Sheffield U v Watford
Wigan Ath v West Ham U

**Coca-Cola Football League
Championship**
Barnsley v Leicester C
Birmingham C v Sheffield W

Cardiff C v Hull C
Coventry C v WBA
Crystal Palace v Derby Co
Leeds U v Ipswich T
Norwich C v Southampton
Plymouth Arg v Preston NE
Southend U v Luton T
Stoke C v Colchester U
Sunderland v Burnley
Wolverhampton W v QPR

Coca-Cola Football League One
Blackpool v Scunthorpe U
Bournemouth v Gillingham
Brentford v Port Vale
Brighton & HA v Oldham Ath
Carlisle U v Swansea C
Chesterfield v Bradford C
Crewe Alex v Tranmere R
Leyton Orient v Nottingham F
Millwall v Bristol C
Northampton T v Huddersfield T
Rotherham U v Cheltenham T
Yeovil T v Doncaster R

Coca-Cola Football League Two
Accrington S v Macclesfield T
Boston U v Torquay U
Bristol R v Swindon T
Chester C v Peterborough U
Grimsby T v Lincoln C
Hereford U v Shrewsbury T
Mansfield T v Barnet
Notts Co v Darlington
Rochdale v Hartlepool U
Stockport Co v Bury
Walsall v Wrexham
Wycombe W v Milton Keynes Dons

Saturday, 5 May 2007
Barclays Premiership
Arsenal v Chelsea
Aston Villa v Sheffield U
Charlton Ath v Tottenham H
Everton v Portsmouth
Fulham v Liverpool
Manchester C v Manchester U
Newcastle U v Blackburn R
Reading v Watford
West Ham U v Bolton W
Wigan Ath v Middlesbrough

Coca-Cola Football League One
Bradford C v Millwall
Bristol C v Rotherham U

Cheltenham T v Brighton & HA
Doncaster R v Northampton T
Gillingham v Yeovil T
Huddersfield T v Leyton Orient
Nottingham F v Crewe Alex
Oldham Ath v Chesterfield
Port Vale v Bournemouth
Scunthorpe U v Carlisle U
Swansea C v Blackpool
Tranmere R v Brentford

Coca-Cola Football League Two
Barnet v Wycombe W
Bury v Mansfield T
Darlington v Stockport Co
Hartlepool U v Bristol R
Lincoln C v Chester C
Macclesfield T v Notts Co
Milton Keynes Dons v Accrington S
Peterborough U v Rochdale
Shrewsbury T v Grimsby T
Swindon T v Walsall
Torquay U v Hereford U
Wrexham v Boston U

Sunday, 6 May 2007
Coca-Cola Football League
Championship
Burnley v Coventry C
Colchester U v Crystal Palace
Derby Co v Leeds U
Hull C v Plymouth Arg
Ipswich T v Cardiff C
Leicester C v Wolverhampton W
Luton T v Sunderland
Preston NE v Birmingham C
QPR v Stoke C
Sheffield W v Norwich C
Southampton v Southend U
WBA v Barnsley

Sunday, 13 May 2007
Barclays Premiership
Blackburn R v Reading
Bolton W v Aston Villa
Chelsea v Everton
Liverpool v Charlton Ath
Manchester U v West Ham U
Middlesbrough v Fulham
Portsmouth v Arsenal
Sheffield U v Wigan Ath
Tottenham H v Manchester C
Watford v Newcastle U

CONFERENCE NATIONAL FIXTURES 2006–2007

Saturday, 12 August 2006
Aldershot T v Gravesend & N
Altrincham T v Stevenage B
Cambridge U v Northwich Vic
Crawley T v Rushden & D'monds
Forest Green R v Dagenham & Red
Grays Ath v Stafford R
Kidderminster H v St Albans
Morecambe v Burton Alb
Oxford U v Halifax T
Southport v Woking
Tamworth v Weymouth
York C v Exeter C

Tuesday, 15 August 2006
Burton Alb v Kidderminster H
Dagenham & Red v Oxford U
Exeter C v Forest Green R
Gravesend & N v Tamworth
Halifax T v Southport
Northwich Vic v Morecambe
Rushden & D'monds v Grays Ath
St Albans v Cambridge U
Stafford R v Altrincham T
Stevenage B v York C
Weymouth v Aldershot T
Woking v Crawley T

Saturday, 19 August 2006
Burton Alb v Oxford U
Dagenham & Red v Tamworth
Exeter C v Altrincham T
Gravesend & N v York C
Halifax T v Grays Ath
Northwich Vic v Kidderminster H
Rushden & D'monds v Forest Green R
St Albans v Aldershot T
Stafford R v Southport
Stevenage B v Crawley T
Weymouth v Cambridge U
Woking v Morecambe

Saturday, 26 August 2006
Aldershot T v Dagenham & Red
Altrincham T v St Albans
Cambridge U v Halifax T
Crawley T v Stafford R
Forest Green R v Gravesend & N
Grays Ath v Woking
Kidderminster H v Weymouth
Morecambe v Stevenage B
Oxford U v Northwich Vic
Southport v Rushden & D'monds
Tamworth v Exeter C
York C v Burton Alb

Monday, 28 August 2006
Burton Alb v Southport
Dagenham & Red v Cambridge U

Exeter C v Crawley T
Gravesend & N v Altrincham T
Halifax T v Morecambe
Northwich Vic v Grays Ath
Rushden & D'monds v York C
St Albans v Tamworth
Stafford R v Aldershot T
Stevenage B v Forest Green R
Weymouth v Oxford U
Woking v Kidderminster H

Saturday, 2 September 2006
Tamworth v Stevenage B

Sunday, 3 September 2006
Aldershot T v Halifax T
Altrincham T v Dagenham & Red
Cambridge U v Exeter C
Crawley T v Northwich Vic
Forest Green R v Woking
Grays Ath v Burton Alb
Kidderminster H v Rushden & D'monds
Morecambe v Weymouth
Oxford U v St Albans
Southport v Gravesend & N
York C v Stafford R

Saturday, 9 September 2006
Burton Alb v Weymouth
Crawley T v York C
Exeter C v Aldershot T
Forest Green R v Cambridge U
Grays Ath v Southport
Halifax T v Gravesend & N
Kidderminster H v Tamworth
Morecambe v Oxford U
Northwich Vic v St Albans
Rushden & D'monds v Altrincham T
Stevenage B v Stafford R
Woking v Dagenham & Red

Tuesday, 12 September 2006
Aldershot T v Stevenage B
Altrincham T v Halifax T
Cambridge U v Kidderminster H
Dagenham & Red v Crawley T
Gravesend & N v Grays Ath
Oxford U v Exeter C
Southport v Northwich Vic
St Albans v Woking
Stafford R v Burton Alb
Tamworth v Rushden & D'monds
Weymouth v Forest Green R
York C v Morecambe

Saturday, 16 September 2006
Aldershot T v Northwich Vic
Altrincham T v Woking
Cambridge U v Stevenage B

Dagenham & Red v Morecambe
Gravesend & N v Exeter C
Oxford U v Grays Ath
Southport v Crawley T
St Albans v Burton Alb
Stafford R v Rushden & D'monds
Tamworth v Forest Green R
Weymouth v Halifax T
York C v Kidderminster H

Tuesday, 19 September 2006
Burton Alb v Cambridge U
Crawley T v Oxford U
Exeter C v St Albans
Forest Green R v Altrincham T
Grays Ath v Aldershot T
Halifax T v Dagenham & Red
Kidderminster H v Southport
Morecambe v Tamworth
Northwich Vic v Stafford R
Rushden & D'monds v Gravesend & N
Stevenage B v Weymouth
Woking v York C

Saturday, 23 September 2006
Altrincham T v Tamworth
Burton Alb v Northwich Vic
Cambridge U v Aldershot T
Crawley T v Grays Ath
Dagenham & Red v Weymouth
Exeter C v Stevenage B
Halifax T v Forest Green R
Morecambe v Kidderminster H
St Albans v Gravesend & N
Stafford R v Oxford U
Woking v Rushden & D'monds
York C v Southport

Saturday, 30 September 2006
Aldershot T v Altrincham T
Forest Green R v Stafford R
Gravesend & N v Dagenham & Red
Grays Ath v Morecambe
Kidderminster H v Crawley T
Northwich Vic v Woking
Oxford U v York C
Rushden & D'monds v Burton Alb
Southport v Exeter C
Stevenage B v Halifax T
Tamworth v Cambridge U
Weymouth v St Albans

Tuesday, 3 October 2006
Aldershot T v Tamworth
Burton Alb v Crawley T
Cambridge U v Altrincham T
Grays Ath v Exeter C
Halifax T v Kidderminster H
Morecambe v Rushden & D'monds
Northwich Vic v York C
Oxford U v Southport
St Albans v Forest Green R

Stafford R v Dagenham & Red
Stevenage B v Woking
Weymouth v Gravesend & N

Saturday, 7 October 2006
Tamworth v Stafford R

Sunday, 8 October 2006
Altrincham T v Weymouth
Crawley T v Morecambe
Dagenham & Red v Northwich Vic
Exeter C v Halifax T
Forest Green R v Oxford U
Gravesend & N v Cambridge U
Kidderminster H v Grays Ath
Rushden & D'monds v Stevenage B
Southport v St Albans
Woking v Burton Alb
York C v Aldershot T

Tuesday, 10 October 2006
Altrincham T v Morecambe
Crawley T v Weymouth
Dagenham & Red v St Albans
Exeter C v Northwich Vic
Forest Green R v Burton Alb
Gravesend & N v Stafford R
Kidderminster H v Oxford U
Rushden & D'monds v Halifax T
Southport v Stevenage B
Tamworth v Grays Ath
Woking v Aldershot T
York C v Cambridge U

Saturday, 14 October 2006
Aldershot T v Kidderminster H
Burton Alb v Gravesend & N
Cambridge U v Crawley T
Grays Ath v Forest Green R
Halifax T v Tamworth
Morecambe v Exeter C
Northwich Vic v Rushden & D'monds
Oxford U v Altrincham T
St Albans v York C
Stafford R v Woking
Stevenage B v Dagenham & Red
Weymouth v Southport

Saturday, 21 October 2006
Aldershot T v Morecambe
Altrincham T v Southport
Cambridge U v Oxford U
Dagenham & Red v Kidderminster H
Exeter C v Stafford R
Forest Green R v Crawley T
Gravesend & N v Woking
Halifax T v Burton Alb
St Albans v Grays Ath
Stevenage B v Northwich Vic
Tamworth v York C
Weymouth v Rushden & D'monds

Friday, 3 November 2006
Burton Alb v Stevenage B

Saturday, 4 November 2006
Crawley T v St Albans
Grays Ath v Cambridge U
Kidderminster H v Forest Green R
Morecambe v Gravesend & N
Northwich Vic v Halifax T
Oxford U v Aldershot T
Rushden & D'monds v Dagenham & Red
Southport v Tamworth
Stafford R v Weymouth
Woking v Exeter C
York C v Altrincham T

Saturday, 18 November 2006
Aldershot T v Southport
Altrincham T v Crawley T
Cambridge U v Morecambe
Dagenham & Red v Burton Alb
Exeter C v Kidderminster H
Forest Green R v Northwich Vic
Gravesend & N v Oxford U
Halifax T v Stafford R
St Albans v Rushden & D'monds
Stevenage B v Grays Ath
Tamworth v Woking
Weymouth v York C

Saturday, 25 November 2006
Burton Alb v Exeter C
Crawley T v Halifax T
Grays Ath v Altrincham T
Kidderminster H v Stevenage B
Morecambe v Forest Green R
Northwich Vic v Gravesend & N
Oxford U v Tamworth
Rushden & D'monds v Aldershot T
Southport v Cambridge U
Stafford R v St Albans
Woking v Weymouth
York C v Dagenham & Red

Saturday, 2 December 2006
Aldershot T v Crawley T
Altrincham T v Burton Alb
Cambridge U v Stafford R
Dagenham & Red v Southport
Exeter C v Rushden & D'monds
Forest Green R v York C
Gravesend & N v Kidderminster H
Halifax T v Woking
St Albans v Morecambe
Stevenage B v Oxford U
Tamworth v Northwich Vic
Weymouth v Grays Ath

Saturday, 9 December 2006
Burton Alb v Aldershot T
Crawley T v Tamworth

Exeter C v Dagenham & Red
Forest Green R v Southport
Grays Ath v York C
Halifax T v St Albans
Kidderminster H v Altrincham T
Morecambe v Stafford R
Northwich Vic v Weymouth
Rushden & D'monds v Oxford U
Stevenage B v Gravesend & N
Woking v Cambridge U

Tuesday, 26 December 2006
Aldershot T v Forest Green R
Altrincham T v Northwich Vic
Cambridge U v Rushden & D'monds
Dagenham & Red v Grays Ath
Gravesend & N v Crawley T
Oxford U v Woking
Southport v Morecambe
St Albans v Stevenage B
Stafford R v Kidderminster H
Tamworth v Burton Alb
Weymouth v Exeter C
York C v Halifax T

Saturday, 30 December 2006
Aldershot T v Grays Ath
Altrincham T v Forest Green R
Cambridge U v Burton Alb
Dagenham & Red v Halifax T
Gravesend & N v Rushden & D'monds
Oxford U v Crawley T
Southport v Kidderminster H
St Albans v Exeter C
Stafford R v Northwich Vic
Tamworth v Morecambe
Weymouth v Stevenage B
York C v Woking

Monday, 1 January 2007
Burton Alb v Stafford R
Crawley T v Dagenham & Red
Exeter C v Oxford U
Forest Green R v Weymouth
Grays Ath v Gravesend & N
Halifax T v Altrincham T
Kidderminster H v Cambridge U
Morecambe v York C
Northwich Vic v Southport
Rushden & D'monds v Tamworth
Stevenage B v Aldershot T
Woking v St Albans

Saturday, 6 January 2007
Aldershot T v Exeter C
Altrincham T v Rushden & D'monds
Cambridge U v Forest Green R
Dagenham & Red v Woking
Gravesend & N v Halifax T
Oxford U v Morecambe
Southport v Grays Ath
St Albans v Northwich Vic

360

Stafford R v Stevenage B
Tamworth v Kidderminster H
Weymouth v Burton Alb
York C v Crawley T

Saturday, 20 January 2007
Burton Alb v St Albans
Crawley T v Southport
Exeter C v Gravesend & N
Forest Green R v Tamworth
Grays Ath v Oxford U
Halifax T v Weymouth
Kidderminster H v York C
Morecambe v Dagenham & Red
Northwich Vic v Aldershot T
Rushden & D'monds v Stafford R
Stevenage B v Cambridge U
Woking v Altrincham T

Tuesday, 23 January 2007
Burton Alb v Tamworth
Crawley T v Gravesend & N
Exeter C v Weymouth
Forest Green R v Aldershot T
Grays Ath v Dagenham & Red
Halifax T v York C
Kidderminster H v Stafford R
Morecambe v Southport
Northwich Vic v Altrincham T
Rushden & D'monds v Cambridge U
Stevenage B v St Albans
Woking v Oxford U

Saturday, 27 January 2007
Aldershot T v Burton Alb
Altrincham T v Kidderminster H
Cambridge U v Woking
Dagenham & Red v Exeter C
Gravesend & N v Stevenage B
Oxford U v Rushden & D'monds
Southport v Forest Green R
St Albans v Halifax T
Stafford R v Morecambe
Tamworth v Crawley T
Weymouth v Northwich Vic
York C v Grays Ath

Saturday, 3 February 2007
Burton Alb v Halifax T
Crawley T v Forest Green R
Grays Ath v St Albans
Kidderminster H v Dagenham & Red
Morecambe v Aldershot T
Northwich Vic v Stevenage B
Oxford U v Cambridge U
Rushden & D'monds v Weymouth
Southport v Altrincham T
Stafford R v Exeter C
Woking v Gravesend & N
York C v Tamworth

Saturday, 10 February 2007
Aldershot T v Oxford U
Altrincham T v York C
Cambridge U v Grays Ath
Dagenham & Red v Rushden & D'monds
Exeter C v Woking
Forest Green R v Kidderminster H
Gravesend & N v Morecambe
Halifax T v Northwich Vic
St Albans v Crawley T
Stevenage B v Burton Alb
Tamworth v Southport
Weymouth v Stafford R

Saturday, 17 February 2007
Burton Alb v Dagenham & Red
Crawley T v Altrincham T
Grays Ath v Stevenage B
Kidderminster H v Exeter C
Morecambe v Cambridge U
Northwich Vic v Forest Green R
Oxford U v Gravesend & N
Rushden & D'monds v St Albans
Southport v Aldershot T
Stafford R v Halifax T
Woking v Tamworth
York C v Weymouth

Saturday, 24 February 2007
Aldershot T v Rushden & D'monds
Altrincham T v Grays Ath
Cambridge U v Southport
Dagenham & Red v York C
Exeter C v Burton Alb
Forest Green R v Morecambe
Gravesend & N v Northwich Vic
Halifax T v Crawley T
St Albans v Stafford R
Stevenage B v Kidderminster H
Tamworth v Oxford U
Weymouth v Woking

Saturday, 3 March 2007
Burton Alb v Altrincham T
Crawley T v Aldershot T
Grays Ath v Weymouth
Kidderminster H v Gravesend & N
Morecambe v St Albans
Northwich Vic v Tamworth
Oxford U v Stevenage B
Rushden & D'monds v Exeter C
Southport v Dagenham & Red
Stafford R v Cambridge U
Woking v Halifax T
York C v Forest Green R

Tuesday, 6 March 2007
Altrincham T v Cambridge U
Crawley T v Burton Alb
Dagenham & Red v Stafford R
Exeter C v Grays Ath

361

Forest Green R v St Albans
Gravesend & N v Weymouth
Kidderminster H v Halifax T
Rushden & D'monds v Morecambe
Southport v Oxford U
Tamworth v Aldershot T
Woking v Stevenage B
York C v Northwich Vic

Saturday, 10 March 2007
Aldershot T v York C
Burton Alb v Woking
Cambridge U v Gravesend & N
Grays Ath v Kidderminster H
Halifax T v Exeter C
Morecambe v Crawley T
Northwich Vic v Dagenham & Red
Oxford U v Forest Green R
St Albans v Southport
Stafford R v Tamworth
Stevenage B v Rushden & D'monds
Weymouth v Altrincham T

Tuesday, 13 March 2007
Aldershot T v Woking
Burton Alb v Forest Green R
Cambridge U v York C
Grays Ath v Tamworth
Halifax T v Rushden & D'monds
Morecambe v Altrincham T
Northwich Vic v Exeter C
Oxford U v Kidderminster H
St Albans v Dagenham & Red
Stafford R v Gravesend & N
Stevenage B v Southport
Weymouth v Crawley T

Saturday, 17 March 2007
Altrincham T v Oxford U
Crawley T v Cambridge U
Dagenham & Red v Stevenage B
Exeter C v Morecambe
Forest Green R v Grays Ath
Gravesend & N v Burton Alb
Kidderminster H v Aldershot T
Rushden & D'monds v Northwich Vic
Southport v Weymouth
Tamworth v Halifax T
Woking v Stafford R
York C v St Albans

Sunday, 25 March 2007
Burton Alb v Morecambe
Dagenham & Red v Forest Green R
Exeter C v York C
Gravesend & N v Aldershot T
Halifax T v Oxford U
Northwich Vic v Cambridge U
Rushden & D'monds v Crawley T
St Albans v Kidderminster H
Stafford R v Grays Ath
Stevenage B v Altrincham T

Weymouth v Tamworth
Woking v Southport

Tuesday, 27 March 2007
Aldershot T v Weymouth
Altrincham T v Stafford R
Cambridge U v St Albans
Crawley T v Woking
Forest Green R v Exeter C
Grays Ath v Rushden & D'monds
Kidderminster H v Burton Alb
Morecambe v Northwich Vic
Oxford U v Dagenham & Red
Southport v Halifax T
Tamworth v Gravesend & N
York C v Stevenage B

Saturday, 31 March 2007
Aldershot T v St Albans
Altrincham T v Exeter C
Cambridge U v Weymouth
Crawley T v Stevenage B
Forest Green R v Rushden & D'monds
Grays Ath v Halifax T
Kidderminster H v Northwich Vic
Morecambe v Woking
Oxford U v Burton Alb
Southport v Stafford R
Tamworth v Dagenham & Red
York C v Gravesend & N

Saturday, 7 April 2007
Burton Alb v York C
Dagenham & Red v Aldershot T
Exeter C v Tamworth
Gravesend & N v Forest Green R
Halifax T v Cambridge U
Northwich Vic v Oxford U
Rushden & D'monds v Southport
St Albans v Altrincham T
Stafford R v Crawley T
Stevenage B v Morecambe
Weymouth v Kidderminster H
Woking v Grays Ath

Monday, 9 April 2007
Aldershot T v Stafford R
Altrincham T v Gravesend & N
Cambridge U v Dagenham & Red
Crawley T v Exeter C
Forest Green R v Stevenage B
Grays Ath v Northwich Vic
Kidderminster H v Woking
Morecambe v Halifax T
Oxford U v Weymouth
Southport v Burton Alb
Tamworth v St Albans
York C v Rushden & D'monds

Saturday, 14 April 2007
Burton Alb v Grays Ath
Dagenham & Red v Altrincham T

Exeter C v Cambridge U
Gravesend & N v Southport
Halifax T v Aldershot T
Northwich Vic v Crawley T
Rushden & D'monds v
  Kidderminster H
St Albans v Oxford U
Stafford R v York C
Stevenage B v Tamworth
Weymouth v Morecambe
Woking v Forest Green R

Saturday, 21 April 2007
Aldershot T v Cambridge U
Forest Green R v Halifax T
Gravesend & N v St Albans
Grays Ath v Crawley T
Kidderminster H v Morecambe
Northwich Vic v Burton Alb
Oxford U v Stafford R

Rushden & D'monds v Woking
Southport v York C
Stevenage B v Exeter C
Tamworth v Altrincham T
Weymouth v Dagenham & Red

Saturday, 28 April 2007
Altrincham T v Aldershot T
Burton Alb v Rushden & D'monds
Cambridge U v Tamworth
Crawley T v Kidderminster H
Dagenham & Red v Gravesend & N
Exeter C v Southport
Halifax T v Stevenage B
Morecambe v Grays Ath
St Albans v Weymouth
Stafford R v Forest Green R
Woking v Northwich Vic
York C v Oxford U

OTHER FIXTURES — SEASON 2006–2007

AUGUST 2006

Tue 1	UEFA Champions League 2Q (2)
Wed 2	UEFA Champions League 2Q (2)
Sat 5	FL Season Commences
Tue 8	UEFA Champions League 3Q (1)
Wed 9	UEFA Champions League 3Q (1)
Thu 10	UEFA Cup 2Q (1)
Sun 13	FA Community Shield
Wed 16	England v Greece (F)
Sat 19	FA Cup EP
	PL Season Commences
Tue 22	UEFA Champions League 3Q (2)
Wed 23	FL Cup 1
	UEFA Champions League 3Q (2)
Thu 24	UEFA Cup 2Q (2)
Fri 25	UEFA Super Cup

SEPTEMBER 2006

Sat 2	FA Cup P
	England v Andorra – EURO 2008 Qualifier
Wed 6	Macedonia v England – EURO 2008 Qualifier
Sat 9	FA Vase 1Q

Mon 11	FA Youth Cup P**
Tue 12	UEFA Champions League MD 1
Wed 13	UEFA Champions League MD 1
Thu 14	UEFA Cup 1st Rd (1)
Sat 16	FA Cup 1Q
Wed 20	FL Cup 2
Sat 23	FA Vase 2Q
Sun 24	FA Sunday Cup P
Mon 25	FA Youth Cup 1Q**
Tue 26	UEFA Champions League MD 2
Wed 27	UEFA Champions League MD 2
Thu 28	UEFA Cup 1st Rd (2)
Sat 30	FA Cup 2Q

OCTOBER 2006

Sat 7	FA Trophy P
	FA Vase 1P
	England v Macedonia – EURO 2008 Qualifier
Sun 8	FA County Youth Cup 1*
Mon 9	FA Youth Cup 2Q**
Wed 11	Croatia v England – EURO 2008 Qualifier
Sat 14	FA Cup 3Q
Sun 15	FA Sunday Cup 1

Tue 17	UEFA Champions League MD 3
Wed 18	FL Trophy 1
	UEFA Champions League MD 3
Thu 19	UEFA Cup MD 1
Sat 21	FA Trophy 1Q
Mon 23	FA Youth Cup 3Q**
Wed 25	FL Cup 3
Sat 28	FA Cup 4Q
Tue 31	UEFA Champions League MD 4

NOVEMBER 2006

Wed 1	FL Trophy 2
	UEFA Champions League MD 4
Thu 2	UEFA Cup MD 2
Sat 4	FA Trophy 2Q
Sun 5	FA County Youth Cup 2*
	FA Sunday Cup 2
Wed 8	FL Cup 4
Sat 11	FA Cup 1P
	FA Youth Cup 1P*
Wed 15	Holland v England (F)
Sat 18	FA Vase 2P
Tue 21	UEFA Champions League MD 5
Wed 22	FA Cup 1P-R
	UEFA Champions League MD 5
Thu 23	UEFA Cup MD 3
Sat 25	FA Trophy 3Q
	FA Youth Cup 2P*
Sun 26	FA Sunday Cup 3
Wed 29	FL Trophy AQF
	UEFA Cup MD 4
Thu 30	UEFA Cup MD 4

DECEMBER 2006

Sat 2	FA Cup 2P
Tue 5	UEFA Champions League MD 6
Wed 6	UEFA Champions League MD 6
Sat 9	FA Vase 3P
Sun 10	FA County Youth Cup 3*
Wed 13	FA Cup 2P-R
	UEFA Cup MD 5
Thu 14	UEFA Cup MD 5

Sat 16	FA Trophy 1P
	FA Youth Cup 3P*
Wed 20	FL Cup 5

JANUARY 2007

Sat 6	FA Cup 3P
Wed 10	FL Cup SF1
	FL Trophy ASF
Sat 13	FA Trophy 2P
Sun 14	FA Sunday Cup 4
Wed 17	FA Cup 3P-R
Sat 20	FA Vase 4P
	FA Youth Cup 4P*
Wed 24	FL Cup SF2
Sat 27	FA Cup 4P
Sun 28	FA County Youth Cup 4*
Wed 31	FL Trophy AF1

FEBRUARY 2007

Sat 3	FA Cup 3P
	FA Youth Cup 5P*
Wed 7	International Friendly
Sat 10	FA Cup 4P-R *(option 2 for clubs in UEFA Cup)*
	FA Vase 5P
Tue 13	FL Trophy AF2
Wed 14	FA Cup 4P-R
	UEFA Cup Rd of 32 (1)
Thu 15	UEFA Cup Rd of 32 (1)
Sat 17	FA Cup 5P
	FA Youth Cup 6P*
Tue 20	UEFA Champions League 1st KO Rd (1)
Wed 21	UEFA Champions League 1st KO Rd (1)
Thu 22	UEFA Cup Rd of 32 (2)
Sat 24	FA Trophy 4P
Sun 25	FA Sunday Cup 5
	FL Cup Final
Wed 28	FA Cup 5P-R

MARCH 2007

Sat 3	FA Vase 6P
Sun 4	FA County Youth Cup SF*
Tue 6	UEFA Champions League 1st KO Rd (2)
Wed 7	UEFA Champions League 1st KO Rd (2)
Thu 8	UEFA Cup Rd of 16 (1)
Sat 10	FA Cup 6P
	FA Trophy SF1
	FA Youth Cup SF1*

Wed 14	UEFA Cup Rd of 16 (2)	Sat 14	FA Cup SF
Thu 15	UEFA Cup Rd of 16 (2)	Tue 24	UEFA Champions League
Sat 17	FA Trophy SF2		SF (1)
Sun 18	FL Trophy Final	Wed 25	UEFA Champions League
Mon 19	FA Cup 6P-R		SF (1)
Sat 24	FA Vase SF1	Thu 26	UEFA Cup SF (1)
	FA Youth Cup SF2*	Sun 29	FA Sunday Cup Final (prov)
	Israel v England –		
	EURO 2008 Qualifier	**MAY 2007**	
Sun 25	FA Sunday Cup SF	Tue 1	UEFA Champions League
Wed 28	Andorra v England –		SF (2)
	EURO 2008 Qualifier	Wed 2	UEFA Champions League
Sat 31	FA Vase SF2		SF (2)
		Thu 3	UEFA Cup SF (2)
APRIL 2007		Sat 5	FL Season Ends
Tue 3	UEFA Champions League	Mon 7	Bank Holiday
	QF (1)	Sat 12	FA Vase Final
Wed 4	UEFA Champions League		PL Season Ends
	QF (1)	Wed 16	UEFA Cup Final
Thu 5	UEFA Cup QF (1)	Sat 19	FA Cup Final
Fri 6	Good Friday	Sun 20	FA Trophy Final
Sat 7		Wed 23	UEFA Champions League
Mon 9	Easter Monday		Final
Tue 10	UEFA Champions League	Sat 26	FL2 Play-off
	QF (2)	Sun 27	FL1 Play-off
Wed 11	UEFA Champions League	Mon 28	FL Championship Play-off
	QF (2)		Bank Holiday
Thu 12	UEFA Cup QF (2)		

* closing date of round
** ties to be played in the week commencing

DATES TO BE CONFIRMED
FA Women's Cup – all rounds
FA Youth Cup Final 1
FA Youth Cup Final 2
FA County Youth Cup Final

FURTHER INTERNATIONAL DATES – 2007
Wed 6 Jun	Estonia v England – EURO 2008 Qualifier
Sat 8 Sep	England v Israel – EURO 2008 Qualifier
Wed 12 Sep	England v Russia – EURO 2008 Qualifier
Sat 13 Oct	England v Estonia – EURO 2008 Qualifier
Wed 17 Oct	Russia v England – EURO 2008 Qualifier
Wed 21 Nov	England v Croatia – EURO 2008 Qualifier

STOP PRESS

Marcello Lippi (Italy) resigns, Jurgen Klinsmann (Germany) resigns ... Juventus, Fiorentina and Lazio relegated in Italy over match fixing, AC Milan deducted points ... Rooney says stamping was an accident ... Owen has to wait for his operation.

Summer transfers completed and pending: **Premier Division: Arsenal:** Tomas Rosicky (Borussia Dortmund) £7,000,000; Joe O'Cearuill (Watford); Vincent Van den Berg (Heerenveen). **Aston Villa:** Damian Bellon (St Gallen); Yago Bellon (St Gallen). **Blackburn R:** Francis Jeffers (Charlton Ath); Jason Roberts (Wigan Ath) £1,000,000; Jason Brown (Gillingham). **Bolton W:** Idan Tal (Maccabi Haifa); Dietmar Hamann (Liverpool); Abdoulaye Meite (Marseille). **Charlton Ath:** Simon Walton (Leeds U) £500,000; Gonzalo Sorondo (Internazionale) (after loan); Jimmy Floyd Hasselbaink (Middlesbrough); Cory Gibbs (Den Haag). **Chelsea:** Andriy Shevchenko (AC Milan) £29,500,000; Jon Obi Mikel (Lyn) £16,000,000; Michael Ballack (Bayern Munich); Hilario (Nacional); Salomon Kalou (Feyenoord) £3,500,000. **Everton:** Tim Howard (Manchester U) Loan; Andy Johnson (Crystal Palace) £8,600,000; Joleon Lescott (Wolverhampton W) £5,000,000; Scott Spencer (Oldham Ath). **Fulham:** Jimmy Bullard (Wigan Ath) £2,500,000; Darren Pratley (Brentford); Gabriel Zakuani (Leyton Orient); Bjorn Runstrom (Hammarby). **Liverpool:** Fabiano Aurelio (Valencia); Craig Bellamy (Blackburn R) £6,000,000; Mark Gonzalez (Banfield) £4,000,000 after year loaned out; Gabriel Paletta (Banfield) £2,000,000. **Manchester C:** Ousmane Dabo (Lazio); Paul Dickov (Blackburn R); Joe Hart (Shrewsbury T) £600,000; Dietmar Hamann (Bolton W). **Middlesbrough:** Herold Goulon (Lyon). **Portsmouth:** Glen Johnson (Chelsea) Loan. **Reading:** Sam Sodje (Brentford); Ki-hyeon Seol (Wolverhampton W). **Sheffield U:** Mikele Leigertwood (Crystal Palace) £600,000; Claude Davis (Preston NE); Chris Lucketti (Preston NE) £300,000; David Sommeil (Manchester C); Christian Nade (Troyes). **Tottenham H:** Benoit Assou-Ekotto (Lens); Dimitar Berbatov (Leverkusen) £10,900,000; Dorian Dervitte (Lille); Didier Zokora (St Etienne) £8,200,000. **Watford:** Chris Powell (Charlton Ath); Sheku Kamara (Charlton Ath); Claude Seanla (Tottenham H); Scott Loach (Lincoln C); Damien Francis (Wigan Ath). **West Ham U:** Carlton Cole (Chelsea); Tyrone Mears (Preston NE) £1,000,000; Lee Bowyer (Newcastle U); Jonathan Spector (Manchester U) £500,000. **Wigan Ath:** Emile Heskey (Birmingham C) £5,500,000; Tomasz Cywka (Gwarek Zawrze); Fitz Hall (Crystal Palace) £3,000,000; Chris Kirkland (Liverpool).

Football League Championship: Barnsley: Michael Coulson (Scarborough); Michael McIndoe (Doncaster R); Sam Togwell (Crystal Palace). **Birmingham C:** Brno N'Gotty (Bolton W); Stephen Kelly (Tottenham H); Neil Danns (Colchester U) £850,000. **Burnley:** Alan Mahon (Wigan Ath); Steve Jones (Crewe Alex); Steve Foster (Crewe Alex); Andy Gray (Sunderland). **Cardiff C:** Roger Johnson (Wycombe W) £275,000; Nick McKoy (Milton Keynes D); Malvin Kamara (Milton Keynes D); Mark Howard (Arsenal); Kevin McNaughton (Aberdeen); Michael Chopra (Newcastle U); Stephen McPhail (Barnsley); Glenn Loovens (Feyenoord). **Colchester U:** Johnnie Jackson (Tottenham H); Jamie Cureton (Swindon T). **Coventry C:** Jay Tabb (Brentford); Mikkel Bischoff (Manchester C); Colin Cameron (Wolverhampton W); Elliott Ward (West Ham U) £1,000,000; Wayne Andrews (Crystal Palace); David McNamee (Livingston); Andy Marshall (Millwall). **Crystal Palace:** Leon Cort (Hull C); Scott Flinders (Barnsley); Mark Kennedy (Wolverhampton W). **Hull C:** Michael Turner (Brentford) £350,000; Sam Ricketts (Swansea C); Dean Marney (Tottenham H). **Leeds U:** Sebastien Carole (Brighton & HA). **Leicester C:** Darren Kenton (Southampton); Andy Johnson (WBA); Josh Low (Northampton T); Gareth McAuley (Lincoln C). **Luton T:** Richard Langley (QPR). **Plymouth Arg:** Sylvan Ebanks-Blake (Manchester U). **Preston NE:** Sean St Ledger-Hall (Peterborough U) £225,000; Jason Jarrett (Norwich C); Kelvin Wilson (Notts Co); Danny Pugh (Leeds U); Liam Chilvers (Colchester U). **QPR:** Damion Stewart (Bradford C). **Sheffield W:** Wade Small (Milton Keynes D); Kenny Lunt (Crewe Alex); Madjid Bougherra (Gueugnon); Yoann Folly (Southampton). **Southampton:** Bradley Wright-Phillips (Manchester C); Grzegorz Rasiak (Tottenham H) £2,000,000; Jermaine Wright (Leeds U); Peter Madsen (Cologne); Marcelo Sarmiento (Racing Cordoba). **Southend U:** Jamal Campbell-Ryce (Rotherham U); Steven Hammell (Motherwell); Michael Ricketts (Leeds U); Simon Francis (Sheffield U); Steven Collis (Yeovil T). **Stoke C:** Vincent Pericard (Portsmouth). **West Bromwich Albion:** Chris Perry (Charlton Ath); John Hartson (Celtic); Pascal Zuberbuhler (Basle).

Football League 1: Blackpool: Marcus Bean (QPR); Paul Tierney (Livingston); Rhys Evans (Swindon T). **Bournemouth:** Danny Hollands (Chelsea); Daryl Taylor (Walsall). **Bradford C:** Matthew Clarke (Darlington); Jermaine Johnson (Tivoli Gardens); Eddie Johnson (Manchester U). **Brentford:** Chris Moore (Dagenham & R); Joe Osei-Kuffour (Torquay U); Adam Griffiths (Bournemouth). **Brighton & HA:** Alex Revell (Braintree T). **Bristol C:**

Liam Fontaine (Fulham); Philip Jevons (Yeovil T); Chris Weale (Yeovil T); Enoch Showunmi (Luton T); Jamie McCombe (Lincoln C). **Carlisle U:** David Raven (Liverpool); Kevin Gall (Yeovil T). **Chesterfield:** Paul Shaw (Rotherham U); Phil Picken (Manchester U). **Crewe Alex:** Julian Baudet (Notts Co); Darran Kempson (Morecambe). **Doncaster R:** James O'Connor (AFC Bournemouth); Kevin Horlock (Ipswich T); Adam Lockwood (Yeovil T); Bruce Dyer (Sheffield U). **Gillingham:** Kelvin Jack (Dundee); Clint Easton (Wycombe W); Mark Bentley (Southend U); Duncan Jupp (Southend U); Dean McDonald (Ipswich T); Gary Mulligan (Sheffield U); Guylain Ndumbu-Nsungu (Cardiff C). **Huddersfield T:** Luke Beckett (Oldham Ath); Matthew Glennon (St Johnstone). **Leyton Orient:** Wayne Corden (Scunthorpe U). **Millwall:** Derek McInnes (Dundee U); Chris Day (Oldham Ath); Richard Shaw (Coventry C); Tom Brighton (Clyde); Filipe Morais (Chelsea); Zak Whitbread (Liverpool); Lenny Pidgeley (Chelsea); Gavin Grant (Gillingham); Adam Cottrell (Charlton Ath). **Northampton T:** Joe Burnell (Wycombe W); Sam Aiston (Shrewsbury T); Andy Holt (Wrexham). **Nottingham F:** Paul Smith (Southampton). **Oldham Ath:** Craig Rocastle (Sheffield W); John Mullin (Burnley); Leslie Pogliacomi (Blackpool); Gary McDonald (Kilmarnock). **Port Vale:** Colin Miles (Yeovil T); Danny Whitaker (Macclesfield T); Paul Harsley (Macclesfield T); Akpo Sodje (Darlington); Jason Talbot (Mansfield); Richard Walker (Crewe Alex). **Rotherham U:** Delroy Facey (Tranmere R); Justin Cochrane (Crewe Alex); Ian Sharps (Tranmere R); Ritchie Partridge (Sheffield W); Scott Wiseman (Hull C); Pablo Mills (Derby Co). **Scunthorpe U:** Ramon Calliste (Liverpool); David Mulligan (Doncaster R); Joe Murphy (Sunderland). **Swansea C:** Darren Pratley (Fulham); Dean Leacock (Fulham). **Tranmere R:** Chris Shuker (Barnsley); Paul McLaren (Rotherham U); Gavin Ward (Preston NE); Kevin Ellison (Hull C); Robbie Stockdale (Hull C). **Yeovil T:** Chris Cohen (West Ham U); Terrell Forbes (Oldham Ath); Jean-Paul Kamudimba Kala (Grimsby T); Wayne Gray (Southend U); Steve Mildenhall (Grimsby T); Darren Behcet (West Ham U); Stephen Maher (Dublin C).

Football League 2: Accrington S: Julien N'Da (Rouen); Andrew Todd (Burton Alb); Sean Doherty (Port Vale). **Barnet:** Lee Harrison (Peterborough U). **Boston U:** Paul Tait (Chester C); David Farrell (Peterborough U); Andy Marriott (Torquay U); Francis Green (Lincoln C); Mark Albrighton (Doncaster R); Tim Ryan (Peterborough U); Anthony Elding (Stevenage B). **Bristol R:** Andrew Sandell (Bath C); Ryan Green (Hereford U); Oliver Barnes (Bristol C). **Bury:** Marc Goodfellow (Grimsby T); Alan Fettis (Macclesfield T); Andy Bishop (York C); Richard Baker (Preston NE). **Chester C:** Ashley Westwood (Northampton T); Graham Allen (Rushden & D); Ricky Ravenhill (Doncaster R) £50,000; Glenn Cronin (Exeter C); Kevin Sandwith (Macclesfield T); Jonathan Walters (Wrexham); Dean Bennett (Wrexham); Drewe Broughton (Rushden & D); Jermaine McSporran (Doncaster R); Graham Allen (Rushden & D); Jamie Hand (Northampton T); Laurence Wilson (Everton); John Danby (Kidderminster H); Phil Bolland (Peterborough U). **Darlington:** Patrick Collins (Sheffield W); Martin Smith (Northampton T); Barry Conlon (Barnsley); Michael Cummins (Port Vale); Gaetano Giallanza (Young Boys). **Grimsby T:** Phil Barnes (Sheffield U); Isaiah Rankin (Brentford); Gary Harkins (Blackburn R). **Hereford U:** Richard Rose (Gillingham); Tim Sills (Oxford U); John Wallis (Gillingham); Gareth Sheldon (Kidderminster H); Wayne Brown (Chester C); Dean Beckwith (Gillingham). **Lincoln C:** James Sherlock (Gainsborough C); Adrian Moses (Crewe Alex); Jamie Forrester (Bristol R). **Macclesfield T:** John Heath (Chesterfield); Carl Regan (Chester C); Marvin Robinson (Lincoln C); Matt McNeil (Hyde U); Tommy Lee (Manchester U). **Mansfield T:** Matthew Hamshaw (Stockport Co); Johnny Mullins (Reading). **Milton Keynes D:** Drissa Diallo (Sheffield W); Sean O'Hanlon (Swindon T); Jon-Paul McGovern (Sheffield W); Joe Tillen (Chelsea). **Notts Co:** Austin McCann (Boston U); Tom Curtis (Chester C); Lawrie Dudfield (Boston U); Alan White (Boston U); Junior Mendes (Huddersfield T); Tcham N'Toya (Chesterfield); Andy Parkinson (Grimsby T); Stephen Hunt (Colchester U); Gary Silk (Portsmouth); Jason Lee (Northampton T); Matt Somner (Aldershot T). **Peterborough U:** Jude Stirling (Lincoln C); Richard Butcher (Oldham Ath); Justin Richards (Woking). **Rochdale:** Adam Rundle (Mansfield T). **Shrewsbury T:** Ryan Esson (Aberdeen); Ben Davies (Chester C); Chris Mackenzie (Chester C); Stuart Drummond (Chester C); Dale Williams (Yeovil T); Daniel Hall (Oldham Ath). **Stockport Co:** Gareth Owen (Oldham Ath); Michael Rose (Yeovil T); Tony Dinning (Port Vale). **Swindon T:** Folawiyo Onibuje (Cambridge U); Adrian Williams (Coventry C); Andy Monkhouse (Rotherham U); Gustavo Poyet (player-coach); Dennis Wise (Coventry C, Player-Manager). **Torquay U:** Lee Mansell (Oxford U); Jamie Ward (Aston Villa); Lee Andrews (Carlisle U); Mickey Evans (Plymouth Arg); Stephen Reed (Yeovil T). **Walsall:** Clayton Ince (Coventry C); Tony Bedeau (Torquay U); Michael Dobson (Brentford); Martin Butler (Rotherham U). **Wrexham:** Neil Roberts (Doncaster R); Chris Llewellyn (Hartlepool U); Steve Evans (TNS); Ryan Valentine (Darlington). **Wycombe W:** Chris Palmer (Notts Co).

Now you can buy any of these other bestselling sports titles from your bookshop or *direct from the publisher.*

FREE P&P AND UK DELIVERY
(Overseas and Ireland £3.50 per book)

Sky Sports Football Yearbook 2006–2007	Glenda Rollin and Jack Rollin	£20.00
1966 and All That	Geoff Hurst	£7.99
Psycho	Stuart Pearce	£7.99
Vinnie	Vinnie Jones	£7.99
Left Foot Forward	Garry Nelson	£6.99
My Autobiography	Tom Finney	£7.99
The Autobiography	Niall Quinn	£7.99
Fathers, Sons and Football	Colin Shindler	£6.99
Cloughie	Brian Clough	£7.99
My World	Jonny Wilkinson	£6.99
Gazza: My Story	Paul Gascoigne	£7.99
Right Back to the Beginning	Jimmy Armfield	£7.99
George Best and 21 Others	Colin Shindler	£7.99
Life Swings	Nick Faldo	£8.99
The Autobiography	Martin Johnson	£7.99
My Autobiography	George Cohen	£7.99
Pointless	Jeff Connor	£7.99

TO ORDER SIMPLY CALL THIS NUMBER

01235 400 414

or visit our website:

www.madaboutbooks.com

Prices and availability subject to change without notice.